EAST ASIAN HISTORICAL MONOGRAPHS

General Editor: WANG GUNGWU

Malay Society in the Late Nineteenth Century

EAST ASIAN HISTORICAL MONOGRAPHS

General Editor: WANG GUNGWU

When this series was first introduced in the late 1960s studies of Asian history were still seen to be too closely identified with Western activities and enterprise and to reflect too little either Asian viewpoints or the economic and social factors which lay behind political events.

As the series moves into its third decade, another generation of historians has emerged who by their researches have opened up entirely new perspectives and charted new courses in the study of the historical process in the region.

It is the hope of the publishers that the East Asian Historical Monographs series will, against this background of innovative scholarship, continue to play a role in meeting the need and demand for historical writings on the region, and that the fruits of the new scholarship will thus reach a wider reading public.

Other titles in this series are listed at the end of the book

Malay Society in the Late Nineteenth Century

The Beginnings of Change

J. M. Gullick

SINGAPORE
OXFORD UNIVERSITY PRESS
OXFORD NEW YORK
1987

Oxford University Press
Oxford New York Toronto
Petaling Jaya Singapore Hong Kong Tokyo
Delhi Bombay Calcutta Madras Karachi
Nairobi Dar es Salaam Cape Town
Melbourne Auckland

and associates in
Beirut Berlin Ibadan Nicosia

Published in the United States by
Oxford University Press, Inc., New York

OXFORD is a trademark of Oxford University Press

ISBN 0 19 588850 2

Library of Congress Cataloging-in-Publication Data

Gullick, J. M.
Malay society in the late nineteenth century.

(East Asian historical monographs)
Bibliography: p.
Includes index.
1. Malaya—Social conditions. 2. Malaya—Economic conditions. I. Title. II. Series.
HN700.6.A8G85 1987 306'.09595'1 87–5806
ISBN 0-19-588850-2

British Library Cataloguing in Publication Data

Gullick, J. M.
Malay society in the late nineteenth century: the beginnings of change.—(East Asian historical monographs).
1. Malaya—Social life and customs
I. Title II. Series
959.5'103 DS594

ISBN 0-19-588850-2

Printed in Singapore by Kim Hup Lee Printing Co. Pte. Ltd.
Published by Oxford University Press Pte. Ltd.,
Unit 221, Ubi Avenue 4, Singapore 1440

Preface

I was first drawn into the study of Malay social history in 1945. The Undang of Jelebu, one of the six Negeri Sembilan dignitaries who sign treaties affecting the State, had died in the last weeks of the Japanese occupation. As he had held office for more than thirty years none of the lesser chiefs of Jelebu had been involved in the process of his election. In spite of the authoritative account of Jelebu *adat* by Sir Andrew Caldecott, there was in 1945, as on subsequent occasions, lively argument as to the rules affecting the choice of a successor. Yet the impending arrival of Sir Harold Macmichael with a treaty which he was to get signed on behalf of all the Malay States made it an urgent matter to arrange the election of a new Undang of Jelebu to complete the constitutional college of Negeri Sembilan rulers. It fell to me in the course of official duties to act as conciliator between the rival schools of thought in Jelebu and a new Undang was duly elected. That hectic but fascinating episode introduced me to Malay history, which has been an absorbing interest for the ensuing forty years.

In 1948 I began a period of study leave at the Department of Social Anthropology of the London School of Economics and this led to the writing of a dissertation which was published under the title of *Indigenous Political Systems of Western Malaya*. At that time there was much discussion among social anthropologists about the proper method of study of social change in traditional societies exposed to powerful external forces by colonial rule or other Western domination. It was generally agreed that a useful first step was to construct a 'zero point' study of a society as it was on the eve of colonial rule. This was essentially a synchronic 'snapshot' of the situation to provide a starting point for the examination of the ensuing changes.

Indigenous Political Systems was merely an academic exercise, based on documentary sources and limited in scope—partly by the availability of source material. Its subject was Malay political institutions as they appear to have been in Perak, Selangor and Sungei Ujong around 1870. It was not propounded as a more comprehensive study of what some other writers have perceived as 'Malay political culture' in the 'Malay world'.

For most of my adult life since then I have been absorbed in other activities. But I have always hoped that there would be time and opportunity to go on from the 'zero point' to an account of the ensuing changes. Returning to this task after so long an interval, a broader approach seemed more useful. It would, in any case, be difficult to construct a picture of Malay political institutions under colonial rule which had emptied them of much of their significance and diverted their development into ceremonial and religious activities rather than the exercise of governmental powers. The theme of this book is therefore an examination of a wider subject area, with an extension in time and space to the latter part of the nineteenth century and the Malay Peninsula.

This book and *Indigenous Political Systems* do have a sequential connection in my mind but this book is not a simple successor to the earlier one. It stands on its own feet as a description and some analysis of what was happening in Malay society during the first generation of its experience of colonial rule and related influences.

It only remains to express my thanks for the help and encouragement which have materially assisted me in writing this book. The publishers, Oxford University Press, responded most positively to my tentative suggestions for a book on these lines and have been very helpful as the book moved into the publishing process. In 1984 I had the good fortune to be invited to spend a period of study at the Research School of Pacific Studies of the Australian National University at Canberra. I am most grateful to Professor J. A. C. Mackie, who was my principal sponsor and who made the visit possible, and to many other friends, old and new, among the specialists in Asian studies at the universities of Australia. My visit was an intellectual stimulus to me, at a time when this book was taking shape, as well as a pleasureable experience.

In a book which derives its material from books and documentary sources the author is always much in the debt of libraries and their staffs. In London I have had a great deal of help at the Public Records Office, the British Library, the India Office Library and Records, the Library of the School of Oriental and African Studies, and the old Colonial Office Library. In Australia I made extensive use of the libraries of the Australian National University and the Australian National Library in Canberra. For the help so willingly given in that context I am most grateful.

This book includes numerous quotations so that the reader may have the flavour of the original observation of what is described where that is likely to be useful. Much of this quoted material is, or was at one time, subject to copyright. In accordance with convention in these matters I have obtained formal permission from a number of publishers and agents to include quotations in the text of the book. These permissions are acknowledged on another page. Throughout the book the source of every quotation is given in a note. Again I would like to express my thanks and my sense of obligation to earlier writers whose work has been so useful as a source for this book. I hope that I have adequately discharged my indebtedness to them and acknowledged what I have derived from them.

Woodford Green,
Essex
June 1986

J. M. GULLICK

Acknowledgements

THE author and the publishers wish to thank the following for formal permission to reproduce copyright material:

Allen & Unwin (Publishers) Ltd.: *British Malaya* by Sir Frank Swettenham (1948 ed.);

A & C Black (Publishers) Ltd.: *In a Corner of Asia* by Sir Hugh Clifford;

Century Hutchinson Ltd.: *Footprints in Malaya* by Sir Frank Swettenham;

The Bodley Head Ltd.: *Malay Sketches*, *Unaddressed Letters* and *The Real Malay*, all by Sir Frank Swettenham; and *The Magic of Malaya* by C. W. Harrison;

Heinemann Educational Books (Asia) Ltd.: *Memoirs of a Menteri Besar: Early Days* by Tan Sri Datuk Dr Mohamed Said;

The Editor, *The Journal of the Royal Asiatic Society, Straits/Malayan/Malaysian Branch*: articles by various contributors;

Macmillan Publishers Ltd.: *Malay Magic* by W. W. Skeat;

John Murray (Publishers) Ltd.: *Malayan Monochromes*, and *In Days that are Dead* both by Sir Hugh Clifford; *Peoples and Places* and *Trifles and Travels* both by A. L. Keyser; and *The Life of Sir Frederick Weld* by Alice Lovat;

The Royal Geographical Society: 'A Journey through the Malay States of Trengganu and Kelantan', by Sir Hugh Clifford, published in *The Geographical Journal*, 1897;

Miss Tessa Sayle: *In Court and Kampong*, *Studies in Brown Humanity*, *In a Corner of Asia*, *The Further Side of Silence*, *A Prince of Malaya*, and *Bushwhacking*, all by Sir Hugh Clifford.

Contents

Preface v
Acknowledgements viii
Abbreviations x

1. Introduction 1
2. The Ruler in Public Life 20
3. The Ruler in Private Life 48
4. A Ruling Class in Search of an Occupation 71
5. The Village Community 98
6. The Village Economy 124
7. The Malay Village and the External Economy 150
8. The Malay Style of Living 181
9. Inequality in Malay Society 210
10. The Maintenance of Order 238
11. New Influences: Medicine and Education 258
12. The Organization of Islam 277
13. The Use of Magic 316
14. Sports, Amusements, and Recreations 329
15. The Stability of Malay Society 363

Appendix 370
Glossary 377
Bibliography 390
Index 412

Abbreviations

AR	Annual Report
BKI	*Bijdragen tot de Taal-, en Volkenkunde van Nederlandsch-Indie*
Cmd.	Command Paper laid before Parliament
CO	Colonial Office
FMS	Federated Malay States
FO	Foreign Office
IOL	India Office Library and Records
JIA	*Journal of the Indian Archipelago and Eastern Asia* (1847–59)
JMBRAS	*Journal of the Malayan/Malaysian Branch of the Royal Asiatic Society*
JSBRAS	*Journal of the Straits Branch of the Royal Asiatic Society* (1878–1922)
JSEAS	*Journal of South-East Asian Studies*
MAJ	*Malayan Agricultural Journal*
MHJ	*Malayan Historical Journal* (1955–6)
NSGG	*Negeri Sembilan Government Gazette* (from 1896)
PCE	Perak Commission of Enquiry 1876
PGG	*Perak Government Gazette* (from 1888)
PMS	*Papers on Malay Subjects*
PRO	Public Records Office
PSCM	*Perak State Council Minutes*
SGG	*Selangor Government Gazette* (from 1890)
SJ	*Selangor Journal* (1892–7)
SS	Straits Settlements
SSD	Despatch from Governor SS to Secretary of State for Colonies
UMS	Unfederated Malay States

1
Introduction

At first sight, Malay society in the nineteenth and then the twentieth century presents a sharp contrast. The nineteenth century appears to have been the last age of unchanging stability and the twentieth century marks the beginning of accelerating processes of social change which continue down to modern times. There is some truth in this view. The end of an epoch and the beginning of another cannot be dated precisely. But one can recognize that by, say, 1920 an age had ended and another had begun. By that date, the Malay community had set aside its initial doubts about the lay education of its sons (and its daughters)—so much so that the Malays were demanding that the network of vernacular schools, a powerful instrument of change, should be extended throughout the Malay states. It was also the time when rubber cultivation, originally confined to plantations, had become widespread among Malay smallholders, thereby offering an opportunity of economic advance. The motor car, and the rural bus service running on all-weather roads, had begun to narrow the gap between countryside and town. The end of World War I introduced a period of economic instability such as Malaya had never experienced before.

These and other factors of change did not have a clear-cut beginning in 1920. On the contrary, one can find their origins in the twenty years which began at the turn of the century. So 1900–20 may be regarded as a watershed. This is perhaps the period when the modern Malaya (and later Malaysia) began to take shape.

Yet if one goes back a little further into the last years of the nineteenth century, is it true to say that the condition of Malay society was at that time static? Was unchanging custom still king? To move back to 1874, when British political control was first imposed on some Malay states, does not provide a satisfactory bench-mark for the measurement of change. Political control of the Malay states by the colonial regime was not completed until 1914. British intervention in 1874 was itself a response to processes of change in the Malay states which had begun in mid-century or even earlier. The leading study of that theme argues that 185[illegible] or thereabouts was the time when 'dynamic economic energies began to penetrate ever more deeply into the Peninsula'.[1] It was therefore necessary to go back to the beginning of the nineteenth century to find a time when 'traditional Malay society, in general, had not been structurally altered'.[2]

It was in the aftermath of the Napoleonic War in Europe that external forces began to make an impact on South-East Asia. The Anglo-Dutch Treaty of 1824 and the Anglo-Siamese Treaty of 1826 conceded to the East India Company its hold on what became the Straits Settlements and a rather imprecise hinterland of influence in what was to be 'British Malaya' later on. The lifting of restrictions on emigration of Chinese from the south-east provinces of China provided an immigrant labour force at the same time as Western industrialization began to make much increased demands on South-East Asia for raw materials. The export trade in British manufactures and the trade with China led to a complex pattern of economic relationships between South-East Asia, India, China and, of course, Europe and America. The Christian missionaries may have had little success in proselytizing the Muslim peoples of the region but they introduced vernacular education and the use of books. These and other factors afford grounds for suggesting that change towards the pattern of the twentieth century began to make way, hesitantly and unevenly at first, about 1820.

The purpose of this study is to describe and, so far as the available material permits, to analyse the processes of change in Malay society in the second half of the nineteenth and the early years of the twentieth century.

In introducing that main theme, this chapter essays to define in terms of time and place and subject-matter what the book is about, where the source material is to be found, and how it is treated. It will be apparent that there are considerable limitations and problems of one kind or another. But it is suggested that a picture can be built up.

First, what should be the area of study? A recent analysis of 'Malay political culture' of this period suggests that there was a 'Malay world' in which a 'sense of Malay-ness' created a cultural unity despite the absence of political unity.[3] This Malay world covered the Malay Peninsula and the north-east of Sumatra. In this region a number of separate communities or states shared a common language, religion, way of life, agricultural economy, and political culture (in the sense that the presence of a Malay *raja*—the situation of *kerajaan*—was indispensable).

One can accept the argument for a 'Malay world' thus defined and yet insist, as this author is disposed to do, that within this Malay world there were subcultures and a strong sense of cultural differences amounting to antagonism. Of the Perak Malays in 1890 it was written that they had 'an exceeding dislike for and jealousy of all foreigners (including Malays not of Perak)'.[4] The Terengganu and Kelantan Malays recruited into the Pahang police force at about the same time were 'somewhat looked down on by the Malays of Pahang'.[5] In Selangor the Kedah men who settled down after the civil war (1867–73) were 'looked down upon . . . as aliens and strangers'.[6] Many more like instances could be given. The study is therefore concerned with communities which had elements in common and yet a strong sense of local identity.

In determining the geographical limits of this study the author has decided to confine himself to the Malay Peninsula. This omits the Malay communities at the frontier of the Malay world, where Malay culture was in conscious opposition to alien cultures such as that of the Batak people of the interior of Sumatra. It also excludes the Malay, or at least Muslim, settlements around the coast of Borneo. The area chosen includes the nine states which in 1948 became the Federation of Malaya, uniting with the settlements of Penang and Melaka, where there were large Malay settlements. It also permits the inclusion of the small Malay states of southern Siam, which were akin in culture to 'British Malaya' though never united with it.

It is an area which comprehended a wide variety of Malay communities and so provides material for comparison. As a very round figure there were about a million and a quarter Malays living in this area in 1900.[7]

The largest concentration, perhaps half a million, was in the north-east (Kelantan, Terengganu and the small states into which ancient Patani had been divided by the Siamese). Here there was little external pressure until the Siamese attempted to exert control in the 1890s. When Kelantan and Terengganu came under British suzerainty in 1909 they had changed very little since 1850. Hence the British reports are a useful guide to these communities as they had been a generation earlier. Essentially they were traditional Malay monarchies, in which Islam was exceptionally strongly established at all levels of society.

The other major area of Malay settlement, which comprised perhaps a quarter of the whole Peninsular population, was Perak, Selangor, Negeri Sembilan and Pahang (grouped to form the Federated Malay States (FMS) in 1896). These were Malay states which had come under British control at various dates from 1874 to 1889. Although the alien administration was relatively uniform the underlying Malay societies differed among themselves. Perak, Selangor and Sungei Ujong had been much affected by external economic penetration from about 1850 onwards as the exploitation of their tin deposits gathered momentum. Perak was an ancient Malay state in the traditional style but Selangor was a kingdom founded by the Bugis a century before and Negeri Sembilan was a confederacy of small states peopled by settlers from Menangkabau, who brought with them their traditional matrilineal (*adat perpatih*) social and political system. Pahang was another traditional Malay kingdom, though its resident dynasty did not obtain recognition as royalty until the 1880s. Unlike Perak it had been an autocracy, though a civil war (1857–63) and a rising (1892–4) had caused upheavals in the pattern. In economic terms Pahang was a backward, sparsely populated state and, in contrast to the north-east region, Islam did not play a dominant part in its social system.

Kedah (and its small offshoot, Perlis) and Johor were also Malay states but their social pattern was quite different from that of the FMS. Both remained formally outside the British colonial system until the beginning of the twentieth century. In Kedah and Perlis the Siamese occupation of 1821–42 had almost destroyed one of the most ancient communities in the Peninsula. Many of the Kedah Malays who fled from the Siamese settled in Province Wellesley and never returned. In reaching an accommodation with the Siamese the Kedah dynasty managed to preserve the substance of its independence until financial chaos brought in a European adviser appointed by the Siamese in 1905 and then transfer to British control in 1909. The rulers of Kedah returned from twenty-one years' exile in the Straits Settlements (SS) imbued with many of the tastes and ideas of the Straits Settlements regime. They developed close economic ties with Penang, which was the principal export market for Kedah's exports of rice and cattle; by this means they offset their formal political submission to Siam. The government of Kedah and the life-style of its ruling class incorporated many European elements. Yet it was still, defiantly and proudly, a Malay state with many traditional features.

Towards the end of the nineteenth century the Malay, predominantly Indonesian, population of Johor was probably not much more than 50,000 but it was rising fast by migration. With some difficulty the ruler obtained general recognition as Malay royalty late in the century. Close economic ties with Singapore and Chinese agricultural development made Johor a very different Malay state from any other in the Peninsula. The ruler himself, and also many of the bureaucrats who served under him, were of Singapore origin.

The Malay population of Penang (including Province Wellesley) and Melaka numbered about 175,000 and the greater part of it lived in rural areas. The Singapore population of some 40,000 had a much larger urban and Indonesian element. In the countryside village communities lived in a very similar style to that of the western Malay states. But there was no Malay ruling class above them to provide a traditional political structure. The urban population had intermarried extensively with immigrant Arabs and Indian Muslims. The celebrated Malay writer Abdullah Munshi was a Malay of mixed Arab and Tamil descent.

Although the Malay population of the FMS was only a quarter of the total, it is at the centre of this study. The preponderance of source material from the FMS makes this an unavoidable result. There is, however, sufficient information on the other Malay communities elsewhere to permit a comparison at least. On some themes, such as the Malay legal system and the position of Islam, it is the 'outlying' communities which supplement the deficiencies of information from the central FMS zone. In any event the Malay communities of the FMS are a particularly interesting case-study since it was in this area that the Malay way of life was in clear-cut interaction with external influences.

The main focus of this study is on the period between 1870 and about 1905. Yet, to provide as complete a picture as possible of Malay society in the early stages of transition from a traditional style of life to something more mixed, it is necessary to bring in information from the records of earlier and later years as well. Within a single community the progress of change was not uniform in every aspect of social life and there was often a marked contrast between different states at the same point in time. A couple of examples may illustrate this point.

Sultan Zainal Abidin III of Terengganu was a very conservative ruler whose object throughout his long reign (1881–1918) was to preserve unchanged the traditions of his community. In this policy he was generally successful. Yet he had inherited from an energetic predecessor, Baginda Omar (r.1839–76), a state economy which had elements of capitalist enterprise in its vigorous cottage industries. When Hugh Clifford was in Kuala Terengganu in 1895 he found that, among other exports, imitation Arab turbans were 'annually despatched to Mecca, where they are retailed to confiding Malay pilgrims as real Arabic manufacture'.[8] The general result of Zainal Abidin's regime was that, when the first British Agent arrived in 1909 (the ruler had declined to accept a British *Adviser*), Terengganu probably had more in common with Perak at the time of James Low's visit in 1826, than with the contemporary West Coast society where in 1922 Malays 'alas! ride in motor cars, wearing patent leather shoes and spats'.[9]

Sultan Abu Bakar of Johor (r.1862–95) early in his reign had earned the British accolade that 'in tastes and habits he is an English gentleman'.[10] Since his Malay fellow rulers were reluctant to accept him as one of their number, he set out to secure recognition as royalty at European courts. The Malay title 'Seri Maharaja Temenggong', to which he was entitled, was abbreviated to 'Maharaja' with its Indian princely connotations and he assiduously cultivated Europeans of title. When in 1889 the Duke of Sutherland brought a yachtload of London socialites to Singapore, Abu Bakar (by now recognized by Britain as Sultan and elevated to Knight Grand Cross of the Order of St. Michael and St. George and also Knight Commander of the Order of the Star of India) entertained them at the *istana* (palace) in royal style, bringing forth the gold dinner service which had originally been made for a viceroy of India.[11] When he visited Europe, he sought introductions at court in London and other capitals, and created Johor decorations to offer to those who assisted him.[12] All this was in total contrast with the situation in Kelantan, which in the early 1890s suffered a period of strict Islamic orthodoxy enforced by the ruler and his controversial minister, the Maha Menteri.[13] A visitor to Kota Bharu in 1894 was told of the punishment of seven women suspected of adultery. Their heads were shaved and their ordeal continued with 'nailing them all by the ear to trees, in which position they remained for several days'.[14]

It is not practicable to measure the progress of change in decades or even in the span of generations. It is better to consider the elements of each situation. Often the same occasion presents its own contrasts. When, for example, a new ruler of Perak was installed in

1889, the ceremonies included a pagan invitation to 'the spirits of the country' to ward off evil, and also a state banquet at which the new ruler proposed the health of Queen Victoria.[15] The period over which material is drawn for the purpose of this study begins as early as 1826 (though most of it is later than 1847) and it extends to about 1920.

The compilation of this study of Malay society in early stages of change is essentially an eclectic search for relevant material of many kinds. The availability, or lack, of suitable material must obviously determine what can be done. Hence a review of the main sources at this point is a necessary preliminary to considering what can be made of it, and what methods used in doing so.

Broadly the information available can be divided into two classes—records of personal experience and observation of specific events and situations, and more general descriptions of Malay society and behaviour. A single work may often provide material of both kinds. The celebrated Victorian lady traveller, Isabella Bird, gave an account of six weeks' travel along the West Coast of Malaya. Yet, at suitable points, the author interposes a chapter of general description of the state which she is about to visit.[16] It is the nature of the information, not the form in which it is presented, which is significant for this purpose.

The Malay contribution to the record of personal experience is only a small part of the whole. Abdullah Munshi visited the East Coast states in 1838 and his son, Ibrahim Munshi, made several journeys up the west coast in 1871–2. There are one or two autobiographies or fragments of personal reminiscence of the writer's 'life and times'. These Malay sources, although small in bulk, are of special value. Take, for example, Mahmud bin Mat's description of growing up in an aristocratic household in Pahang which had been deprived of its domestic staff by the abolition of slavery and debt-bondage. He recollects, as a young child, that 'two or three young slave girls attended on him at play, at meal time and at bed-time. Then after a year to two they disappeared. . . Later on at the age of nine or ten years the writer had, after school hours, to bear his share of the household drudgery while the elder members of his family had to bear the full burden of the labour on the farm which formerly was done by slaves.'[17]

To the direct testimony of Malays one may add European records of statements made by Malays. They range from evidence (in English translation) taken down at trials and enquiries, to shorter and less exact notes of information given in conversation.[18] The best of it is excellent material. Early in the twentieth century the rulers of Kedah, Selangor and Pahang seem to have commissioned members of their households to write state chronicles (*hikayat*), which, in so far as they relate to the nineteenth century, are rather stiff political narratives. Yet one can sometimes glean information from them.[19]

Frank Swettenham wrote that, 'In 1874, the ignorance of all Europeans in the colony [Straits Settlements] concerning their near neighbours in the Malay Peninsula almost passes belief. . . . Mysterious Malaya was *terra incognita* to official and trader alike.'[20] Yet, there is evidence that amid the general ignorance there was a small group who had visited the western Malay states at least. T. J. Newbold and P. J. Begbie wrote comprehensive accounts in the 1830s of the states of the Malay Peninsula.[21] A few years later, between 1847 and 1859, J. R. Logan published the *Journal of the Indian Archipelago and Eastern Asia* to which he and other visitors to the Malay states, notably Thomas Braddell and James Low, contributed accounts of their experiences. Another notable contributor, writing on the Malays of Province Wellesley, was J D. Vaughan. After an interval, a later group of enthusiasts, among whom W. E. Maxwell was prominent, established the *Journal of the Straits Branch Royal Asiatic Society* (*JSBRAS*) in 1878. Re-named the *Journal of the Malayan Branch of the Royal Asiatic Society* (later 'Malaysian Branch'), it has continued and flourished down to our day. In its early days, *JSBRAS* published accounts by Swettenham and W. E. Maxwell, among others, of journeys into what were then unknown parts of the Malay Peninsula.[22] Finally, in this category, when W. W. Skeat led a party to the north-east states, including those in Siam, in 1899–1900, he and F. F. Laidlaw wrote a lengthy account of life in remote Malay communities which is a most valuable source.[23]

With the extension of British rule to the western Malay states in 1874 a new type of firsthand experience enters the records. The administrators were required to maintain journals of their daily working activities. In the first year or two of his arrival, the administrator was concerned to explore his territory by extensive tours, and he noted down in his journal (supplemented by reports) what he saw at a time when the new regime had hardly begun to alter the Malay society in which he was now a potent instrument of change. J. W. W. Birch and Bloomfield Douglas are generally regarded as men insensitive to the Malays and their way of life. But both were careful men who have left a substantial record in journal form.[24] Swettenham's journals for 1874–6 and Hugh Low's journal of his first two months in Perak in 1877 are the work of the two outstanding administrators of their day.[25] Lastly, in this category, when Hugh Clifford went as British representative to the court of Pahang in 1887, he wrote a series of reports which, although not in the form of a journal, are a firsthand record of his experiences. Later, when he led an expedition to Terengganu and Kelantan in 1895, he wrote a report on its activities which is an excellent source of information on Terengganu and, to a lesser extent, on Kelantan.[26] Another notable foray into almost unknown territory was C. F. Bozzolo's journey overland from Upper Perak to Kelantan in 1888.[27]

In the 1890s the state governments of Perak and Selangor published their own official gazettes. For some years it was the practice to include in these gazettes extracts from monthly reports by district officers, relating mainly to tours in their districts. Much useful information, especially on the Malay village economy, can be obtained from these reports.[28] There are some other reports on specific subjects.

The Golden Chersonese is an outstanding example, but not the only one, of a book in the form of a 'traveller's tale'. The *Voyages* of Abdullah Munshi and Ibrahim Munshi, also mentioned above, fall into this group. Although Emily Innes was not a traveller, her riposte to Isabella Bird, *The Chersonese with the Gilding Off*, is in part an account of her daily life in Selangor and Perak. W. T. Hornaday's *Two Years in the Jungle*, Henry Norman's *Peoples and Politics of the Far East*, and Florence Caddy's *To Siam and Malaya* are essentially travel books recording the impressions of a journey. The writers lacked intimate knowledge of Malaya and the Malays and to that extent their impressions are less reliable. J. F. A. McNair's *Perak and the Malays*, A. B. Rathborne's *Camping and Tramping*, Swettenham's *About Perak*, J. H. M. Robson's *Peoples in a Native State*, and A. L. Keyser's *People and Places* are books written by men who had lived for long periods in the Malay states, and who incorporate in their general descriptions, varying amounts of anecdote and reminiscence which is firsthand reporting of particular events.[29]

Among the sources which offer a general description of Malay society or some aspect of it, the collections of stories by Clifford and

Swettenham are outstanding.[30] They also, in their capacity as British Residents, wrote annual reports which contain passages giving their view of Malay society; both gave a lecture (Clifford gave two) to the Royal Colonial Institute in London in a similar vein.[31] In a rather different vein, but still essentially general description, are the many articles and notes contributed to *JSBRAS* (and some other journals) from 1878 onwards. The outstanding contributor to *JSBRAS* in the last quarter of the nineteenth century was W. E. Maxwell, who rivalled Swettenham and Clifford in his knowledge, gained at first hand, of Malay society.[32] The *JSBRAS* material is serious ethnography, written for the minority who might be interested in it. In this respect it contrasts with the books for the general reader of which a sufficiently representative sample has been given above. About 1900 a later generation, W. W. Skeat, R. J. Wilkinson and R. O. Winstedt, began to produce a considerable collection of books and essays on the same subjects—Skeat's *Malay Magic* and the *Papers on Malay Subjects*, edited by Wilkinson, are works of real scholarship.[33] Although it comes after the period of this study, Gimlette's *Malay Poisons and Charm Cures* is an account of its subject based on material collected over the previous twenty years.[34] It is a faithful picture of the late nineteenth-century Malay practices.

It would not be useful to extend further the list of descriptive works, since they are cited as sources where necessary and included in the bibliography. In contrast to the record of particular impressions and experiences, the author of general descriptive writing is, in each case, making an attempt to assemble, interpret, and present his information in a comprehensive and coherent form. As such it is indispensable. It is hardly possible to build up a complete picture from individual cases alone. Yet precisely because there is a conscious effort at interpretation, there is a much greater risk of distortion. Apart from his subconscious assumptions, the author is shaping his picture to present what he now regards as the correct image. Swettenham provides a neat example. In the latter part of 1874, Swettenham was in pursuit of the fugitive Raja Mahmud of Selangor, who had gone across the border into Sungei Ujong to assist one of its chiefs in resistance to British intervention. It was Swettenham's task to find Raja Mahmud and persuade him to give himself up. They met for the first time on 5 December 1874, when Swettenham noted in his journal that 'Raja Mahmud is a small, well-built man with anything but a prepossessing face'. Swettenham later notes with contempt that Mahmud had casually killed a man for a trivial reason—'this is merely one specimen of the ordinary habits of this interesting creature, the Salangor Raja'.[35] However, a year later in Perak, Mahmud by his cool courage saved Swettenham's life and the two men became firm friends. In writing his *British Malaya* thirty years later, Swettenham retells the story of his first encounter with Mahmud in a very different tone—'he had a fine open face, looked you straight and fearlessly in the eyes'. It is a sympathetic, indeed a very romantic, portrait.[36]

Both types of material have their uses. In combination each can provide a check on the accuracy of the other. It is the aim in this study—though it is not always possible—to find specific instances to set against general propositions. For example, the European accounts of Malay slavery and debt-bondage undoubtedly reflect the very strong feelings of Victorian England against the brutal trade in African slaves. The numerous stories of the individual experiences of Malay men and women in debt-bondage make it possible to form an impression of what this Malay institution really meant. That is not to justify it nor to prove that the reports are wrong. But it puts the picture in better balance.

A cross-check of this kind is particularly useful when it is clear that a European informant is seeking to make a case on some aspect of Malay culture or society on which he has a committed view. Swettenham's argument for 'regeneration' of the Malay character arises from his opposition to opening English language schools which, in his opinion, had been so disastrous in India. In asserting that, by custom, the cultivator must pay a tithe of his crop to the Malay ruler, W. E. Maxwell was seeking to strengthen his case for *variable* land rents, under the Torrens system of tenure, which he was then introducing into Malaya. In this contention he persisted in face of awkward facts and his colleagues' criticism. In each case, and one could cite others, one can find firsthand description and individual instances which qualify or correct the general assertion made.[37]

It may be objected that the record of actual observation is anecdotal. It merely tells a story of some Malay individual or local community in a particular situation. That need not be so. No man is an island. The action which he takes, the treatment which his community accords to him, the reasons which he gives, and the aspirations which motivate him reflect the society in which he lives. It is evidence of values and norms as much as an individual episode.

In selecting and presenting this contemporary material relating to late nineteenth-century Malaya the modern writer is just as much likely to err as the observer or writer on whom he draws. Thirty years ago the leading historian of South-East Asia wrote that 'the completely objective history has never been produced, nor are one man's knowledge and judgment adequate for a fully satisfactory treatment of so vast a subject as the present one'.[38] This study is on a very modest and restricted scale, but in so far as it assembles material from many sources, the author subscribes with respect to Hall's verdict. It is unavoidable that one should bring to the task the intellectual baggage, in the way of theories or assumptions or values, with which one travels. Given the same source material different writers would produce very different studies and conclusions.

What must remain paramount are the facts—in so far as one can determine what they were. If one brings to the facts a theory as an hypothesis to be confirmed or rejected by that test, it may help one to understand the subject-matter and perceive the underlying relationships. Functional anthropology has always seemed to the author a possible line of approach to understanding rather than a preconceived theory of what is significant in any society or culture. No doubt it can be usefully supplemented, especially in an essay in historical reconstruction, by other methods, some of which have been touched on earlier in this chapter. The wrong use of a theory is to assume that by reference to it one may determine, in advance of an examination of the facts, what is the nature and structure of a culture or society. With such preconceptions, selected facts, if considered in detail at all, are automatically slotted into place to support the theory. It is hoped that this methodological error has been avoided in the present work. If what is written here leads others to work over the material and offer better conclusions, it will have served a useful purpose.

It does not seem necessary or useful to attempt a definition of what is meant by 'Malay society' and in consequence what should be included or omitted from this study. The central theme is how the Malays of the Peninsula lived in the latter part of the nineteenth century. The study has to be limited to a reasonable length and also kept in balance. There are elements of Malay culture which have been studied in depth by other writers and which would need a monograph to themselves if fully analysed here. Such topics as Malay law and the legal digests, the many aspects of Islamic doctrine and rules of conduct in Malay society, and the elaborate magical rituals of the *pawang* find their place in one or other of the chapters which follow but are treated as marginal, not principal, themes. It may occur to the reader that there was already a large Chinese population in the SS and FMS. Yet it is surprising how little their presence seems to have affected Malay life and attitudes in this period. It would be an anachronism to let Sino-Malay relations cast a shadow on Malay society of the nineteenth century. At this time the Malays seem to have perceived the Chinese merely as aliens, despised like other foreigners, who could be left to their own devices.

It is clear from some of Clifford's stories that in Pahang Malay relations with the aborigine peoples of the jungle were a significant element in village life. Malay villagers traded with them, sometimes intermarried with them, and sometimes organized slave raids against them.[39] This situation does not appear to have had as much importance anywhere else but in inland Pahang. The *adat perpatih* of Negeri Sembilan and Naning is another essentially local culture trait. As such they are not appropriate in a general study of this kind.

The policies of the colonial regime were not the only external influence on Malay society but they were often a powerful factor in particular fields such as land tenure or education. It is the influence which they exerted and the effect which they produced on the Malay way of life, not the policies themselves with all their reasons and details, which find a place here.

36. Khoo Kay Kim, *The Western Malay States 1850–1873: The Effects of Commercial Development on Malay Politics*, Kuala Lumpur, Oxford University Press, 1972, p. 2

37. Ibid., p. 1. These comments relate of course to the situation in Perak, Selangor and Sungei Ujong only.

38. A. C. Milner, *Kerajaan: Malay Political Culture on the Eve of Colonial Rule*, Tucson, University of Arizona Press, 1982, p. 9.

39. *AR Perak 1890*; N. Annandale and H. C. Robinson, *Fasciculi Malayenses: Anthropological and Zoological Results of an Expedition to Perak and the Siamese Malay States 1901–1902, Anthropology—Part 1*, London, University Press of Liverpool, 1903, pp. 68–9, to the same effect.

5. *AR Pahang 1889*.

6. J. F. A. McNair, *Perak and the Malays: Sarong and Keris*, London, Tinsley Bros., 1878, reprinted Kuala Lumpur, Oxford University Press, 1972, p. 202, and also p. 131 on the aloofness of the Bugis, who were 'very distinct' from neighbouring settlements.

7. The earliest comprehensive population figures for 'British Malaya' are those of the 1911 census, which reported a Malay population (including 'Other Malaysians', i.e. Indonesians) by areas as follows:

Area	*1911 Malay Population*	*1901 Population*
Straits Settlements	232,595	212,85[illegible]
Federated Malay States	425,707	316,07[illegible]
Johor	110,047	n.a.
Kelantan and Terengganu	414,233	n.a.
Kedah and Perlis	227,300	n.a.
	1,409,882	

Source: M. V. del Tufo, *Malaya: A Report on the 1947 Census of Population*, London, Crown Agents, 1949, Appendix C, 'Former Population Counts', pp. 584–8.

A comparison of the SS and FMS figures for 'Other Malaysians' in 1901 and 1911 shows that in the FMS there was substantial Indonesian immigration in the first decade of the twentieth century—it increased from 27,288 in 1901 to 80,362 in 1911 for the FMS as a whole. It is known that there was a similar influx into Johor at that time. The estimate of 1¼ million for Malaya around 1900 is obtained by working back from the 1911 census figures and making a rough allowance for Malay population in southern Siam. It is merely a global figure for the purpose of a breakdown of estimated population by areas.

8. H. C. Clifford, 'Report: Expedition to Trengganu and Kelantan', *JMBRAS*, 34(1), 1961, p. 92, originally printed in 1895. His lecture, 'A Journey through the Malay States of Trengganu and Kelantan', *The Geographical Journal*, 9(1), 18[illegible], is a slightly shortened version but with some interesting extra introductory material. Shaharil Talib, *After Its Own Image: The Trengganu Experience 1881–1941*, Singapore, Oxford University Press, 1984, is a valuable study of the political and economic situation (hereafter cited as *The Trengganu Experience*); one chapter was previously published as 'The Trengganu Ruling Class in the Late Nineteenth Century', *JMBRAS*, 50(2), 1977; also Heather Sutherland, 'The Taming of the Trengganu Elite', in Ruth T. McVey (ed.), *Southeast Asian Transitions: Approaches through Social History*, New Haven and London, Yale University Press, 1978; M. C. ff. Sheppard, 'A Short History of Trengganu', *JMBRAS*, 22(3), 1949; J. de V. Allen, 'The Ancien Regime in Trengganu 1909–1919', *JMBRAS*, 41(1), 1968.

9. A. L. Keyser, *People and Places: A Life in Five Continents*, London, Murray, 1922, p. 104; J. Low, 'Observations on Perak', *JIA*, 4, 1850, pp. 497–504.

10. SSD 10 February 1868. See p. 55 below for details.

11. F. Caddy, *To Siam and Malaya in the Duke of Sutherland's Yacht 'Sans Peur'*, London, Hurst and Blackett, 1889, p. 235.

12. In 1866 Sultan Abu Bakar applied to the Colonial Office for presentation at court in London (CO 273/15, p. 220). In 1893 he visited Cairo and Carlsbad, both fashionable resorts of European high society (SSD 20 February 1893: CO 273/192, p. 21). In 1868 he sent a present of cigars to the Prince of Wales (CO 273/[illegible], p.

3–9). The award of the GCMG and KCSI had a 'great effect upon the Malays' (SSD 2[illegible] January 1882). In 1894 he offered Johor decorations to 'certain high personages and court officials' at Constantinople and Vienna who had received him in 1893 (CO 273/201, p. 6). In addition to the Duke of Sutherland, he entertained both the Duke of Edinburgh in 1869 and Prince Henry of Prussia in 1880 (SSD 16 December 1869 and 16 July 1880).

13. Clifford, 'Expedition', pp. 116–17; Hugh Clifford, *Studies in Brown Humanity being Scrawls and Smudges in Sepia, White and Yellow*, London, Grant Richards, 1898, p. 24. See also p. 283 below.

14. Henry Norman, *The Peoples and Politics of the Far East: Travels and Studies in the British . . . Colonies and Malaya*, New York, Scribner, 1895, p. 583.

15. SSD 15 April 1889. See p. 33 below.

16. Isabella L. Bird, *The Golden Chersonese and the Way Thither*, London, Murray, 1883, reprinted Kuala Lumpur, Oxford University Press, 1967 and 1980; J. M. Gullick, 'Isabella Bird's Visit to Malaya: A Centenary Tribute', *JMBRAS*, 52(2), 1979, describes how she constructed her narrative from letters written to her sister from Malaya. The original letters are held by her publisher, John Murray.

17. Datuk Mahmud bin Mat, CMG, OBE, 'The Passing of Slavery in East Pahang', *MHJ*, 1(1), 1954, p. 10. See p. 214 below for a further extract.

18. The largest single record of evidence given by Malay deponents, much of it of great value, was compiled by the Perak Commission of Enquiry (PCE) which investigated the events in Perak leading to the death of J. W. W. Birch in November 1875 and by the court which subsequently tried the Datuk Maharaja Lela and his associates on charges of killing Birch. The PCE records (SSD 14 December 1876) fill three bulky volumes at PRO (CO 273/86–88). The record of the trial was enclosed (SSD 11 January 1877). Another substantial document of this type is the record of the Kuala Langat piracy trial of February 1874 (enclosed with SSD 24 February 1874: printed in Cmd. 1111).

19. Muhammad Hassan bin Dato' Kerani Muhammad Arshad, *Al-Tarikh Salasilah Negeri Kedah*, published in *Rumi* in Kuala Lumpur, Dewan Bahasa dan Pustaka, 1968, previously published in *Jawi*, 1926; Wan Mohamed Amin bin Said, *Pesaka Selangor*, edited by Abdul Samad Ahmad, Kuala Lumpur, Dewan Bahasa dan Pustaka, 1966; *Hikayat Pahang*, author unknown, is an important source quoted extensively in translation by W. Linehan, 'A History of Pahang' (hereafter cited as 'Pahang'), *JMBRAS*, 14(2), 1936. See also Milner, *Kerajaan*, p. 37, for a discussion of the authorship of this history which is the basis of some chapters of Milner's book.

Wan Mohamed Amin was at the siege of Klang in 1870 and includes reminiscences of this and later stages of his career in his book. He was *penghulu istiadat* in the household of Sultan Sulaiman of Selangor (r.1898–1938) and much concerned with the royal installation ceremonies of 1903.

20. F. A. Swettenham, *The Real Malay: Pen Pictures*, London, John Lane Bodley Head, 1900, p. 7. Swettenham's general point is supported by the practice of SS governors in the late 1870s of consulting a select panel of experts on the Malay states whenever some question arose which required background knowledge. If available, the panel seems to have comprised A. Anson (Lieutenant-Governor, Penang), Thomas Braddell (Attorney-General), J. F. A. McNair (Colonial Engineer), C. J. Irving (Auditor-General), and of course Swettenham himself, who became Assistant Colonial Secretary, Native States, between 1876 and 1882. The other leading

experts, who were away in Perak at this time, were Hugh Low and W. E. Maxwell. J. G. Davidson, a Singapore lawyer who acted as Resident of Selangor and then of Perak (1875–7) for a time, had extensive knowledge of Selangor owing to his business interests from at least 1872 onwards.

21. T. J. Newbold, *Political and Statistical Account of the British Settlements ... with a History of the Malayan States on the Peninsula in the Straits of Malacca*, 2 vols., London, Murray, 1839, reprinted with the title *British Settlements in the Straits of Malacca*, Kuala Lumpur, Oxford University Press, 1971; P. J. Begbie, *The Malayan Peninsula Embracing the History, Manners and Customs of the Inhabitants, Politics, Natural History etc. from Its Earliest Records*, Madras, Vespery Mission Press, 1834, reprinted as *The Malayan Peninsula*, Kuala Lumpur, Oxford University Press, 1967. Also relevant are G. W. Earl, *The Eastern Seas—Or Voyages and Adventures in the Indian Archipelago in 1832–33–34 ... Commercial Resources of the Archipelago*, London, W. H. Allen & Co., 1837, reprinted as *The Eastern Seas*, Singapore and Kuala Lumpur, Oxford University Press, 1971; J. Cameron, *Our Tropical Possessions in Malayan India: Being a Descriptive Account of Singapore, Penang, Province Wellesley, and Malacca, their Peoples, Products, Commerce and Government*, London, Smith Elder & Co., 1865, reprinted as *Our Tropical Possessions in Malayan India*, Kuala Lumpur, Oxford University Press, 1965; J. T. Thomson, *Some Glimpses into Life in the Far East*, London, Richardson, 1864, reprinted as *Glimpses into Life in Malayan Lands*, Singapore, Oxford University Press, 1984; J. Low, *A Dissertation on the Soil and Agriculture of the British Settlement of Penang or Prince of Wales Island in the Straits of Malacca Including Province Wellesley on the Malayan Peninsula ..., with ... Incidental Observations, etc.*, Singapore, 1836, reprinted as *The British Settlement at Penang*, Singapore, Oxford University Press, 1972. This is not an exhaustive list.

22. W. E. Maxwell, 'A Journey on Foot to the Patani Frontier in 1876 being a Journal Kept during an Expedition Undertaken to Capture Datoh Maharajah Lela of Perak', *JSBRAS*, 9, 1882; he also contributed some shorter travel notes to other issues. F. A. Swettenham, 'From Perak to Slim and Down the Slim and Bernam Rivers', *JSBRAS*, 5, 1880; and 'Journal Kept during a Journey across the Malay Peninsula', *JSBRAS*, 15, 1885. Various other contributors provided other travel notes of varying interest. In time, however, the material published in the journal became predominantly articles and notes rather than accounts of journeys.

23. W. W. Skeat and F. F. Laidlaw, 'The Cambridge University Expedition to Parts of the Malay Peninsula 1899–1900: Personal Accounts', *JMBRAS*, 26(4), 1953.

24. J. W. W. Birch, *The Journals of J. W. W. Birch First British Resident to Perak 1874–1875* (hereafter cited as *Birch Journal*), edited by P. L. Burns, Kuala Lumpur, Oxford University Press, 1976. The extant volumes of the private diary (probably written to record material for use in his official journal) of W. Bloomfield Douglas cover most of the years 1876–82 in which he was Resident of Selangor. Extracts have been published in J. M. Gullick, 'Selangor 1876–1882—The Bloomfield Douglas Diary', *JMBRAS*, 48(2), 1975. On J. W. W. Birch in Perak see R. O. Winstedt and R. J. Wilkinson, 'A History of Perak', *JMBRAS*, 12(1), 1934, pp. 102–14, and F. A. Swettenham, *Malay Sketches*, London, John Lane Bodley Head, 1895, pp. 227–47. A xerox copy of the complete Bloomfield Douglas Diary is now held at Rhodes House Library, Oxford.

25. F. A. Swettenham, *Sir Frank Swettenham's Malayan Journals 1874–1876* (cited hereafter as *Swettenham Journal*), edited by P. L. Burns and C. D. Cowan,

Kuala Lumpur, Oxford University Press, 1975. This edition of Swettenham's Journals of 1874–6 comprises all the extant material. It does incidentally reprint, with a revised editorial commentary, the text of material previously published in 'Sir Frank Swettenham's Perak Journals 1874–1876', edited by C. D. Cowan, *JMBRAS*, 24(4), 1951. Citations from *Swettenham Journal* throughout this book are from the 1975 edition. See also Hugh Low, 'The Journal of Sir Hugh Low, Perak 1877' (hereafter cited as 'Low Journal'), edited by E. Sadka, *JMBRAS*, 27(4), 1954.

26. Two reports by Clifford on Pahang were enclosed with SSD 28 April and 3 August 1887; see also Clifford, 'Expedition'.

27. A printed copy of Bozzolo's lengthy report was enclosed with SSD 31 January 1889.

28. Bound volumes of the published Perak and Selangor gazettes are series CO 467 and 469 respectively at PRO. As the research did not extend to Malaysia itself, the author has been unable to consult the Selangor Secretariat and other like records now held at the Arkib Negara. The author did, however, work on the Selangor records of 1875–86 in 1950 and has been able to draw on them indirectly through E. Sadka, *The Protected Malay States 1874–1895*, Kuala Lumpur and Singapore, University of Malaya Press, 1968, and Rex Stevenson, *Cultivators and Administrators: British Educational Policy towards the Malays 1875–1906*, Kuala Lumpur, Oxford University Press, 1975. Both authors cite extensively from material on the files.

Another valuable series of periodic reports came from the British Advisers in Kedah and Perlis and the British Agent in Terengganu from 1909 onwards. Copies of monthly reports, minutes of state council meetings and the like were sent to London under cover of SSD of various dates from late 1909 onwards and are enclosed in the CO 273 series at PRO.

29. Emily Innes, *The Chersonese with the Gilding Off*, 2 vols., London, Richard Bentley and Son, 1885, reprinted (in one vol.) Kuala Lumpur, Oxford University Press, 1974; William T. Hornaday, *Two Years in the Jungle: The Experiences of a Hunter and Naturalist in India, Ceylon, the Malay Peninsula and Borneo*, New York, Scribner, 1885; Ambrose B. Rathborne, *Camping and Tramping in Malaya: Fifteen Years' Pioneering in the Native States of the Malay Peninsula*, London, Swan Sonnenschein, 1898; reprinted Singapore, Oxford University Press, 1984; F. A. Swettenham, *About Perak*, Singapore, Straits Times, 1890; J. H. M. Robson, *People in a Native State*, Singapore, Singapore Free Press, 1894.

30. Their numerous works are listed in the bibliography. Some of Clifford's later books are essentially reprints of material which had appeared earlier in books or magazines. Selections from both have been edited by W. R. Roff, and published in Kuala Lumpur by Oxford University Press, as *Stories by Sir Hugh Clifford*, 1966, and *Stories and Sketches by Sir Frank Swettenham*, 1967.

31. The relevant annual reports of Residents, district officers, and heads of departments are cited individually in later chapters. Until the state governments began to publish their own official gazettes from around 1890, the more important annual reports were published in the *SS Gazette*. See also P. H. Kratoska (ed.), *Honourable Intentions—Talks on the British Empire Delivered at the Royal Colonial Institute 1874–1928*, Singapore, Oxford University Press, 1983, for a verbatim record (reprinted from the *Proceedings of the Royal Colonial Institute*) of the talks and the ensuing discussion at each meeting.

32. The bibliography lists all of W. E. Maxwell's literary output except some minor essays in *JSBRAS*—see *JMBRAS*, 36(4), 1970, pp. 84–5 for a complete list. His

two outstanding essays are 'The Law and Customs of the Malays with Reference to the Tenure of Land', *JSBRAS*, 13, 1884, and 'The Law Relating to Slavery among the Malays', *JSBRAS*, 22, 1890. He wrote some important official reports including *Memorandum on the Introduction of a Land Code in the Native States in the Malay Peninsula*, Singapore, Government Printer, 1894, which assembles the memoranda of his critics (on land questions) as well as his covering memorandum. *The Selangor Gazette* (1890–2) includes several major reports written while Maxwell was British Resident there.

33. W. W. Skeat, *Malay Magic: Being an Introduction to the Folklore and Popular Religion of the Malay Peninsula*, London, Macmillan, 1900; reprinted Singapore, Oxford University Press, 1984. His other notable contribution to Malay ethnography is his account, written jointly with F. F. Laidlaw, of the expedition to the north east in 1899–1900 (cited in note 23). He also wrote works on the aboriginal people of Malaya. Individual essays in the *Papers on Malay Subjects* series are cited in notes to later chapters as appropriate. A large selection of *PMS* was reprinted as *Papers on Malay Subjects Selected and Introduced by P. L. Burns*, Kuala Lumpur, Oxford University Press, 1971. Two of Wilkinson's own contributions are reprinted in *JMBRAS*, 30(4), 1957—'The Incidents of Malay Life' and 'Malay Beliefs'. In notes to later chapters of this study, citations refer to pages of these reprints. There is a list of the prodigious output of R. O. Winstedt in J. Bastin and R. Roolvink (eds.), *Malayan and Indonesian Studies: Essays Presented to Sir Richard Winstedt on His Eighty-fifth Birthday*, London, Oxford University Press, 1964. 'Report by Mr. R. O. Winstedt . . . on Vernacular and Industrial Education in the Netherlands East Indies and the Philippines', *Proceedings of the Legislative Council, Straits Settlements*, Paper No. 22 of 1917, is his major contribution to the policy on Malay education, on which he had had some influence in earlier years as an associate of R. J. Wilkinson. The greater part of Wilkinson's work was published either in *JSBRAS/JMBRAS* (and is listed in *JMBRAS*, 36(4), 1970, pp. 151–2) or as essays in the *PMS* series. He is perhaps best remembered for his dictionary—R. J. Wilkinson, *A Malay–English Dictionary*, 2 parts, Singapore, Kelly & Walsh, 1901 (revised as *A Malay–English Dictionary (Romanised)*, 2 parts, Mytilene, Salavopoulos & Kinderlis, 1932). His official writing includes 'The Education of Asiatics', *Special Reports on Educational Subjects*, Cmd. 835, Vol. 8, 1902.

34. J. D. Gimlette, *Malay Poisons and Charm Cures*, London, Churchill, 1915 (3rd ed. 1929), reprinted Kuala Lumpur, Oxford University Press, 1971, and Singapore, Oxford University Press, 1985. See also J. D. Gimlette and H. W. Thomson, *A Dictionary of Malayan Medicine*, London, Oxford University Press, 1939; reprinted Kuala Lumpur, Oxford University Press, 1971, and 1983.

35. *Swettenham Journal*, pp. 167 and 169.

36. F. A. Swettenham, *British Malaya: An Account of the Origin and Progress of British Influence in Malaya*, London, John Lane Bodley Head, 1907 (revised edition London, Allen & Unwin, 1948), p. 191 (revised edition). Raja Mahmud's career is described in Chapter 4.

37. Swettenham, *The Real Malay*, p. 261. A few pages later Swettenham faces the underlying question of European understanding of Malay character—'It is often said that a European cannot understand the character of an Eastern, or follow the curious workings of his brain' (p. 265). He goes on to argue that 'if you make yourself familiar with the language . . . then the reading of their character is no longer an impossible task'. J. de V. Allen, 'Two Imperialists: A Study of Sir Frank Swettenham

and Sir Hugh Clifford', *JMBRAS*, 37(1), 1964, studies in depth the views of the two men on Malay character and society, making full use of their lectures to the Royal Colonial Institute which are reprinted in Kratoska, op. cit.

On W. E. Maxwell and Malay land tenure see note 32. Swettenham (*AR Perak 1890*) had publicly contradicted him, saying that 'there was not in the pre-Residential period any system of payment by tenths'. W. E. Maxwell himself had to concede that 'the exaction of a tithe is by no means a universal tax in the Malay States' (*Memorandum on the Land Code*, p. 98). In fact it was nowhere collected except in the Krian district of Perak where there were particular historical reasons and the land had only come under cultivation in recent years.

38. D. G. E. Hall, *A History of South-East Asia*, London, Macmillan, 1955, preface to first edition and reprinted in fourth edition, 1981, p. xxix. This began a long debate, much of it in early issues of *JSEAH*, on 'Europe-centric' history and the desirability of 'studying Malaya from within, looking outwards' (K. G. Tregonning (ed.), *Papers on Malayan History*, Singapore, University of Malaya, 1962, preface). That is not quite the issue raised in this chapter, i.e. looking at Malay culture from a European standpoint, but it is close to it.

39. H. C. Clifford, *In Court and Kampong, Being Tales and Sketches of Native Life in the Malay Peninsula*, London, Grant Richards, 1897, pp. 97–110 (2nd ed. with autobiographical preface, London, Richards Press, 1927); *Studies in Brown Humanity*, pp. 1–21, 243–64; *In a Corner of Asia being Tales and Impressions of Men and Things in the Malay Peninsula*, London, Fisher Unwin, 1899, pp. 65–96; and *The Further Side of Silence*, New York, Doubleday, Page & Co., 1927, pp. 3–39, 77–102, 166–86, 215–71, are some of Clifford's stories on various aspects of Malay relations with aborigines in Ulu Pahang. (Some of the stories appear in more than one collection.)

2
The Ruler in Public Life

THE number of nineteenth-century Malay rulers about whom anything significant is known is very small. Many reigned only for a few years and for that or other reasons little is recorded about them. It was, moreover, the Malay convention that in public the ruler should be an impersonal symbol. Hence 'the sultans and rulers remain colourless and shadowy—history lacks a personality base'.[1]

This chapter and the next therefore deal with a mere handful of rulers whose eccentricity or close contact with European observers make them the exception, i.e. their circumstances and personalities are well documented in contemporary records. The justification for giving so much prominence to them is that they played a leading part in their communities. By virtue of their office, they were men of influence whose precept and example had a widespread effect especially on the upper class of Malay society which came into close contact with them, and related their own status to ties of kinship with the royal dynasty or the holding of court office. The rulers were also more exposed than most of their subjects to external influences. They received foreign visitors and if they adopted alien habits, as they sometimes did, it was a powerful recommendation to others to do likewise.

The main theme of this study is social, not political, history. Yet the essential role of a ruler was political even if it had atrophied before colonial rule deprived it of what might have remained of real power. Under the new regime the ruler continued to be a public figure. Hence this chapter begins with the public life of a ruler in the pre-colonial period before coming later to his activities under the new regime. The new alien rulers still treated him as titular head of state and accorded him a position of honoured impotence in the public life of his community. The ruler himself reacted to the new situation in which he found himself.

In the pre-colonial period a few rulers dominated their states and actively governed their subjects. One such case is Sultan Ahmad of Pahang of whom Clifford wrote that no man in his state 'dared think above a whisper without his leave'.[2] Behind a mask of languid courtesy, Ahmad governed by methods which Clifford observed with fascinated horror. In contrast to this autocratic regime, other rulers, such as Sultan Abdul Samad of Selangor, resigned all power to turbulent chiefs, saying 'they are both young men and should fight it out'.[3] Whether or not they attempted to govern, all rulers had public duties to perform, since they were, in every state, symbols of dignity and authority from whom lesser potentates derived formal recognition of their own status. Convention required that the most turbulent of chiefs should preserve the appearance of acting under royal command and should pay formal respect to the ruler in public.[4]

The essential point of contact between a ruler and his subjects was his hall of audience (*balai*). This was a wing or, more often, a separate structure erected in front of or somewhere alongside the ruler's residence (*istana*). Although there were many differences of detail, every *balai* exhibited two essential features in its construction. First, it had open sides, except on the side where it adjoined the *istana*, and it often had a raised floor. By this means a large assembly of people outside could view the proceedings within and perhaps hear what was said. The *balai* was a stage for the performance of public and ceremonial acts.

Secondly, the floor of the *balai* did not continue at one level but rose in steps. The ruler was seated at the highest level and other dignitaries took their place at the level appropriate to their status. Distinctions of rank were of much importance and relative height was a symbolic means of expressing status in visible form. As an example, when J. R. Logan visited Kedah in 1850, he and the ruler sat on chairs placed on the dais at the highest level; the ruler's four adolescent sons 'decked out for the occasion with gold chains, cloth of silk and gold etc. were placed on the carpet beside us, while Wan Mat and some other *mentris* occupied the lower floor'.[5] Yet this was a quite informal occasion by Malay court standards; the ruler was away from his state capital and Logan, a friend and former legal adviser, was on a private visit.

The significance of these seating arrangements is clear from Henry Norman's account of his reception in the *balai* at Kota Bharu in Kelantan. When Norman entered the hall the ruler 'was already seated upon a deer-skin on a raised platform, surrounded by his ministers and a dozen heavily-armed men. Behind him stood officials bearing his golden *keris* and other insignia of royalty . . . he had intended that I should take a seat upon the bare floor in front of him by which arrangement my head would have been just at the height of his feet.' Norman, however, came prepared to frustrate what he deemed an unseemly arrangement; his servant followed him with a camp-stool upon which Norman took his seat.[6]

It can be seen that in the Kelantan encounter, unlike that in Kedah at a much earlier date, the ruler did not sit on a chair. A ruler might without loss of dignity sit cross-legged provided that the floor on which he sat was at an appropriate level. However, the Malays had long been acquainted with the use of chairs—the Malay word '*kerusi*' is of Arabic origin—and James Low, visiting Perak in 1826, notes that 'a sopha and chairs were placed' on the ruler's dais in the *balai*, though this may perhaps have been done to accommodate him as he sat with the ruler.[7] The Kelantan ruler seems to have been ultra-conservative in his seating arrangements.

If a Malay ruler did seat himself on a chair in some informal encounter he used it as a means of emphasizing his superior status. For example, when Syed Hamid, chief of the Tampin district (Negeri Sembilan), met that very Europeanized ruler, Sultan Abu Bakar of Johor, the latter was already seated on a chair—probably in an ordinary room with a single-level floor. Abu Bakar did not offer Syed Hamid a chair and Syed Hamid declined to squat on the floor with the Maharaja's entourage. He remained standing 'till at last the Maharaja who evidently expected him to squat down with the others, felt obliged to get another chair for him'.[8]

There could also be difficulties when a ruler had dealings with a European official or other visitors in a room furnished with a table and chairs. As a normal rule a Malay chief did not presume to sit at the same table, and therefore at the same level, as his ruler. On one such occasion in 1872, C. J. Irving called on the powerful chief of Larut, usually known by his Perak state title as 'the Mantri', and they sat down together at a table. Irving relates that the Raja Muda (later Sultan) Abdullah entered and 'he came down and sat by me at the top of the table, the Tunku Mantri getting up and taking his seat in a chair by the wall'.[9]

There was a well-recognized etiquette, quite apart from seating arrangements, for proceedings in the *balai*. The ruler propounced a question and invited the views of his chiefs and other officers of state. The latter in turn gave their replies with due deference—'Pardon, my lord, a thousand pardons . . .'—but eventually gave their advice taking into account what the ruler appeared to expect. To argue with the ruler to his face or even to put forward proposals which he was unlikely to accept was contrary to convention. The ruler closed the discussion by stating his decision that it was proper (*patut*) to adopt a certain course and the assembled magnates formally concurred—'baik, Tuanku'.[10] Clearly this was not a debate but an act of public consensus (*kebulatan*) to which Malay constitutional convention attached the utmost importance. One might compare it with the final act of legislation in English parliamentary procedure, when spokesmen for the absent monarch announce to the Upper House that royal assent has been given to a Bill, which thereby becomes an Act of Parliament.

Yet few rulers were absolute autocrats who could simply impose a royal decision on powerful chiefs without any real consultation. Even Sultan Ahmad of Pahang, whose domination so impressed Clifford, found it expedient to make soundings before taking a decision; Ahmad told a visiting governor in 1875 that 'he must ask the opinion of the Chiefs of the Ulu'.[11] This stage of actual consultation and exchange of views took place in private and was conducted without the formality of its subsequent ratification in the *balai*.[12]

In this respect also, the appearance of the first British officials at Malay courts with awkward innovations to propose, gave rise to difficulties of procedure. Convention required that when a foreign envoy arrived the ruler should transact business with him in the *balai*. But such business was not of a traditional nature and so the royal decision did not have to be promulgated in the *balai*. Hence the order of events was reversed. The visitor was received in the *balai* and 'a few preliminary observations' of a non-committal nature were exchanged. The ruler then invited the visitor to withdraw with him into the *istana*, ostensibly to partake of refreshments—and the real talking began.[13]

Any departure from the strict formality of proceedings in the *balai* was a gross breach of decorum. The assembled crowd of onlookers took their places 'in total silence . . . not a soul speaks but in a whisper, even during the temporary absence of their Sultan or Raja; there is no bustling or pushing, but everybody seems contented with the position he may have taken up, although it may be some distance off'.[14] If the ruler himself chose to breach the convention it was a mark of his displeasure, in the oblique fashion which Malay convention required. James Low witnessed such an occasion in 1826, when the ruler of Perak conferred titles of honour on chiefs who had intrigued against him during the recent Siamese intervention in Perak. 'The new ministers and other officers then approached and had the oath tendered to them. This oath consists in two parts and is very short. The first part is the promise of fidelity, the second imprecates every calamity to afflict the juror and his family to remote generations should he betray the trust and confidence reposed in him ... the Raja and some of the chiefs indulged their mirth occasionally to the evident mortification of some of his chiefs then present whose gravity was ludicrously contrasted with it. Several of those who had intrigued with the Siamese betrayed evident symptoms of alarm. Indeed, under a less indulgent prince, they might have lost their heads.'[15]

In this episode one has an example of a general proposition, i.e. that the conventions enjoined by tradition are not unbreakable but their breach can be made to bear its own significance.

The state councils established in Selangor and Perak in 1877, and later in other states by the colonial regime, were an innovation in outward form and procedure. Yet they were—unknowingly perhaps—built upon foundations of Malay practice of informal consultation between a ruler and his court officers and chiefs. In the generation before Kedah established its state council in 1905, a previous ruler, Sultan Ahmad Tajuddin, had a circle of officers to whom he turned for advice. When the first British Agent reached Kuala Terengganu in 1909, he found that the ruler had an informally constituted state council of about a dozen members and summoned on each occasion those of its members with whom he wished to consult. In the West Coast states also, there was a group of confidants available if the ruler felt the need for advice. The new state councils of the colonial regime combined the practice of confidential consultation between ruler and chiefs with a European type of procedure. The ruler sat at the head of the table with the Resident at his right hand and the members ranged down the table. Proposals were made and minutes were kept. In this respect it borrowed something of the formal atmosphere of the *balai*. Wilkinson makes this point clear with an anecdote of a Malay member of the Perak State Council who was invited to open the discussion of an item of business without knowing, as he would have done if it had been the final act of state in the *balai*, what view the ruler took. He rose and spoke at length with eloquence which earned him a round of applause when at last he sat down. Wilkinson continues: '"An excellent speech", said the Sultan, when the applause had subsided. "But what did he say?" enquired the bewildered Resident. "Oh, he did not say anything at all, but the way he said it was magnificent!"' In the end Malay members of council resolved their problems by treating these occasions as something non-Malay in character. Although the debates were conducted in Malay, the Malay members, from the ruler downwards, attended wearing European clothes.[16] In this way any awkwardness over sitting at the same table with the ruler was also removed. It was simply not an occasion to which Malay etiquette applied.

In the traditional working procedure of Malay government, letters and other written documents were an essential part of the system. When a ruler received a letter from another Malay ruler or from a foreign power such as the King of Siam or the Governor in Singapore, the letter was carried with pomp and ceremony through the capital and then read aloud in the *balai*. The outward form of such a letter, especially if it were written in Malay as it usually was, received the closest scrutiny. The opening compliments (*terasul*), the colour of the paper on which it was written, and the calligraphy 'must reflect the respective status of sender and recipient'.[17] Sultan Zainal Abidin III of Terengganu, who was particularly insistent that he ranked above all other Malay rulers, addressed the ruler of Kelantan, whom he considered junior to him, as '*paduka anakanda*' and sent his letters to him in envelopes of white calico. He expected that the replies should address him as '*paduka ayahanda*' and be enclosed in an envelope of yellow silk.[18]

The sender might well be unable to sign his name but he signified his authority for the issue of the letter by instructing his clerk to affix his seal.[19] If he had a personal as well as a state seal it was essential that the latter should be affixed to an official missive. If the wrong seal were used, it cast doubt on the authenticity of the letter.[20] The extreme attention given to matters of form was in marked contrast to the indifference of the sender to the content of his letters. The normal procedure was to instruct a confidential clerk to prepare the letter. When the letter was ready it might be read aloud for approval but in some cases the clerk merely sealed it and handed it to the messenger or recipient.[21] If the clerk misrepresented the ruler's intentions, or if he breached his confidence by unauthorized disclosure of the contents, he risked suffering a drastic punishment.[22] Yet the more probable error lay in slovenly or imprecise wording due to the scribe's disinterest or failure to understand the instructions given to him. For example, Ahmad of

Pahang, who was illiterate, issued large mining concessions in the 1880s in 'very indefinite terms'.[23] A generation of modern historians has puzzled over the real intention of the letter which Abdul Samad of Selangor gave to his son-in-law, Tunku Kudin of Kedah, in June 1868, by which the latter obtained British recognition as 'Viceroy' of all Selangor.[24] In these matters one may discern the Malay concern with status and formality and the disinterest of Malay rulers and chiefs, even if they were literate, in paperwork. It was simply not a task for a gentleman.

Except in Johor and Kedah, states where some of the staff were recruited from the ranks of the clerical service of the SS government, there was apparently no systematic preservation of records.[25] Much, however, depended on the individual ruler or chief. One of the leading chiefs in Pahang seems to have kept a considerable collection of state papers.[26] The clerk to the ruler of that state kept copies of the concessions which had been issued—presumably so that the terms on revenue collection might be enforced. In an earlier period, the exiled ruler of Kedah apologized to Newbold for his inability to produce his state papers since they had been lost in the flight from the Siamese in 1821.[27] The Malay *hikayat* written early in this century cite dates of public events of the last century which suggests that there may have been some record in the form of a state calendar.

Public business in the *balai* occupied only a small part of the ruler's day. There were individual rulers whose pleasure was the hunting of big game, or the active encouragement of Malay agriculture or industry.[28] Zainal Abidin III of Terengganu spent his time in 'book-reading, eating sweetmeats and attending to his womenfolk'.[29] He, and some other rulers too, was notably pious, spending much of the day in prayer and coming forth to attend Friday prayers at the town mosque. James Low mentions that the ruler of Perak in 1826 came regularly to pray with the local congregation.[30]

Apart from Friday prayers at the mosque it was customary for his subjects to pay their respects to a ruler on the occasion of the major festivals (*hari raya*) of the Muslim calendar.[31] The public ceremonies of the reign—the installation or funeral of a ruler, a royal marriage, or even the reception of a foreign ruler or envoy—might include an Islamic element, but essentially they were public rather than religious occasions. A modern writer has commented that apart from 'the Muslim justification of rule by Sultans, the use of Muslim prayers in some rituals at the court and the ruler's obserance of Muslim practices in his private life Islam was not a pillar of royal authority'.[32]

British control of external relations deprived the Malay ruler of another important ceremonial function, i.e. the public reception of foreign envoys or of letters from foreign powers. Such occasions could be major events. In 1909 suzerainty over Kedah was transferred from Siam to Britain without reference to the ruler of Kedah. He made the best of an embarrassing situation by according to the official communication of the decision all the traditional pomp of former days. 'The letters were placed in a golden tray and a procession was formed. The royal drum beaters led the way followed by a court official carrying the golden tray which was shadowed by a large yellow umbrella. . . .' This display reflected the personal tastes of the rather extravagant ruler and had no parallel elsewhere. In the neighbouring state of Perlis the new British Adviser limited the hand-over to counting the cash at the state treasury.[33]

In place of foreign envoys came British governors on tour, who were received with a different style of public ceremony, organized on European lines by resident British officials.[34] The traditional practice of receiving visits by foreign rulers and paying visits to their capitals was made easier by the use of the small steamers which now plied along Malayan coasts. There was a tendency, however, for such occasions to be assimilated in style to the colonial model. As part of the Siamese policy of asserting its doubtful authority over the northern Malay states, King Chulalongkorn, who had himself adopted a very European style of public life, invited the ruler of Kedah to Bangkok and he visited the capitals of Kedah, Kelantan and Terengganu. When he came to Terengganu in 1887, 'the visit lasted two days and the King marked the occasion by bestowing Siamese decorations on the Sultan and the Raja Muda and distributing many gifts of gold embroidered cloth. He also presented the Sultan with a gold-hilted and gold-sheathed sword, and gold ornaments to Tunku Long and the other members of the royal family.'[35]

The exchange of gifts was of course as much part of the traditional as of the European practice but there had been some misunderstandings as to what were appropriate gifts. In 1869 Queen Victoria's presents to the ruler of Terengganu were an oil painting and a silver ink-well, which were later described by a perplexed Raja Muda as 'a picture of an animal and an ink bottle'.[36]

As the royal families of different states sometimes intermarried, a ruler would often be visiting kinsmen when he went abroad. It was, none the less, considered essential that he should make a proper display of his status by the traditional means of bringing a large retinue with him. When Sultan Zainal Abidin III of Terengganu set off for Mecca in 1913, he broke his journey at Singapore, staying with his relative, the ex-ruler of Riau, 'which was a great strain on the latter's resources as there were 150 persons to be fed every day'. This was a larger party than usual. For some reason forty followers seems to have been the generally acceptable minimum. A brief visit to Singapore or to Penang to do business with the British authorities, or merely as a break in a journey, brought the ruler into an unfamiliar, but generally agreeable, environment and must have made him more susceptible to changes of life-style.[37]

In the pre-colonial period it was not common practice, however, for a ruler to visit the outlying districts of his state. When, for example, the ruler of Selangor visited the inland mining town of Kuala Lumpur in 1879, it was said that no ruler had come to the interior in the past hundred years. Again, in 1874, a report notes that Malay rulers 'know nothing whatever of the interior of their countries' and might in consequence be unable to state exactly where the boundaries of the state were situated.[38] The ruler probably remained at his state capital because, if he toured the state he would have to take a large following and household with him to safeguard his dignity and perhaps his personal safety. It would be beyond the resources of the small villages of the interior to accommodate, feed or transport so large a party. It certainly was a major operation when it did occur. In 1889, for example, the ruler of Pahang removed himself from his state capital to Pulau Tawar on the middle reaches of the Pahang River to put himself at a distance from the unwelcome new British regime. He took with him his household which included 300–400 women.[39]

Wherever he might be, the ruler kept possession of his regalia (*kebesaran*), since this was an essential mark of his position as the established ruler. The regalia were exhibited at the installation of a ruler and on other formal occasions. The account of the Perak ruler's conferring titles on chiefs in 1826 has been quoted above. James Low also wrote that 'in front of the sopha on which the Raja sat were arranged the following articles, a low stool on which stood the Koran, and a large jar of consecrated water, on top of which was a model of a crown. The Raja advanced dipping the regalia, consisting of armour in the water, and placed them against a pillow. The ceremony then began.'[40]

The regalia included musical instruments—drums, gongs, trumpets—and receptacles for the ingredients used in making betel quids for chewing. In all classes of society the offer of betel was a mark of friendship and—on the part of a ruler—favour. The musical instruments (*nobat*) were played on ceremonial occasions and in some states there were regular performances by the royal musicians.[41] When Skeat was in Kedah in 1899 he found that the band performed 'once every Friday, as well as on feast days throughout the year . . . every performance of this band had to end before twelve o'clock, because noon itself is a dangerous moment, when mens' [*sic*] shadows are at their shortest, and his hold on life is at its most tenuous'.[42]

Much of the supernatural power which surrounded the person of the ruler was concentrated in his *nobat*. Only members of the royal band might handle or play them and it was believed that sickness or other dire consequences would befall anyone who broke the taboo. Even a practice session, which Skeat attended, was begun with a propitiatory ritual. 'All except the gong were covered with the yellow cloth of Malay royalty; so was the spring carrying-bar shaped to rest on two mens' [*sic*] shoulders, and used for transporting the gong. There was also a curious staff (*tongkat*) of rattan which was supposed to possess great, though ill-defined, miraculous powers. Upon the ground close to the gong lay packets of saffron rice and *lauk*.' When the band had finished its performance a sample of the rice was placed on the drums and on the mouthpiece of each wind instrument. The musicians then relaxed; they consumed the remainder of the food and invited Skeat to join them. They also told him that the instruments should only be taken with the Sultan if he made a state progress and not on a less formal journey—'it would be *lese-majeste* to disturb them for so little; they were the servant greater than the master'.[43] This passage is the more striking because Kedah was a state in which the ruler had adopted much of the European life-style. The musicians of the royal band were chosen from certain families in Kedah which had a hereditary right to these posts. The musicians ranked as members of the ruler's ceremonial entourage and enjoyed appropriate privileges.[44]

Although British officials intended to preserve and enhance the influence of the ruler in whose name they governed the state, the general effect of colonial rule was to disrupt the public and ceremonial life of a Malay ruler. Ceremonial was diminished. To preside at meetings of a state council, seated round a table behind closed doors, was no substitute for the visible majesty of an assembly in the *balai*. There might occasionally be a gathering in the *balai* to confer a title on the successor to a chieftainship or court office but the interplay, formal as it may have been, between ruler and royal court had lost its significance. Even the most impotent of rulers had been the apex, the 'organising principle' of Malay aristocratic life and also the symbol of the state to the general body of his subjects (*rakyat*).[45] It was necessary for the most powerful chiefs to attend upon the ruler, and thus to demonstrate their relative status by participation in the gatherings at the *balai* to promulgate royal decrees (*titah*) or other public acts of formal consensus. If the ruler had exercised real power he and his chiefs had occasion to meet for consultation.[46]

British policy was to concentrate power at the centre, to suit colonial requirements and because administrators perceived this situation as the restoration to the ruler of powers which he had lost in the recent past.[47] As a result the ruler was now left suspended in a vacuum without any real contact with the chiefs—except in the alien ambience of the state council chamber. The ruler was thus deprived of the public role, centred on the *balai*, accorded to him by the traditions of the past. The reaction of rulers to this new situation, which is the main theme of the remainder of this chapter, depended on individual circumstances and personalities. In particular, a distinction must be drawn between the older men who were in office when the new regime took over and those who succeeded to their thrones in the first generation of colonial rule. Something can also be learnt from the situation of rulers of states which retained a nominal independence until 1909 since there were similar trends, actuated perhaps by different causes, in their case also. One should not over-emphasize the impact of colonial rule; it was only one form of external pressure.

The older men tended to relieve the emptiness of their lives by adopting a role in public which was traditional in form, but eccentric in the lengths to which they sometimes carried it. Sultan Ahmad of Pahang is a striking example of this tendency. Although it had suited him to mask his personality behind an 'air of languor and grace . . . quiet and almost melancholy gentleness', he was a man of action who had won a civil war a quarter of a century before and then ruled his sprawling state with a strong and ruthless hand. Then came British rule which led Clifford to observe 'the downfall of his power . . . with sympathy and understanding'.[48] As already mentioned, he avoided the open humiliation of his new position by withdrawing up-river to find an outlet for his energy in hunting *seladang*, the wild ox which is the most dangerous of Malayan big game. In his retreat he maintained an enormous household of several hundred, mainly women domestics, though described by Europeans as a 'harem'. Then the uprising in Pahang in the early 1890s provided a different kind of outlet for his skill in action. While the British floundered, the ruler raised and deployed with great skill, a force of Malay irregulars. He captured no less than twelve stockades—but suspended operations during the Muslim month of fasting. The harassed Resident paid tribute to his 'scouting and attacking parties' and 'the excellence of his men as guerrilla soldiers when fighting in dense jungle' and also to the ruler's skill in 'organising commissariat services for Malays'. He must have been one of the best Malay field commanders of his time. For a few months the adrenalin ran again in his veins but it was over all too soon. He withdrew again into a morose retirement, made worse by increasing ill-health due to opium smoking. Although he delegated such powers as he had to his son, he fought a rearguard action over the small things and yet sought—and eventually obtained—the customary British accolade of a KCMG. At the investiture in 1903 he provided splendid entertainment in the Malay style, ending with 'a *joget* gracefully performed by His Highness's dancing girls'. He died in 1914 at the age of about eighty, having outlived the world in which he had played such a strenuous part long ago.[49]

Another representative of the disgruntled older generation was Raja Yusuf of Perak, described as 'obstinate, tyrannical, vindictive . . . a strong man with a will and not fond of innovation'.[50] He was willing to co-operate with the new regime since he well knew that he owed his position as Regent, and ultimately Sultan, to British support. But he found its constraints very trying. In his case release from tension came in exhibitionism of various types. When the governor visited Perak, Yusuf came a long distance to receive him 'with elephants most gorgeously and artistically decorated and caparisoned in gold and embroidery and silk and flowers'.[51] In his dress he 'affected gay colours . . . a tartan silk jacket, combining many violent colours [with] a high collar which enclosed the wearer's bull neck and reached to the ears. The nether garment was a pair of very wide and loose silk trousers fastened by many yards of a scarlet silk waistcloth . . . sky-blue canvas shoes which encased stockingless feet. On his head tilted rakishly over one ear . . . a wonderful round bright yellow cap, flat on the top with stiff sides on which were sewn in Arabic characters of black cloth, a verse from the Koran.'[52]

Sultan Abdul Samad of Selangor was already seventy years old when the new regime relieved him of such residual responsibility as he had not already relinquished to the protagonists of the Selangor Civil War (1867–73). Yet he showed 'occasional signs that he felt the loss of dignity entailed on him by his revenue being collected and his laws altered and administered for him by aliens'. He, too, was eccentric in his dress but in a different style—he was 'hardly distinguishable from a Malay peasant' except on ceremonial occasions in his *balai*. The traditional pursuit in which he absorbed himself was Malay agriculture. On various occasions his visitors observed him down in the flooded padi-fields, sawing timber and joining in the pursuit of a goat which he wished to present for meat to his guest.[53]

Sultan Zainal Abidin III came to his throne at the age of seventeen in 1881 and was deprived of power, which he did not want, by greedy relatives instead of British administrators, who did not arrive until towards the end of his reign in 1909—he lived until 1918. By disposition he was a devout and scholarly recluse. He therefore dedicated himself to his studies and devotions and was 'much addicted to concubinage with young debt-slaves'. As a formality he married some of them and later divorced them; it was said in 1918 that he had thirty-seven ex-wives living in Kuala Terengganu.[54] However, in the latter part of his reign he seems to have become more active, though unchanged in his tastes. In his final years (1909–18) he successfully held back the pressures of change introduced by the presence of a British Agent.

The new generation of rulers were more disposed to look for outlets in the one field of activity reserved to them by treaty—'questions touching Malay Religion and Custom'.[55] By elaboration in this area they found compensation for what they had lost elsewhere. In addition, they more readily came to terms with the new life-style of the British officials in their states, and so they adopted selectively some of the practices and habits of the Europeans, more especially those which gave them an opportunity of returning to the conspicuous position which their predecessors had held in the days of traditional rule. In this chapter the aspect for consideration is the ruler's involvement in ceremonial and other public activity, partly traditional, partly Islamic, and partly colonial.

Although 'custom' (*adat*) is an imprecise term that could include the Malay system of government, which the colonial regime had dismantled, it gains more exact meaning (in one of its senses) when linked with *istiadat*. '*Adat istiadat*' means 'traditional ceremony'; in this field the ruler had a free hand, subject only to the financial constraints on what might be spent on it from his privy purse or state revenues. It was all the easier to elaborate in this area because many British officials had an aesthetic appreciation of Malay ceremonies and so were very willing to assist in organizing a major ceremony.[56] With such combined enthusiasm, public ceremonies tended to become ever more lavish—and expensive.

As an example, take the installation of Sultan Idris of Perak in 1889. Idris was himself one of the leading Malay authorities on traditional subjects and his Resident was Hugh Low. The installation ceremony, attended by the Resident and other European officials as well as a large concourse of Malays, took place at Bukit Chandan, which was the residence of the new ruler. Here he was publicly 'invested with the ancestral sword of state' and took his place on the royal dais (*singgasana*) 'with the regalia displayed on the *peterana* (mat of honour) before him'. He then signed an oath of office, like a colonial governor on taking up his appointment, and this was subsequently published in the official *Perak Gazette*. A proclamation of accession was read aloud and the appropriate salute of seventeen guns was fired. The new ruler 'descended from the royal seat' and when he was in that less exalted position 'European officers and gentlemen were presented to him'. The Sultan then made a formal speech. In the evening there was a banquet and a fireworks display. The Sultan proposed 'the loyal toast', i.e. the health of Queen Victoria, and the band played 'God Save the Queen'. The Resident made a speech in reply.

After this ceremony there was five days of rejoicing with an 'abundance of sports and races, plays, shooting and rowing matches with feasts for the chiefs and people who are said to have numbered more than 15,000'.[57] Thus ended the officially sponsored ceremonies.

Malay tradition, however, called for additional rites.[58] Idris had prepared himself for his installation by a retreat of several days spent 'in fasting and prayer'. The installation itself had included the speaking of a formula by which the ruler was recognized as a temporal representative of divine authority. It was still necessary to invoke supernatural powers of a different kind.[59]

'On the 8th [January] a number of Malay chiefs and *rayats* assembled in the grounds of the *istana* for the purpose of erecting a "*balai mandi*" or "*balai hantu*", the spirits of the country having been invoked and propitiated some days previously, with a view to securing long life and prosperity to His Highness the Sultan. The *balai*, the building of which was commenced at daybreak and completed a little after midnight, was about forty feet in height, and composed of eleven tiers or "*tingkats*". The topmost tier was covered with an ornamental roof, in each corner of which a large bamboo stem filled with water had been fixed. Several small boxes covered with red and gilt paper, containing *sireh* and cakes, propitiatory offerings from the chiefs and *penghulus*, were suspended from the awnings and posts of the "*balai*". The usual ceremonies attending the invocation of the spirits were continued throughout the night, a number of skilled *pawangs* having been summoned from all parts of the state for the occasion. At 4 a.m. the Sultan, attended by a number of Rajas, and Malay ladies, ascended the *balai*. The bamboo cisterns were then broached, and His Highness and certain members of his family proceeded to bathe themselves in the water that flowed from them. This concluded the ceremony, which although incompatible with the tenets of the Mohammedan religion is one that is always performed by the Perak Malays on a Sultan's accession to the throne, and on those occasions when they consider the intervention of the spirits would be beneficial to the country.'[60]

There was still one more ritual to follow. The twenty-eighth ruler of Perak, Idris went to visit the tombs of his ancestors at Ayer Mati on the Perak River. With his 'whole family' he went to 'a sandspit at the mouth of the Perak river, where the rites necessary to the final ceremony of his installation were duly performed'.[61]

Throughout his reign Sultan Idris was punctilious in his observance of Islamic religious practice and let it be seen that he was devout. In 1889 he may have had to suppress internal doubts about the propriety of continuing rituals which, however ancient, accorded recognition to pagan deities. As will be recounted in the chapter on Islam he was attended by Muslim divines who were becoming intolerant of such practices. However, whatever internal or verbal disputes there may have been, Idris was a ruler in the mainstream of the Malay tradition of which he was a staunch upholder. After the tolerant fashion of the time, he probably concluded that the ceremonies need not be regarded as heretical, since their function was not to express belief, but to present to the general body of his subjects the symbolism of a ruler now invested with majesty (*daulat*) as the human vessel of the fortunes of the state.

Although the contemporary account of the lustration ceremony states that it was 'always performed' it is unlikely that the three rulers of Perak before Idris had been installed with so much ceremony. At all events there was no mention of it. Ismail and Abdullah had both come to the throne in circumstances of controversy unattended, so far as the records go, by the general rejoicings of 1889. Sultan Yusuf was installed with some European ceremonial but apparently without Malay traditional rites.[62] In 1889, for the first time in a generation, opportunity and inclination combined in the full traditional ceremonies of the occasion, to which were added elements of European practice, that marked the different circumstances in which the new reign began.

The next major installation of a Malay ruler came in Selangor in 1903.[63] When Sulaiman succeeded his grandfather, Abdul Samad, in 1898, there was no one alive who had witnessed the installation of a ruler of Selangor, as there had been no such ceremony since 1826.[64] Abdul Samad had let most of the high offices of state fall vacant by failing to appoint successors when the incumbents died during his long reign (1857–98). The court historian states that no regalia had been preserved since a Muslim zealot from Sumatra had decreed the destruction of these impious baubles. However, Skeat, who had been District Officer at the royal capital in the 1890s, includes a photograph of the regalia in his book on Malay magic.[65] Skeat's photograph discloses that the surviving regalia were neither very splendid nor of the type which Malay court pretensions now required. That may explain the contradiction in the contemporary sources.

The new ruler of Selangor, like Idris of Perak, was both a traditionalist and a devout Muslim. His confidant and kinsman, Raja Bot, was all too ready to act as master of ceremonies for a really sumptuous occasion. Swettenham, who was governor at the time, described Raja Bot as 'a busybody, well-meaning perhaps . . . the Sultan of Selangor's principal adviser and sadly wanting in discretion'.[66] There was a mass appointment of court officers to make up the complement, and new regalia were designed and made on a lavish scale. Raja Bot himself went off to Riau, whence the Selangor dynasty had come as Bugis interlopers a century and a half before, to obtain from that source authentic information of the proper ceremonial for installing a ruler of Bugis descent. Earlier precedent, if any, was dismissed with contempt—'before this there was no proper procedure or protocol of installation—everything was done according to the whims and fancies of the Rajas'.

The ceremony was in two parts. The first stage took place on a dais in public view before the *istana* at Klang. One of its most striking features was a procession of more than sixty Malay ladies of aristocratic family all dressed in white scarves. Others brought in the regalia. The local defence force, the Malay States Guides, were in 'brilliant scarlet uniforms' and the Sultan's bodyguard were 'clad in yellow tunics with dark blue sarongs and white trousers'. The entry of the ruler and his consort was preceded by the arrival of the court musicians 'who bore curious looking drums and silver trumpets'. The ruler himself was attended by six men carrying 'six gigantic yellow umbrellas'. Behind him came 'thirty-eight young girls, some of whom were clad in light blue and yellow and some in pink and yellow. These bore unlighted tapers.' The ruler's salute of seventeen guns was fired no less than five times. In addition the military band and the royal musicians on their Malay instruments provided musical honours.

The central feature of the ceremony was the ritual anointing of the hands and feet of the ruler and his consort. In all this the Raja Muda, who was an elderly relative of the ruler, and Raja Bot took a prominent part.

The second part of the ceremony took place within the *istana*, which had been recently built in the Moorish style, 'flanked by towers capped by cupolas'. Here in the throne-room the ruler and his consort were formally crowned by Raja Bot. At the end of the proceedings the ruler entertained his guests, who included the Resident-General and the Resident, to a banquet 'in European style'. The guests also included visitors from the royal families of Kedah and of Perak. This, too, was a mark of a different age. With the exception of the installation of the first Selangor ruler in 1766 it had not been the practice for members of the ruling family of one state to attend an installation of the new ruler of another. Such a ceremony, however important, had been previously a domestic event within the state.[67]

Without knowledge of the information, whether authentic or not, of Bugis practice which Raja Bot may have obtained at Riau, it is difficult to assess the significance of this lavish ceremony. The impression which it makes is that it was lavish for its own sake. It was also an attempt to outdo the neighbouring state of Perak. The Selangor celebrations of 1903, for example, were spread over a month as compared with the five days of the Perak ceremonies and jollifications of 1889.

There was a similar elaboration in the celebration of royal marriages and funerals. For example, when the ruler of Terengganu came to Pahang to marry the daughter of the ruler of that state, he brought with him 1,400 persons as his retinue. The supply of loaves and fishes to this multitude was such a burden that the hosts soon withdrew from it. The bridegroom, however, remained in Pahang for a year and the Malay account of the sequence of ceremonies runs to 2,500 words.[68]

In addition to ancient ceremonies some rulers developed a new one—the royal progress through the state after the style of a governor on tour. Sultan Idris of Perak, more than most of his contemporaries, perceived the possibility of projecting the royal presence by this means. When he drove out from his *istana* on a local call, he rode in a carriage with an escort of mounted police.[69] If he made a trip down the Perak River, he was received on his return 'at the Bukit Chandan jetty with a salute of 17 guns and a guard of honour; a number of the principal European and Malay officials having assembled at the landing place to meet him'.[70]

Appendix: The Rulers of This Period

State	*Ruler*	*Regnal Years*
Johor	Abu Bakar	1862–95
	Ibrahim	1895–1959
Kedah	Ahmad Tajuddin II	1854–79
	Zainal Rashid II	1879–81
	Abdul Hamid	1882–1943
Kelantan	Mohamed II	1839–86
	Ahmad	1886–9
	Mohamed III	1889–91
	Mansur	1891–1900
	Mohamed IV	1900–20

(*continued*)

Appendix (*continued*)

State	*Ruler*	*Regnal Years*
Negeri Sembilan	Antah	1872–88
	Mohamed	1888–1933
Pahang	Ahmad	1863–1914
Perak	Ismail	1871–6
	Abdullah	1874–6
	Yusuf (originally Regent)	1876–87
	Idris	1887–1916
Selangor	Mohamed	1826–57
	Abdul Samad	1859–98
	Sulaiman	1898–1938
Terengganu	Baginda Omar	1839–76
	Ahmad II	1876–81
	Zainal Abidin III	1881–1918

1. J. Bastin, 'Problems of Personality in the Reinterpretation of Malayan History', in J. Bastin and R. Roolvink (eds.), *Malayan and Indonesian Studies: Essays presented to Sir Richard Windstedt on His Eighty-fifth Birthday*, London, Oxford University Press, 1964, p. 152.

2. H. C. Clifford, *Bushwhacking and Other Asiatic Tales and Memories*, New York, Harper, 1929, pp. 178–9. Clifford had seen Ahmad's written orders for the assassination of chiefs whom he distrusted (SSD 28 April 1887: CO 273/14[illegible], p. 512). Linehan, 'A History of Pahang', *JMBRAS*, 14(2), 1936 (hereafter cited as 'Pahang'), p. 103, suggests that these orders may have been issued without authority by applying the royal seal to them without his knowledge—he was illiterate (SSD 15 June 1886). Weld lends a little support to this possibility—'as the "Sultan" of Pahang can neither read nor write he may not always be well-informed as to what he signs' (SSD 15 June 1886). If, however, the notorious orders to kill had been issued in this fashion, it is unlikely that Clifford would not have heard of it. On strong rulers generally, see note 46.

3. SSD 24 February 1874, enclosure 3, a report by Thomas Braddell on Clarke's negotiations with the Sultan at Kuala Langat in February 1874 (printed in Cmd. 1111), para. 50.

4. 'Each party in turn made periodical visits to the old Sultan. To all comers, from whatever quarter, the Sultan seemed to signify his approval, and, with strict impartiality, made gifts of some sort' (F. A. Swettenham, *British Malaya: An Account of the Origin and Progress of British Influence in Malaya*, London, John Lane Bodley Head, 1907 (revised editions 1929 and 1948, London, Allen & Unwin), p. 130,

referring to the Selangor Civil War (1867–73)). As to whether Swettenham misread the Sultan's character, see J.M. Gullick, 'A Careless, Heathen Philosopher?', *JMBRAS*, 26(1), 1953. The significant point here is that both sides felt the need to obtain the ruler's formal approval.

5. J.R. Logan, 'Notes at Penang, Kedah etc.', *JIA*, 5, 1851, pp. 55–65. On the context of this meeting see J.M. Gullick, 'Kedah 1821–1855: Years of Exile and Return', *JMBRAS*, 56(2), 1983. Abdullah Munshi, visiting Kelantan in 1838, noted that 'the floor was laid at varying heights to facilitate audiences' and 'there were a lot of other people but they all sat on the lower staging' (Abdullah bin Abdul Kadir, Munshi, *Kesah Pelayaran Abdullah*, translated by A.E. Coope, *The Voyage of Abdullah: A Translation from the Malay*, Singapore, Malaya Publishing House, 1949, pp. 31 and 39).

6. H. Norman, *The Peoples and Politics of the Far East: Travels and Studies in the British ... Colonies and Malaya*, New York, Scribner, 1895, p. 582. McNair relates a story told by A.R. Wallace of an Indonesian chief who rejected the European carriage which he had ordered from England when he found, on its arrival, that his coachman would be seated on the driving seat well above the level at which the owner would ride in the body of the carriage (J.F.A. McNair, *Perak and the Malays: Sarong and Keris*, London, Tinsley Bros., 1878, reprinted Kuala Lumpur, Oxford University Press, 1972, pp. 297–8).

7. J. Low, 'Observations on Perak', *JIA*, 4, 1850, p. 503.

8. SSD 23 February 1883, enclosing a report by D.F.A. Hervey on his recent visit to Rembau and Tampin. This passage relates to a hostile meeting between two Malays, each anxious to assert his status.

9. SSD 24 February 1874, enclosure 2, report by C.J. Irving on his visit to Perak in April 1872, para. 25. McNair, op. cit., p. 297, provides a picture of Sultan Abdullah and a number of Perak chiefs, probably from the famous meeting on the S.S. '*Pluto*' in January 1874 at which the Pangkor Engagement was signed. He comments: 'In this case the Sultan is seated on a chair, and as is always observed, no other chief can take such a seat unless it is of a lower level than that of his lord, and consequently they all sit or crouch upon their hams.' Another report notes generally that Malays 'never appeared gauche or awkward except when sitting on a chair for the first time' (A.B. Rathborne, *Camping and Tramping in Malaya: Fifteen Years' Pioneering in the Native States of the Malay Peninsula*, London, Swan Sonnenschein, 1898, reprinted Singapore, Oxford University Press, 1984, p. 53). Clifford tells how a Malay visitor invited to take a chair made 'half-hearted curtseys in the direction of the floor' before committing himself to this unfamiliar contraption (H.C. Clifford, *In Days that are Dead*, London, Murray, 1926, p. 287). It was often European insistence which overcame Malay diffidence over chairs—'he was given a chair, sitting beside Mr Raffles and Mr Farquhar' (Raja Ali Haji ibn Ahmad, *Tuhfat al-Nafis*, translated and annotated by Virginia Matheson and Barbara Watson Andaya, *The Precious Gift*, Kuala Lumpur, Oxford University Press, 1982, p. 228), and 'he was not comfortable on a chair if his seniors were on the ground' (ibid., p. 283). Ibrahim Munshi, said, 'I sat in the middle between the Yam Tuan and Mr. Irving in order to interpret for them' (Mohamed Ibrahim bin Abdullah, Munshi, *The Voyages of Mohamed Ibrahim Munshi*, translated by Amin Sweeney and Nigel Phillips, Kuala Lumpur, Oxford University Press, 1975, p. 79).

10. A.C. Milner, *Kerajaan: Malay Political Culture on the Eve of Colonial Rule*, Tucson, University of Arizona Press, 1982, p. 74. See also Sultan Abdullah's

discussion with the Perak chiefs at p. 318 below and also McNair, op. cit., p. 204.

11. SSD 7 August 1875. Ahmad was here making an excuse for resisting an unwelcome suggestion about reform of revenue collection. None the less, there are signs that on occasion chiefs did disagree with a ruler in discussion with him. See, for example, Raja Ali Haji ibn Ahmad, op. cit., p. 63, and Linehan, 'Pahang', p. 70.

12. The evidence given to PCE includes some accounts of informal discussions of this kind. It was said of Sultan Abdullah that he 'is always influenced by the chiefs around him . . . he generally listens to the counsels of a set of scamps, who fight his cocks and smoke opium with him' (SSD 16 October 1875). Clifford's reports on Pahang in 1887 also mention a circle of advisers around the ruler and in particular the influence of his secretary, Wan Hitam (SSD 28 April 1887: CO 237/144, p. 544; and SSD 15 October 1887: CO 273/148, pp. 228–31).

13. R.H. Vetch, *Life of Lieutenant General Sir Andrew Clarke*, London, Murray, 1905, p. 172. When Jervois visited Pahang in August 1875 the same invitation was made to him (SSD 7 August 1875). When Sultan Abdul Samad wished to avoid frank discussion with Weld in October 1882 he continued the meeting in open *balai* so as to constrain the discussion (SSD 27 October 1882).

14. SSD 7 August 1875.

15. J. Low, 'Observations on Perak', p. 504. Low's visit was part of a British move to oust Siamese envoys from Perak where they had been building a pro-Siam party (L. A. Mills, 'British Malaya 1824–1867', *JMBRAS*, 3(2), 1925; reprinted in *JMBRAS*, 33(3), 1960, p. 183 (citations from the 1960 reprint)).

16. On the speech and the clothes see R. J. Wilkinson, 'The Incidents of Malay Life', *Papers on Malay Subjects, Life and Customs*, Part 1, Kuala Lumpur, Government Press, 1908, reprinted in *JMBRAS*, 30(4), 1957, p. 49, and 'Some Malay Studies', *JMBRAS*, 10(1), 1932, p. 89. On Kedah see Muhammad Hassan bin Dato' Kerani Muhammad Arshad, *Al-Tarikh Salasilah Negeri Kedah*, Kuala Lumpur, Dewan Bahasa dan Pustaka, 1968 (previously published in *Jawi*, 1926), p. 221; and on the Terengganu State Council, SSD 22 September 1909: CO 273/351, p. 223; see also Shaharil Talib Robert, 'The Trengganu Ruling Class in the Late Nineteenth Century', *JMBRAS*, 50(2), 1977, *passim*. On Perak before 1874 see note 12 above. On Perak and Selangor State Councils see E. Sadka, 'The State Councils in Perak and Selangor 1877–1895', in K. G. Tregonning (ed.), *Papers on Malayan History*, Singapore, University of Malaya in Singapore, 1962. The Perak State Council minutes for 1877–82 are reprinted in Burns (ed.), *PMS*.

17. R. J. Wilkinson, 'Letter Writing', *Papers on Malay Subjects, Literature*, Part 3, pp. 21–4. 'Then he ordered the letter to be read aloud in the presence of the people' (Abdullah Munshi, op. cit., p. 31).

18. SSD 17 November 1909. The ruler of Terengganu here assumed a classificatory status of parent, i.e. senior, towards the ruler of Kelantan. '*Anakanda*' and '*ayahanda*' (with the honorific prefix '*paduka*') are the respective terms for 'child' and 'parent' used in the formal language of court correspondence (R. J. Wilkinson, *A Malay–English Dictionary*, 2 parts, Singapore, Kelly & Walsh, 1901, revised as *A Malay–English Dictionary (Romanised)*, 2 parts, Mytilene, Salavopoulos & Kinderlis, 1932), Pt. 1, pp. 28 and 55).

19. In 1878 Raja Yusuf, the Regent of Perak, was required to put his signature to a document. As he was illiterate he had never done this before. His son-in-law, Raja Idris, wrote it for him and Yusuf touched the pen in motion so that it would be regarded as his signature (*PSCM*, 26 June 1878, *PMS*, p. 169). Raja Ali Haji ibn

Ahmad, op. cit., p. 246, also mentions the signature of a letter which may have been written in Dutch.

20. SSD 6 September 1882. See Gullick, 'A Careless, Heathen Philosopher?', p. 101, for the background.

21. Mohamed Ibrahim Munshi, op. cit., p. 80, describes such an episode with mild surprise as if it were normal for a letter to be read to its author before despatch. PCE has numerous references to the issue of letters (CO 273/86, pp. 339, 470, 480 and 500; CO 273/87, pp. 315, 368, 370, 381, 390, 490, 563 and 580). In two cases the witness states that he wrote the letter at dictation (CO 273/86, pp. 454 and 501); and in another that he was told 'to draft a suitable letter in reply' (CO 273/87, p. 390). In another situation an envoy brought with him three blank sheets of paper which had been sealed in advance (CO 273/87, p. 489). This story is confirmed in J. W. W. Birch, *The Journals of J. W. W. Birch First British Resident to Perak 1874–1875* (hereafter cited as *Birch Journal*), edited by P. L. Burns, Kuala Lumpur, Oxford University Press, 1976, p. 303.

22. In PCE Sultan Abdullah is said to have ordered the killing of his clerk 'who has been revealing secrets' (CO 273/87, p. 53, confirmed in *Birch Journal*, p. 332).

23. *AR Pahang 1888*, para. 23.

24. C. D. Cowan, *Nineteenth Century Malaya: The Origins of British Political Control*, London, Oxford University Press, 1961, p. 71; Khoo Kay Kim, *The Western Malay States, 1850–1873: The Effects of Commercial Development on Malay Politics*, Kuala Lumpur, Oxford University Press, 1972, pp. 154–5; R. O. Winstedt, 'A History of Selangor', *JMBRAS*, 12(3), 1934, p. 21. All comment on Kudin's letter.

25. E. Thio, *British Policy in the Malay Peninsula, Vol. 1: The Southern and Central States*, Kuala Lumpur and Singapore, University of Malaya Press, 1969, p. 233, cites CO 273/294 of 19 October 1903 for Swettenham's inspection of the Johor government departments. He called the Secretariat 'a farce'. On the state secretariats of Kedah and Johor see p. 84 below. The personnel held office by royal favour and served as personal staff of the ruler. Yet they were evolving towards a bureaucracy on the SS model.

26. Linehan, 'Pahang', pp. 201–23, reprints a selection of the large number of papers on state matters preserved by the Maharaja Perba of Jelai, one of the territorial magnates of Pahang. Note 23 above on the concessions.

27. T. J. Newbold, *Political and Statistical Account of the British Settlements ... with a History of the Malayan States on the Peninsula in the Straits of Malacca*, London, Murray, 1839, reprinted as *British Settlements in the Straits of Malacca*, Kuala Lumpur, Oxford University Press, 1971, Vol. 2, p. 224.

28. There are references later in this chapter and also in the next chapter to Sultan Ahmad's addiction to big-game hunting in Pahang, to the preoccupation with agriculture of Sultan Abdul Samad of Selangor, and to the interest taken in local industry by Sultan Ahmad Tajuddin of Kedah.

29. J. de V. Allen, 'Sultan Zainal Abidin III of Trengganu', *Malaya in History*, 1, 1968, p. 6.

30. J. Low, 'Observations on Perak', p. 502, quoted at p. 280 below.

31. When Negeri Sembilan was reunited in 1898 under the Yam Tuan as paramount ruler the territorial ruling chiefs (*Undang*) stipulated that their status in their own districts should be marked by remaining in their districts (*luak*) to receive the loyal salutations of their subjects on Muslim holidays (J. de V. Allen, A. J. Stockwell and L. R. Wright (eds.), *A Collection of Treaties and Other Documents*

Affecting the States of Malaysia 1761–1963 (hereafter cited as *Treaties*), New York, Oceana Publications, 1981, Vol. 1, p. 326).

32. G. P. Means, 'The Role of Islam in the Political Development of Malaysia', *Comparative Politics*, 1(2), 1969, p. 269.

33. SSD 3 August 1909.

34. When Weld visited the Malay states in the 1880s he was received in much the same style as in a visit to Penang or Malacca. These occasions are described both in his official despatches and in his biography (A. Lovat, *The Life of Sir Frederick Weld: A Pioneer of Empire*, London, Murray, 1914). Yet only a few years before, Sultan Ahmad of Pahang received Jervois (in 1875) 'surrounded by many chiefs and some 300 Malays, sitting in solemn conclave in and about the *balai*' (SSD 7 August 1875). As Jervois moved on to visit Kuala Terengganu he was received by 'a guard of honour of some sixty spearmen who upon either side escorted him in Indian file' (ibid.).

35. M. C. ff. Sheppard, 'A Short History of Trengganu', *JMBRAS*, 22(3), 1949, p. 37. Tunku Long, of the Pahang royal family, was one of the wives of the Terengganu ruler.

36. CO 273/42, p. 623—a Foreign Office report.

37. SSD 25 November 1913. He took only 15 of this large party with him on the next stage of his journey. He stopped at Klang where he was taken for 'a motor drive round Klang by the Tunku Mahkota of Selangor' (ibid.). He got as far as Cairo where an illness prevented him from going on to Mecca. But he was much impressed by the strength of Islam in the Middle East (Sheppard, 'History of Trengganu', p. 55; H. Sutherland, 'The Taming of the Trengganu Elite', in R. T. McVey (ed.), *Southeast Asian Transitions: Approaches through Social History*, New Haven and London, Yale University Press, 1978, p. 38, citing CO 273/412, p. 318). SSD 27 May 1909 describes an earlier visit to Singapore en route to Riau, where the ruler had relatives. In spite of its decline in the last years of the nineteenth century Riau was the hub of a network of kinship ties extending northwards to the Malay states. Long before, a ruler of Selangor had been to Riau in 1839 and again in 1846—and had almost fallen into the clutches of his creditors at Melaka (SSD 2 August 1878; see also Raja Ali Haji ibn Ahmad, op. cit., p. 284).

In 1875 when Jervois visited the east coast of Malaya the rulers of both Kelantan and Terengganu told him that they would like to re-visit Singapore (SSD 7 August 1875).

The ruler of Kedah, who had been born in exile in Penang, maintained a town house there in later years—as did other leading members of the Kedah royal family (A. E. Anson, *About Others and Myself 1745–1920*, London, Murray, 1920, p. 313).

The ruler of Johor also had a house in Singapore, the celebrated 'Tyersall', where his principal wife lived (F. Caddy, *To Siam and Malaya in the Duke of Sutherland's Yacht 'Sans Peur'*, London, Hurst & Blackett, 1889, p. 236).

The conventional forty followers is considered in the next chapter (see p. 51). It was one of the grievances of the exiled ruler of Kedah when compelled to move from Penang to Melaka in 1831 that 'we were not permitted to take more than 10 of our slaves with us' (Gullick, 'Kedah', p. 42, citing India Office Library Board Collections, Vol. 1480, Item 58164).

In his travels abroad a ruler was expected to behave with decorum: to 'go on the town' was a disgrace (Raja Ali Haji ibn Ahmad, op. cit., p. 227).

38. SSD 24 February 1874. In 1875 the ruler of Terengganu said that 'nobody ever visited the interior and he was unaware of the position of his boundaries' (SSD

7 August 1875). On the royal visit to the interior of Selangor in 1879 see J.M. Gullick, 'Selangor 1876–1882: The Bloomfield Douglas Diary', *JMBRAS*, 48(2), 1978, p. 32.

39. *AR Pahang 1889*. In this case the move was made along a major waterway, on which large boats could be poled upstream (see below, p. 158). Pulau Tawar was a large settlement in the centre of a productive area, described by Swettenham as 'a fine kampong' (F.A. Swettenham, 'Journal Kept during a Journey across the Malay Peninsula', *JSBRAS*, 15, 1885, p. 20). In other cases a royal journey inland with a 'patriarchal following of women and slaves' was a cumbersome operation, as in the case of Sultan Ismail's flight from Perak to Kedah in 1876 (W.E. Maxwell, 'A Journey on Foot to the Patani Frontier in 1876 being a Journal Kept during an Expedition Undertaken to Capture Datoh Maharajah Lela of Perak', *JSBRAS*, 9, 1882, p. 22). If a ruler went abroad on a visit he often chartered a small steamer to transport the entire party, as when the ruler of Terengganu visited Singapore in 1910 (SSD 28 June 1910).

40. J. Low, 'Observations on Perak', p. 503. According to R.O. Winstedt and R.J. Wilkinson, 'A History of Perak', *JMBRAS*, 12(1), 1934, p. 163, a distinction was drawn between those articles, such as the sword of state, with which the ruler could be invested at his installation by attaching them to his person, and 'other heirlooms' which were not strictly regalia. Whether the magic passed from the regalia to the ruler or vice versa, it appears that contact was essential. W.W. Skeat, *Malay Magic: Being an Introduction to the Folklore and Popular Religion of the Malay Peninsula*, London, Macmillan, 1900, reprinted Singapore, Oxford University Press, 1984, pp. 23–42, and R.J. Wilkinson, 'Some Malay Studies', *JMBRAS*, 10(1), 1932, pp. 87–8, also describe regalia in detail.

41. Winstedt and Wilkinson, op. cit, p. 59.

42. W.W. Skeat and F.F. Laidlaw, 'The Cambridge University Expedition to Parts of the Malay Peninsula 1899–1900: Personal Accounts', *JMBRAS*, 26(4), 1953, p. 127.

43. Ibid., p. 127. *Lauk* was solid food, usually fish, eaten with rice as a relish (Wilkinson, *1932 Dictionary*). Skeat tells how he breached the taboo by handling the Selangor *nobat*. When he fell ill his Malay friends regarded this as the predictable consequence of 'an act of extraordinary rashness' and one of them vowed 'to make sacrifices at the shrine of a famous local saint' for his recovery (Skeat, *Malay Magic*, p. 40).

44. SSD 24 November 1909 on the Kedah royal household.

45. Milner, *Kerajaan*, p. 96. J.M. Gullick, *Indigenous Political Systems of Western Malaya*, London, Athlone Press, 1958, Chapter 8.

46. The rulers of Kedah, Pahang and Terengganu, down to 1876, were all described as strong rulers. J. de V. Allen, 'The Elephant and the Mousedeer—A New Version: Anglo-Kedah Relations 1905–1910', *JMBRAS*, 41(1), 1968, p. 82, citing Sir John Anderson's letter of 1910 on Ahmad Tajuddin of Kedah (r.1854–79); Clifford, *Bushwhacking*, p. 178, cited in note 2 above (Ahmad of Pahang); Sheppard, 'History of Trengganu', p. 37 (Baginda Omar).

The territorial chiefs did not remain in constant attendance on the ruler but spent much of their time in their districts. If the ruler was a powerful autocrat it was worth sacrificing status at court in order to keep at a safe distance. A Pahang chief told Clifford that he 'had never been to see the Sultan though he had been repeatedly called. He said that if he went there he might be kept against his will' (SSD 28 April

1887: CO 273/144, p. 477—at p. 497 there is mention of a chief who was detained at Pekan for two years). In Perak in the years 1871–4 the up-river and down-river chiefs supported different claimants to the throne and neither group saw much of the other's candidate.

47. 'The Raja element must come down and the real government must be the Sultan . . . and the Resident' (Douglas Diary, 14 April 1876).

48. Clifford, *Bushwhacking*, p. 178–80. It is likely that the ruler (father of the principal character) who is so unsympathetically portrayed in the second part of Clifford's *A Prince of Malaya*, New York, Harper, 1926 (originally published as 'Sally' in *Blackwoods Magazine*, February 1904, and *Saleh: A Sequel*, London, Blackwood, 1908) is Clifford's view of Ahmad of Pahang on his home ground at Pekan.

49. *AR Pahang 1889* and *AR Pahang 1891* (harem and military prowess); SSD 16 October 1874, and Swettenham, 'Journey across the Malay Peninsula', p. 30 (opium); *AR Pahang 1897* and SSD 27 January 1909 (delegation and succession). His disputes with the colonial regime included preservation of religion and custom (SSD 17 May 1900); choice of Resident (SSD 18 April 1901); abolition of slavery (SSD 23 August 1906). The despatch about his approach to secure the award of a KCMG depicts an embittered old man—'the other day he told me that he could not afford to do any of the things which he thought befitted and were incumbent on his station' (SSD 6 October 1902). His investiture is described in the *Malay Mail*, 9 April 1903. In 1913 there is a report that he 'attended in his brass tub' the farewell ceremony of the ruler of Terengganu who was visiting Pekan. Presumably Ahmad was now unable to walk and the brass tub was some form of carrying-chair (SSD 21 August 1913).

50. SSD 19 August 1876 and SSD 23 January 1882. In the 1850s when Raja Yusuf was a young man, his father, Sultan Abdullah, had been embroiled in a civil war with the Perak chiefs in which Yusuf, fighting for his father, made many enemies. When the throne fell vacant in 1857, 1865, and 1871, the chiefs took their revenge by excluding Yusuf from the place to which he was entitled, as son of a ruler, in the complex Perak succession scheme. He withdrew into embittered seclusion so that British officials in the early 1870s were unaware even of his existence and pretensions. Sultan Abdullah (r.1874–6) for his own purposes purported to appoint Yusuf to the office of Raja Muda about 1873 and this led to him becoming Regent when Abdullah was removed to the Seychelles; in 1886 he was accorded the title of Sultan but he died a year later. He impressed British officials as obstinate, quarrelsome but—in his fashion—a man with whom they could do business and on whom they could rely. Clifford, *Bushwhacking*, pp. 170–8, and F. A. Swettenham, *Malay Sketches*, London, John Lane Bodley Head, 1895, pp. 161–78, give colourful accounts of him. See also H. Low, 'The Journal of Sir Hugh Low, Perak 1877' (hereafter cited as 'Low Journal'), edited by E. Sadka, *JMBRAS*, 27(4), 1954, pp. 38, 70, 98 and 103; *Swettenham Journal*, pp. 71–3; *Birch Journal*, p. 76; the 1876 and 1882 despatches above, and SSD 3 April 1886.

51. SSD 21 September 1881.

52. Swettenham, *Malay Sketches*, p. 163. McNair, op. cit., p. 444, has a portrait of him—if only it were in colour!

53. E. Innes, *The Chersonese with the Gilding Off*, London, Richard Bentley, 1885; reprinted Kuala Lumpur, Oxford University Press, 1974, Vol. 1, pp. 39 and 44. Douglas Diary, 2 October 1878. The goat was caught for presentation to

Birch—a story worth reading (*Birch Journal*, p. 51). Among other eccentricities he had a marked dislike of wearing any clothing on the upper part of his body (Innes, op. cit., p. 39). The *Selangor Journal* often refers to this—'the old man struggling into his *baju* walked slowly past the guard of honour with his innumerable attendants following behind' (*SJ*, 11 November 1892, on a royal visit to Kuala Lumpur). 'He generally carries his coat over one shoulder' while out for a walk (*SJ*, 23 September 1892). He 'received us in a *sarong* ... he had no other clothes on' (*SJ*, 4 September 1896). Keyser, who first met him when he was about 90, said that he became uncharacteristically 'peevish' if invited to exercise any of his 'royal prerogatives' (A. L. Keyser, *Trifles and Travels*, London, Murray, 1923, p. 133). But he took part in public ceremonies and showed general interest in the progress of Selangor and its people. He was hardly the irresponsible old hedonist depicted by Swettenham (*British Malaya*, p. 128).

54. Shaharil Talib Robert, 'The Trengganu Ruling Class', p. 33. There is a brief but illuminating character study in J. de V. Allen, 'Sultan Zainal Abidin III of Trengganu', *Malaya in History*, 1, 1968, p. 4. There are many references to him in the reports of the British Agents for the period 1909–18 and H. C. Clifford, 'Report: Expedition to Trengganu and Kelantan', *JMBRAS*, 34(1), 1961, originally printed for Colonial Office use in 1895, reprinted Kuala Lumpur, Government Press, 1936, pp. 66–7, explains the circumstances of his accession. The quotation is from the *Bucknill Commission Report* of 1918, p. 160, repeated by Shaharil Talib Robert, op. cit.

55. Allen, Stockwell and Wright (eds.), *Treaties*, Vol. 1, p. 391. Although some other states, notably Selangor, did not enter into a similar treaty the Pangkor formula was generally applied (F. A. Swettenham, *About Perak*, Singapore, Straits Times, 1890, p. 14).

56. The installation of Sultan Idris of Perak, described below, was organized by a committee consisting of the commandant of police, the district officer and the Sultan's English tutor (SSD 15 April 1889).

57. SSD 15 April 1889; see also *PGG* 1890, pp. 89 and 301.

58. R. O. Winstedt, 'Kingship and Enthronement in Malaya', *JMBRAS*, 20(1), 1947; and *The Malays: A Cultural History*, Singapore, Kelly & Walsh, 1947, Chapter 4 and p. 55 (lustration); Wilkinson, 'Malay Studies', pp. 82–8; Winstedt and Wilkinson, op. cit., p. 175, 'The Chiri or Coronation Address'.

59. SSD 15 April 1889.

60. *PGG* 1890, p. 89.

61. *AR Perak 1890*. There are genealogies at pp. 131–3 of Winstedt and Wilkinson, op. cit.; Idris appears as the twenty-eighth Perak Sultan at p. 133.

62. Sultan Yusuf, the immediate predecessor of Sultan Idris, was installed as ruler after a long period (1876–87) as Regent; he was old, infirm, and extremely unpopular (note 50 above). His installation lacked the elaboration and popular celebration incidental to that of Idris two years later. With characteristic flamboyance (p. 31) Yusuf emerged 'wearing a dress decorated by a profusion of beautiful diamonds'. He took his seat with the regalia (*kebesaran*) on a 'richly ornamented *peterana* or low table before him'. The 'proper officers' then invested him with the regalia. His oath of office was read aloud and he signed it. A proclamation was read; a seventeen-gun salute was fired; a guard of honour presented arms. Idris as Raja Muda called for 'cheers for the prosperity' of the ruler and there were cries of '*daulat! daulat!*' Hugh Low, the Resident, made a speech and the new Sultan replied. He then retired, 'feeling fatigued'. There were sports and refreshments—

'sherbet as the only beverage'. At the state dinner in the evening Idris presided but Yusuf appeared and made a speech; there were prayers led by the Chief Kathi (SSD 25 May 1887).

63. When Sultan Ibrahim succeeded his father, Sultan Abu Bakar, as ruler of Johor in 1895, there were elaborate ceremonies, described as 'a curious mixture of Oriental and European customs' (SSD 4 November 1895).

64. On the death of Sultan Mohamed of Selangor in 1857 the chiefs refused to accept the late ruler's young son, Raja Mahmud (not to be confused with the more celebrated Raja Mahmud mentioned at p. 81 below). After a period of intrigue the son-in-law of the late ruler, Raja Abdul Samad, became Sultan a few months later on the understanding that he would make way for the late ruler's son when the latter had grown up; when the claim was made, however, in 1864 Abdul Samad clung to his throne and lived on to die in 1898 still the ruler of Selangor. It is unlikely that Abdul Samad's accession was celebrated with the full pomp. On that assumption there was no ceremony of accession between 1826, when Sultan Mohamed came to the throne, and 1898 when Sultan Abdul Samad died. On the disputed succession see Winstedt, 'History of Selangor,' p. 19, and Khoo Kay Kim, *Western Malay States*, pp. 140–1.

65. Wan Mohamed Amin bin Said, *Pesaka Selangor*, edited by Abdul Samad Ahmad, Kuala Lumpur, Dewan Bahasa dan Pustaka, 1966, pp. 75 and 89, describes the appointment of eight *orang besar* in October 1898 to offices which had fallen vacant in the previous reign. He also tells of the destruction of all the regalia, except a *songkok leleng*, which was later lost, in the reign (1826–57) of Sultan Mohamed. This was the work of, or decreed by, one Sheikh Abdul Ghani, '*sa-orang ulama*', from Bima in Sumatra. At about the same time a man of Arab descent, Abdul Ghani by name, was 'endeavouring to gain the ascendency' in Province Wellesley, where he became one of the leaders of the opposed Muslim factions and purported to appoint a number of *kadi* to whom he issued his personal warrants (J. D. Vaughan, 'Notes on the Malays of Pinang and Province Wellesley', *JIA*, n.s., 2, 1857, p. 153). See also the scathing passage on Haji Abdul Ghani of Province Wellesley in W. E. Maxwell's memorandum enclosed with SSD 7 June 1892—see p. 286 below. 'Abdul Ghani' is quite a common name but the coincidence of two religious leaders of this type with the same name at about the same time is notable. It could be that they are one and the same. Skeat's photograph of the surviving Selangor regalia is in *Malay Magic*, p. 40. There are two small drums, various weapons, and a trumpet.

66. SSD 11 December 1902. Mohamed Amin Hassan, 'Raja Bot bin Raja Jumaat', *JMBRAS*, 40(2), 1967, is an interesting short biography. The description of the Selangor installation of 1903, from which the quotations are taken, is from the *Malay Mail*, 6 November 1903—an unsigned article probably by J. H. M. Robson, reprinted in *JMBRAS*, 58(2), 1985, 'Coronation of H. H. Sultan Alauddin Sulaiman Shah, 1903' (Appendix to Khoo Kay Kim, 'Raja Lumu—Sultan Salehuddin: The Founding of the Selangor Dynasty', ibid.).

67. B.W. Andaya, 'The Installation of the First Sultan of Selangor in 1766', *JMBRAS*, 47(1), 1974, describes the very unusual circumstances of that occasion. The Bugis ruler of the Selangor coast wished to assume the status of a royal ruler to which he had no hereditary claim. His installation in the presence of representatives of an ancient Malay ruling dynasty added weight to his pretensions.

68. Sheppard, 'History of Trengganu', pp. 70–4, is a translation of the Malay account of the marriage. J. C. Pasqual, in an article published in the *Singapore*

Sunday Times, 28 October 1934, describes how the body of Tunku Kudin of Kedah, the former Viceroy of Selangor who died in exile in Penang in 1909, was brought back with much pomp for burial in the Kedah royal burial ground. (Pasqual is cited hereafter by reference to the *Singapore Sunday Times* and the date of issue). The Kedah royal marriages of 1904 cost $125,000 and caused a financial crisis (Allen, 'The Elephant and the Mousedeer', p. 62). The wedding of Raja Muda (later to be Sultan) Sulaiman of Selangor in 1891 and the funeral of the venerable Sultan Abdul Samad in 1898 were both conducted with much expensive ceremony (*SGG* 1891, pp. 228–30, and *SGG* 1898, p. 71; SSD 10 March 1898).

69. P. Morrah, 'The History of the Malayan Police', *JMBRAS*, 36(2), 1963, p. 90.

70. *PGG* 1890, p. 269.

3
The Ruler in Private Life

In the middle of the nineteenth century the life-style of a Malay ruler was plain and at times austere. Baginda Omar of Terengganu was described in 1846 as a 'fine-looking man very plainly dressed in a *sarong*, white *baju* and black velvet jacket slashed with gold thread, very shabby and worn-out'.[1] There was little difference between classes in the food which they ate.[2] In Perak in 1826 'the Raja gave a feast to his people—five or six huge iron pots were placed over the fires. In each of these about thirty fowls were boiled.'[3]

No doubt a ruler ate substantial meals, had more clothes and lived in a larger house than his *rakyat*, but the difference was not a wide one. The most significant difference between the ruler and other members of the ruling class on one side, and the mass of peasant cultivators on the other, lay in the command of services of men and women which the former possessed and the latter made possible.

The outward and visible sign of high social status was a large household and personal following. Debt-bondage and corvée labour (*kerah*), which will be considered in a later chapter, were the basis of the personal and domestic service at the disposal of a person of position. There were obligations on both sides. The great man protected and sometimes supported those who served him. His greatness gave them a special position within their own class which they valued.

Just as the *balai* was the focus of a ruler's public position, his household was the centre of personal privileges. Its importance is apparent from the number of people it included and sometimes from an elaborate organization of duties. The rulers of Kedah, despite their Western tastes, lived in a traditional style. The royal servants (*orang balai*) numbered about 600. They did not, however, all attend at the *istana* at the same time. There was a rotation system by which the royal servants lived in their villages and performed a tour of duty of about fifteen days at a time in working groups of about ten. By this means, the burden of service was reduced and most of the household were self-supporting. They were not paid for their work but were exempt from the unpopular land tax.

In addition to general domestics of both sexes there were some special categories. The *orang lepau* prepared the royal meals—'*lepau*' means a back verandah or kitchen. There were some twenty-five or thirty night-watchmen (*orang tunggu*) who guarded the *istana* at night. The royal musicians (*orang nobat*) have already been described.[4] Although there is no mention of such formal organization in other states, there was a general practice of assigning specific tasks. Among the women who gave evidence to the Perak Commission of Enquiry in 1876 were members of Sultan Abdullah's household. One said that 'at first I had all kinds of different employments, but afterwards I was employed in making cakes'; another said, 'I was close to Sultan Abdullah because I was looking after his child.'[5] Perhaps because each individual did his or her own work and no other, it was impossible for the head of the household to travel without a large domestic following. When, for example, old Sultan Abdul Samad of Selangor attended the first gathering of FMS rulers at Kuala Kangsar in Perak he preferred not to attend his host's banquet 'in European style' but 'dined by himself in Malay style, . . . and he was waited on in royal style with rice-attendants, and attendants for his drinks and others with similar duties'.[6]

There was a wide variety of work, some of it heavy and monotonous chores. The women of the Terengganu royal household were employed in 'chopping firewood, drawing water, washing clothes, marketing, nursing, needlework, serving at meals and massage'.[7] It was unthinkable that an aristocrat of either sex should do these things for themselves. For this reason some of the older rulers clung to the privilege of service by bondswomen long after they had been legally set free. In 1906 the Resident-General of the FMS felt obliged to represent to Sultan Ahmad of Pahang that he really must comply with the law of his own state. The old man protested that his male retainers (*budak dalam*) were now 'few in number' and if his maidservants were set free 'he would be left without anyone even to cook his rice'.[8] It was one of the cherished differences between a secondary wife (*gundik*) and a mere concubine in a royal household that the former did 'no menial work at the palace'.[9]

The traditional method of recruiting royal domestic staff was to round up young women from the villages for service at the *istana*, sometimes for the rest of their lives.[10] Mention has been made in the previous chapter of the 'harem' of 300 or 400 women in the household of Ahmad of Pahang and of the numerous concubines of the uxorious Zainal Abidin of Terengganu.[11] European prurience may have exaggerated the sexual aspect of the conscription of women to serve in the *istana*.[12] If a girl was attractive she might share the ruler's bed until he grew tired of her. She was then relegated to purely domestic service or allocated to a member of the ruler's following as a concubine or wife. Unless given away in this fashion she was, so long as she served in the *istana*, entirely at the ruler's disposal for sexual or other purposes. Death or torture were the expected penalties for both parties if caught in illicit intercourse.[13] A domestic might also be maltreated if the ruler's attentions became so marked as to rouse the resentment or jealousy of his wives.[14]

In addition to domestic staff there were two other categories who gave service. To provide food for his household the ruler needed labourers, men or women, to cultivate his fields. It was more usual, however, to mobilize agricultural labour under the *kerah* system and such workers did not rank as members of the household. The ruler might of course, have debt-bondsmen to provide the core of his field-workers. The other—and more notorious—element were the royal retinue of pages and armed retainers, the much feared *budak raja*.

Some of the *budak raja* were young men of good family for whom service to the ruler afforded an opportunity of making a career at court or at least of earning a living, especially by extortion from the ruler's subjects. Others among them, and these may have been the more numerous, were 'broken men' who had fled from punishment for a crime committed in their native districts and sought protection in the ruler's service. To these were sometimes added men of lower status, often foreigners (*anak dagang*), who had simply drifted into the royal retinue, perhaps hoping thereby to obtain a wife or mistress among the surplus women.

European observers give a harsh picture of the *budak raja* as 'a lawless rabble of male followers'.[15] Without rejecting that version entirely, it is reasonable to take into account the world in which they lived and the norms of conduct to which they were subject. Considerations of prestige, personal safety and the need to prevent crimes of violence from totally disrupting normal life in the state capital, obliged a ruler to have an armed bodyguard at his immediate disposal. The *budak raja* were a palace guard in a society in which violence was common and every adult male carried arms, which he was ready to use. The ruler whom they served did not pay them a regular wage nor even sometimes provide their food. They were then left to forage for themselves. The opportunity came when they went forth to enforce the ruler's authority—'a youngster, brilliantly dressed in silks of many colours, swaggered into the compound. He carried a *keris* in his girdle, and a short sword, with a sheath of polished wood, in his hand.'[16] Such a young man was ready for violence and immune from redress for any wrong he might do. 'He is licensed to commit any act of oppression on any who are not of the same position as himself.'[17]

To expect of men in such a position the discipline of a colonial police force is unreasonable. The peasant might resist the seizure of his women, suicidal as it was likely to be, but he accepted the casual expropriation of his property as part of the way of life to which he had been born. 'When a *raja* helps himself to their goods it gives them a sort of claim on him which, though never put in words, may at some future date be worth a good deal to them in the shape of food, clothing or protection.'[18] The relationship between power and dependence was unequal but it did impose obligations on both sides.

Although the *budak raja* were professional fighting men, they were not numerous enough to form an army. It seems to have been the convention that a ruler or other magnate should not move about unless followed by a minimum of forty followers.[19] On the other hand, he could not control more than 100 or 200 at most, nor expect them to find food from local resources. If he needed an army, he had to mobilize his subjects under the *kerah* system of compulsory service.[20]

It was common practice for a ruler to leave the able-bodied adults of both sexes of his household to fend for themselves. The men robbed and the women were sometimes reduced to prostitution to get their daily rice.[21] The ruler did have a traditional obligation to support men who had been disabled while fighting in his wars and the dependants of men who had died or been killed.[22] There was also a more general obligation to relieve the suffering of the destitute of the community. Sultan Idris said that 'he was expected to have an open hand and appeals to his charity were numerous indeed'.[23] Failure to respond to such appeals was unseemly and could make the ruler very unpopular. It was one of the many reproaches against the detested Raja Yusuf, Regent and then Sultan of Perak (r.1876–87), that he was mean and miserly.[24]

The ruler was also obliged to support his wives and their personal retinue even if he turned a blind eye to the prostitution of the domestic staff of lower degree. As a Muslim, a ruler might have as many as four wives, but it was unusual for all the wives to enjoy the same status. A distinction was drawn between a royal consort, on whom the title 'Tunku Puan' might be conferred, and a secondary wife (*gundik*).[25] A secondary wife might have some prestige and exercise influence over her husband.[26] She was usually of a very respectable family but not of royal or high aristocratic descent. In theory at least, her sons would not have the same claim to succeed their father as his sons by a royal consort. If two of the wives ranked as royal consorts—it was unusual to accord this status to more than two—there could be bitter competition between the wives and their respective sons for the throne when it fell vacant. There was such a conflict in Kedah in 1879–81.[27]

Polygamy was more common among rulers than their subjects but it has been left for consideration in a later chapter since it was not a royal monopoly. Royal wives submitted reluctantly to polygamous marriage as a price to be paid for their privileged position.[28] To relieve the inevitable jealousy between wives, and because convention required it, a ruler usually accommodated his wives in different places. At the very least, he kept them apart by giving them separate wings of the *istana*.[29] More usually, like Sultan Idris, he maintained 'entirely different establishments' so that each wife had her own house.[30] Sultan Abdul Samad, ever a practical farmer, built a house for his second wife adjacent to a new area of padi land which he had developed and 'she now lives there and superintends operations'.[31]

In addition to suitable and separate accommodation, a royal wife was entitled to a domestic staff of appropriate size. It was also expected that the ruler would avoid showing so much favour to one wife as to inflict a public affront on the others. If each wife appeared to receive a minimum of sexual and other attention from her royal husband, she had to be content with that.[32] Many wives concentrated their efforts on extracting jewellery and other gifts of tangible value as a consolation for having to share their husband with other wives. It is not only in twentieth-century America that 'diamonds are a girl's best friend'. The trophies could be displayed on the lady's person on formal court occasions.

These various commitments—the support of dependants, gifts to charities, satisfying the claims of war veterans and wives—constituted a considerable burden on the ruler's resources. He could, of course, mobilize the services of his subjects as debt-bondsmen or under the *kerah* system to meet some demands. In so far as he needed cash, he usually made no distinction between household consumption and his outlay as a ruler. The concept of a privy purse entered into the Malay ruler's scheme of things only when a colonial regime deprived him of the right to collect revenues, relieved him of the provision of public services (if any) and made him a 'political allowance' for his personal needs. In the earlier period the ruler had various sources of cash income. In addition to his receipts from taxes, whether directly collected or remitted to him from districts, he might draw profits from monopolies of the import or export of specific commodities. In Pahang, for example, gold had to be sold to the ruler at a fixed price of $22 per ounce, compared with the market value (in 1887) of $30–40 in Kuala Lumpur.[33] The ruler of Terengganu drew part of his income in 1909 from the profits of his pepper plantations.[34] In the West Coast states, export duties on tin and import duties on opium for the Chinese miners were an important part of royal revenues.[35] In Kedah in 1889, total state revenue of about $170,000 per annum came from export duties on padi and rice and from the import of opium and spirits.[36] In those states where the machinery for the collection of revenue was rudimentary, the ruler—and the local chiefs—were disposed to tax 'everything that moved' since goods in transit were most susceptible to their imposts. In Pahang, for example, Clifford received many complaints of the high price of 'common necessaries such as tobacco, gambier ... even such articles as needles and thread, and such common necessaries as onions and curry-stuffs being heavily taxed'. Imported Javanese tobacco cost $1 per pound in Pahang but only 40–50 cents in Perak. In addition, the ruler levied a poll-tax on adult males and required the local chiefs to accept imported cloth by compulsory purchase (*serah*) at a high price for resale in their districts at prices which were about double the normal market price. Yet this ruler's revenues totalled only about $120,000 per annum—though a good deal more must have been retained by those who collected the taxes for him, whether as intermediaries or contractors to whom the right to collect a specific tax was 'farmed', i.e. let for a fixed sum.[37] It seems a fair general conclusion that, in an independent Malay state, the ruler obtained with some difficulty an annual revenue of $100,000 or a little more, but much of it was committed to existing outgoings, personal or public.

A few rulers managed none the less to accumulate a surplus. There was a disposition to hoard these savings in realizable but unproductive form as a reserve against the crises which experience showed could befall a ruler at short notice. When the ruler of Kedah fled through the jungle to escape the Siamese in 1821 he scattered rupee notes from his elephant howdah so that the pursuing Siamese would halt to look for the money; later he raised a war chest by pledging a variety of gold ornaments and utensils to the money-lenders of Melaka.[38] When Raja Mahdi was driven out of the rich tin district of Klang in 1870, he took his hoard of $100,000 in notes.[39] Raja Yusuf of Perak, a notorious miser, did not conceal his wealth but occasionally indulged his taste for striking costume by 'appearing effulgent in a blazing diadem of gold and diamonds'.[40] Sultan Abdul Samad was another ruler who managed to accumulate wealth. When, for example, he visited Kuala Lumpur in 1892, he brought with him $8,000 in notes so that he might exchange the money into silver dollars in which he had more confidence.[41] He 'was supposed to have a very large store [of tin ingots] buried under his house'[42] and '$30,000 in two iron chests under his bed'.[43] At his death in 1898 his treasure, mainly in dollars and jewellery, was valued at about $200,000.[44] But unlike Yusuf, he was ready to draw on his wealth to make loans to peasant cultivators and for other forms of agricultural development.[45]

As recounted in the previous chapter the rulers reacted to colonial rule by seeking new activities. They also showed their interest in Islam in various ways.[46] The loss of free services due to the abolition of debt-bondage and the limitation of *kerah* service to public activities, imposed on them for a time a reduction in the scale of their private and personal interests.[47] In time, however, their 'political allowances' from the state treasuries grew sufficiently to give them scope for new recreations. Contact with European visitors and officials opened up new vistas.

As early as 1826 James Low, on a visit to Perak, invited the ruler to afternoon tea—'he partook of coffee, biscuits and confections. He amused himself with music particularly that of the violin.'[48] In adopting new habits, a ruler did not abandon old traditions. Idris of Perak, for example, followed the hallowed practice of putting his children into the hands of foster-parents to avoid the ill fortune which might befall those who had charge of rearing royal children.[49] But when it came to furnishing his new *istana* in the 1890s he obtained the china, glass and crockery from Maples Store in Tottenham Court Road in London—'very handsome, each piece has a wavy Malay *keris* engraved on it'.[50] It was sometimes necessary to restrain the eagerness of British officials who foisted on Malay rulers articles for which they had no use, such as the piano supplied to Sultan Abdul Samad—neither he nor any member of his household could play it.[51]

Abu Bakar of Johor was not accepted by his fellow rulers as one of their number and so he sought acceptance in European circles by adopting a European life-style.[52] When Florence Caddy stayed with him 'the Sultan appeared dressed for dinner in a monkey jacket, with the order of the Star of India, and a black fez, with an *aigrette* of large diamonds in front; half-a-dozen gipsy-rings on each hand, almost covering his fat little fingers; the rings all rubies and diamonds on one hand, and emeralds and diamonds on the other . . . we pulled crackers and the Sultan's band played during dinner'. The gold dinner service included wine-coolers and 'the smaller pieces of this service in the Neo-Pompeian style are very elegant'.[53] Another observer wrote that 'the Sultan kept a splendid stud of horses, drove a four-in-hand (as did also Governor Weld), played cricket and billiards, and was generally a good sportsman'.[54] His first venture in the ownership of a steam-yacht ended in disaster. On her arrival at Singapore from Scotland, where she had been built, she was prepared for an inaugural voyage up the coast with the Governor and other leaders of local society as the ruler's guests. Before the distinguished passengers had embarked the engine-room blew up, killing thirty people, including four European mariners who had been wrestling with the recalcitrant engines.[55] Undeterred, however, he obtained a replacement and on occasion lent it to the Governor, since it was more comfortable than the government launch. This did not save him from a rebuke on his extravagance; if he spent money on the development of his state, said Weld, it would 'make the Maharaja's name more illustrious than palaces, and plate and entertainments'.[56]

The object of this lavish hospitality was always to impress. Florence Caddy overheard Abu Bakar speaking 'sharply' to his nephews—'Now mind you talk to these English people; if you can't talk sense, talk nonsense, only talk plenty.'[57] Yet Abu Bakar had his reservations. He provided fine wines for his guests but as a

Muslim drank only water at the dinner table. When he travelled abroad he took his own cooks to prepare his meals, using meat slaughtered in the Muslim fashion.[58]

The only other Malay ruler of this period who openly adopted a European life-style, though in a more restrained fashion, was Ahmad Tajuddin II of Kedah (r.1854–79) whose early years had been spent in the SS.[59] He habitually wore European clothes, drank alcohol, and made frequent visits to Penang.[60] He also made periodic visits to Bangkok to do business with the King of Siam, whose vassal he was, and the King's ministers.[61] He seems to have been a gifted musician and he employed a European music master with whom he played the violin each evening.[62] In spite of these various proclivities the ruler of Kedah was unquestionably a scion of an ancient dynasty which retained its Malay character.

The traditional form of royal transport by land was—in North Malaya at least—the domesticated elephant. The European carriage was a much more comfortable means of transport but it could only be brought into use as the rulers began to build roads in and around their capitals. Towards the end of the nineteenth century the carriage was making its appearance even in unlikely places such as Kuala Terengganu, where Skeat found in 1899 that 'Trengganu in fact showed more European influence than the other Malay states. A Victoria, a dog-cart and several horses were landed by the *Neera* on her arrival at Trengganu even during our visit; pneumatic-tyred bicycles were already being used by the Sultan's entourage, and a few rickshaws had been imported.'[63] Bicycles were probably the fashionable novelty of the time. A few weeks later in Alor Star, Skeat wrote that 'I saw the Sultan flash past, mounted on a bicycle and followed closely by one of his body-guard'.[64] It has been mentioned above that Abu Bakar of Johor drove a four-in-hand. When Swettenham visited Alor Star in 1889, he went snipe-shooting with Sultan Abdul Hamid 'driving to the ground—the Sultan himself drives tandem but uses on state occasions a regular English state carriage drawn by 17 hand horses and driven by an Indian coachman'.[65] With horses came a variety of related innovations. Skeat noted 'the Raja's palm-thatched stables' in Perlis;[66] Norman found that in southern Siam the ruler of Legeh had a 'large racecourse' in front of his *istana*.[67]

Few rulers could match the affluence, or extravagance, of Abu Bakar in owning a yacht but Ahmad Tajuddin II of Kedah owned and built vessels mainly as a commercial enterprise. In 1863 he bought a two-masted sailing ship and manned her with a Malay captain and crew. He also owned a paddle-steamer, suitable for rapid transit in the sheltered waters between Kedah and Penang. When he visited Bangkok in 1865, he went overland to Singgora (Songkhla) and went on by sea in his own ship, which he used as his base during his stay in the Siamese capital. King Mongkut, not to be outdone, placed a state barge at his disposal in which he was rowed along the canals of Bangkok.[68]

Ahmad Tajuddin of Kedah also established a shipbuilding yard for the construction and enlargement of wooden vessels and took much personal interest in its operations.[69] The main centre of Malay shipbuilding was Kuala Terengganu. Here, too, local industries had been established or developed by an energetic ruler, Baginda Omar. A visitor in 1846 described a wooden schooner built by Malay craftsmen trained in Singapore and assisted by Chinese carpenters as 'a very creditable piece of workmanship'. The Malay shipbuilders were astonished that a visiting cruiser, built of iron, could float.[70]

No distinction can be made between these commercial enterprises and the traditional role of a Malay ruler in encouraging local agriculture and industry. The more businesslike rulers saw their opportunities and took them. 'At his court [at Raman, north of Perak, in 1883] are workmen skilled in the manufacture of spears, *krises*, parangs and other weapons, they are good carvers in wood and workers in gold. The Raja himself makes very handsome howdahs of fine wrought *rotan* for his elephants.'[71] The craftsmen at such a court worked partly for the adornment of the ruler's household and partly for export. Moreover, a ruler might, without loss of dignity, work as a craftsman. Baginda Omar of Terengganu sent wood carvings which were the work of his own hands to Sir Harry Ord, the Governor in Singapore.[72] Later Sultan Sulaiman of Selangor 'carved the ornamental wood-work and extracts from the Kuran which can be seen at the top of the *mimba*, the pulpit in the mosque from which he on occasion preaches to his people'. He had also been 'seen on his hands and knees measuring the size of the prayer-mats which would be required in the new mosque'.[73] In this, he was following the example of his grandfather and immediate predecessor, Sultan Abdul Samad, whose habit it was to carry a *parang*, the all-purpose Malay chopping knife, when taking his daily walk, to demonstrate that he could do agricultural work, as indeed he did when so disposed.[74]

One may here discern some subtle distinctions. The work of a craftsman carried some prestige, even though most craftsmen were of the subject class, and so a ruler might join in such work without loss of dignity. But domestic chores of preparing a meal and serving it were, by tradition, the task of slaves or bondswomen.[75] No aristocrat would willingly do such things for himself. There were some rare exceptions. Raja Arfah, wife of Tunku Kudin and daughter of Sultan Abdul Samad of Selangor, was imperious and quite as cranky as her father. She cooked her own meals but this was regarded as eccentric.[76]

Monopolies of the export or import of commodities were a traditional method of raising revenue, as described above. The ruler generally delegated this prerogative, where it existed, to a tax farmer or—in earlier times—to an Indian merchant as *saudagar raja*.[77] Royal trade monopolies soon disappeared. Straits Settlements merchants pressed for their abolition and in any case a ruler had difficulty in maintaining an effective commercial monopoly with the limited means of control at his disposal. However, the tradition of royal involvement in business enterprises persisted and found new outlets, some of which have already been described.

When Weld visited Johor in 1882 he was taken to see Abu Bakar's tea, coffee and cocoa plantations and sampled his tea, which he pronounced to be of 'excellent quality'.[78] In Kedah, Ahmad Tajuddin II began to plant coffee as early as 1870.[79] When the rubber boom began, Idris of Perak formed a consortium of 'native gentlemen' with a view to planting 15,000 acres. This would have been a huge estate by the standards of the time but nothing seems to have come of the project.[80]

There was a general disposition among rulers to adopt a European life-style in such things as dress and housing. When Abdul Hamid of Kedah visited London in 1911 to attend the Coronation, he brought no Malay costume with him. Buckingham Palace, however, indicated that if he was to ride in the procession he must wear his national dress. He then arranged with a London tailor to make what was required, including a folded head-cloth—it must have been an interesting commission for Savile Row.[81] Even on formal public occasions in his own state, or elsewhere in Malaya, it was normal practice for the ruler to wear a European suit. But, as will be explained in a later chapter, Malay ideas of decency require that the male thighs shall be veiled in a very loose garment. Sultan Sulaiman of Selangor therefore wore a *sarung* over his trousers.[82]

Suit, *sarung* and—usually—a Turkish-style fez combined to provide a new and mixed style of Malay formal dress. In the same spirit of compromise, a ruler might preserve the austere Malay domestic furnishings for the interior of his *istana* but equip his public rooms, where he received guests, who were often European, in Western fashion. Alternatively, he had a separate guest-house built for the accommodation of his visitors and they found that 'everything was done as in a European's house'.[83]

Visits to Singapore or Penang gave a ruler the opportunity of observing how the Europeans lived. One of the most striking cultural encounters of this kind was the visit to Singapore in April 1910 of Sultan Zainal Abidin III of Terengganu, who was a pious recluse and had had little previous contact with European society. On his arrival 'a motor car was placed at his disposal' and 'he visited the Alhambra Theatre that evening and witnessed a cinematograph exhibition'—we are not told, however, what the programme was. Later he saw a balloon ascent and parachute jump and a military parade.[84] It was not the technical novelties which impressed him. On his return, the British Agent reported that 'the Sultan and his followers were greatly impressed by this parade of British and Indian troops and have frequently since our return expressed their astonishment at the sight of so many men acting as one simply on a word of command . . . in fact they derived more pleasure from this parade than from anything else they witnessed in Singapore'.[85] The parade was sufficiently like Malay ceremonial with its lines of spearmen along the route to the *balai* to be within the range of experience of the Terengganu party.[86] The technological marvels were just too strange to be comprehensible.

Delicate questions of precedence could arise when rulers paid visits to each other or met on neutral ground since, according to Clifford, 'each state holds that its ruling house should by right take precedence of all others'. When the four rulers of the newly established FMS gathered for the first time at a durbar at Kuala Kangsar in 1897, it was feared that this might lead to 'some unpleasant incident'. However, Sultan Idris of Perak played the role of host with such 'courtesy and tact' and splendid hospitality that everyone was in high good humour.[87] If one ruler visited another, the host felt that he must outshine his guest in the lavishness of his royal hospitality.[88] Competition of this kind brought Kedah and Johor, still independent of British financial control, to the verge of bankruptcy.[89]

Sultan Abu Bakar of Johor, in his persistent search for foreign kudos to offset the lack of it at home, made several visits to Europe—the Continent as well as Britain—and he also visited India, China, and Japan. In his last visit abroad—he died in London—he met the Emperors of Germany and Austria, the King of Italy, and the Sultan of Turkey.[90] Sultan Idris of Perak was the only other Malay ruler of this period who travelled to Europe. He visited London four times. On his first visit in 1884 'what struck him most was the fact that in London there were "ten thousand times ten thousand carriages"'. He was also interested in the technology—the casting of big guns at the Woolwich ordnance factory, the telegraph instrument room at the General Post Office, and even the lavatories.[91]

Foreign travel, in particular a visit to London including meetings with Colonial Office officials and others who dwelt in the corridors of power, did more for Sultans Abu Bakar and Idris than enhance their prestige and widen their horizons. It gave them an insight into the structure of British imperial policy-making. Abu Bakar, and after him his son Sultan Ibrahim (r.1895–1959), learnt how to play off London against Singapore—to the fury of a succession of governors. Idris built up his influence by subtler and more effective means.[92] He kept the confidence and goodwill of powerful men in the colonial regime, especially Swettenham, and learnt how to communicate with them in terms of their own assumptions. In this fashion he was able to secure the adoption, in the teeth of much official scepticism, of R. J. Wilkinson's scheme for a Malay College at Kuala Kangsar.[93] In his own backyard in Perak he could manipulate British power to get his way in the prolonged intrigues of the early twentieth century over the choice of a successor to himself.[94]

Sultan Idris, and also Sultan Sulaiman of Selangor, had been educated to read and write Malay in their boyhood or early manhood.[95] Both realized that a command of English would be useful in developing their lines of communication with the British bureaucracy and they set about learning English—Idris when he had already come to the throne, and Sulaiman when, as Raja Muda, he was already performing public duties for his aged grandfather, Sultan Abdul Samad.[96] When Swettenham was in Kedah in 1889, he found that the young Sultan Abdul Hamid spent two hours every evening with his English tutor, and his brother, Raja Muda Abdul Aziz—'a very intelligent young fellow—studies for four hours every day and already speaks English tolerably fluently'.[97] They did not generally speak English in public—they may have preferred not to do so in an imperfect fashion.[98] The proceedings of their state councils were conducted in Malay and Residents and district officers were required to be proficient in Malay, but it must have been useful to a ruler to be able to follow an English conversation or read an English document.

New tastes and activities added to the ruler's personal expenditure without diminishing his traditional obligations. Wives, too, had expensive tastes and yet expected to be supplied with the same number of personal servants as in the old days when slaves or bondswomen worked without being paid. Sultan Idris reckoned that in providing 'three entirely different establishments' for his wives he employed between sixty and one hundred domestic staff as paid servants.[99] 'Besides these expenses and a carriage and horses His Highness is expected to have an open hand and the appeals to his charity are very numerous indeed . . . a principal feature of Malay society has always been the feudal system . . . the people look to their chiefs and especially to the Sultan for assistance whenever they are in difficulty and they expect to receive it.'[100]

Fortunately this was a period of increasing public revenues from the growing prosperity of the Malay states. In states such as Johor or Kedah, royal expenditure might exceed available income. In the states under colonial rule, the ruler's problem was to persuade the authorities that his allowance from public funds should be increased as public revenues themselves increased.[101] Most Residents, anxious to preserve the ruler's goodwill and well aware of his embarrassment, were sympathetic. But Colonial Office approval for a periodic increase was sometimes more difficult to obtain.

From one of these official dialogues, over a proposed increase in the allowance to Sultan Sulaiman of Selangor in 1909, it is possible to build up a picture of the calls on a ruler's income. The Resident (H.C. Belfield) borrowed the Sultan's account books to extract figures with which to convince the curmudgeons of Downing Street. The Sultan spent $2,060 per month on 'allowances to the ladies of his household and to his children, the cost of their maintenance, the wages of political officials, attendants, servants and watchmen, in his own household and those of the ladies and divers other calls upon his purse'. The ruler's allowance from state funds was only $2,000 per month. On that alone Micawber's principles of domestic finance would have predicted misery in the *istana*. But there was worse to come, for the Sultan had also to provide for 'the cost of personal maintenance of the Sultan himself, whether by way of food or clothing, the education of his sons . . . the upkeep of his private garden and estate at Langat'. One may here interpose that the ruler's plantation was not a commercial success. In addition to these personal and family commitments, and charitable doles for which a supplementary allowance was already provided, the ruler had to respond to appeals for donations to funds for the building of mosques, the opening of village schools and other public good causes. It was not difficult to demonstrate that the ruler was 'in really straitened circumstances'.[102] It was all very different from the time when his grandfather had been able to hoard tin or dollars in a box under the bed.

Some parts of this chapter are equally applicable to the changing circumstances of members of royal families and holders of high traditional offices. The special problems of the Malay upper class in general are considered in the next chapter.

1. Anon., 'Journal Kept on Board a Cruiser in the Indian Archipelago in 1846', *JIA*, 8, 1854, p. 179.

2. J. R. Logan, 'The Manners and Customs of the Malays—Meals', *JIA*, 1850, pp. 433–5.

3. J. Low, 'Observations on Perak', *JIA*, 4, 1850, p. 502. Food was plain.

4. SSD 24 November 1909, where W. G. Maxwell describes a system which had probably been introduced by a previous ruler, Sultan Ahmad Tajuddin II (r.1854–79), who was an energetic organizer.

5. CO 273/87, pp. 229–39 and 333–7: evidence of witnesses to PCE.

6. *Malay Mail*, 29 July 1897.

7. Shaharil Talib Robert, 'The Trengganu Ruling Class in the Late Nineteenth Century', *JMBRAS*, 50(2), 1977, p. 28.

8. SSD 23 August 1906. See also p. 7 above for Mahmud bin Mat's account of his childhood.

9. R. J. Wilkinson, *A Malay–English Dictionary*, 2 parts, Singapore, Kelly & Walsh, 1901 (revised as *A Malay–English Dictionary (Romanised)*, 2 parts, Mytilene, Salavopoulos & Kinderlis, 1932), Part 1, p. 381.

10. Report by J. W. W. Birch dated 28 July 1875, enclosed with SSD 29 July 1878, printed in Cmd. 3285 and also in J. W. W. Birch, *The Journals of J. W. W. Birch First British Resident to Perak 1874–1875* (hereafter cited as *Birch Journal*), edited by P. L. Burns, Kuala Lumpur, Oxford University Press, 1976, pp. 100–4. See also H. C. Clifford, *Studies in Brown Humanity being Scrawls and Smudges in Sepia, White and Yellow*, London, Grant Richards, 1898, p. 210.

11. *AR Pahang 1889*; Shaharil Talib Robert, 'Trengganu Ruling Class', writes that Sultan Zainal Abidin 'was something of a sybarite and was known for his love of food and his sexual prowess' (p. 32).

12. 'The women in the palace were not the Sultan's concubines and owed no money, but were shut up by him, forbidden to marry and severely punished if they misbehaved' (Linehan, 'A History of Pahang', *JMBRAS*, 14(2), 1936, p. 124 (hereafter cited as 'Pahang'). This is probably the more typical situation.

13. 'It is death for anyone to go into the Sultan's house at night' (F. A. Swettenham, *Sir Frank Swettenham's Malayan Journals 1874–1876* (hereafter cited as *Swettenham Journal*), edited by P. L. Burns and C. D. Cowan, Kuala Lumpur, Oxford University Press, 1975, p. 282). See also Clifford's report enclosed with SSD 3 August 1887, para. 6; H. C. Clifford, *In Court and Kampong, Being Tales and Sketches of Native Life in the Malay Peninsula*, London, Grant Richards, 1897 (2nd ed. with autobiographical preface, London, Richards Press, 1927), pp. 182–95, for a gruesome account of the consequences of being caught.

14. E. Innes, *The Chersonese with the Gilding Off*, 2 vols., London, Richard Bentley and Son, 1885, reprinted Kuala Lumpur, Oxford University Press, 1974, Vol. 1, pp. 92–5, describes such an episode.

15. *AR Pahang 1889*; Linehan, 'Pahang', p. 129.

16. The *budak raja* is thus described in H. C. Clifford, *The Further Side of Silence*, New York, Doubleday, Page & Co., 1927, p. 66 (also included in *Studies in Brown Humanity*, p. 203, and H. C. Clifford, *Stories by Sir Hugh Clifford*, edited by W. R. Roff, Kuala Lumpur, Oxford University Press, p. 136). This is the beginning of a story of the brutal killing of a young villager who resists the abduction of his wife.

17 Report by Hugh Clifford on conditions at the royal capital of Pahang, enclosed with SSD 15 October 1887 (CO 273/148, p. 234). See also *AR Pahang 1889*; p. 238 below; and Innes, op. cit., Vol. 1, p. 182, cited in note 18.

18. Innes, op. cit., Vol. 1, pp. 182–3. On the general practice of expropriation (*merampas*), see A. C. Milner, *Kerajaan: Malay Political Culture on the Eve of Colonial Rule*, Tucson, University of Arizona Press, 1982, Chapter 2. The general effect was to discourage the peasant cultivator from producing a surplus.

19. Tunku Kudin arrived to stay as the house guest of Emily Innes with forty armed followers (Innes, op. cit., Vol. 1, p. 177). When Sultan Abdullah came to dinner with Birch he also brought forty followers (*Swettenham Journal*, p. 60). Kudin said that if he visited the hostile state capital of Selangor during the Civil War he took between 100 and 200 men for his personal safety (SSD 23 March 1875).

20. Ahmad of Pahang mobilized 4,000–5,000 men for his intervention in the Selangor Civil War in 1872 (Linehan, 'Pahang', p. 95). They were, however, divided up into contingents of about 1,000—perhaps because of problems of supply. In 1891 he raised 1,000 men to assist in suppressing the rising in Semantan (*AR Pahang 1891*, and Linehan, 'Pahang', pp. 143–4). When it was proposed to abolish *kerah* in Kedah in 1909 the Sultan's first reaction was to ask for an assurance from the British that if they thus deprived him of his conscript forces they would assist him in dealing with any local rising (SSD 16 September 1909).

21. Birch report cited in note 10; J. M. Gullick, *Indigenous Political Systems of Western Malaya*, London, Athlone Press, 1958, p. 103, citing PCE evidence; Swettenham's report of 30 June 1875, printed in Cmd. 3285 of 1882.

22. SSD 5 June 1875 and SSD 26 October 1877 refer to recognized obligations of this kind in Pahang and in Kedah, arising in both cases out of the Selangor Civil War in which men from both states had taken part.

23. SSD 24 September 1890.

24. 'The most penurious man in the state ... did nothing to uphold the dignity of his office' (SSD 24 September 1890).

25. Although *gundik* normally denoted a wife (note 9 above), it was used in Pahang to include a concubine as well as a wife (Linehan, 'The Bendaharas of Pahang', *JMBRAS*, 4(3), 1926, p. 337). In Terengganu there was no royal consort or principal wife among the ruler's numerous spouses and so all his children ranked as *anak gundik*. This status did not disqualify a son from succeeding to the throne, but if there were younger half-brothers born to a royal wife, they took precedence (SSD 22 September 1909: CO 273/351, p. 217). In the Selangor succession dispute of 1857–9 (Chapter 2, note 64 above) the late ruler's sons by *gundik* were passed over altogether in favour of a young boy but he in turn was displaced by a cousin. A consort of royal birth had the title '*raja perempuan*' (or '*puan*') but a principal wife of non-royal birth was '*raja permaisuri*' (Wilkinson, *1932 Dictionary*, Part 2, p. 280).

26. One such was Che Uteh, the formidable secondary wife—among several—of Sultan Idris of Perak. Anderson, on leave in London in 1909, wrote to the Colonial Office that 'the Sultan's second wife gives the Sultan no rest over the matter' (the choice of a successor) (CO 273/355, p. 269). On the marriages of the uxorious Sultan Idris—there were seven—see Hussain bin Mahmud, 'Sultan Idris of Perak', *Malaya in History*, 13(1), 1970, and W. E. Maxwell, 'The History of Perak from Native Sources', *JSBRAS*, 14, 1884, p. 319.

27. Ahmad Tajuddin II had two royal wives. At his death his eldest son succeeded him as Sultan Zainal Rashid II but died within two years in 1881. There was then a bitter dispute as to whether the next son, in order of age, born of the same wife should succeed or whether the succession should pass—as in the end it did—to the eldest son of the other royal wife. This was Sultan Abdul Hamid (r.1882–1943), whose mother was the sister of the powerful chief minister, Wan Mat Saman, who played a leading part in the struggle. Sultan Ahmad of Pahang (r.1863–1914), who usurped the throne from his elder brother, Wan Mutahir, sought to justify his action by asserting that his (Ahmad's) mother was of higher status: she had been a secondary wife whereas Mutahir's mother was a mere concubine of their father and so he had 'superior legitimacy' (Linehan, 'Bendaharas of Pahang', p. 337). It does not matter whether the claim was factually correct: the fact that it was made shows the importance of the issue.

28. In all walks of life Malay women had a 'strong objection to being one wife of many' (F. A. Swettenham, *British Malaya: An Account of the Origin and Progress of British Influence in Malaya*, London, John Lane Bodley Head, 1907 (revised editions 1929 and 1948, London, Allen & Unwin), p. 154. Polygamy is considered at p. 217 below.

29. Ahmad Tajuddin of Kedah allotted separate wings of the same *istana* to his two wives (Muhammad Hassan bin Dato' Kerani Muhammad Arshad, *Al-Tarikh Salasilah Negeri Kedah*, Kuala Lumpur, Dewan Bahasa dan Pustaka, 1968 (previously published in *Jawi*, 1926), p. 207).

30. SSD 24 September 1890.

31. *SGG* 1893, p. 609.

32. It was inevitable that some wives should receive more favour than others.

Florence Caddy wrote of Abu Bakar's principal wife that 'he esteems her highly and consults her in everything' (F. Caddy, *To Siam and Malaya in the Duke of Sutherland's Yacht 'Sans Peur'*, London, Hurst & Blackett, 1889, p. 236). At the other extreme, Ahmad of Pahang complained to Swettenham that his brother ruler and son-in-law, Sultan Zainal Abidin III of Terengganu, treated Tunku Long, daughter of one and wife of the other, 'like a kept woman' (SSD 24 June 1895). In the end there was a divorce 'owing to incompatibility of temper—the pleasure loving blood in the Pahang royalties did not mate well with the religious and austere blood of the Trengganu family' (SSD 21 August 1913). It appears that after the marriage the ruler of Terengganu returned to his own state leaving his bride behind (in 1886). Her father declined to send her to join her husband, arguing that the latter should return to escort his wife to his country (SSD 25 July 1893). When she did take up residence in Kuala Terengganu her husband so much neglected her as to give public affront. Since he later pleaded that he had been ill, it appears that he did not cohabit with her in the sexual sense—at all events not as often as decorum required. She then returned to Pahang (SSD 26 August 1895). Dynastic marriages could be prickly affairs, especially if the wife was disposed to stand on her dignity. In Jelebu, Keyser (*Trifles and Travels*, London, Murray, 1923, p. 89) met the Undang (ruling chief) 'reclining in a bullock cart, while on his way from the district where the relations of one wife were paramount to another where the claims of spouse No. 2 had to be put on an equally satisfactory footing. "And after that," he sighed wearily, "there are two more."' In Jelebu, only the Undang and the Yam Tuan Muda (royal chief) were permitted to depart from the norm of monogamy (p. 111).

33. On the Pahang revenues the principal source of information is the reports by Clifford in 1887 enclosed with SSD 28 April 1887: CO 273/144, pp. 466–70, and SSD 3 August 1887: CO 273/146, pp. 100–1.

34. In Terengganu the ruler's income in 1909 was about $100,000 per annum, which he shared with the Raja Muda and 'a cloud of chiefs' (SSD 22 September 1909: CO 273/351, p. 216).

35. During his time (1874–5) in Perak, J. W. W. Birch collected material for detailed reports of 14 December 1874, enclosed with SSD 14 December 1876, and 2 April 1875 enclosed with SSD 26 April 1875; both are reprinted in *Birch Journal*, pp. 378–98. *Birch Journal*, *Swettenham Journal*, and H. Low, 'The Journal of Sir Hugh Low, Perak 1877' (hereafter cited as 'Low Journal'), edited by E. Sadka, *JMBRAS*, 27(4), 1954, abound with references to particular aspects of the revenues of rulers and chiefs in Perak and Selangor.

36. Report by W. G. Maxwell, who visited Kedah in 1889, enclosed with SSD 17 May 1889.

37. See reports cited in note 33 above.

38. J. M. Gullick, 'Kedah 1821–1855: Years of Exile and Return', *JMBRAS*, 56(2), 1983, pp. 31 and 46.

39. Memorandum by C. J. Irving enclosed with SSD 18 June 1878.

40. SSD 5 February 1886. At his death his estate included $30,000 in cash and jewellery estimated to be worth $50,000, plus some items in the possession of 'the ladies of the family' (SSD 20 August 1887). Another source mentions a 'diamond kopiah, *sirih* box and house property at Kuala Kangsar' (*PSCM*, *PGG* 1892, p. 703).

41. *SGG* 1892, p. 930.

42. Swettenham, *British Malaya*, p. 128.

43. Douglas Diary, 13 May 1878.

44. *Malay Mail*, 7 February 1898. At the Sultan's death a worried district officer took charge of the boxes of valuables held in a wooden building at the *istana*, made a rough inventory and sealed them up (*SGG* 1898, p. 70). The financial problems of his grandson and successor, Sultan Sulaiman, referred to below, were due in part to the fact that he inherited nothing from this large estate. Under Islamic law of inheritance the widows and surviving children alone shared in it. Sulaiman had no entitlement, as he would have had if English law of intestate distribution had applied, to the share of his father who had died in 1884, i.e. before Sultan Abdul Samad.

It was rumoured in the 1890s that Sultan Abdul Samad had 5 hundredweight of gold ornaments—*sirih* boxes, *pinding* (waist buckles), ear-rings, bracelets, and brooches. One of the largest brooches weighed 5 pounds and was made of pure gold with a large uncut sapphire in the centre. The gold *sirih* boxes and *keris* handles were 'very beautifully wrought' (*SJ*, 23 September 1892, probably written by J. H. M. Robson, who had been the local district officer in his time).

45. As one example of Abdul Samad's willingness to put money into agriculture he made loans of $2,000 to smallholders in 1892 (*AR Selangor 1892*). See also *AR Selangor 1886* and *AR Selangor 1892* and various entries in the Douglas Diary.

46. Chapter 2, p. 32, and Chapter 12, p. 293.

47. Chapter 9, pp. 213–14.

48. J. Low, 'Observations on Perak', p. 503.

49. R. J. Wilkinson, 'The Incidents of Malay Life', *Papers on Malay Subjects, Life and Customs*, Part 1, Kuala Lumpur, Government Press, 1908; reprinted in *JMBRAS*, 30(4), 1957, p. 44. If the foster-parents survived their perilous task they might expect compensation in exceptional good fortune in later life. Wilkinson suggests that the real reason was to remove royal children from the risk of death at the hands of another wife, jealous of their mother.

50. E. Thio, *British Policy in the Malay Peninsula*, Vol. 1: *The Southern and Central States*, Kuala Lumpur and Singapore, University of Malaya Press, 1969, p. 164; *PGG* 1896, p. 678.

51. SSD 24 August 1882, on the enforced retirement of Bloomfield Douglas, who had broken the rule against selling goods to the ruler of his state. The piano was said to have been a present but the Sultan had paid, by deduction from his political allowance, for a uniform, horses, carriages, and picture. His account books, enclosed with the despatch, are interesting reading.

52. Norman noted that the other rulers 'do not regard him as an equal, on account of his far from royal birth' (*The Peoples and Politics of the Far East: Travels and Studies in the British ... Colonies and Malaya*, New York, Scribner, 1895, p. 63). This is confirmed in respect of a number of individual rulers—Yusuf of Perak (SSD 3 April and 28 August 1886); Ahmad of Terengganu (SSD 14 August 1878); Abdul Samad of Selangor (SSD 23 January 1882). Zainal Abidin of Terengganu once refused to sit at table with Abu Bakar (R. O. Winstedt, 'A History of Johore', *JMBRAS*, 10(3), 1932, p. 119). In the same passage Winstedt lists the foreign rulers and courts where Sultan Abu Bakar had met with acceptance (p. 60) on his final burst of visiting foreign capitals.

53. Caddy, op. cit., p. 235.

54. Roland St. J. Braddell, 'The Good Old Days', in Walter Makepeace, Gilbert

E. Brooke and Roland St. J. Braddell (eds.), *One Hundred Years of Singapore*, London, Murray, 1921, Vol. 2, p. 522.

55. Charles Burton Buckley, *An Anecdotal History of Old Times in Singapore 1819–1867*, Singapore, Fraser & Neave, 1902, reprinted Kuala Lumpur, University of Malaya Press, 1965, and Singapore, Oxford University Press, 1984, Vol. 2, pp. 720–1.

56. The loan of the yacht and Weld's rebuke (SSD 8 July 1883 and SSD 10 January 1884).

57. Caddy, op. cit., p. 265.

58. Ibid., p. 242.

59. Gullick, 'Kedah', p. 34. J. M. Gullick, 'Kedah in the Reign of Sultan Ahmad Tajuddin II (1854–1879), *JMBRAS*, 58(2), 1985, p. 116.

60. A. E. Anson, *About Others and Myself 1745–1920*, London, Murray, 1920, p. 313.

61. Muhammad Hassan, op. cit., pp. 201 and 214, mentions visits to Bangkok in 1855 and 1865, but there were probably others as well. The King of Siam visited Kedah in or about 1874 (Muhammad Hassan, op. cit., p. 227).

62. Muhammad Hassan, op. cit., p. 225.

63. W. W. Skeat and F. F. Laidlaw, 'The Cambridge University Expedition to the North-eastern Malay States, and to Upper Perak, 1899–1900', *JMBRAS*, 26(4), 1953, p. 124.

64. Ibid., p. 126.

65. SSD 23 November 1889.

66. Skeat and Laidlaw, op. cit., p. 135.

67. Norman, op. cit., p. 553. When J. S. Mason, the first British Adviser to Kelantan, arrived to take up his post in 1909, he and his Siamese-appointed predecessor, W. A. Graham, rode to the *balai* for the hand-over ceremony in the Sultan's carriage (SSD 3 August 1909). By this time it had become accepted that in a European carriage the distinguished royal passenger might be seated at a lower level than his coachman (see p. 39, note 6 above).

68. Muhammad Hassan, op. cit., pp. 211–15. This was not the ruler's first venture as a ship-owner. In 1856 he bought a British barque, the *Gratitude*, and entrusted the 'entire management' of the vessel to a Penang merchant, L. Nairne. In April 1857 she was chartered to a Chinese for a voyage to China but was lost by shipwreck off the coast of China (J. W. Norton-Kyshe, *Cases Heard and Determined in H.M. Supreme Court of the Straits Settlements 1808–1884*, Singapore, Singapore and Straits Printing Office, 1885, Vol. 1, p. 145, reporting *Nairne* v. *Sultan of Kedah*). See also Khoo Kay Kim, *The Western Malay States 1850–1873—The Effects of Commercial Development on Malay Politics*, Kuala Lumpur, Oxford University Press, 1972, pp. 65–6, on Nairne, and Gullick, 'Sultan Ahmad Tajuddin', p. 115.

69. Gullick, 'Sultan Ahmad Tajuddin', p. 115.

70. Anon., *Journal Kept on a Cruiser*. In 1875 Swettenham saw a three-masted schooner belonging to the ruler of Terengganu (*Swettenham Journal*, p. 266).

71. J. Cameron, 'On the Patani', *JSBRAS*, 11, 1883, p. 130. Clifford described the economic role of a Malay ruler as—'he was the principal trader, the richest man, the banker and advancer of capital to his people' (H. C. Clifford, 'Life in the Malay Peninsula: As It Was and Is', in P. H. Kratoska (ed.), *Honourable Intentions: Talks on the British Empire in South-East Asia Delivered at the Royal Colonial Institute, 1874–1928*, Kuala Lumpur, Oxford University Press, 1983 (reprinted from the

Proceedings of the Royal Colonial Institute, 1899), p. 230).

72. 'Specimens of the Sultan's skill as a carver of which he is very proud' (SSD 22 December 1869).

73. *Singapore Sunday Times*, 9 September 1934, p. 13. Winstedt wrote that the Sultan's 'hobbies were religion, cookery and wood-carving' (Richard Winstedt, *Start from Alif, Count from One: An Autobiographical Memoire*, Kuala Lumpur, Oxford University Press, 1969, p. 5).

74. *SJ*, 23 September 1892.

75. See notes 4–9 above.

76. Innes, op. cit., Vol. 1, p. 97.

77. Milner, *Kerajaan*, Chapter 2. B.W. Andaya, 'The Indian "Saudagar Raja" (The King's Merchant) in Traditional Malay Courts', *JMBRAS*, 51(1), 1978. On Pahang monopolies see note 33 above. On the Kelantan monopolies of the mid-nineteenth century, see SSD 14 October 1867: CO 273/15, p. 427; CO 273/23, p. 280. On Terengganu royal monopolies see Shaharil Talib, *After Its Own Image: The Trengganu Experience 1881–1941* (hereafter cited as *The Trengganu Experience*), Singapore, Oxford University Press, 1984, p. 48.

78. SSD 3 October 1882.

79. Muhammad Hassan, op. cit., p. 220.

80. *AR Perak 1898*; J.C. Jackson, *Planters and Speculators: Chinese and European Agricultural Enterprise in Malaya 1786–1921*, Kuala Lumpur and Singapore, University of Malaya Press, 1968, p. 221. In 1905 the Sultan was a buyer of shop property in Kuala Kangsar (*AR Perak 1905*).

81. Mubin Sheppard, *Tunku: A Pictorial Biography 1903–1957*, Petaling Jaya, Malaysia, Pelanduk Publications, 1984, p. 20. See note 59 on Sultan Ahmad Tajuddin II.

82. *Malay Mail*, 18 February 1898. He normally dressed in this style on formal but less important occasions. When European visitors arrived to see his grandfather, Sultan Abdul Samad, at Kuala Langat, it was the duty of Sulaiman, then Raja Muda, to receive them at the entrance to the *istana* compound. He was 'dressed in European fashion with the *sarong* added' (*SJ*, 23 September 1892). He was, however, accompanied by some forty or fifty followers in traditional fashion—see note 19 above and p. 189 below.

83. SSD 23 November 1889—an account by Swettenham of his reception during a visit to Alor Star. Muhammad Hassan, op. cit., p. 209, mentions that a house built by Tunku Kudin, then Raja Muda of Kedah, was by arrangement between him and his elder brother, the ruler, used for the accommodation of foreign visitors.

84. SSD 27 April and 28 June 1910.

85. SSD 28 June 1910.

86. See p. 42, note 34, above for the reception given to Jervois in Terengganu in 1875. Sultan Zainal Abidin III, as a boy of ten, may well have witnessed it.

87. *AR Pahang 1897*. The real disaster of the Kuala Kangsar durbar was the programme of entertainments. 'A great fish drive' was a fiasco as the fish took refuge in deep water. Few competitors entered for the athletic sports but the traditional rock-slide (*menggeluncur*), described at p. 347 below, was much more popular. Boat races could not take place as planned, since the large influx of visitors led to the occupation of the boats as temporary accommodation. Finally, someone set off the fireworks before the distinguished guests had gathered to watch the display. Idris, however, gave a series of splendid dinner parties and then took the party, which

included many chiefs attending on their rulers, on late night rounds of the theatrical and other popular entertainments in the town. They all seem to have enjoyed themselves, except old Sultan Abdul Samad who was within a few months of his death at the age of ninety-three and was not equal to the strain of the occasion. (SSD 20 August 1897 forwarding a report by Swettenham).

88. In asking for an increase in his political allowance, Sultan Idris argued that he needed houses, carriages, etc., suitable for the entertainment of the Sultan of Kedah and the King of Siam, both of whom had recently visited Perak. Idris himself had been lavishly entertained by the extravagant Sultan Abdul Hamid when Idris visited Kedah (SSD 24 September 1890).

89. On the death of Sultan Abu Bakar in 1895 the state treasury was almost empty (Gaddy, op. cit., p. 236; Thio, op. cit., p. 227). On the Kedah crisis arising from the royal marriages of 1904, see p. 47 above. Neither Johor nor Kedah was at this stage under colonial rule, but both were so much permeated by European influence in the royal life-style that 'pre-colonial' is hardly a meaningful distinction in this context of social behaviour.

90. Winstedt, 'History of Johore', p. 119.

91. Norman, op. cit., p. 61. H. Clifford, *Bushwhacking and Other Asiatic Tales and Memories*, New York, Harper, 1929, pp. 191–6; *Malayan Monochromes*, New York, Dutton, 1913, pp. 149–58, describes Sultan Idris's 1902 visit to London. During the visit an emotional outburst by the Sultan's son, Raja Alang Iskander, who had been a student in England for some years before, prompted Clifford to write his novel, *A Prince of Malaya*, on the impact of Western culture on an impressionable young Malay aristocrat (see. P. C. Wicks, 'The Malayan Novels of Sir Hugh Clifford', *Malaya in History*, 27, 1984, p. 14). Clifford may have over-dramatized his main theme but in the second half of the novel, originally published as *Saleh: A Sequel*, he provides an absorbing picture of domestic life and intrigue within a royal *istana*. This is no doubt based on his observation of Ahmad's household at Pekan in 1887–9.

92. Sultan Idris was the only one of the four FMS rulers who was able to take part in the debates at the first meeting of the new FMS Federal Council in 1909 (SSD 2[illegible] December 1909). Although the short study by Hussain bin Mahmud, op. cit., is useful, the political career and personal development of Sultan Idris merit a full-length study. As a young man he was one of the rather raffish circle around his cousin, Sultan Abdullah (see p. 40, note 12 above). He was an opium smoker whom Birch judged 'rather a debauchee' (*Birch Journal*, p. 58). The turning point perhaps came with the arrival in Perak of Hugh Low in 1877. Within weeks Low concluded that this was a prominent figure whom he would recommend—'a good berth to be provided for him' ('Low Journal', p. 81). Thereafter, there was an unbroken flow of high praise from senior figures of the colonial regime—'stands for all that is best in the Malay ruling class . . . intelligence . . . experience . . . great charm of manner . . . a fluent speaker . . . a very earnest Muhammadan, without a trace of bigotry . . . a high authority on questions of Muhammadan law and religion' (Swettenham, *British Malaya*, p. 343). Significantly Swettenham continues that 'In all the Malay states there is no one who . . . has done so much to promote the success of the new system of administration' (ibid.). Clifford's verdict is in similar terms—'among the most enlightened rulers of the Native States of the East, and a convinced apostle of British rule' (*Bushwhacking*, p. 192). 'Enlightened' is a sort of 'code word' used by British administrators of this period to mean that a Malay shared their ideas on government.

It was also applied to Tunku Kudin in his time (1868–78) as Viceroy of Selangor (SSD 18 June 1878: memo by Anson). F. A. Swettenham, 'Some Account of the Independent Native States of the Malay Peninsula Especially the Circumstances Which Led to the More Intimate Relations Recently Adopted towards Some of Them by the British Government', *JSBRAS*, 6, 1880, p. 171, writes of the 'enlightened views' of the Kedah royal family.

93. R. Stevenson, *Cultivators and Administrators: British Educational Policy towards the Malays 1875–1906*, Kuala Lumpur, Oxford University Press, 1975, Chapter 8.

94. CO 273/355, pp. 270A–270G, contains a long, handwritten letter from Ernest Birch, then Resident of Perak, to Sir John Anderson, who was on leave in London (in 1909). Birch reports an interview with Sultan Idris, from which it is clear that with consummate skill, Idris manoeuvred the colonial regime into blocking the pretensions of his pushing son-in-law, Raja Chulan, a son of ex-Sultan Abdullah, for appointment to one of the Perak royal offices leading to the succession. Idris, himself, could not afford to be seen in open opposition to this pressure. On the Perak succession generally see Jagjit Singh Sidhu, *Administration in the Federated Malay States 1896–1920*, Kuala Lumpur, Oxford University Press, 1980, pp. 112–18.

95. Hussain bin Mahmud, op. cit., on the education of Sultan Idris. Stevenson, op. cit., p. 169, mentions that during three years spent in Singapore, when his father Raja Muda Musa was in virtual exile, Sulaiman attended the Raffles Institution. He, none the less, also went to school as a young adult when the English-language Raja School opened in Kuala Lumpur in late 1890 (Stevenson, op. cit., p. 152). On the education of Malay boys of aristocratic birth, see pp. 269–70 below. The teaching was provided by Muslim *ulama*, in addition to instruction in reading the Koran (Hussain bin Mahmud, op. cit., referring to Idris). 'Low Journal', p. 86, identifies one as Sheikh Hassan of Lambor; Abdul Rahman of Kota Lama is mentioned in PCE. See also p. 264.

96. Idris, on becoming ruler, had tuition in English from a sequence of British officials (*PGG* 1890, p. 169). On Sulaiman see note 95 above.

97. SSD 23 November 1889.

98. Idris 'briefly addressed the assemblage in Malay, the British Resident interpreting in English' (*PGG* 1889, p. 302).

99. See p. 52 above on royal polygamy.

100. SSD 24 September 1890. The rulers of Perak and Selangor received a special allowance to cover their obligations to support the poor. See p. 285 below.

101. SSD 24 September 1890 cited above was written with reference to a request by Idris for an increase. Generally they obtained something but not all for which they asked.

102. SSD 1 June 1909. See also note 44 above. Unlike Sultan Idris, who had substantial income from ancestral mining lands (*PGG* 1890, p. 247), Sultan Sulaiman had no substantial private fortune. His plantation at Kuala Langat, planted mainly with coconuts, did not prosper—'has an appearance of neglect' was the verdict in 1891 (*AR Selangor 1891*).

'. . . if a man had twenty pounds a year for his income, and spent nineteen pounds nineteen shillings and sixpence, he would be happy, but that if he spent twenty pounds one he would be miserable. After which he [Micawber] borrowed a shilling of me for porter . . .' (Charles Dickens, *David Copperfield*, Chapter 11).

4
A Ruling Class in Search of an Occupation

'THERE was, in 1874, a very broad line indeed between the ruling classes in Malaya and the *raiats*, the people.'[1] This accepted picture of Malay class structure distracts attention from the gradations of status within each of the two main classes and also from the possibility, occasionally realized by an exceptional individual, of rising from the lower to the upper class. Swettenham's 'broad line' was very real but somewhat blurred at the edges.

Within the ruling class the use of honorific prefixes to personal names made it easy to distinguish the two main groups.[2] A man or woman, if descended in the male line from a former ruler of the state was royal (*anak raja*) however many intervening generations there might be, and bore the title 'Raja' or 'Tunku', e.g. 'Raja Hamid' or 'Tunku Hamidah', without distinction of sex. In most states there was an established practice of using one prefix or the other exclusively but they were of similar connotation. The other group were the notables (*orang besar* or *orang kaya*) of aristocratic but non-royal descent; they bore titles such as 'Datuk' (especially a man who was a chief of a district or the holder of a court office) or 'Wan' or, less often, 'Megat' as an indicator of general status.[3] Arabs who claimed descent from the Prophet had the title 'Sayid' (men) or 'Sharifa' (women) and were of quasi-royal status. In Perak especially, 'scions of the Sayid house were sought for eagerly in marriage and married into the families of all the greater Perak chiefs'.[4] As a result of intermarriage some Malay aristocrats bore these Arab titles.

Among those of royal descent there was often a distinction made between the close relatives of the ruler or his predecessor, from whom the ruler drew his personal aides and advisers, and those who were more distant. In Terengganu, for example, this 'royal family' (*kerabat diraja*) was distinguished from remoter kinsfolk of the ruler (*kerabat am*).[5] In Perak the inner group of royalty were classified as '*waris negeri*'.[6] It was usual for a brother or son of the ruler to bear the title 'Raja Muda' which sometimes—but not, for example, in Kedah—indicated an heir apparent. The general function of a Raja Muda was to assist the ruler in his political functions.[7]

Each of the non-royal lineages usually had a local base in some outlying district of the state, if not in the capital itself, and a semi-hereditary entitlement to a title (*gelaran*) bestowed on a leading male member of the lineage by the ruler. Clifford wrote that 'the officers were hereditary, but succession was subject to the sanction of the *Raja*, who personally invested and ennobled each chief, and gave him, as an ostensible sign of authority, a warrant and a state spear, both of which were returned to the Raja on the death of the holder'.[8] Swettenham adds that 'it was an accepted custom of the country that certain high [court] offices carried with them control over districts'.[9] These offices, or chieftainships, were conventionally graded in status into four of the first rank, eight of the second, and so on.[10]

The members of the lineage derived their aristocratic status from descent and from relationship to the current holder of the office in which they had a corporate interest. Just as the ruler was the apex and point of reference of the entire system, the ennobled holder of chiefly office (*orang bergelar*) of the lineage was the patron and protector of his kinsmen. Unless estranged by family feud, they gave him personal service and support. In return he helped them to find a livelihood, often by allocating to them a duty, such as collection of revenue or control of part of the ancestral fief, which gave them a recognized position and source of income.

The main basis of status was descent but there were some individuals who achieved high status—or higher status than that to which they had been born—as trusted aides of the ruler (*orang keistimewaan*) or as authorities on religious doctrine (*ulama*).[11] A young man might embark on a career at court by joining the *budak raja*, or royal bodyguard, and perhaps progress to higher status by distinction as a field commander (*panglima*). In difficult times, such as the period (1857–63) of the Pahang Civil War, even a commoner might rise to power from obscurity. In the 1880s royal favour had made the detested To Gajah, son of a Rawa immigrant, the most powerful man in the state after the ruler and given him charge of the important Temerloh and Lipis districts.[12] However, it was not often that a ruler could loosen the rigidity of a system of status ascribed by birth to reward a favourite in this way.

Despite the minute gradations of status within the upper class, all members of it demanded absolute respect from the subject class (*rakyat*). In addressing his superior, the peasant referred to himself either as '*patek*', when speaking to a prince, or as '*hamba datuk*', when addressing a non-royal aristocrat. If he met either on a path he squatted down to put himself on a lower level. When Abdullah Munshi was out with one of the Kelantan Rajas during the troubled times of 1838, 'we met a party of eighty men carrying a large gun to the stockade, and, when they saw us with the young Raja, they cast the gun on the ground, squatted down and did obeisance'. He also noted that when a peasant passed before the house of a *raja* in the rain, he furled his umbrella.[13]

As with the ruler himself, the key indicator of status was control of men and women as attendants. 'Every Malay chief of importance has a considerable following, both in his house and outside it. There is his family—often several families—his servants and hangers on, his relatives, some of whom are sure to live with him, and in return for food and other benefits, perform services of various kinds, ranging from the care of his estates, investments, money, or valuables, to the veiled surveillance of his wives and the running of messages.'[14] Some of these attendants and domestics were in debt-bondage. In Kuala Terengganu, for example, as late as 1918 each *kerabat* (princely) household had between five and ten debt-bondsmen or women.[15]

To be without a following was an admission of distress. At the end of the Selangor Civil War in 1873 Syed Mashhor, a leader in the defeated faction, 'took refuge in Perak where he is living on charity, having no followers and no money'.[16] Money and followers went together because the one was needed for the support of the other.

The aristocrat who had charge of a district or even of a few villages called on his subjects to work in his padi-fields under the customary labour service obligation (*kerah*).[17] J. W. W. Birch noted in 1875 that the Maharaja Lela of Pasir Salak in Perak 'can command the services of about 150 men at his village'; on a later visit the chief 'was at the paddy fields'.[18]

He might also help himself to the peasant's crops. '"Go fetch me that corn," said the Tunku to his followers, and the men immediately broke through the poor man's fence, tore up the corn and brought it to their master. No compensation whatever was offered.'[19] If the district produced tin, even on a limited scale, he could use his control of *kerah* labour and his political authority to obtain substantial revenues from Malay or Chinese sources. For example, in 1876 Tunku Ahmad Tunggal of Kuala Pilah in Negeri Sembilan obtained 25–30 *bahara* of ore monthly, say 4 tons, from the seven mines which he had opened with capital borrowed in Melaka. In addition he took one-tenth of the output of other mines in his district by way of a tax on them.[20]

With these resources at his disposal he could live in a large house, often protected against attack by a surrounding stockade. McNair wrote that 'it is in the building of a chief's house that the best efforts are put forth'. The walls of split reed would be 'woven into a neat check pattern, red and white; while other parts are strips of bamboo neatly interlaced'.[21] When the Maharaja Lela of Pasir Salak realized that in avenging the death of Birch the British would burn his house—'the best house in Perak'—he entered it for the last time in tears.[22]

With prestige and wealth and an armed following, an aristocrat might consolidate his position within his class by judicious matrimonial ties with other men of influence. The Menteri of Larut, for example, was the wealthiest man in Perak in the 1860s from the revenues of the tin mines. His father had been a very minor connection of the local potentates of western Perak but the Menteri had married a daughter of the Laksamana of Perak, the leading territorial magnate of Lower Perak, and he was the brother-in-law of the Temenggong, chief of Kota Lama, one of the principal villages on the Perak River.[23] The upstart To Gajah of Pahang, mentioned above, was 'a great warrior, the Field Marshal of Pahang and ranks with the *Orang Besar Ampat* or chiefs of the first class'.[24] There was more than one avenue to success but the rewards were generous—above all they gave prestige, the most prized possession of all in aristocratic life.

The imposition of colonial rule, with its concentration of power in alien hands at the centre, destroyed the foundations of the traditional aristocratic way of life and 'pulled their house down about their ears'.[25] The state council, meeting behind closed doors, was no substitute for the public demonstration of status at gatherings in the *balai*; moreover, only a handful of Malay chiefs were members of these new-fangled bodies.[26] The links of authority and obedience between chiefs and peasantry were also severed. Debt-bondage was outlawed and *kerah* restricted to the needs of the new state government.[27] Swettenham summed it up—with some exaggeration of past abuses—by saying that a chief 'could not levy taxes as he pleased; could not kill without enquiry, ravish or rob without imprisonment, requisition the labour of the *rakyats* without payment'.[28]

These changes were a public humiliation of the former ruling class. Even their prized possessions were at risk. In 1874 few of the high-handed acts of J. W. W. Birch outraged Malay feeling in Perak so much as the burning down of the house of the Tunku Panglima Raja who had been 'collecting bad characters'.[29] Swettenham was told that Sultan Ismail, the patron of the delinquent chief, 'was very angry about it'.[30]

Deprived of their customary perquisites, the aristocrats were in many cases reduced to poverty. 'Dris wants money,' wrote Hugh Low in his journal, 'as all the Rajas do, they have now no means of living.[31] Two other entries read—'the Sri Maharaja Lela sent a letter begging for *belanja*', and 'Raja Hussain . . . came to ask for some money, saying that the family had not rice to eat'.[32] No one felt the disgrace of poverty more keenly than the wives of great men. Of the wife of the Menteri of Larut, whose life story will be described in Chapter 9, Swettenham wrote that 'as the principal wife of the wealthiest and most powerful chief in the land, her every wish had been gratified . . . her wishes were numerous and expensive . . . she suddenly found herself deprived of all that had helped to make her one of the greatest ladies in the land'.[33] In time, those members of the upper class who had clearly defined traditional rights to revenues were compensated by the grant of fixed allowances from state funds. But some got nothing, and all were bitter. There was 'the feeling of the loss of real power, possibly national dignity, of constraint and forced obedience to the law, compensated for only by a moderate salary or pension'.[34]

Perforce they now reduced their style of living. The gradual prohibition of the carrying of arms, combined with the abolition of debt-bondage, at least relieved them of the need to support an armed retinue. When the Datuk Seri Lela of Kota Lama, stronghold of resistance to the British forces in 1875, came to pay a call on Hugh Low and Swettenham at the Residency in 1878, he came with only 'three or four followers'. He came in peace but also in reduced circumstances.[35]

The new regime set about drawing the more amenable members of the former ruling class into working association with them.[36] Although membership of the state councils was restricted and its proceedings unglamorous, it proved 'satisfactory to the native members in the consideration shown to them and their prejudices, and the importance attaching to their membership'.[37] Those of them who had hereditary claims to traditional offices were duly appointed to fill the vacancies with much pomp—perhaps more than in earlier times since ceremony had become an object in itself.[38]

In the administrative districts into which the states were now divided, men who might have been local chiefs in former times were, in some cases, appointed to the position of Native or Malay Magistrate. In that capacity they sat in court alongside European officials—an arrangement which sometimes made manifest a divergence of values between two contrasting cultures. The story is told of an accused whose guilt of the offence charged was clear beyond doubt. 'What do I care for evidence?' said the Malay Magistrate, adding, 'He belongs to my tribe.'[39] The most significant contribution of Malay Magistrates was in informal conciliation to settle Malay disputes before they came to court. As an example, Wan Mohamed Isa, son of the exiled Menteri of Larut, eventually became Malay Magistrate of Selama—and also a member of the Perak State Council. It was said of him that he was 'a powerful influence for good not only in his district but throughout the state'.[40] Others were less successful. Two were dismissed from their posts in Negeri Sembilan in 1899 for taking bribes.[41] The local Kinta chiefs were reproached with 'partiality' in their magisterial role because, it was said, they were 'wrapped up in speculations'.[42]

Although a Malay Magistrate had no executive duties, he was also expected to assist the European district officer as his adviser on Malay affairs and as a government spokesman to his own community on such unpopular innovations as vaccination against smallpox. Open opposition was a rare event but it was understood well enough that it would not be tolerated. When two Negeri Sembilan chiefs petitioned a Turkish admiral, who was then visiting Singapore, 'for the removal of British influence', one was dismissed from his traditional office and the other was publicly rebuked by the ruler of the state.[43]

In addition to membership of state councils and appointment as Malay Magistrate, there was a third avenue of entry to the pay-roll of the new regime—the office of *penghulu*, or subdistrict headman under the district officer. This was, of course, a traditional office adapted to the requirements of a new system of government. In former times the *penghulu* had been a village headman. He was a man of standing in his own community, usually a member of one of the founder families of the village and comparatively well-to-do. He was always drawn from the village and not superimposed upon it—though he owed his appointment to the recommendation of the district chief to the ruler, with whom the formal power lay.

In the western Malay states in the troubled years before 1874, many villages had been left without a *penghulu* when the position fell vacant or someone had become recognized informally as successor.[44] The colonial regime perceived the *penghulu* as a useful and inexpensive means of extending its control to the villages. In keeping with the tradition that a *penghulu* must be formally appointed by the ruler, candidates to fill vacant places, or requiring confirmation of their *de facto* position, were proposed to meetings of the state councils.[45] The Malay members of the upper class, who made up the Malay element in the councils, were not disposed to object to the innovation of appointing to the office of *penghulu*, men of their own class who in former times might have had charge of some part of the territory of the chief who was the head of their lineage. In Selangor, for example, thirteen out of twenty-four *penghulu* appointed at one meeting of the state council were men of the *raja* class.[46]

As in the case of Malay Magistrates, there were difficulties in reshaping traditional roles in new, bureaucratic forms. The aristocrat who became a *penghulu* was disposed to regard his official position as a source of income rather than a working responsibility. 'The Malay *rajas* who receive the highest salaries', it was said in 1884, 'are decidedly the most inefficient *penghulus*.'[47] This was a situation which became steadily more difficult as the new regime loaded on to the *penghulu*, of whatever class, a variety of new tasks.[48]

The sheer constraint of financial need induced some members of the upper class to demean themselves by manual labour in the road construction gangs, which even a peasant would have despised a decade earlier. Others earned a living as fishermen or woodcutters or took minor government posts as forest rangers, village schoolteachers or even office messengers.[49]

Although so many aristocrats found it far from easy to adapt to the requirements of a new occupation, some made a success of it. Take the case of Wan Mat Salleh. His father had been Seri Adika Raja, warden of the northern marches of Perak and a great territorial magnate of a remote area. The father died in his escape from the British reprisals which followed the death of Birch in 1875. As a young man, Mat Salleh decided to make a career in association with the new regime, which helped him with a period of attachment to the Resident's office so that he might learn their unfamiliar ways. Then in local administration within the family fief, he worked his way up to become—in the early 1890s—a quasi-district officer in charge of three *mukim* along the upper reaches of the Perak River. His annual reports (in English translation) were published in the official gazette along with the reports of European district officers. They 'reveal a trained and energetic administrator [who] undertook strenuous tours of inspection which involved days of walking over rough country; he collected rents, reported on mining and planting, assisted settlers from Patani, made bridlepaths to the mines of his own district, cut irrigation channels, enforced quarantine regulations' and so on.[50] He became Seri Adika Raja in succession to his father in 1891 and a member of the Perak State Council in 1894.

When Swettenham went on a difficult mission to Pahang in 1885, he took Mat Salleh with him and years later he wrote that Salleh was 'the ablest Malay in the Peninsula'.[51] Yet those who admired him most felt that he was too narrowly confined within the limits of the Malay tradition in which he had grown up. When his ruler, Sultan Idris, decided to attend the coronation in London in 1902, he 'uprooted him sorely against his will' to come with him. According to the Malay tradition a royal command, however unwelcome, must be obeyed—*titah dijunjung*. He loathed London. Clifford found him in a hotel bedroom in a very cold June 'swaddled up to the chin in an ulster, and his bare feet were flap-flapping on the carpet. "What are you doing?", I asked. "I am walking from Kuala Kangsar to Bukit Gantang," he replied.' Clifford adds that he 'detested the whole experience' though the hotel had done its best, supplying a Malay cuisine, curry and rice with chicken killed in the Muslim fashion.[52] A younger generation might be attuned to a new world by means of its education—a theme to be considered in a later chapter.[53]

Even within their own community the upper class found that the situation was changing. The *rakyat* continued to show deference since their own code of good manners required it. Clifford wrote of a Malay peasant in prison in a colonial gaol in company with a chief that 'respect to chiefs and elders . . . represent more to the ordinary Malay than to any other human being'.[54] Yet, relieved of the fear of reprisals, 'Malays in the Protected Malay States are no longer very backward in making complaints'[55] and they were 'far less submissive to ill-treatment and extortion on the part of their headmen'.[56] The abject submission of squatting by the roadside when a man of superior rank was passing was, at first, reserved to much respected figures such as the elderly Sultan Abdul Samad, and gradually fell into abeyance altogether.[57] However, the former rulers were not without means of demanding respect and it was unwise to push things too far. 'A chief with a head on his shoulders can always make things hot for his enemies, can trump up a case against them and have them put in gaol, can raise local opinion against them so that their neighbours look askance at them, and can worry and irk in a hundred minor ways.'[58]

The economic expansion of the period offered opportunities to men of all walks of life, if they had the wit to take them. It created a new form of class mobility for the commoner who made money. But it was only a limited opening. One such was Karim bin Ibrahim of Selama, who had come over from Sumatra as a young man in 1855 to work as a clerk for the chiefs of the prosperous Larut mining district. In the disturbances of the early 1870s Karim lived by his wits and obtained from the impecunious Sultan Abdullah a territorial grant of the remote Selama district in the north-west of Perak. Here, in 1876, W. E. Maxwell visited him—'a bright and intelligent little man, rather dark for a Malay and with a larger share of moustache and whiskers than usually fall to the lot of his race'. He was living 'in a simple and unpretentious wood and *atap* house'.[59] To develop his district he had borrowed $25,000 from Penang financiers on which he paid annual interest of 24 per cent. The two or three thousand Sumatran and Chinese miners of Selama bought their foodstuffs and opium from him at high prices, and sold their tin to him at a fixed low price.[60] He sat as a magistrate and maintained a Malay school. At the instance of Hugh Low he became a member of the Perak State Council. Yet, even in this non-traditional position, he was uneasy and preferred to absent himself from council meetings rather than sit at the same table with hereditary grandees.[61] When the price of tin fell in the late 1870s his highly geared financial regime collapsed and he vanished again into his natural obscurity.[62]

Syed Musa, *penghulu* of Chigar Galah, had an illustrious pedigree—in contrast to Karim. When Weld visited him, he proudly displayed his family pedigree showing that he was descended through thirty-five generations from the Prophet Muhammad; by intermarriage his family were well connected with the Perak aristocracy.[63] Perhaps his Arab descent gave him unusual commercial acumen; Hugh Low regarded Syed Musa and his kinsmen as 'an intelligent and scheming looking lot'.[64] Partly for that reason Low arranged to risk $8,000 in a government loan to Musa to finance the opening of a pepper plantation—16 acres worked by Acehnese and Javanese labour on a share-cropping basis.[65] Syed Musa was 'very much in the hands of the Achehnese coolies working on contract' but found time to attend to the marketing of his pepper in Penang.[66] For a time his pepper was a show-piece though not very profitable. When he died, the government bought his plantation to avoid having a bad debt.[67]

In the rich tin-mining district of Kinta in Perak, there were about 400 Malay 'ancestral mines' in the foothills which their owners had worked on a small-scale and intermittent basis in previous years. When new techniques made it possible to exploit the potential of the swampy Kinta valley in the 1880s, these fortunate land-owners were suddenly elevated from relative poverty to affluence; some of them received mining royalties of $500–1,000 per month.[68] The Datuk Panglima Kinta had the additional good fortune of owning the land on which the new mining centre of Ipoh was built. He laid out his land in building plots and erected shophouses 'which would be a credit to Singapore or Penang' or sold off the vacant plots to Chinese traders for $25 each.[69]

With these abundant resources, the Kinta Malay aristocrats went into a variety of new enterprises, including hiring out elephants to work on the mines.[70] Another commercial adaptation of a traditional practice was the construction of irrigation works. In one of the more ambitious projects of this kind, $40,000 was expended to build a 200-acre reservoir behind a dam 780 feet long. From this supply, four miles of distribution channels would carry water to 2,000 acres of padi land. The promoter 'does not expect to make a large income from this source [by levying water rates on the cultivators] but will be satisfied if his name goes down to posterity as the creator of the work'[71]—an interesting combination of traditional and commercial objectives. Members of the same group of aristocratic entrepreneurs also took up land 'to cut drains and introduce settlers'.[72] In the end, however, little came of these schemes.[73]

The plutocrats built spacious villas in Ipoh. Weld was accommodated in 1882 in 'a very pretty [room] hung in silk, carpeted and with lovely embroidered cushions'.[74] The Datuk Panglima Kinta was the wealthiest Malay in Perak at his death in 1902 and his spacious Ipoh mansion was purchased for use as a courthouse.[75] While it lasted, they enjoyed the *dolce vita* of affluence in Malay style—'it is for them that the richest silks of Trengganu and Batu Bara are woven, it is they who vie with each other in the building of expensive houses and the possession of horses and carriages, while many of them own residences in the sacred city of Mecca'.[76]

There were very few of the Malay upper class on whom fate showered material blessings with this abundance. The life story of Raja Mahmud of Selangor is a more representative picture of the experiences of a Malay aristocrat adapting himself to a changed world. Raja Mahmud was born in the mid-nineteenth century. His father, Raja Saman, who was nicknamed Raja Berkat, was both cousin and brother-in-law of Sultan Abdul Samad, ruler of Selangor from 1857 to 1898. As young men they had fought together and in later years Raja Berkat bore the title 'Tunku Panglima Raja', 'royal commander', and was the ruler's closest confidant.[77] Raja Mahmud grew up in a martial tradition.

When he was a boy of eleven or twelve years of age, 'his father bade him try his prentice hand' at killing a man, selecting for this experiment a decrepit Chinese labourer who was too feeble to resist the attack even of a small boy.[78] Twenty years later Mahmud claimed to have 'slain two hundred men—not counting Chinamen'.[79] On the outbreak of the Selangor Civil War in 1868 he joined Raja Mahdi's party 'for friendship's sake and because he liked fighting'.[80] He soon became 'Mahdi's best fighting man' because he enjoyed it—'his eyes were wont to dance and [his] mouth smiled cheerily when danger was afoot'.[81] He became famous—'equally noted for his cruelty and his fighting qualities'.[82]

In an earlier chapter Swettenham's immediate and subsequent recollections of his first meeting with Raja Mahmud in 1874 have been described.[83] After an initial adverse impression Swettenham concluded that Raja Mahmud had been 'the tool of others' and was now 'a reformed character'.[84] He took Mahmud with him, to command his Malay scouts, during the military operation known rather grandly as the 'Perak War'. A few weeks before, Swettenham had narrowly escaped death at the time of the killing of Birch, and Mahmud had saved his life. Swettenham and his party, including Mahmud, were on a boat on the Perak River at Blanja. When they anchored, one Haji Ali came on board to invite Swettenham to land. Mahmud, who well knew the guile which preceded an attack in traditional style, was quicker than Swettenham to discern the murderous intent of that invitation. 'Thereupon,' said Mahmud later, 'I tied up my *keris* and put on my trousers in front of Haji Ali and said to him that he had better return ashore as we were going downstream.' Putting on trousers was a sign of determination to stand and fight. Mahmud's bluster disconcerted Haji Ali, who withdrew; under cover of darkness Swettenham's boat slipped away downstream to safety.[85]

Raja Mahmud's services in the Perak War were marred by looting and burning as he led his irregulars up the Kinta valley ahead of the ponderous British advance. But he was rewarded with a sword of honour, a small pension from the Perak government, and permission to return to his native Selangor from which he had been exiled since 1874.[86] Swettenham was able to overrule the objections of the Resident of Selangor and secure for Mahmud an appointment at $50 per month as *penghulu* of Sepang, just south of his father's ancestral village of Kanchong on the Selangor coast.[87]

Gone were the days of casual killing, of risking one's life on being quicker in thought and action than one's opponent—the very essence of Malay military skill. The path of peace was a stony road for Raja Mahmud. He neglected his official duties and abandoned his family.[88] Somehow he endured the notorious rudeness of Bloomfield Douglas, Resident of Selangor, who records complacently in his diary that he used 'plain words' in rebuking Mahmud, 'told him a good many truths' and even sent a detachment of police to Sepang as 'an army of occupation'.[89]

In 1882 Swettenham replaced Douglas in Selangor just after Mahmud had been moved to become *penghulu* of Kuala Selangor, the ancient but now rather run-down former capital of the state. The local administrators found Mahmud a stiff-necked and unreasonable champion of the local Malay community, especially in disputes over sending their children to the local Malay school.[90] Mahmud's side of the story is not available; Swettenham had to extricate all parties from these encounters without too much loss of dignity. There was probably relief in 1887 when Mahmud was recalled to active service as escort commander and adviser to Hugh Clifford, with whom he spent most of the next two years at Pekan, the state capital of Pahang. The intrigue and the threat of danger made the hot blood run again in Mahmud's veins. In the long intervals of tense inactivity, Clifford 'by means of cunning coaxing . . . led him on to talk of his lurid past . . . the glow of excitement [was] engendered by his awakened memories'.[91]

Then disaster struck again. Late in 1888 news reached Pekan of the death of Mahmud's father. Clifford wrote later that 'I spent two nights awake by the side of Raja [Mahmud], with difficulty restraining him from running *amok* in the streets of Pekan, because his father had died a natural death in Selangor'.[92] To this frustrated, unstable man, violence was a means of release from tension. When he had recovered his balance Raja Mahmud returned to Selangor to take his father's place as Tunku Panglima Besar and as a member of the Selangor State Council.[93] He was drawn, perhaps again 'the tool of others', into a pointless but very damaging quarrel with Raja Muda Sulaiman, the heir apparent to the aged Sultan Abdul Samad. The Resident was now W. E. Maxwell, an autocrat and a bitter critic of Swettenham and his works. Maxwell decreed, though it was formally the ruler's decision, that Raja Mahmud should be deprived of his official position and exiled for life from Selangor.[94]

Thereafter until 1910 Mahmud lived mainly in the Straits Settlements. In 1892 he engaged in a mining venture in Melaka, financed with money borrowed from the old Johor ruling family of Kampung Glam in Singapore. This ended in failure and recrimination against a British official. He was once permitted to revisit Selangor briefly for business reasons as in November 1891 he was in Klang 'to settle my case with Raja Laut'.[95]

With the accession of Sultan Sulaiman to the throne of Selangor in 1898, the old quarrel of 1890 was healed. When the anniversary of the new ruler's accession was celebrated at Klang in April 1902, the entertainments included 'sword dancing at which Raja Mahmud distinguished himself as greatly as in his fighting days'.[96] A few months later he appeared again in the celebrations in Kuala Lumpur of the end of the Anglo-Boer War—'now advancing now retreating, with one foot gracefully poised, hands working and eyes always watchful . . . the four cuts and single thrust of native swordsmanship were exhibited with their accompanying guards'. Although now an elderly man, he showed 'agility by leaping out of reach from time to time' as he danced to the accompaniment of 'beating drums and playing trumpets'.[97] The fighting man had become an entertainer.

As always he was short of money. In 1907 he invited the SS government to accept a return of his sword of honour in return for an increase in his pension of $162.50 per month. In 1910 he asked that his pension might be paid to him in Jeddah, where he was still living in 1912. In offering to return his sword, he wrote that 'I am old now and unable to help the Government'.[98] Thereafter no more is heard of him. The old soldier simply fades away. In the early 1890s he had sent two of his sons to attend the Raja School in Kuala Lumpur.[99] He must have perceived that for them the best opportunity of a career lay in learning the ways of the new regime.

In the states of northern Malaya and Johor, the future Unfederated Malay States (UMS), formal independence of colonial rule lasted into the early years of the twentieth century, and the process of adjustment of Malay aristocratic values and roles took a different and less painful form. It was none the less a trend in the same direction towards selective adoption of some elements of an alien culture. It is necessary to describe each of these states separately according to their respective circumstances.

In Kedah the ruler between 1854 and 1879 was the energetic and hard-working Sultan Ahmad Tajuddin, assisted by one or other of his younger brothers as Raja Muda.[100] He had been born in Penang and maintained close personal, social and economic ties with Penang.[101] In keeping with his general disposition to adopt Western ideas, he remodelled the government of his state. The traditional high offices of Bendahara, Laksamana and the like had been allowed to lapse by not appointing successors when the incumbent died. Yet the ruling class, and in particular the 'Wan family' which had provided many holders of these offices in the past and intermarried with the royal family, continued to be associated with the ruler in his essentially Malay government.[102]

An outstanding—but not the only—instance of this arrangement is the career of Wan Mat Saman. When the throne of Kedah fell vacant in 1854, there was a succession dispute within the royal family and Ahmad Tajuddin owed his position as ruler to the support of the influential Wan Ismail, a son of a former Laksamana of Kedah. The alliance was confirmed by the subsequent marriage of the young Ahmad Tajuddin to a daughter, Wan Hajar, of Wan Ismail. Wan Mat Saman, a son of Wan Ismail, was therefore a brother-in-law of the ruler. Mat Saman was a man of great ability—Swettenham called him 'the most intelligent man in the state'—and he, like the ruler, had absorbed some external culture traits. He spoke Hindustani fluently and understood some English.[103] He is best known as the man who was able to mobilize traditional resources, in the form of *kerah*, as well as capital and Chinese contract labour to build the canal, the *sungai korok*, which bears his name and which opened up much of the southern plain of Kedah.[104] He was Chief Minister of Kedah from about 1870 until his death in 1898. In the 1870s he was close to the ruler; in the regency period of the 1880s he was a power in the land; but his influence seems to have waned in his last years, possibly due to ill-health. Other members of the Kedah ruling class were drawn into the new style of government as bureaucrats and not as hereditary grandees. In so far as the ruler perceived needs which his own ruling class could not meet, he employed foreigners such as a European chief of police and an Indian doctor.[105]

The achievements of Ahmad Tajuddin's very personal regime down to 1879 were clouded by the financial chaos of the early years of his son and successor, Sultan Abdul Hamid (r.1882–1943). Yet when the British took control in 1909, they found 'a fully organised central administration composed of Malays some of them men of considerable ability and individuality . . . they are very tenacious of power and privilege and no doubt the agitation and intrigues which preceded the transfer were largely due to the apprehension that those in power would be reduced to the position of pensioners with only titular authority and duties'.[106] It is a passage which neatly contrasts the essential FMS and UMS role of the local ruling class of different states.

In spite of the style of government and the related economic development—the ruler laid out towns, built roads and promoted plantation development—much of the old traditional style of government was preserved. The new bureaucrats, for example, did not draw fixed salaries but were rewarded by the grant (*ampun kurnia*) of state revenue from particular sources. The grant of the revenues of a *mukim* carried with it the right to appoint a *penghulu* of the grantee's choice to collect the revenues for him. Of these appointees 'some few are honest and reliable men of good family but the majority are illiterate scoundrels'.[107] The peasant cultivator either paid a land rent or, if he did not, was liable to compulsory (*kerah*) service. The holder of revenues of a *mukim* converted the right to *kerah* service into money by selling the peasant's labour to whoever might be willing to buy it. As a result of these abuses *kerah* in Kedah became 'an object of dread to Malays'.[108]

Johor resembled Kedah in its deliberate, if selective, adoption of bureaucratic methods of government and programmes of economic development. It differed from Kedah in its lack of a traditional

Malay society as the starting point. In the 1830s P. J. Begbie estimated that the Malay population of Johor was no more than a thousand.[109] The story of the Temenggongs' rise to the dignity of Sultans is well told elsewhere, and the expedients to which Maharaja Abu Bakar resorted have been mentioned in earlier chapters.[110] As in Kedah, the regime in Johor was personal to the ruler, who appointed men of his choice to positions, high and low in his central government. The Johor bureaucrats were 'new men', many of them from the Singapore Malay middle class and educated at Christian mission schools. For example, Mohamed Salleh bin Perang, who became Datuk Bentara Luar of Johor, was born in the Malay settlement of Teluk Belanga in Singapore in 1841. He had entered the service of Temenggong Ibrahim as a clerk in the chief minister's office.[111] Ibrahim Munshi, son of the celebrated Abdullah Munshi, began his career as a language teacher to European officials, travelled in the 1870s as interpreter, and eventually became Johor State Secretary with the title of 'Datuk Bentara Dalam'.[112] A third instance is provided by the Sultan's nephew, Abdul Rahman, who had been educated in England. He became the ruler's private secretary with the title 'Datuk Seri Amar di Raja'.[113]

It is worth noting how these bureaucrats in the course of their careers were equipped with high-sounding Malay titles to give them status. Thus ennobled, they claimed precedence, among members of the Johor State Council, over the handful of minor hereditary dignitaries. Some of them were men of ability but the general standard of performance was probably not as high as in Kedah. Swettenham described the Johor Secretariat as 'a farce, but the personnel is just clever enough to make it look like reality to the general spectator'.[114]

In contrast to Johor, Terengganu was a bastion of ancient Malay tradition. In this it owed something to the personal character of two long-lived rulers, Baginda Omar and Sultan Zainal Abidin III, to whom reference has been made in earlier chapters. In Clifford's opinion the former 'ruled the country with a hand of iron, but with not a little wisdom and intelligence'.[115] In his time power, and the collection of revenue, was in the hands of the ruler to whom his kinsmen of the royal family looked for support. On the accession of Sultan Zainal Abidin III—'a weak, studious boy ... shy and nervous' there was a reaction—'a partition of the revenue of the state was arranged, by which the Sultan was left with only a slender income derived from a small portion of his state, the rest being divided among his relations'.[116] Yet the ruling group around the throne remained concentrated in the state capital. They collected their revenues through local agents or sent emissaries out for that purpose. In Baginda Omar's reign the traditional system of decentralized rule through district chiefs had been allowed to die out, as in Kedah, by not appointing successors to these positions when the incumbents died. There was no intermediate link between the village headman and the state capital. To some extent the Islamic hierarchy filled the gap but the local *ulama*, as will be explained in a later chapter, were mere clients of religious authorities of higher status in and around the capital. It was a very personal, and in some respects arbitrary, system. Yet, in spite of its essentially Malay character, the Terengganu regime introduced some devices of colonial government such as a land system and, in particular, the grant of concessions to foreign entrepreneurs.[117]

In Kelantan, as in Terengganu, it is difficult to present a social analysis which is not a recapitulation of political and dynastic history.[118] In the period down to 1903, members of the royal family obtained from the ruler authority to govern outlying districts in his name. But, unlike Terengganu, these grants did not carry the right to retain the revenues collected in each district, except for those parts of the revenues which the ruler allocated to the district chiefs. In this respect Kelantan seems to have had a system more like that of Kedah than of neighbouring Terengganu. In the villages of Kelantan, however, authority was exercised by *imam*, who had temporal as much as religious influence. Later the Siamese, who made much more progress in penetrating Kelantan than Terengganu, induced the creation of an intermediate level of local government in the form of 'circle' or subdistrict headmen, somewhat like the reformed system of administration through *penghulu* of *mukim* in the FMS. Then in 1903, the appointment of a European adviser (W. A. Graham) by the Siamese marked the first move, at a slower pace than in the FMS, towards a centralization of authority at the capital.[119] The Kelantan ruling class reacted by strengthening the machinery of religious administration in such a fashion as to retain for themselves something of their traditional influence in the community.[120]

In closing this review of the position of the Malay ruling class in the different states one may note a general tendency, arising from different local factors, towards the replacement of traditional patterns of authority by bureaucratic methods of government of one kind or another. The establishment of the Malay College at Kuala Kangsar in 1905 was the decisive move towards the creation of a professional cadre of Malay administrators, drawn mainly from the old ruling class. In this fashion new bottles were filled with old wine.[121]

1. F.A. Swettenham, *British Malaya: An Account of the Origin and Progress of British Influence in Malaya*, London, John Lane Bodley Head, 1907 (revised editions 1929 and 1948, London, Allen and Unwin), p. 141.

2. It is convenient, though not strictly in accordance with accepted usage, to apply the term 'lineage' to Malay aristocratic families (J.M. Gullick, *Indigenous Political Systems of Western Malaya*, London, Athlone Press, 1958, preface). The Malay aristocratic group comprised individuals related by common descent but lacked any corporate structure in the general sense.

3. In rare cases an aristocrat of non-royal descent but very high status was addressed in royal style. The Maharaja Perba Jelei, the leading magnate of Ulu Pahang, was addressed as 'Engku' (H.C. Clifford, *In Court and Kampong, Being Tales and Sketches of Native Life in the Malay Peninsula*, London, Grant Richards, 1897 (2nd ed. with autobiographical preface, London, Richards Press, 1927), p. 113). The Menteri of Larut (see note 23 below) had 'a right to the designation of *tengku*, a title generally given to royalty but in Perak to the highest commoner chiefs' (R.O. Winstedt and R.J. Wilkinson, 'A History of Perak', *JMBRAS*, 12(1), 1934, p. 81). Yet Irving wrote that 'the *Tunku Mantri* himself said to me that he was not a raja but an officer of state of the Sultan of Perak' (report enclosed with SSD 24 February 1874).

4. R.O. Winstedt, 'The Hadramaut Saiyids of Perak and Siak', *JSBRAS*, 79, 1918, p. 49. 'The Malays observe the same reverence in dealing with them as with *rajas*' (Abdullah bin Abdul Kadir, Munshi, *Kesah Pelayaran Abdullah*, translated by A.E. Coope, *The Voyage of Abdullah: A Translation from the Malay*, Singapore, Malaya Publishing House, 1949, p. 10).

5. Shaharil Talib Robert, 'The Trengganu Ruling Class in the Late Nineteenth Century', *JMBRAS*, 50(2), 1977, p. 27.

6. Minutes of the Perak State Council, 26 October 1882, reprinted in *Papers on Malay Subjects*, edited by P.L. Burns, Kuala Lumpur, Oxford University Press, 1971, p. 265. Perak State Council Minutes are hereafter cited as *PSCM*; minutes of meetings held after 1882 were published in the Perak Government Gazette (*PGG*) from 1888 onwards.

7. On *Raja Muda* meaning 'heir apparent' see R.J. Wilkinson, *A Malay–English Dictionary*, 2 parts, Singapore, Kelly & Walsh, 1901 (revised as *A Malay–English Dictionary (Romanised)*, 2 parts, Mytilene, Salavopoulos & Kinderlis, 1932, Pt. 1, p. 301). The description of the status and functions of the Raja Muda of Kedah, in *AR Kedah 1909*, p. 11, states that 'the succession to the throne is from father to son, and the second brother of the Sultan is appointed Raja Muda . . . to take the drudgery of routine administration' off the shoulders of the Sultan.

8. Clifford, *In Court and Kampong*, p. 4.

9. Swettenham, *British Malaya*, p. 137, referring to the states of western Malaya, in particular Perak. It was not universally true of the East Coast states.

10. Winstedt and Wilkinson, op. cit., Appendix D. The third and fourth classes of the sixteen and thirty-two chiefs are an example of the Malay disposition to juggle with numbers. There was never a full complement and in some cases it was uncertain which chieftainships fell into which class (J. W. W. Birch, *The Journals of J. W. W. Birch First British Resident to Perak 1874–1875* (hereafter cited as *Birch Journal*), edited by P. L. Burns, Kuala Lumpur, Oxford University Press, 1967, p. 108). In this century there was a tidying up operation in which official lists were drawn up but they were 'in no sense historical' (Winstedt and Wilkinson, op. cit., p. 155).

11. Shaharil Talib Robert, 'Trengganu Ruling Class', p. 27.

12. 'A very energetic man who performs any work given to him faster and better than most Malays', according to Clifford (SSD 15 October 1887). He was unpopular both as an upstart chief, which offended Malay ideas of what was proper, and as a harsh and oppressive administrator. To Bahman, who began the 1891 uprising, had once been the Sultan's 'dog boy' (*AR Pahang 1890*). He owed his rise to a high position to his prowess as a leader, especially in the Selangor Civil War (W. Linehan, 'A History of Pahang' (hereafter cited as 'Pahang'), *JMBRAS*, 14(2), 1936, pp. 94–7 and 139. On the *budak raja* see p. 50 above.

13. Abdullah Munshi, op. cit., pp. 16, 36 and 41.

14. F. A. Swettenham, *The Real Malay: Pen Pictures*, London, John Lane Bodley Head, 1900, p. 143.

15. Shaharil Talib Robert, 'Trengganu Ruling Class', p. 28.

16. F. A. Swettenham, 'Some Account of the Independent Native States of the Malay Peninsula especially the Circumstances Which Led to the More Intimate Relations Recently Adopted towards Some of Them by the British Government', *JSBRAS*, 6, 1880, p. 189.

17. *Kerah* is explained in Chapter 5.

18. *Birch Journal*, pp. 114 and 128. Clifford's story, 'The Weeding of the Tares', in *Studies in Brown Humanity being Scrawls and Smudges in Sepia, White and Yellow*, London, Grant Richards, 1898, pp. 202–10 (reprinted as 'Droit Du Seigneur', in *The Further Side of Silence*, New York, Doubleday, Page & Co., 1927, pp. 65–76) is set in the context of a village called out to work in the padi-fields of the local chief.

19. E. Innes, *The Chersonese with the Gilding Off*, 2 vols., London, Richard Bentley, 1885, reprinted Kuala Lumpur, Oxford University Press, 1974, Vol. 1, p. 182. 'Using their power to rob the people', F. A. Swettenham, *Sir Frank Swettenham's Malayan Journals 1874–1876* (hereafter cited as *Swettenham Journal*), edited by P. L. Burns and C. D. Cowan, Kuala Lumpur, Oxford University Press, 1975, p. 275.

20. Report of 8 February 1876 enclosed with SSD 19 August 1876. The Shahbandar of Perak in 1874 had 20–30 Malays at work on his mines and was about to recruit Chinese (*Birch Journal*, p. 260). When the Datuk Bandar of Sungei Ujong abandoned his stockade at Kepayang in December 1874 he left behind 60 lb. of gold dust and 1,700 pieces of tin worth about $20,000 (*Swettenham Journal*, p. 168).

21. J. F. A. McNair, *Perak and the Malays: Sarong and Keris*, London, Tinsley Bros., 1878, reprinted Kuala Lumpur, Oxford University Press, 1972, pp. 167–8.

22. Gullick, *Indigenous Political Systems*, p. 111; evidence to PCE in CO 273/88,

p. 13—'Maharaja Lela went into his house and cried because he said, "The white men will burn it"'.

23. Gullick, *Indigenous Political Systems*, pp. 82–8, on intermarriage among aristocrats. On the question of the Menteri's descent, see Winstedt and Wilkinson, op. cit., p. 78. His detractors spread reports that he was merely the son of a 'shrewd trader from Penang or Province Wellesley' (ibid.). These tales no doubt reflected the jealousy of an aristocrat who had risen within the ruling class to higher status. On his other connections, see Gullick, *Indigenous Political Systems*, p. 87, and *PSCM*, 4 March 1879; Burns (ed.), *PMS*, p. 192 and *Swettenham Journal*, p. 31 (editor's note).

24. F. A. Swettenham, 'Journal Kept during a Journey across the Malay Peninsula', *JSBRAS*, 15, 1885, p. 20. F. A. Swettenham ('The Passing of Panglima Prang Samaun', *Malay Sketches*, London, John Lane Bodley Head, 1895, pp. 112–46) describes another celebrated fighting man. See also the account of Raja Mahmud's career below at p. 81.

25. Swettenham, *The Real Malay*, p. 17.

26. The original members of the Perak State Council comprised only three Malay chiefs plus Che Karim (see p. 79 below), who had been preferred to the Datuk Panglima Kinta, whose loyalty to the new regime was suspect. The Selangor State Council also had four Malay members—a son, son-in-law (Tunku Kudin—the Viceroy), and brother-in-law of the ruler and Syed Zin, who had been associated with Kudin during the civil war (E. Sadka, 'The State Councils in Perak and Selangor 1877–1895', in K. G. Tregonning (ed.), *Papers on Malayan History*, Singapore, University of Malaya, 1962, pp. 96–9). Although a reputed descendant of the Prophet, Syed Zin, like Che Karim, was a *parvenu*; his brother was master of a vessel belonging to the ruler of Kedah (Muhammad Hassan bin Dato' Kerani Muhammad Arshad, *Al-Tarikh Salasilah Negeri Kedah*, Kuala Lumpur, Dewan Bahasa dan Pustaka, 1968 (previously published in *Jawi*, 1926), p. 223).

27. See p. 100 below.

28. Swettenham, *The Real Malay*, p. 17. Clifford, *Studies in Brown Humanity*, p. 228.

29. *Birch Journal*, pp. 98 and 143–7.

30. *Swettenham Journal*, p. 185.

31. H. Low, 'The Journal of Sir Hugh Low, Perak 1877' (hereafter cited as 'Low Journal'), edited by E. Sadka, *JMBRAS*, 27(4), 1954, p. 64.

32. Ibid., pp. 75 and 78. On *belanja* meaning 'money to live on' (literally 'expenses'), see A. C. Milner, *Kerajaan: Malay Political Culture on the Eve of Colonial Rule*, Tucson, University of Arizona Press, 1982, pp. 24–5.

33. Swettenham, *The Real Malay*, pp. 203–4. See p. 218 below on Toh Puan Halimah.

34. SSD 21 October 1880—Weld relaying Low's assessment of the situation. Tunku Kudin told Bloomfield Douglas that although 'the lower class would gladly see the country under the British flag' he knew that 'the Rajahs found their prerogatives lessened' (Douglas Diary, 15 June 1878).

35. Swettenham's report of his tour of 1878 enclosed with SSD 6 March 1879. On the conventional forty followers see p. 51 above.

36. 'The period of "passive resistance" was eventually overcome by infinite patience and consistent firmness, so that in the end the ever-decreasing band of irreconcilables found themselves without either sympathy or support' (Swettenham,

British Malaya, p. 221; see also p. 179 of that work). H. C. Clifford, 'Life in the Malay Peninsula: As It Was and Is' and 'British and Siamese Malaya', in P. H. Kratoska (ed.), *Honourable Intentions: Talks on the British Empire in South-East Asia Delivered at the Royal Colonial Institute, 1874–1928*, Kuala Lumpur, Oxford University Press, 1983 (reprinted from the *Proceedings of the Royal Colonial Institute*, 1899) p. 265. J. de V. Allen, 'Two Imperialists: A Study of Sir Frank Swettenham and Sir Hugh Clifford', *JMBRAS*, 37(1), 1964, *passim*, and H. C. Clifford, *A Prince of Malaya*, New York, Harper, 1926 (originally published as 'Sally' in *Blackwoods Magazine*, February 1904, and *Saleh: A Sequel*, London, Blackwood, 1908) deal at length with various aspects of the Anglo-Malay accommodation of this period.

37. SSD 10 September 1878.

38. E. Sadka, *The Protected Malay States 1874–1895*, Kuala Lumpur and Singapore, University of Malaya Press, 1968, p. 278, and p. 35 above (on Selangor) and p. 76 on Wan Mat Isa, son of the exiled Menteri of Larut.

39. A. B. Rathborne, in *Camping and Tramping in Malaya: Fifteen Years' Pioneering in the Native States of the Malay Peninsula*, London, Swan Sonnenschein, 1898, reprinted in Singapore, Oxford University Press, 1984, p. 203. Douglas Diary, 18 June 1878 (cited in J. M. Gullick, 'Selangor 1876–1882: The Bloomfield Douglas Diary', *JMBRAS*, 48(2), 1975, pp. 25–6) relates a story to a similar effect.

40. SSD 4 May 1917. On his career *PSCM*, 20 August and 2 November 1895, in *PGG* 1895.

41. *AR Negeri Sembilan 1899*. However, *AR Negeri Sembilan 1891* praises Malay Magistrates who were of 'great assistance in settling all petty disputes'.

42. *AR Kinta 1899* in *PGG* 1900, p. 189; Sadka, *Protected Malay States*, p. 263. In 1911 Raja Chulan, well known as the first Malay unofficial member of the FMS Federal Council, applied for leave to retire from the government service in Perak. He pleaded that 'as a Native Chief he had so many calls on his time that he could not do his work properly' and that his salary was insufficient for the support of a large family. In conversation Sultan Idris, who was his father-in-law, and the Resident (E. W. Birch) agreed that Chulan had showed little energy in his official duties but had 'rendered useful service' as a member of the state council. A Colonial Office minute notes that Chulan as a magistrate 'is unable to resist pressure from litigants who are related to him or to his friends' and describes him as 'too fat and lazy to do a land officer's work' (SSD 10 January 1911). It may be an unsympathetic assessment but it brings out the various difficulties of a Malay aristocrat in coming to terms with the civil service career in which he was a pioneer (he was a son of ex-Sultan Abdullah and had been in the Perak government service since the early 1890s).

43. *AR Negeri Sembilan 1892*. On the vaccination campaign see p. 260 below. A Sungei Ujong chief who led local opposition to the unpopular land registration system (see p. 109 below) was 'temporarily removed' to Singapore (*AR Sungei Ujong 1884*, published in *SS Gazette 1885*, p. 390).

44. 'Very few regularly appointed Pungulus existed' (Report of 2 April 1875 by J. W. W. Birch enclosed with SSD 26 April 1875, para 41. Printed in Cmd. 1320 and in *Birch Journal*, pp. 388–98).

45. Sadka, *Protected Malay States*, pp. 14, 113, 187, 276–83 and elsewhere, is a valuable source of material on official policy in appointing *penghulu*. Characteristically she took immense pains to get the facts, and addressed some trenchant queries to the author.

Before submitting names to state councils for approval British administrators enquired to find out which candidate had most local support (SSD 27 August 1878). See 'Low Journal', pp. 37 and 46–7, on the vexed question of choosing a *penghulu* for Chigar Galah.

This passage deals with *penghulu* in the general sense of the term. In Negeri Sembilan '*penghulu*' is used also to denote a major or a minor territorial chief, holding a traditional office filled from among eligible lineages only. That is something quite different. In Selangor, the Menangkabau settled at Ulu Klang resisted the appointment of a government *penghulu*, Raja Shaban, and demanded recognition of their own headman (Douglas Diary, 28 June 1879).

46. Sadka, *Protected Malay States*, p. 276. The practice, once established, died hard. As late as 1906 'there is a natural desire to promote and appoint *anak raja*' (*AR Perak 1906*).

47. *AR Selangor 1884*.

48. Swettenham, *British Malaya*, p. 228. This theme is developed at p. 110 below.

49. *SGG* 1893, p. 123, report from Kuala Langat. Sadka, *Protected Malay States*, p. 276. In Kuala Selangor, an *anak raja* 'who was even well educated, applied for a *peon*'s place, but a *peon* must do menial work here, so I did not care to give it to him' (*SGG* 1890, p. 305). Times change, however; when the author was in Seremban in 1945–8 the senior peon at the Residency was a 'Raja' and the British Adviser was punctilious in addressing him with the appropriate honorific term for Malay royalty.

50. Sadka, *Protected Malay States*, p. 280. His annual reports are printed in *PGG*.

51. SSD 22 October 1902 reporting on a trip to north-eastern Malaya with Mat Salleh. In the context of the 1885 expedition, he is called 'a young and highly intelligent Malay' (F. A. Swettenham, *Footprints in Malaya*, London, Hutchinson, 1942, p. 89).

52. H. C. Clifford, *Bushwhacking and Other Asiatic Tales and Memories*, New York, Harper, 1929, p. 190; *Malay Mail*, 11 July 1902.

53. See p. 269 below.

54. H. C. Clifford, *In a Corner of Asia, Being Tales and Impressions of Men and Things in the Malay Peninsula*, London, Fisher Unwin, 1899, p. 116: 'in common with most Malay peasants, his awe of the chiefs was still intense'.

55. Report by Swettenham of 6 June 1883, printed in *SS Legislative Council Proceedings 1883*, Paper No. 23, 'Local District Administration'.

56. *AR Pahang 1891*.

57. *SJ* 23 September 1892 on the respect still shown by squatting down to the aged Sultan Abdul Samad. L. Richmond Wheeler, *The Modern Malay*, London, Allen & Unwin, 1928, p. 199, on the desuetude of this custom in 1928.

58. H. C. Clifford, *In Days that are Dead*, London, Murray, 1926, p. 286. Syed Hussein Alatas, 'The Grading of Occupational Prestige Amongst the Malays in Malaysia', *JMBRAS*, 41(1), 1968, p. 153, analyses the contrasting value systems of aristocratic and peasant society; in the latter 'conformity' was prominent. This of course was part of the tradition; it may have faded somewhat but it did not disappear at once.

59. W. E. Maxwell, 'A Journey on Foot to the Patani Frontier in 1876 being a Journal Kept during an Expedition Undertaken to Capture Datoh Maharajah Lela of Perak', *JSBRAS*, 9, 1882, pp. 6 and 8. See also 'Low Journal', pp. 52–3.

60. Wong Lin Ken, *The Malay Tin Industry to 1914*, Tucson, University of Arizona Press, 1965, p. 87. The Perak government collected a tenth of Karim's revenues and so it can be calculated that these were about $40,000 in 1874, $80,000 in 1875 but declined to about $20,000 in 1878 (SSD 3 August 1879).

61. Report by Swettenham enclosed with SSD 6 March 1879. *SS Legislative Council Proceedings 1878*, Paper No. 5, 'Report Showing the Constitution of the Court of Justice in Perak, Selangor and Sungei Ujong'. See also Sadka, *Protected Malay States*, p. 178, on Karim's career and note 26 above on membership of the Perak State Council.

62. *PSCM*, 23 March 1880 (and some later meetings), Burns (ed.), *PMS*, p. 225, record discussion of Karim's financial problems and the settlement reached.

63. Winstedt, 'Hadramaut Saiyids', p. 49; A. Lovat, *The Life of Sir Frederick Weld: A Pioneer of Empire*, London, Murray, 1914, p. 331, on the pedigree.

64. 'Low Journal', p. 48.

65. Low's policy was to 'support such undertakings' in the hope that their success would encourage European investment in pepper growing in Perak (*AR Perak 1888*). See also J. C. Jackson, *Planters and Speculators: Chinese and European Agricultural Enterprise in Malaya, 1786–1921*, Kuala Lumpur and Singapore, University of Malaya Press, 1968, p. 91.

66. *AR Kuala Kangsar 1890*, printed in *PGG* 1891, p. 798.

67. There are numerous references to the fluctuating fortunes of Syed Musa's small pepper estate, including Sadka, *Protected Malay States*, p. 360; *PSCM* 18 February 1889, in *PGG* 1890, p. 147; *PGG* 1889, pp. 61 and 147; *PGG* 1890, pp. 27, 270 and 395; *PGG* 1891, p. 798; *PGG* 1892, pp. 69 and 809; *PGG* 1894, p. 118; *PGG* 1895, pp. 423 and 674; *PGG* 1897, p. 138.

68. *AR Kinta 1888* in *PGG* 1889, p. 337; SSD 14 September 1886; 'large lumps of tin ore were found only a foot below the surface' (*PGG* 1892, p. 679).

69. SSD 26 September 1892; *AR Kinta 1888* in *PGG* 1889, p. 341.

70. See p. 199 below.

71. SSD 26 March 1899. The project had been under construction for several years but lack of expertise in the construction work caused a series of collapses in the dam (*AR Kinta 1896* in *PGG* 1897, p. 338; further information in *PGG* 1897, p. 714).

72. *AR Lower Perak 1896* in *PGG* 1897, p. 83.

73. 'Has done little good owing to the greater attractions attending mining' (*AR Perak 1900*).

74. Lovat, op. cit., p. 351.

75. *AR Perak 1903*.

76. *AR Perak 1894*.

77. Innes, op. cit., Vol. 1, p. 100, and Vol. 2, p. 6, gives a vivid picture of Raja Berkat with whom she, rather unexpectedly, struck up a firm friendship. See also *Swettenham Journal*, pp. 110 and 143. Bloomfield Douglas expelled Raja Berkat from the Selangor State Council in 1878 for attempting to bribe a magistrate. This precipitated a famous crisis in the evolution of the Residential system—Cmd. 2410 of 1879; C. D. Cowan, *Nineteenth Century Malaya: The Origins of British Political Control*, London, Oxford University Press, 1961, p. 251; Gullick, 'Douglas Diary', pp. 19–24.

78. Clifford, *In Court and Kampong*, p. 152. At p. 30 Clifford identifies 'Raja Haji Hamid' as Raja Mahmud by mentioning that he was the Selangor *raja* who

headed the Malay party which accompanied Clifford to Pahang in 188[illegible]. In the 'autobiographical preface' added to the 1927 edition (p. 16), Clifford explicitly identifies Raja Haji Hamid as the historical Raja Mahmud. He also describes him: 'He was the finest Malay swordsman and fencer I have ever seen, he was deeply versed in all manner of warriors' lore (*ilmu hulubalang*) and was believed and believed himself to be invulnerable. He had the silkiest, most conciliatory manner of any Malay I have ever known, the quickest eye and hand, and the stoutest heart ... one of the staunchest friends that any man ever had.'

79. Clifford, *In a Corner of Asia*, p. 197. The twenty-year period must be 1867–87, i.e. down to the time of the conversation between them. Clifford, however, refers to a period 'preceding the advent of the British', which suggests 1854–74—if applied to Mahmud's home state of Selangor.

80. Swettenham, 'Independent Native States', p. 188.

81. Clifford, *Studies in Brown Humanity*, p. 42 (reprinted in W. R. Roff (ed.), *Stories by Sir Hugh Clifford*, Kuala Lumpur, Oxford University Press, 1966, p. 160).

82. Rathborne, op. cit., p. 91. Like most local heroes Mahmud's reputation travelled with him. In Sungei Ujong, 'Raja Mahmud appeared and all the Malays fled' (*Swettenham Journal*, p. 158 citing Pickering). In Perak in 1875 he was known as 'a dangerous man, he has already killed many people' (Evidence to *PCE*, CO 273/87, p. 362).

83. See above p. 11.

84. *Swettenham Journal*, p. 311.

85. SSD 28 February 1912; Mahmud's story is reprinted in *Peninjau Sejarah*, 3(1), 1968, pp. 65–70. On the significance of putting on trousers in preparation for a fight, see Clifford, *Studies in Brown Humanity*, p. 37; see also p. 192 below on the conventional dress of a Malay fighting man. Swettenham's account of this celebrated incident is in *Malay Sketches*, pp. 203–5, and in *Footprints*, pp. 57–60.

86. SSD 29 September 1877.

87. SSD 6 March 1877; Douglas Diary, 1 May 1876, and 24 and 25 October 1876.

88. The passages from Douglas are cited in Gullick, 'Douglas Diary', pp. 28–9. The relevant diary entries are 3 February 1877; 12 and 13 May 1878; 27 February, 1 March and 6 August 1879; 19 June, 31 August, 7 October and 21 December 1881.

89. Douglas Diary, 24 October 1876, 14 May 1878, and 24 August 187[illegible]. The despatch of the police to Sepang was part of Douglas's maladroit handling of his celebrated encounter with Mahmud's father, Raja Berkat (see note 77 above). Douglas 'was simply struggling with the problem of fitting a restless, extravagant young dandy into a sober new world where krises had to be turned into pegs and fighting-cocks into farmyard roosters' (Sadka, *Protected Malay States*, p. 211, citing a note of a conversation between Douglas and Mahmud in Sel/Sec 69/79 in March 1979).

90. The story is well told in R. Stevenson, *Cultivators and Administrators: British Educational Policy towards the Malays 1875–1906*, Kuala Lumpur, Oxford University Press, 1975, pp. 121–5. See also Philip Loh Fook Seng, *The Malay States 1877–1895: Political Change and Social Policy*, Kuala Lumpur, Oxford University Press, 1969, p. 165.

91. Clifford, *In a Corner of Asia*, p. 197. See also Clifford, *In Court and Kampong*, pp. 30–6, for one of the episodes in Mahmud's 'lurid past'.

92. Clifford, *In Court and Kampong*, p. 79. Raja Berkat died in 1887 (*AR Selangor 1887*).

93. The correct title was 'Tunku Panglima Besar' but Raja Berkat had been permitted the 'personal styling' of Tunku Panglima Raja (*Swettenham Journal*, p. 110 editor's note)).

94. *AR Selangor 1890*, para. 176. The ostensible cause of the rift was over the choice of a new Capitan China (Sadka, *Protected Malay States*, p. 305). The deeper cause was probably Mahmud's jealousy of Raja Muda Sulaiman and his antagonism towards the latter's confidant (see above, p. 35), Raja Bot, with whom Mahmud had clashed during the Selangor Civil War (*Swettenham Journal*, p. 285).

95. SSD 14 April 1894 on the Melaka affair. The quarrel was with Ernest Birch who, with characteristic imprudence, was dabbling in the affairs of a rival mining syndicate.

96. *Malay Mail*, 14 April 1902.

97. *Malay Mail*, 30 June 1902.

98. SSD 28 February 1912.

99. Stevenson, op. cit., p. 170.

100. Muhammad Hassan, op. cit., Chapters 14–16 on the reign of Sultan Ahmad Tajuddin II. Tunku Kudin, the original Raja Muda of the period, was absent in Selangor from 1868 until 1878. The next younger brother, Tunku Yakob, replaced him as Raja Muda in 1873. See J. M. Gullick, 'Kedah in the Reign of Sultan Ahmad Tajuddin II', *JMBRAS*, 58(2), 1985, and 'Tunku Kudin in Selangor 1868–1878', *JMBRAS*, 59(2), 1986.

101. A. E. Anson, *About Others and Myself 1745–1920*, London, Murray, 1920, p. 313. See p. 56 above on the ruler's general life-style.

102. See note 100 above. Sharom Ahmat, *Tradition and Change in a Malay State: A Study of the Economic and Political Development of Kedah 1878–1923*, MBRAS Monograph No. 12, 1984, Chapter 4, describes an initial situation in 1878 which had been established during the reign of Sultan Ahmad Tajuddin II in the years before.

103. SSD 23 November 1889.

104. *AR Kedah 1909*; R. D. Hill, *Rice in Malaya: A Study in Historical Geography*, Kuala Lumpur, Oxford University Press, 1977, p. 57; Sharom Ahmat, 'The Structure of the Economy of Kedah 1879–1905', *JMBRAS*, 43(2), 1970, pp. 4–5.

105. Muhammad Hassan, op. cit., Chapter 15.

106. SSD 1 September 1909.

107. *AR Kedah 1905*. See also Sharom Ahmat, *Tradition and Change*, pp. 81–2, which gives much interesting detail on the appointment and functions, partly religious, of the Kedah *penghulu*.

108. SSD 24 November 1909. Sharom Ahmat, *Tradition and Change*, pp. 38–41, describes how the *kerah* system worked in Kedah. It was the arbitrary exercise of power as 'the system of land administration . . . was very largely theoretical'.

109. P. J. Begbie, *The Malayan Peninsula Embracing the History, Manners and Customs of the Inhabitants, Politics, Natural History etc. from its Earliest Records*, Madras, Vespery Mission Press, 1834; reprinted as *The Malayan Peninsula*, Kuala Lumpur, Oxford University Press, 1967, p. 272.

110. C. A. Trocki, *Prince of Pirates: The Temenggongs and the Development of Johor and Singapore 1784–1885*, Singapore, Singapore University Press, 1979; E. Thio, *British Policy in the Malay Peninsula*, Vol. 1: *The Southern and Central States*, Kuala

Lumpur and Singapore, University of Malaya Press, 1969, Chapters [illegible] and 9; Winstedt, 'A History of Johore', *JMBRAS*, 10(3), 1932, Chapters 11 and 12. See above pp. 6 and 55.

111. Mohamed Salleh bin Perang, *Reputations Live On: An Early Malay Autobiography*, edited and translated by Amin Sweeney, Berkeley, University of California Press, 1980, p. 51.

112. Mohamed Ibrahim bin Abdullah, Munshi, *The Voyages of Mohamed Ibrahim Munshi*, translated by A. Sweeney and Nigel Phillips, Kuala Lumpur, Oxford University Press, 1975, Introduction, p. xxvi.

113. Thio, op. cit., p. 225.

114. Ibid., p. 233.

115. H. C. Clifford, 'Report: Expedition to Trengganu and Kelantan', *JMBRAS*, 34(1), 1961, p. 61. Clifford's Report (hereafter cited as 'Expedition', with page references to the *JMBRAS* reprint) was originally printed for Colonial Office use in 1895; reprinted Kuala Lumpur, Government Press, 1936.

116. Clifford, 'Expedition', p. 67. This passage in the text is only a brief summary of Clifford, 'Expedition', pp. 61–88. The main theme, explored in much detail, of Shaharil Talib, *After Its Own Image: The Trengganu Experience 1881–1941* (hereafter cited as *The Trengganu Experience*), Singapore, Oxford University Press, 1984, is the use by the Terengganu ruling class, especially the Sultan and his close kinsmen (*kerabat diraja*), of their political power to buttress their control of the economy against expropriation by the new colonial rulers (after 1909) and the gradual erosion none the less of their privileges. The most effective device was the royal grant of large territorial concessions (*cap zuriat* or *dzuriat*) to the ruler's children and other relatives so that they might garner the revenues to be obtained from subletting agricultural or mining rights to foreign concessionaires. There were also grants in respect of revenue collection (*pajak*) and land rents (*cap kurnia*). See also M. C. ff. Sheppard, 'A Short History of Trengganu', *JMBRAS*, 22([illegible]), 1949, pp. 37–54. On Sultan Zainal Abidin III see pp. 32 and 59 and on village administration in Terengganu see p. 113 below.

117. This is fully described by Shaharil Talib, *The Trengganu Experience* cited in note 116 above. See also H. Sutherland, 'The Taming of the Trengganu Elite', in R. T. McVey (ed.), *Southeast Asian Transitions: Approaches through Social History*, New Haven, Yale University Press, 1978. Under the pressure of tighter colonial control the ruling class of Terengganu were gradually deprived of their privileges but were to some extent consoled by their new status as 'a salaried class' (Shaharil Talib, *The Trengganu Experience*, p. 176).

118. A. Rentse, 'A History of Kelantan', *JMBRAS*, 12(2), 1934. W. R. Roff (ed.), *Kelantan: Religion, Society and Politics in a Malay State*, Kuala Lumpur, Oxford University Press, 1974, is a most valuable collection of essays in which the earlier contributions cover the social history of this period.

119. W. A. Graham, *Kelantan—A State of the Malay Peninsula: A Handbook of Information*, Glasgow, James MacLehose & Sons, 1908, is written more as a handbook than an account by Graham of his work and experiences. He also wrote annual reports from 1904 onwards; his initial report is in CO 273/314. See also Roff (ed.), *Kelantan* and Clive S. Kessler, *Islam and Politics in a Malay State: Kelantan 1838–1969*, Ithaca, Cornell University Press, 1978. It appears that by the end of the nineteenth century Kelantan had begun to establish a central government which, like that of Kedah and Johor, had some Western elements. Graham, op. cit., p. 35,

mentions that in his time (1903–8) the state secretariat had invested in a *Jawi* typewriter.

120. Mohamed bin Nik Mohamed Salleh, 'Kelantan in Transition 1891–1910', in Roff (ed.), *Kelantan*, p. 44, is the main source for this passage. For subsequent developments see W. R. Roff, 'The Origins and Early Years of the Majlis Ugama', in Roff (ed.), *Kelantan*.

121. Stevenson, op. cit., Chapter 8. Khasnor Johan, *The Emergence of the Modern Malay Administrative Élite*, Singapore, Oxford University Press, 1984, is a comprehensive study in depth of the emergence of the new professional class of Malay administrators (see p. 227 below also). J. M. Gullick, 'The Malay Administrator', *Merdeka Outlook*, 1(1), 1957, is an impressionistic attempt to trace the theme. For the wider issues and the theme of Malay nationalism see W. R. Roff, *The Origins of Malay Nationalism*, New Haven, Yale University Press, 1967, which is the definitive study of that aspect.

5
The Village Community

THERE were many different kinds of Malay village community. If Anderson's rough population estimates are to be accepted, Perak in the 1820s had just under a hundred villages, of which three-quarters had between ten and fifty houses.[1] Those who travelled in the Malay states in the mid-nineteenth century rarely mention a solitary house or a hamlet of less than five houses.[2] Evidently life in a community, even a small one, was an imperative of Malay existence. These communities were generally established on the banks of rivers.[3]

There was a significant difference in socio-economic structure between a large settlement, almost a town, such as Klang in Selangor or the three or four largest villages along the Perak River, and the outlying, smaller villages. In the larger villages there was likely to be the household of a chief, as local administrator with his armed followers and his domestic staff. Traders, shopkeepers and artisans added another special element to the composition of the larger village. The Malay population, in the broad sense of 'Malay', would include some who were not of local origin.

By contrast a small village or hamlet was essentially a homogenous, agricultural community. All the population would be natives of the state or immigrants of the same cultural group, since there was much antipathy between local and foreign Malays and between immigrants of different origins.[4] The description which follows relates especially to the smaller villages, since it was in these settlements that the majority of the Malay population lived.

The basis of the village economy, to be examined in a later chapter, was the use of land for agriculture. 'The people occupied and cultivated such lands as they chose, and paid nothing for them (indeed, they had no known value) but the authorities . . . dispossessed the occupants at pleasure, or helped themselves to any produce that they thought worth having whenever they felt able and inclined. . . . In those days every able-bodied *raiat* (unless specially exempted) had on demand to give so many days forced labour to the Sultan or local chief or pay recognised compensation . . . this was not a land tax, for it applied equally to those who occupied or cultivated land and to those who did neither.'[5] The main theme of this chapter is the transition from this initial situation of feudal service to the peasant ownership of land.

Compulsory labour was a much more onerous and disruptive burden than slavery and debt-bondage. Slavery in the strict sense was restricted to non-Muslims, such as captured aborigines and Africans purchased by pilgrims to Mecca in the slave markets of Arabia.[6] A Malay villager might go raiding to capture aborigines, especially in inland Pahang, or own a foreign slave, but this was not typical.[7] The incidence of debt-bondage varied between states. It existed on a significant scale in Perak and Pahang, and to a lesser extent in the northern states.[8] It was not a purely economic institution but served to attach debtors to creditors to enhance the prestige of the latter. It also brought into the house of a ruler or a chief the domestic servants whose services he required in order to live in traditional style. To that extent debt-bondage disrupted village communities by withdrawing individuals, particularly young women, from the families to which they belonged. It could be a disruptive influence and yet it was part of the traditional way of life.

Some creditors, however, permitted debtors to live in their villages, supporting themselves but also working on the land of the creditor. In Kedah, for example, the work of bondsmen could be *kerja dalam bendang* (work in the fields) but also—more significantly—*kerja tunggu dusun*, 'which is merely the performance of the duty of a caretaker in a fruit orchard'.[9] Sadka concludes that in the FMS area debt-bondsmen were not 'used on any significant scale to develop mining and commercial agriculture; their importance was to help provide subsistence and personal attendance for the chief's household . . . they added to the prestige of the chief without doing any productive work'.[10]

The mechanism by which members of the ruling class obtained services of economic value from the peasants was compulsory *kerah* service.[11] It was a flexible system which could be adapted as required. In some instances there was a regular and continuing demand. Skeat, in Jambu in southern Siam in 1899, noted that 'the working of the *Raja*'s land was parcelled out among various headmen, a single job being assigned to each *penghulu*; it might consist of ploughing, sowing, planting out or reaping'.[12] It was also possible to mobilize labour, sometimes for a long period or for work at a distance from the village, for a particular task such as poling a boat on a journey or carrying loads as porters, to clear a river of fallen trees or to build a road. In contrast to the debt-bondsmen, the conscripted labourer was expected to bring with him his own provisions for his maintenance during the working period. Abdullah Munshi in Kelantan in 1838 was told 'every day we serve the *Raja* . . . I have to bring my own food, leaving my family with no certainty of getting anything to eat . . . this is the usual oppression of us Malays'.[13]

The hardship in *kerah* service was not so much the work itself, as the incidental disruption of the peasant's working routine on his own land, which resulted from sudden arbitrary calls, often at seasons of peak agricultural activity. It was detested. Even when a colonial regime had reduced the service obligation to a mere six days in each year, Perak villagers were prepared to resist by force until overawed by a detachment of a hundred armed police.[14]

In the harsher days of pre-colonial rule the peasant resorted to indirect means of evading the impositions and demands of his betters. If the seizure of his crops or possessions or the burden of *kerah* service became intolerable, he abandoned his plot of land and fled to make a new home elsewhere.[15] A visitor to Jelebu in Negeri Sembilan in 1884 wrote that 'the whole land is waste . . . mile after mile of deserted *kampongs* with fine *padi* land all round in abundance and with fruit trees still in bearing'.[16] The uncertainty, the risk that they might be forced to abandon everything, cast a blight over village life in normal times. 'The people are afraid to cultivate more than enough for their actual necessities, or to keep cattle other than sufficient to plough their fields.'[17]

Until—if ever—it was time to flee, the peasant hoped to keep at a safe distance from his superiors. Even in later times 'his awe of the chiefs was still intense'.[18] Thus, one of the several functions of the village headman (*penghulu*) was to stand as an intermediary between his village and the arbitrary higher authority to which it was subject. His other main duty was to preserve order within a community in which neighbours and even kinsfolk might sometime quarrel. 'They want a *penghulu* or *orang tua* appointed by government to regulate their petty affairs.'[19]

Swettenham described the various qualifications of the *penghulu* of the traditional type as follows: 'this office he has probably inherited (at least he looks upon it partly as inheritance) from his father or other near relation. The sympathies of the villagers are with him, he is personally known to all, related to many, his influence is greater or smaller in proportion to the number or fewness of his relations or following, the character he bears, the years he has been in office, the position he holds in the esteem of his *Raja*, and the amount of his private property.'[20] It was a position in which personality counted for more than executive efficiency. 'The old-fashioned *penghulu* is delightful to meet, courteous, full of quaint sayings and fascinating superstitions ... he owned much land and overlooked the lethargy of his relations and lifelong associates ... was sympathetic and settled his little world's disputes without friction.'[21]

From this picture of the *penghulu* another fact of village life emerges. He was usually a man of comparative wealth but there were other well-to-do villagers. Indeed the evidence, though it is scanty for this period, suggests that the *penghulu* relied on the support of an embryonic village middle class. Later on, when the colonial regime introduced an unpopular system of quit-rent as land revenue, it was said that the village headman 'had been afraid to tax the richer peasants'.[22] Even in 1878 one reads of 'a foreigner of great influence among the trading community and what may be called the middle classes of Perak'.[23]

This middle class is difficult to define and identify since it was small in number and deliberately inconspicuous. These men took no overt part in political life and preferred to conceal rather than to flaunt their possessions—lest this should lead to expropriation.[24] Yet the ruling class had need of their support, and often transacted its business dealings through them. They were sometimes traders rather than land-owners and so they were often found in the larger settlements. Some of them were foreigners. Yet they were essentially a middle class in the sense that they were a middle stratum of Malay society. Whether as village headmen, emissaries or advisers, they were commoners in direct contact with the traditional rulers. Their position gave them status and influence among the peasant cultivators who made up the majority of the village communities.

Since there is little general description, a picture of the middle class can be constructed from individual cases. Nakhoda Ketek, a man from Siak in Sumatra, said that he had traded for the past five years in Perak: 'I have a boat of about 2 *koyans* burden and I trade in a small way in rice between Perak and Pulo Pinang. I make advances of provisions to some mines at Batang Padang and am paid back in tin.'[25] Another Sumatran said that he 'traded on a small scale in rice, salt, piecegoods etc. up the country being assisted by Panglima Prang Mat Alee'.[26] Another, Haji Ali, lived at Blanja 'under the protection of the Sultan and traded on a small scale'.[27] The information given by these men about themselves discloses incidentally the trade pattern of the up-country villages which were not self-sufficient but imported salt, textiles and sometimes rice for local consumption.[28]

Some traders were specialists. J. W. W. Birch mentions a Terengganu man who travelled in Perak with a stock of *keris* blades for sale.[29] Others brought in textiles—'certain garments, trousers of fine silk texture, very wonderfully made'.[30] Not all the traders were Malays of foreign origin and some traded on a larger scale. Haji Mat Yassin of Durian Sabatang in Lower Perak was connected by marriage with the Datuk Laksamana, the leading chief of that part of Perak, and his half-brother was a member of Sultan Abdullah's household. Mat Yassin's father, a trader before him, had left him a substantial fortune—perhaps $30,000 or $40,000—and he engaged in involved transactions with Sultan Abdullah, giving rise to a claim for $23,000, which was a very large sum in the 1870s.

When Mat Yassin went up-river to prospect for tin and to trade, the party travelled in three boats. His own boat carried 500 *gantang* of rice as well as tobacco, oil, gambier, and four balls of opium. For the personal protection of a crew of six he took two swivel cannon, eight or nine muskets, nine spears, seven *keris*, and three large daggers. The other two boats carried rice, coconut oil, and also weapons. While up-river he sold rice on credit to Panglima Prang Samaun, a celebrated warrior, and bought tin.[31]

There were also trade links with the SS ports. On 5 December 1873 a prahu left Kuala Langat in Selangor for Melaka with a Malay crew of four and four fare-paying passengers. The master, a Bugis called Toolak, was in the service of Raja Yakob, a son of the Sultan. Yakob owned the boat but Toolak had a share in it. Before his departure Toolak obtained an advance of $20 from Yakob for trade purchases of coconuts, oil and tobacco, and also $4 for his personal expenses. At the time of his arrest on suspicion of piracy he had $63 in his possession.[32] J. W. W. Birch, in Perak in 1875, came across a Javanese who lived at Sayong on the Perak River. He traded in partnership with his two brothers, one from Singapore and the other from Penang—'we bought a lot of goods and then all three came by the Qualla and arrived at Sayong. I took my things to my house and my two brothers . . . bought a raft and lived in that with their property. They sold all their things, and they purchased 20 *pikuls* of bones at 75 cents a *pikul*, and they bought a *bahara* of tin for $70.' However, the venture ended tragically with the murder of the two brothers.[33]

Profit-sharing was a regular feature of these voyages. Nakhoda Ketek, mentioned above, sold a consignment of tin for $150 but shared two-thirds of the profit on the deal with his crew of six.

From this sort of material one derives a picture of active but generally small-scale trade. The traders—often Hajis or Nakhodas—were more often than not Malays of foreign origin, who may have retained links with their homes in modern Indonesia, but were none the less established in the Malay states or the SS ports. They were a focus of influence and commercial know-how in the larger villages of western Malaya. At this time they adopted a low profile, preferring to do business with the local aristocracy as their clients, but their connections and standing made them a potential alternative leadership of the village communities with which they traded and in which they lived.

The previous chapter has explained how, in the western Malay states, colonial rule deprived the ruling class of its effective control of the subject class and indeed almost severed the links between them. The Malay trading class seems to have lost ground to Chinese in dealings between the states and the SS. But the destruction of the traditional leadership of the Malay peasant class created a vacuum into which the middle class could direct its entrepreneurial skills. The particular opportunity which opened itself before them was the mass migration into western Malaya, mainly from the north-east, which was a feature of the last quarter of the nineteenth century.[34]

The existing Malay village population did not respond with any vigour to the new situation. With good reason, this period has been called 'the years of uncertainty'.[35] Old habits and attitudes persisted for some time. For years padi cultivation was 'merely carried on from habit and with no zest'.[36] The disincentive features of the old system of Malay rule had been removed but their effects persisted. The villagers were suspicious of the new land tenure introduced by the colonial regime, and they resented the prohibition against shifting cultivation of dry padi on hillsides, which they much preferred to wet padi cultivation. These are themes to be considered in the next chapter. Meanwhile the dynamism in the Malay economy, the leadership and organization, was supplied by the immigrants, both as entrepreneurs and as settlers.

The new regime was desperately aware of the wide open spaces, albeit still covered in jungle. 'I maintain that the first essential in these states is population, the second population and the third population. I reiterate my conviction that to prepare the land for the reception of settlers is the surest way of inducing them to come in.'[37] The greatest inducement was perhaps the political stability of western Malaya but there were other, more specific attractions such as improved access by paths and roads, and settlement grants. Yet it is doubtful whether there would have been so large a response—Perak alone received 2,000–3,000 settlers each year—if there had not been a powerful pressure to emigrate from the north-east.[38]

Kelantan, which had the largest concentration of Malay population in the mid-nineteenth century, suffered a series of disasters in the 1880s. A tornado, the legendary *angin besar* of modern Kelantan tradition, destroyed much of the coconut groves which were the mainstay of the peasant economy. Then an epidemic disease killed more than half the cattle and halted the export trade in livestock to Singapore, Patani, and elsewhere. It also deprived many cultivators of the means of tilling their padi-fields. Earlier there had been an outbreak of cholera and a serious fire which destroyed much of the state capital, Kota Bharu.[39] The ruling class exploited the misery of their subjects, forcing many of them into debt-bondage or flight. Bozzolo, who visited Kelantan in 1888, estimated that the population had been reduced by two-thirds within the space of six years. This may exaggerate what happened but there was certainly a mass movement out of Kelantan.[40]

Another major inflow of settlers to western Malaya came from Patani which had been subject to Siamese pressure and interference since the failure of an uprising in the 1830s.[41] A third source of settlers was Aceh, in northern Sumatra, which was gradually subjugated by the Dutch, at the cost of much fighting and disruption.[42] In addition, the records speak of Javanese, Menangkabau, Mandiling and other Sumatran settlers as well as Bugis, Banjarese and other migrants from the 'outer islands'.

Some migrant groups comprised complete families of men, women and children. In other cases the men came alone, intending to return to their original homes eventually but taking wives from the local communities and so founding local families meanwhile.[43] They travelled in parties and they settled down together. In this way new villages emerged which, like the existing settlements, were communities in which there was cultural homogeneity within the village. There is no information on how they travelled to the promised land. The government subsidies sometimes included an element for 'passages', i.e. travel expenses, and it may be assumed that they came by sea in small boats if that was practicable. But the migrants from north-eastern Malaya must have plodded on foot over jungle paths, bringing what they could carry.

In some cases they were led by one of themselves, a Moses bringing his people out of Egypt. There are, however, numerous references in the records to applications by village headmen or other notables, already settled in Perak or Selangor, to which the main migration flowed, for government aid to enable them to bring in settlers. As one example, Che Mat, himself of Kelantan origin, obtained a government loan of $300 in 1893 and went off to recruit padi planters to settle on land along the Selangor River which had been abandoned during the civil war twenty years before. On their arrival the settlers planted coffee and maize as well as padi. Che Mat may have been a semi-professional 'migrant broker' since he seems to have introduced settlers to several places, including Batang Berjuntai, Ijok and Ulu Langat.[44]

Another report relates that 'one Sheikh Mat Salleh from Menangkabau has applied for land for himself and thirty followers . . . he proposes to plant coffee on the high ground and padi in the adjoining swamps'.[45]

At their new settlement the migrants began to clear the land and build dwellings. Some Mandiling settlers 'are all working together for the common good, though each man has his lot demarcated . . . they all live in one square house, with rooms all round the outside like a pigeon-cot, and the mosque is upstairs in the centre of the building'.[46]

It was gruelling hard work over the first three years. In the first year they felled the jungle, burnt it and planted a catch crop of maize or some other annual crop. In the second year they rooted out the stumps, burnt the hardwood trees and levelled the ground. In the third year the land was ready for ploughing.[47] If the difficulties proved too severe they might abandon their holdings altogether or neglect the work for some easier alternative. Some of the new villages began to flourish—'many of the headmen have tastefully laid out flower gardens and good clean houses, tokens of a more refined method of living than what is customary to meet with among natives'.[48]

They would not come, or if they came they would not stay,

unless money was available for food and other necessaries during the early years in which they were struggling to establish themselves. Most of the money was provided by the state governments, but a little came from the minority of Malay aristocrats who were able and willing to perform their traditional role of providers of capital, and there is occasional mention of advances from Penang financiers. A government loan was not made direct to the settlers, but always to the headman who had organized their arrival and who supervised or directed their work on the land. He was made liable for the repayment of the loan and so he had an interest in seeing that the money was spent as intended, and that the settlers kept to their work.

As an example, the *penghulu* of Ulu Selama obtained a loan of $15 per family to settle up to 100 families of Patani settlers in his *mukim*. The money was advanced 'for their support until they can get in their first harvest' and the *penghulu* was to be responsible as their surety.[49] In the use of an intermediary there was a risk of exploitation. An administrator warned that 'a particularly watchful eye [should be] kept on their headman over them, lest he be tempted to push his own advantage at their expense'.[50]

Although the work of the first years was strenuous, it did not employ the settlers throughout the twelve months of the year and they demanded the opportunity of earning money as wages during the slack season. The road and railway construction of the period made it possible to offer them work. It thus came to be accepted that new settlers would need to work for a wage for up to six months of each year during the first three or four years after their arrival.[51] In this way they could augment their income and pay back their loans. At Sitiawan, for example, the settlers 'worked off $693.80 by constructing a cart road for the Public Works Department; nearly all the roads in Sitiawan have been made by settlers'. Nearby, the men of a Javanese settlement were working on the railway.[52]

In these arrangements the settlers showed a keen sense of the going market rate. 'The Malays are always crying out for work and complaining of their poverty' but they had refused work on clearing jungle when offered less than the accepted market rate.[53] What began as an urgent need to earn money gradually became a habit and an accepted part of the way of life. As mentioned in Chapter 4, even *anak raja* could be found in the road gangs of the 1890s.[54] It was probably the 'no-nonsense' approach of the foreign settlers which induced this change of attitude since it did not spread to Pahang, where there were comparatively few new settlements.[55]

The attitude persisted that 'no one could be certain that he would not have to fly on the morrow' but this sense of impermanence was now expressed in the choice of crops and the reaction to the new form of land tenure introduced by the state governments.[56] It was the accepted official doctrine that 'no Malay settlement is permanent without *padi*'.[57] The complex factors which made Malay villagers reluctant to practise permanent cultivation of padi are described in Chapter 6.[58] They much preferred to exploit the fertility of newly cleared land by practising shifting cultivation of dry padi, usually on hillsides or undulating land.[59] Officials complained of 'people wandering from place to place',[60] and of 'constant applications from Malays for forest land, for the purpose, they say, of planting coffee, pepper and nutmegs . . . the land is always abandoned after one crop of dry padi has been taken off it, and the applicant surrenders the land, saying the coffee which he has never planted will not grow'.[61] It is noticeable that the strongest resistance to the ban on shifting cultivation (*ladang*) was encountered in Selangor and Pahang, where civil war in the past had disrupted village life. By contrast, Negeri Sembilan, with its tradition that land is an ancestral possession (*harta pesaka*), was already an area of permanent cultivation of wet padi in spite of its narrow valleys and difficult terrain. Cultural factors underlay economic practices.[62]

The immigrant settlers had, as yet, no sentimental attachment to their land. The attitude was essentially practical. 'They give no preference to any particular description of cultivation, planting everything which commands a market. Their cultivation is, however, of a permanent type, generally consisting of fruit-trees, coconuts, betel-nuts and coffee . . . in a sense the Javanese cannot be called permanent settlers, as the majority of them return to their own country; but the result of their stay is of such a substantial type that it soon changes hands and nothing is lost by their departure, nay, rather something is gained, as the story of their success in the country of their stay tends to attract others to it.' The same report on 'the foreign Malay cultivator' continues: 'he is fully aware of the value of his property, and unless he obtains it (which he nearly always does) is quite content to remain and cultivate, and in such a case generally intermarries with the people of the country and settles the property on his wife and children if he returns to Java'.[63]

Sumatrans as much as Javanese, treated their developed land as saleable property. 'Most of the Malay immigrants are natives of Sumatra, who merely come to the state to make money and not to settle permanently. These people find that after four years work they can make a coffee garden some four or five acres in extent which they can sell for $300 to $400. This they promptly do, and return to their own country fairly rich men.' Land as saleable property was not an entirely new concept. Although undeveloped land was abundant and of no value, the occupier might expect to recover the value of improving cultivated land if he sold it. This was the concept of *pulang belanja*—the purchaser 'simply buys out the occupier by compensating him for his labour'.[64] In the past, there had been few such transactions, since the sense of impermanence worked against improving the land and a new settler could invest labour instead of money by taking up undeveloped land (*tanah mati*) and bringing it into cultivation by clearing it.[65]

There was still land in abundance and so no scarcity or pressure of population on the land. But the development of paths and roads and the growth of markets for produce began to give land a consequential value. Land along the Perak River 'although but of small value while inaccessible becomes very valuable as soon as roads or mines are opened near them'. Settlers began to select sites with this factor in view: 'the Javanese ask for no irrigation simply paths to enable them to walk on the land'.[66] The new system of land title, which facilitated sale, responded to rather than created the altered attitude to land-ownership.

There were other commercial developments in the Malay ownership and occupation of land. The largest area of land opened for wet padi cultivation in this period was the vast Krian swamp at the north-west extremity of Perak—the first of the new 'rice bowls'. In the period before 1874, Malay cultivators had crossed the border from Province Wellesley or Kedah to plant a crop of padi on the marshes of Krian, take their harvest, and then return northwards. In the 1880s, however, there began an organized programme of permanent settlement and land alienation at Krian.[67] In this 'a number of the more well-to-do settlers had a good deal more land than they could cultivate themselves; they had, therefore, to find men to rent their land, and for this purpose introduced new settlers to whom they gave advances until the crop was harvested, when the tenants repaid their advances and rent in padi, calculated at a very low rate . . . after repaying the advances and rent in a year or two the tenant had saved sufficient padi to keep himself and his family for a year, and also to acquire a new plot of land for himself. . . . In a couple of years, if he was industrious, he would himself be able to let some of his land to other newcomers.'[68] Some of the Krian landlords were absentees: 'in the early days of Krian [land was given] to men of capital who live out of Perak and sub-let their land to others'.[69]

There were risks as well as profits in ventures of this kind. In the late 1880s Krian was for a time devastated by a padi borer beetle and for several years the crop failed. The expected influx of new settlers did not materialize so that in 1889 much land lay fallow and 'nearly all the land under padi cultivation now has been planted by the owners or their friends, as outsiders, who used to swarm here to rent land, have been scared away'.[70] In good seasons, however, the profit was large—a land-owner might be able to obtain $7–9 per *orlong* as a payment of rent in cash in advance.[71]

Since the burden of *kerah* had been much reduced and the peasant had new opportunities of earning cash, it was deemed reasonable to extract revenue from him in the form of an annual quit-rent or land-tax. For this purpose it was necessary to compile lists of occupiers of developed land. This was the origin, so far as concerns Malay villages, of the system of registered title to land.[72] The peasant, with his practical common sense, could see no advantage in obtaining a piece of paper which stated what land he occupied. It was well enough known to his neighbours in the village. Even those who had at first applied for a documentary title changed their minds when it was realized that by this means they became liable to pay a new-fangled land-rent. 'People who had applied for extracts [from the *mukim* land register] refused to take them when prepared.'[73]

In 1883 the Selangor government waived the hated tax for three years (1884–6) with the exception of landholdings in the Kuala Lumpur district, whose owners had ready access to the largest urban market in the Malay states for the sale of their produce.[74] In Perak, Hugh Low concluded in 1882 that 'the difficulties in the way of the collection of a land-tax are at present insuperable'.[75] Yet the idea of land as a valuable and saleable form of property, to be transferred under the alien system of registered title, did slowly gain ground. 'The natives are also fast beginning to realise the full value of their land; the fact that they pay an annual quit-rent for it, and hold it under title having helped them to become impressed with an idea of its importance.'[76]

By tradition the *penghulu* stood between the village community and higher authority. It was still so but with a difference, since the state governments had in effect co-opted him to be their spokesman to the village rather than the acknowledged representative of the village. Swettenham, writing early in the twentieth century, described the *penghulu* as 'most useful officers ... armed with commissions setting out their manifold duties, which mainly consisted in keeping the peace, arresting offenders, sending them to the nearest police station; reporting accidents and the outbreak of infectious disease, collecting land and other revenues, settling small disputes and dealing with minor offences within their very limited power as magistrates'.[77] One might add that whenever some new problem arose such as mass vaccination, or restriction on the felling of forest timber, or the construction of a new road or bridlepath, the *penghulu* was either the principal or an ancillary arm of the government machine in its dealings with his community.

The men who had been appointed or confirmed in the 1870s on the basis of their traditional claims to the office of *penghulu*, and the men of the upper class appointed to give them status and a salary, simply could not cope with their new, unfamiliar but exacting duties. The *penghulu* was no longer the headman of a single village but placed in charge of a subdistrict (*mukim*) of several villages. He might have in his charge new villages of immigrant settlers with the result that cultural differences created a social as much as a spatial distance between the *penghulu* and his people. Within the village, the traditional role of the *penghulu* devolved on a village headman (*ketua kampung*) recognized informally by the administrative machine.

There was little understanding of the *penghulu*'s predicament. Comments in the reports range from mild disparagement, such as 'unequal'[78] to their work, to outright condemnation—'practically useless'.[79] There are jibes—'they are placed in charge of districts for the purpose of promoting the welfare and prosperity of the people and not merely as recipients of more or less involuntary gifts and for their own aggrandisement'.[80] There are specific complaints of 'receiving money on account of government and not duly accounting for it' and of neglecting official duties in order to pursue private business ventures.[81] Now and again there is a more sympathetic tribute to 'old men accustomed to the old regime' performing as best they could 'multifarious and responsible duties'.[82] The experiment of appointing clerks to assist *penghulu* proved unsatisfactory and so from about 1890 it became the practice, as posts fell vacant to fill them with younger and better educated men.[83] In this way the *penghulu* became a civil servant with a salary and a scheme of service.[84]

The new type of *penghulu* was 'less polished, at times painfully punctilious, rather uninteresting ... as often as not a stranger to his district, an official not a village patriarch, a subordinate not a landed proprietor'. Land work was 'the most important of a *penghulu*'s duties' and in this he was expected to show 'a strictness which is kindness in disguise to the *raiat*'.[85] It was still desirable that 'they should be given their posts in provinces, if not the *mukims*, where they have hereditary claims' but local influence was a subordinate consideration; it was a useful buttress to administrative efficiency which was the prime requirement.[86]

Negeri Sembilan raised special problems. Here the social organization was matrilineal and on marriage a husband usually went to live in his wife's village. The *lembaga* or *ibu-bapa* who headed a major (*suku*) or minor (*perut*) matrilineage found it difficult to exercise authority since the male members of their group were dispersed in their wives' villages. The government *penghulu*, with responsibility for the people of a *mukim*, was not usually a lineage head as well, though he might be a member of a prestigious local lineage. The whole basis of his position, therefore, was at variance with social organization.

The same tendency to convert the *penghulu* from being a leader of a local community to the role of representing higher authority in his locality appears in the states which were not yet under colonial control. It was a consequence of the trend towards bureaucratization which has been noted in describing the position of the Malay upper class.

In Kedah, the grant (*ampun kurnia*) of the revenues of a district carried the right to appoint *penghulu* to collect those revenues or to mobilize the labour of the peasants.[87] The system earned sharp strictures by British officials, though it is probable that the abuses, as is always the case, tended to overshadow the unobtrusive decency of the more satisfactory *penghulu*. The complaints relate to excessive use of compulsory labour (*kerah*), illegal issue of temporary passes to clear land for temporary cultivation (*ladang*) or to carry on various forms of local trade, improper settlement of land disputes, and accepting bribes, among others.

Yet the centralized nature of Kedah government helped to keep the abuses in check. The peasant cultivator was not completely overawed by authority and addressed his complaints direct to the ruler or his deputy (the Raja Muda), who called for an enquiry to be made. Each *penghulu* was also called in to the capital at least once a year for consideration of his estimate of revenue from his *mukim*. It is also significant that the traditional means of escape from oppression in Kedah, i.e. migration across the border into Province Wellesley, dwindled to a trickle in the last years of the nineteenth century. There may of course have been other factors at work in this trend. Vacant land was no longer easy to find in Province Wellesley and irrigation works and roads in Kedah made developed land too valuable for the owner to abandon it without grave reason for doing so. However, an attempt in 1883 to establish 'a proper land office' in Kedah was a failure.[88]

The puritan inclinations of Islamic authorities did not find as much scope in Kedah as in the states of North-east Malaya. But, in contrast to the situation in the states already under colonial rule, the *penghulu* in Kedah combined his lay duties with the enforcement of the Islamic code of conduct. Apart from such worldly matters as theft, robbery or smuggling, the *penghulu* was concerned to restrain breaches of the moral code of Islam—gambling, cock-fighting, drunkenness and 'worshipping of trees and rocks'. Unless his own behaviour was blameless, which was not always the case, it was difficult for him to be strict in these matters.[89]

Johor, like Negeri Sembilan—though in a very different way—was a unique case. The dominant element in local administration in nineteenth-century Johor was the *kangchu* system by which the ruler granted concessions to Chinese entrepreneurs.[90] Until towards the end of the nineteenth century the Malay population of Johor was insignificant, though it then began to grow rapidly by immigration of Javanese and other Indonesians who settled mainly along the west coast.[91] In the mid-nineteenth century the function of the handful of Malay *penghulu* was to collect taxes in the form of export duties on gutta percha, *damar*, rattan and other produce which aborigines collected in the jungle and sold to Malay traders. Many of these local tax-gatherers were Malays from the Temenggong's retinue at Teluk Belanga in Singapore. In accord with the general tendency in Johor to assimilate its peculiar features to the normal Malay model, these headmen were later on equipped with letters of authority, such as it was customary to issue to *penghulu* in other states. They were, however, drafted by the ruler's advisers in 'English legalese'.[92]

Village communities, on the same pattern as in the states of west Malaya, were established along the north coast of Johor. In one such case the original founder was described in the later tradition as a 'Bugis prince'. At a later period migrants from Java, Kelantan and elsewhere settled in the village. These disparate elements gradually united to form a community. However, the descendants of the founder remained a close-knit group in a community 'cemented' by kinship, wealth and local political influence; until very recent times the office of *penghulu* was always held by a member of the founder's family group.[93]

Another Johor village had been founded by Malays from Melaka, but came to be predominantly Javanese in composition. Some of the Javanese were bondsmen (*orang tebusan*), transferred into the service of local landholders by agents (*syaikh*) who supplied labour from Java, including pilgrims repatriated from Mecca on advances—for passage costs—which they repaid by labour.[94] In this way the village developed an economic class structure, wealthy and poorer groups, at an earlier stage than in most Malay villages. The office of *penghulu* was filled from among members of the leading family but from the start he was the representative of the state government rather than a local headman. He was none the less a local man and chosen as an influential figure.[95]

In Terengganu, the accession to the throne in 1881 of Sultan Zainal Abidin III led to the grant of the revenues of various districts to members of the court circle. The grantees continued to reside in the state capital, but sent forth junior members of their entourage who 'tyrannized mercilessly over local headmen and peasants'.[96] It was a very commercial system designed to maximize revenues. For example, villages in areas where there was a valuable stand of hardwood timber were required, under the *kerah* system, to fell a prescribed number of logs, square them and float them to the mouth of the local river, without receiving any payment for the work.[97] During the reign of Baginda Omar the ruler had used his influence to enhance the authority of the local village headmen. He appointed them and they were directly responsible to him.[98] Under the new regime, which began in 1881, the standing and authority of the *penghulu* declined under the pressure exerted on his community by the revenue-collection system. As *penghulu* died, their office was often left vacant and their role was filled by the local Islamic leaders (*ulama*).[99]

In Kelantan the disasters of the 1880s, described above, caused rural depopulation and disrupted village communities. Bozzolo, visiting Kelantan in 1888, wrote that throughout 'my journey I met at various places parties of Kelantan natives, some temporarily settled down, others on the way wandering to some places'. The emigration of adult males to other states led to 'daily increase of destitution amongst women and children'.[100] To some extent, this problem was relieved by offers of employment as agricultural workers or as weavers in the service of the upper class. There was also a general movement away from the densely populated area around Kota Bharu towards Ulu Kelantan in order to garner the quick results of shifting cultivation of new land.[101]

In time, stability and tolerable living conditions were restored. Perhaps because of the disruption of the 1880s there were no village headmen as such, but the *imam* of a village mosque had temporal as well as religious influence or authority within the district in which the congregation lived. Presumably this system was found to be unsatisfactory to the ruler and his government. Late in the nineteenth century, under Siamese influence, a new class of 'circle' (subdistrict) headmen (*To Kweng*), was superimposed on a group of villages (*daerah*). Within the village the *imam* was restricted to his religious functions and a village headman (*To Nebeng*) dealt with lay matters. The arrival in 1903 of W. A. Graham, as Adviser appointed by the Siamese, led to a reorganization of Kelantan into five administrative districts, but the underlying subdistrict and village system, described above, was left undisturbed.[102]

As in the western Malay states, Kelantan introduced a system of registered title to land as a means of extracting revenue from the peasant. 'A person desiring to take up land had to apply, in accordance with a very old-established custom, to the headman of the district in which the land in question was situated, and from him to obtain permission to occupy on payment of a fee which varied according to the nature of the land. The fee was supposed to be paid to the ruler, but was usually retained by the headman.' From 1881 onwards, the grant of occupation rights was registered, and from 1896 title documents were issued from a Land Office. By 1907 some 30,000 titles had been issued.[103] It is likely that pressure of demand for land in the Kelantan plain made it useful to register titles. Graham refers to abuses 'by persons whose high position enabled them to browbeat officials in order to secure to themselves lands to which their right was defective'.[104]

The rural Malay population of Penang, Province Wellesley and Melaka had no traditional political structure over their heads, but as village communities they needed a local headman as much as the villages of the Malay states. It was no less convenient to the colonial administrators of the SS to have *penghulu* through whom to deal with the Malay communities. However, the *penghulu* system of the SS was unsatisfactory to all concerned.[105] In the rural areas of Penang and Province Wellesley the *penghulu* was no more than a village police constable, with an assistant (the *mata-mata*). He was appointed by the district police officer; he received no salary but was exempt from payment of taxes. Neglected by his superiors, the *penghulu* was of little use to them. There were complaints that the *penghulu* 'prefer playing into the hands of the *rakyat* to being of assistance to the government' and that many of them had links with the Malay secret societies which were implicated in the Penang riots of 1867.

There were some sixty-five *penghulu* in the rural districts of Melaka, and they were appointed by the Resident Councillor (the senior administrator of the settlement) on the nomination of a village meeting convened by the district officer or the police officer. Although the system worked better than in Penang, there were again complaints that unless closely supervised, the *penghulu* might be dishonest or provide inaccurate information. One notes the tacit assumption that the *penghulu*'s function was to be the agent and informant of higher authority. One of their administrative duties, for example, was to accompany the district office clerk into the fields to assist him in assessing the crop, on which a tax was levied. W. E. Maxwell relates that 'a little of the *padi* is cut and an estimate formed of the probable yield. The clerk makes a return which purports to state what area is cultivated by each occupier, what is the probable yield and what is the assessed tenth. These clerks are ignorant ... they are entirely dependent on the *penghulu*.'[106] Another complaint was that a *penghulu*, if called upon to mobilize his people for some useful work such as the repair of the local irrigation system, failed to achieve a satisfactory turn-out.

Maxwell ascribed the poor performance of Melaka *penghulu* to the 'mischief and injustice' done by 'men styling themselves *Kadis*'.[107] This is a subject to be considered in a later chapter.[108] By this comment Maxwell, who knew the SS rural districts very well, tacitly acknowledges that a *penghulu* was not simply an official appointee acting in the name of the government. He was a member of a village community sharing his influence with others. In the period covered by this study the *penghulu* had changed from a 'village patriarch' to an 'official' but in that capacity he still needed the status of his traditional role, atrophied as it now was.

The other main theme of this chapter is the change in the nature of the village community itself, its place in Malay society, and its perception of itself. What had been an unstable settlement, subject to the demands of *kerah*, had become a more settled community, aware of the value of its land but subject to a tax upon those rights of ownership. In this situation lay the origins of the smallholder rubber economy and the problems which led to the passing of the Malay Reservations Enactment in 1913.

1. J. Anderson, *Political and Commercial Considerations Relative to the Malayan Peninsula and the British Settlements in the Straits of Malacca*, Penang, 1824, reprinted in *JMBRAS*, 35(4), 1962, pp. 182–6. The capitals of Kelantan and Terengganu were a larger concentration of population than most others. See F. A. Swettenham, *Sir Frank Swettenham's Malayan Journals 1874–1876* (hereafter cited as *Swettenham Journal*), edited by P. L. Burns and C. D. Cowan, Kuala Lumpur, Oxford University Press, 1975, pp. 261 and 268, and W. A. Graham, *Kelantan—A State of the Malay Peninsula: A Handbook of Information*, Glasgow, James MacLehose & Sons, 1908, p. 27. However, Graham (ibid., p. 30) notes that in the country areas the villages ranged in size from 'half a dozen to fifty houses' like those of the West Coast states.

2. F. A. Swettenham, 'From Perak to Slim and Down the Slim and Bernam Rivers', *JSBRAS*, 5, 1880, p. 68, passed fifty or sixty houses, mostly new, on the middle reaches of the Bernam River. These were sited in groups of five or six houses together. But further up the river he had travelled eighty miles without seeing any houses at all. On the other hand, in the Langat valley of Selangor, depopulated by civil war, Thomas Braddell mentions 'numerous detached houses but no villages', as if this was unusual (SSD 24 February 1874).

3. P. Sullivan, *Social Relations of Dependence in a Malay State: Nineteenth Century Perak*, MBRAS Monograph No. 10, Kuala Lumpur, 1982, pp. 19–20, argues that 'colonial observers [who] found access to inland areas difficult' overlooked a substantial degree of Malay settlement away from river valleys. Sullivan can hardly have considered the extent to which Braddell, Logan, Birch, Swettenham, W. E. Maxwell, Clifford, Hugh Low, Bozzolo and Norman made—and left records of—overland journeys in the Malay states. Their evidence is virtually unanimous—villages were on the banks of rivers. As examples—'in the valleys of the large rivers the Malay villages cluster along the banks' (H. C. Clifford, *Studies in Brown Humanity being Scrawls and Smudges in Sepia, White and Yellow*, London, Grant Richards, 1898, p. 153); 'the Malay villages *always* on the banks of a stream' (F. A. Swettenham, *British Malaya: An Account of the Origin and Progress of British Influence in Malaya*, London, John Lane Bodley Head, 1907 (revised editions 192[illegible] and 1948, London, Allen & Unwin), p. 119 (emphasis supplied)). If there had been settlements away from the rivers, they would have shown up in the administrative reports of later

years. But these testify that only the construction of paths would induce Malays to settle anywhere but on a river bank. For example, 'without this [path] they say the land cannot be taken up; there must be a line or path to work from' (*PGG* 1893, p. 300). 'By means of these bridle-paths . . . large tracts of country are opened to the people' (*PGG* 1896, p. 390). On the significance of rivers and streams as lines of communication see p. 179 below.

4. J. F. A. McNair, *Perak and the Malays: Sarong and Keris*, London, Tinsley Bros., 1878, reprinted Kuala Lumpur, Oxford University Press, 1972, Chapter 13. Peter J. Wilson, *A Malay Village and Malaysia*, New Haven, HRAF Press, 1967, pp. 18–23, offers some interesting material on the antagonisms between neighbouring villages in Selangor, founded by different cultural groups a generation or two before. 'The *anak dagang*'s objection to dealing with the *anak negeri* or settling near him' (*AR Kuala Selangor 1892*, para. 46, in *SGG* 1893, p. 502).

5. *AR Perak 1890*. Swettenham is here rebutting the assertion of W. E. Maxwell that, by custom, the Malay cultivator paid, or was at least liable to pay, a tithe of his crop to the ruler in return for the use of his land. Most of the official papers on this prolonged and bitter controversy are collected in W. E. Maxwell, *Memorandum on the Introduction of a Land Code in the Native States in the Malay Peninsula*, Singapore, Government Printer, 1894. W. E. Maxwell, 'The Law and Customs of the Malays with Reference to the Tenure of Land', *JSBRAS*, 13, 1884, is his theoretical exposition of his case. Extracts from the 1884 essay are reprinted in M. B. Hooker, *Readings in Malay Adat Laws*, Singapore, Singapore University Press, 1970, pp. 354–61. David S. Y. Wong, *Tenure and Land Dealings in the Malay States*, Singapore, Singapore University Press, 1975, Chapter 2, gives a most lucid exposition of the issue. R. J. Wilkinson, 'Malay Beliefs', *PMS*, 1906, reprinted in 'Papers on Malay Customs and Beliefs', *JMBRAS*, 30(4), 1957, p. 6, explains how Maxwell went wrong. In brief, a tithe of the crop was originally payable to the *imam* for charitable purposes; the Malay chiefs appropriated this source of revenue to themselves; the colonial regime then laid claim to it as a Malay customary revenue. Apart from his personal feud with Swettenham, Maxwell was concerned to find a justification in Malay custom for imposing a quit-rent which would be subject to revision from time to time, in line with the profitability of the land. He got his way over that but, like most other writers, the author believes that there was no justification for asserting that Malay custom gave the ruler a right to a tithe of the crop as land revenue. As Swettenham says, in the passage quoted in the text, the basic obligation of the *rakyat* to the ruler was service (*kerah*) when demanded.

6. See p. 211 below on slavery and debt-bondage. In many respects the best modern summary is Aminuddin bin Baki, 'The Institution of Debt-slavery in Perak', *Peninjau Sejarah*, 1(1), 1966. Sullivan, op. cit., is interesting but dominated by preconceived *idées fixes*.

7. H. C. Clifford, *The Further Side of Silence*, New York, Doubleday, Page & Co., 1927, pp. 244–71, vividly conveys the desperate flight of the aborigines in a vain attempt to escape capture in such a raid. See also p. 13 above.

8. 'In different states this debtor-bondage is carried to greater or less extremes' (Swettenham report of 30 June 1875 enclosed with SSD 16 October 1875 (printed in Cmd. 3285 of 1882)). See p. 211 below on the extension of debt-bondage in Kelantan during the hard times of the 1880s.

9. *AR Kedah 1909* and p. 212 below.

10. E. Sadka, *The Protected Malay States 1874–1895*, Kuala Lumpur and

Singapore, University of Malaya Press, 1968, pp. 85–6. The author prefers Sadka's view to the 'basic economic fact' asserted by Sullivan and developed in his Chapter 3, especially at p. 54. Two factors probably limited the economic use of debt-bondsmen. The creditor was expected to feed and clothe the debtor, at all events if he called on his services. He had also to organize the work done. By contrast a chief who called on a village for *kerah* did not have to feed them (see below) and the village headman stood in the hot sun and supervised the work.

11. See above, p. 73.

12. W. W. Skeat and F. F. Laidlaw, 'The Cambridge University Expedition to Parts of the Malay Peninsula 1899–1900: Personal Accounts', *JMBRAS*, 26(4), 1953, p. 61. See also p. 50 above.

13. Abdullah bin Abdul Kadir, Munshi, *Kesah Pelayaran Abdullah*, translated by A. E. Coope, *The Voyage of Abdullah: A Translation from the Malay*, Singapore, Malaya Publishing House, 1949. There was a large-scale mobilization of *kerah* labour in Kedah in 1864–5 to build seventy miles of road from Alor Star to the Siamese frontier (CO 273/24—pamphlet by Colonel Man, Resident Councillor of Penang 1860–7), and see R. D. Hill, *Rice in Malaya: A Study in Historical Geography*, Kuala Lumpur, Oxford University Press, 1977, pp. 54 and 75, on the exodus of Kedah peasants to Province Wellesley to escape the call-up and p. 99 above on *kerah* in Kedah in 1909.

14. SSD 25 May 1883.

15. See note 13 above. On resistance to *kerah* in Pahang in 1889 see W. Linehan, 'A History of Pahang' (hereafter cited as 'Pahang'), *JMBRAS*, 14(2), 193[illegible], p. 129.

16. H. A. O'Brien, 'Jelebu', *JSBRAS*, 14, 1884, p. 342.

17. *Swettenham Journal*, p. 303. Abdullah Munshi, op. cit., pp. 15, [illegible]1, 43 and 55, makes repeated references to the disincentive effect of *kerah* on the peasant economy.

18. H. C. Clifford, *In a Corner of Asia being Tales and Impressions of Men and Things in the Malay Peninsula*, London, Fisher Unwin, 1899, p. 116.

19. *SGG* 1891, p. 687, report from Klang.

20. Memorandum of October 1876 enclosed with SSD 28 May 1883.

21. *AR Perak 1909*, quoting R. O. Winstedt as District Officer, Matang.

22. *AR Negeri Sembilan 1893*.

23. SSD 26 March 1878 referring to Sheikh Mat Taib. Hill, *Rice in Malaya*, p. 82, refers to 'the Malay "middle class", the *shaikhs, wans* and *syeds* . . . [who] owned larger farms than the *rakyat*' in Province Wellesley. Against this view is Logan's opinion that 'villagers are usually on nearly the same level . . . a village *penghulu* will seldom try or be allowed to dominate over a score or two of his fellow villagers' (J. R. Logan, 'Plan for a Volunteer Police in the Muda Districts, Province Wellesley, Submitted to Government by the Late J. R. Logan in 1867', *JSBRAS*, 16, 1885, p. 183). Province Wellesley was perhaps not representative of other Malay communities; see p. 115.

24. '. . . wealthy Malay traders were frequently victimized by rajas' (A. C. Milner, *Kerajaan: Malay Political Culture on the Eve of Colonial Rule*, Tucson, University of Arizona Press, 1982, p. 22).

25. Evidence to PCE in CO 273/87, p. 314. A *koyan* at this period varied from 27 to 40 *pikul* (R. J. Wilkinson, *A Malay–English Dictionary*, 2 parts, Singapore, Kelly & Walsh, 1901, revised as *A Malay–English Dictionary (Romanised)*, 2 parts, Mytilene, Salavopoulos & Kinderlis, 1932, Item *koyan* in the 1932 edition). On the

basis of a *pikul* of 100 *kati* (1⅓ lbs.) a *koyan* would have been in the range 1.6–2.4 tons.

26. As for note 25, p. 328.

27. As for note 25, p. 454. This was probably the same Haji Ali who tried unsuccessfully to tempt Swettenham to his death in November 1875: see p. 81 above. Swettenham describes Haji Ali as 'a tall, well-made man in the prime of life ... [a] genial person of evil reputation' (*Malay Sketches*, London, John Lane Bodley Head, 1895, p. 258). He is an interesting example of the dual role of businessman and political agent filled by men of his type. He owned a tin mine at Kinta and was distantly related to Sultan Ismail (PCE loc. cit.).

28. Chapter 6 below deals with the village economy.

29. J. W. W. Birch, *The Journals of J. W. W. Birch First British Resident to Perak 1874–1875* (hereafter cited as *Birch Journal*), edited by P. L. Burns, Kuala Lumpur, Oxford University Press, 1976, p. 125.

30. H. C. Clifford, *Malayan Monochromes*, New York, Dutton, 1913, p. 153.

31. Evidence to PCE in CO 273/87, p. 585. Swettenham, *Malay Sketches*, pp. 112–46, describes one of the adventures of Panglima Prang Samaun.

32. Data on Toolak from the report of the Kuala Langat piracy trial of February 1874 in which he (named as Ma Tyron) was accused No. 1. He was convicted (apparently on false evidence, see *Swettenham Journal*, p. 291) and executed. Report enclosed with SSD 24 February 1874.

33. *Birch Journal*, pp. 298–9.

34. It is not possible to demonstrate that the traders of the 1870s organized the migration of the 1880s and 1890s nor is it suggested that there was continuity of that kind. Occasionally, one encounters an individual, such as Haji Tahir, the agricultural pioneer of Klang, whose personal history bridges the transition from a politico-commercial role in the 1870s to land development in the 1890s (see p. 162 below). The hypothesis advanced and illustrated—it is not fully proved—is that as the traditional aristocratic leadership of Malay society waned the nascent middle class of businessmen, with their contacts in the outside world of the SS and their commercial flair, provided the initiative and the organization which the new situation demanded.

35. Lim Teck Ghee, *Peasants and Their Agricultural Economy in Colonial Malaya 1874–1941*, Kuala Lumpur, Oxford University Press, 1977, Chapter 2. Although Lim is referring to the period 1896–1904, his phrase could fairly be applied to the preceding decade also. See also J. M. Gullick, 'The Entrepreneur in Late 19th Century Malay Peasant Society', *JMBRAS*, 58(1), 1985, which is an earlier account by the author of the developments described in the passage which follows.

36. *AR Tampin 1896*, para. 24, in *NSGG 1897*, p. 87, describing the former attitude of a decade before, i.e. 1887. 'The difference between these *kampongs*, which are all inhabited by Patani Malays, and those of the natives of Perak is striking' (*PGG* 1889, p. 613, report from Kuala Kangsar). Disparagement of the older villages on these lines is common in the reports of this period.

37. *AR Negeri Sembilan 1899*, written by Ernest Birch who was a leading advocate of a programme of government irrigation works, on which he wrote a pamphlet (SSD 17 May 1900).

38. In 1885 Krian and Larut received 3,000 settlers (*AR Perak 1885*). There was a similar influx into Perak as a whole in 1891 (*AR Perak 1891*). In 1907 it was estimated at 2,000 (*AR Perak 1907*). In Selangor there was also a substantial inflow though overall estimates are not given.

A recent study has suggested that the scale of migration from North-east Malaya may have been exaggerated because Newbold's population figures for the 1830s, which are the starting point, may be too low (N. N. Dodge, 'Population Estimates for the Malay Peninsula in the Nineteenth Century, with Special Reference to the East Coast States', *Population Studies*, 34(3), 1980). This is an issue for debate among demographers but the contemporary evidence from the West Coast states clearly shows that substantial numbers were arriving there. Lim Teck Ghee, op. cit., p. 12 and Appendix 1.3, demonstrates 'large numbers of immigrant Malays' for the last decade of the nineteenth century.

39. H. C. Clifford, 'Report: Expedition to Trengganu and Kelantan', *JMBRAS*, 34(1), 1961, originally printed for Colonial Office use in 1895, reprinted Kuala Lumpur, the Government Press, in 1936, p. 116 of *JMBRAS* reprint. SSD 31 January 1889, Bozzolo's report. Dodge, op. cit., p. 447. *Swettenham Journal*, p. 268, on the cattle trade. See also p. 87 above and p. 211 below.

40. Bozzolo, then District Officer in Upper Perak, made an overland journey to Kota Bharu via Ulu Kelantan in 1888 (SSD 31 January 1889). T. J. Newbold, *Political and Statistical Account of the British Settlements . . . with a History of the Malayan States on the Peninsula in the Straits of Malacca*, 2 vols., London, Murray, 1839, reprinted as *British Settlements in the Straits of Malacca*, Kuala Lumpur, Oxford University Press, 1971, Vol. 2, p. 65, had estimated the Malay population of Kelantan in the 1830s at only 50,000, but Dodge, op. cit., doubts this figure. The figure of 100,000 *male* Malays given to Swettenham in 1875, before the exodus, must have been much too large (*Swettenham Journal*, p. 268). But whatever the figures, there is no doubt that severe hardship in the 1880s did induce a large movement in spite of harsh penalties imposed to discourage it (Abdullah Munshi, op. cit., p. 56).

41. After suppressing the rising in Patani in 1832 the Siamese broke up the state into a number of smaller units, so that Patani in the later years of the nineteenth century was a mere fraction of what it had been. Swettenham had noted signs of demoralization in 1875—'the town is cramped and dirty' (*Swettenham Journal*, p. 267). See also p. 367, note 2, below on the appeal to Swettenham by the Raja of Patani in 1901.

42. Dutch military operations against Aceh continued intermittently from 1873 to 1899 (D. G. E. Hall, *A History of South-East Asia*, London, Macmillan, 1955 (4th edition 1981), pp. 619–21).

43. 'Most of them came with their families in their own small boats' (*AR Perak 1885*). But in another case 'mostly Java and Malacca men, only allied to Sungei Ujong by marriage' (SSD 20 August 1880).

44. *SGG* 1893, pp. 124, 327 and 803.

45. *SGG* 1893, p. 263.

46. *PGG* 1895, p. 577. The author has not come across any other reference to a communal dwelling of this kind. It may not be a representative case.

47. 'Reports Furnished by Order of His Excellency the Governor upon the Best Means of Encouraging the Cultivation of Rice in the Malay Peninsula', *Straits Settlements Legislative Council Proceedings 1893*, Paper No. 6 (hereafter cited as 'Rice Cultivation Report 1893'), p. 142. 'It takes three years to convert a forest into a *sawah*' (*SGG* 1893, p. 417, report from Kuala Langat).

48. *SGG* 1890, p. 416, commenting on a Javanese settlement at Tanjong Duabelas in Kuala Langat. The settlers grew fruit which was exported to the Singapore market by local steamers.

49. *PSCM*, 21 August 1881, *PMS*, p. 239. The 'Rice Cultivation Report 1893', p. 135, mentions a *penghulu* who borrowed $485.20 to settle ten or twelve families who had fled from Kedah to escape a cholera epidemic in 1883, and also advances of $7 per acre to Banjarmasin and Javanese settlers to help them clear 2 or 3 acres each. In this instance the *penghulu* was also required to make a personal recommendation of each family. In spite of all the precautions there were defaults; Douglas refers to advances as 'so many losses' (Douglas Diary, 23 July 1879).

50. 'Rice Cultivation Report 1893', p. 112.

51. *AR Kuala Langat 1891* in *SGG* 1892, p. 654.

52. 'Rice Cultivation Report 1893', p. 135.

53. *SGG* 1893, p. 264. This comment refers to a period of hardship when disease had greatly reduced the number of cattle available for ploughing.

54. See p. 77 above.

55. *AR Pahang 1899*, para. 95.

56. *AR Negeri Sembilan 1892*.

57. *AR Perak 1909*.

58. See below, p. 128.

59. *AR Pahang 1898*, para. 13. The preference for growing padi in newly made clearings (*ladang*) is considered in the next chapter; see p. 127 below.

60. *AR Kinta 1888* in *PGG* 1889, p. 339.

61. *AR Kinta 1890* in *PGG* 1891, p. 763. See also *PGG* 1897, pp. 267 and 385 for similar reports from other parts of Perak.

62. In 1902 the almost total absence of padi cultivation in Selangor was attributed to (1) the preponderance of 'foreign' Malays and (2) mining and other activities (*AR Selangor 1902*).

63. *SGG* 1894, p. 117, report from Klang.

64. *AR Ulu Selangor 1894* in *SGG* 1895, p. 212, on Sumatran migrants. W. E. Maxwell, 'The Law and Customs of the Malays with Reference to the Tenure of Land' (cited hereafter as 'Land Tenure'), *JSBRAS*, 13, 1884, p. 121, on *pulang belanja*. Aristocrats as well as peasants dealt in land as saleable property—at all events in the last years of the nineteenth century. 'Raja Bot was very fond of buying pieces of land which he considered would be of higher value and thereby bringing him greater returns; he would thus sell one piece of land for another.' In 1897, for example, he sold land in Kuala Lumpur and invested the proceeds in buying land planted with coffee at Klang. At that stage in the decline of the short-lived coffee boom, it was a disastrous error of judgement (see p. 162 below) (Mohamed Amin Hassan, 'Raja Bot bin Raja Jumaat', *JMBRAS*, 40(2), 1967, p. 92).

65. W. E. Maxwell, 'Land Tenure'; 'it was difficult to get ten dollars an *orlong* for excellent *padi* land by *pulang belanja* but when security of tenure and the full right of alienation of the soil was introduced in the district by the British government, it became possible to sell the same land [at Krian] for $60 or $70 an *orlong*'. He then mentions the government purchase of land at Kuala Kangsar to be the site of the Residency; the price paid was the value of the fruit trees and the houses. The Regent, Raja Yusuf, confirmed that a transfer on the basis of occupier's improvements, as distinct from a sale of the land for its inherent value (if any) was the traditional concept (Maxwell, ibid., pp. 121–2).

66. *AR Lands Department Perak 1888* in *PGG* 1889, p. 251, on land values. *PGG* 1895, p. 395, on paths.

67. Between 1879 and 1891 the Malay population of Krian and the adjacent

Kurau area increased from 6,852 to 14,991. This 120 per cent increase in twelve years was larger than in any other part of Perak (Lim Teck Ghee, op. cit., p. 61, note 44). This owed much to the work of Noel Denison, who was District Officer, Krian, from 1877 to 1881.

68. 'Rice Cultivation Report 1893', p. 118, report by the Commissioner of Lands, Perak.

69. *AR Krian 1894*, para. 31, in *PGG* 1895, p. 405.

70. *AR Krian 1889* in *PGG* 1890, p. 79.

71. *PGG* 1891, p. 623, report from Krian. The fluctuating fortunes of the Krian 'rice bowl' are reflected in the value of its exports which reached $204,405 in 1885 but had fallen by more than 80 per cent to $24,033 in 1890 (Lim Teck Ghee, op. cit., p. 61, note 45). An *orlong* (or *relong*) when applied to an area (see Glossary) is about 1⅓ acres or 0.6 hectare of land.

72. In addition to the sources cited in note 5 above, on the long controversy over the introduction of registered title to land in Malay areas, see Sadka, *Protected Malay States*, pp. 340–4. The Selangor Land Regulations, published in *SGG* 1891, and related directives, were Maxwell's masterly but over-elaborate formulation of the land system which he recommended. Although some changes of detail were made, the uniform land legislation for the FMS enacted in 1897 was substantially on the Maxwell model.

73. *AR Kuala Selangor 1891* in *SGG* 1892, p. 648.

74. *AR Selangor 1884*.

75. *PSCM*, 22 May 1882, *PMS*, p. 248. The Perak government experimented with a complicated compromise by which male Malays between the ages of 15 and 40 were liable to an annual poll-tax of $1 (in substitution for the former obligation to perform 4 days' *kerah* service) but anyone who had paid quit-rent on his land did not also pay poll-tax. This proved just as unpopular as simple quit-rent and Swettenham recommended its total abolition (*AR Perak 1884*, para. 199). See also *PSCM*, 30 December 1880, *PMS*, p. 231, and Douglas Diary, 18 June 1881.

76. *AR Pahang 1897*, para. 9.

77. Swettenham, *British Malaya*, p. 228.

78. *AR Perak 1889*.

79. *AR Selangor 1885*.

80. *AR Selangor 1886*.

81. *PSCM*, 18 November 1879, *PMS*, p. 211. See Douglas Diary, 24 July and 22 August 1879, for two particular instances.

82. *AR Perak 1900*.

83. *AR Selangor 1895*. As a specific instance the Perak State Council in 1895 gave the *penghulu* of Hutan Melintang the choice of employing a clerk at $10 per month or of retiring (*PSCM*, 20 August 1895, *PGG* 1895, p. 526).

84. *AR Perak 1906*.

85. *AR Perak 1909*, quoting Winstedt writing as District Officer, Matang. Contrast the other passage cited in note 21 above.

86. *AR Perak 1906*, citing A. Hale as District Officer, Krian.

87. See p. 85 above on *ampun kurnia* grants in Kedah.

88. Sharom Ahmat, 'The Political Structure of the State of Kedah 1879–1905', *JSEAS*, 1(2), 1970, pp. 119–20. See also source cited in note 89 *passim*.

89. Sharom Ahmat, *Tradition and Change in a Malay State: A Study of the Economic and Political Development of Kedah 1878–1923*, MBRAS Monograph 12, 1984, pp. 81 and 120.

90. A. E. Coope, 'The Kangchu System in Johore', *JMBRAS*, 14(3), 1936; C. A. Trocki, 'The Johore Archives and the Kangchu System 1844–1910', *JMBRAS*, 48(1), 1975. See also C. A. Trocki, *Prince of Pirates: The Temenggongs and the Development of Johor and Singapore 1784–1885*, Singapore, Singapore University Press, 1979, *passim*.

91. R. O. Winstedt, 'A History of Johore', *JMBRAS*, 10(3), 1932; Khoo Kay Kim, 'Johor in the 19th Century: A Brief Survey', *Journal of the Historical Society, University of Malaya*, Vol. 6, 1967–8; Trocki, *Prince of Pirates*.

92. Trocki, *Prince of Pirates*, pp. 80, 82 and 211.

93. K. O. L. Burridge, 'The Malay Composition of a Village in Johore', *JMBRAS*, 29(3), 1956, especially pp. 61 and 77; and 'Managerial Influences in a Johore Village', *JMBRAS*, 30(1), 1957, p. 96.

94. S. Husin Ali, *Social Stratification in Kampong Bagan: A Study of Class, Status, Conflict and Mobility in a Rural Malay Community*, MBRAS Monograph No. 1, 1964, pp. 29–30. However, most of the Javanese labourers who passed through the hands of Singapore brokers at this time were sent to Borneo, Sumatra and other destinations outside Malaya (R. N. Jackson, *Immigrant Labour and the Development of Malaya 1786–1920*, Kuala Lumpur, Government Printer, 1961, p. 127). On repatriated pilgrims as labour see p. 176, note 74, and p. 314 below.

95. S. Husin Ali, *Malay Peasant Society and Leadership*, Kuala Lumpur, Oxford University Press, 1975, pp. 117–18. See also p. 86 above.

96. M. C. ff. Sheppard, 'A Short History of Trengganu', *JMBRAS*, 22(3), 1949, p. 38; Clifford, 'Expedition', p. 73.

97. Clifford, 'Expedition', p. 73.

98. Sheppard, 'History of Trengganu', p. 35.

99. Shaharil Talib, *After Its Own Image: The Trengganu Experience 1881–1941* (hereafter cited as *The Trengganu Experience*), Singapore, Oxford University Press, 1984, p. 27. See also p. 289 below.

100. SSD 31 January 1889. On Bozzolo and his expedition see note 40 above.

101. As note 100.

102. Mohamed bin Nik Mohamed Salleh, 'Kelantan in Transition 1891–1910', in W. R. Roff (ed.), *Kelantan: Religion, Society and Politics in a Malay State*, Kuala Lumpur, Oxford University Press, 1974, p. 44.

103. Graham, op. cit., pp. 92–4.

104. Ibid., p. 94. See also Shaharil Talib, *The Trengganu Experience*, p. 225, on similar abuses in Terengganu.

105. SSD 7 June 1892 on the SS Criminal Procedure Code encloses a long printed memorandum of 1882 on local district administration in rural areas from which the quotations and other material reproduced in this passage are taken. The printed memorandum had been published in *Straits Settlements Legislative Council Proceedings*, 1883, as Paper No. 30.

106. As for note 105 above. Quotation from a memorandum by W. E. Maxwell.

107. As for note 105. Maxwell had served for about ten years (1865–75) in the SS rural districts and had exceptional knowledge but little tolerance of the shortcomings to which he refers.

108. See p. 287 below.

6
The Village Economy

When Midshipman Sherard Osborn took part in the British naval blockade of the Kedah coast in 1838–9, he learnt that its most severe effect was an acute shortage in Kedah of salt.[1] The Malay village did not produce all the basic commodities which it consumed. Most Malay states imported textiles since local production was not adequate to satisfy local needs.[2] When James Low visited Perak in 1826, 'the goods most in request are blue cloth of cotton, Acheen dresses, opium, tobacco, salt, salt-fish, gambier and minor articles'.[3] The contemporary accounts also refer to trade in 'oil', which was presumably coconut oil, pottery, glass and metal utensils. The latter must have been required more by the well-to-do than by the ordinary peasant. Although many villages grew enough rice for their own needs, some did not, and everywhere rice was imported when the local crop failed.

John Anderson's list of the principal exports is tin, bees-wax, birds' nests, cutch, *damar*, fish maws, rice, rattans, sharks' fins, betel-nut, canes, dragons blood, elephant's teeth, gold dust, sago, *agila* and *sapan* woods, hides and skins.[4]

The flow of trade in both directions had important effects on the structure of traditional Malay society and on village life. Taxes on trade, including monopolies, were a source of revenue to the ruling class. The cost of moving goods overland induced settlement along the banks of rivers, which were the main lines of communication.[5] The villager bought and sold goods for money, with the result that he lived in an exchange economy in which money and prices expressed in money were part of his culture.

None the less, a typical village produced a great deal of what it consumed and it had a semi-subsistence economy, in which rice and other local foodstuffs were the essential basis of living. Modern studies have demonstrated that in the nineteenth century padi was grown by several different methods of cultivation.[6] In particular the accumulation of water behind a dam and its transfer to the padi-fields through man-made distribution channels, an irrigation scheme' in the technical sense, was restricted to a few areas, notably Kedah and Negeri Sembilan; elsewhere a variety of other methods were in use.

A broad distinction was made between growing dry padi (also called 'hill padi'—*padi bukit*) and wet padi (or 'swamp padi'). In dry padi cultivation, land was cleared and padi seeds planted to exploit the accumulated fertility of the soil by taking one year's crop. The land was then either abandoned or some more permanent crop was planted on it. This was shifting cultivation of padi which took its name from the Malay word '*ladang*' (clearing). In a country where a hundred inches of rain fall in a year, dry padi could flourish on the moisture retained in the soil.

The essential feature of wet padi cultivation was that during the growing season, which lasted several months, the fields were covered in a shallow layer of standing or running water. To obtain a good crop the padi plants must grow in a suitable and consistent depth of water, neither too much nor too little. It was the general practice to divide up the fields into enclosed level patches (*lopak* or *petak*) separated from adjoining patches by low earth bunds (*batas*). As the soil within each patch was level, the water would be at a uniform depth. If there was a slope in the general lie of the ground, water would seep from the higher to the lower parts of the fields. It was not Malay practice to construct hill-terraces, such as are found in some other parts of South-East Asia. The bunds also served as paths through the flooded fields.

It was sometimes possible to establish padi-fields in areas of permanent swamp (*paya*); the problem then was getting rid of surplus water but there was no need to provide an external supply. This method of swamp cultivation shaded into the use of low-lying land where rain-water would accumulate during the growing season, if the right time for planting was selected. The cultivators might also build a brushwood dam across a stream above the level of their fields and divert the water by natural flow through their fields. In Negeri Sembilan irrigation water was lifted from the stream to the fields by an ingenious waterwheel (*kincir*) which was rotated by the force of the main stream against its projecting paddles; its runnels (usually lengths of hollow bamboo) picked up water as they turned and decanted it into a trough at a higher level.

The common feature of all methods of wet padi cultivation was a thorough preparation of the land before planting. In some areas the cultivator ploughed his land, using buffaloes or even human traction to pull the light plough. A simpler use of buffaloes was to drive them round and round each patch of ground within its encircling bund until the soil had been sufficiently churned up by their hooves. Elsewhere the land was prepared with a draw-hoe (*cangkul*), or the cultivator might be content to cut down the weeds which had grown up since the last harvest, using a slashing-knife (*tajak*). The padi seed was usually planted in a nursery so that the seedlings might be transplanted to the fields, but in some areas, seed was broadcast by hand so that it fell direct upon the surface of the fields.[7] There were two main methods of harvesting. The more traditional method was to cut each ear separately with a small reaping knife (*tuai*); the alternative was to use a sickle (*sabit*).

Contemporary reports follow Malay usage in classifying land under padi cultivation in three categories. First, there was *tanah ladang*, i.e. taking one year's crop on a new clearing and then leaving the land fallow for at least seven or eight years. Secondly, there was *tanah tenggala*, i.e. ploughed land irrigated by rainfall which would yield satisfactory crops for about four or five years but must then lie fallow for two years. Lastly, there was swamp land, *tanah paya* (also called '*bendang*' or '*sawah*'), which was kept in permanent cultivation but required a continuous water supply of some sort.[8] Suitable swamp land was not plentiful since land which was permanently flooded was usually difficult to get into. However, in the latter part of the nineteenth century there was a large-scale move into the Krian swamps, and in Kedah, Wan Mat Saman's canal provided a means of access to a large area.[9]

Malay villagers had definite preferences and it was not easy to persuade them to abandon old or adopt new methods of cultivation. There was a general preference for *ladang* cultivation; it yielded a light crop but it required only a moderate effort and there was less risk of losing the crop. Wet padi cultivation of any kind entailed some measure of investment in land improvement, which ran counter to the prevailing sense of impermanence in pre-colonial village life. It was also vulnerable to a number of hazards—buffaloes, pests, floods, and droughts.

Before coming to these problems, wet padi cultivation needs to be put in its cultural context. It entailed a traditional allocation of tasks between men and women. The planting of seedlings in the fields, for example, was women's work but preparing the fields for planting fell to the men. There were rituals to be performed under the guidance of the *pawang*.[10] Apart from giving reassurance of success, the *pawang* acted as a coordinator. He decided when the sequence of cultivation operations, such as planting or harvesting, should begin since all must conform to his ritual initiation of each stage. Then, in long-settled villages at least, the peasants felt a 'hereditary obligation to occupy and till the ground as their fathers had done before them'.[11] Yet there was the alternative of temporary or shifting cultivation of *ladang* to which no ancestral imperatives attached. The choice of method might be determined partly by terrain but there were other factors.

In Perak and Pahang, both areas of long-established Malay settlement which had been much disturbed by civil war and unrest, Malay villages grew both dry and wet padi, but made little use of artificial methods of irrigation. It was said that in Perak *ladang* cultivation 'on the hillsides is exclusively the native method' and that only villages of Sumatran origin grew wet padi.[12] This statement probably exaggerates the situation. In inland Selangor, where the Malay population was mainly Sumatran, there was little wet padi cultivation until the Malay traders and miners had settled down to agriculture—a complicated process to be examined below.[13] There was certainly no stigma of social disapproval of *ladang* cultivation in these various areas.[14] It was simply perceived as a possible, often more convenient, alternative to wet padi growing. In Kelantan there was a similar combination of methods; in Terengganu at this time not much padi was grown.

From central Kedah southwards through Province Wellesley to the Krian district of Perak, the swampy land was conducive to wet padi cultivation; but in the extreme north of Kedah, beyond the limits of the rice plain, there was dry padi cultivation. In Negeri Sembilan, and to some extent in Melaka, there was a well-established tradition of wet padi growing even though the narrow valleys of Negeri Sembilan were not very favourable terrain.[15]

The new colonial regime sought to restrain and eliminate *ladang* cultivation, since it could lead to soil erosion and silting of rivers. The Malay peasant, however, showed some ingenuity in his pretexts for obtaining temporary permits for *ladang*, and it fell to the harassed *penghulu* to do what he could to enforce the unpopular system, and persuade his people to practise wet padi cultivation to a greater extent than they wished.[16]

Except in Kedah, where padi was grown for export, the peasant tended to limit his rice production to the estimated requirements of his own household—though in bad years he was obliged to buy imported rice.[17] Kedah had better communications than most other states, and so an exportable surplus there could be exported. Elsewhere, the cost of transport made it impracticable to dispose of a surplus. Braddell, on tour in inland Melaka, 'passed a party of 15 Malays carrying rice from Tanka to sell to the miners; the price I heard was 7 *gantangs* to the dollar, an advance which appears to be barely sufficient to remunerate for the labour of carriage on men's backs'.[18]

Yet, if there was an opportunity of sale or barter of rice, the villagers took it. Thus in Upper Perak 'in former days it was the custom for Korinchi pedlars to come to the district, selling cloth to the natives, and fixing such exorbitant prices for the same which was of very inferior quality that the natives, being unable to pay the price asked, used to give in exchange so many gantangs of padi. . . . The natives when their crops were in, had to carry the same to large rafts belonging to these Korinchi who used to wait by the river side to receive the padi. . . . In 1887 I saw as many as 15 large rafts, each containing over 1,000 gantangs of padi.'[19] When improved communications made it less costly to move produce to markets, the Malay villager usually preferred to export fruit and other foodstuffs, since these were less risky to produce and more profitable to grow for sale than rice.[20]

The vicissitudes of padi growing in Selangor in the nineteenth century are an informative case-study. The Bugis who founded Selangor in the eighteenth century were traders and fighting men but, by the second quarter of the nineteenth century, their descendants were a settled community which grew padi on a significant scale. The authority of their ruler was applied to stimulate their efforts. 'In olden times,' wrote Raja Bot in 1902, 'my grandfather, Sultan Mohamed of Selangor, was himself very fond of planting padi and rigorously imposed on all his subjects doing so too . . . those who were slow or who did not toil at padi planting were punished.' Along the Selangor River, 'nothing but padi fields could be seen in those days'.[21] Then the expansion of tin mining drew into the interior of Selangor both turbulent Chinese miners and Sumatran traders and miners. The ensuing civil war (1867–73) disrupted the economy and most of the settled Malay population fled. Into the Klang valley came migrants from Kedah, Pahang, Sumatra and the SS; but at first their interest too was in trade, mining and sometimes production of crops other than rice.[22] As late as 1900 Selangor was reckoned 'almost devoid of a settled Malay population'[23] and in consequence there was little padi—'only small patches grown in a half-hearted manner'.[24]

As related in the previous chapter, the 1880s saw a second wave of immigrant Malay settlers—men from Kelantan, Banjarmasin (Borneo), Java and Sumatra. These men had more of an agricultural tradition, which may explain their better standard of cultivation. In this respect they did better than the 'local Malays', who were 'neither energetic nor industrious nor are they much influenced by the motive which actuates most Mohammedans to make money—namely the desire of making a pilgrimage to Mecca'.[25] The settlers came from padi-growing areas in their homelands, and had command of useful techniques, such as the use of buffaloes or sometimes of waterwheels or constructing rudimentary irrigation works. But they were not interested in growing padi in Selangor unless it paid them to do so. An 1889 report from Klang, where there were many Javanese, states that there was little padi cultivation, 'the Malays preferring to cultivate gardens of cocoanuts, pinangs, and other fruit'.[26] Agriculture was a commercial operation; one could make a better living by growing other crops and using the proceeds of sale to buy rice. If, however, the price of rice became attractive, they grew it along with their other cash crops. A report from Klang in 1897, when the price of rice had risen, notes that 'nearly every garden owner has planted rice in between permanent products, and in most cases good crops have been realised'.[27]

Yet, in their way of life, growing padi was always more than a simple commercial operation. Although some settlers sold their land for cash and returned to their homelands, yet others stayed on. Land, which had been developed as a speculation, became a heritage. Non-economic factors began to modify the attitude to rice. Skeat, in recommending measures to assist padi growers in Ulu Langat in 1896, argued that 'padi planting would very shortly become a securely established industry in this district, it being a form of culture the most congenial both to the Mendiling and Menangkabau Malay, of whom the local Mohamedan population almost entirely consists, and whose zeal for this form of culture is more affected by the results of the harvest than by rising and falling prices as is often supposed'.[28] There was a two-way interaction. Continued occupation of land induced a willingness to grow padi, even if it was less remunerative. Padi growing strengthened the attachment of the cultivator to his land. They 'cling to their rice fields more from association and custom than because they consider it a better investment than any other form of labour' though even in this period the younger generation were not content and tended to 'seek a livelihood beyond the regions of a rice swamp'.[29] Ernest Birch summed it up in 1909—'No Malay settlement is permanent without *padi*.'[30]

This gradual progression towards padi growing as a way of life, rather than a livelihood, was impeded and sometimes held in check by a variety of hazards. Although Skeat discounted market price fluctuations as a factor, he recognized the importance of 'the results of the harvest' and recommended government aid in procuring buffaloes. There are, however, numerous reports of epidemics which killed large numbers of buffaloes.[31] If the peasant then purchased new stock imported from outside the state, they might bring in more disease.[32] In Pahang, despairing villagers threw the carcasses of dead animals into the river regardless of the risk of spreading the disease to villages lower downstream.[33] Unless herded or tethered, a healthy buffalo could do a great deal of damage. Abdullah Munshi in Kelantan in 1838 saw 'cattle and buffaloes and goats by the hundred lying all over the rice fields; they had no pens and no one was looking after them; they just lived on their own . . . no one cared'.[34] This neglect did no harm in the off season between the harvest and the next planting. But buffaloes were also allowed to stray into the standing crops. In 1889 the Orang Kaya of Temerloh told the Pahang State Council that 'disputes between buffalo-owners and padi-planters, sometimes leading to bloodshed, were of frequent occurrence in his district'.[35] Rules requiring that buffaloes be herded or tethered or confined in an enclosure or a shed at night, were more easily made than enforced.[36]

As Islamic orthodoxy strengthened its hold, the *pawang* receded into the background of village life.[37] This may have contributed to the breakdown of the essential system of coordinated padi cultivation within the village fields. When the Pahang State Council discussed making regulations to enforce a programme, there was despondency about the alternative of leaving the matter to the villagers themselves—'the chiefs strongly expressing the opinion that the cultivators were incapable of combining among themselves to agree to any such arrangement as the simultaneous planting of their crops . . . selfish considerations, they said, would always lead some members of the village community to delay planting in spite of any mutual agreement; others fearing the destruction of their crops by vermin if planted before those of their neighbours, would follow their example'. On the other hand 'many years ago His Highness the Sultan issued an order that all crops should be planted simultaneously upon a fixed date' and this had been successful.[38] In passing, one may note that the authority of the *penghulu* and the tradition of co-operation (*gotong-royong*), which had been the cement of village life, may have been weaker in the new era of individual land-ownership.

There was also some confusion about the reckoning of time. By ancient tradition 'the lower classes estimate the year by the fruit seasons and by their crops of rice only'.[39] They also reckoned time by the growing season—a 'year of rice' was six months but 'a year of maize' was only three.[40] The peasant could keep these shorter periods in line with the solar year by noting the position of the stars.[41] Then Islam introduced a year made up of lunar months, totalling 355 days—with the result that the Muslim calendar 'slipped' back by ten days in each solar year. Such months were useless in the agricultural cycle, but 'the Malays still entertain a superstitious fear that rice planted in certain months of the Mohammedan year will bear none but empty ears of grain. If they were at liberty to act as they pleased in the matter, they would be guided in their planting operations simply by the name of the lunar month.'[42] This was a passing problem but an interesting example of culture contact.

Of all the natural hazards, water—or the lack of it—was perceived as the greatest threat to a successful harvest. As an example, take the Kuala Selangor district in the three years from 1900 to 1902. In 1900 a drought prevented the planting of wet padi; in 1902 rats and flooding destroyed the crop.[43] These were not isolated cases; the cultivator was fortunate if his crop was good in one year in three. It was essential to have a controlled water supply. A modern expert has written that 'drainage is often more important than irrigating ... adequate control of drainage throughout the season should be designed to supply adequate water during seasonal shortages and to drain sufficiently rapidly in periods of excessive rain'.[44]

The colonial government completed one major project at Krian, designed to provide a controlled water supply to 50,000 acres at an estimated cost of $300,000; in the event, the completed scheme cost $1,600,000 and in theory provided a controlled supply to 70,000 acres.[45] There were also a few government schemes on a much smaller scale. The Kuang scheme in Selangor, built between 1900 and 1902, was designed to supply water to 430 acres but in 1902 only 320 acres were actually irrigated and of that area only 200 acres were occupied by cultivators.[46] The Selangor government also experimented with grants to enable villagers to construct small schemes; if they lacked the necessary expertise, they hired Kelantan Malays to do it for them. Thus, a small grant was made in 1902 for irrigation of 60 acres at Dusun Tua.[47] It soon came to be realized that without expert help the money would be wasted. For example, at Lobok Salah in the Kinta district, 'a Malay had made a dam of considerable size, and a long *tali ayer* over ten feet deep in places, but the dam leaked and the *tali ayer* was faulty in its levels'.[48]

Maintenance of existing works could be a burden. After the death of Wan Mat Saman of Kedah in 1898, his canal, the greatest achievement of Malay hydraulic engineering in the nineteenth century, was neglected, with the result that 'the canal lock gates broke down and the canal itself partially silted' but it was still useful as 'a navigable waterway for the greater part of its length over which a large traffic in timber from Kedah Peak and a quantity of *padi* is carried'.[49] In Perak, the Menteri of Larut had constructed a canal which was a deep cutting through sandy soil; the banks tended to erode and fall in. After a period of disuse, it was deepened and widened in 1880, but this added the new problem of tidal flooding. It ran for about four miles and served to irrigate land in the area of Simpang and Sungai Limau. In 1894 it was supplying water on an adequate scale but 'requires constant attention'.[50]

Rather like the pretty daughter and her plain sister, padi was given too much attention and the useful coconut palm, too little. The coconut was an easy crop to grow, though the palm required about five years from planting to reach maturity and begin to yield nuts. Perhaps for that reason it did not, in the early years of the west coast immigration, appeal to the footloose settler. It was already a familiar sight along the coast when Abdullah Munshi made his trip up the east side of Malaya in 1838: in Pahang 'cultivation ... consisted chiefly of coconut and betelnut trees ... eight coconuts cost a dollar'; at Kuala Terengganu 'one can see nothing but coconut trees and white sandy beaches'; at the mouth of the Kelantan River 'there are houses on both sides of the river, surrounded by coconut trees and bamboos'.[51] A generation later, his son travelled up the west coast, noting 'most of all coconut and areca palms' near Batu Pahat and 'a village with coconut palms etc.'

at Muar.[52] Although the coastal zone was best suited to the coconut, it did grow inland; J. W. W. Birch, on the Perak River, noted that the coconuts 'are remarkably fruitful for trees so far from the sea air'.[53]

In the nineteenth century, the Malay peasant grew coconut palms more as a source of food for himself than as an export crop. Among other uses, it provided cooking oil, fuel and sugar; it was, of course, an essential ingredient in foodstuffs such as sweetmeats. A Malay villager living on the coast of Selangor in the 1890s was likely to have some coconut palms and a fishing boat but he had lost interest in padi growing.[54] If he grew padi it was often supplemented with a few coconut palms; 5 acres of padi land and twenty-five palms was reckoned to provide a family with all it needed.[55] Land under coconut came to have a high value—as much as $200 per acre in 1896.[56] The export trade in copra, which began to grow rapidly at the end of the century, must have contributed to this trend.[57]

The smallholder was not, however, to be hustled by the 'powers that be' into planting coconuts. In 1880 the Perak State Council issued an order that every householder should plant twenty-five coconut palms in that year and twenty-five more in 1881. However, in 1882 it was recognized that the planting programme had failed due to 'lack of supervision'.[58] In good time and in the coastal districts, which were best suited to it, the coconut became the predominant crop. In 1892 Kuala Selangor had 3,000 acres under coconut, much of its planted since 1888.[59] In 1904 the state of Selangor had twice as much land under coconut as under padi.[60]

With large contiguous areas under coconut, the peril of monoculture, the spread of pests and diseases, took its toll. It was found necessary to introduce compulsory measures to contain the attacks of red and black coconut beetle.[61] Coconuts, 'the consols of the East', were a more reliable crop than speculative products such as coffee—and later rubber.[62]

The role of the buffalo in padi growing has been described. It was also a source of meat, though Malays slaughtered buffaloes for food only when preparing for a feast. In the meantime, a well-to-do peasant invested his savings in buffaloes, so that he might sell them to raise money for the expenses of the pilgrimage. The hide of the buffalo was used to provide the membrane which covered large, ceremonial drums, part of the ruler's regalia.[63] Buffalo horn could be shaped to make part of the handle of a *keris*, and calcined buffalo bones provided manure for a rice nursery. On the East Coast buffalo fights were a public entertainment.[64] J.W.W. Birch in Perak noted that 'buffaloes are very plentiful but they seldom milk them'.[65] Buffalo's milk contains more fat than cow's milk, but Malays had small need of either as food, though they made cement by mixing buffalo's milk with fresh lime.[66] Although the Malays made little use of cattle for their own purposes, they raised them for export to the markets of the SS towns.[67] In Perak in 1875, J.W.W. Birch saw few cows and bulls but 'goats are to be seen in all the villages and flourish'.[68] Apart from the use of buffaloes for ploughing, livestock were a less important part of the Malay village economy than might have been expected. This may have been due in part to the comparative scarcity of good grazing land.[69]

The animal protein in the Malay diet was obtained by eating fish, fowls and eggs, and the meat of wild animals trapped or killed in hunting. 'Ducks thrive remarkably well on these rivers,' wrote Birch, 'and are bred in large numbers by the Malays. They readily sell them as well as their eggs; a duck is 50 cents. Fowls are also plentiful . . . but it is very difficult to induce them to sell even one fowl's egg.' Hens' eggs had ritual and ceremonial uses, and perhaps for that reason they were not treated as an ordinary trade commodity.[70]

To supplement their basic diet of rice, the villagers grew maize, cassava, sago, sweet potato, egg-plant, pumpkin and gourds, banana, mango, jack-fruit, durian and a number of other fruits, coffee, areca, sugar-cane and also the 'jaggary palm'.[71] They were 'inordinately fond' of raw sugar-cane, 'taking lengths of it, to peel off the silicious skin, and then cut it in convenient pieces for chewing'.[72] The juice of the sugar-cane could be extracted by crushing it between rotating wooden rollers; the syrup was then converted to a coarse brown sugar for local consumption.[73] This sugar (jaggery) was an essential ingredient of many Malay sweetmeats.

Malay technical ingenuity was seen at its best in the manifold devices used to catch fish. In the sheltered waters of the Straits of Melaka 'fishing stakes', fixed fish-traps in shallow water, could yield as much as 25 *pikul* of fish in one cycle.[74] 'The stakes are driven into the sea-bed on the edge of a bank, where there is a sudden drop into deep water. For deep-sea nets, they are in about 36 feet of water at high tide, with six feet of their length above water. They are round jungle poles, straight and strong, with the bark unstripped; they are fixed in the form of a pair of compasses, opened to include an angle of about 40°, the legs of the compasses so laid that the rising tide sweeps full into them. The stakes are bound securely together with rattans, and, at the hinge of the compasses, there is a submarine gate, the latticed doors of which open into a small enclosure, also made of stakes, but carefully encased, from sea-bed to high-water mark, with latticed lining through which no fish can escape.' The whole structure was braced with crossbars and above it stood a 'tiny crows nest' in which the fishermen sat and watched. When they judged that the right moment had come they raised the net laid on the sea-bed of the inner compartment, using rattan ropes running over wooden pulleys, to lift the catch to the surface.[75] They supplemented their main catch by fishing with hook and line from boats.[76]

Even in these calm waters there were perils. In the troubled times of the past, fishermen feared lest passing pirates should capture them on their exposed offshore fishing-stakes or in their boats, and sell them as slaves.[77] In the peaceful times which followed, the risk was that a small steamship or sailing vessel would crash into the fishing-stakes at night. Such a collision was very dangerous to the ships' crews also since the impact often canted the vertical stakes to a horizontal position so that they swept across the decks of ships like spears. Fishermen showed a red lamp at night to give warning of their position.[78]

On the exposed East Coast, fixed fishing-stakes would have been destroyed in the storms of the monsoon season and so the fishermen went out to sea in boats, to catch fish with nets.[79] The East Coast fishermen 'were once pirates to a man' and in later days they were 'a rough, hard-bit gang, ignorant and superstitious beyond belief, tanned to the colour of mahogany by exposure to the sun, with faces scarred by rough weather and hard winds'. They were 'plucky and reckless ... full of resource ... bound fast by a hundred immutable customs'. When the north-east monsoon kept them ashore they suffered privation, but in the fishing season they could earn as much as $8 a month, a high wage, in their dangerous calling.[80]

Inland villages obtained their fish from the rivers and streams, from the flooded padi-fields and even from artificial fish-wells. Skeat in Patani in 1899 'came on a party of Malays clearing the fish out of what is here called a fish-well (*telaga ikan*) ... when there were only a few inches [of water] left, everybody went down into the mud at the bottom and groped for fish, which were thrown into baskets and passed up . . . these fish-wells were emptied four times a year and a large number of fish taken on each occasion'.[81]

The most common method of getting fish from a river was an organized fish-drive, sometimes called a *relap besar*. In Upper Perak in 1894, there was a *relap* in which the fish were driven four miles down the river to Chigar Galah where '*belats* (traps) and other fishing stakes had been erected, and they were there speared and netted. Some hundreds of Malays—men, women and children—took part in the sport and a large number of fish were caught.'[82] It was easier to catch the fish if they were rendered insensible. 'In days gone by the method would have been to *tuba* the stream above a pool, but this poisoning of the water affects the river for miles, and dynamite which is not nearly so destructive is preferred. The plan is to select a large and deep pool round which the men stand ready to spring in, while the women make a cordon across the shallow at its lower end, ready to catch the fish that escape the hands of the swimmers. Two cartridges of dynamite with a detonator and a piece of slow match are tied to a stone and thrown into the deepest part of the pool, there is an explosion sending up a great column of water, and immediately the dead fish come to the surface and begin to float downstream. Twenty men spring into the pool, and with shouts and laughter struggle for the slippery fish; those which elude the grasp of the swimmers are caught by the women.'[83] A fish-drive could be a fiasco in which the fish escaped—as at the durbar of FMS rulers at Kuala Kangsar in 1897—but if they did not surface, 'the boldest and best divers will search the bottom of the pool'.[84] Dynamite caused less general damage but it was much more dangerous than the stupefying *tuba*; there is an 1890 report of a Malay whose two hands were blown off when the dynamite exploded too soon.[85] In addition to collective fishing of this type, an individual might go fishing in the river with a casting net (*jala*).

Fresh fish rotted within a few hours unless preserved by salting them in brine or drying them. J. W. W. Birch, travelling along the West Coast in April 1874, found 'salt fish in great abundance, which is collected and salted, all along the beach [at Sepang in Selangor] from here to the Jugra river, principally by Malacca Chinese and Malays'. Further on he again found 'any amount of fish salted and most of it ready for sale'. In a third stop, at Tumboh, 'there are 30 Malacca Malays . . . there also was a very large stock of salt fish and they intended to remove it to Sungei

Ujong by Sungei Sappan the next day'. It was a profitable trade since the salted fish found a ready market at the nearby mining camps. At Dindings on the Perak coast, Birch 'found 3 or 4 boatloads of salt fish waiting to go to Penang'.[86] Salting fish on a commercial scale and then moving it to a market was a major operation, and so it was presumably beyond the resources of local fishing communities; they sold their fish to middlemen for curing.

Abdullah Munshi, in Kelantan in 1838, came on a large estuarial lake from which the local people obtained 'hundreds of *pikuls* of prawns every year and also great quantities of gray mullet'. They preserved the prawns by boiling them, then drying them in the sun and finally they sold the dried prawns to Chinese for $8 a *pikul*.[87] At Kuala Terengganu he noted 'the smell of rotting fish' and the local preference for 'evil-smelling things, such as pickled durians and fish-preserve'.[88] Neither Abdullah nor Swettenham (in 1875) includes fish in the list of East Coast exports, but in 1895 Clifford found that large quantities of fish were exported from Terengganu to Singapore annually. He too comments on 'the penetrating odour of fish—fresh, dry, or in the process of being dried' and 'the immense quantity of the Malay caviare called *blachan* [prawn paste]'.[89] Imported salt was often subject to an import duty, which in Perlis in 1889 was 'so prohibitory that fish cannot be salted'.[90]

Fish, which deteriorated so swiftly, is an extreme example of a general problem of the Malay village economy. The producer could never match his output to his own needs. Sometimes, as with the East Coast fisherman, his whole livelihood consisted in producing a surplus, for disposal either within his own community or, after curing, by export. In a more typical case the peasant might find that a bumper or a disastrous harvest of rice, or fruit or other produce created an unmarketable surplus or a desperate shortage, to be satisfied by bringing in supplies from elsewhere. There was no easy means of dealing with these erratic swings from abundance to scarcity and back again—especially in rural areas which had poor internal communications. Bloomfield Douglas, on tour in Ulu Selangor in 1876, slept in Malay huts surrounded by heaps of fruit and saw piles of durian rotting on the ground.[91]

The Malay traditional expertise in trade and exchange sufficed to produce a rudimentary distribution and marketing system, especially in the East Coast states, but it is not possible from the available records to describe it in detail.[92] Wholesale transactions, especially in external trade, were often a royal monopoly since the ruler could by this means secure useful revenues for himself.[93] In Kelantan, tobacco, opium, gambier, coconut oil, betelnut and textiles were trade monopolies of the ruler.[94] In Pahang, all gold and gutta-percha were sold to the ruler at fixed prices below the external market level.[95]

Even if he did not have a monopoly, a ruler or some member of the ruling class found it profitable to trade on a substantial scale, often using agents for the purpose. Sultan Abdullah of Perak sent Nakhoda Ketek to Penang with $2,000 with which to buy muskets and gunpowder, and also sugar, dates and biscuits, cloth-goods, gold thread, etc.[96] Daga, a Sumatran trader, came across to Kuala Langat in Selangor in 1873 with a cargo of fish and sold two *pikul* of fish (presumably dried or salted) to Raja Yakob, a son of the Sultan, for $10.[97] This must have been a purchase for resale; Raja Yakob's entourage could not have consumed so much in a short time.

Mat Yassin of Batak Rabit, whose trading expedition up the Perak River has been described in Chapter 5, 'kept the ordinary Malay books' for the purpose of his business, and denied that he had concocted 'a regular set of accounts' as false evidence. In another context there is mention of 500 *gantang* of rice and 50 *gantang* of salt loaded into a boat as supplies sent by Sultan Abdullah to the Maharaja Lela, to augment his stores for the uprising against Birch in November 1875.[98]

Retail trade, even if supplied from these upper-class sources, took place in the villages. Supplies were sometimes brought to the villages by travelling traders, who moved along the rivers with cargoes for sale at villages along their route. In October 188[illegible], for example, 'hawkers who sold their goods from boats, obstructed the landing place, paid no dues, and damaged the profits of the local traders' were banned from Batu Gajah in Perak.[99] In Ulu Kelantan, Skeat found that 'there were about ten small raft-shops here, moored to the bank. Once a month the owners went the long journey down the river to re-stock at the Kelantan capital.' At a 'general store' Skeat bought rice, sugar, *pulut* (glutinous rice), torches, Japanese calico, salt, matches, mats and boat-awnings. Other shops sold coconuts, salted anchovies in large jars, dried fish and coconut oil, among other things.[100]

There were also shopkeepers permanently established in the villages. Logan, in Kuala Kedah in 1850, saw 'dirty, slovenly *atap* shops on each side of a long narrow muddy lane in several of which cloths were piled up while most exhibited only the usual Malay commodities'.[101] Douglas, at Kajang in Ulu Langat in 1876, found Menangkabau and Mandiling settlers, 'all planting rice . . . except two or three who have shops'.[102] The Korinchi shopkeepers at Kuala Kangsar, who had been there for seven or eight years, shut their shops and threatened to depart in a body when the tax on their shops was increased from $2 to $6 per month for each shop.[103]

The East Coast states had established markets for produce in which the vendors were usually women. Skeat came upon 'a landing place . . . where a brief market was held daily between 9 and 10 a.m.' and further on 'there were several hundred people at the stalls in the main street and on the foreshore . . . many more must sometimes collect there from the country round about'.[104] Many years before, Abdullah Munshi at Kuala Terengganu found that 'the market is held only in the evening. And the sellers and hawkers of various kinds of food and clothing are all women. When the sun begins to decline, the women in the town and in the orchards and up-country come with baskets of food and clothing on their heads. They come to the market, sit and sell . . . and at sunset all go home and the market is deserted until next evening.'[105] A visitor in 1889 wrote that 'at a small market that was being held, the sales were conducted by women. I noticed in several places in the town, large quantities of salted limes put out in the sun to dry . . . coconuts too were numerous.'[106]

The precise timing of the markets may reflect other factors, such as the return of the fishing boats with catches which the fishermen usually sold for cash immediately on arrival. At Kota Bharu, 'at the break of day the ferry boats . . . began bringing from the opposite shore an average of 30 women each trip, keeping going backwards and forwards all day, as well as a number of small *sampans* coming from every direction containing women with their goods for the market . . . I was very much tempted to stop and buy fruits and flowers . . . most neatly made up in small bouquets, and in different shapes. . . . Amongst the variety of fruits I noticed for sale were the water-melon, oranges, limes and mangoes. . . . Every article of food (Malay) that could be imagined may be found every day in the market. A covered market is reserved for the sale of cloth . . . another which is also covered are brass and iron-ware including crockery and other nic-nacs [*sic*]. . . .'

'In the middle of the day a movement begins by those who have completed the sale of their goods going into the river to wash themselves.... At about 3.20 p.m. the market begins to close, and almost at the same time the fishing boats commence to arrive landing near the sandbank, in a short space of time groups of hundreds of women are seen surrounding the fishing boats ... at 4.30 p.m. the majority of them begin to start for their homes carrying a small basket containing an assortment of things for their supper, and before 5.30 the market is altogether abandoned.'[107] These markets in East Coast centres served to meet the needs of substantial non-agricultural producers, fishermen or artisans, such as did not exist elsewhere.

Even in the remote East Coast states as early as 1838, prices were quoted to Abdullah Munshi in dollars and cents.[108] There were, however, more than one species of dollar and a conservative prejudice in inland districts in favour of the oldest and most familiar kinds. Henry Norman, preparing to visit inland Kelantan in the 1890s, had to pay a premium of 9 per cent over face value in Penang, to obtain a supply of 'the once famous Maria Theresa dollar with two pillars on the reverse ... the only civilised coin that the Malays of the interior will accept'.[109] In Terengganu this type of dollar 'is never seen' and the local preference was for 'the Mexican dollar'.[110]

The cent was too large a unit for convenience and also difficult to obtain. In the East Coast states the rulers produced a smaller denomination coin of tin, called variously a *keping* or *pitis*; there was also a *kupang*, which was an eighth of a dollar. There was no fixed rate of exchange between these local currencies and the dollar, of whatever variety; the dollar itself fluctuated in value according to changes in the price of silver.[111] In Terengganu in 1895, the rate was 960 *pitis* to the dollar; in Kelantan the rate in 1900 was 720, but it had fallen to 480 in 1907.[112] The Kelantan *pitis* was 'an alloy of tin and lead ... a small circular coin pierced in the centre and carried in bundles threaded on a string ... the currency chiefly in use in the bazaars and markets' of Kelantan early in this century.[113] There must in effect have been a number of different local currency zones in which certain coins circulated at generally recognized rates of exchange with others. By the beginning of the twentieth century, however, the dollar, divided into a hundred cents, was displacing the local alternatives.

Although it was the generally accepted practice of Malay villagers to express values and buy and sell in terms of money prices, there were vestiges of an older system preserved in transactions between members of the same village community. In Negeri Sembilan, supply of rice to a neighbour was 'subject to a convention or customary price which is fixed, and is always lower than the price which could be got in an open competitive market. The market price of *padi* being 5 to 7 cents a *gantang*, the customary price in the villages . . . is 3 cents only.'[114] The same conventional price system also extended to foodstuffs such as sugar, coconuts, and eggs. Clifford mentions a loan of buffaloes for safekeeping on terms that the borrower might use them as recompense for his trouble but made no hire payment—'such arrangements are very common among Malayan villagers'.[115] The observance of these conventional bargains was enforced by the belief that ill luck would visit anyone who broke the code. Thus the sharing of the catch among Trengganu fishermen was 'determined by immutable custom . . . which no Malay would be so impious as to contravene'.[116]

The conventional prices and the like are a limited exception to the general picture of the village economy which emerges from the material in this chapter. In no society does the individual behave as an 'economic man' without regard to other conventions, but the Malay villager was much more businesslike and commercial in his dealings than is sometimes believed.

Another feature of village life, which is illustrated by some of the material, is the general acceptance of co-operation with one's neighbours and the pleasure which men and women obtained from it. The allocation of work between the sexes, the communal fishing drives like the accounts of *atap* making and timber felling given in the next chapter, show people at work in groups and enjoying themselves because it was so. It has been rightly observed that the value system of Malay villages stressed 'cooperation, *gotong-royong*, *usaha* (labour), and conformity'.[117] The individual ownership of land and the general use of money in exchange transactions did not significantly detract from it.

1. S. Osborn, *Quedah: Or Stray Leaves from a Journal in Malayan Waters*, London: Routledge, 1857 (2nd ed. entitled *My Journal in Malayan Waters, or the Blockade of Kedah*, London and New York, 1861), p. 123. On the naval blockade, see J. M. Gullick, 'Kedah 1821–1855: Years of Exile and Return', *JMBRAS*, 56(2), 1983, p. 47.

2. See p. 163 below on local textile production.

3. J. Low, 'Observations on Perak', *JIA*, 4, 1850, p. 498. Gambier was one of the ingredients of a betel quid (p. 195 below).

4. J. Anderson, *Political and Commercial Considerations Relative to the Malayan Peninsula and the British Settlements in the Straits of Malacca*, Penang, 1824, reprinted in *JMBRAS*, 35(4), 1962, p. 124. Those items, which were of economic importance in the latter part of the nineteenth century, are described elsewhere in this chapter or the next. Cutch (Malay '*kachau*') (*Acacia catechu*) is an Indian rather than a Malayan product: a tanning substance is obtained from it by boiling the chopped-up wood. 'Elephant's teeth' is of course ivory. '*Agila*' is difficult to identify; if it is the botanist's '*aglaia*' then it is a hardwood timber, for which there are several Malay names, used in Malaya in the interior woodwork of houses. '*Sapan*' is presumably the Malay '*sapang*' (*Kurrimia*), which is also a source of building timber (I. H. Burkill, *A Dictionary of the Economic Products of the Malay Peninsula*, 2 vols., London, published on behalf of the SS and FMS Governments, Crown Agents, 1935, pp. 15, 72–3 and 1288).

Abdullah Munshi mentions *kemuning* wood, resins, rattans, gold, tin, coffee and textiles as the exports of the East Coast states (Abdullah bin Abdul Kadir, Munshi, *Kesah Pelayaran Abdullah*, translated by A. E. Coope, *The Voyage of Abdullah: A Translation from the Malay*, Singapore, Malaya Publishing House, 1949, pp. 8, 19 and 44). *Kemuning* (*Murraya exotica*) is best known as a source of decorative hard yellow wood, used in making the handles of *keris*. It is also a source of essential oils (Burkill, op. cit., pp. 1505–6).

5. See p. 98 above on riverine settlement.

6. R. D. Hill, *Rice in Malaya: A Study in Historical Geography*, Kuala Lumpur, Oxford University Press, 1977, *passim* but especially pp. 36–46; James C. Jackson, 'Rice Cultivation in West Malaysia: Relationship between Culture History, Customary Practices and Recent Developments', *JMBRAS*, 45(2), 1972; H. Fukui, 'An Agro-environmental Consideration', in M. Kuchiba, Y. Tsubouchi and N. Maeda (eds.), *Three Malay Villages: A Sociology of Paddy Growers in West Malaysia*, translated by P. Hawkes and S. Hawkes, Honolulu, University Press of Hawaii, 1979. In addition to these modern works there is an extensive body of writing about padi cultivation in Malaya, much of it in the *Malayan Agricultural Journal*. See also Zaharah Haji Mahmud, 'The Pioneering of Wet-rice Growing Traditions in West Malaysia—A Restudy with Special Reference to the State of Kedah', *Geographica*, Vol. 5, 1969, and 'The Period and Nature of "Traditional" Settlement in the Malay Peninsula', *JMBRAS*, 43(2), 1972; E. M. Cooke, *Rice Cultivation in Malaya*, Singapore, Eastern Universities Press, 1961; Burkill, op. cit., p. 1592; R. G. Cant, *An Historical Geography of Pahang*, MBRAS Monograph No. 4, 1973, Chapters 3–7; R. D. Hill, 'The History of Rice Cultivation in Melaka', in K. S. Sandhu and P. Wheatley (eds.), *Melaka: The Transformation of a Malay Capital c.1400–1980*, Kuala Lumpur, Oxford University Press, 1983.

7. F. A. Swettenham, 'Journal Kept during a Journey across the Malay Peninsula', *JSBRAS*, 15, 1885, p. 21, describes the method of sowing by broadcasting seed in the fields as 'strange', which suggests that in the course of 15 years' service in Malaya he had not seen it anywhere else before.

8. SSD 1 February 1900; H. C. Clifford, 'Report: Expedition to Trengganu and Kelantan', *JMBRAS*, 34(1), 1961, originally printed for Colonial Office use in 1895, and reprinted Kuala Lumpur, Government Press, 1936, pp. 95–6.

9. J. C. Jackson and also Hill, cited in note 6, give a full account of the

different types of cultivation and of the Malay terminology used in connection with them.

10. See p. 317 below.

11. *AR Selangor 1902*, para. 15.

12. J. F. A. McNair, *Perak and the Malays: Sarong and Keris*, London, Tinsley Bros., 1878, reprinted Kuala Lumpur, Oxford University Press, 1972, p. 71. R. D. Hill, *Rice in Malaya*, describes padi growing in Perak, distinguishing between irrigation ('not widely used', p. 98) and trapping rain-water. 'In most districts of Pahang the areas of readily available *paya* and *tenggala* land would have been adequate for the needs of all, but hill or dry *padi* grown in *ladangs* required less sustained effort and was favoured by the people in spite of much lower yields' (Cant, op. cit., p. 35).

13. R. D. Hill, *Rice in Malaya*, p. 145. Bloomfield Douglas found between 400 and 500 *ladang* at one village in Ulu Selangor in 1879 (Douglas Diary, 28 July 1879).

14. Padi growing in Perak was 'coming more and more into fashion with the people, especially the dry ground, or mad *padi*, which yields a crop in the shortest time' (McNair, op. cit., pp. 158–9).

15. R. D. Hill, *Rice in Malaya*, Chapters 4–6, is the main source for this brief summary. See also Hill, 'Rice Cultivation in Melaka'.

16. See p. 107 above.

17. In 1889 the export duty on rice and padi in Kedah had been let to a revenue farmer for $17,000 per annum and represented about a tenth of total state revenue. The rates were $5 per *koyan* for unhusked padi and $8 on rice. The main market was Penang (SSD 17 May 1889). Among many other passages *AR Pahang 1898*, para. 13, states that it was general practice for Malay growers to produce padi only for their own needs.

18. T. Braddell, 'Notes of a Trip to the Interior of Malacca', *JIA*, 7, 1853, p. 82. On Kedah in 1874 see SSD 24 February 1874, para. 23, and F. A. Swettenham, *British Malaya: An Account of the Origin and Progress of British Influence in Malaya*, London, John Lane Bodley Head, 1907, (revised editions 1929 and 1948, London, Allen & Unwin), p. 311.

19. *AR Perak 1889*, in *PGG* 1890, p. 231, citing a report by Bozzolo. He persuaded 'the natives' to ship their padi down-river for sale for cash at Kuala Kangsar.

20. See p. 157 below.

21. Raja Bot bin Raja Jumaat, 'Rice Cultivation in the States', a letter published in the *Malay Mail*, 14 November 1902, and reprinted in *Peninjau Sejarah*, 1(2), 1966, p. 71. He says that in the Langat valley 'Malays worked at their ladangs and there were no sawahs . . . no foreign rice was consumed in Selangor' (ibid., p. 72). However, an epidemic of rinderpest killed many buffaloes in 1859 and caused a severe setback to wet padi cultivation in the Selangor valley; this, of course, was aggravated later by the civil war. Sultan Abdul Samad, like his predecessor, was an enthusiast for padi cultivation (see p. 32 above) but 'was not powerful enough to insist on the work being continued for though he himself liked padi planting he could not enforce it upon the *raiat* of the country' (ibid.). The whole passage is an interesting picture of the Malay ruler in his role of promoting economic development (see p. 57 above).

22. 'Owing to [the Klang] district having been the scene of disturbances for

about 7 years, nearly the whole of the original population left it. The present population are for the most part males, foreigners from Sumatra, Pahang and Kedah, and traders from the Straits Settlements—only now beginning to settle themselves permanently' (initialled 'W. J. F. D.' (Sir William Jervois, Governor SS) and dated 16 October 1875). This was a footnote to a report of 23 August 1875 by J. G. Davidson, then Resident of Selangor, to the effect that there were few debt-slaves in Selangor. See Cmd. 3285 of 1882 for the report, with its footnote.

23. *AR Selangor 1900*.

24. *AR Selangor 1902*.

25. *AR Selangor 1895*.

26. *AR Klang 1889* in *SGG* 1890, p. 280.

27. *AR Klang 1897*, para. 37, in *SGG* 1898.

28. *AR Ulu Langat 1895* in *SGG* 1896, p. 486.

29. *Malay Mail*, 30 December 1896, unsigned but almost certainly by the editor and proprietor, J. H. M. Robson, who had been a district officer in Selangor between 1889 and 1896. See also J. H. M. Robson, *People in a Native State*, Singapore, Singapore Free Press, 1894, for his general impressions of Selangor Malays.

30. *AR Perak 1909*. Birch was contemplating the likely effects of the coming boom in rubber cultivation. It was no coincidence that the Malay Reservations Enactment of 1913, intended to restrain Malay sales of land, came soon afterwards.

31. See p. 104 above on Kelantan; SSD 23 February 1883 on Rembau; *PGG* 1898, p. 895, on Lower Perak; *PGG* 1888, p. 174, on Selama; and *SGG* 1890, p. 332, on Ulu Selangor.

32. In 1881 the import into Selangor of buffaloes from Sungei Ujong was banned as a quarantine measure (Douglas Diary, 14 and 20 September 1881).

33. *AR Pahang 1892*, para. 10.

34. Abdullah Munshi, op. cit., p. 51.

35. W. Linehan, 'A History of Pahang' (hereafter cited as 'Pahang') *JMBRAS*, 14(2), 1936, p. 133. See also *SGG* 1892, p. 727, report from Kuala Selangor. A. L. Keyser, *Travels and Trifles*, London, Murray, 1923, p. 93.

36. Douglas Diary, 1 August 1879.

37. On the role of the *pawang* generally see p. 324 below. On the sequence of rice rituals which fixed the planting calendar, see W. W. Skeat, *Malay Magic: Being an Introduction to the Folklore and Popular Religion of the Malay Peninsula*, London, Macmillan, 1900, reprinted Singapore, Oxford University Press, 1984, pp. 218–49; C. O. Blagden, 'Notes on the Folkore and Popular Religion of the Malays', *JSBRAS*, 29, 1896. 'The exact day for each event is fixed by the pawang' (R. J. Wilkinson, 'The Incidents of Malay Life', *Papers on Malay Subjects, Life and Customs*, Part 1, 1908, reprinted in *JMBRAS*, 30(4), 1957, p. 46).

38. *AR Pahang 1897*. See also *PSCM*, 4 March 1879, *PMS*, p. 19; SSD 28 April 1887. At the Perak State Council meeting the regulations were described as the 'revival of an old custom'.

39. *AR Pahang 1898*.

40. T. J. Newbold, *Political and Statistical Account of the British Settlements ... with a History of the Malayan States on the Peninsula in the Straits of Malacca*, 2 vols., London, Murray, 1839, reprinted as *British Settlements in the Straits of Malacca*, Kuala Lumpur, Oxford University Press, 1971, Vol. 2, p. 357; H. C. Clifford, *In a Corner of Asia being Tales and Impressions of Men and Things in the Malay Peninsula*,

London, Fisher Unwin, 1899, p. 102. R. J. Wilkinson, *A Malay–English Dictionary*, 2 parts, Singapore, Kelly & Walsh, 1901 (revised as *A Malay–English Dictionary (Romanised)*, 2 parts, Mytilene, Salavopoulos & Kinderlis, 1932), Part 2, p. 515, '*tahun padi*' and '*tahun jagung*'.

41. G. E. Shaw, 'Rice Planting', *Papers on Malay Subjects, Malay Industries*, Part 3, 1911 p. 4 (not reprinted in P. L. Burns (ed.), *Papers on Malay Subjects*, Kuala Lumpur, Oxford University Press, 1971). They watched the height of the Pleiades and of the sun at midday.

42. *AR Pahang 1898*. But Shaw, op. cit., p. 3, states that although the Malays refer to the Islamic lunar calendar, they do not plant in the same lunar month of each year.

43. *AR Kuala Selangor 1900*, para. 22, and *AR Kuala Selangor 1902*, paras. 23–4. Other examples in *AR Kinta 1896* in *PGG* 1897, p. 337; *AR Pahang 1893* and *AR Pahang 1895*; and p. 109 above (on padi borer beetle at Krian).

44. D. H. Grist, 'The Rice Problem', *Journal of Tropical Geography*, Vol. 5, 1955, p. 21.

45. D. E. Short and J. C. Jackson, 'The Origins of an Irrigation Policy in Malaya', *JMBRAS*, 44(1), 1971, pp. 92–3. R. D. Hill, *Rice in Malaya*, pp. 108–15.

46. *AR Selangor 1900*, para. 25; *AR Ulu Selangor 1902*, para. 25.

47. *AR Ulu Langat 1902*, para. 22. *SGG* 1893, p. 714, has a report on another small scheme of this kind in Kuala Selangor.

48. *PGG* 1898, p. 291; *PGG* 1895, p. 349; *AR Pahang 1893*. See also p. 80 above on irrigation schemes promoted by Perak aristocrats. On Pahang village irrigation schemes executed by Kelantan Malays, at a cost much in excess of estimate, see Pahang *Annual Reports* for 1891, 1893 and 1898. Really effective drainage and irrigation schemes, still relatively costly, began in the 1930s when a specialist Drainage and Irrigation Department was established (Short and Jackson, op. cit.). Only gradually did the authorities accept that they were unlikely to recover a direct return in water-rate payable by cultivators which would match the capital outlay and maintenance costs.

49. *AR Kedah 1906–1908*. See p. 85 above.

50. *AR Larut 1890* in *PGG* 1891, p. 338; *PGG* 1894, p. 441; *AR Matang 1895*, in *PGG* 1896, p. 210; R. D. Hill, *Rice in Malaya*, p. 107; Cheng Siok Hwa, 'The Rice Industry of Malaya: A Historical Survey', *JMBRAS*, 42(2), 1969, p. 135.

51. Abdullah Munshi, op. cit., pp. 8, 16 and 26. On Singapore Island coconut cultivation began in the 1840s and 'was rapidly on the increase' in 1865 (J. Cameron, *Our Tropical Possessions in Malayan India: Being a Descriptive Account of Singapore, Penang, Province Wellesley, and Malacca, Their Peoples, Products, Commerce and Government*, London, Smith Elder & Co., 1865, reprinted Kuala Lumpur, Oxford University Press, 1965, p. 170).

52. Mohamed Ibrahim bin Abdullah, Munshi, *The Voyages of Mohamed Ibrahim Munshi*, translated by A. Sweeney and Nigel Phillips, Kuala Lumpur, Oxford University Press, 1975, pp. 7, 46 and 74. At pp. 74 and 77 he implies that the absence of coconuts at Klang and Kuala Langat was a consequence of the recent civil war.

53. Report of 2 April 1875 enclosed with SSD 26 April 1875, para. 48, printed in Cmd. 1320 and in J. W. W. Birch, *The Journals of J. W. W. Birch First British Resident to Perak 1874–1875* (hereafter cited as *Birch Journal*), edited by P. L. Burns, Kuala Lumpur, Oxford University Press, 1976, pp. 388–98.

54. *AR Kuala Selangor 1896* in *SGG* 1879, p. 463.

55. C. W. Harrison, *Some Notes on the Government Services in Malaya*, London, Government Information Agency, 1929, p. 48.

56. An offer of $200 per acre for land under coconut palms, only half of which were in bearing, had been refused (*SGG* 1897, p. 761).

57. Abdullah Munshi, op. cit., pp. 8, 19 and 44, does not mention copra in his list of exports from East Coast states in 1838, and Swettenham does not mention copra in his list of exports from Kelantan and Terengganu (F. A. Swettenham, *Sir Frank Swettenham's Malayan Journals 1874–1876* (hereafter cited as *Swettenham Journal*), edited by P. L. Burns and C. D. Cowan, Kuala Lumpur, Oxford University Press, 1975, pp. 262 and 268). But in 1895 Clifford found that 'a considerable quantity is annually exported to Singapore' and in 1908 Graham described copra as one of the 'chief exports' of Kelantan (Clifford, 'Expedition', p. 97, and W. A. Graham, *Kelantan—A State of the Malay Peninsula: A Handbook of Information*, Glasgow, James MacLehose & Sons, 1908, p. 60).

58. *PSCM* 22 May 1882, *PMS*, p. 249. Regulations on coconut cultivation were made at the Council meeting on 25 February 1880 but these have been omitted from the 1971 *PMS* reprint of the minutes of that meeting.

59. *AR Kuala Selangor 1892*, para. 46.

60. Eighteen thousand and eight hundred acres of coconuts and 8,000 acres of padi land, most of which were in the inland Ulu Selangor district, where many of the Malays were settlers of Menangkabau origin with a cultural tradition of wet padi growing (*AR Selangor 1904*). This coconut acreage may have included plantations as well as smallholdings. But the planters were now hastening to replace coconut with rubber, of which Selangor had 15,000 acres in 1904. See Lim Teck Ghee, *Peasants and Their Agricultural Economy in Colonial Malaya 1874–1941*, Kuala Lumpur, Oxford University Press, 1977, pp. 50–2, on smallholder coconut planting generally at this time.

61. Under an enactment of 1898 there was an inspector; by 1902 there was a complete Coconut Department to enforce the legislation (A. Wright and H. A. Cartwright (eds.), *Twentieth Century Impressions of British Malaya: Its History, People, Commerce, Industries and Resources*, London, Lloyds, 1908, p. 503 (an article contributed by L. C. Brown, Inspector of Coconut Plantations FMS)).

62. From about the mid-1880s it was official policy to encourage smallholders to plant coconuts (*AR Selangor 1884*; Lim Teck Ghee, op. cit., p. 51).

63. See p. 29 above.

64. See p. 352, note 13, below.

65. As for note 53 above, para. 49.

66. Burkill, op. cit., p. 381.

67. See p. 156 below.

68. As for note 65 above.

69. 'The climate and vegetative characteristics of Malaya are not congenial to livestock production' (International Bank for Reconstruction and Development, *The Economic Development of Malaya*, Baltimore, Johns Hopkins, 1955, p. 26).

70. As for note 65 above, para. 51. See also p. 141 below on the sale of produce, including eggs, at conventional fixed prices.

71. Birch report cited in note 65, para. 48; McNair, op. cit., pp. 56–7 and 177; *SGG* 1892, p. 812, report from Kuala Langat; Abdullah Munshi, op. cit., pp. 43–4; SSD 31 January 1889 (Bozzolo's Kelantan report). The 'egg-plant'—also called

'*brinjal*'—is '*terung*' (Malay); 'areca' is of course betel-nut. 'The jaggary palm', mentioned by Birch (loc. cit.), was probably *Caryota urens* (*gula kabong*), i.e. the toddy palm from which sugar could be obtained.

72. McNair, op. cit., p. 177.

73. W. W. Skeat and F. F. Laidlaw, 'The Cambridge University Expedition to Parts of the Malay Peninsula 1899–1900: Personal Accounts', *JMBRAS*, 26(4), 1953, p. 89, give a description and a drawing of a Malay sugar mill of this type; Clifford, 'Expedition', p. 97.

74. *AR Kuala Selangor 1890* in *SGG* 1891, p. 636. These Selangor fishing villages were communities of fair size; Douglas found 46 houses on Pulau Angsa in 1879 (Douglas Diary, 15 August 1879).

75. F. A. Swettenham, *The Real Malay: Pen Pictures*, London, John Lane Bodley Head, 1900, pp. 119–20, describing fishing-stakes off the coast of Province Wellesley. T. W. Burdon, 'The Fishing Methods of Singapore', in T. W. Burdon and M. L. Parry (eds.), 'Papers on Malayan Fishing Methods', *JMBRAS*, 27(2), 1954, is a detailed account of modern West Coast fishing-stakes and other devices.

76. *SGG* 1893, p. 327, report from Kuala Selangor of *rawei* (long line of baited hooks) fishing with five hooks per fathom; Burdon and Parry (eds.), 'Papers on Malayan Fishing Methods', *JMBRAS*, 27(2), 1954, p. 19.

77. *SGG* 1893, p. 506, report from Kuala Selangor.

78. Swettenham, *The Real Malay*, pp. 119–20.

79. H. C. Clifford, *In Court and Kampong, Being Tales and Sketches of Native Life in the Malay Peninsula*, London, Grant Richards, 1897 (2nd ed. with autobiographical preface, London, Richards Press, 1927), pp. 134–50, is a colourful contemporary account. Raymond Firth, *Malay Fishermen: Their Peasant Economy*, London, Kegan Paul, 1946 (revised edition 1966), is the authoritative modern anthropological study. Burdon and Parry (eds.), op. cit., pp. 77–144, describe the methods in use on the East Coast in detail. C. A. Gibson-Hill, 'The Boats of Local Origin Employed in the Malayan Fishing Industry', *JMBRAS*, 27(2), 1954, pp. 145–74, is a valuable account illustrated with photographs and drawings.

80. Clifford, *In Court and Kampong*, pp. 136, 139 and 150.

81. Skeat and Laidlaw, op. cit., p. 30.

82. *PGG* 1894, p. 201, report from Kuala Kangsar. On *relap besar* see Glossary.

83. F. A. Swettenham, *Malay Sketches*, London, John Lane Bodley Head, 1895, p. 20. *Tuba* is a poison obtained by pounding the root of *Derris elliptica* and soaking it before throwing it into the water (Burkill, op. cit., p. 687).

84. Swettenham, *Malay Sketches*, p. 21. On the fish drive at the Kuala Kangsar durbar see p. 68, note 87, above.

85. *PGG* 1890, p. 447, report from Kuala Kangsar. Accidents of this kind were frequent since it was easy enough to obtain dynamite from the stocks held by road construction contractors for rock blasting, and those who used it for fishing did not understand the necessary safety measures. The *penghulu* were often the 'worst offenders' in encouraging the illicit and dangerous use of dynamite for village fish drives (ibid.).

86. *Birch Journal*, pp. 43, 45 and 86.

87. Abdullah Munshi, op. cit., p. 49.

88. Ibid., p. 19.

89. *Swettenham Journal*, pp. 262 and 268. Clifford, 'Expedition', pp. 75 and 91, and also p. 116 on the export of fish from Kelantan.

90. SSD 17 May 1889.

91. Douglas Diary, 23 and 24 July 1876.

92. The passage which follows does not seek to distinguish between internal and external trade. The same commodities were sometimes moving in both types of trade. The export of Malay products to external markets is one of the main themes of the next chapter.

93. A. C. Milner, *Kerajaan: Malay Political Culture on the Eve of Colonial Rule*, Tucson, University of Arizona Press, 1982, Chapter 2. B. W. Andaya, 'The Indian "Saudagar Raja" (The King's Merchant) in Traditional Malay Courts', *JMBRAS*, 51(1), 1978.

94. SSD 14 October 1867 in CO 273/12, p. 222; see also CO 273/15, p. 427, and CO 273/23, p. 280, on Kelantan trade.

95. SSD 3 August 1887. *AR Pahang 1894*, para. 14. See Clifford, 'Expedition', p. 74, on royal trade monopolies in Terengganu. Even in Perlis the export of hides was a royal monopoly (SSD 17 May 1889).

96. Evidence of Nakhoda Ketek to PCE (CO 273/87, p. 315). 'He gave me a written list of the things I was to buy' and for this Ketek was to have a 10 per cent commission. See also the evidence to PCE of Mahlim, an acquaintance of Nakhoda Ketek and the husband of one of the ruler's slave-girls (CO 273/87, p. 328). Haji Ali (see above, p. 102) traded 'under the protection' of Sultan Ismail (CO 273/87, p. 484).

97. Daga gave evidence at the Kuala Langat piracy trial; report enclosed with SSD 24 February 1874. He said that he pressed Raja Yakob to pay his debt and it was this which precipitated the piracy, i.e. Raja Yakob needed money. Raja Yakob in his evidence denied the whole transaction.

98. On Mat Yassin see p. 102 above. Evidence to PCE in CO 273/87 pp. 533, 549, 585 (and also p. 68 on trade goods shipped by Sultan Abdullah). Although he was himself a commoner, Mat Yassin was a Haji, a man of wealth, and connected by marriage with the powerful Datuk Laksamana, the leading chief of Lower Perak. His father had married a cousin, on the mother's side, of Sultan Abdullah (Evidence to PCE in CO 273/87, pp. 532–3).

99. *PSCM*, 21 October 1882, *PMS*, p. 262. See also p. 128 above on the barter trade (textiles for rice) organized by the Korinchi traders at Chigar Galah.

100. Skeat and Laidlaw, op. cit., p. 97. Skeat includes in his list 'coconut called *budu* in large jars' but this must be an error in transcription since '*budu*' is the term for pickled anchovies (Wilkinson, *1932 Dictionary*, Part 1, p. 158). See p. 101 above for other examples.

101. J. R. Logan, 'Notes at Penang, Kedah, etc.', *JIA*, 5, 1851, p. 57.

102. Douglas Diary, 18 July 1876.

103. *Swettenham Journal*, p. 315.

104. Skeat and Laidlaw, op. cit., p. 63. In Pahang Malays sold sugar, coconut and areca-nut at local markets along the Pahang River (*AR Pahang 1889*, para. 13).

105. Abdullah Munshi, op. cit., p. 19.

106. W. Davison, 'Journal of a Trip to Pahang with H. E. the Governor', *JSBRAS*, 20, 1889, p. 86.

107. Bozzolo's report enclosed with SSD 31 January 1889. These accounts of markets at Kota Bharu and Kuala Terengganu relate to town rather than village markets but both were situated in the centre of agricultural districts and drew in people from surrounding villages. There are descriptions of East Coast markets in

Raymond Firth, *Malay Fishermen*, and in Rosemary Firth, *Housekeeping among Malay Peasants*, London, Athlone Press, 1943 (revised edition 1966), and Thomas M. Fraser, *Rusembilan: A Malay Fishing Village in Southern Thailand*, Ithaca, Cornell University Press, 1960.

108. Abdullah Munshi, op. cit., pp. 9, 19 and 37.

109. H. Norman, *The Peoples and Politics of the Far East: Travels and Studies in the British . . . Colonies and Malaya*, New York, Scribner, 1895, p. 536.

110. Clifford, 'Expedition', p. 79, and *Studies in Brown Humanity being Scrawls and Smudges in Sepia, White and Yellow*, London, Grant Richards, 1898, p. 31—'pillar dollars . . . the standard currency' of Kelantan. Malaya suffered from an abundance of competing currencies, including 'trade dollars' minted in Japan, USA, and France (Chiang Hai Ding, 'The Origins of the Malayan Currency System', *JMBRAS*, 39(1), 1966, p. 3). For a general history of Malayan coinage see Chiang Hai Ding, op. cit., and F. Pridmore, *Coins and Coinages of the Straits Settlements and British Malaya 1786 to 1951*, Singapore, Memoirs of the Raffles Museum, Singapore, No. 2, 1955, reprinted Singapore, National Museum of Singapore, 1975.

111. Clifford, 'Expedition', p. 76, describes the Terengganu currency system at length. Abdullah Munshi, op. cit., p. 19, at a much earlier stage, gives a rate of 3,840 *pitis* to the dollar.

112. Clifford, 'Expedition', p. 76; Skeat and Laidlaw, op. cit., p. 68. Graham, op. cit., p. 62, describes the Kelantan tin coin as a *pitis* but Clifford, 'Expedition', p. 115, calls it a *keping*, worth 480 to the dollar. For good measure, Abdullah Munshi, op. cit., p. 9, found a local coin in Pahang called a *tampang* worth 16 to the dollar.

113. Graham, op. cit., p. 62.

114. *AR Malacca 1892*, p. 575, cited in R. D. Hill, *Rice in Malaya*, pp. 137–8.

115. H. C. Clifford, *Malayan Monochromes*, New York, Dutton, 1913, p. 170.

116. Blagden, op. cit., p. 7; Clifford, 'Expedition', p. 90.

117. Syed Hussein Alatas, 'The Grading of Occupational Prestige amongst the Malays of Malaysia', *JMBRAS*, 41(1), 1968, p. 153.

7
The Malay Village and the External Economy

THE previous chapter was an examination of the Malay village as a producer of commodities such as rice, mainly for its own consumption or for sale within the same locality. Yet, as the opening passage indicated, the village could not produce all which it needed—salt and textiles, for example, were generally imported. The ruler or district chief, and later on the state government, levied taxes in money or extracted resources from the village in various other ways. Hence, the village economy was based on monetary values for its transactions. The villager had to earn money with which to pay his outgoings.

There were traditional sources of income such as the production of tin and the collection of jungle produce for sale. Towards the end of the nineteenth century the villager produced other commodities which he did not himself consume and, in some cases, he worked for a wage. The main theme of this chapter is the links between the village economy and the external economic system and the responses to it.

It is not suggested, however, that it is useful to separate different forms of output into subsistence and export commodities. Even rice was sometimes sold, and there were a number of products such as woven palm-thatch (*atap*), which could roof a village house or yield a cash income on sale.

Tin mining had been a small-scale, intermittent activity. Then, the arrival of Chinese tin miners in large numbers towards the middle of the nineteenth century introduced new methods of mining to obtain much larger quantities of tin. Malay mining did not cease altogether and it continued to be a useful source of income. The presence of Chinese mining communities created markets for Malay produce and opportunities of earning money by rendering services to the Chinese miners.[1]

In the traditional Malay economy the normal time for tin mining was after the rice harvest, when there was a lull in agricultural work and usually a dry season. 'It is then that the black tin ore, found in the sands and shingles of the river bed is most accessible, and the Malays come hither, in little family parties, to wash for it. Men, women and little children stand in the shallows, deftly shaking their great flat wooden trays, with a circular motion, and storing small pinches of tin in the hollow of bamboos.' Clifford adds that 'the amount of their earnings is very small, but Malays are capable of a great deal of patient labour when it takes a form that, for the moment, they happen to find congenial'.[2]

The attraction of this activity was that it made a family outing in the slack season—with the added inducement of being something of a gamble on one's luck in finding tin. Using this simple method, the mining party could begin or give up its search for tin at will, since no preliminary labour was needed to excavate a mine. It was necessarily limited to places where ore lay at or near the surface. The Malays prudently tapped the knowledge of aborigines in selecting a spot for mining.[3]

There were also mining operations organized by aristocrats, sometimes by the use of debt-bondsmen as labour and sometimes on a more commercial basis. They asserted exclusive rights to 'ancestral mines'. Later on, under the colonial regime, continued claims by Malay land-owners to mining lands caused much trouble.[4] Perak was the main centre of Malay mining since it had the richest deposits but there are also reports of Malay mines, large or small, in Selangor, Negeri Sembilan and Melaka—'worked in the most laborious manner'.[5]

In former times, when the Malays were the only producers of tin, they had built large dams to provide a head of water for a primitive form of hydraulic mining. They may have dug the pits, the famous *lombong siam*, to reach the deeper deposits.[6] The Malay villagers of the second half of the nineteenth century still occasionally used these workings of former times, but they were regarded as almost superhuman, and legendary origins were attributed to them. 'The rock looks as though it had been levered out with crowbars so as to make the water race,' said a report of 1889, 'but the Malays say there was a clever *pawang* who cut the rock away with the stalk of a succulent plant called *dedap*, and that when he had finished the work he was taken up to heaven.'[7] Swettenham, visiting Ulu Selangor in 1875, saw the disused remains of a late eighteenth-century mine which was 'gigantic compared to the mines of today and ... worked entirely by Malays'. To provide powerful streams of water through 'two long and deep sluices', a dam had been built across a valley. The dam itself was 200 yards long, and the stretch of water behind it extended for more than a mile, with a width of 100–200 yards, back to the foothills.[8] More typical of late nineteenth-century Malay mining, where it persisted at all, was the mine operated by the *penghulu* of Trong in 1897; he got 20 *pikul* of ore each month unless heavy rain interrupted his operations.[9]

There was also some Malay gold mining—mainly in the hinterland of Melaka and in Pahang, around Raub. 'The Malay process of gathering the gold dust is very simple. They dig till they come to the rock, then break and pound it, carry it to a stream and wash off the gold dust . . . the gold gathered is 24 *katis* annually which is all brought to Melaka.'[10]

Few communities had the good fortune of living near a rich deposit of tin or gold. Most villages relied on the sale of jungle produce, timber, or agricultural products later on, to obtain a cash income. The numerous references to rattan suggest that it was an important element in the Malay cash economy.[11] There were many different kinds of rattan (Malay '*rotan*'); they were distinguished by their Malay names and they had many uses. Rattan was exported through Singapore to industrial countries for use, as 'split cane', in making baskets and furniture. In South-East Asia rattan was often used as a substitute for string or rope. 'Houses, fences, fish-traps, and even boats are bound together with rattan, often without the use of a single nail. Ropes for tethering buffaloes, drag-ropes for hauling timber, mooring ropes, anchor cables, bridge cables and deer-snares are still made from rattans. . . . Baskets, bird-cages, mats, sun-blinds and (in the towns) cane furniture are amongst the many other local uses.'[12]

To obtain rattans, the collector had first to identify in the jungle whatever type of creeper was suitable for his purpose. It might be a thick stem adhering to the trunk of a tree, or be intertwined among the branches. He cut it at the base and pulled it down. This stage could bring down a rotten branch or the creeper itself on the head of the collector and do him serious injury. When the creeper was on the ground, the collector stripped away the thorny outer sheath with his chopper (*parang*) or by pulling the creeper across a branch or other projection. He cut off the upper portion which was too soft to be of use. The usable part was dried over a fire or in the sun to preserve it.[13]

There was a good deal of skill in collecting rattan, but it was not a specialist activity. Any able-bodied man could master it and go out collecting intermittently when he had time and inclination. However, each collector usually brought in only a limited quantity. To obtain a large quantity he would have to go further afield and then carry or drag his stock over a longer distance to bring it in. Demand for rattan fluctuated with general economic conditions. In 1890, a slump period in Malaya, 'quite a number of foreign Malays left the [Ulu Langat] district, giving as their reason for doing so that they could not live by agriculture alone, and that, owing to the lessened activity in mining matters they did not get as ready a sale for jungle produce, such as rattans and other building materials as formerly'.[14]

Forest timber was also in demand as a building material and for other uses. Malays usually felled the trees and floated the logs down a river for sale to a Chinese buyer.[15] When they went logging, 'a company of six to ten is made up; they are generally friends and relations; a headman is selected, and he is generally responsible for the advances of money that are made to them . . . they purchase a boat and lay in a stock of provisions, tools etc. . . . wives and children accompany their husbands, and frequently lend a hand in hauling or rolling the logs out of the forest. They live in the jungle in huts while the trees are being felled, and in huts on the rafts when they are made up and in transit to the mills.'[16]

This was work which required skill and could be dangerous. It also required a knowledge of the many species of jungle trees in selecting them for felling. There were about seventy different kinds of trees, and each had its appropriate uses—for door frames, poles for pepper vines, rudders, Chinese coffins, planks, masts, charcoal burning, rafters, laths, incense burning, furniture, oars, firewood, bark for roofs, sheaths for *keris*, crooked joints for ships' frames, and so on.[17] As industrial demand grew, new uses for forest wood were found. In 1885 'many of the cultivators [in Selangor were] engaged in cutting timber for building purposes and railway sleepers and firewood for the numerous brick-kilns and mining engines'.[18]

By the end of the nineteenth century, the depletion of standing timber within easy reach of villages was causing concern, which led to the establishment of forest conservation departments in the FMS in 1893. The long-term aim of this policy was to preserve timber for village use, but its immediate effect was to restrain a profitable village industry in supplying wood to commercial consumers.[19]

Among other forest trees, the Malays used the wood of the *taban* or *taban merah* species to make keels of boats and planks for housebuilding. The tree could also be a source of latex (*getah taban*) known to the industrial world as 'gutta percha'. It has the property of being soft when heated but it hardens again as it cools. It was found to be very suitable for insulating submarine cables, and demand increased rapidly as the programme of laying telegraph cables on the sea-bed to link distant countries proceeded apace. This demand led to a short and destructive boom in the extraction of gutta percha from Malayan forests.

It is possible to extract the latex by means which do not destroy the tree but these methods are less productive since the latex does not flow freely. The maximum yield could be obtained by felling the tree. A collector selected a mature tree of at least 3 feet in circumference and felled it at about 6 feet above ground. He then cut off the branches to reduce loss of moisture by evaporation and made rings around the trunk by incision with a knife at intervals of 5–15 inches. The latex was collected in empty half coconut shells or folded palm leaf cups and boiled for an hour to prevent it becoming brittle. In this fashion a tree would yield, say, 10 pounds, as compared with between 1 and 3 pounds obtained by tapping the bark of the standing tree.[20] The product could be sold for $45–50 per *pikul* according to quality.

Extraction of gutta percha was so profitable that outsiders moved in to join the local Malay producers. The coast of Pahang became accessible during the season of the south-west monsoon. There was then an influx of Chinese, of Malays from Singapore and Indonesia, and of Dayaks from Sarawak.[21] When Bloomfield Douglas visited Ulu Bernam in July 1876, he found that a quarter of the Rawa settlement of about 300 people, men, women and children, were engaged in collecting gutta percha. Significantly, they did not produce enough rice for their own consumption.[22] As the stock of trees diminished, Malays arranged with aborigines to collect gutta percha in the remoter part of the country and sell it to them.

There was no practicable way of restraining the destruction of trees in the forests. For a time during the 1880s there was an official ban, which was difficult to enforce, on the export of gutta percha from the FMS. Meanwhile, the botanical experts and others wrote papers on improved methods of extraction and so on. But it was all to no avail; in 1889 the ban was relaxed and by the end of the century Malayan stocks of wild trees had been virtually exhausted.

Gutta percha production continued thereafter only as a small-scale plantation crop.[23]

The Malay word '*damar*' means both 'resin' and 'a torch', since the Malays carried a bundle of wood and leaves impregnated with resin as a light at night. Among the variety of resins obtainable from jungle trees, some had a market value which made it worthwhile to collect them for sale. In particular, 'wood oil' (*minyak keruing*) was extracted from the *keruing* tree by cutting a large hole in the trunk and lighting a fire in it. It was exported for use as a wood preservative, a varnish, and an ingredient in the manufacture of paint.

To obtain *damar*, the collector had sometimes to climb the trunk of the tree to a height of 100 feet above the ground. As he climbed, he made footholds by driving stakes into the tree and he steadied himself with a hanging rope. It was dangerous work but well-paid—up to $5 per day. The Malay showed characteristic *sang-froid*—'I watched a man make the perilous ascent of a tall tree—as he climbed he sang.' Once at the top, he slung a rattan rope over the branch above his head in case the branch on which he sat should break.[24]

One of the essential building materials of this period, in towns as well as in Malay villages, was palm-thatch (*atap*) made from the leaves of the *nipah* palm (*Nypa fruticans*), which grows wild, especially around river estuaries. The Malay villager also planted *nipah* palm to augment the natural supply. The main leaf stems grow up to 20 feet in length with a line of short pinnate fronds on either side which can be stitched together to form roof shingles. If laid in overlapping horizontal layers across a roof frame, the *atap* thatch has a useful life of about two years on a low sloping roof and five years on a steep roof.

Rathborne's picture of this village industry is 'the Malay drifts up with the flowing tide in his little dug-out boat . . . he lands, and wading through the mud amidst his grove of palms, cuts off the largest branches, and denudes them of their leaves until sufficient have been collected and loaded when he . . . drifts home with the ebbing tide, smoking the while and paddling leisurely along. The next process is relegated to the women and children, and occupies their spare time, as sitting and chatting they deftly double the leaves over a small lath cut from the trunk of the *nebong* palm, sewing them together with rattan to keep them firm and in position.'[25]

Like many other traditional Malay crafts, local small-scale output was developed in some places to become an export industry, supplying distant markets such as the tobacco plantations of the Dutch in eastern Sumatra, who used *atap* to roof their drying sheds.[26] The sale of *atap* was one of the points at which the Malay producer bargained with the Chinese middleman—and was not always the loser. Thus, at Tanjong Karang in Selangor in 1897, the Chinese dealer offered $3.50 per thousand *atap*, to be paid not in cash but in kind. The local producers, however, held out for $5, which was the going market price in the district headquarters of Kuala Selangor.[27] Kota Setia at the mouth of the Perak River was another main centre of *atap* production.

A man produced 200 *atap* in a day and sold them for perhaps 55 cents per 100, which was about half the price which they would realize when re-sold in a main market.[28] A commercial buyer demanded *atap* of rather higher quality than was acceptable for local use.[29]

The stimulus to Malay production of goods of any kind for export was access to a market through the link provided by adequate communications. Thus, the export of dried or salted fish and of copra from Kelantan and Terengganu towards the end of the nineteenth century owed much to improved sea communications with Singapore through the coastal steamers. When Bozzolo was at Kota Bharu in 1889, he wrote that 'during my stay in Kota Bharu I have seen very little loading and unloading from sailing vessels and judging from this I should say the trade in Kelantan is very insignificant at present; the steamer which was then running every fortnight was ample enough to carry all the products of export as well as import'.[30] But less than twenty years later, Graham observed that 'the carrying trade to and from Kelantan, which was formerly done by means of sailing vessels, has now passed in great measure to the coasting steamers which visit the state in increasing numbers every year'. He gives the shipping tonnage entering and leaving the port in 1906 as more than 52,000. In addition, sailing vessels carried cargoes along the coast to Terengganu and Patani—'the river, from the capital to the sea, is thronged with these at all times during the season when the monsoon regime permitted vessels to enter and leave the port'.[31] By this time the Kelantan fishing industry, including fish curing, employed 30,000 people.[32]

The economy of Kedah benefited greatly from the road built in the 1860s to provide a link between the east coast of the isthmus at

Singgora (Songkhla) in southern Siam and the Kedah coast.[33] Kedah itself was one of the few states with a regular export surplus of rice; in 1888 it exported 7,000 tons of padi to Penang.[34] The other main export commodity was cattle on the hoof. Much of the stock exported from Kedah had come in from Patani and Ligor to the north-east.[35] Maxwell, on his trek to the Patani frontier in 1876, met a party of Patani Malays with twenty or thirty cattle, heading for Larut, the largest mining centre in Perak at that time. In the drovers' camp 'large fires were kept burning all night under the coconut trees to keep away tigers', which would no doubt be tempted by so much succulent meat on the hoof.[36] In 1886 buffaloes for ploughing were being imported into Selangor from Pahang at the rate of 100 a month in spite of a Pahang export duty of $5 per head.[37]

The supply of fruit, vegetables, poultry and eggs grew more slowly since they were difficult to move to a market and their value would not support heavy transport costs. Initially, it was difficult to find a surplus in the villages. 'As for food,' wrote Swettenham, 'the traveller or his people carried it and even in villages it was practically impossible to buy anything except an old hen.'[38] However, during the 1880s, the extension of Chinese tin mining, especially in the Kinta valley, brought new markets to existing centres of production. Bridlepaths or roads were built to cover the short distances between them.[39] The effect was dramatic. In Lower Perak in 1886, for example, 'a great improvement in the circumstances of the people has taken place by the ready market that now exists for everything they produce, all kinds of property have enormously increased in value, and their fruit, their grain, their buffaloes, goats and poultry sell for more than four times the price at which they could have been purchased' in earlier years.[40]

Immigrant Malay settlers were quick to see the importance of a near-by market for their produce. At Sitiawan 'they all looked very contented but a better outlook for their produce is required'.[41] The proximity of a mining village was a factor to be weighed in selecting a site for a village of agriculturalists.[42] In districts where there were no mines, better communications opened up trade routes. Sri Menanti, the royal district of Negeri Sembilan, shut away in a remote valley, benefited from the new road links with Melaka built in the 1880s with SS financial aid, and the value of produce exported increased to $750 per month.[43] Yet twenty years before, Cavenagh had written that 'when I first visited Melaka there were districts . . . in which roads were utterly unknown. Fruit was allowed to rot wholesale for want of means of conveying it to a mart.'[44]

The changing modes of transport available to villagers are worth describing. In the traditional Malay economy, goods could be moved by elephant, or by boat on a river, or by men carrying loads on their backs. The elephant is an aristocratic perquisite to be examined in a later chapter.[45] The river was much the most convenient means of transport—'in the broad Perak valley no man foots it when there is a boat at hand'.[46] The majestic main rivers of Perak and Pahang were indeed navigable waterways of much commercial value.[47]

On these rivers 'huge freight barges' might be 40 or even 50 feet long, poled by a crew of four or six men. They were 'long flat *perahus* . . . decked right over the gunwale, and—fore and aft—two broad stages extend beyond the stern and bow respectively, whilst the centre is covered by a low deckhouse about five feet in height at the ridge. This deckhouse is often about twenty feet long and is divided into two compartments, one for the men and the other for the master or *nakhoda*, the latter facing the foremost part of the *perahu* . . . the front stage is used as a platform for the boatmen or polers, and that at the stern for the steersman and also for cooking operations.'

The polers used poles of 12- to 14-foot length, or even more in deep water, sheathed with 'a strong, sharp iron ferrule', and fitted at the top end with a curved wooden block to fit the chest of the poler, who walked the length of the boat pushing with the weight of his body, and then returning to the bow to make another thrust. 'The action is rhythmical and calls to mind one of the figures in Sir Roger de Coverley. Where the current is strong, there is a great strain on the men, and every muscle shows out in strong relief, their eyes seem starting out of their sockets, their bodies are bent forward until almost horizontal and with toes and hands they grip and clutch at every projection they can lay hold of to help push and pull themselves along often uttering all the while wild and unearthly cries.' By dint of strength and fitness the polers could keep up this 'tremendous labour' for hours on end with only short breaks to chew a betel quid. Sustained over-exertion sometimes broke their health, but they were a proud profession who 'will not settle down to any other kind of work'. One of these large river boats could move as much as 100 *pikul*, i.e. about 6 tons of cargo.[48]

On the lesser rivers and tributary streams, the boats were much smaller and the boatmen were recruited from the local villages. On the Linggi River, for example, a Malay mine-owner had 'a fleet of fairly large boats which were poled downstream ... tin ingots and ore were unloaded at his godown there. Those boats were then loaded with bags of rice, opium, salt, bales of *kain belacu* (unbleached cotton cloth) and other textiles and poled upstream.'[49] For passengers the small boat was a very uncomfortable means of travel. Emily Innes never forgot her first experience of a boat 'which reminded me of the oubliettes that I had seen in the dungeons of the Inquisition at Rome ... I resolved that it should be my last ... it was impossible to sit or stand in it at all, on account of the very low palm-leaf awning; one could only lie down in it and that in a very uncomfortable position'.[50]

Everyone who could, made his home on a river bank to avoid the difficulty and expense of overland travel. However, mines had to be opened in the places where nature had placed deposits of tin ore—this could be at the head of a valley beyond the navigable stretch of any local stream. In such cases the tin ore was carried out on the backs of porters. A district officer mentions meeting a party of Malays each carrying an 80-pound slab of tin down to Tanjung Malim. For this 5-mile carry over a muddy and uneven track they earned 80 cents.[51] It was sometimes cheaper to hire an elephant or a buffalo which could carry loads of 3½–5 *pikul* and 1 *pikul* respectively.[52]

Any kind of path, properly cleared and perhaps levelled, was a great improvement over jungle tracks, which were generally first opened by the elephants crashing through the undergrowth. Tracks used by elephants, whether improved or not, were a sequence of potholes since it was the habit of elephants to put each foot down in the same spot as all the elephants which had passed that way before.[53] At this period, however, a path was wide enough if a man or a loaded beast of burden could get through. When Swettenham was on one of his early tours, local Malays told him that 'a narrow path would be quite sufficient and that there would be no need of a 'carriage road' for years to come.[54]

In fact the progress towards a system of rural roads was more rapid than seemed likely in 1878. What began as 'bridlepaths', for the passage of a mounted rider, became rough tracks suitable for bullock-carts. The economies were considerable; the cost of moving a slab of tin from Kuala Pilah to Melaka on a man's back was $2.50

but by bullock-cart only $1.[55] With the bullock-cart came a new Malay occupation, and the travelling bullock-cart driver, who often covered long distances, became a familiar sight. He might, for example, take a load from Melaka to Pahang and bring another back. Each night he camped by the roadside and sometimes he took his wife and children with him—'the lady often reclines at her ease in a hammock under the tilt, sleeping continuously . . . anyhow, up there she is out of mischief'.[56] As a means of transporting people the bullock-cart enlarged the horizon of the proverbial village 'frog under a coconut shell'.[57] Bullock-carts developed into regular passenger services—in 1890, Swettenham wrote that 'there are a number of bullock busses [*sic*] running on the main road in Perak now that carry passengers 23 miles for fifty cents a head'. Later on, competition between the bullock-bus and the subsidized 'horse coach' reduced fares to a mere 10 cents. In moving goods, the bullock-cart, which could deliver from door to door, held its own against the new railway system.[58]

New systems of road and rail transport diverted traffic from the traditional river highway. Clifford lamented that 'the river is no longer alive with crafts as it was in the days of old, and the sleepy villager, whose patient eyes watch life indolently from the water's brink, wonders why the land has fallen to sleep'.[59] But in this Clifford was wrong. New communications opened the village to a variety of cultural as much as economic innovations. The land did not sleep but awoke to new opportunities; in particular to new crops.

Much of the story of the search for economic crops suitable to be grown in Malayan conditions belongs to the history of plantations.[60] There is, however, a Malay-village facet to the subject. Tobacco was not perhaps a real cash crop, since the cultivator sometimes consumed his own product or bought imported tobacco. According to McNair, 'as a rule the Malay prefers Javanese tobacco, but failing this he uses his own coarse preparation of the leaf, grown on his own patch of garden, with very little trouble . . . he takes the *rokok*, or outer sheath of the palm-leaf, or else the thin sheath of the plantain, or *pisang*, rolls in it a little tobacco, forming rather a large cigarette, and smokes in peace'.[61] But there was also a market demand even for locally grown Malay tobacco despite its poor quality; immigrant settlers sometimes grew it as a cash crop.[62]

Gambier was another product on the borderline of commercial production. In Malay villages it was sometimes grown for use in making the indispensable betel quid for chewing. A decoction of gambier leaves was used in tanning leather but Malay production did not supply this market. Although many districts produced some gambier there were particular areas which specialized in it. Along the upper reaches of the Tembeling River in Central Pahang, for example, 'the Malays plant enough *gambir* to supply the wants of the whole betel-chewing population of Pahang'.[63] However, an attempt by some Malays from Melaka at gambier growing on a commercial scale in Negeri Sembilan was a failure.[64] Gambier was not a money-spinner.

When J. W. W. Birch first came to Perak in 1874 he had high hopes of transferring traditional Acehnese expertise in pepper growing to the state. 'It is a class of cultivation to which the Perak Malay might gradually be brought to turn his attention and I think it would be worth the while of the government of Perak to import a village of Acehnese and a village of Bugis, giving them the necessary advances, and attempt thus to introduce the cultivation.'[65] Nothing came of it at the time, but a decade later, Dutch pressure on Aceh created just such an opportunity which was taken by Hugh Low—though not with any lasting success.[66]

The coffee boom of the 1890s was another story of disappointed hopes.[67] The greater part of the coffee planting was done on plantations, but Sumatran and Javanese immigrants also gave it their attention.[68] As already related, many of them planted coffee and other crops, not as a continuing venture, but with a view to selling off the land to take a quick profit.[69]

Although coffee growing is a short episode in the history of Malay peasant agriculture, it affords some interesting insight into the trends of the time. In Selangor the pioneer was Haji Tahir, 'our most enterprising Malay planter', who had been a prominent figure in Selangor since the Selangor Civil War in which he had taken a leading part.[70] He began to grow coffee, and also indigo, about 1884. In 1887 he obtained a $4,000 loan from the state government to develop his land by planting areca palm, durian, mangosteen, and coconut. Areca, however, proved unprofitable and so Haji Tahir 'with extraordinary energy, for a native, . . . drained his land, and planted up a portion with coffee, which . . . proved so successful that he has been able to cut up most of his land into blocks, averaging from three to five acres, which he sub-lets at 50 cents an acre for coffee gardens, to Chinese and foreign Malays'.[71]

His example induced Europeans as well as Malays to take up

other low-lying, swampy ground for coffee growing around Klang in the early 1890s. The land was unsuitable and this use of it led to the 'Klang fiasco' which 'considerably undermined the confidence that planters ... had felt hitherto in the Selangor government'.[72] Haji Tahir was adroit enough to keep out of this affair, though he was a respected adviser on agricultural matters to the government and to the European planters. The latter disparaged Haji Tahir's methods of cultivation as untidy—though economical—but he made a commercial success of his coffee so long as anyone could do so.[73] As such, he is an interesting example of a new type of Malay capitalist, using commercial methods of management.[74] He died—with a characteristically good sense of timing—just before a world slump in coffee prices and local disease brought the Selangor coffee boom to its close.

There was much criticism of the standards of cultivation of Malay coffee planters. For example, 'coffee bushes need careful handling throughout the time of their growth and the Malay understands planting but does not realise what cultivation means'.[75] Again, 'So naturally I expected an estate worth seeing. But it was completely suffocated in deep undergrowth ... nobody on the estate knew how to prune the trees when planted.'[76] However, the European disasters in planting on unsuitable land and a reference to 'clean weeding', applied later with such unfortunate effects to rubber, suggest that Malay methods of coffee cultivation may have been sounder than their critics recognized. At all events, the price of coffee fell and the Malay grower rapidly lost interest in it.[77]

Manufactured goods imported from the factories of industrialized countries, and the arrival in Malaya of Chinese artisans, destroyed the indigenous Malay crafts with but few exceptions. Rathborne wrote in 1898 that 'Malay silversmiths, blacksmiths and carpenters are fast being superseded by Chinese, and as the villagers have no trades to give them occupation during the time there is nothing doing in the fields, many of the men leave their homes in search of employment, returning at frequent intervals, for they are able by working three months in the year to supply themselves with all the necessaries they require for the remaining nine. The women stay at home ... they do not weave, and sew but little, as they usually purchase their apparel ready made.'[78]

In Kedah in 1906 'cloth and silk are no longer woven, as sarongs and piecegoods can be far more cheaply obtained from Birmingham and India, carpentry and brick-laying are almost entirely in the hands of Chinese, Malay blacksmiths and potters still exist but ironmongery is now usually imported, as are the earthenware pots and cooking utensils required for household use'.[79]

Just as access to markets stimulated the output of agricultural produce, lack of a market probably contributed to the decline of Malay village industries. The craftsman did not usually have enough customers at hand to keep him fully occupied and so able to perfect his skill. With only intermittent demand, it was not worthwhile to hold a large stock of materials or a wide variety of tools.[80]

Handwoven textiles were perhaps the product most widely made until imported machine-made cloth supplanted them. Skeat, who was a persistent and careful collector of Malay artefacts of all kinds, had little success in Raman, north of Perak, in 1899. 'During the afternoon I searched for old sarongs, and was able to buy samples of two kinds, a *kain chawi* and a *kain Bali telepok*, both of which I had earlier found rare on the west coast. Apparently they had gone out of fashion here also, and like the *kain chindai* were no longer in current use. It is difficult to know when, and why, this process of elimination began. I had noticed it in Selangor, and it was apparent again here in the Patani states, and later in Kelantan. New, recent work seemed to be much more limited in range than the older pieces that one could occasionally unearth, after much searching. Possibly it was due to a quickening of tempo; the people now wanted to appear in new cloths more frequently, and that could only be done if they were quicker to make and cheaper to buy.'[81]

As a result of the decline in output, skill in weaving, which had been passed from mother to daughter in many households, became a rarity which was demonstrated in school classrooms by the elderly survivors of the craft. In 1897, for example, the District Officer at Kuala Selangor came on 'an aged Malay woman named Baiedah at work at her loom manufacturing kain belabas'. He proposed that she should teach her skill at the local girls' school lest it should die with her.[82]

The cost of materials restricted the work of the silversmith to the courts and the houses of great men.[83] However, the craft of the metalworker, skilled in making weapons, was more widespread. It was a society in which it was a sign of cowardice for a man to go unarmed, and so there was a wholesale demand for the Malay *keris*.[84] Imports from Java, Sumatra or the Celebes satisfied part of that demand since blades from those celebrated sources were much prized.[85] It was a specialized craft and so it was concentrated at particular places in the Malay states. In April 1874 Birch and Swettenham made two visits to Kampung Korinchi and Sungei Siput, which was 'renowned for its spears and knives'.[86] Swettenham's comment—'they make the most beautifully shaped spears I have ever seen'—suggests that in his extensive travels in Selangor and Perak he had not come across any other metalworking of this calibre. Elsewhere he wrote that 'the smith, the maker of spears and daggers and lethal weapons generally did a good business, and skilled men made reputations for themselves'.[87] It was the work of a small élite of specialist craftsmen.

Imported weapons were distributed by travelling traders; their stock often consisted of blades, which were of special value, without handles, which could be added by local craftsmen. Birch in Perak had a complaint from a trader whose stock comprised 7 *keris panjang*, 2 short *keris* with sheaths, 34 *keris* with handles or sheaths, 1 *badik* without handle or sheath and plenty more *keris* without handles.[88] Once a *keris* came into the ownership of a famous warrior, it might acquire a reputation—and a scarcity value—from its use and the user. 'No money would buy it; a common saying was "money will buy gold, but it will not buy a lucky keris".'[89]

Many of the weapons which Malay men carried must have been ordinary products of no special value, since they were so numerous. 'Every Malay man was armed, he went everywhere with a *keris* in his belt, one or two spears in his hand, a gun over his shoulder, and perhaps a sword slung somewhere where he could carry it.'[90] In addition 'the peasant's regular cutting instrument, one which serves the purpose of both knife and weapon, is the *parang* which he wears slung at his left side like a short sword; and the dexterous way in which this is used in cutting a way through the jungle is often the admiration of the European'.[91] Another Malay tool which was much admired was the *beliung* 'made of iron, and . . . so constructed that it can be shifted in its rattan socket, and becomes either adze or hatchet at the workman's pleasure'.[92] The 'extremely pliable handle' of the Malay axe gave it a spring effect which added to the cut of the blade on impact. With such a tool, even large jungle trees could be felled with remarkable rapidity.[93]

Workaday tools of this kind were made by village smiths and kept sharp by the owner. Norman wrote of the *parang* that 'the blade is home-made, of soft iron, with a very sharp thin edge. This naturally is soon blunted, but a bit of sandstone and a bowl of water suffices to put a razor edge on it again in a few minutes.'[94]

The equipment of the village smith was simple but he showed much ingenuity in the use of it. 'The smith's forge consists of a circular semi-open hearth of hard, dried mud, built under a slight shed.' He burnt charcoal, raising an intense heat by the use of bellows.[95] Maxwell saw an ingenious piston pump in use by Malay iron workers—'two upright wooden cylinders about 2½ feet high placed side by side. A piston . . . was worked perpendicularly in each by a man standing between them. He grasped a handle in each hand and worked them up and down quickly, one rising as the other descended. Both cylinders communicated with the furnace by the same nozzle. . . . This is the national Malay bellows.'[96] The smith could not smelt iron ore but made use of imported material. 'Hammers used for breaking road metal were often stolen, and one end forged into an axe edge . . . a nasty ripping knife is sometimes made by fixing an old razor blade into a *tumbok lada* hilt . . . small knife blades, four or five inches long, often of European manufacture are fitted with hilts and loose wooden scabbards.' The same ingenuity of adaptation was applied to non-metallic materials; gramophone records, crushed and melted, were used to provide an adhesive to fix the tang of the blade into the handle. In addition to weapons for men, the local smith made spurs for fighting cocks and 'a curious kind of scissor [*sic*] used for slicing betel nut'.[97]

In contrast to the special skill of the metal-smith, most Malay men could use their tools, the *parang* and the *beliung*, to do rough carpentry and in particular to build houses.[98] The women could make *atap* thatch, and mats of woven bamboo and other materials such as pandanus or screw-pine (*mengkuang*). A superior house, however, would require planks to be purchased from a sawyer or sawmill.

Swettenham came across an 'excellent Malay pottery' in central Pahang in 1885.[99] Significantly, he adds that as there was no regular market, 'the potters keep no stock and make only what is ordered. The shapes of the jars I ordered are all good, and the decoration, done with a sharp tool before the firing, is most artistic.' However, this renowned centre of pottery manufacture was perhaps the only one of its kind. Again, one notes the lack of regular demand and the Malay flair for good design.

In sharp contrast to these small, scattered industries elsewhere was Kuala Terengganu, 'the Birmingham of the Peninsula'.[100] Here, there were 5,000 artisans, one-eighth of the adult male population, in 1895. It was the legacy of a former ruler, Baginda

Omar, who 'took an immense interest in learning and trade . . . and by introducing foreign skilled artisans to teach his people, he left an indelible mark on the intellect and industries of the state'.[101] The most important industries were the manufacture of textiles, weapons and other artefacts of wood or metal.

In the textile industry women worked the looms, but men prepared the vegetable dyes, devised the patterns, set up the looms and marketed the output. Terengganu metal products included brass utensils and also articles made of *tembaga putih*, an alloy made by a process 'the secret of which is jealously preserved by those who hold it'. There were also knives, daggers, swords, spears, pruning-knives, and choppers. The Terengganu *parang* was 'especially cheap and good'.[102]

The woodwork included elegant *sirih* boxes, indispensable for the ceremonial of offering and consuming betel quids. These boxes were veneered with thin strips of *kemuning* wood selected for their patterns. When the local supplies of this wood were exhausted, stocks were imported from Sumatra. The woodworkers also made handles and hilts, designed and shaped with much artistry, to be fitted to the *keris* and other metal blades made by the metalsmiths. There was a flourishing boat-building industry, which supplied craft to the local fishing industry, but Terengganu boats were rated not quite equal to those of Pahang.[103] The prestige of the craftsman was enhanced by the direct participation of the former ruler, as related in Chapter 3.

There was an impressive commercial expertise to support the industrial skills of the Terengganu craftsmen. Clifford wrote that 'much ingenuity is displayed by Terengganu weavers in imitating the manufactures of Pahang. A large number of Terengganu *kain sarong* are now sold as Pahang cloths, and it is not until the dyes begin to run and fade after a week's wear, that the deception is detected.' The Terengganu weavers also made turbans of 'white cloths shot with gold thread' for export to Mecca 'where they are retailed to the confiding Malay pilgrims as real Arabic manufacture'.[104] Similar skill was applied to the production of imitations of the prestigious *keris* blades of Celebes and Java. 'Nevertheless the Terengganu metal-smiths can turn out very excellent work when it is worth their while to do so.' On receiving an order it was their practice to ask whether the customer required the goods for personal use or for re-sale in the market—and their standards were adapted accordingly.[105]

'Boats are also built on a European pattern, the art having been first taught by one of the Baginda's workmen, who was presented with a Singapore-built gig for use as a model . . . and the boats in model, in workmanship, and in finish are infinitely superior to anything which the dock-yards of the Straits are accustomed to produce.'[106]

One would like to know how the production and marketing of this considerable output were organized—but the reports are silent on these matters. As there is no mention of central factories, it may be assumed that production was decentralized to the houses or worksheds of individual craftsmen. Factory methods would have been alien to the Malay work ethos of the time. But one cannot even guess how orders were obtained from distant markets, who provided the working capital, and how the finished goods were shipped.

The Terengganu industries were geared to supplying distant markets; the small production of other states was sold in local markets. But both were vulnerable to the competition of cheaper, if inferior, mass-produced articles from industrialized countries which began to flood the South-East Asian markets at this time. Artistic excellence and local tradition saved these industries from total extinction, but in time, they shrank to a small fraction of what they had been. The market for *keris* and other weapons dwindled to a connoisseurs' demand for *objets d'art*, as the wearing of weapons was prohibited, to diminish the risk of affrays.

In a passage quoted above, Rathborne noted how the decline of village crafts led to a temporary exodus of the men in search of work with which to earn money to spend on imported goods. It was a change of occupation made possible by a change of attitude. As early as 1880 the future Sultan Idris of Perak, an expert on the Malay tradition, said, 'People in Perak once thought it a disgrace to work for wages, but the feeling is rapidly dying out.'[107] In Chapter 5, it has been suggested that the example of immigrant Malay settlers, responding to their own need of money, may have contributed to this change; it was certainly not universal.[108] It reflected the circumstances of the case and even men of the upper class were affected by it.[109]

Although it was a short-term, seasonal exodus it tended to disrupt the pattern of village life. 'A great many of the men were away from home, leaving their wives and children behind,' reported an administrator in Kuala Langat in 1884, 'they go away to find work, and then when they have made a little money return and do little or nothing all day until the money is finished when they go away again—this accounts for most of the kampongs being in such a state of neglect.'[110] A report from Krian, however, is more sympathetic—'as each dry season comes round a great many people leave the coast district, where there is nothing for them to do during that season, to seek means of livelihood elsewhere; they return to the district when they hear that sufficient rain has fallen to render planting operations possible'.[111]

There was a considerable variety in the wage-earning activities which they pursued. In some cases Malays made use of a traditional skill in a new environment. Malay expertise in felling jungle was legendary.[112] The French planter, Henri Fauconnier, noted how his Malay gangs first observed the line and angle of the standing trees and the links between them made by strong jungle creepers. In this way they could work out how the felling of one tree would bring down several more—all in a predictable direction. They then cleared away the undergrowth, and built a platform against the trunk of the tree selected for felling, so that they could cut through it at a height from the ground where the broad base of the tree had begun to taper a little. For hours 'the axes thud against the stems before a single tree falls' but now and again the tree fellers paused to listen to the vibration of their blows, to note the tension of the creepers, the rustle of the foliage and the strength and direction of the wind. In the very dangerous game of giant dominoes which they were playing, these were essential precautions. Then—when the trees were about to go over—they jumped clear amid the rending shriek of a tornado'. Fauconnier noted that 'they seem positively to enjoy the risk'.[113]

On the tin mines there was sometimes work for both men and women. The men cleared jungle, split the logs into rough uneven planks or squared them into beams and rafters, hitched the wood to buffaloes to pull it out and built houses and sheds, and in addition found 'many little odd jobs' to do.[114] Their wives 'obtain a fair livelihood from re-panning and re-washing tailings'.[115] The extensive railway construction in the West Coast states created a large demand for railway sleepers and here, too, Malay woodcraft was put to good use.[116]

As related in Chapter 6, Kelantan men, who moved to Pahang to escape the hardships following the Kelantan disasters of the 1880s, found work in building irrigation dams and distribution channels, work in which they were experts.[117] In 1897 three-fifths of the boatmen who poled the heavy barges along the Pahang River were Kelantan Malays, using another of their particular skills.[118] Yet another instance of Kelantan expertise was the training of buffaloes imported into Selangor for ploughing.[119]

There were some unusual combinations of village life and outside activities—'the entire personnel of a Malay theatrical group from Penang have settled comfortably down to plant at Telok [in Kuala Langat] making (no doubt) very pleasant addition to their income by giving theatrical representations at Jugra in the evening'.[120]

Wherever they went in search of work, they preferred to live and share their tasks as a group, allocating the work between them as they saw fit. When W. E. Maxwell set out for Patani in 1876 with a party of Malay porters, 'out of the forty men about 15 carried smooth-bore carbines, others had spears or *ladings* (a formidable short sword); all carried the national *keris*. They arranged among themselves who should carry the cooking pots of each mess; the betel nut, *sirih*, tobacco and other luxuries were entrusted to the leaders.'[121]

Apart from new applications of traditional skills there were entirely new occupations, such as driving bullock-carts, referred to above.[122] A rough count in 1897 of the occupations of former pupils of Malay schools in Perak found that they included teachers, clerks, *penghulu*, orderlies, domestic servants, syces, sailors, constables, fishermen, gardeners, labourers, shopkeepers, and traders. But by far the largest proportion were classified as '*padi* planters' or just 'at home'.[123] By this time it was official policy to encourage the recruitment of Malays to subordinate positions in the expanding government services. The Education Department was pressing for the reservation to Malays of positions of 'clerks, orderlies, messengers or punkah-pullers'. It was also suggested that Malays should be recruited to the government hospital staff in the hope of thereby overcoming Malay patients' distrust of these strange institutions.[124]

Another alien organization, the police force, still had difficulty in attracting recruits from the villages of the Malay states. The peasant distrusted a body which he regarded as successor to the oppressive *budak raja*. Even in the 1890s 'a respectable man did not care for a constable to come near his house, whilst he would have refused to entertain the idea of giving his daughter in marriage to a man who wore the objectionable uniform'.[125] This was a prejudice which was beginning to fade, but there was some way to go before a career in the police was a much prized opportunity for a young man of spirit.

There is no denying the strength of tradition in the economic as in the other elements of Malay life of this period. But this chapter also contains some striking examples of the wide range of practical skills and knowledge, the adaptability and versatility of the villager in seeking his livelihood in the changing circumstances of the time.

1. Until the arrival of Chinese miners in large numbers beginning in the 1840s tin mining was a Malay activity, organized on the lines described in the text. There was a transitional period in which Malay chiefs employed Chinese miners but within a few years the predominant pattern was mining organized, financed and manned by Chinese but yielding revenue in taxes (and providing markets for produce) to the Malay community. Malay mining continued, but only a few small sites, on the old lines (Wong Lin Ken, *The Malayan Tin Industry to 1914*, Tucson, University of Arizona Press, 1965, pp. 29–35; P. Sullivan, *Social Relations of Dependence in a Malay State: Nineteenth Century Perak*, MBRAS Monograph 10, 1982, pp. 29–35).

2. H.C. Clifford, *Studies in Brown Humanity being Scrawls and Smudges in Sepia, White and Yellow*, London, Grant Richards, 1898, p. 4. If the party hit a rich deposit they might earn for themselves as much as $2 each per day, which was three times a day's wage on a Chinese mine (J. Errington De La Croix, 'Some Account of the Mining Districts of Lower Perak', *JSBRAS*, 7, 1881, p. 4). Douglas was told that Malay women washing tailings on Chinese mines in Ulu Selangor earned up to 80 cents per day but he thought 13–14 cents was a more realistic general figure (Douglas Diary, 25 July 1879). If a party of villagers joined in mining it was organized as a cooperative—'sometimes the concern is a general one, and is divided into shares of fifteen dollars each' (J. Low, 'Observations on Perak', *JIA*, [illegible], 1850, p. 498).

3. *PGG* 1889, p. 633, and *PGG* 1894, p. 126.

4. See pp. 74 and 80 above. *AR Kinta 1888* in *PGG* 1889, p. 33[illegible] (ancestral mines); *PSCM*, 3 March 1879, *PMS*, pp. 190–1 (claims).

5. H. Crookewit, 'The Tin Mines of Malacca', *JIA*, 8, 1854, p. 12[illegible]. J. W. W. Birch noted 'some tin mines worked entirely by Malays' in Ulu Langat (J. W. W. Birch, *The Journals of J. W. W. Birch First British Resident to Perak, 1874–1875* (hereafter cited as *Birch Journal*), edited by P. L. Burns, Kuala Lumpur, Oxford University Press, 1976, p. 50). Khoo Kay Kim, *The Western Malay States 1850–1873: The Effects of Commercial Development on Malay Politics*, Kuala Lumpur, Oxford University Press, 1972, p. 145.

6. A. Hale, 'On Mines and Miners in Kinta, Perak', *JSBRAS*, [illegible], 1885, p. 304, describes pits of 8 feet in diameter and 20 feet in depth which he believed had not been worked for at least a century. There were similar old workings in Pahang (*AR Pahang 1893*, para. 14). Wong Lin Ken, op. cit., pp. 44–5, describes the methods used to dewater the pits and extract ore. He comments, of the workings at Selinsing in Pahang, that they 'required greater mechanical skill than the Malays were observed to possess'. But the origin of *lombong siam* was a mystery.

7. *PGG* 1889, p. 633, referring to a Malay mine at Juang in the Kinta valley.

The report adds that the Malays obtained much of their tin by buying it from aborigines.

8. F. A. Swettenham, *Sir Frank Swettenham's Malayan Journals 1874–1876* (hereafter cited as *Swettenham Journal*), edited by P. L. Burns and C. D Cowan, Kuala Lumpur, Oxford University Press, 1975, p. 226 (sketch at p. 227).

9. *SGG* 1892, p. 679.

10. B. Westerhout, 'Notes on Malacca', *JIA*, 2, 1848, p. 171. F. A. Swettenham, 'Journal Kept during a Journey across the Malay Peninsula', *JSBRAS*, 15, 1885, p. 33. Khoo Kay Kim, *Western Malay States*, p. 107.

11. J. Anderson, *Political and Commercial Considerations Relative to the Malayan Peninsula and the British Settlements in the Straits of Malacca*, Penang, 1824, reprinted in *JMBRAS*, 35(4), 1962, p. 124. J. Low, 'Observations on Perak', p. 499. 'When rice is insufficient he ekes out a living by working rattan, gutta and other jungle produce' (*AR Pahang 1891*). In Singapore trade circles, rattan was referred to as '*rotan Pahang*'. However, Swettenham, during his trip up the East Coast in 1875, noted that these states did not export rattan in quantity (*Swettenham Journal*, pp. 262 and 268).

12. J. G. Watson, 'Rattans', in I. H. Burkill, *A Dictionary of the Economic Products of the Malay Peninsula*, 2 vols., London, published on behalf of the SS and FMS Governments, Crown Agents, 1935, Vol. 2, p. 1874.

13. Ibid. Later aborigines seem to have been the suppliers (*AR Kuala Langat 1899* in *SGG* 1900).

14. *AR Ulu Langat 1890* in *SGG* 1891, p. 489.

15. *PGG* 1888, p. 148. *SGG* 1893, p. 506. R. G. Cant, *An Historical Geography of Pahang*, MBRAS Monograph 4, 1973, p. 40. *AR Selangor 1885*, para. 19. H. C. Clifford, 'Report: Expedition to Trengganu and Kelantan', *JMBRAS*, 34(1), 1961, originally printed for Colonial Office use in 1895 and reprinted Kuala Lumpur, Government Press, 1936, p. 73.

16. F. Caddy, *To Siam and Malaya in the Duke of Sutherland's Yacht 'Sans Peur'*, London, Hurst & Blackett, 1889, p. 253, describing Malay logging in Johor.

17. E. F. de Bruijn Kops, 'Sketch of the Riau-Lingga Archipelago', *JIA*, 8, 1854, p. 100. J. Low, 'Observations on Perak', p. 499. Elsewhere Low differentiates among 120 varieties of timber and specifies their uses, no doubt drawing on Malay information (J. Low, *A Dissertation on the Soil and Agriculture of the British Settlement of Penang or Prince of Wales Island in the Straits of Malacca Including Province Wellesley on the Malayan Peninsula ..., with ... Incidental Observations, etc.*, Singapore, Singapore Free Press, 1836, reprinted as *The British Settlement at Penang*, Singapore, Oxford University Press, 1972, pp. 199–206).

18. *AR Selangor 1885*, para. 19. The anonymous author of the 'Journal Kept on Board a Cruiser in the Indian Archipelago in 1846', *JIA*, 8, 1854, p. 176, mentions that the ship stopped to pick up firewood.

19. S. W. Jones, *Public Administration in Malaya*, London, Royal Institute of International Affairs, 1953, pp. 35 and 74–7. Lim Teck Ghee, *Peasants and Their Agricultural Economy in Colonial Malaya 1874–1941*, Kuala Lumpur, Oxford University Press, 1977, pp. 46–8 and 54.

20. I. H. Burkill, *A Dictionary of the Economic Products of the Malay Peninsula*, 2 vols., London, published on behalf of the SS and FMS Governments, Crown Agents, 1935, Vol. 2, pp. 1623–38 on gutta percha generally. H. J. Murton, 'Notes on Gutta and Caoutchouc in the Malay Peninsula', *JSBRAS*, 1, 1878, and Burkill,

op. cit., p. 1636, on yield. De Bruijn Kops, op. cit., p. 400, puts the yield at between 15 and 20 *kati* per tree, if felled as described. C. B. Buckley, *An Anecdotal History of Old Times in Singapore 1819–1867*, 2 vols., Singapore, Fraser & Neave, 1902, reprinted Kuala Lumpur, University of Malaya Press, 1965, and Singapore, Oxford University Press, pp. 402–4, reprints a useful article from the *Singapore Free Press* on the economic history of gutta percha; at pp. 76, 482 and 57[illegible] he gives information on the trade in it.

21. *AR Pahang 1891* and *AR Pahang 1898*. *AR Lower Perak 1888* in *PGG* 1889, P. 511. *AR Ulu Selangor 1889* in *SGG* 1890, p. 332. *SGG* 1892, p. 358, report from Kuala Selangor. *Swettenham Journal*, p. 262. Douglas Diary, 22 and 24 July 1876.

22. Douglas Diary, 25 July 1876.

23. On conservation see SSD 18 July 1891, and 21 March 18[illegible] and 14 December 1899, and sundry articles in *JSBRAS*, Nos. 3, 5 and 12. Hugh Low, who was a botanist before becoming an administrator, was unable during his long tenure in Perak (1877–89) to devise any workable conservation measures.

Gutta percha is now only a minor Malayan product obtained by controlled tapping of trees grown or preserved as a plantation resource. There are about 4,0[illegible]0 acres of gutta percha forest in Perak and Pahang (Ooi Jin-Bee, *Land, People and Economy in Malaya*, London, Longmans, 1963, p. 273).

24. De Bruijn Kops, op. cit., p. 401. Burkill, op. cit., pp. 757–66 (*damar*) and pp. 838–42 (*dipterocarpus*). W. W. Skeat and F. F. Laidlaw, 'The Cambridge University Expedition to Parts of the Malay Peninsula 1899–1900: Personal Accounts', *JMBRAS*, 26(4), 1953, p. 145. *Negeri Sembilan Gazette 1896*, p. [illegible]02, report from Kuala Pilah. Camphor (*kapur barus—Dryobalanops aromatica*) was another forest product 'in great demand by the Chinese' for embalming and for use as incense and medicine (H. Lake, 'Johore', *The Geographical Journal*, 3, 18[illegible], p. 286). Malay camphor collectors resorted to magic to ward off perils in the forest. But over-exploitation had made it scarce and difficult to find (Burkill, op. cit., p. [illegible]55).

25. A. B. Rathborne, *Camping and Tramping in Malaya: Fifteen Years' Pioneering in the Native States of the Malay Peninsula*, London, Swann Sonnenschein, 1898, reprinted Singapore, Oxford University Press, 1984, pp. 259 and 284.

26. Ibid., p. 284, and *PGG* 1892, p. 679. The value of *atap* exports from Lower Perak to Deli in 1886 was $102,033 (*AR Perak 1886*).

27. *SGG* 1897, p. 936, report from Kuala Selangor.

28. *AR Kuala Selangor 1893* in *SGG* 1894, p. 299.

29. Skeat and Laidlaw, op. cit., p. 63, referring to Jering in southern Siam. The price was 1 *kupang* (12½ cents) for forty slats.

30. SSD 31 January 1889.

31. W. A. Graham, *Kelantan—A State of the Malay Peninsula: A Handbook of Information*, Glasgow, James MacLehose & Sons, 1908, p. 60. He also op. cit., p. 58) refers to 'regular weekly mails' to Singapore and Bangkok.

32. Ibid., p. 66. A few years before, in 1895, Clifford reported that 'the bulk of the population is engaged in agriculture' (Clifford, 'Expedition', p. 116). It may be inferred that in 1895 the export of fish and copra was not yet on a significant scale (see Chapter 6, note 57).

33. See p. 118, note 13, above.

34. SSD 23 November 1889 covering a report of a visit to Kedah by Swettenham who wrote that 'the flat country (a green extent covering many thousands of acres) is all under rice cultivation from the sea to the hills and on both sides of the Kedah

river'. In 1906 the Yen district, described as 'the garden of Kedah', exported large quantities of fruit to Penang (*AR Kedah 1906–1908*).

35. CO 273/15, p. 401. This file (No. 15) in the CO 273 series comprises India Office papers transferred to the Colonial Office in 1868 as background material.

36. W. E. Maxwell, 'A Journey on Foot to the Patani Frontier in 1876 being a Journal Kept during an Expedition Undertaken to Capture Datoh Maharajah Lela of Perak', *JSBRAS*, 9, 1882, p. 12. Later the Perak government restricted the import of cattle from the north-east because of the risk of disease (*PGG* 1888, p. 174, report from Selama, and *PGG* 1896, p. 677, report from Kuala Kangsar).

37. *AR Selangor 1886*. In 1879 Douglas had noted that many buffaloes were coming into Ulu Selangor from Pahang (Douglas Diary, 28 July 1879).

38. F. A. Swettenham, *British Malaya: An Account of the Origin and Progress of British Influence in Malaya*, London, John Lane Bodley Head, 1907 (revised editions 1929 and 1948, London, Allen & Unwin), p. 119. 'There was nothing but fowls to be had' (E. Innes, *The Chersonese with the Gilding Off*, 2 vols., London, Richard Bentley, 1885, reprinted Kuala Lumpur, Oxford University Press, 1974, Vol. 2, p. 29). She says (op. cit., Vol. 1, p. 126), that she needed three fowls every two days for her household. She raised her own chickens, giving them the names of her fashionable friends in Singapore, and grew her own vegetables at Kuala Langat (Vol. 1, pp. 112 and 114, and Vol. 2, p. 30). This was done partly to relieve the crushing tedium of her lonely existence. Birch (see p. 134 above) had less difficulty in obtaining local produce other than hens' eggs.

39. Wong Lin Ken, op. cit., Chapter 2, on the expansion of mining. In the 1870s Yap Ah Loy of Kuala Lumpur encouraged the surrounding Malay villages to produce food for sale as it was cheaper than importing supplies (S. M. Middlebrook, 'Yap Ah Loy', *JMBRAS*, 24(2), 1951, p. 90).

40. *AR Perak 1886*. On rising land values see p. 108 above.

41. SSD 28 January 1889.

42. In Ulu Selangor the District Officer expected the population of a Malay village to increase 'as long as the mining lands hold out' (*SGG* 1894, p. 302).

43. SSD 24 December 1886. On SS financial aid towards road construction in the Melaka hinterland see SSD 26 March 1885, 19 February 1886, 9 March 1886, and 24 March 1889.

44. O. Cavenagh, *Reminiscences of an Indian Official*, London, W. H. Allen & Co., 1884, p. 262. He was Governor SS from 1859 to 1867. See also Douglas Diary, cited at p. 137 above, on surplus fruit rotting in Ulu Selangor.

45. 'When *people of consideration* had to journey by land, they travelled on elephants' (Swettenham, *British Malaya*, p. 119) (emphasis supplied). On elephants generally see p. 197 below.

46. Clifford, *In Days that are Dead*, London, Murray, 1926, p. 281. On bamboo rafts see p. 179 below. Malays made dugout canoes (*jalur*) for use on narrow streams by felling a large tree and hollowing out its inside by the use of fires, with some final trimming with an axe (*beliung*). Very large canoes carried 20–30 men but the more usual and smaller-sized, only two or three. Their buoyancy made them suitable for streams where it was necessary to pass rapids (Lake, op. cit., p. 284).

47. Cant, op. cit., p. 30, gives an interesting account of traffic on the Pahang River.

48. W. Cameron, 'On the Patani', *JSBRAS*, 11, 1883, pp. 127–9, is the source of the quotations and other material used in this passage. J. Low, 'Observations on

Perak', p. 500, gives a shorter but similar account of boats on the Perak River. See also H. C. Clifford, *Bushwhacking and Other Asiatic Tales and Memories*, New York, Harper, 1929, p. 84. Sir Roger de Coverley, to which Cameron refers, is the name of an English traditional dance in which the dancers move in set patterns.

49. Datuk Mohamed Said, *Memoirs of a Menteri Besar: Early Days*, Singapore, Heinemann, 1982, p. 26. See also p. 240 below, where the aggrieved husband was cuckolded while absent on river trading expeditions.

50. Innes, op. cit., Vol. 1, p. 10. Her real complaint (p. 14) was lack of privacy—to relieve the calls of nature. Isabella Bird, and the two daughters of the Resident Councillor, Melaka, made an uncomfortable journey by launch up the Linggi River to Seremban. She too is reticent on this delicate subject. She mentions incidentally observing 'canoes hollowed out of tree trunks' and large and small native boats covered and thatched with *atap*' on the river (I. L. Bird (Mrs Bishop), *The Golden Chersonese and the Way Thither*, London, Murray, 1883; reprinted Kuala Lumpur, Oxford University Press, 1967 and 1980, pp. 164 and 167).

51. *PGG* 1893, p. 305, report from Tanjong Malim. In 1876 it cost $40 per *koyan* to move rice from the river mouth to Ulu Bernam (Douglas Diary, 24 July 1876). See p. 179 below on practicable loads on a long trip.

52. W. Cameron, op. cit., p. 132.

53. 'The path was among bogs and twisted gnarled roots, making progress difficult and most fatiguing' (Douglas Diary, 24 July 1876). 'A sheet of muddy, prismatic water, over which the large branches formed a kind of network, while the trunks lay, some in the water, some out' is Emily Innes's description (op. cit., Vol. 1, p. 137) of a path made by Malay wood-cutters. On elephant tracks see Rathborne, op. cit., p. 236, and H. Norman, *The Peoples and Politics of the Far East: Travels and Studies in the British ... Colonies and Malaya*, New York, Scribner, 1895, pp. 543–4.

54. Report enclosed with SSD 6 March 1879.

55. SSD 19 February 1886. In 1892 the cost of a final 2-mile carry by porters to an estate was $7.50 per bag of rice (J. C. Jackson, *Planters and Speculators: Chinese and European Agricultural Enterprise in Malaya, 1786–1921*, Kuala Lumpur and Singapore, University of Malaya Press, 1968, p. 179).

56. C. W. Harrison, *The Magic of Malaya*, London, John Lane, 1916, p. 131.

57. C. C. Brown, *Malay Sayings*, London, Routledge & Kegan Paul, 1951, p. 164 — '*saperti katak di-bawah tempurong*'.

58. Swettenham, *About Perak*, Singapore, Straits Times, 1890, p. 2[illegible]. He is probably referring to the buses which plied between Kuala Kangsar and Taiping.

59. Clifford, *Studies in Brown Humanity*, p. 154.

60. Jackson, *Planters and Speculators*, is the authoritative study of nineteenth-century plantation agriculture. See also Lim Teck Ghee, op. cit., on Malay involvement in the latter part of the century in the search for new cash crops.

61. J. F. A. McNair, *Perak and the Malays: Sarong and Keris*, London, Tinsley Bros., 1878, reprinted Kuala Lumpur, Oxford University Press, 1972, p. 1[illegible].

62. *AR Selangor 1884*. Swettenham saw 'some fine tobacco' at Kota Lama in Perak in 1875 (*Swettenham Journal*, p. 304).

63. H. C. Clifford, *In Court and Kampong, being Tales and Sketches of Native Life in the Malay Peninsula*, London, Grant Richards, 1897 (2nd ed. with autobiographical preface, London, Richards Press, 1927), p. 197. They sold the gambier and used

the proceeds to buy rice. It was a 'long-standing' centre of gambier production (*AR Pahang 1890*, para. 24).

64. *AR Negeri Sembilan 1899*.

65. Report of 2 April 1875 enclosed with SSD 26 April 1875 and reprinted in Cmd. 1320 and in *Birch Journal*, p. 393, para. 46.

66. See p. 80 above. Another enterprising Syed, Syed Yahya, *penghulu* of Cheras in Ulu Langat, was 'a great advocate of pepper planting' and had planted 3 acres of his own land. But the local Malays would not follow his example (*SGG* 1890, p. 417, report from Ulu Langat).

67. J. C. Jackson, *Planters and Speculators*, Chapter 9, 'European Coffee Estates'. See also J. M. Gullick, 'Kuala Lumpur 1880–1895', *JMBRAS*, 28(4), 1955, pp. 62–5 (a passage written by C. A. Gibson-Hill).

68. *AR Selangor 1885* and *AR Selangor 1892*. 'On the coffee gardens in the Ulu the owners and labourers are almost always without exception natives from Java and Sumatra' (*AR Pahang 1897*).

69. See above, p. 108, on sales of land. *AR Ulu Selangor 1894* in *SGG* 1895, p. 212. Although the boom in coffee did not begin until the late 1880s coffee had been grown in Malaya since 1779 at least (Burkill, op. cit., p. 621). Swettenham mentions coffee in his list of Terengganu exports in 1875 (*Swettenham Journal*, p. 262). It is not in Clifford's list of Terengganu agricultural products in 1895 (Clifford, 'Expedition', p. 35). J. W. W. Birch reported that in 1875 coffee was growing well in Perak (report cited in note 65).

However, these earlier reports relate to the species *Coffea arabica*. The start of the later boom was the introduction in 1875 of *Coffea liberica*. It was hoped that this new variety would be immune to the devastating fungus disease, *Hemileia vastatrix*, which ravaged the coffee estates of Ceylon in the 1870s and led to the migration of European coffee planters from Ceylon to Malaya (Burkill, op. cit., pp. 621–3). In the end Malayan coffee succumbed to disease and a fall in world prices.

70. He was originally named Nonggek; according to Malay tradition he became headman of the Batu Bahara or Mandiling Sumatran Malays in the Klang valley in the late 1860s (Wan Mohamed Amin bin Said, *Pesaka Selangor*, edited by Abdul Samad Ahmad, Kuala Lumpur, Dewan Bahasa dan Pustaka, 1966, p. 16; Haji Buyong bin Adil, *Sejarah Selangor*, Kuala Lumpur, Dewan Bahasa dan Pustaka, 1971, p. 52). In the records of the Selangor Civil War he is often referred to as the Datuk Dagang of Klang (or of Kuala Lumpur), the title conferred on him by the Sultan in recognition of his position as leader of the Sumatran Malays of the Klang valley (E. Sadka, *The Protected Malay States 1874–1895*, Kuala Lumpur and Singapore, University of Malaya Press, 1968, p. 14). For his services he was entitled, until 1877, to a levy of $1 per *bahara* on tin exported from Kuala Lumpur. At some stage, perhaps when his fortunes were at a low ebb—he was on the losing side in the war—he must have made the pilgrimage to Mecca. Thereafter, he is named as Haji Tahir. He died about 1894. Sadka (ibid.) says that in 1969 his descendants were still living at Klang.

71. Resident's tour notes 22 June 1894, in *SGG* 1894, pp. 368–9. *AR Selangor 1894*. He exported 200 *pikul* of indigo in 1888 (*AR Selangor 1888*, para. 18). He is there dubbed by Swettenham 'our most enterprising Malay planter, the Datuk Dagang of Klang'.

72. J. C. Jackson, *Planters and Speculators*, pp. 196–7, tells the sad story of the Klang fiasco.

73. *AR Selangor 1894*, para. 75.

74. Two other such cases, drawn from different social categories, are Tunku Kudin and Syed Alsagoff. Tunku Kudin of Kedah, son-in-law of the ruler of Selangor and at one time Viceroy of the state, in later years owned a plantation of about 2,000 acres on the north bank of the Klang River opposite Klang town. He employed Javanese labourers, supervised for him by the Javanese *penghulu* of Klang, Sheikh Abdul Mohet (*AR Selangor 1890*).

Syed Alsagoff owned a 10,000-acre estate on Kukub island off the coast of Johor and worked it with indentured Javanese labour. As a Singapore shipowner and merchant, he paid the passages of Javanese pilgrims, stranded at Jeddah without money, and required them to work off the debt by labour on his estate: vols. 216 and 217 of the CO 273 series contain a number of papers on this dubious arrangement. His estate is described in an anonymous article entitled 'A Monster Estate' in the *Singapore Free Press*, 13 December 1892.

75. *AR Selangor 1897*, para. 14.

76. Skeat and Laidlaw, op. cit., p. 52.

77. *AR Batang Padang 1895* in *PGG* 1896, p. 347. *AR Selangor 1895*, para. 9.

78. Rathborne, op. cit., p. 34.

79. *AR Kedah 1906–1908*, p. 3.

80. In addition to G. E. Shaw, 'Rice Planting', *Papers on Malay Subjects, Malay Industries*, Part 3, 1911, Winstedt wrote two monographs in the 'Malay Industries' section of *PMS*: these are not included in the reprint of selected *PMS* material edited by P. L. Burns and published in 1971. Winstedt's monographs are entitled 'Arts and Crafts', 1909, reprinted 1925, and 'Fishing, Hunting and Trapping', 1911, reprinted 1929. There are also a large number of specialist monographs, many of them in *JSBRAS* or in the *Journal of FMS Museums*.

81. Skeat and Laidlaw, op. cit., p. 88. Skeat goes on to speculate that the Malay man was losing 'some of his peacock-pride in his appearance' and that this factor contributed to the decline in Malay hand-woven textiles on which he comments. Elsewhere he wrote that in Kedah 'sarongs are made only by the up-country Malays' (p. 128) and that 'the cloth here was coarse, and the colours inferior . . . many of the women wore Penang sarongs' (p. 141). The general picture which emerges is of a loss of interest in the Malay community as much as a simple displacement by a cheaper competitive product. *Kain telepuk* is cloth on which designs have been imprinted, sometimes in gold foil, by means of wooden blocks. *Kain cindai* was an Indian cloth imported for use as sashes. Imitations of it were made in Java by a 'tie and dye process' (R. J. Wilkinson, *A Malay–English Dictionary*, 2 parts, Singapore, Kelly & Walsh, 1901 (revised as *A Malay–English Dictionary (Romanised)*, 2 parts, Mytilene, Salavopoulos & Kinderlis, 1932), pp. 227 (Part 1) and 554 (Part 2). *Kain cawi* has not been identified.

82. *SGG* 1897, p. 113, report from Kuala Selangor. *Kain belabas* was a fabric of silk and gold thread, used for borders, caps, etc. (Wilkinson, *1932 Dictionary*, note 81, Part 1, p. 102).

83. Mubin Sheppard, *Taman Indera: Malay Decorative Arts and Pastimes*, Kuala Lumpur, Oxford University Press, 1972, reprinted as *A Royal Pleasure Ground*, Singapore, Oxford University Press, 1986, p. 150. Swettenham was 'a persistent collector of Malay silver vessels' and preserved a valuable collection to the time of his death in 1946; F. A. Swettenham, *Footprints in Malaya*, London, Hutchinson, 1942, pp. 118–20, is a useful short description of Malay silverwork.

84. Europeans who . . . go about unarmed make a great mistake, since a Malay is apt to interpret such action as being dictated by cowardice' (Clifford, *In Court and Kampong*, p. 158).

85. Ivor H. N. Evans, *Papers on the Ethnology and Archaeology of the Malay Peninsula*, Cambridge, Cambridge University Press, 1927, p. 55.

86. *Birch Journal*, pp. 71 and 74. *Swettenham Journal*, pp. 66 and 68. Elsewhere Swettenham refers to Rembau and Patani, as well as Terengganu, Perak and Kedah, as centres of renowned metalwork.

87. Swettenham, *Footprints*, p. 51.

88. *Birch Journal*, p. 125. A *keris panjang* is a long straight dagger, sometimes used for executions; a *badik* is a short dagger with a handle like a cross-saw.

89. Swettenham, *British Malaya*, p. 146.

90. Swettenham, *Footprints*, pp. 50–1. See also p. 238 below.

91. McNair, op. cit., p. 248.

92. Ibid., p. 166. Rathborne, op. cit., p. 134. S. Osborn, *Quedah: Or Stray Leaves from a Journal in Malayan Waters*, London, Routledge, 1857 (revised 1860 and 186 and published as *My Journal in Malayan Waters or the Blockade of Kedah*), p. 117.

93. P. J. Begbie, *The Malayan Peninsula Embracing the History, Manners and Customs of the Inhabitants, Politics, Natural History, etc. from Its Earliest Records*, Madras, Vespery Mission Press, 1834, reprinted as *The Malayan Peninsula*, Kuala Lumpur, Oxford University Press, 1967, p. 207—'the cutters erect a temporary stage around the tree to be felled at the height of about three feet from the ground, upon which they stand, and cut with astonishing rapidity'.

94. Norman, op. cit., p. 542.

95. Evans, *Papers on the Malay Peninsula*, p. 56.

96. W. E. Maxwell, *Journey to Patani*, p. 9. He says, however, that this form of bellows was a Chinese device adopted by Malay iron workers and tin miners for smelting

97. G. B. Gardner, *Keris and Other Malay Weapons*, Singapore, Progressive Publishing Co., 1936, pp. 21 and 113. See Glossary on meaning of *tumbok lada* (a form of dagger).

98. See below, p. 183.

99. Swettenham, 'Journal Kept during a Journey across the Peninsula', p. 18.

100. Clifford, 'Expedition', p. 78.

101. Ibid., p. 61.

102. Ibid., pp. 92–3.

103. Ibid., p. 94.

104. Ibid., p. 92.

105. Ibid., p. 93.

106. Ibid., p. 94.

107. *PSCM*, 30 December 1880, *PMS*, p. 231.

108. See p. 106 above. Pahang retained the traditional prejudice against wage labour (*AR Pahang 1899*, para. 95).

109. See p. 77 above.

110. Unpublished diary of District Officer, Kuala Langat, 12 March 1884 (probably at the Arkib Negara).

111. *PGG* 1896, p. 754, report from Krian. The Krian district had a long tradition of seasonal movement. In the middle of the nineteenth century, before

there was permanent settlement on the Krian marshes, Malays came in from Kedah and Province Wellesley to plant a rice crop, tend it to maturity and then return home after taking the harvest. 'Persons living in Penang ... annually cultivated lands in Krian ... living part of the year in that district and resorting during the remainder of the year to Pulau Pinang' (report of 4 February 1848 cited in R. D. Hill, *Rice in Malaya: A Study in Historical Geography*, Kuala Lumpur, Oxford University Press, 1977, p. 94). The passage from the 1896 report cited in the text relates, of course, to a later period when Malay cultivators who had made their permanent homes in the Krian district went forth to find off-season work at a wage elsewhere.

112. Rathborne, op. cit., p. 34.

113. Henri Fauconnier, *The Soul of Malaya*, translated by Eric Sutton, London, Elkin, Mathews and Marrot, 1931, reprinted Singapore, Oxford University Press, 1985, pp. 177–9. The entire passage in Fauconnier is worth reading. He was a planter in the Kuala Selangor district in the early years of this century, growing rubber and later oil palm, as described in his book.

114. Rathborne, op. cit., p. 134.

115. Ibid., p. 132. Douglas in Ulu Selangor in 1879 noted that 'a good deal of tin washing is done by [Malay] women in this district' (Douglas Diary, 25 July 1879).

116. *AR Selangor 1885*, para. 19. 'Rice Cultivation Report 1893', p. 15.

117. 'Malays from the neighbouring state of Kelantan are often hired by the natives of Pahang to do necessary manual labour of digging trenches for purposes of irrigation' (*AR Pahang 1891*). Clifford attributes this practice to 'the natural indolence' of the Pahang Malays, but the superior expertise of the Kelantan Malays, in work which required much skill, was probably a more important consideration.

118. *AR Pahang 1897*. Clifford adds that some of the remaining two-fifths, who did not hail from Kelantan, were boatmen from states other than Pahang.

119. *AR Kuala Selangor 1893* in *SGG* 1894, p. 296.

120. *SGG* 1896, p. 493, report from Kuala Langat.

121. W. E. Maxwell, *Journey to Patani*, p. 6.

122. See p. 161 above. There was a regular flow of bullock-cart traffic up the new road built along the Linggi valley to Seremban. The river silted up, owing to tin mining upstream, and ceased to be navigable (*AR Sungei Ujong 1892*).

123. *AR Education Department Perak 1897* in *PGG* 1898, p. 179.

124. *PGG* 1896, p. 818, quarterly report of the Education Department. See also pp. 259 and 271 below.

125. J. H. M. Robson, *People in a Native State*, Singapore, Singapore Free Press, 1894, p. 23. Robson had had administrative charge of local police in his time as a district officer in Selangor in the early 1890s. See also P. Morrah, 'The History of the Malayan Police', *JMBRAS*, 36(2), 1963, especially at p. 102, and J. M. Gullick, 'Syers and the Selangor Police Force 1875–1897', *JMBRAS*, 51(2), 1978, pp. 24, 43 and 50. Chapter 10 gives further material on the hostile attitude of Malay villagers to 'foreign' Malays (i.e. Malays recruited from outside the state) in the local police.

Supplementary Note
Travel in the Interior of the Malay States

In 1895 Clifford took a party overland from the interior of Pahang into Terengganu and Kelantan by an overland route (see Clifford, 'Expedition', paras. 1–96). In his lecture to the Royal Geographical Society in 1897, he repeated most of the text of his official report but omitted some passages and prefaced the lecture with an account of the constraints of inland travel in Malaya, as he had experienced them. This passage is such a vivid and detailed account of—among other things—the factors which obliged travellers, and most settlers, to keep close to a watercourse of some kind, even if it was not navigable by boats or canoes (see note 3 to Chapter 5) that the author feels it deserves quotation (in part). Communications dictated the pattern of settlement.

The passages below are taken from *The Geographical Journal*, 9(1), 1897, pp. 5–10.

'The rivers are the highways of uncivilised Malaya. In the lower reaches, huge boats, whose occupants are shielded from the sun by thick palm-mat roofs, are poled and punted up-stream until the river narrows. Then the big boats are exchanged for small dug-outs, which in their turn are used until the shallow waters become quite unnavigable. Even then the Malay traveller does not wholly desert the river, for in the jungle it is the only real landmark and guide. The paths lead up the river banks crossing the stream frequently, until the hills are reached. Then the ascent is made, and the traveller passes down into the basin of another stream, which is followed in the same way until it too becomes navigable. . . .'

'The average Malay cooly on a long march can carry only about 5 *gantang* of rice, that is to say a weight of about 35 lbs. This quantity, which is equivalent to five bushels, is sufficient to supply one full ration for twenty days. The cooly who carries this load will himself consume one-half of his pack of rice in ten days, leaving only ten full rations to be devoted to the common use. Thus every cooly who carries ammunition, or any load that is not rice, requires another cooly to carry his rations for ten days. . . .'

Clifford later states with reference to overnight camps that: 'The place chosen is always on the banks of a small stream, and at a spot where some of the many wild palms grow in abundance. Each hut is formed of a couple of forked uprights driven into the earth, and another pole laid across and rested horizontally upon them, at a height of about 4 feet from the ground. Palm fronds are then rested upon this cross-piece so that the end of the fronds hangs over, and thus form at once a back wall and a roof to the hut. Each shed will hold about four men and their loads. . . . The palm-leaves are woven into a mat about 8 feet long by 5 feet wide, and this mat is rested slantwise against the wooden cross-piece. . . . Beds of boughs and leaves, soft and springy . . . are made inside each shed and on these the mats are laid.'

Clifford relates that huts of this type for 300 men could be made within half an hour; they were fairly water-proof.

When they had passed over the watershed and reached navigable streams on the far side the party used 400 bamboos (large ones) to make 50 rafts, each capable of carrying four men and their baggage. It may be that some bamboo were cut in half since he later refers to rafts of 8–10 bamboos, lashed together with rattan. Four Malays could make such a raft in half an hour.

He mentions the many other uses of bamboo in Malay technology—to build houses, to make candlesticks, baskets, fishtraps, fences, cups, cooking pots and pickle-jars.

To the various uses of watercourses—as a means of transit, an aid to following a route, a source of useful materials—one must add, for village settlement, that land suitable for wet padi cultivation by one method or another, was normally found only in a river valley.

Small numbers of people, more especially if they wished to conceal their presence, may have taken to the upland zone away from the rivers, but the cost in money or human effort of moving inward supplies and outward produce for sale, was a powerful disincentive (see p. 159 above).

8
The Malay Style of Living

THE Malay house is a useful introduction to the general subject of the Malay style of living, since the house stands at the centre of Malay traditional culture and reflects many of its facets.

There was a wide variety in the details of Malay houses. They were different in size, in design, in the materials used in their construction, in the particular elements which distinguished houses built, say, in Perak from houses in Negeri Sembilan or in Melaka. Yet beneath the differences, all houses shared common elements and so it was possible for the author of a modern study to entitle his essay 'The Basic Malay House'.[1]

A Malay house was raised on wooden or brick pillars so that its floor stood at about 4 or 5 feet above ground level, and it comprised three functional parts—'a place for the reception of visitors, a sleeping place, and a place for cooking'.[2]

A verandah (*serambi*), along the front of the house or projecting from it (*anjung*), was the only part to which male visitors were ordinarily admitted. Here the master of the house entertained guests and adult unmarried sons slept at night. Any handiwork which the occupier was engaged on, such as a fish-trap, would be found here.

The central part of the house (*ibu rumah* or *tengah rumah*) was essentially the women's part of the house though the husband slept in it. The connubial sleeping place was usually curtained off and it might be a low wooden platform, with sleeping mats unrolled at night and a mosquito net unfurled over it. The unmarried daughters were accommodated in a semi-attic (*para*), which was an open-ended platform built from one side to project into the main room at head height. Women guests also were accommodated in the central room. Spare clothing was stored here in baskets and the family kept its most precious possessions in this room.

The kitchen (*dapur*) was at the back. It could be a separate hut, open-sided and linked with the house by a covered gangway, which was at a lower level than the house floor. Here there was a simple hearth of large stones, a collection of cooking and water pots, and culinary implements such as a coconut rasp or a mortar for grinding chillies.

Around the house, or possibly on the ground under the raised floor of the house, there was a rice granary (*kembung*), which like the house stood clear of the ground on supporting posts, an open shed sheltering a rice mortar (*lesung*), and perhaps a raised hen-house or goatshed. At the nearby river's edge was a floating bath-house and latrine.

This is merely a description of the standard elements of a simple peasant's house in a village. Depending on the resources and status of the householder, he might have a larger house with additional but ancillary features, or add to or extend his original house. Houses did not usually stand alone and the word for a village (*kampung*) conveys the basic idea of 'grouping' together.[3]

Building a house to make a dwelling was an important family event, which required ritual to ward off the evil influences which might otherwise bring ill luck to the inmates. As with so much else in their culture, the Malays blended Islamic and pagan elements of ritual. An account of the building of a house at Endau in Johor in 1917 begins with the assembly, at the invitation of the builder and prospective occupier, of a working group of neighbours. They dug the holes in which the main posts would be placed and put together the posts and horizontal crossbars, which at this stage were left lying on the ground. A broken silver coin and other objects were thrown into each hole, and packets of rice were attached to each recumbent main post. The village magician (*pawang*) and his assist-ant went round and poured water and a mixture of rice flour and water on to the timbers. All then partook of a preliminary feast of glutinous and parched rice before raising the first pair of upright posts and their crossbar into position, with 'loud shouts of "Mohamed rasul' Allah"'. While this was going on, the *lebai* of the mosque, who shared the ritual with the *pawang*, recited prayers.[4] The final stage of the ritual came before the owner moved into his new house; he fired 'several volleys to drive away the evil spirits'.[5]

The posts and cross-beams, which were the essential structure of the house, were jungle trees felled by the house-owner and dragged by buffalo to the site. They were then lashed together with ties of rattan. As a result, the house was not a rigid structure. If, however, it slipped a little the householder 'accommodates himself . . . to the want of horizontal in his dwelling'.[6] Burglars in Aceh 'begin by shaking the house to discover whether the inmates are sound enough asleep'.[7] To the basic structure of poles it was necessary to add floor, walls and roof. Springy split bamboo or *nibung* stems were laid as a floor. Sheets of woven bamboo matting made the walls. The roof was *atap* thatch but in inland areas, where the *nipah* palm did not always flourish, it might be a thatch of the leaves of the *bertam* palm.

The building of a house was a straightforward and inexpensive use of local materials to a design which was part of the cultural heritage of the community. Everyone learnt how to build a house by lending a hand at the job. The Malay house of this type was not, however, durable. The *atap* thatch soon ceased to be waterproof. The roof was usually set at an angle of 45° or less (*tara*); its life could be extended by setting it at a steeper angle (*giruf*) but only at the cost of using longer central posts and more *atap*.[8] When the breezy American naturalist, William Hornaday, was accommodated on a front verandah in Selangor in 1879, he complained of 'a roof of thatch which had several holes large enough to have thrown a dog through ... like the man from Arkansaw, when it rained they couldn't fix the roof, and when it did not rain they didn't need to'.[9] If the main posts were buried in the damp ground they soon rotted. But this could be avoided by supporting them above the ground on plinths of hard wood or laterite.[10]

If the householder wished to move, he could take his house to pieces and reassemble the materials on another site. However, 'to pull it down is considered unlucky, as it is also to repair any house that has been seriously damaged'.[11] It was normal practice simply to abandon an old house and leave it to fall down. The spirits, which would be outraged by disturbance, were indifferent to human neglect.

The short life of the Malay house was in part a consequence of the sense of impermanence which also affected the approach to agricultural technique. In many parts of Malaya there was a greater sense of security as the nineteenth century drew towards its close. Better materials also became available. The well-to-do villager began to use sawn timber for the framework of his house and employ a carpenter to make mortise joints. He might also have sawn planks for walls and roof. The supporting plinths were of concrete. If he preferred it, he could roof his house with the more durable corrugated iron 'which turns the house into an oven at midday' or use tiles, which were now manufactured in quantity to roof houses in towns—as a fire precaution.[12]

As might be expected, the upper class led the way in the use of these materials. Thomas Braddell at Muar in 1853 found Sultan Ali's mother 'living in a comfortable but small plank house'.[13] This was an innovation to which custom had not attached any restrictions, and there was no objection later to a peasant copying the example of his betters in his choice of materials. But the design of the house remained subject to traditional prohibitions. Winstedt wrote in 1909 that 'there are still types of house no peasant would erect in the proximity of his chief'.[14] Yet the peasant might escape from the net of custom, by building a house which was not in the Malay fashion at all. The purse-proud *penghulu* of Klang, Sheikh Abdul Mohet, built a mansion on a conspicuous site which was described as the 'peacock blue palace' with 'a really fine room on the first floor which serves as a hall'.[15] Plainly this was not a house built to a Malay design, yet there was a certain unease; when the same man 'usurped certain royal privileges or prerogatives on the occasion of his daughter's wedding' and died suddenly, there was a general belief that supernatural sanctions had struck him down.[16]

Like the house itself, the furnishings were often spare, inexpensive and obtained by use of local materials. Mats were made of *mengkuang*, utensils of half coconut shells, and so on. In the house there might be wooden shelves and racks, but woven baskets served in place of cupboards. It was not usual to have a bedstead, table or chairs since Malays did not use such things.[17] Yet even in the 1830s there were differences between a well-off and a poor peasant in the scale of their possessions. The former might own 'a Kuran, also brass kitchen utensils, cuspidors of brass, about a dozen china cups and plates, bedding and mosquito curtains of coarse muslin, and mats, water jars—often of Peguan manufacture—a chest, rice-mortars and sieves, betel box and apparatus of brass, fishing apparatus, grain and oil measures, a spear and a *keris*, a knife or *parang*, baskets of rattan work, a boat when close to the sea or on the bank of a river; massive gold earrings for the women of the family, also gold and silver buttons and silver bracelets, charms and ornaments; silk and cotton dresses'. The total value of these possessions would be in the range of $10–100. This account relates to a peasant who owned between 2 and 5 acres of land in Province Wellesley. At the other extreme a tenant farmer, tilling no more than 1½ acres, would own property worth no more than $10 with a house valued at $5–6.[18] Although this comparison, with its details, was originally made by James Low in the 1830s, it was repeated, as apparently still valid, in a report of the 1890s.[19]

The Malay peasant came gradually to use a variety of articles of European or Chinese manufacture in replacement for the traditional artefacts of his own culture. Instead of a resin (*damar*) torch in a wooden holder to light the house at night, he bought candles and stuck them in a half coconut shell. The ultimate luxury was a candlestick or even a brass paraffin lamp imported from India. In 1909 Winstedt wrote that 'cheap Chinese earthenware is common everywhere now'. The family rice was cooked in a clay or metal pot instead of a green bamboo stem. There is mention of cupboards, cradles, spoons, and other useful implements.

In the inner room the furnishings and possessions, pride of the housewife, became more elaborate. Mats were edged with borders of gold thread, and pillows had embroidered or gold and silver 'ends'. The sleeping platform, when not in use, was a place of display.[20] Bedding was exhibited in other ways. When Tunku Kudin, the Viceroy of Selangor, made his departure from the house of Emily Innes, she notes that 'when his bedding was carried Malay fashion, publicly down to his boat, I noticed that the pillows were of mauve satin, the round ends being almost entirely pure gold'.[21]

In some respects the householder, especially if he was in contact with Europeans, added European articles to his possessions. Winstedt, whose work brought him into close touch with Malay schoolteachers, wrote that a schoolmaster's house would have 'crocheted antimacassars and bentwood Austrian chairs, photos of the owner by a Chinese perpetrator and oleographs of Queen Victoria or of the Sultan of Turkey'.[22]

The villager lived his life around his house as much as in it. There was a Malay theory that in Perak a house should face the river, but in Kedah it should be built 'according to the points of the compass'.[23] There was also a tradition that in times gone by, groups of houses faced inwards round the sides of a quadrangle and were surrounded by a defensive fence. There were traces of such things in the nineteenth-century *kampung*. The houses commonly stood at the edge of a river or stream and were sometimes built on an east–west axis, perhaps to avoid too much sunshine when the sun was low in the sky.[24] William Maxwell wrote that 'the *kampungs* are surrounded on the land side by ditches and banks to keep out the buffaloes, of which there are great numbers. These earthworks may easily be mistaken for works of defence or stockades and will serve as such in case of need.'[25]

A peasant did not surround his own house with a separate stockade, for that was the privilege of a man of rank, but he often had a space in front (*halaman*) edged with herbs or flowers.[26] The steps, wooden or later concrete, leading up to the house were a point of vantage—'here he sits and looks patiently out at life . . . it is here that his neighbour comes to gossip with him'.[27] The women, too, did much of their work, such as pounding the padi to remove the husk, out of doors. Here the 'poultry seldom in excess of household needs' scratched for a frugal living.[28]

The residence of a chief or local magnate was a much larger and more pretentious dwelling. Swettenham describes such a place in later days as: 'there was a hill, a slight elevation, planted with palms and fruit trees, under the shade of which were dotted the dwellings of the chief, his wives and people. Their houses and gardens and orchards, occupying the whole of the rising ground, were surrounded by a high brick wall, through which gates and doors led, on one side to the main road, and on another to a lake, the water lapping the western base of the hill.' This, 'the residence of the most wealthy chief in Perak', was 'one of the best-built places in Perak'.[29] The brick wall was unusual; in former times the barrier would have been 'a stout fence of split bamboo . . . so strong that they will throw off a musket ball'.[30] Another of these strongholds in the troubled times of 1875 was 'the Maharaja Lela's own dwelling, a large and comparatively new building of more than ordinarily substantial kind, round which he had for months past been digging a great ditch and throwing up a formidable earthwork crowned by a palisade'.[31] Alas! it never stood a siege and the Maharaja Lela left it in tears, knowing that the vengeful British would burn it.[32]

Not everyone of rank had a large house, however. The house of the principal wife of Raja (later Sultan) Abdullah of Perak was 'a very modest dwelling . . . a building of mat sides and thatched roof raised from the damp and muddy earth on wooden piles, a flight of steps led into the front of the house and a ladder served for exit at the back. The interior accommodation consisted of a closed-in verandah, one large room, and a kitchen tacked on behind.'[33] So also Abdullah Munshi, visiting one of the Kelantan *raja* wrote 'I couldn't see any difference between his house and its surroundings and those of the peasants—they were as alike as two pins'.[34]

The essential difference, whether the house was large or small, was that an aristocrat had a domestic staff and a following. Even Raja Mahmud, living in straitened circumstances at Sepang, dwelt among a group of four families, 'Raja Mahmud's own people and followers'.[35] As in the household of a ruler there were female domestics, but there was less elaborate organization of their duties. One was described as 'a sort of maid-of-all-work and general drudge ... when not employed in the house cooking, sewing, pounding rice, or carrying water—at every one's beck and call—she was made to work in the ricefields; hoeing, planting, reaping or gleaning, according to the season'.[36] The ending of debt-bondage did not entirely disperse the domestic staff from aristocratic households. Some at least remained, from force of habit and having nowhere else to go as much as under the inducement of a wage.[37]

The upper class, like the peasants, tended to build more elaborate houses when the resources became available. A man born in 1907 in the house of his grandfather, a territorial chief in Negeri Sembilan, remembers it as one of the largest houses in the district, with a central room which had sixteen pillars to support the roof, roofed with tiles, and a cooking 'range' in the kitchen.[38] Yet its design was still essentially in the traditional pattern.

In places where there had been fighting during the civil wars the magnates continued for some time to live in baronial style. One such area was Ulu Selangor, in which the invading Pahang forces stayed on for many years after the fighting of 1872–3.[39] When Douglas visited one of the Pahang chiefs 'a somewhat irregular salute was fired from some old guns in honour of our arrival', and when he departed his host escorted him, carrying 'a long sword and a revolver'. The Datuk Panglima Garang, who outlasted the rest, was eventually absorbed into the Selangor establishment as *penghulu* of Ulu Selangor. But it was not a task for which he was well suited; he went off on trading expeditions and was far from impartial in dealing with the people under his charge.[40] One may contrast the reception of W. E. Maxwell by Che Karim in the equally remote Selama district of Perak in 1876. Che Karim's background was commercial rather than martial. Maxwell related that 'sitting on a comfortable carpet spread in the narrow room, which forms the front of most Malay houses, Che Karim and I discussed native politics, to the accompaniment of some very good tea (the milk was Swiss, the biscuits English)'.[41]

In general, the Malay upper class retained the essential features of the traditional house and furnishings, but made use of new materials and found new uses for them. In 1874 the *istana* of Sultan Abdul Samad of Selangor was built of squared timbers, had a tiled roof, and was 'raised from the muddy ground on short brick pillars'. The compound was surrounded by a stout fence and the entrance to it closed by a strong gate.[42] In more peaceful times he moved to Jugra hill, where his new residence comprised three separate buildings, linked by a passage, and appropriated as his personal quarters (approached through a porch), his audience hall (*balai*) and the 'womens' [*sic*] house or harem'. The porch was 'a convenient reception room' where the ruler gave interviews to European callers.[43]

The interior of the rambling residence of a ruler or chief could be dark and claustrophobic. Clifford described the *istana* at Pekan as: 'a sort of rabbit-warren of a place, with narrow crooked passages, the floors of yielding bamboo laths, the walls of plaited wattle and it was so dark that it was with difficulty that Saleh could see his way [to] a big room, the centre of which was filled by a great square platform raised about two feet above the level of the floor. Upon this was spread a flock sleeping mat, covered with crimson silk, with a stack of square impossible-looking pillows piled at its head, and with ample curtains looped up into untidy, twisted knots.' There was no other furniture except a 'vast brass vessel . . . intended for a spittoon'.[44]

When Isabella Bird paid a courtesy call on the principal wife of Sultan Abdul Samad at Kuala Langat, she was received in an apartment divided off by heavy silk curtains. At one end was a two-tier dais covered with fine mats and with Persian carpets. They all sat on chairs. 'Two guards sat on the floor just within the door, and numbers of women, some of them in white veils, followers of the Sultana, sat in rows also on the floor.'[45]

The price which aristocratic women paid for their higher rank and freedom from domestic chores, was confinement within the silken walls of their quarters. It was a boring and sometimes frustrating existence.

A claim by a chief for compensation for property looted from his house by a raiding party provides an interesting list of the possessions of a fairly well-to-do Malay aristocrat whose tastes were more European than some of his contemporaries. Apart from the loss of cannon, muskets, spears, swords and gunpowder, the property taken or destroyed included eight bronze hanging lamps, two wall lamps, a large round ship's clock, a large Turkish carpet and five or six smaller carpets, a large gong and two smaller ones, five boxes of cloths, some tables and chairs, and various gold ornaments and items of jewellery.[46] Only a small minority of the upper class went so far as to adopt a predominantly Western style of living.[47]

In their dress the Malays showed the same artistry and variety, blending tradition and innovation. Fashions varied and changed so much that Sultan Idris of Perak once gave his state council a fascinating review of the subject, concluding that 'Malay costume might be anything and everything'.[48]

Yet there were certain overriding rules on dress. 'Islam is against nakedness, be it of arms, legs or body; it looks on dress as meant to be decent ... and insists that garments shall be loose and as unsuggestive of bodily shape as they can be.'[49] The main application of this rule to masculine attire was that the wearer must, by his dress, avoid any suggestion of the existence of his private parts. The original Malay garment around the middle was the *sarung* worn as a waist cloth.[50] This was quite sufficient for decency unless a man was likely by his exertions to reveal his body beneath. As a fight was essentially an athletic encounter of rapid movement, a warrior put on trousers in preparation for a fight. If, in a situation of conflict, a man did not wear or don trousers, it was—like failure to carry arms—interpreted as a sign of cowardice. Trousers (*seluar*) had been introduced by Indian Muslims to South-East Asia via Aceh as Middle Eastern 'baggy garments with trouser legs extending to below the knee'. Later came trousers of European type with a much tighter fit. If a Malay man wore trousers of this type, decency required that he should wear a *sarung* over them.[51] In one of Clifford's stories of late nineteenth-century Pahang, an officious police constable, in uniform trousers or shorts, is put to shame when a bystander addresses him as 'man without a waist skirt'.[52]

The ordinary costume of a man also included 'a short loose jacket of silk or cotton' (*baju*).[53] However, propriety did not require that a man should wear a jacket and he often dispensed with it, especially when at work. In Kelantan 'that garment is never used, except by the nobles on official occasions'.[54] It is significant that Emily Innes, describing Sultan Abdul Samad's habit of carrying and not wearing a jacket, says that he was 'hardly distinguishable from an old Malay peasant'.[55]

The cut and style of a man's jacket reflected many foreign influences. The Chinese style was double-breasted and tied at the waist: down the front there were frogged buttons. The Dutch style was high at the neck and tight at the wrist.[56]

Another part of a man's dress in which tradition and high fashion might blend or conflict, was the headgear of a square headcloth (*saputangan* or *tengkolok*). There was 'much rivalry' in the choice of patterns in the cloth, and even more care was given to the way the headcloth was folded. 'Sometimes with one point waxed and sticking up; sometimes with two points aloft; sometimes prominent in front; sometimes protruding behind . . . it could be made to convey a hint of a man's rank or even a promise of "unchanging love" to someone whom the wearer was anxious to court.'[57] These of course were the affectations of men of status on occasions of display. The peasant wore a casually folded cloth to shade his head from the sun. An old man might wear a black skullcap and a *haji* was entitled to sport a turban of Arab style. The modern Malay cap (*songkok*) is considered later.

At the other extremity of the body, Malay peasants did not usually wear shoes on their feet but 'people with means liked to wear them as a sign of superiority'.[58] The peasant, if he wore any footgear at all, had only rough sandals but a Malay gentleman, especially if he had occasion to don Arab robes, wore sandals or loose slippers of the appropriate kind.[59]

For a woman a *sarung* hitched up under the armpits to fall loosely over her body down to the knees sufficed as the minimum for decency. Girls up to the age of eleven and women in the privacy of their own house need wear this much only.[60] To expose the bare shoulders in a public place was apparently considered immodest but not indecent. During the period of Muslim puritanism in Kelantan in the 1890s, women who appeared in this fashion were liable to have black resin daubed on their exposed shoulders.[61] To avoid the reproach of immodesty a woman, on leaving the house, put over her shoulders—sometimes over her head to fall over her shoulders—a veil (*selendang* or *tudung*). If she met a male stranger she might draw it across the lower part of her face. The effect was not always modest—'they however display a good deal of the upper part of the body, only throwing their upper dress, which is a narrow piece of cloth, carelessly across the breast'. At the lower end a woman might put on a second *sarung* hanging from the waist so that she was covered from head to ankles.[62]

Although this style of women's clothing is seen in photographs taken in the twentieth century, it seems that many women had adopted the alternative of a jacket or coat on the upper part of the body and a *sarung* from the waist to the lower leg.[63] In its original form, the feminine tunic (*baju kurung*) had no opening in front and was pulled over the head like a loose jersey. As a minimum length it fell to cover the top of the *sarung* at the waist, but it could be longer 'reaching to a little above the ankle, its cuffs fastened with buttons of gold and sometimes with diamonds'. This was a common form of apparel in Melaka in the mid-nineteenth century. Then, if not before, feminine fashion—in the towns at least—substituted the long, flowing tunic-coat (*kebaya*) or a tunic (*baju belah*) which was divided in front, put on like a coat and fastened with brooches, which were part of the wearer's jewellery. Winstedt suggests that the *baju kurung* lost favour because it disarranged the hair when put on or taken off. He also says that the *kebaya* was worn out of doors and the short open jacket, which he calls '*baju jipun*', was 'now universally worn by women' indoors.[64] The *kebaya* was not always a becoming garment. Thomson, viewing some plain girls, adds unkindly that 'their figures were not improved by being encased in a long *baju* or species of bottomless sack which envelopes the whole body, and flattens, distorts or conceals the shape'.[65]

When dressing for a special or public occasion, a Malay woman put on her jewellery—brooches to fasten the tunic, pins in her hair, rings, bracelets, etc. The ladies were 'not above the use of powder on their faces' and in the SS towns 'seldom appear abroad without a European umbrella or parasol'.[66] Wilkinson tells a story of a group of Perak ladies invited to a royal wedding in Pahang who came prepared for 'the purpose of outshining the Pahang ladies in the matter of silks and diamonds'. Not to be outmanoeuvred, their hostesses stipulated that at the wedding all should appear in 'ancient Pahang costume; no jewellery'.[67]

More typical, however, of the dress of both sexes—of the peasant class—on a working day, is Clifford's account of 'a party of Malay weeders, men and women' in Pahang in 1897. They 'were all dressed in upper garments of coarse cotton stuff, dyed blue with indigo. The men wore short trousers of bleached cotton, stained all imaginable colours by much wear ... the women wore their skirts hanging from waist to ankle ... both men and women alike wore cotton sarongs twisted turban-wise about their heads' hanging down to protect their necks and backs from the sun as they stooped at work.[68]

James Low estimated that in the 1830s 'a substantial *rakyat* ... will wear out yearly 2 sarongs, two long sashes called *kain panjang*, two bajus or jackets, 2 pairs of pantaloons, two kerchiefs, two handkerchiefs besides keeping by him a complete festival suit of clothes'. The finery of a woman would include a *sarung* of silk with gold thread, costing $30–40, gold earrings costing $15 per set; an oblong sash buckle 'often set with stones of small value' worth between $20 and $60; gold hair pins worth $3–6 and 'gold or silver rings set with precious stones of moderate value'.[69] The difference between these prized possessions of a woman of the 'yeoman class' and those of her aristocratic sister, as described above, lay in the individual value of the trinkets. They were of much the same type in either case.

Apart from class distinctions clothes served to display differences of occupation. The full 'rig' of the fighting man was unmistakable.[70] Apart from the trousers, essential for decency, he wore a tight tunic under his loose jacket, a sword belt over his sash into which two or three *keris* were thrust, and usually shoes or sandals in case his opponents had placed sharp spines (*ranjau*) on the line of approach—or retreat.[71]

For the returned pilgrim to Mecca, the great day of the year was *Hari Raya Haji* when he donned Arab clothes to display his status. A *raja* who was not a *haji* might demonstrate exceptional piety by similar sartorial splendour but this was considered rather affected.

Malay sailors were well known for their conspicuous style of dress—and seem to have been uninhibited by the general ban on tight trousers. 'The nautical Malay adopts the English trousers, and wears them so tight to the skin, that every movement on his part threatens to send the buttons flying.' One Malay sailor was such a dandy that he had twenty-seven 'monkey jackets'. It was said that 'their vests generally are made of silk, satin or velvet, with edging and lining of other colours, gilt buttons, green pantaloons, glengarry caps, several sashes of different gay colours, flashy handkerchiefs etc'.[72]

The Malay seamen, described above, could abandon the traditional conventions on Malay dress because they served on European ships and came ashore at cosmopolitan ports. The Malay student at an English-language school was also outside his normal cultural environment, and tempted to imitate European fashions, much admired at this period. 'The young Malays, who may be educated by Europeans, adopt the trousers, socks, shirts and boots of their teachers, and to show that they are not completely converted, they wear the *kebaya* or rather loose Arab cloak and turban.'[73] In the towns of the FMS in the 1890s young Malays appeared in the new garments required at *Hari Raya*—but with a difference—'stiff shirt collar and polished black shoes' but with trouser ends tucked into their socks. At the top end they wore a 'gorgeously embroidered smoking cap' and 'blue tinted goggles'.[74]

In these touches, as in much else, one senses a conflict between an inclination to adopt European clothing and a need to preserve a Malay identity. The story of Malay headgear illustrates a tendency to adaptation. As described above, the traditional headgear for a Malay man was an elaborately folded 'headkerchief' or a workaday head-cloth. Towards the end of the century, it became common for rulers and other notables to appear in public in European suits. But they also took to wearing the Turkish tarboosh which had Islamic associations. When Sultan Abu Bakar of Johor entertained European guests at dinner, he wore 'his best black velvet tarboosh with a still more magnificent *aigrette* enriched with the Johor star and crescent in brilliants'.[75] When Tunku Kudin of Kedah, living in exile in Penang, took his evening drive he passed through Penang 'in a brougham drawn by a pair of prancing bays, his two coachmen in livery and fez perched on the high seat'.[76] It may be that the general adoption of the tarboosh—the '*songkok Turki*'—encouraged the Malay middle class to wear the *songkok*, a modified form, as formal headgear.[77]

An earlier chapter described the example set by Sultan Sulaiman of Selangor (r.1898–1938). Malay traditions of decency impelled him to wear a *sarung* over the European suit in which he generally appeared.[78] This was not unusual; Florence Caddy wrote that 'white or black jacket and a sarong is the costume of Malays of the upper class'.[79] At the funeral of his grandfather in 1898, Sultan Sulaiman appeared as chief mourner on a ceremonial state occasion 'in a black suit, sarong round waist, silk socks, silk shirt and pumps with a black head cloth'.[80] Although he wore a head-cloth, it was of black instead of the conventional Malay mourning colour, which was white.[81] At his installation, postponed until 1903, he wore 'green and white' at the first public ceremony, and 'robes of state' at the coronation in the *istana*.[82]

There were of course individual eccentricities of dress. It was not usual at this period, though it sometimes happened, that a ruler appeared in European-style military uniform.[83] One also reads of a village headman who decked out his son for a circumcision ceremony with a laurel wreath on his brow 'made entirely of the leaves of the coconut tree'.[84]

After houses and dress we come to the third main element in the

Malay life-style—meals.[85] For all classes the basic foodstuff was rice, cooked with care so that the water in the pot simmered rather than boiled. Rice was supplemented by fish or occasionally meat (*lauk*), vegetables, either cooked (*sayur*) or uncooked (*hulam*), and sometimes condiments (*sambal*). It was Malay custom to cook and consume a meal at convenient times and not at a fixed hour. In a peasant household, however, the family normally took a light meal soon after rising at dawn, a more substantial meal between 8.00 a.m. and 10.00 a.m., and another in the late evening between 7.00 p.m. and 10.00 p.m. If the family were alone they might eat together in the kitchen. A well-to-do family would eat 'in one of the middle rooms' of the house. If there were guests, the men ate on the verandah and the women in the central room.[86]

At all meals, however simple and informal, there were rules of etiquette to observe. Before beginning to eat 'the right hand must be washed and thoroughly cleansed' as it was this hand which must be used to take food from the dish to the mouth.[87] It was extreme bad manners to eat with the left hand. After washing 'each person then says, "*Bismillah hirahman irraheem*"—"In the name of God, the compassionate, the merciful" and proceeds to eat'.[88] 'There is very little ceremony . . . the rice is put in a large plate or bowl, with dried fish or curry in small cups which are placed on a mat spread on the floor, and four or five eat of the same dish, each helping himself to curry as needed. Water is always placed handy in pots.'[89] The men sat cross-legged (*bersila*) and the women with both legs bent back together at one side (*bertimpoh*).[90]

On a special occasion, such as a village feast (*kenduri*) for a religious occasion or a wedding, the guests were seated in groups, each supplied with appropriate dishes. It was permissible to use a spoon (*sudu*) to take meat or fish from the central dish to mix with the rice on an individual plate from which the food, rolled into a ball, was carried by the fingers to the mouth. Malays regarded their habit of eating with the fingers as much cleaner than the European use of implements.[91] When Emily Innes entertained a Malay chief, he 'apologised gracefully for eating with his fingers, saying he was an old man and could not learn new ways'. He added that he did not 'know the history of this fork. It has been in a hundred, perhaps a thousand mouths.'[92]

At the end of the meal, water was poured over the right hand to cleanse it and it was wiped dry on a towel.[93] If it was a feast, the host then supplied the materials for making a betel quid for chewing or, if it was the harvest season, some *pulut* rice.

Betel chewing was until late in the nineteenth century an essential part of Malay life, to which ritual or traditional importance often attached. Norman, travelling by raft on the Kelantan River in 1894, relates that 'every now and then the rowers would lay down their oars . . . and . . . would remark with a smile "*Makan pinang, tuan*", literally "Eat betel, sir." The little pot of *chunam* or lime, would be produced, a *sireh* leaf selected and coated with it, a bit of betel-nut chipped off and rolled in the leaf, and the package chewed with every sign of gratification and refreshment. The *pinang* is to the Malay what the cigarette and brandy-and-soda are to the Englishman at home.'[94]

The peasant kept his materials in simple containers. But in upper-class society, and especially in royal households, the betel casket (*bekas* or *tempat sirih*) was a work of art made of silver and prized as an heirloom. The offer of betel had a symbolic significance in diplomacy. Even among villagers it was part of the delicate preliminaries to arranging a betrothal. 'What could be more innocent than the position of the little silver vase containing the *sirih* that is offered to a visitor? Yet if this vase is upset and left lying on its side, the quick-eyed enquirer knows that his quest is useless; the lady's people do not desire the marriage.'[95]

As with some other elements of Malay culture, the symbolic use of betel outlasted its general consumption. Swettenham wrote in 1900 that 'the practice is now in many places becoming confined to old people. The teeth of the betel-chewer become black, and the "new woman" of Malaya has determined that black teeth do not improve her appearance; while the Malay youth, who smokes either the home-made or the foreign cigarette, has no craving for the astringent flavour of the areca-nut, and looks with less than admiration at the crimson lips and blackened teeth of his old folks.'[96]

Apart from the humdrum routine of family meals, there were special occasions to celebrate by giving a feast and entertaining one's neighbours or other guests. In the last months of 1875 the Maharaja Lela, chief of Pasir Salak in Perak, gave at least three feasts. Sultan Abdullah came to Pasir Salak, when the chief celebrated the ear-piercing of his daughter and the festivities included a *ma'yong* performed by local dancers. The great Islamic feast of *Hari Raya* fell at the beginning of November and the Maharaja Lela gave a feast to his people early that day to celebrate the end of the month of fasting. The next day saw the death of Birch at Pasir

Salak. On the day following, the chief gave another feast to celebrate the elimination—so he thought—of alien oppression. Yet tension was already rising; 'there were only men present, all the women ran away to a place far inland'.[97]

There were many humbler occasions for a feast. Family events such as the birth of a child in a peasant family, the puberty ceremonies of sons and daughters, a wedding or a funeral, were usually marked by a feast. There were also Islamic occasions to be celebrated.[98] So far as one can judge from the extant accounts, there was little change in the manner or regularity of these festivities. Yet there were subtler alterations of attitude. What had been done because its due observance was deeply significant, was continued because it was conventional and a source of enjoyable entertainment.[99] Wilkinson deplored the tendency to introduce 'improvements of a most deadly character.... Anyone who attends a modern Malay ceremony, be it a wedding or an ear-boring or even the installation of a prince, will be struck by the inevitable confusion between the new and the old. Not even Malay conservatism will suffice to preserve the old customs of the country from the disintegrating influence of modern improvements.'[100] In this comment Wilkinson shows less sympathetic insight than is his wont. Custom which lives is custom which changes.

Not every change was for the worse. There will be no regret for the passing of the cruel practice of filing down a girl's teeth to one-quarter of their original height on the eve of marriage—'a peculiarly harsh and unpleasant sensation'.[101] There were equally gruesome rituals of purification for the mother after the birth of a child, including roasting her over a fire. Skeat says that 'on one occasion a poor woman was brought to the point of death' and, in fact, she went out of her mind for several months.[102] It was the custom and it cannot have been a unique consequence.

Other innovations were harmless enough. The traditional method of inviting a guest to a ceremony was to call on him in person or to send a messenger to perform that office. Then upper-class Malay society adopted the European formality of issuing printed invitation cards. However, the significance of the letters 'RSVP' was less readily understood. 'Most Malays do not trouble to reply ... they come or do not come to attend the party after receiving the invitation as they like or as circumstances dictate.'[103]

The last topic of this chapter is transport. Enough has been said in previous chapters of the horse-drawn carriage and of the bullock-cart and bullock-bus. The late nineteenth century was also a period of railway construction in western Malaya. But to judge from the absence of mention of trains in contemporary records, few Malays ventured on to these steaming monsters. They watched them hurtle—at perhaps 30 miles an hour—past their villages and derisively called them '*kereta sombong*'—too proud for us.[104]

The domesticated elephant was in its day a useful means of transport, and the story of its gradual displacement incidentally illustrates the adaptability of Malay culture. Although the wild elephant lived its sometimes destructive life in Malayan forests, it is probable that the art of capturing and taming it came to Malaya from elsewhere centuries ago.[105] In the heroic age of the fifteenth-century Melaka Sultanate, the tame elephant had ceremonial and perhaps warlike uses. The last ruler of Melaka rode out to meet the Portuguese invaders in 1511 mounted on his war elephant.[106] By the nineteenth century the use of elephants had declined but it was still an essential and prestigious form of overland transport in some parts of Malaya.[107] It moved at no more than 3 miles per hour and travelled only 15 miles in a day, but it could get through almost pathless country.[108] A ride on an elephant was less exhausting than plodding on foot 'over the roots, through the thorns, wading or swimming rivers and streams, ploughing through miles of bogs and mud in the heat and the rain, stung by everything that stings (their name is legion)'.[109] The elephant was a very sagacious mount, which tested the strength of an improvised bridge before putting its weight on it and balancing its way along a single fallen tree trunk across a swamp.[110]

None the less, a ride on an elephant over jungle paths was usually very uncomfortable. Passengers were carried in 'a pair of rattan panniers slung across the animal's back by stout cords'. Only 'when women or persons of rank are carried, a dome-shaped hood or cover, is placed over the panniers'.[111] From the many European travellers' tales, take Isabella Bird, whose elephant squirted muddy water 'with a loud noise over himself and his riders . . . when I hit him with my umbrella he uttered the loudest roar I ever heard'.[112] There were of course Malay mahouts, like river boatmen, a caste apart, who communicated with their beasts by a special language—'Hee' means 'Quick' and 'Haw', 'Stop'.[113]

The use of the elephant was limited to 'people of consideration' who travelled in northern Malaya. In Selangor and further south, there were wild elephants in the jungle but they were not captured and tamed.[114] The geographic limit strengthens the theory that this was a culture trait borrowed from Siam. Apart from the tradition which restricted the use of elephants to rulers and aristocrats, it was beyond the resources of a peasant to capture, tame or maintain them. In the first stage of trapping elephants a large number of men built a stockade of jungle logs, 20 or 25 feet long and sunk in the ground to a depth of 5 feet or so, lashed together with rattans and buttressed with more jungle logs. Into this vast trap the beaters cautiously edged the elephant herd. There was a serious risk that the enraged animals would turn back, trampling or goring their pursuers as they escaped. Once trapped by the dropping of the huge gate, the female elephants were isolated, hobbled and 'confined by ropes in strong timber stalls, and behind the ears stout timber uprights prevented the head being drawn back'.[115] By this means, 'with painstaking exactness' over a period of months, continued imprisonment and occasional kindness broke the spirit of the animal and it could then be taught to work. Male elephants might be similarly subdued, but they were often killed at once since the ivory of their tusks would fetch as much as the live animal when tamed. In captivity mortality was high; the tight bonds often caused wounds in the skin which easily became gangrenous. That also could happen if the working harness chafed the skin.[116]

Only a ruler or other magnate could mobilize men for *kerah* work of this kind, and so the capture of elephants was a 'sport of kings'. When J. W. W. Birch came to Blanja in March 1875, he found that Sultan Ismail was absent 'and is said to have gone to capture elephants at Kampar'.[117] To maintain an elephant it was necessary to employ a mahout and to feed it; an elephant ate about thirty coconut fronds each day.[118] Although the use of elephants as personal transport continued into the 1880s—Weld rode on elephants when he visited Perak[119]—the more convenient pony or horse-drawn vehicle was beginning to displace it.[120]

The use of the elephant to move goods also had a long history, and this continued to the end of the nineteenth century. In 1875 Birch found that Sultan Ismail 'keeps his elephants, or some of them here, ready to be hired out when anyone wants them. $2 to this place from Gopeng for 100 *gantangs*, and $2½ for 4 *pikuls* of tin.'[121] An elephant could carry as much as half a ton of tin but Birch's figure, equivalent to about a quarter of a ton, was more general.[122] In 1877 the value of an elephant was about $300–50.[123] Later on, the Malay plutocrats of Kinta hired out their elephants to

Chinese miners but set the rate of charge so high that the miners found it cheaper to employ labourers to push wheelbarrows.[124] The high rate of charge for the use of elephants may well have been due in part to the growing scarcity of wild elephants for trapping in Perak. The State Council found it necessary to restrict trapping by a licensing system.[125] Perak imported elephants from Raman to the north, which was a main centre of elephant taming, but competition from abroad forced up the price. In 1902 Indian importers were sending their mahouts to Penang to offer as much as $1,000 for an elephant and there was also a demand from zoos and menageries in the West.[126]

Although the elephant had ceased to be an economic means of transport by 1900, its ceremonial use continued into the 1920s. In 1909 the FMS Federal Council held its inaugural meeting at Kuala Kangsar. Sultan Idris arrived riding at the head of a procession of fifty elephants—Cecil B. de Mille, making a Hollywood spectacular, could hardly have done more.[127] As late as 1922 when Sultan Iskander, son of Sultan Idris, brought the King of Thailand to visit the Malay College at Kuala Kangsar, they rode in together on 'a grandly caparisoned elephant with a beautifully decorated howdah on its back'.[128] Yet this was not the same as in former times. The stately ride was a preservation of a cherished tradition but it was also a conscious revival of the pageantry of the past. That was something new.

1. R. N. Hilton, 'The Basic Malay House', *JMBRAS*, 29(3), 1956. See also R. O. Winstedt, 'The Circumstances of Malay Life: The Kampong, The House, Furniture, Dress, Food', *Papers on Malay Subjects, Life and Customs*, Part 1, 1909; reprinted 1925, pp. 1–30 (hereafter cited as 'Malay House'), not included in P. L. Burns (ed.), *Papers on Malay Subjects*, Kuala Lumpur, Oxford University Press, 1971.

2. Winstedt, 'Malay House', p. 14.

3. Hilton, op. cit., *passim*, gives an excellent account, with a number of drawings and illustrations, of the various types of Malay house. R. O. Noone, 'Notes on the Kampong, Compounds and Houses of the Patani Malay Village of Banggul Ara, in the Mukim of Batu Kurau, Northern Perak', *JMBRAS*, 21(1), 1948, is a detailed description of the houses of a particular village with drawings. J. R. Logan, 'Five Days in Naning', *JIA*, 3, 1849, pp. 28–9, gives a very detailed account of a headman's house in Naning in the mid-nineteenth century. The passage which follows in the main text is concerned with the use of a Malay house rather than its structural details. On groups of houses see p. 98 above; on *kampung*, see R. J.

Wilkinson, *A Malay–English Dictionary*, 2 parts, Singapore, Kelly & Walsh, 1901 (revised as *A Malay–English Dictionary (Romanised)*, 2 parts, Mytilene, Salavopoulos & Kinderlis, 1932), Pt. 1, p. 503.

4. I. H. N. Evans, 'Ethnological Miscellanea—Setting up the Posts of a Malay House', *Journal of the FMS Museum*, 7(4), 1918, p. 211. W. W. Skeat, *Malay Magic: Being an Introduction to the Folklore and Popular Religion of the Malay Peninsula*, London, Macmillan, 1900, reprinted Singapore, Oxford University Press, 1984, pp. 141–6.

5. O. Cavenagh, *Reminiscences of an Indian Official*, London, W. H. Allen & Co., 1884, p. 316.

6. J. F. A. McNair, *Perak and the Malays: Sarong and Keris*, London, Tinsley Bros., 1878, reprinted Kuala Lumpur, Oxford University Press, 1972, p. 164.

7. C. S. Hurgronje, *The Achehnese*, translated by A. W. S. O'Sullivan, London, Luzac, 1906, Vol. 1, p. 42. Hilton, op. cit., p. 137, in describing a modern house built of squared timber with mortise joints, tightened with wedges, brings out very clearly how the intersections and joints are placed to give complete rigidity and stability to the framework.

8. Hilton, op. cit., p. 139. I. H. Burkill, *A Dictionary of the Economic Products of the Malay Peninsula*, 2 vols., London, published on behalf of the SS and FMS Governments, Crown Agents, 1935, p. 1558. It was possible to combine a steep roof of the central room with a flatter extension roof to cover the verandah and kitchen.

9. W. T. Hornaday, *Two Years in the Jungle: The Experiences of a Hunter and Naturalist in India, Ceylon, the Malay Peninsula and Borneo*, New York, Scribner, 1885, p. 304.

10. Hilton, op. cit., p. 137.

11. T. J. Newbold, *Political and Statistical Account of the British Settlements ... with a History of the Malayan States on the Peninsula in the Straits of Malacca*, 2 vols., London, Murray, 1839, reprinted as *British Settlements in the Straits of Malacca*, Kuala Lumpur, Oxford University Press, 1971, Vol. 2, p. 194; Noone, op. cit., p. 126. However, in 1879 Raja Muda Yusuf proposed to the Perak State Council that a large house should be moved from Bukit Gantang and re-erected at Sayong (*FSCM*, 4 March 1879, *PMS*, p. 195). In 1953 the Malayan High Court recognized 'the customary principle that the Malay-style wooden house resting on stilts is movable not immovable property' (M. B. Hooker, *Islamic Law in South-East Asia*, Singapore, Oxford University Press, 1984, p. 142, citing *Kiah binte Hanapiah* v. *Som binte Hanapiah* [1953] MLJ 82). 'The whole house belongs in Aceh to the category of movable property' (Hurgronje, *The Achehnese*, p. 42).

12. Noone, op. cit., p. 132. Winstedt, 'Malay House', p. 18, mentions the use of 'improved materials' but he adds that 'the vast majority of huts are still untouched or touched but imperceptibly by modern influences'. Against this, one must set W. E. Maxwell, who said in 1891 that 'good plank walls and floors are now much more often seen in their houses than in the old times' (P. H. Kratoska (ed.), *Honourable Intentions: Talks on the British Empire in South-East Asia Delivered at the Royal Colonial Institute 1874–1928*, Singapore, Oxford University Press, 19[illegible], p. 140, reprinting the *Proceedings of the Royal Colonial Institute*, 1891).

13. T. Braddell, 'Notes of a Trip to the Interior of Malacca', *JIA*, 7, 1853, p. 104.

14. Winstedt, 'Malay House', p. 18.

15. *SJ*, 21 October 1892 and 4 October 1895.

16. Skeat, *Malay Magic*, p. 38.

17. See p. 22 above on chairs.

18. J. Low, *A Dissertation on the Soil and Agriculture of the British Settlement of Penang or Prince of Wales Island in the Straits of Malacca including Province Wellesley on the Malayan Peninsula ..., with ... Incidental Observations, etc.*, Singapore, Singapore Free Press, 1836, reprinted as *The British Settlement at Penang*, Singapore, Oxford University Press, 1972, p. 87.

19. 'Rice Cultivation Report 1893', p. 158, where W. E. Maxwell, who also knew the Province Wellesley of his day very well, cites James Low at length. In giving a long and detailed list of Malay domestic utensils and furnishings, Winstedt, 'Malay House', pp. 19–30, adds 'not a tithe of them will be found in the ordinary house'.

20. Winstedt, 'Malay House', pp. 19–29, lists these among other items. 'Chinese earthenware' at p. 23.

21. E. Innes, *The Chersonese with the Gilding Off*, 2 vols., London, Richard Bentley, 1885, reprinted Kuala Lumpur, Oxford University Press, 1974, Vol. 1, p. 179.

22. Winstedt, 'Malay House', p. 19. He was Assistant Inspector of Schools, Perak, in the early years of the twentieth century; later he became Assistant Director and then Director of Education, SS and FMS.

23. Ibid., pp. 1–2, discusses Hurgronje's theories.

24. Hilton, op. cit., p. 136, on the east–west axis, which was the traditional orientation. At p. 143 he discusses how 'accretions' (additions to the original structure) were placed.

25. Report by W. E. Maxwell, dated 17 November 1875, enclosed with SSD 2 December 1875, printed in Cmd. 1505.

26. Winstedt, 'Malay House', pp. 3 and 5.

27. H. C. Clifford, *Studies in Brown Humanity being Scrawls and Smudges in Sepia, White and Yellow*, London, Grant Richards, 1898, p. 49.

28. Winstedt, 'Malay House', p. 7.

29. F. A. Swettenham, *The Real Malay: Pen Pictures*, London, John Lane Bodley Head, 1900, pp. 191–2. 'A large brick house at Permatang' (*PSCM*, 4 March 1879, *PMS*, pp. 192–3).

30. McNair, op. cit., p. 168.

31. F. A. Swettenham, *Malay Sketches*, London, John Lane Bodley Head, 1895, p. 235. The fortification of this house was one of the main topics considered in the evidence (of intention) at the trial of the Maharaja Lela for the murder of Birch (SSD 11 January 1877).

32. See p. 74 above and J. M. Gullick, *Indigenous Political Systems of Western Malaya*, London, Athlone Press, 1958, pp. 106–7.

33. Swettenham, *Malay Sketches*, p. 184, where—under the thin disguise of different names—he tells the story of the elopement of the wife of Sultan Abdullah with Raja Daud of Selangor.

34. Abdullah bin Abdul Kadir, Munshi, *Kesah Pelayaran Abdullah*, translated by A. E. Coope, *The Voyage of Abdullah: A Translation from the Malay*, Singapore, Malay Publishing House, 1949, p. 50.

35. Douglas Diary, 19 June 1881. See p. 82 above on the career of Raja Mahmud.

36. Swettenham, *The Real Malay*, p. 187.

37. See p. 214 below.

38. Datuk Mohamed Said, *Memoirs of a Menteri Besar: Early Days*, Singapore, Heinemann, 1982, p. 2.

39. W. Linehan, 'A History of Pahang' (hereafter cited as 'Pahang'), *JMBRAS*, 14(2), 1936, pp. 99–100.

40. Douglas Diary, 23 and 24 July 1876 and 24 July 1879. He was still *penghulu* of Ulu Selangor in 1882 (SSD 28 May 1883).

41. W. E. Maxwell, 'A Journey on Foot to the Patani Frontier in 1876, being a Journal Kept during an Expedition Undertaken to Capture Datoh Maharajah Lela of Perak', *JSBRAS*, 9, 1882, p. 8. On Che Karim see p. 79 above.

42. Swettenham, *The Real Malay*, p. 65.

43. I. L. Bird, *The Golden Chersonese and the Way Thither*, London, Murray, 1883, reprinted Kuala Lumpur, Oxford University Press, 1967, and 1980, p. 230. It would be inappropriate to describe the European furniture, including a piano, since much of this had been foisted on the ruler by Bloomfield Douglas (SSD 24 August 1882). A. B. Rathborne, *Camping and Tramping in Malaya: Fifteen Years' Pioneering in the Native States of the Malay Peninsula*, London, Swan Sonnenschein, 1898, reprinted Singapore, Oxford University Press, 1984, p. 112, has a photograph taken in front of the *balai*, of which some details can be seen in the background.

44. H. C. Clifford, *A Prince of Malaya*, New York, Harper, 1926 (originally published as 'Sally' in *Blackwoods Magazine*, February 1904, and *Saleh: A Sequel*, London, Blackwood, 1908), p. 140, is here plainly describing the *istana* at Pekan, where the second part of the novel is set (under the fictitious name of 'Pelesu' instead of 'Pahang'). At p. 143 he describes the room of the ruler's principal wife, which was similar but smaller and darker, stuffy and lit only by a lamp.

45. Bird, op. cit., p. 233.

46. SSD 23 February 1883. The owner of these possessions was the ruling chief of Tampin, a district of Negeri Sembilan, adjoining the frontier of Melaka, where the chief had a town house inherited from his father, who had lived there before him. On the background see J. M. Gullick, 'The Tampin Succession', *JMBRAS*, 49(2), 1976.

47. See pp. 54 and 80 above.

48. R. J. Wilkinson, 'Some Malay Studies', *JMBRAS*, 10(1), 1932, p. 89. The State Council was considering a proposal that all Malay officials in Perak should be required to wear the *songkok* at their place of work. The Sultan and the other Malay members of the Council were wearing, as was their habit, European suits and so found it difficult to insist on others adopting Malay headgear. Wilkinson follows his anecdote with a note on Malay dress. R. O. Winstedt, 'The Circumstances of Malay Life ... Dress', *PMS*, *Life and Customs*, Part 1, 1909, reprinted 1925 (hereafter cited as Winstedt, 'Malay Dress'); J. R. Logan, 'The Manners and Customs of the Malays: Dress', *JIA*, 3, 1849 (hereafter cited as 'Manners and Customs: Malay Dress'); and J. D. Vaughan, 'Notes on the Malays of Pinang and Province Wellesley', *JIA*, n.s., 2, 1857, also describe Malay dress in some detail. As with houses, the purpose of the passage in the text which follows is to examine the social aspects of dress rather than its details.

49. Wilkinson, 'Some Malay Studies', p. 90.

50. Wilkinson, *1932 Dictionary*, Pt. 2. p. 390, points out that in Malay idiom a waist-cloth is '*kain*' since '*sarong*' means any kind of sheath or wrapping. *Kain sarung* is explicit but not usual. The use of 'sarong' in English is an interesting example of how a word can shift its precise meaning when adopted for use in another language.

Cf. 'actual' meaning 'real' in English and '*actuel*' meaning 'modern' or 'current' in French; both are derived from the same Latin root.

51. Wilkinson, *1932 Dictionary*, Pt. 2, p. 415, on '*seluar*' from '*shalwar*' (Persian) or '*shilwar*' (Indian). Swettenham, *The Real Malay*, p. 117, indicates that the absence of trousers was imputed to a notorious lecher as a matter of indecency.

52. See H. C. Clifford, *Malayan Monochromes*, New York, Dutton, 1913, p. 147, for the anecdote about the police constable. See also Clifford, *In a Corner of Asia being Tales and Impressions of Men and Things in the Malay Peninsula*, London, Fisher Unwin, 1899, p. 164, 'shameless folk who wore trousers but no protecting *sarong*'; and Vaughan, op. cit., p. 151. See p. 58 above on the apparel of Sultan Sulaiman.

53. F. A. Swettenham, *Footprints in Malaya*, London, Hutchinson, 1942, p. 50. 'Loose blouse' (H. C. Clifford, *The Further Side of Silence*, New York, Doubleday, Page & Co., 1927, p. 5). The *baju*, like the trousers, was a garment of Middle Eastern origin—'*bazu*' (Persian) (Wilkinson, *1932 Dictionary*, Pt. 1, p. 68).

54. Clifford, *Studies in Brown Humanity*, p. 31. Malays went coatless in much earlier times (Winstedt, 'Malay Dress', citing James Low, p. 37).

55. 'Usually dressed in nothing but a very scanty little cotton kilt' (Innes, op. cit., Vol. 1, p. 38). *SJ*, 23 September 1892 and 7 October 1892 and 4 September 1896. See also p. 32 above.

56. Winstedt, 'Malay Dress', p. 39. McNair, op. cit., p. 444, has a drawing of Raja Yusuf of Perak wearing a conventional type of *baju*.

57. Wilkinson, 'Some Malay Studies', p. 92. 'Something like a bishop's mitre', was the description of Innes, op. cit., Vol. 1, p. 100; she had grown up as a canon's daughter in the precincts of Canterbury Cathedral. 'Handkerchief twisted round his head' (Newbold, op. cit., Vol. 2, p. 178). Winstedt, 'Malay Dress', p. 44. See Wilkinson, *1932 Dictionary*, Pt. 2, p. 569, on the origin of '*tengkolok*', etc. Florence Caddy was told (*To Siam and Malaya in the Duke of Sutherland's Yacht 'Sans Peur'*, London, Hurst & Blackett, 1889, p. 237) that as a Muslim a Malay might not wear a hat with a brim. But Sultan Idris of Perak, a staunch upholder of the tradition, appeared at the Kuala Lumpur durbar of 1903 in uniform, surmounted by a cocked hat, which he doffed as he entered (*Malay Mail*, 21 July 1903).

58. Swettenham, *Footprints*, p. 50. Logan, 'Manners and Customs: Malay Dress', p. 274.

59. Wilkinson, 'Some Malay Studies', p. 93. Winstedt, 'Malay Dress', pp. 43–4.

60. McNair, op. cit., p. 274, mentions no other female garment but the *sarung* worn in this fashion. Very young children of both sexes wore no clothes at all (R. J. Wilkinson, 'The Incidents of Malay Life', *PMS, Life and Customs*, Part 1, 1908, reprinted in *JMBRAS*, 30(4), 1957, p. 44).

61. Mubin Sheppard, *Taman Indera: Malay Decorative Arts and Pastimes*, Kuala Lumpur, Oxford University Press, 1972, reprinted as *A Royal Pleasure Ground*, Singapore, Oxford University Press, 1986, p. 113. Abdullah Munshi, op. cit., p. 45, comments on 'an exceedingly large number of loose women' at Kota Bharu. 'They had their *sarongs* tied high above their breasts and wore no jackets.' It was probably at this class that the authorities aimed their severe sanctions.

62. J. Low, 'Observations on Perak', *JIA*, 4, 1850, p. 503. F. A. Swettenham, *British Malaya: An Account of the Origin and Progress of British Influence in Malaya*, London, John Lane Bodley Head, 1907 (revised editions 1929 and 1948, London, Allen & Unwin), p. 152.

63. R. J. H. Sidney, *Malay Land—Tanah Melayu: Some Phases of Life in Modern British Malaya*, London, Palmer, 1926, p. 164, has a photograph of an elderly Malay woman at work at the front of her house wearing a *sarung* at the armpits with shoulders bare. W. A. Graham, *Kelantan—A State of the Malay Peninsula: A Handbook of Information*, Glasgow, James MacLehose & Sons, 1908, p. 22, has a photograph of a group of Kelantan peasant women clad in double *sarung* and veil.

64. For a general account of these changes see Winstedt, 'Malay Dress', p. 39, and Wilkinson, *1932 Dictionary*, Pt. 1, p. 68. The 1901 edition of Wilkinson's dictionary does not include this information. In a general description of current fashion in a basic reference book it was said in 1908 that 'the women wear a longer coat [than Malay men] which is fastened down the front' (B. O. Stoney, 'The Malays of British Malaya', in A. Wright and H. A. Cartwright (eds.), *Twentieth Century Impressions of British Malaya: Its History, People, Commerce, Industries and Resources*, London, Lloyds, 1908, p. 223). This article, and Swettenham, *British Malaya*, p. 209, and *Footprints*, pp. 45 and 49, have photographs, offered as typical of the time, of Malay women wearing the *kebaya*. Vaughan, op. cit., writing in 1857, refers to the *kebaya* as normal wear for Malay women. Wilkinson, *1932 Dictionary*, loc. cit., says that 'women used to wear jackets . . . but in the towns the *kebaya* is now general'. One may assume that in the towns Malay women adopted the *kebaya*, worn by Straits Chinese *nonya* and Portuguese Eurasians, at an earlier date; it then spread gradually to the Malay states.

65. J. T. Thomson, 'Pulau Aur', *JIA*, 4, 1850, pp. 191–2. There may be something of prejudice here in the eye of the beholder. The culture to which Thomson belonged tended to emphasize the outline of the female bust by tight bodices, etc., at this period.

66. Swettenham, *British Malaya*, p. 153. See also CO 273/24, Colonel Man's memorandum on Province Wellesley Malays.

67. Wilkinson, 'Some Malay Studies', p. 91. Pahang costume was supplied to the guests for the occasion—an interesting example of the introduction of 'period costume' into a Malay ceremonial occasion.

68. Clifford, *In a Corner of Asia*, pp. 203–4.

69. J. Low, *Dissertation*, p. 87.

70. G. B. Gardner, *Keris and Other Malay Weapons*, Singapore, Progressive Publishing Co., 1936, Appendix B on Malay war dress, gives a full description and catalogue. The supply of fighting clothes by a commander to his levies was a call to arms (Linehan, 'Pahang', p. 68). See also p. 82.

71. A fighting man was expected to be colourfully and smartly dressed for battle 'with silk trousers and a silk sarong' (Swettenham, *British Malaya*, p. 19), describing Raja Mahmud. His garments might also be adapted to give him invulnerability, by embroidering on them texts from the Koran and having a neck of the fighting jacket which had been made of 44 pieces stitched together by 7 maidens on 7 successive Fridays (W. E. Maxwell, *Notes and Queries*, issued with *JSBRAS*, 15, 1885, p. 53).

72. Vaughan, op. cit., p. 150. D. J. Macgowan, 'Notes on the Maritime Malays', *JIA*, 4, 1850, p. 691.

73. Vaughan, op. cit., p. 152.

74. *SJ*, 20 April 1894.

75. Caddy, op. cit., p. 239. She also wrote (p. 237) that in the open he wore a pith helmet and that 'most of the Malay gentlemen wear billy-cock hats'.

76. J. C. Pasqual, article published in the *Singapore Sunday Times*, 28 October 1934, quoted in S. M. Middlebrook, 'Yap Ah Loy', *JMBRAS*, 24(2), 1951, p. 88. Tunku Kudin himself also wore a tarboosh and a European suit.

77. See note 48 above on official encouragement of the *songkok*. The link is apparent in the term for a tarboosh—'*songkok Turki*' (Wilkinson, *1932 Dictionary*, Pt. 2, p. 487).

78. Malays 'consider the ordinary costume of white *men* so immodest as to be almost indecent' (Sir Frank Swettenham, *Unaddressed Letters*, London, John Lane Bodley Head, 1900, p. 14). See also citations from Clifford in note 52 above and p. 58 above on Sultan Sulaiman's attire.

79. Caddy, op. cit., p. 240.

80. *Malay Mail*, 18 February 1898. When Weld visited Alor Star in 1882 he was received by the young Sultan Abdul Hamid and his uncle, the Regent, who wore 'London made clothes, with a *sarong*, and were very civilised in appearance' (A. Lovat, *The Life of Sir Frederick Weld: A Pioneer of Empire*, London, Murray, 1914, p. 307). See also p. 58 above on Abdul Hamid in London.

81. His subjects still followed Malay convention in their mourning for the late ruler—'the white head mourning is generally observable throughout the district' (*SGG* 1898, p. 141, report from Kuala Selangor). When the popular Resident of Negeri Sembilan, Martin Lister, died, the Malays of the Tampin district also wore Malay mourning bands (*Negeri Sembilan Gazette* 1897, p. 126).

82. *Malay Mail*, 6 November 1903. See p. 36 above on this ceremony.

83. European military uniform was one of the obsessions of the young Sultan Abdullah of Perak (J. W. W. Birch, *The Journals of J. W. W. Birch First British Resident to Perak 1874–1875* (hereafter cited as *Birch Journal*), edited by P. L. Burns, Kuala Lumpur, Oxford University Press, 1976, pp. 161, 203, 253, and 339, and various references in PCE (CO 273/86–88)). His successor, Sultan Idris, indulged a similar taste though with more discretion—see note 57 above. When Isabella Bird visited Kuala Langat in 1879, Sultan Abdul Samad wore 'something like a loose hussar jacket' and 'trousers with a broad gold stripe on the outside' (Bird, op. cit., p. 231). However, the Resident, Bloomfield Douglas, had obtained it for him (see note 43 above)—and described the ruler on this occasion as 'radiant in the new clothes made for him in Singapore' (Douglas Diary, 4 February 1879). It was not by any means the old man's natural style. Before she departed, Isabella Bird caught a glimpse of the Sultan 'lounging at ease in a white shirt and *sarong*, all his gorgeousness having disappeared' (Bird, op. cit., p. 234).

84. 'Notes of a Trip to Kedah', *Malay Mail*, 20 April 1900: anonymous but probably by J. H. M. Robson.

85. J. R. Logan, 'The Manners and Customs of the Malays: Meals', *JIA*, 4, 1850, pp. 433–5; Winstedt, 'The Circumstances of Malay Life . . . Meals', *PMS, Life and Customs*, Part 2, 1909, reprinted 1925; Vaughan, op. cit., p. 147; Zainal Abidin bin Ahmad, 'Malay Manners and Etiquette', *JMBRAS*, 23(3), 1950, pp. 49–52, all describe Malay habits and etiquette at meals.

86. Logan, 'Manners and Customs: Malay Meals', p. 433.

87. Zainal Abidin bin Ahmad, 'Malay Manners', p. 49.

88. Logan, 'Manners and Customs: Malay Meals', p. 433.

89. Vaughan, op. cit., p. 148.

90. Zainal Abidin bin Ahmad, 'Malay Manners', p. 52.

91. Logan, 'Manners and Customs: Malay Meals', p. 433; Winstedt, 'Malay

Meals', p. 57; Zainal Abidin bin Ahmad, 'Malay Manners', p. 50. The passage in the main text, derived from these sources, is intended to describe an informal gathering at a family meal or when only one or two guests were present; for a large feast there were necessarily much more elaborate arrangements for serving the food.

92. Innes, op. cit., Vol. 1, p. 102. She adds, 'I confess that he had rather the best of the argument'. Her guest was the father of Raja Mahmud (see p. [illegible] above). See also Winstedt, 'Malay Meals', p. 57, to the same effect. The successful but rather unlikely friendship of Emily Innes and the Tunku Panglima Raja is one of the more relaxed passages in her embittered chronicle. She found that 'his favourite beverage was not tea, but Bass's pale ale, which however, he took in homoeopathic doses' (p. 101). She also taught him to play tennis—'he flew about the ground with his petticoats tucked up . . . hitting the ball straight up into the air as high as he possibly could' (Vol. 2, p. 6). There must have been many more of these fascinating episodes of culture contact as the Europeans brought their way of life to the Malay states but no one has told of them as well as Emily Innes.

93. Zainal Abidin bin Ahmad, 'Malay Manners', p. 56, on the etiquette of washing the hands.

94. H. Norman, *The Peoples and Politics of the Far East: Travels and Studies in the British . . . Colonies and Malaya*, New York, Scribner, 1895, p. 56[illegible]. *Cunam* ('*chunam*' in Norman's text) is lime (*kapur makan*) for use with betel. McNair, op. cit., pp. 180–5.

95. Wilkinson, 'Incidents', p. 51; Sheppard, *Taman Indera*, pp. 16[illegible]–7. The Perak royal heirlooms included a pair of betel boxes which were carried in procession behind the ruler and his wife (R. O. Winstedt and R. J. Wilkinson, 'A History of Perak', *JMBRAS*, 12(1), 1934, p. 163).

96. Swettenham, *The Real Malay*, pp. 114–15, and *Footprints*, p. 120; Sheppard, *Taman Indera*, p. 170.

97. Evidence to PCE in CO 273/87, pp. 34–50, and in CO 273/88, p. 1[illegible]. On the trial see SSD 11 January 1877 in CO 273/90, pp. 143, 180 and 189. The *Hari Raya* feast comes at the end of the Muslim month of fasting.

98. Wilkinson, 'Incidents', describes the ritual of the *rites de passage* of Malay life—p. 42 on birth, pp. 47 and 49 on sending a son to a Koran teacher, p. 54 on betrothal, pp. 56–8 on weddings, pp. 63–4 on *Hari Raya Besar*, and p. 73 on funerals. Skeat, *Malay Magic*, also deals with these rites at length. See also Winstedt, especially *The Malays: A Cultural History*, Singapore, Kelly & Walsh, 1947. Limitations of space preclude a detailed description here. Chapter 9 pursues the topic of Malay marriage and Chapter 11, religion and magic.

99. See p. 320 below on this theme.

100. Wilkinson, 'Incidents', p. 78.

101. Newbold, op. cit., Vol. 1, p. 253 (*asah gigi*). Men also sometimes had their teeth filed: Skeat, *Malay Magic*, pp. 355–9, describes the filing of the teeth of a youth of about fifteen. Although the practice gradually died out, it was still common to see Malays with filed teeth in the early years of the twentieth century. 'The majority of women have their teeth filed down to the gums. The men however prefer the saw-tooth pattern. The rich Malays often have expensive gold ornaments inserted in the centre of each tooth' (*Malay Mail*, 3 January 1901).

102. Skeat, *Malay Magic*, p. 343, quoting Vaughan, op. cit. Skeat's whole account (pp. 332–52) of ceremonies at and after the birth of a child is distressing reading.

103. Zainal Abidin bin Ahmad, 'Malay Manners', p. 52. He wrote in 1948 but attributes the Malay adoption of the practice to Western influence within the previous fifty years. 'RSVP' are the initial letters of *repondez, s'il vous plaît*, a polite request for a prompt reply. It may be that the technique of a reply in the form of a 'third person note' was as baffling to the Malays as, say, the opening compliments of a conventional Malay letter are to a European.

104. See pp. 56 and 160 above. Wilkinson, *1932 Dictionary*, Pt. 2, p. 486, translates '*kereta sombong*' as 'mail train—train too "arrogant" to pay attention to small stations'.

105. '*Gajah*' (elephant) is a word of Sanskrit origin (Burkill, op. cit., p. 908). But the literary synonym—'*biram*'—may be Malay (Wilkinson, *1932 Dictionary*, Pt. 1, p. 144). W. G. Maxwell, 'Mantra Gajah', *JSBRAS*, 45, 1906, suggests that despite Malay tradition—*keturunan daripada Siam* (of Siamese origin)—the domestication of elephants came to Malaya from India via Sumatra. Barbara Watson Andaya, *Perak: The Abode of Grace*, Kuala Lumpur, Oxford University Press, 1979, pp. 401–3, gives a most interesting account of elephants in Perak down to the beginning of the nineteenth century. See also W. E. Maxwell, *Notes and Queries*, issued with *JSBRAS*, 15, 1885, p. 32, and J. M. Gullick, 'The Elephants of Syed Zin', *JMBRAS*, 59(1), 1986.

106. *Sejarah Melayu or Malay Annals*, Raffles MS 18, trans. C. C. Brown, *JMBRAS*, 25(2–3), 1952, p. 168.

107. Swettenham, *British Malaya*, p. 119.

108. *PGG* 1891, p. 370, report from Kurau; Norman, op. cit., p. 540; and W. E. Maxwell, *Notes and Queries*, issued with *JSBRAS*, 15, 1885, p. 58, give data in different forms, which, however, are all consistent with an elephant's progress at 3 miles per hour over 15–18 miles per day of 6 hours.

109. Swettenham, *British Malaya*, p. 119. In 1821 the ruler of Kedah fled southwards to Province Wellesley pursued by the Siamese. The members of the party who were mounted on elephants got through but those 'who had not the advantage of being mounted perished [from] fatigue, hunger and exposure' (P. J. Begbie, *The Malayan Peninsula Embracing the History, Manners and Customs of the Inhabitants, Politics, Natural History, etc. from its Earliest Records*, Madras, Vespery Mission Press, 1834, reprinted as *The Malayan Peninsula*, Kuala Lumpur, Oxford University Press, 1967, p. 110).

110. *Swettenham Journal*, p. 10; *Birch Journal*, p. 288; J. T. Thomson, *Some Glimpses into Life in the Far East*, London, Richardson, 1864, reprinted as *Glimpses into Life in Malayan Lands*, Singapore, Oxford University Press, 1984, p. 122.

111. W. E. Maxwell, *Notes and Queries*, issued with *JSBRAS*, 15, 1885, p. 52.

112. Bird, op. cit., p. 303. See also Norman, op. cit., pp. 543–5; F. A. Swettenham, *Sir Frank Swettenham's Malaya Journals 1874–1876* (hereafter cited as *Swettenham Journal*), edited by P. L. Burns and C. D. Cowan, Kuala Lumpur, Oxford University Press, 1975, p. 30; J. R. Logan, 'Notes at Penang, Kedah, etc.', *JIA*, 5, 1851, p. 56. In 1886 the elephant was 'still a valuable and indeed indispensable means of transport' (W. E. Maxwell, cited in note 111 above). 'Regular communication by means of elephant' in Kedah (J. Anderson, *Political and Commercial Considerations Relative to the Malayan Peninsula and the British Settlements in the Straits of Malacca*, Penang, 1824, reprinted in *JMBRAS*, 35(4), 1962, p. 98). 'No elephants, so there was nothing for it but to start on a walk thro' the jungle' (*Swettenham Journal*, p. 19).

113. Norman, op. cit., p. 544; W. G. Maxwell, 'Mantra Gajah', *passim*, McNair, op. cit., p. 117.

114. Swettenham, *Footprints*, p. 42, and report of 8 April 1875 enclosed with SSD 27 April 1875. Rathborne, op. cit., p. 180. The main area for trapping and taming elephants was Perak and Raman to the north of it. Bozzolo went to Kelantan for the purpose of buying elephants, but had difficulty in getting any (SSD 3[illegible] January 1889). Mayer (see note 115 below) had no difficulty in finding Malays in Terengganu to help him trap elephants but one does not read of the use of domesticated elephants in Terengganu.

115. SSD 14 September 1896. The account of trapping elephants is based on Charles Mayer, *Trapping Wild Animals in Malay Jungles*, London, Fisher & Unwin, 1922, Chapter 3, where he gives a graphic and detailed account of the capture of about sixty elephants in Terengganu early in the twentieth century, using traditional Malay methods. See also W. G. Maxwell, 'Mantra Gajah'.

116. H. C. Clifford, *Bushwhacking and Other Asiatic Tales and Memories*, New York, Harper, 1929, pp. 246–64, gives a sombre account of trapping elephants in the dry zone of Ceylon by the same method of driving them into a trap. He wrote of a captured female that 'maybe she was doomed to die of heartbreak and gangrene, as is the fate of a large percentage of captured elephants'. Mayer (note 115 above) captured about sixty elephants, male and female, adult and small, but exported only sixteen tame females. He killed the males for their tusks.

117. *Birch Journal*, p. 240. The Raja of Raman seems to have been one of the most active organizers of the trade, exporting elephants to Perak or Penang for shipment to India (SSD 17 April 1883, 21 June 1886 and 3 October 189[illegible]: *PGG* 1898, p. 348). See also note 126 below.

118. W. W. Skeat and F. F. Laidlaw, 'The Cambridge University Expedition to Parts of the Malay Peninsula 1899–1900: Personal Accounts', *JMBRAS*, 26(4), 1953, p. 141. As a mature coconut palm carried about 24 edible fronds, the feeding of an elephant was equivalent to complete defoliation of five palms every four days.

119. SSD 23 February 1881. Lovat, op. cit., p. 350—Weld and his party travelling in the Kinta valley on twenty-three elephants.

120. Until 1880 Bloomfield Douglas had his Residency at Klang but made regular visits to Kuala Lumpur, travelling by launch as far as Damansara on the Klang River. In 1876 he had to complete his journey on foot (Douglas Diary, [illegible]4 July 1876). Three years later, however, he took ponies on the launch with him and rode on to Kuala Lumpur over the 'Damansara road' then under construction (Douglas Diary, 7 May 1879).

121. *Birch Journal*, p. 269. The Datuk Panglima Kinta told Birch that Sultan Jaafar (r.1857–65) 'took great care of his elephants and he, Panglima Kinta, used to look after them'. The Panglima had at least three elephants of his own (ibid., p. 268). Sultan Ismail owned between fifty and sixty elephants (*Swettenham Journal*, p. 194).

122. McNair, op. cit., p. 118: 'They are the chief beasts of burden of the country, and will walk away comfortably with half a ton of tin; but where the load is of a bulky nature, from four to six hundredweight is considered sufficient. They are naturally the property of the Sultan and his chiefs, and elephants are looked upon as part of the Sultan's regalia, fifty being reckoned in his regal list.'

123. H. Low, 'The Journal of Sir Hugh Low, Perak 1877' (hereafter cited as 'Low

Journal'), edited by E. Sadka, *JMBRAS*, 27(4), 1954, pp. 70 and 99. Hugh Low offered elephants for sale at $600 each (p. 102).

124. Governor Mitchell, visiting mines at Ipoh in 1894, 'found a parade of 52 elephants awaiting me' (SSD 22 March 1894). *PGG* 1890, p. 570, report from Kinta. See also p. 80 above.

125. *PSCM*, 23 March 1880 in *PMS*, p. 225. *PGG* 1896, p. 678, report from Kuala Kangsar.

126. The Raja of Raman came to a meeting at the Perak frontier in 1886 bringing a hundred elephants. He may have done it to impress the British officials but it indicates the size of his stock (SSD 21 June 1886). On Indian purchases see SSD 21 June 1902. In a protracted dispute over the theft of elephants from Perak, which eventually engaged the attention of the Governor SS (Swettenham), King Chulalongkorn of Siam and two of his Ministers, the Colonial Office and the Foreign Office, the owner of the elephants claimed—and was paid—compensation at the rate of $400 per annum for the period in which the working elephant was detained in Raman (SSD 3 October 1899 (and eight subsequent despatches)): the story is told in Gullick, 'The Elephants of Syed Zin', cited in note 105 above.

127. SSD 20 December 1909.

128. Datuk Mohamed Said, op. cit., p. 156.

9
Inequality in Malay Society

INEQUALITY was perceived as one of the facts of life. It was neither approved nor disapproved. It simply happened and one must learn to live with it. There was the major cleavage—Swettenham's 'broad line' between the ruling class and the *rakyat*. But the latter had its own subdivisions. Slaves in the strict sense, since they were generally not Malays, but aliens brought into the Malay community by capture or purchase—aborigines, Batak from Sumatra, or Africans imported through the Middle East—were a small and insignificant class. A peasant who owed only a general fealty to his chief was in a better situation than a debt-bondsman who, however much a free man in theory, was at the immediate beck and call of the creditor. Women were regarded as vulnerable rather than inferior beings, but certainly they were different in social status and role. Everyone owed loyalty to the ruler but he could be arbitrary and it was most unwise to appeal to him for redress against one of his more powerful subjects. 'Large fish ate small ones.'[1]

In those states which came under colonial rule, the new regime was ideologically committed to the preservation of 'Malay custom'—and this was expressed in the terms of the treaties upon which the new system was founded.[2] Even in 1927 Clifford disclaimed any 'mandate' to alter the political—and he might have added the social—framework of the Malay states.[3]

Yet in all the states, protected or still independent, there were new ideas and to some extent new institutions at work. The colonial regime equated debt-bondage with slavery and was resolved to sweep away both together.[4] New institutions, such as courts of law, an administrative framework for Islam, and registered title to land, took root in the protected states and were to some extent copied in the others. By asserting a general superiority over Malay society as a whole, the alien regime unintentionally set to work forces, such as education, which in the long run would have some levelling effect. One should not exaggerate these tendencies—but they are not to be ignored because they were tentative and had little immediate effect.

The abolition of slavery and debt-bondage was generally not accompanied by any examination of the circumstances which had created them. In forwarding a report on this subject to the Colonial Office, Governor Jervois noted that the absence of debt-bondage, on any significant scale, in the Klang valley of Selangor, was correlated with the departure of the settled Malay population during the civil war and its replacement by immigrant Malays from other states. There was no settled population yet.[5] Swettenham carried the argument a little further with 'the system of debt-slavery ... is only seen in its worst light where a *raja* or chief is a creditor and a subject the debtor'.[6] Although debt-bondage had an economic basis its real significance was as part of a political relationship.[7]

Kelantan supplies an example of how it came into being. The disasters of the 1880s have been described in Chapter 5. The men went off to seek a livelihood in the western states, leaving the wives and children behind—temporarily at least. Bozzolo relates that 'The Sultan taking advantage of these hard times commenced to lend out money but at a very high rate of interest and from this source the number of his slaves increased; those who had means also imitated the Sultan's way in lending out money but only for short periods, with the result that a number of families, the majority being women and children, submitted to slavery for small sums ... for some time the upper class derived great profit from this source by employing these poor destitute people, some at weaving, others at work in the *padi* fields.'[8] In hard times the peasant had no reserves; 'few subjects in a Malay country are well off', wrote Swettenham, as they would be deprived of any surplus cash by a *raja*.[9]

The origin of debt-bondage was some urgent need of money, either to survive in bad times or perhaps to meet extra expenditure such as a feast to celebrate a wedding. In those times of need, the well-to-do were ready—at a stiff price—to provide the money on loan. Hugh Low noted that a prominent Malay lady of the upper class 'had invested most of her private money in advances of this description, which up to the time of British interference, was the favourite form of security, and she is now the largest claimant in the country for the repayment of her money'.[10]

Unsecured personal loans to Malay peasants were a risky form of 'investment'. Why none the less was it 'a favourite form of security' in Perak? The creditor could call on the debtor and his family to render services—this might either be at the creditor's place of residence or elsewhere. Debt-bondsmen may therefore be divided broadly into two groups—those who formed part of the personal entourage and household of the creditor, and those who 'lived out'. The latter seem to have been less numerous and they were usually recruited into debt-bondage more as clients than as servants. Haji Dris conceded that he was 'slave debtor to Haji Mat Yassin' but added with hauteur that 'a man like him is not expected to do menial work. He has opportunities of trading on his own account, and the only way his master requires his services is that he is obliged to attend on him.'[11] Much depended on the debtor's status. There were debtors who lived at a distance, but were required to do 'menial work' such as herding the creditor's buffaloes entrusted to them or even working his mines. However, the case of Haji Dris illustrates the practice by which people of wealth increased their prestige by enlisting respectable clients whose service lay merely in forming part of the creditor's 'following' when required to do so.

The majority of references to debt-bondsmen (and women) relate to members of the creditor's household. Many of the women were simply domestic servants whose work was cooking, cleaning, looking after the younger children of the creditor's family, or occasionally light field-work such as planting or weeding. The men often found wives among the creditor's domestics and made themselves useful to him as messengers, boatmen or servants. As an example, Indut, who came from Siak, 'took up with one of Sultan Abdullah's women Si Long Mahnoon' and worked as one of the Sultan's boatmen.[12] No doubt these attendants, male and female, had to render constant service but it was not a heavy duty for many of them.

The benefit to the creditor of having so many people in his household was twofold. Their mere numbers enhanced his standing. They also sufficed to relieve the creditor and his family of kinds of work which, as aristocrats, they regarded as beneath them. A son of such a family wrote that 'having got slaves to attend to the agricultural drudgery and other household works, the master and members of his family were able to command a considerable degree of leisure', including 'various forms of amusement and idle pastime' or attendance on the ruler at court with a view to making a political career. These aristocrats 'were not used even to ordinary manual labour which they naturally disdained'.[13]

Debt-bondage was born of the desperate financial need of the peasant class, but it yielded to the creditor not an economic return but higher social standing. The services of the debtor were regarded as of 'scarcely more than nominal value'. Hence it was logical that those services did not discharge the debt. (In this respect Kedah was a limited exception but it was a much more commercial economy than most). The abolition of debt-bondage in the early years of colonial rule exposed a conflict, which was only half understood on either side, of Malay and European values. In European eyes the debtor owed money and it was fair to him and the creditor that he should work off his debt. In Pahang, for example, the work of a male debtor was valued at $2 per month and that of a female at $1.50. By working they could pay off the debt, limited to a maximum of $100 for this purpose, over a period of time.[14]

The creditors were none the less aggrieved. Those of their debtors who lived 'in entire freedom in different parts of the country' were not accustomed to 'work regularly' for the creditor. The creditor could not find productive work for them to do, unless the government lent them money 'to enable them to open mines or gardens in which they could employ their debtors'. Domestic bondsmen, accustomed to the light work of old servants, showed 'an unwillingness . . . to go and work for a living which involved greater exertion'. The creditors deemed it unfitting that the relationship should be dissolved by treating it as repayment of a debt. 'How can we take money for our friends who have so long lived with us, many of them born in our houses? We can sell cattle, fruit or rice, but not take money for our friends.' Again 'many slave children whose own mothers are dead, always call their mistress "Mother", and the attachment is reciprocal'.[15] It was not always such an affectionate relationship. Many in bondage complained of ill-treatment, and some creditors alleged idleness or depravity on their part. Yet, for good or ill, it was a personal, not an economic, relationship, based on political status.

The formal release of the bondsmen therefore had little immediate effect. 'The slaves did not find it convenient to leave the premises of their masters altogether. Their living quarters were built around or near their master's house on their master's land. They had no land of their own. They were so used to depending upon rations—food and clothing—supplied by their master. Remunerative employment was not available anywhere. Some of the older ones had become really attached to their masters and regarded themselves as part of the family establishments. They continued to be attached to the establishment of their masters, enjoying most of their benefits but avoiding much of the work.'[16] Those final words do serve to reveal a change of attitude. The bondsmen and women wished to remain in the familiar environment but they were also conscious of the change in their position. Some did in fact go out into the world. Datuk Mahmud continues his above-quoted account with recollections of an aristocratic household which had to cook its own rice and till its own fields because the bondswomen in particular had elected to go off and get married to live in their own homes. Generally the effect of abolishing debt-bondage was to reduce the size of aristocratic households without entirely changing their character. In Alor Star, for example, 'most Malay middle-class families had some man, woman or child as an unpaid domestic servant for his or her lifetime, and the upper class families had several of them'.[17] In Kuala Terengganu in 1918 a relative of the ruler was likely still to have five or even ten women domestics.[18]

The abolition of debt-bondage did not eliminate the occasional financial crises of peasant life, which in former times had been relieved by acceptance of bondage. The villager could no longer look to his upper-class patron for help, since the latter had no inducement to lend money and often had no money to lend. But a well-to-do villager might still be looking for cheap domestic labour. Clifford tells a story of two Malay girls, 9 and 11 years old—'When their parents died he had forced them to come and live with him, alleging that some old debt of which the children knew nothing, gave him the right to claim their services. He had fed and clothed them after a fashion, simply because it was necessary to keep the little wretches in some sort of health if they were to work for him to the extent that he considered necessary.' It was hardly possible for a remote colonial regime to discover and suppress practices of this kind in up-country villages.[19]

Later on, when it was no longer possible to pledge services in return for a loan, the villager, now the registered owner of a plot of land, was tempted to pledge or sell his land as security. Out of these transactions came the gradual stratification of village society into wealthy land-owners, middle-category tenants or share-croppers, and landless labourers disclosed by modern field studies.[20]

Women had been particularly vulnerable to being drawn into debt-bondage. They might be rounded up by a ruler or chief for concubinage or domestic service in his household. They might be involved through connection with a husband or father. 'The debtor's wife, his children, his grandchildren all become equally bound with himself to the payment of this debt.'[21] In debt-bondage, domestic service was probably a more continuous and demanding subordination than any other. Although the passing of debt-bondage benefited women more perhaps than men, there were other continuing disadvantages of their sex.

On reaching puberty a young woman was segregated. 'Until she marries she is not supposed to have any conversation with men, and when out of doors (never alone, of course) she meets a man she covers her face with extreme ostentation. Sometimes the effort is so great that her face is for a moment entirely disclosed. It is no doubt the result of excessive modesty and nervousness.'[22] Marriages were, by convention, to be arranged between the elders of the two families of the spouses and the bride might never have seen her husband before the wedding day. She would not have been alone with him. She herself took no part in the Islamic ceremony by which the marriage contract was made. Yet in a society in which arranged marriage was the accepted norm, it often settled down to a tolerable match. Although convention frowned on any open display of affection between spouses, there was sometimes deep feeling beneath the surface.[23]

Clifford tells a story of a young girl married to a stranger, 'a typical villager of the interior, good natured and easy going'. After the 'initial paralysis of fear' at being in the power of a man, 'her gratitude to her man had been extravagant and passionate in its intensity when she found he was consistently kind and tender to her'.[24] But compatibility was a minor consideration for their elders in choosing a partner for a son or daughter. Marriage, even in village society, could be a search for status or the confirmation of a useful alliance.

In aristocratic society status was all important. In particular a woman of royal blood, even if only distantly related to the ruler, was expected to marry an *anak raja*. 'A woman of the blood,' wrote Clifford, 'no matter how remote her connection with the ruling house, can wed only with one of her own clan, or with a *sayid*.' In the state capital a young woman of the *raja* class could usually be paired with a husband of that class, though perhaps only as a second wife. In the remoter districts, however, such women might be 'so utterly alone that they were forced to labour unremittingly to keep the rice-bin stocked and their backs covered with patched garments'. For them, the choice lay between 'the existence of the wanton and the drudge'. A wanton might suffer death at the hands of an outraged kinsman. Menial labour in obscurity was less disgraceful than a *mésalliance* with a peasant.[25]

Married life, however, could be dull—especially for a young wife of aristocratic birth with no chores to take her out of the house, and perhaps a husband who was pursuing his amours elsewhere and already neglecting her. There was then a 'chafing under the monotony of existence' for which flirting or even adultery was a welcome but very dangerous escape. If the lovers were discreet, the husband might remain in ignorance or choose to ignore the signs of his wife's infidelity. If, however, the affair became an open scandal, the society in which they lived demanded that the husband should kill his wife's paramour; if he did not kill her, too, he must at the least divorce her.[26] Yet, in spite of the consequences, some wives took the risks and even showed a 'growing longing for notoriety'.[27] If they had real or imagined grounds for jealousy, they found release in the violence to which their menfolk were too much addicted. 'The younger women resorted to weapons for the settlement of their quarrels, and a girl would stab a rival, or a faithless lover, as soon as not.'[28]

If a woman was disgraced for unchastity, she hoped that her lover, if he survived the husband's revenge, would marry her. To remain an abandoned woman was an almost ineradicable disgrace. In the harsh words of the proverb, the woman was like a piece of sugar-cane which had been chewed and spewed out.[29] The husbands, for whom conventional morality had a more tolerant standard—do not get caught in adultery—took elaborate precautions to deny to their wives the liberty which they took as their right. They returned home unexpectedly, or kept a watchful eye on the wife's movements. In upper-class society the husband arranged to provide his wife with a 'companion' who would in fact be a caretaker.[30] If he suspected infidelity or had other reasons for disapproval of his wife's conduct, he yielded to 'the Malay man's unshakeable belief in the ability of the rod to inspire in a wife a proper sense of subordination'.[31] If, however, the matter had become a scandal, he was likely to resort to the ultimate sanction of divorce.

Malay women of all classes were at a disadvantage in the facility with which a husband could divorce his wife by pronouncing the conventional three *talak*. He need not have or specify grounds for divorce, though in practice he might be constrained by the risk of a quarrel with the wife's family or the financial consequences of a division of the marital property. A wife often feared that as she grew to middle age and lost her youthful attractions, her husband might discard her by divorce or, a possibility which she resented still more, enter into a polygamous marriage with a younger woman, while retaining her in the domestic responsibilities of her household.[32]

Except in the upper levels of the aristocracy, polygamous marriage was not common in Malay society. Convention required that the husband should 'provide a separate house and establishment for each additional lady'. To avoid a serious quarrel with the first wife, he usually continued to treat her as 'the principal wife' and entered into short-lived marriages with other wives.[33] Hence the position of a second wife, unless she was of lower social status than the husband, was unattractive. Some ladies, invited to become a second wife, responded by insisting that the husband should divorce the first wife.[34] Financial factors and the emotional wear and tear detracted from the joys of polygamy.

The wife was entitled under Islamic rules to a divorce at her instance if she could satisfy a *kadi* that her husband had ill-treated her, or failed to support her, or was an imbecile and mentally incapable.[35] In practice she could sometimes compel her husband to divorce her, either by making his life at home unendurable or by shaming him before the neighbours. If the marriage ended by death of the husband, the Islamic rules for division of his property gave a share to the wife, with the children, but in practice rules of custom or an informal agreement within the family often decided how the property should be divided.[36]

In spite of their difficulties Malay women usually held their own in whatever walk of life they found themselves. Clifford commented that women 'very soon acquire an extremely good notion of how to look after themselves'.[37] Swettenham too wrote that 'once a woman has married, and so obtained a certain amount of independence, she will, especially if she is of strong character, develop into a considerable power in her own household, and often exert her influence in many directions beyond those limits'. Among the aristocracy, 'titles held by the husband confer rank and title on his principal wife'.[38] Women did not attend the mosque but custom required that they should be present at many non-Islamic ceremonies and festivals. It was the women who did much of the cooking and other preparations for such occasions. They also had an essential role to play in the sequence of operations in the padi-fields.

In mixed company the women could often close ranks to establish a sort of feminine cameraderie. 'Their bright and amusing conversation, carried on in allusions and cryptic references', could mystify a stranger and deflate the male ego.[39] There was a less attractive side to the assertiveness of upper-class women. They could be arrogant to their equals and harsh to their inferiors. A debt-bondswoman in domestic service said 'and yet withal she could bear with the Bandar but his wife she says she can stand no longer. Not only does she set her hard work, and much of it, but this is always with abuse both to herself and her children.'[40]

The influence of aristocratic wives often depended on their wealth. One such was the celebrated Che Mida (Hamidah), sister of the Datuk Seri Maharaja Lela of Sayong and at one time married to the Datuk Laksamana of Perak. British officials who consulted her on their early visits to Perak make many references to her as a shrewd personality. She eventually sold her house, which was very large, to Hugh Low as the original Residency at Kuala Kangsar.[41] Another 'very famous old lady' was Wan Teh Sapiah, who had wealth, connections, and political influence. Her brother, Wan Abu Bakar, held a royal grant (*kuasa*) as chief of Ijoh; she herself had the unusual distinction of becoming *penghulu* of Ulu Kurau in 1878.[42]

The story of Toh Puan Halimah provides some interesting details of the position and resources of a Malay *grande dame*. She was the daughter of the Datuk Laksamana of Perak, the leading magnate of Lower Perak in the 1860s and early 1870s. She became the principal wife of the Tengku Menteri, chief of the important mining district of Larut and a key figure in the complicated political situation leading to the Treaty of Pangkor. In accordance with Malay custom her husband assigned a large house to her for her use; this she was entitled to retain if the marriage ended in divorce. It was a large brick house, i.e. a more substantial and expensive dwelling than most, and it had been specially built for her at Permatang in Larut at the time of her marriage. It was surrounded by 'extensive fortifications', perhaps as a sign of status more than for defensive purposes.[43] The Menteri may have given her these special perquisites to provide compensation for his second, polygamous marriage to a celebrated Perak beauty, who was younger than Toh Puan Halimah and of lower social status.[44]

Toh Puan Halimah herself was 'a woman of remarkable appearance' with a 'striking face'. Swettenham 'used to imagine she might resemble Cleopatra though that was no great compliment to the Egyptian queen'. As a personality she was 'a very determined, masterful and extravagant lady' whose husband satisfied her 'numerous and expensive' demands. She bore her husband two sons.[45] In the 'very real rivalry between these two wives' she held her own. On the whole fortune had smiled on Toh Puan Halimah in the early years of her marriage.

Then in the early 1870s disasters befell her. Civil war broke out again in Larut and her fine house 'was rendered uninhabitable during the Chinese disturbances'. The new colonial regime carried out some inadequate repairs but in the aftermath of the disturbances of 1875 the house was 'temporarily used as a barrack for soldiers and a court for the trial of the Maharaja Lela and others'. There was some doubt as to whether it was her property or that of the state government, but Hugh Low decided not to claim it.[46]

At the same time Toh Puan Halimah's father and husband were deprived of office, and with it lost any entitlement to the political allowances from state revenue paid as compensation for the loss of the right to levy local taxes. They were shipped off to the Seychelles on account of their complicity in the events leading to the death of J.W.W. Birch in 1875. A sum of $300 per month was allocated for the support of the Menteri, his two wives, children and other dependents, a total of about thirty people.[47] The two wives refused to go into exile with the Menteri but they then had to live in Perak in much reduced circumstances. The humiliation was savagely resented. Swettenham said that Toh Puan Halimah showed 'uncompromising hostility to the British Government, to its officers and all their works'.

Adversity, however, is a test of character and Toh Puan Halimah showed her resolve and skill. In the early days of her tribulation she went to see Hugh Low over her financial position. At first there was some nervousness, but later she showed more confidence in her complaints against her husband's business agents. One of them 'puts too many restrictions on her liberty and will never let her have an elephant or a horse to go anywhere and she won't stand it'.[48] She salvaged from the wreck of her fortunes whatever property she could lay claim to. In addition to the house at Permatang, she claimed to own the local mosque.[49] It was Toh Puan Halimah to whom Low referred, in a passage cited above, as the largest single 'investor' in debt-bondage.[50] Until debt-bondage in Perak was abolished in 1883, she was entitled to use her debt-bondsmen 'in any legitimate employment' and—difficult was it may have been to organize—she presumably did so. She also received, like other creditors, the sums per head paid by the state government as compensation for the unpaid debts of the bondsmen.[51] She also went into business and submitted a tender of $120 per month for the right to collect taxes on *atap* exported from Larut.[52]

Her relations with her absent husband and with her fellow wife were strained. The Menteri refused to divorce either of them, but the other wife persuaded the ruler to grant her a divorce so that she might remarry. Toh Puan Halimah was 'full of scorn for the backsliding of this weaker vessel'. However, as the years went by, 'the smart, high-born wife' also sought divorce on the grounds of prolonged separation. But the Menteri refused, saying that she could end their separation by joining him in the Seychelles. Halimah went off to protest to the Resident, who was now Swettenham. There were stormy interviews. She was now becoming a little eccentric. If her request was refused 'she would be transported to Bombay'—but Swettenham doubted whether she knew what Bombay was, still less where it was. The ruler could not refuse her the divorce which he had granted to the other wife, and so in time she got her way.

She now had a taste for arguments with the powers that be and began to take up other people's causes. 'She used to come weekly, almost daily,' said Swettenham, 'as a sort of professional intermediary.' It gratified her sense of her own importance.

Eventually the Menteri, in failing health, was allowed to come back as far as Singapore to die in 1895. Whatever her feelings about that event, Halimah must have had much satisfaction in the appointment of her elder son to the vacant office of Menteri. He was already *penghulu* of Bukit Gantang and the younger son was made his assistant. The new Menteri, unlike his formidable mother, had come to terms with the new regime and made a very successful career in public life.[53]

There were other Malay women of the aristocratic class with no less determination than Toh Puan Halimah. Raja Arfah, the daughter of Sultan Abdul Samad of Selangor and wife of Tunku Kudin, the Viceroy, impressed Emily Innes as 'a stronger character' than either of them. She came to James Innes to argue that her monthly allowance was payable thirteen times in the year which, under the Muslim calendar, is divided into lunar months of twenty-nine days.[54]

Control of property was often the buttress which supported the position of a Malay woman of the upper class. Whatever property they obtained on marriage from fathers or husbands was usually safeguarded by 'written conditions of marriage, "settlements" of a kind';[55] if the marriage ended in divorce there was a formal division of property. Hugh Low had to deal with a claim for $245 by a divorced wife against her husband 'in place of jewels of hers which he has gambled away'.[56] The principal wife of Sultan Abu Bakar of Johor was reported to make him an allowance out of her resources since she had most of the money.[57]

Yet, as Emily Innes shrewdly noted, there were 'artificial disabilities' which prevented a Malay woman of the upper class from playing an *overt* political role.[58] She might, however, exercise influence behind the scenes. Che Mida, for example, on one occasion acted as a go-between.[59] The wives of rulers were sometimes able to promote the interests of sons or sons-in-law by intrigue in the court circle.[60]

Women of any class appeared at social occasions, such as a wedding, though they generally kept together as a group and did not mix with the male guests. There is also evidence that, as the nineteenth century drew on to its close, there was a relaxation of the prohibition against their presence at formal official ceremonies. When James Low visited Perak in 1826, 'the Raja's wife and her attendants peeped through the partition at the end of the room'.[61] But half a century later, when Andrew Clarke visited Pahang, 'His Highness conducted us into an inner apartment where his wives and children were assembled'.[62] Then in 1880 when Weld made his first visit to Perak, 'all the native ladies had congregated in a kind of open pavilion close to the Residency, in order to see the procession up to it. I was told afterwards that they would have been highly pleased if I had gone in and spoken to them. The "Robber Datoh", Toh Seri Lela, told me he would have made no objection; however on such a complicated subject as the Eastern code of etiquette, it was better to keep on the safe side.'[63]

In village society the basic rules of feminine decorum were modified by local practices. The village women took their produce to sell at the local markets of the East Coast states and chaffered readily with prospective customers.[64] Winstedt, when posted for the first time to Negeri Sembilan, stronghold of the Menangkabau social system in which women had a prominent position, noted that 'in other Malay states the men visit government offices, and if they have to bring their women-folk, bring them veiled and demure. There is order and decorum and no jostling. In Kuala Pilah my office was always thronged with eager, loud and persistent ladies.'[65]

Even where etiquette prescribed restraint, the ice broke very easily. An earlier chapter has mentioned the American naturalist Hornaday's stay on a village front verandah. When the time came for his departure he made a present to the headman's wife in appreciation of her hospitality—'a very nice figured sarong, which pleased her mightily'. She responded by providing him with a 'hot dinner—a very nice and highly palatable meal of fried bananas, preserves of nutmeg and pomegranate, and a dry short-cake to eat with butter and sugar . . . it was a feast, for it was the very best the house could offer'. Hornaday continues that 'the mother-in-law and daughter had often peeped through the door at me, but had never shown themselves until I sent in to the old lady, a knife, fork and spoon, as a present, instead of the spoon she had craved as a curiosity; whereupon she forthwith donned her best sarong and jacket and came into the room where I was to thank me for her presents and her daughter's . . . but her daughter's face I never saw.'[66]

It may be that the wife was sulking. When Bloomfield Douglas came to the same house three years later, he noted that the headman 'is a very decent civil fellow with an intriguing restless Penang woman for a wife, and they don't pull together and I hear the Datuk wishes to make a change in his domestic arrangements'. The headman wished to retire to Penang but 'his wife is a very active busybody and says she fears the Datuk will divorce her when he goes to Penang and take a younger wife. I think it is very likely as Mrs. Datuk must be a very fatiguing woman to live with, her tongue and its incessant use is something fearful.'[67] There were different facets of Malay domestic life in the villages.

Over the last quarter of the nineteenth century there was a small but growing community of Malay households in the towns. It is among this group that one may best observe the first signs of changing matrimonial relationships. In the course of his career as teacher and then pilgrimage commissioner, Haji Abdul Majid bin Zainuddin had varied marital experience. He remained married to his first wife—'a good old soul'—for over thirty years; he ventured into a serious but disastrous experiment in polygamy in Malaya;

and making his annual stay of seven months in Arabia during the pilgrimage season he married briefly six 'cooks and household keepers'.[68] He was an early specimen of the Malay 'intellectual' and his reflections on marriage are of much interest.

When he married in the early years of the twentieth century, convention still required that a marriage should be arranged between the respective parents. However, Abdul Majid was attracted to a girl when he first saw her passing in the distance, veiled and in the company of relatives, as was proper (*patut*). He married her within a few days without the formality of consulting his parents.[69] Yet years later when a suitor for the hand of Abdul Majid's daughter approached him direct, just as he had done, he rebuffed him—'I told him in reply that it was not according to the established Malay custom for him to ask me in person for my daughter in marriage'—and he insisted that a conventional approach must be made 'by sending to me someone responsible from his family'.[70]

In his own sequence of marriages, he was pursuing 'an insatiable quest for the *kindred spirit* in the fair sex' and in his first marriage he treated his wife as 'an unrefined diamond' to whom he would 'be useful in the refining process of her spirit'.[71] However, he had to admit that 'God's own scheme' simply required a mating between them. In spite of his high-faluting notions, he was put out when his wife proved progressive enough to consult a European woman doctor for advice on birth control or sterilization.[72] He also recognized that polygamy was a form of exploitation of women—'grab, grab, grab'—and he knew that his decision to take a second wife in Malaya caused great distress to his first wife. Yet he married a second time, consoling himself with the thought that 'polygamy is destined to become extinct when woman is taught to believe that she is the equal of man'.[73] With the same honesty as Samuel Pepys, he did what was wrong and committed to paper his uneasiness of conscience over it. He does at least recognize a different set of values as an intellectual proposition.

Abdul Majid was not alone in moving towards ambivalence over arranged marriage without regard to the inclinations of the spouses. Swettenham wrote that although marriages were still arranged 'the most enlightened Malay parents would not press a girl to marry if she expressed strong objection to the suitor'.[74] The anonymous writer of a newspaper article relates how he and the girl of his choice contrived to set out from their homes at the same time on the road to school. They did not actually walk together but they could look at each other. In the end, each was married off to another partner chosen for them by the parents and he acknowledges that it would have been 'disgraceful and unbecoming for a Malay youth if it had been discovered that he was looking for a girl of his own choice for a mate, when he was still a schoolboy, the more so for a Malay girl.... We had neither courage nor means to inform our parents of what was in our minds and hearts.' His marriage to the wife chosen for him by his parents a year or two later was a happy one.[75]

Even married couples were subject to strict conventions of conduct. If they went out together 'it is considered more seemly if they take with them at least a child to show that they are husband and wife'.[76] Moreover, the wife walked a few paces behind her husband; to walk side by side was considered improper.[77] Any open show of affection in public would have been indecent.

Although polygamy was rare, except in the upper class, a well-to-do villager might indulge himself in this way. Sometimes the wives made the best of the situation with fair harmony. A caller at a villager's house in Kedah in 1900 wrote that 'at the time of our visit one wife was weaving a sarong, chatting merrily the while to another who was preparing two big river fish for her lord's dinner.... His third wife we did not see.'[78] More often, however, the first wife demanded a divorce as soon as the second marriage took place. If there was a dispute she could expect little help from the *kadi* to whom polygamy was a normal incident of Muslim life. It had become the convention that if the wife tendered the fee for registration of a divorce by the husband, she should have it. But a district officer in Pahang told how 'a Malay woman came to him with $60 in her hand saying that she wished to pay this sum to her husband, who had just married a co-wife, and to obtain a divorce. The *kadi* acknowledged that legally the woman could claim a divorce on payment of the necessary fees and that he must take official cognisance of it, "But, Tuan," he said, "how can I assist her?"' He went on to allege that a Chinese with whom the woman wished to cohabit had given her the money.[79]

There is a story of a prudent village wife who made a contract with her husband by which, if he married a second time and she tendered the $60 fee, he must then divorce her or pay $1,000 if he did not. She registered the contract. In another case the wife of a *penghulu* objected to his proposed second marriage on the grounds that a Muslim may take another wife only if he can support both wives and their children. 'His salary', she said, 'is only $15 per month and on that he cannot support just me alone—I have to go out and work to supplement our income.'[80] Polygamy, always resented, was no longer accepted as something which a man might indulge in at his discretion.

In upper-class society too, where polygamy had been more common because there were fewer financial constraints, there was growing resistance. Around the turn of the century there was a rift, discreetly concealed, between Sultan Sulaiman and his first and principal wife, Tunku Maharum. Soon after his accession he took a second wife. Tunku Maharum then went off to Penang to live with her father and, despite the dispatch of a succession of envoys to reason with her, refused for two years to come back. In the meantime the preparations for the new ruler's accession ceremony, for which her presence as Tunku Ampuan was deemed essential, were delayed. Eventually the Sultan, a quiet man, hinted that there might be a divorce—and she came back.[81]

Earlier chapters have offered examples of men rising from the subject class to partial acceptance as members of the upper class. There were also *anak raja* driven by financial need to earn a livelihood in tasks which convention reserved to the peasant class. Swettenham's 'broad line' could be crossed.[82] Yet so long as the Malay community perceived itself as divided into these two main classes, the crossing of the dividing line by a few individuals merely reduced the significance of the distinction without abolishing it. To some extent that situation continued—and continues to this day.[83]

There were, however, new elements emerging in Malay society which *as groups* did not fit neatly into the upper or lower strata of the traditional structure. Here there was the beginning of a third or middle class. One such element is found in those of the immigrants, from Sumatra or other parts of modern Indonesia, who did not become quickly assimilated into the Malay peasant class but pursued a business career in the towns or larger villages. Enough has been said in earlier chapters of the first appearance of such men—Che Karim, Haji Tahir, Sheikh Mohet, Che Mat, and others.[84] Although mining and trade were the normal basis of their rise from the ruck, they were versatile as well as mobile. Sheikh Mahomed Taib, who came from Padang in Sumatra, had 'a great deal of influence' in Perak but has also been in both Pahang and Selangor. He eventually became chief *kadi* in Perak and a member of the state council.[85] Haji Mohamed Taib from Menangkabau pursued a more conventional business career in Selangor from 1876 until his death in 1925. He became 'one of the richest Malays in Selangor, owning tin-mines, plantation land and large numbers of houses and shops in Malay Street and the environs of Kuala Lumpur'.[86]

In so far as they came into contact with the two established classes of Malay society they were upstart interlopers. Clifford has a couple of stories of successful traders and capitalists in conflict with village leaders.[87] Their pretensions were also resented by the aristocracy whose antagonism found expression in dwelling on their 'foreign' origins; they were *anak dagang*, not natives of the state. In 1890 Swettenham wrote that Perak Malays had 'an exceeding dislike for and jealousy of all foreigners (including Malays not of Perak)'.[88] As it happens, Abdul Majid, whose matrimonial experiences have been related above, was an *anak dagang* in Perak during the early years of this century and bears testimony to his uneasy position. He had been born in 1887 at Pudu, a suburb of Kuala Lumpur, a son of a Menangkabau trader who kept a provision shop. Abdul Majid obtained entry to the Malay College at Kuala Kangsar in 1905 by the patronage of its founder, R. J. Wilkinson. After a short period of study he stayed on as the only Malay teacher on the staff. Sultan Idris, like Wilkinson, recognized the young man's talent, but conservative constraints in the royal circle obliged the ruler to adopt a most circuitous method of drawing Abdul Majid into that circle. In the course of his weekly visit to the town mosque at Kuala Kangsar, Idris contrived to include the young schoolmaster, whom he professed not to know, in a collective invitation to a feast at the *istana*. Abdul Majid concedes that he did not enjoy the grand occasion as much as he had hoped. After the meal the party took it in turn to read the Koran 'in which I did not particularly shine'. Moreover, he was not fully accepted—'I was regarded as an "*anak dagang*" more than as an *orang Perak*.' However, he had his moments of social triumph such as the 'Motor Car Procession' which formed part of the celebrations of the Sultan's Silver Jubilee in 1912. Abdul Majid was one of the party of four who rode in 'the most beautiful and the biggest car in the state' lent for the occasion by the Chinese millionaire, Eu Tong Seng. 'As we were moving slowly towards the *astana*, Haji Mohamed Noor remarked to me slowly, "Think of the irony of fate—the Perak Malays always look down upon the *anak dagang*; and yet here we are as the representatives of their most exclusive

Club—all four are *anak dagang*."'[89] The bourgeoisie had broken through the barrier.

Abdul Majid is typical of another slow-moving social change. His father was a trader but Abdul Majid was a civil servant. In time, the growing number of Malay civil servants in the expanding middle ranks of the bureaucracy became the predominant element of the middle class. To some extent these positions were filled by sons of the aristocracy. Among the young men who attended the Selangor Raja School during its brief existence from 1890 to 1894, two became 'apprentice tracers' in technical departments and a third, a municipal health inspector.[90] Yet many of the teachers, clerks, *penghulu*, police constables and the like were of the peasant class—but in a different occupation. Some of these were very lowly positions but they formed the base of a new urban class at the apex of which stood the Malay administrators.[91]

The emergence of the Malay administrator took different forms in different parts of the Peninsula.[92] In the FMS, especially in Perak, there had been some tentative and very limited experiments in appointing Malays to administrative posts in the 1890s.[93] The origin of the FMS Malay Administrative Service is to be found in the establishment of the Malay College at Kuala Kangsar in 1905 since the service was recruited from its students. This is a subject which lies beyond the time limits of the present study, but it is worth a brief examination since it brings out conflicts which had their origins in earlier years.

Members of the Malay Administrative Service held assistant district officers' posts. In authority they were a mere shadow of the former district chiefs but they constituted a Malay 'presence' in country districts which continued a ruling class tradition.[94] The upper class was therefore disposed to regard entry to the Malay College as an aristocratic perquisite. Yet from the start, the College did admit a few pupils of the subject class—Abdul Majid was such a case. However, there were protests. When a ruler learnt that a descendant of a slave had been selected for the College he made his displeasure known.[95] In Selangor, the committee which selected boys for the College restricted its choice to boys born in the state and came close to ruling that sons of immigrants (*anak dagang*) were ineligible.[96]

In the states, a Malay administrative officer occupied an ambivalent position. He was a civil servant and yet an aura of traditional status—or the lack of it if he was a commoner by birth—surrounded him. One admitted that he was uneasy when posted to serve at the district office at Pekan, the royal capital of Pahang. In Selangor, Malay administrators, when invited to ceremonies at the *istana*, were expected to sit on the floor with the general body of the ruler's subjects. Some preferred to find diplomatic excuses for declining the invitation.[97]

It was a society moving slowly towards a structure of achieved status by role—but yet it could not overlook status ascribed by birth.

1. F. A. Swettenham, *British Malaya: An Account of the Origin and Progress of British Influence in Malaya*, London, John Lane Bodley Head, 1907 (revised editions 1929 and 1948, London, Allen & Unwin), p. 141. '*Anak ikan di-makan ikan*': C. C. Brown, *Malay Sayings*, Routledge & Kegan Paul, London, 1951, p. 94.

2. 'Malay religion and custom' were by clause 6 of the Pangkor Engagement of 20 January 1874 excluded from the matters on which the ruler of Perak was obliged to act on British advice (J. de V. Allen, A. J. Stockwell and L. R. Wright (eds.), *A Collection of Treaties and Other Documents Affecting the States of Malaysia 1761–1963*, 2 vols., New York, Oceana Publications, Vol. 1, p. 391).

3. *Proceedings of the Federal Council of the FMS 1927*, 16 November 1927.

4. By Islamic law it was unlawful to enslave a fellow Muslim. Malays distinguished between a slave (*abdi*) and a debt-bondsman (*orang berhutang*), who was still a free man (*orang merdeka*).

W. E. Maxwell, 'The Law Relating to Slavery among the Malays', *JSBRAS*, 22, 1890, is a clear statement of the traditional rules relating to both categories. In their campaign to eliminate these practices the European administrators wrote a series of reports between 1875 and 1883 on the current situation in the western Malay states. These were published in Cmd. 3285 and Cmd. 3429 of 1882; much of this material has been reprinted as Appendix B to Chai Hon-Chan, *The Development of British Malaya 1896–1909*, Kuala Lumpur, Oxford University Press, 1964. The reports on Pahang come later: SSD 15 October 1887, 28 August 1889 and especially 17 January 1890. *AR Kedah 1909* summarizes the position and practice in Kedah at that time. On Terengganu see SSD 23 July 1909 and Shaharil Talib Robert, 'The Trengganu Ruling Class in the Late Nineteenth Century', *JMBRAS*, 50(2), 1977, p. 28, and SSD 23 December 1918, and Shaharil Talib, *After Its Own Image: The Trengganu Experience 1881–1941*, Singapore, Oxford University Press, 1984 (hereafter cited as *The Trengganu Experience*). On Kelantan: SSD 31 January 1889. On Singapore and Johor: C. B. Buckley, *An Anecdotal History of Old Times in Singapore 1819–1867*, 2 vols., Singapore, Fraser & Neave, 1902, reprinted Kuala Lumpur, University of Malaya Press, 1965, and Singapore, Oxford University Press, 1984, pp. 159 and 210.

The best modern study is Aminuddin bin Baki, 'The Institution of Debt-Slavery in Perak', *Peninjau Sejarah*, 1(1), 1966. See also P. Sullivan, *Social Relations of Dependence in a Malay State: Nineteenth Century Perak*, MBRAS Monograph 10,

1982, *passim*; J. M. Gullick, *Indigenous Political Systems of Western Malaya*, London, Athlone Press, 1958, pp. 98–105; P. Loh Fook Seng, 'The British Approach to Slavery in the Straits Settlements and the Malay States 1819 to 1910', *Journal of the Historical Society, University of Malaya*, 3, 1964–5; M. Yegar, 'The Abolition of Servitude in British Malaya: An Historical Analysis', *Israeli Yearbook on Human Rights*, 5, 1975; W. Linehan, 'Reinstatement of an *Orang Hulur*', *JMBRAS*, 4(2), 1926; Mahmud bin Mat, 'The Passing of Slavery in East Pahang', *MHJ*, 1(1), 1954, and 'Some Features of Malay Life in East Pahang at the Close of the 19th and the Beginning of the 20th Centuries', *Malaysia* (formerly *Malaya*), May 1964; J. W. W. Birch, *The Journals of J. W. W. Birch First British Resident to Perak 1874–1875* (hereafter cited as *Birch Journal*), edited by P. L. Burns, Kuala Lumpur, Oxford University Press, 1976; F. A. Swettenham, *Sir Frank Swettenham's Malayan Journals 1874–1876* (hereafter cited as *Swettenham Journal*), edited by P. L. Burns and C. D. Cowan, Kuala Lumpur, Oxford University Press, 1975; Douglas Diary; and the literary work of Clifford and Swettenham: H. C. Clifford, 'Two Little Slave Girls', *Malayan Monochromes*, New York, Dutton, 1913, pp. 119–48, and F. A. Swettenham, *British Malaya*, pp. 195–6.

5. See p. 144, note 22, above.

6. Report of 30 June 1875 by Swettenham in Cmd. 3285.

7. This view is supported by the situation in Negeri Sembilan where most of the states had a settled population but no *raja* class—and very little debt-bondage (SSD 28 April 1882 and 4 May 1882). In the royal domain of Sri Menanti, on the other hand, there were some debt-bondsmen who were set free in 1887 (SSD 4 July 1887).

8. SSD 31 January 1889 and see p. 104 above. Bozzolo adds that the obvious alternative of flight into Ulu Kelantan was frustrated by 'want of road'.

9. As for note 6.

10. Report of 14 December 1878 in Cmd. 3285. Another Perak lady 'has also claims of a like nature on several families' (ibid.). Later, when the Perak State Council discussed the ending of debt-bondage in 1882, Raja Dris (later Sultan Idris) 'states that he has already freed all his own slaves and slave-debtors ... but he cannot however include in this manumission the slaves who are the personal property of his wife' (*PSCM*, 10 October 1882, *PMS*, p. 253).

11. Evidence to PCE in CO 273/87, p. 585. See p. 102 above on Haji Mat Yassin.

12. Evidence to PCE in CO 273/87, pp. 209–39. Si Mahnoon was the royal pastrycook: see pp. 49 and 73 above. W. Linehan, 'A History of Pahang' (hereafter cited as 'Pahang'), *JMBRAS*, 14(2), 1936, pp. 124 and 129—'few of them were royal concubines'.

13. Mahmud bin Mat, 'Passing of Slavery', p. 9. See p. 7 above for his description of his personal experience of deprivation of attendant nursemaids.

14. SSD 17 January 1890. 'Scarcely more than nominal value' was the opinion of a Perak aristocrat expressed to Hugh Low (report cited in note 10). See Loh, 'British Approach to Slavery', and Yegar, 'Abolition of Servitude', on the details of the arrangements for setting free the bondsmen and slaves. In some states the government paid sums to the creditors by way of discharge of that part of the debt which was not repaid by service. See Sharom Ahmat, *Tradition and Change in a Malay State: A Study of the Economic and Political Development of Kedah 1878–1923*, MBRAS Monograph 12, 1984, p. 134, on Kedah.

15. Hugh Low's report—see note 10 above.

16. Mahmud bin Mat, 'Passing of Slavery', and see. p. 7 above.

17. W. G. Maxwell, 'Memories of the First British Adviser Kedah', *Malaya in History*, 4, 1958, pp. 14–15.

18. Shaharil Talib Robert, 'Trengganu Ruling Class', p. 28. The number had been much larger in earlier times.

19. Clifford, *Malayan Monochromes*, p. 131. The story, presumably based on an actual episode, tells how the two girls escape down-river by boat, make an 80-mile journey to Pekan and, after various encounters with officialdom, get in to see the Resident who summons their master and 'puts the fear of death into what did duty within him for a soul'. He suffers a fine and returns to his up-river village 'a wiser and sadder man'. Douglas has entries in his diary between June and November 1876 on a rather similar if less colourful affair. See also Douglas Diary, 23 July 1878, for another case.

20. S. Husin Ali, *Social Stratification in Kampong Bagan: A Study of Class, Status, Conflict and Mobility in a Rural Malay Community*, MBRAS Monograph No. 1, 1964, especially p. 135. M. G. Swift, 'Economic Concentration and Malay Peasant Society', in M. Freedman (ed.), *Social Organisation: Essays Presented to Raymond Firth*, London, Frank Cass, 1967.

21. As for note 6. Swettenham adds that if a free man marries a bondswoman, he and their descendants enter into bondage. There was no sex discrimination over this.

22. Swettenham, *British Malaya*, p. 152. Weld, travelling by river, 'met a boat full of women, who all turned their faces to the jungle, as was right and proper, in passing us. But . . . I looked suddenly around, and found Eve was looking and was very much abashed indeed' (A. Lovat, *The Life of Sir Frederick Weld: A Pioneer of Empire*, London, Murray, 1914, p. 309). A. L. Keyser, *Trifles and Travels*, London, Murray, 1923, p. 111.

23. R. J. Wilkinson, 'The Incidents of Malay Life', *Papers on Malay Subjects, Life and Customs*, Pt. 1, 1908, reprinted in *JMBRAS*, 30(4), 1957, pp. 51–5 (betrothal), pp. 56–60 (marriage); Zainal Abidin bin Ahmad, 'Malay Manners and Etiquette', *JMBRAS*, 23(3), 1950, p. 70. M. G. Swift, 'Men and Women in Malay Society', in B. Ward (ed.), *Women in the New Asia*, Paris, UNESCO, 1963, p. 281, emphasizes the 'discrepancy between appearance and reality' in matrimonial relations. Although no affection is displayed even in private this may mask the real feelings. J. Cameron, *Our Tropical Possessions in Malayan India: Being a Descriptive Account of Singapore, Penang, Province Wellesley, and Malacca, their Peoples, Products, Commerce and Government*, London, Smith, Elder & Co., 1865, reprinted as *Our Tropical Possessions in Malayan India*, Kuala Lumpur, Oxford University Press, 1965, p. 130, writes of 'a sincere and generally lasting attachment' between spouses.

24. H. C. Clifford, *In a Corner of Asia, being Tales and Impressions of Men and Things in the Malay Peninsula*, London, Fisher Unwin, 1899, p. 149. The husband contracts leprosy but the wife continues to nurse him although both become outcasts from their village in consequence. Clifford's account of the process of adjustment in the early years of an arranged marriage (ibid., pp. 147–9) is too long to quote but is worth reading. The story is reprinted in *The Further Side of Silence*, New York, Doubleday, Page & Co., 1927, pp. 182–214. Although a little sentimental in tone, it is a very moving account of something which Clifford himself had witnessed.

25. H. C. Clifford, *Bushwhacking and Other Asiatic Tales and Memories*, New York, Harper, 1929, p. 145 (W. R. Roff (ed.), *Stories by Sir Hugh Clifford*, Kuala Lumpur, Oxford University Press, 1966, p. 114). The story is about a girl who flouted the convention—and what happens to her. See also Gullick, *Indigenous Political Systems*, pp. 66, 78 and 86.

26. Swettenham, *Malay Sketches*, London, John Lane Bodley Head, 1895, pp. 179–91, tells the story (with the identities thinly disguised by altering the names) of the elopement of Raja Tipah, wife of Raja (later Sultan) Abdullah of Perak, with Raja Daud of Selangor. Abdullah divorced his wife in her absence but made no attempt to pursue the runaway pair. 'This conduct earned him not the admiration but the contempt of his people' (p. 189). The quotation is from p. 186. See also R. O. Winstedt and R. J. Wilkinson, 'A History of Perak', *JMBRAS*, 12(1), 1934, p. 94; Swettenham, *The Real Malay: Pen Pictures*, London, John Lane Bodley Head, 1900, p. 147; H. C. Clifford, *Studies in Brown Humanity being Scrawls and Smudges in Sepia, White and Yellow*, London, Grant Richards, 1898, p. 172.

27. H. C. Clifford, *In Court and Kampong, being Tales and Sketches of Native Life in the Malay Peninsula*, London, Grant Richards, 1897 (2nd ed. with autobiographical preface, London, Richards Press, 1927), p. 191, and see p. 240 below.

28. Swettenham, *The Real Malay*, p. 71, and *Malay Sketches*, p. 68; *British Malaya*, p. 126; *Swettenham Journal*, p. 207. E. Innes, *The Chersonese with the Gilding Off*, 2 vols., London, Richard Bentley, 1885, reprinted Kuala Lumpur, Oxford University Press, 1974, Vol. 1, pp. 92–4, tells the story of the maltreatment and eventual killing of a slave girl by a jealous wife.

29. '*Seperti tebu, ayer-nya di-makan, hampas-nya di-buang*' (Brown, *Malay Sayings*, p. 186). The judgement on unchastity of a single woman was equally harsh—'*sunggoh bersubang, tidak berdarah*' (ibid., p. 151—she wears the maiden's earrings but is no virgin). See also ibid., pp. 81, 115, 137, 183 and 215 for other sayings which express bitter disapprobation of the 'fallen woman'. It was obviously a dominant theme of Malay morality.

30. Swettenham, *The Real Malay*, p. 144; Brown, *Malay Sayings*, p. 122, 'sniffing the air like a buffalo behind the herd'. Haji Abdul Majid bin Zainuddin, *The Wandering Thoughts of a Dying Man*, edited by W. R. Roff, Kuala Lumpur, Oxford University Press, 1978, pp. 141–3.

31. Clifford, *Further Side of Silence*, p. 15 (for indecency), *In Court and Kampong*, p. 32 (to quell a wife's protest). In *Bushwhacking*, p. 144, a brother beats his sister (in the episode referred to in note 25 above). The term '*panjat angkara*' was applied to the abduction of a girl by her lover from her home (W. E. Maxwell, *Notes and Queries* No. 4, issued with *JSBRAS*, 17, 1886, p. 118). Violence was not far below the surface of sexual relationships (see Chapter 10). The women could be violent too—see note 28 above and Swettenham, *British Malaya*, p. 126; Clifford, *In Court and Kampong*, p. 40.

32. Swettenham, *British Malaya*, p. 154, says that wives 'seem quite reconciled' to being divorced at the husband's will but object strongly to 'sharing a man with several other women'. On divorce generally see p. 220 below and W. E. Maxwell, 'Malay Proverbs, Part 3', *JSBRAS*, 3, 1879, p. 44.

33. 'That he should have other wives and concubines was of course only what she had been educated to expect' (Swettenham, *Malay Sketches*, p. 182). In this particular case (see note 26) the husband's conduct led to the breakup of the marriage. H. C. Clifford, *A Prince of Malaya*, New York, Harper, 1926 (originally published as 'Sally' in *Blackwoods Magazine*, February 1904, and *Saleh: A Sequel*, London, Blackwood, 1908), p. 148, brings out the savage resentment of a royal consort now neglected by her husband in favour of younger women.

34. '*Sayangkan kain, buangkan baju*'—discard one garment to get another (Maxwell, cited in note 32 above).

35. J. D. Vaughan, 'Notes on the Malays of Pinang and Province Wellesley', *JIA*, n.s., 1857, p. 143.

36. M. B. Hooker, *Adat Laws in Modern Malaya*, Kuala Lumpur, Oxford University Press, 1972, especially Chapter 10.

37. Clifford, *In Court and Kampong*, p. 199.

38. Swettenham, *British Malaya*, p. 155.

39. F. A. Swettenham, *Footprints in Malaya*, London, Hutchinson, 1942, p. 51; *British Malaya*, p. 148: 'amusements and social intercourse . . . open to them'.

40. *Swettenham Journal*, p. 282. In evidence to PCE another domestic said that she was sharply reproved by a chief's wife—'What are you doing there, go to your work' (CO 273/88, pp. 5–15). See Clifford, *Bushwhacking*, p. 147, and Swettenham, *The Real Malay*, pp. 269–89, on the hard side of female character.

41. *Swettenham Journal*, pp. 34, 36 and 65. Some of her wealth was derived from tin mines (ibid., pp. 92 and 192, and *PSCM*, 12 March 1882, *PMS*, p. 244); J. F. A. McNair, *Perak and the Malays: Sarong and Keris*, London, Tinsley Bros., 1878, reprinted Kuala Lumpur, Oxford University Press, 1972, p. 131; Gullick, *Indigenous Political Systems*, p. 85; *Birch Journal*, pp. 70, 75–6. McNair, op. cit., has a picture of Che Mida as his frontispiece, and another of her house at p. 169.

42. *PSCM*, 4 February 1878—the appointment is not included in the Burns reprint of *PSCM* but she is mentioned later at p. 165 thereof. In 1879 the Perak State Council had to deal with her claim to a house at Bukit Gantang (*PSCM*, 4 March 1879, *PMS*, p. 195).

43. *PSCM*, 4 March 1879, *PMS*, pp. 192–3. The issue which came before the Perak State Council was whether the house was family property, to which Halimah might lay claim as donee from her husband, or a state residence which he had built for the Sultan's use when visiting Larut. See note 46 below.

44. Swettenham, *The Real Malay*, p. 205. Most of the information on Halimah's situation after 1875 comes from ibid., pp. 201–9, augmented by specific references in H. Low, 'The Journal of Sir Hugh Low, Perak 1877' (hereafter cited as 'Low Journal'), edited by E. Sadka, *JMBRAS*, 27(4), 1954, and *PSCM*, cited as required in various notes. Quotations in the text are from Swettenham, *The Real Malay*, unless otherwise identified.

45. In 1877 she brought her two sons, aged eleven and seven, to see Hugh Low: 'Low Journal', p. 97; Swettenham, *The Real Malay*, p. 206.

46. *PSCM* cited in note 43 above. Low advised the Council to relinquish its claim to the house as the government had no further use for it and—significantly—since it would cost a great deal of money to repair and then maintain it. There is no further record of what Halimah did with it.

47. 'Low Journal', p. 39: SSD 14 June and 21 July 1877. In the end the Menteri took six attendants with him to the Seychelles and each of his two wives received $75 per month from his total allowance for himself and his family.

48. 'Low Journal', pp. 98 and 103. She continued to fight her husband's battles by presenting petitions (SSD 20 July 1878).

49. The Perak State Council ruled that the mosque was not her property (*PSCM*, 5 January 1881, *PMS*, pp. 234–5).

50. Low report of 14 December 1878 cited in note 10 above.

51. The Perak scheme for the enfranchisement of debt-bondsmen set a maximum of $60 for a man and $30 for a woman as the reckonable debt. The debtor was to pay off half the debt by service to the creditor and the state government paid the rest

(*PSCM*, 9 October 1882, *PMS*, p. 251). See p. 213 above on the Pahang scheme.

52. Her tender was rejected as there 'was reason to believe that it would pass into the hands of a Chinaman' if the contract were awarded to her (*PSCM*, 18 November 1879, *PMS*, p. 210). The episode does suggest that she was not in penury and was capable of negotiating business arrangements.

53. *PSCM*, 20 August 1895, *PGG* 1895, p. 526. On the career of the elder son, Wan Mohamed Isa, see p. 76 above. The exiled husband and former Menteri was allowed to return to live in Sarawak in 1889 and then permitted to come to Singapore in 1893. At the end of his life he was planning to spend his last years in Mecca—an interesting example of the pilgrimage as an outlet from humiliation (SSD 5 September 1894).

54. Innes, op. cit., Vol. 1, pp. 88–9 and 96–7.

55. Swettenham, *Malay Sketches*, p. 9.

56. 'Low Journal', p. 103. Hugh Low added a footnote to a decision of the Perak State Council on a claim by the daughter of Raja Yusuf, the Regent, writing that 'the income of a woman from her own private property or settlements is independent of any control by her husband' (*PSCM*, 26 October 1882, *PMS*, p. 266). Keyser, *Trifles and Travels*, p. 93, to the same effect.

57. E. Caddy, *To Siam and Malaya in the Duke of Sutherland's Yacht 'Sans Peur'*, London, Hurst & Blackett, 1889, p. 236. She was no beauty; see Lovat, op. cit., p. 376, where she is described as half-Malay and half-Chinese, 'coarse featured and square built, very homely in appearance but pleasing in manner and quite unaffected'. Abu Bakar was extravagant and she was careful with money.

58. Innes, op. cit., Vol. 1, p. 89.

59. At her own suggestion she undertook to persuade her foster-son, Bendahara Osman, to co-operate with Swettenham, who joined them later (*Swettenham Journal*, p. 305).

60. Wan Hajar, the widow of Sultan Ahmad Tajuddin II of Kedah (r. 1854–79), was a considerable power in Kedah, both by force of personality and as the sister of the chief minister, Wan Mat Saman, during the first twenty years of the reign of her son, Sultan Abdul Hamid (1882–1943), who was mentally unstable. The Siamese government recognized this fact by inviting her to come to Bangkok in 1890 with her son (Muhammad Hassan bin Dato' Kerani Muhammad Arshad, *Al-Tarikh Salasilah Negeri Kedah*, Kuala Lumpur, Dewan Bahasa dan Pustaka, 1968 (previously published in *Jawi*, 1926), p. 240). In 1905 the Raja Muda of Kedah went to Bangkok to negotiate the $2.6 million loan which was necessary to rescue Kedah from insolvency. By this time Wan Hajar had suffered a stroke and was confined to a wheelchair but she was one of the signatories of the formal letter requesting the loan (Allen, 'The Elephant and the Mousedeer—A New Version: Anglo-Kedah Relations 1905–1915' (hereafter cited as 'Anglo-Kedah Relations 1905–1915'), *JMBRAS*, 41(1), 1968, p. 66). 'Mak Wan Besar', as she was known, was an exceptional case but it illustrates how far the overt exercise of power by a Malay woman close to the throne could go. Kedah was still a very traditional Malay state in 1909, the year of her death. See also Shaharil Talib, *The Trengganu Experience*, p. 14.

The wife of Sultan Mohamed of Selangor (r.1826–57) was able to secure the title of Raja Muda for her son, Raja Mahmud, although he was only a young boy at the time. It did not, however, secure the succession to him as she had hoped (R. O. Winstedt, 'A History of Selangor', *JMBRAS*, 12(3), 1934, p. 19).

In Kedah Wan Maheran, the wife to Sultan Zainal Rashid II (r.1845–54), arranged the marriage of her eldest son, Ahmad Tajuddin, to the daughter (Wan Hajar mentioned above) of the influential Wan Ismail and thereby secured for her son the succession to the throne although he was a very young man in 1854. Later in 1867 she had a part in the decision that her second son, Tunku Kudin, should marry the daughter of Sultan Abdul Samad of Selangor, from which Kudin was able to attain the position of Viceroy of Selangor (1868–78). She also lent him $60,000 towards his war chest in the Selangor Civil War (Muhammad Hassan bin Dato' Kerani Muhammad Arshad, op. cit., p. 200; J. C. Pasqual, *Singapore Sunday Times*, 28 October 1934; SSD 18 June 1878). Wan Hajar, one of the two principal wives of Sultan Ahmad Tajuddin II of Kedah (r.1854–79), was a leading figure in the Kedah succession dispute of 1879–81 and was successful in securing the succession to her son, Sultan Abdul Hamid, against the sons of the other wife (Allen, 'Anglo-Kedah Relations 1905–1915', pp. 58–61; Muhammad Hassan, op. cit., p. 240).

In Perak Wan Teh Sapiah (see note 42 above) spread rumours that the reason for the British plan to educate the two sons of ex-Sultan Abdullah at English schools was to ensure that one of them would succeed Sultan Idris in due course (see note 93 on their actual careers as civil servants—and also p. 91, note 42 above on Raja Chulan). Later, in 1909, one of the wives of Sultan Idris pressed him to appoint Raja Chulan to the office of Bendahara, so as to bring him into the line of succession—he was her son-in-law (CO 273/355, pp. 270A–270G, letter from E. W. Birch, Resident of Perak, to Sir John Anderson)—an absorbing picture of palace intrigue in the early years of the twentieth century. See p. 52 also.

61. J. Low, 'Observations on Perak', *JIA*, 4, 1850, p. 501.

62. SSD 16 October 1874. However, when Jervois visited Terengganu and Kelantan, strongholds of tradition, in the following year (1875) the rulers apparently did not permit him to meet their wives (SSD 7 August 1875). Although women attended 'great entertainments' (Swettenham, *British Malaya*, p. 148) decked out for the grand occasion it was bad form for them to comment on each other's clothes (ibid., p. 155).

63. Lovat, op. cit., p. 298. The 'Robber Datoh' was chief of Kota Lama which had been the main centre of Malay resistance to the British advance in 1875.

64. See p. 139 above.

65. R. O. Winstedt, *Start from Alif, Count from One: An Autobiographical Memoir*, Kuala Lumpur, Oxford University Press, 1969, p. 143. In Negeri Sembilan the women were often the owners of 'tribal lands' and it was their property about which they came to the district office.

66. W. T. Hornaday, *Two Years in the Jungle: The Experiences of a Hunter and Naturalist in India, Ceylon, the Malay Peninsula and Borneo*, New York, Scribner, 1885, pp. 312–13.

67. Douglas Diary, 31 August 1881 and 18 September 1881. The contrast between the two pictures of the wife—demure and retiring in Hornaday's eyes, but a termagent to Douglas—causes doubt as to whether the two passages refer to the same family. However, both identify the husband as 'Datoh Puteh' (Hornaday, op. cit., p. 304, and Douglas cited above) and there was only three years between the two visits. It is possible that Douglas, hearing the voices of the women inside the house, may have confused the mother-in-law with the wife. His command of Malay was poor (J. M. Gullick, 'Selangor 1876–1882: The Bloomfield Douglas Diary', *JMBRAS*, 48(2), 1975, p. 1).

68. Abdul Majid bin Zainuddin, *Wandering Thoughts*, pp. 34–5. He lived from

1887 to 1943. The title ('Dying Man') refers to the incurable diabetes from which he suffered when, at the end of his life, he wrote his autobiography—down to 1923—and left it unpublished and written in English. Apart from his great rival, Zainal Abidin bin Ahmad ('Zaba'), he was perhaps the leading Malay writer of his day.

69. Ibid., p. 24. His father-in-law was an Indian Muslim to whom Malay etiquette may have been unimportant (p. 31).

70. Ibid., p. 142.

71. Ibid., p. 24.

72. Ibid., p. 34. She had had a sequence of difficult and painful confinements. He refers to an 'operation' which seems to have prevented further pregnancies.

73. Ibid., pp. 21 and 28.

74. Swettenham, *British Malaya*, p. 153.

75. *Singapore Sunday Times*, 21 April 1935. He does not say how old he was at the time when the article was written. It may relate to the inter-war period. It seems clear that the pair came from middle-class and probably urban families. His opinion is that it is an advantage in an arranged marriage if the spouses 'have known and understood each other first' and he is opposed to 'forcing of any sort'.

76. Zainal Abidin bin Ahmad, 'Malay Manners', p. 70.

77. Hashimah Roose, 'Changes in the Position of Malay Women', in B. Ward (ed.), *Women in the New Asia: The Changing Social Roles of Men and Women in South and South-East Asia*, Paris, UNESCO, 1964, p. 290. Although this was written in 1964 it is expressed to refer to conduct 'at the turn of the century' (p. 288).

78. 'Notes of a Trip to Kedah', *Malay Mail*, 19 April 1900.

79. 'Pahang Notes', *Malay Mail*, 1 April 1901. There was apparently no convention against the remarriage of a widow. In the Pahang Civil War a dying warrior summoned his four wives to stand two on each side of his deathbed. 'If I die, don't you marry again,' he said; they dutifully replied, 'Very well, Dato'!' (Linehan, 'Pahang', p. 80, apparently repeating a tale from the *Hikayat Pahang*). He would not have issued the injunction if by custom they had been prohibited from remarrying.

80. 'Pahang Notes', *Malay Mail*, 1 April 1901, for both anecdotes. These contributions are anonymous. It is unlikely that the author, who was evidently resident in Pahang, was J. H. M. Robson, who may well have written the Kedah item while on tour (note 78 above).

81. Wan Mohamed Amin bin Said, *Pesaka Selangor*, edited by Abdul Samad Ahmad, Kuala Lumpur, Dewan Bahasa dan Pustaka, 1966, pp. 79–86. As *penghulu istiadat* (master of ceremonies) in the royal household, Amin was a horrified witness of the affair. It fell to him to escort the lady back to Selangor. She was the daughter of Tunku Kudin, the former Viceroy of Selangor, and Raja Arfah (see p. 220 above). She seems to have inherited the imperious temperament of her mother, who was dead by this time. Kudin, who had been defeated in a bid for power in Kedah in 1881 (see note 60 above), lived in Penang, though he had often visited Selangor in the 1880s and 1890s. As Kudin had married wives in Kedah and Selangor he was in no position to support his daughter in a crusade against polygamy. He seems to have been rather embarrassed by the whole business but, as he said to Amin, it was pointless for him to order his daughter to return if the underlying estrangement remained.

82. Swettenham, *British Malaya*, p. 141.

83. Chandra Muzaffar, 'Continuity and Change in Malay Ideas of the Melakan

Period', in K. S. Sandhu and P. Wheatley (eds.), *Melaka: The Transformation of a Malay Capital c.1400–1980*, Kuala Lumpur, Oxford University Press, 198[illegible], Vol. 2, explores the theme of the persistence of traditional aristocratic ideas in the conduct of the modern United Malays National Organisation (UMNO). See also the same author's *Protector? An Analysis of the Concept and Practice of Loyalty . . . within Malay Society*, Penang, Aliran, 1979; Syed Husin Ali, *Stratification*, and *Malay Peasant Society and Leadership*, Kuala Lumpur, Oxford University Press, 1975; Syed Hussein Alatas, 'The Grading of Occupational Prestige amongst the Malays in Malaysia', *JMBRAS*, 41(1), 1968. In the space available the author has not explored the concept of class in its application to Malay society. Syed Husin Ali, *Stratification*, pp. 4–12, gives an excellent short introduction to these theoretical issues.

84. See pp. 79 and 187 (Karim); p. 161 (Tahir); p. 184 (Mohet); and p. 105 (Che Mat).

85. *Swettenham Journal*, p. 220, editorial note; 'Low Journal', p. 99; E. Sadka, *The Protected Malay States 1874–1895*, Kuala Lumpur and Singapore, University of Malaya Press, 1968, pp. 112, 161, 179 and 182. Although he was related to Sultan Abdullah by marriage and had high status as a *syaikh* he does not appear to have been an aristocrat in the normal sense. There are several references to him in the Douglas Diary between 1876 and 1879. Even when he had finally departed for Perak he seems to have maintained his business connections with his fellow countryman, Sheikh Mat Ali, headman of the Sumatran mining community of Ulu Klang near Kuala Lumpur. Hugh Low may have appointed him to the Perak State Council to use his enmity with the Regent, Raja Yusuf, to hold the latter in check (Sadka, op. cit., p. 112).

86. W. R. Roff, 'The Life and Times of Haji Othman Abdullah', *Peninjau Sejarah*, 1(2), 1966, p. 62. The subject of Roff's study, Othman, born in 1905 in Jalan Pudu, Kuala Lumpur, was the grandson of Haji Mohamed Taib.

87. In one instance the *parvenu* boasts to the village *imam* of his power over the villagers, all of whom are indebted to him. However, his pride is humbled—see note 19 above. In the other story, the man has travelled abroad and 'garnered a fair stock of worldly goods . . . a very rich man'. He shocks the village by his atheism—and he too comes a cropper (Clifford, *Malayan Monochromes*, pp. 134 and 163).

88. *AR Perak 1890*. It is perhaps significant that Swettenham found it apposite to emphasize this aspect of Perak behaviour at a time when foreigners were coming to the fore. On the hostility between groups who had different cultural origins see p. 3 above.

89. Abdul Majid bin Zainuddin, *Wandering Thoughts*, pp. 72, 74, 80 and 82. Before World War I there were few motor cars in Malaya. J. H. M. Robson, *Records and Recollections 1889–1934*, Kuala Lumpur, Kyle Palmer, 1934, has a chapter on early motoring in Malaya. A. L. Keyser, *People and Places: A Life in Five Continents*, London, Murray, 1922, p. 104, writes as if by 1922 it was not unusual for Malays of the upper class to use cars; see p. 6 above. Eu Tong Seng was a prominent Perak miner and the Chinese unofficial member of the FMS Federal Council. The club was the Perak Malay Club (*Kastan Zarian*) of which Abdul Majid was at the time the secretary (Abdul Majid bin Zainuddin, *Wandering Thoughts*, p. 79).

90. R. Stevenson, *Cultivators and Administrators: British Educational Policy towards the Malays 1875–1906*, Kuala Lumpur, Oxford University Press, 1975, p. 154.

91. *AR Perak Education Department, 1897* in *PGG* 1898, p. 179, gives a list based

on a rough count of the occupations of former pupils of Malay schools. See p. 169 above.

92. See Chapter 4.

93. See Khasnor Johan, *The Emergence of the Modern Malay Administrative Élite*, Singapore, Oxford University Press, 1984, especially Chapter 2 on the early moves; Sadka, *Protected Malay States*, pp. 104–6.

On the two sons of ex-Sultan Abdullah, Raja Mansur and Raja Chulan, see p. 91, note 42 above and Sadka, *Protected Malay States*, pp. 253, 263–4 and 278–9. Isabella Bird met them when they were schoolboys in 1879 and gave a vivid picture of them (I. Bird, *The Golden Chersonese and the Way Thither*, London, Murray, 1883, reprinted Kuala Lumpur, Oxford University Press, 1967 and 1980, p. 281).

One may contrast these two young men who did not fit in easily with the *mores* and practices of the foreign administrators with the case of Wan Mat Salleh, the Seri Adika Raja, who was given charge of three remote *mukim* in an area of Upper Perak where his forebears had been the district chiefs. See p. 78 above.

94. On the continuity of tradition between the Malay district chief and the Malay administrator of the colonial period see J. M. Gullick, 'The Malay Administrator', *Merdeka Outlook*, 1(1), 1957. See also Syed Hussein Alatas, op. cit., p. 149, and Chandra Muzaffar, cited in note 83 above.

95. R. O. Winstedt, *The Malays: A Cultural History*, Singapore, Kelly & Walsh, 1947, p. 43. On investigation it was found that the head of the aristocratic family which had owned the boy's slave ancestor had specially recommended his admission to the Malay College.

96. Khasnor Johan, op. cit., pp. 55–7.

97. Ibid., Chapter 10, 'Malay Officers and the Malay Society', *passim*. Same author's 1974 thesis, p. 222. A Malay officer posted for service outside his native state was made 'to feel like a stranger', and any severity on his part in dealings with the *rakyat* was readily resented as arrogance. But by punctilious observance of the prescribed Islamic rules, e.g. attendance at the mosque for Friday prayers, he might be able to break down the prejudice against a 'foreigner' (ibid., p. 180). See also ibid., p. 173, on relations with the ruler and his court.

10
The Maintenance of Order

'THERE was little fault to be found with the constitution of Perak; the trouble was with the holders of office, the disappointed, the unruly, and the foreign freelances, who found the place exactly to their taste; while the poor groaned and suffered, and there was no one to listen to their exceeding bitter cry.' So wrote Swettenham of Perak in 1872.[1] There is probably considerable exaggeration in these accounts of Malay rule, prompted in part by a desire to justify British intervention. When, for example, the first British Agent at Kuala Terengganu inspected the gaol, the subject of one of Clifford's most horrific descriptions, he noted that it was 'a dilapidated structure' from which 'escapes are frequent'; none of the prisoners had 'been incarcerated for more than a year'.[2] In Kelantan in 1904 the penalty for murder was a fine of between $50 and $1,000.[3]

Except in royal capitals, where intrigue and the excesses of the *budak raja* led to many crimes of violence, the Malay community lived fairly peaceable lives troubled mainly by their own quarrels over adultery and the like, and by the depradations and demands of the local chief. There were two underlying problems—the lack of a framework of law and the means of enforcing it, and, secondly, the readiness to resort to violence. 'Murder was frequently done for the most trivial causes, and a Malay often drew a knife, when an Englishman would have been content to drop a damn.'[4] These are the main topics of this chapter.

'In 1874 no Malay man was ever seen unarmed. The men usually carried from three to eight weapons and boys of a few years old two or three.'[5] Three daggers, two spears, a sword and a gun were the normal personal armament.[6] Carrying arms was both the cause of and a reaction to the frequency of an affray. In June 1874, Swettenham witnessed a dispute at Kuala Kangsar over a debt, which itself resulted from the purchase of a *keris* two years before. 'I found each man surrounded by a small group of partisans, everyone armed with two *keris* and a spear. I expressed some slight surprise at one man wanting to kill another for $4, but I was told it was usual to pursue the same course in the case of 4 cents. I asked the man if he was not afraid of being hanged had he killed his man. He said, "Oh no, we never hang people in Perak." He spoke with a certain amount of confidence as he had already killed four men for no particular reason.'[7]

With weapons at hand it was all too easy to use them. In 1881 two brothers, young men of about twenty, 'were flying kites when the string of Jamil's kite fouled the string of Hitam's kite and severing it the kite was lost in the jungle'. Hitam hit Jamil 'who snatched his brother's small dagger (tumbok lada) from the folds of his sarong and stabbed him in the side. Hitam was taken home but died in two days. The Sultan heard of it and said as it was only a family quarrel it should be hushed up.' But Jamil came to trial before the Resident's court, where he admitted the facts, saying, '"I have killed my brother. He is dead. What can I do now?" . . . He appeared strangely callous and indifferent.'[8]

Under the colonial regime there was a gradual enforcement of a ban against the carrying of weapons.[9] The greater personal security may have made the change less unwelcome but there was some evasion. It was still permissible to carry a *parang* as the essential omni-purpose tool. Some Malays fitted a heavy *keris* blade to a *parang* handle and carried it concealed in a sheath. Others fitted handles to razor blades or to small knives of European manufacture and hid them in their clothing.[10] There were still violent quarrels but they became less lethal. In 1894 one-quarter of the crimes tried before courts in Pahang were cases of assault; but in the majority of cases the assailant had used his fists or a stick.[11]

The traditional admiration of a fighting man, even if—like Raja Mahmud of Selangor—he was a bloodthirsty killer, was another cultural factor conducive to violence. Apart from charismatic war leaders like Raja Mahmud, there was a grim type of 'Malay freebooter'. One such 'was a big man, darker than the average Malay, with a thick moustache and a strong Patani accent. He was naked from the waist upwards, but for a handkerchief knotted round his head, and he deposited a musket outside the door as he entered . . . he spoke of the crimes he had committed with a modesty and candour hardly to be expected from one who so evidently excelled in his own particular line.'[12] Men of this kind were often hired to commit murders for others. In 1876 Douglas tried Panglima Kakab, 'one of the most determined ruffians I ever met. He states he was put up to the murder for the sake of $6—that he is an hireling assassin—and coolly stated he was open to any offer. It was his trade.'[13] It was, however, a trade destined to disappear and the practitioners went with it.

In the villages, where the incidence of violent crime was low, its cause was usually sexual, i.e. jealousy or revenge against an adulterer.[14] As an example, take a case reported in 1901. The husband was 'a typical down-river man', who owned a herd of buffaloes and an orchard; 'above all he had many boats, carrying merchandise between Kuala Lipis . . . and Kuala Pahang'. His wife, who had aristocratic connections, found village life dull and the husband, returning unexpectedly, caught her consoling herself with a lover. There was a savage fight and a divorce. At the husband's trial, on a charge of causing grievous bodily hurt, the wife 'told the unlovely tale with the frank directness of a Malay woman proud of the notoriety she had achieved, and far from regarding the intrigue as a disgrace'.[15]

The injuries were often horrific. 'A man and a woman were brought in from up river with terrible wounds in their legs and arms. The husband of the woman found the couple in the act of adultery and hacked them with a heavy chopper.'[16] Family disapproval could be as violent as marital revenge. In 1898 'a Malay woman, who had been living in concubinage with a Chinese trader in a village in the Temerloh district, was murdered by her relations, after they had vainly tried to induce her to leave her paramour'. The whole community, led by the *penghulu*, then conspired to give false evidence against a Chinese hawker, accusing him of the murder so that the real culprits might escape.[17]

The fear of retribution restrained theft or robbery; if the wrongdoers were local men they were unlikely to escape identification. There are no rational factors of that kind apparent in cases where a man 'runs amuck' (*amuk*) and creates havoc by mindless multiple slaughter until he himself is killed.[18] Yet as the years went by, the number who ran *amuk* diminished—and for this there must be some explanation, not necessarily operative on the mind of a potential *amuk* case.

Swettenham, adopting the opinion of Sultan Idris, suggested that *amuk* was brought on when an acute sense of grievance (*sakit hati*) was combined with an existing but latent disposition to insanity.[19] The grievance might arise from a sense of shame (*malu*) which was quite as intolerable, in the Malay scale of values, as suffering a wrong without redress.[20] There was also a theory that an element of calculation could, in spite of appearances, enter into outbursts of *amuk*—'I have heard it more than once stated by Malays that in these cases of *amuk*, the man is not really mad . . . this man in the first instance, often from jealousy, murdered the person against whom he had a spite. Then knowing that he could not suffer a greater penalty than death, even if he killed half a dozen people, he set about doing so on the off chance that he would be brought in as insane and simply detained.'[21] This explanation could only apply in later days when courts could find the accused 'guilty but insane'. *Amuk* cases had occurred long before that. It also does not fit the killer who turns on his own family, like the case in 1897 of 'a Malay [who] while seated at his food with his family suddenly developed insanity and attacked his wife and two men'.[22] It is true, however, that in some cases of *amuk*, the killer first attacked the object of his resentment before turning on others.[23]

Where the facts were discoverable it was generally found that the killer's rage was touched off by some specific cause of grievance or shame. In the most celebrated *amuk* case in modern times, the mass murder on the coastal steamship *Klang* as she left Singapore in 1925, the killer slew thirteen people and badly injured five more, including the ship's master and members of the crew who were complete strangers. After embarking he had found that he had lost the present which he had bought to give to his wife on his return home; this apparently sufficed to start him off.[24]

The wider meaning of the word '*amuk*', i.e. reckless courage in attacking in battle, may contribute its quota to explaining *amuk* murders. It was killing almost as a form of suicide.[25] As an act of courage it was much admired. In different circumstances a man, for whom there was no other relief from shame or grievance, might throw away his life in this way. It cost the lives of others but this was a society, as the passages above disclose, in which everyone's life was held cheap. When social conditions changed and the sense of helplessness in face of intolerable wrong or disgrace was relieved, if not removed, by effective means of legal or other redress, the recourse to suicide by killing others became infrequent. James Low wrote that in the course of seventeen years, mainly among the Malays of Province Wellesley, he recollected only three cases of *amuk*.[26] Two generations later in 1894, Dennys stated that 'British rule has almost exterminated *amuk* in the Settlements, the prospect of being hanged in cold blood causing a disinclination to run the risk'.[27] Without statistics of a more exact and comprehensive kind, it is difficult to judge.

In and around a state capital or a mining camp, there was a much greater incidence of violent crime, caused by social conditions and arising from motives and emotions which are readily understood. Robbers, thieves, and murderers were drawn to these areas 'like vultures to a carcase'.[28] However, even country villages could suffer a raid. 'It is no uncommon thing for the inhabitants of one village to make a raid on the dwellers in another who are weaker, and carry off their herds.'[29] When the entire household went forth to work in the fields, there was a risk that professional thieves would carry out 'a housebreaking job in a fairly workmanlike manner'.[30]

Most of all, the villager feared a night attack by armed robbers. In some parts of Malaya the villages were isolated settlements, separated from each other by long distances. But areas of relatively dense settlement, such as Province Wellesley, were more vulnerable. 'When a house is attacked,' wrote Logan, 'the neighbours usually remain aloof' lest they be wounded or killed by the robbers or even suspected by the victims of complicity in the crime. 'The robbers have, in almost all cases, firearms, which very few Malays possess; their attacks are sudden, they discharge muskets and use savage threats.' The raiders were sometimes led by the dreaded professional *Panglima* already described with an awesome reputation both for ferocity and invulnerability. There was little that the householder could do. 'One of my Malay tenants', wrote Logan, 'had had his house burnt down in the previous night. Whilst he was asleep someone first planted bamboo spikes along the path leading to the house to lame the inmate in escaping or his neighbours should they come to his assistance and had then set fire to it.' If the householder made a successful resistance, he might find that the raiders returned on a later occasion to take reprisals. As a result, 'a gang of ten or twenty robbers may march through the most populous villages, plunder houses and retire with complete immunity'.[31]

The situation which Logan described in 1867 was much improved by the posting of detachments of the new colonial police to rural areas. In Selangor in the late 1870s, 'the mere fact of small bodies of police being stationed in the interior of the country has a tendency to check crime not from their active interference but from it being known that ... the sufferer has some chance of obtaining redress on the spot'. The village police station could support the *penghulu* in his task of dealing with 'cases of simple assault and other trivial offences'.[32]

On the other hand, there was also hostility to the police as 'foreign' Malays. Clifford, who had seen it happen in Pahang in 1889, wrote that 'the Malays loathe and detest men of their own race who flock into a newly protected state at the heels of their white masters. In the villages . . . the Malay policeman is treated with elaborate courtesy. They call him "*Che' Sarjin*"—which means Mr. Sergeant—defer to him on almost every point, give him their daughters to wife, if he so wills it, and do all they can to propitiate him . . . at the king's court men hate him more and fear him less.'[33]

Not for nothing did the Malays call the police 'Eyes' (*mata-mata*). In some respects they were too inquisitive. Swettenham relates that 'an intelligent Malay sergeant of police proceeded to the spot (Lambor on the Perak river) and discovered a murder which the local people had concealed. The dead man's relatives, however, suspected foul play and reported the death to the police.'[34]

The Malays in the police were 'foreign' because there was a strong prejudice in the FMS against enlisting in the new colonial police force. In Selangor, for example, it was necessary to recruit the state police from Melaka. In Pahang, many of the police came from Kelantan and Terengganu and were 'somewhat looked down on by the Malays of Pahang'.[35] It was not until the beginning of the twentieth century that the old prejudice was broken down, and a career in the police became a respectable, indeed an esteemed, career for a local man.[36]

The 'foreign' police, dispersed into village police stations and working with the *penghulu*, were the first instance of 'culture contact' between Malays of different cultural traditions, as the immigrant settlers kept to themselves in their own new villages. The police constable as a potential son-in-law presented the villager with problems of adjustment. Clifford, quoted above, suggests that such alliances were made to 'propitiate' these newcomers. Robson, who had observed what happened in Selangor villages in the 1890s, noted some reluctance.[37] Possibly there is a distinction to be made between the first marriage of a village maiden, for whom the best possible partner must be found from among the local swains, and a second or later marriage of a woman who was in the distressing situation of being a widow or a divorcee (*janda*). Robson refers, a little unkindly, to 'policemens' [*sic*] wives, with their plain, plain faces, their cheap old garments, and their interesting pasts!' It was not that policemen 'prefer middle-aged ladies with a past, but simply because their financial resources will not run to the "young and beautiful" and it has to be said because they know their unmarried comrades will be less susceptible to the charms of a middle-aged lady'.[38] A police constable was liable to be posted to a number of different places in the course of his service. His wife would move on with him to some other station where the local community did not know her 'interesting past'.

At all events the village police station of the SS and FMS gave more security than a village home guard equipped with muskets supplied by Francis Light.[39] The hours of darkness were still the time of greatest risk and it was normal practice to stay behind closed doors at night. 'No respectable Malay is ever out at night . . . at dark they fasten themselves securely in their own houses, to be safe from marauders of all kinds.'[40] Anyone who moved about at night in the village was deemed to be an enemy until identified. In Kedah, a royal decree authorized the villagers to open fire on 'any person who enters a village or enclosure by night without warning and without a light'.[41] In Perak in 1878, the State Council noted 'the frequency of night robberies in the various kampongs'. At the request of the *penghulu*, a regulation was made by which any person found out of doors after 9.00 p.m. without a torch or other light might be arrested and fined up to $6.25.[42]

Apart from gang robbery, Province Wellesley, Kedah, Perak and even Melaka were penetrated to some extent by the rival 'Red Flag' and 'White Flag' Malay secret societies which had their origin and headquarters in Penang.[43] The urban criminal made other occasional forays into the quiet country villages of western Malaya. There are scattered reports of falsified accounts, impersonation, and the passing of forged notes.[44]

The remainder of this chapter is concerned with the legal system and the courts of pre-colonial Malay society. Anyone who had a complaint, whether of a crime or a disputed ownership of property and the like, could approach the authorities—the village headman, the district chief or even the ruler, or a judge appointed by the ruler, to petition for a remedy. Few in fact did so. 'If there was a complaint (poor people knew better than to make one) and the parties were hailed before some chief or *raja* . . . the result was usually that everybody returned poorer than he went.'[45] The law was arbitrary and uncertain. 'The penghulus and datus fine whenever they like, and with no regard to the law, pocket the fines, or if large ones, give part to the Sultan.'[46] Even the ruler of Johor, who prided himself on maintaining a European style of government, 'confessed that there were no rules, and that sentences were passed according to his own judgment'.[47]

Like much else in the pre-colonial Malay system of government, the Malay legal system is described by European observers with a fair amount of prejudice. Clifford said that 'the Sultan was the supreme judge ... [but] the right to judge was generally deputed to more or less incompetent persons, most often selected from among the number of the royal favourites ... all who came to the judges brought gifts ... roughly equivalent to our fees of court'. It was not usual to hear evidence. Either the complainant's statement was accepted and an order made against the other party, or it was rejected. This procedure, Clifford concludes, produced 'a long list of strange judgements'.[48]

What can one make of this? Stripped, as far as may be, of Clifford's European preconceptions of a 'proper' legal system, the picture is of the law treated as an exercise of authority in the name of the ruler. There were old legal digests but there was no written *code* of law. The basis of the English legal doctrine of 'precedent' (which is not the basis of many European legal systems) is that each case should be decided in conformity with earlier decisions on similar facts. Malay legal theory acknowledged no such principle, and had no means of adopting it since there were no records of earlier decisions. The other bed-rock principle of English law was that each side should have the opportunity of putting his case, hearing the other side's case, and producing his own evidence and testing the opponent's evidence, mainly by questioning witnesses. This, too, was alien to Malay legal practice.

The best approach to a further consideration of the Malay legal system is to search for information, which is not easy to find, of what actually happened when a case came before an authority for decision. The best information comes from Kedah and Terengganu, where the law was administered in Malay courts until 1909 at least. There is also some scanty information of practice in other states.

The legal digests (*undang-undang*), of which several versions have been preserved, were valued as repositories of ancient traditions. The possession of a manuscript of a prestigious digest was on a par with ownership of a treasured heirloom. But there is little to suggest that *in practice* the digests were used as sources of law in the nineteenth century. In 1878 the Perak State Council, whose members included the two Malay judges who sat in 'the chief court of Kuala Kangsar', noted that this court 'administers, as far as it will go, the law of the country, and this law, *though unwritten*, is very generally understood and appears to differ little from the code of laws formerly in force in great Malay kingdoms' (emphasis supplied).[49] Unfortunately this guarded passage does not specify which parts of the ancient codes were found suitable. No less an authority than Winstedt has pointed out that no judge in Perak could 'prescribe a white camel (that does not figure in Malayan *fauna*) for the funeral feast in case of manslaughter'.[50] It may be inferred that if a Malay judge knew of a relevant principle which seemed to him also to be in accord with oral and customary traditions, he applied it. A great deal depended, as it always does, on the calibre of the judge.

In Kedah, a body of local law had begun to develop by the making of royal edicts. However, these had been issued with reference to particular problems or cases, and no record had been kept of them to which convenient reference could be made.[51] In Terengganu, also, the ruler occasionally promulgated regulations but these were concerned mainly with minor matters such as port administration. They were essentially regulations, not laws. The 'interpretation of all difficult legal matters' was delegated to the influential *ulama*, Ungku Said Abdul Rahman.[52]

In Terengganu, unlike most other states, a ruler, Baginda Omar, elected to administer the law in person, sitting in public 'to dispense justice to his people, all of whom had free access to him'. In a state which was famous as a centre of Islamic learning, he chose to apply the savage penalties of the *Hukum Syarak* in 'the strictest spirit . . . making grim jests for which he was famous'. This regime produced sentences of death, mutilation, or 'imprisonment in gaol-cages which was worse than death'.[53] Yet his nephew, Sultan Zainal Abidin III (r.1881–1918), who succeeded him after a short interval and who was no less devout, was a recluse who left the administration of justice—and much else—to others. It was said of the English medieval court of Chancery that equity varied with the length of the Chancellor's foot. In a similar fashion, Malay royal justice was an individual thing.

Royal justice was concerned with maintaining authority and order. A very different type of legal system was evolved in dealing with property matters such as inheritance or disputed ownership. There is little reference to this before the last quarter of the nineteenth century. It was only when land, which was the most important form of property, came to have a value, that it was worth going to law over it. In village communities there was an inclination, which can be demonstrated from modern land registers, to work out a '*pakat* or family agreement'.[54] It was probably in the well-to-do families of the state capitals that there was occasional resort to litigation of this kind.

The first British Agent in Kuala Terengganu described the system which he found as follows: 'When the owner of land dies his land is either divided among his heirs or if this is inconvenient it is sold and the proceeds divided by the court, a lengthy and expensive proceeding known in some cases to occupy 16 or 17 years without arriving at finality. Disputes and suits involving the ownership of land provide the bulk of the court work. . . . The *hakim* is the judge and is provided with a *naib* or bailiff to enforce his decrees; a council to assist his deliberations, and an officer to administer oaths . . . the practice of the courts in deciding cases is to search the *Kuran* and its commentaries for a law or precept having explicit or constructive reference to matters similar to that in dispute. . . . Ten per cent *ad valorem* seems to be the court charge in all suits; this is payable after recovery by the plaintiff; to this is added a fee of 75 cents for a summons or *subpoena* payable in advance.' In addition to these prescribed fees the litigants might find it expedient to offer presents as 'refreshers' to rouse the court to activity after a period of adjournment.[55]

The Terengganu court may have been more bureaucratic, dilatory, and preoccupied with points of Islamic law than the courts of other states. James Low wrote that the ruler of Perak in 1826 'hears complaints and settles business early in the morning'. It does not sound as though it took long to settle these matters.[56] A visitor to Rembau in Negeri Sembilan in the mid-nineteenth century witnessed a public hearing in the court of the ruling chief (*Undang*). The chief sat on a dais on his verandah with a Muslim dignitary (described as 'the high priest') standing at one side but not on the dais itself. 'Many persons placed themselves in the verandah.' The parties to the dispute made obeisance to the chief before the hearing began. The chief 'appeared to pay great attention to the cause, hearing both parties in silence; he afterwards put several questions to them, and, having received their answers, he became exceedingly angry'. In their anger, the chief and the *ulama* shouted 'high and strongly', apparently by way of reprimand. 'The whole was ended by condemning the guilty party to pay a fine.'[57]

In other states, minor disputes were usually brought before the *penghulu*, sitting as a court. A Kedah *penghulu* 'held court that evening in the *penghulu*'s house sitting on a mat in the middle of the verandah while the men squatted tailor fashion in a semi-circle before him.... [It was] more the form of a discussion than the stiff and formal procedure one is accustomed to in our law courts, justice being administered more or less on patriarchal lines.' In this instance, the *penghulu* was not a patriarch but a young man of about twenty who owed his position and personal authority to a 'good connection and high position' combined with his own tact and fairness.[58]

If the evidence was challenged, the usual method of testing its veracity was ordeal by oath. 'The oath is effected by taking the plaintiff or defendant, in a case where there is some doubt, to the mosque, and there one or other may clinch his arguments by solemnly swearing forty times with the *Kuran* on his head that his story is true. When this is done the opposite party in the suit usually accepts the oath without demur.'[59] In some courts including those in the SS, a witness was required to say, with the *Kuran* on his head, 'There is no God but God and Mohamed is his Prophet.'[60] The sanction against false testimony was the belief that divine retribution would befall the perjurer. However, if he was detected by earthly means 'a false witness was punished by having his face blackened. He was then gonged, and at the same time flogged, through the streets.'[61] British administrators continued to accept ordeal by oath since they recognized that Malay fear of retribution was a very real deterrent.[62]

As an alternative to ordeal by oath there were tests of physical endurance. In Perak, the ruler might order an ordeal by immersion (*bertangkap mangmang*). As the litigants were permitted to delegate the test to others, it was more of a gamble than a true test by ordeal. Two boys jumped into the river and plunged below the surface. Each held a bamboo tube. One tube contained a statement that the testimony on the disputed point was true and the other that it was false. It was not disclosed in advance which boy had the 'true' or 'false' verdict. Whichever of the boys remained longer under the water than the other was the winner and the statement in his bamboo tube was accepted.[63] Bloomfield Douglas witnessed a trial by immersion on simpler lines in Selangor in 1878.[64] As late as 1897 a man accused of theft at Tampin in Negeri Sembilan ate a cupful of raw rice which had been impregnated with incense. It was believed that if he had lied he would be unable to avoid vomiting up the rice.[65]

Although a few Malay rulers, such as Baginda Omar, ordered savage punishments, there was a disposition to impose fines even for homicide; it had the incidental effect of producing revenue for the royal privy purse.[66] The amount of the fine could be a deterrent or a humiliation. In the colonial period, when a cuckolded husband could no longer kill his wife's lover with impunity, it was necessary to find methods of punishing an adulterer whose *amours* would otherwise disrupt the peace of the court circle. Swettenham tells a story of such a man summoned into the royal presence for rebuke and sentence. The ruler fined him $2,000, which was 'the extreme penalty sanctioned by ancient usage'. As he withdrew, the offender is said to have whispered, 'I was afraid His Highness would fine me fifty cents.'[67]

There was also a customary procedure of pre-colonial times by which an aristocrat who had committed a serious offence, such as murder, formally abased himself before the ruler's *istana* and petitioned for royal pardon. He appeared with his hands loosely tied behind him with his own 'headkerchief'—hence it was called '*ikat diri*'—and repeatedly asked for pardon—'*ampun, Tuanku, beribu-ribu ampun*'. When the ruler judged that there had been sufficient expression of contrition, he sent his herald forth from the *istana* bearing the regalia (*kebesaran*) to announce that pardon had been duly granted.[68] This was obviously not a procedure which the colonial regime was willing to permit.

The introduction of European legal procedure into the Malay states had only a limited effect on Malay life, but there were some problems of adjustment. In a prosecution where it seemed that a conviction was 'a foregone conclusion', Swettenham relates that 'the majority of the jurors declined the responsibility of a verdict of guilty, lest that should lead to hanging; for they believed that ghosts of the hanged would haunt those who condemned them'.[69] But in a more general way, British officials sitting in court recognized that they must take account of matters outside their own perception, and so they 'avail themselves, when possible to do so, of the assistance of one of the local *rajas*'.[70]

Until 1896, the FMS did not permit professional lawyers to appear in the new courts which the state governments had established.[71] It was at about that time also that registered land titles, and all which went with the system, became well established. Until then, there was little scope in the states for a rural advocate or agent—the 'bush lawyer' (*loyar buruk* or *loyar keledek*)—whose activities incurred much official disapproval in the rural districts of Penang and Melaka. W. E. Maxwell described them as 'a mischievous class . . . who make a living by practising on the credulity and fears of the ignorant when business obliges them to apply to the government authorities or to the courts or lawyers in the town'.[72] In another context, however, Maxwell gives a more sympathetic portrait of 'a good specimen of the native lawyer and politician . . . one of the class created by English civilisation and law courts. On the passive cunning of his race many years of intercourse with Europeans and of loitering in the passages and verandahs of the colonial courts have grafted much worldly wisdom and not a little familiarity with business. A journey to Mecca gave him a title and a turban, and added polish to his manners. He had a fluent tongue and a lively imagination, knew the weaknesses of his countrymen well, and was not slow to turn them to his own pecuniary advantage; finally he was one of the most entertaining companions I ever met among Malays, though, I fear, he was not burdened with too much principle.'[73]

Maxwell's pen portrait incidentally discloses the villagers' need of an intermediary or communicator who could deal with the authorities on their behalf. This was the traditional role of the *penghulu*, but as he became an 'official not a village patriarch' and preoccupied with many official duties, he ceased to be an effective spokesman.[74]

To be sent to prison under the new regime was no great hardship. 'The hours of the meals were the great events in the prison day, and the convicts ate heartily.'[75] To have infringed some alien law was also no disgrace—'incarceration does not degrade the victim. A man will, on his release, speak quite openly to strangers of his experiences while in gaol . . . he regards the time spent in captivity as a payment exacted for the sin of discovery.'[76] Malay convicts sometimes asked to be sent to a prison near their homes so that family visits were easier to make.[77] If imprisonment befell an aristocrat, his relatives' 'one idea was how to compass his release' and thereafter perhaps to send him on the pilgrimage to Mecca so that he might repair the slight dent to his reputation.[78] The worst ordeal for him might be the derision and disrespect to which he would be subject at the hands of some, but not all, of his fellow Malays in the prison population.[79]

1. F. A. Swettenham, *British Malaya: An Account of the Origin and Progress of British Influence in Malaya*, London, John Lane Bodley Head, 1907 (revised editions 1929 and 1948, London, Allen & Unwin), pp. 120–1. H. C. Clifford, 'Life in the Malay Peninsula: As It Was and Is', in P. H. Kratoska (ed.), *Honourable Intentions: Talks on the British Empire in South-East Asia Delivered at the Royal Colonial Institute, 1874–1928*, Kuala Lumpur, Oxford University Press, 1983 (reprinted from the *Proceedings of the Royal Colonial Institute*, 1899), pp. 225–43, offers an extended description of anarchy and oppression as he perceived it in Pahang in 1887. As examples see 'Droit du Seigneur' and 'A Malayan Prison' in Clifford's *The Further Side of Silence*, New York, Doubleday, Page & Co., 1927, pp. 65–76 and 135–47 respectively. 'Droit du Seigneur' was originally printed under the title 'The Weeding of the Tares' in Clifford's *Studies in Brown Humanity being Scrawls and Smudges in Sepia, White and Yellow*, London, Grant Richards, 1898, pp. 202–10, and is reprinted (as 'The Weeding of the Tares') in W. R. Roff (ed.), *Stories by Sir Hugh Clifford*, Kuala Lumpur, Oxford University Press, 1967. These stories are no doubt based on actual observations but that leaves open how far they were typical. Both Hugh Low and William Treacher gave a discreet warning that they felt that he exaggerated (P. H. Kratoska (ed.), *Honourable Intentions: Talks on the British Empire in South-East Asia Delivered at the Royal Colonial Institute 1874–1928*, Singapore, Oxford University Press, 1983, pp. 249 and 251).

2. SSD 22 September 1909 in CO 273/351, p. 210. Clifford, 'A Malayan Prison', cited in note 1. Conlay also found that in a reign which had then lasted twenty-eight years the ruler had passed sentence of death only five times—on three Malays and two Chinese (SSD 22 September 1909).

3. *AR Kelantan 1903–1904* in CO 273/314, p. 15. In 1909, when the first British Adviser Kelantan, took over, he inspected the prison and ordered that the practice of keeping the prisoners, male and female, in fetters should end. He made no other comment (SSD 8 September 1909).

4. H. C. Clifford, *In Court and Kampong, being Tales and Sketches of Native Life in the Malay Peninsula*, London, Grant Richards, 1897 (2nd ed. with autobiographical preface, London, Richards Press, 1927), p. 151. On general conditions see pp. 51 and 73 above.

5. F. A. Swettenham, *The Real Malay: Pen Pictures*, London, John Lane Bodley Head, 1900, pp. 24–5.

6. F. A. Swettenham, *British Malaya*, p. 135; J. W. W. Birch, *The Journals of J. W. W. Birch First British Resident to Perak 1874–1875* (hereafter cited as *Birch Journal*), edited by P. L. Burns, Kuala Lumpur, Oxford University Press, 1976, pp. 69 and 384. On the 'blooding' of a young *raja* (Raja Mahmud) see p. 81 above.

7. F. A. Swettenham, *Sir Frank Swettenham's Malayan Journals 1874–1876*, (hereafter cited as *Swettenham Journal*), edited by P. L. Burns and C. D. Cowan, Kuala Lumpur, Oxford University Press, 1975, p. 92 and p. 169 on the casual killing of a man by Raja Mahmud (p. 11 above).

8. Douglas Diary, 10 October 1881. Douglas sentenced him to ten years' imprisonment but with the intention of 'a large commutation' if he behaved well. On concealment of crimes see pp. 240 and 243 below.

9. In August 1880 Hugh Low issued an administrative order which forbade carrying weapons into the jungle except with a permit from the *penghulu*. This was presumably done to test the reaction as Low issued his order before asking the state council to ratify what he had done (*PSCM*, 20 September 1880, *PMS*, p. 230).

'The carrying of arms was gradually forbidden' (Swettenham, *The Real Malay*, p. 25). He adds that 'a *keris*, which used to be a Malay's most prized possession, has now very little value'. It is not clear, however, whether he here refers to economic or sentimental value.

10. G. B. Gardner, *Keris and Other Malay Weapons*, Singapore, Progressive Publishing Co., 1936, p. 113.

11. *AR Pahang 1894*, para. 44.

12. W. E. Maxwell, 'A Journey on Foot to the Patani Frontier in 1876 being a Journal Kept during an Expedition Undertaken to Capture Datoh Maharajah Lela of Perak', *JSBRAS*, 9, 1882, p. 20. W. Linehan, 'A History of Pahang' (hereafter cited as 'Pahang'), *JMBRAS*, 14(2), 1936, Chapters 7 and 8, has numerous references to Pahang *Panglima* as junior fighting commanders. Some of them, such as To Gajah and To Bahman, rose from obscurity to positions of political power by prowess in the wars (see p. 74 above). On Mahmud see p. 81 above.

13. Douglas Diary, 6 July 1876. He was convicted and hanged for murder.

14. In 1889 there were eight reported cases of stabbing in Pahang and five of them were fatal. They were 'usually caused by jealousy' (*AR Pahang 1889*). As this was the first year of British rule there may well have been additional unreported cases of the same kind. In 1897 in Pahang 'in the country districts, which are inhabited by purely agricultural classes, there is little or no crime'. But 'foreign' Malays from Kelantan or from the West Coast states had a higher crime rate—suggesting that the stability of village life induced more peaceable behaviour (*AR Pahang 1897*). In Negeri Sembilan in 1886 'the amount of crime in the country may be considered small' (SSD 24 December 1886). 'This disturber of domestic peace was carried home with a broken head, due to a blow from a revengeful husband who, armed with a bottle, had hidden in the bushes for his chance' (A. L. Keyser, *Trifles and Travels*, London, Murray, 1923, p. 92)—probably a representative example of these episodes.

15. *Malay Mail*, 4 February 1901.

16. SSD 24 January 1918, report from Terengganu.

17. *AR Pahang 1898*. Clifford tells the whole story in detail in *In a Corner of Asia being Tales and Impressions of Men and Things in the Malay Peninsula*, London, Fisher Unwin, 1899, pp. 197–214.

18. The literature on *amuk* includes Swettenham, *The Real Malay*, pp. 232–57, where he quotes at length from Crawfurd and Logan; *Malay Sketches*, London, John Lane Bodley Head, 1895, pp. 4, 38 and 253; *Footprints in Malaya*, London, Hutchinson, 1942, p. 52; and *British Malaya*, p. 143; H. C. Clifford, *Malayan Monochromes*, New York, Dutton, 1913, p. 300; T. J. Newbold, *Political and Statistical Account of the British Settlements . . . with a History of the Malayan States on the Peninsula in the Straits of Malacca*, 2 vols., London, Murray, 1839, reprinted as *British Settlements in the Straits of Malacca*, Kuala Lumpur, Oxford University Press, 1971, Vol. 1, p. 185; J. Cameron, *Our Tropical Possessions in Malayan India: Being a Descriptive Account of Singapore, Penang, Province Wellesley, and Malacca, Their Peoples, Products, Commerce and Government*, London, Smith, Elder & Co., 1865, reprinted as *Our Tropical Possessions in Malayan India*, Kuala Lumpur, Oxford University Press, 1965, pp. 258–62; J. Low, *A Dissertation on the Soil and Agriculture of the British Settlement of Penang or Prince of Wales Island in the Straits of Malacca Including Province Wellesley on the Malayan Peninsula . . ., with . . Incidental Observations, etc.*, Singapore, Singapore Free Press, 1836, reprinted as *The British*

Settlement at Penang, Singapore, Oxford University Press, 1972, p. 296; A. B. Rathborne, *Camping and Tramping in Malaya: Fifteen Years' Pioneering in the Native States of the Malay Peninsula*, London, Swan Sonnenschein, 1898, reprinted Singapore, Oxford University Press, 1984, pp. 233 and 273; *PGG* 1890, p. 246, report from Kinta, and p. 131, report from Lower Perak; *PGG* 1897, p. 970, report from Kuala Kangsar; *AR Kuala Kangsar 1895* in *PGG* 1896, p. 336.

19. Swettenham, *The Real Malay*, pp. 249–50.

20. A. L. Keyser, *People and Places: A Life in Five Continents*, London, Murray, 1922, p. 105; Clifford, *In Court and Kampong*, p. 79.

21. *AR Kuala Kangsar 1895* in *PGG* 1896, p. 336.

22. *Malay Mail*, 4 November 1897. He might of course have suspected his wife of adultery with one or both the men, but the report does not suggest this explanation.

23. H. Fauconnier, *The Soul of Malaya*, translated from French by E. Sutton, London, Elkin, Mathew & Marrot, 1931 (originally published as *Malaisie*, Paris, Librairie Stock, 1930), pp. 221–38, where the killer's approach to the father of a girl whom he wishes to marry is rejected.

24. L. R. Wheeler, *The Modern Malay*, London, Allen & Unwin, 1928, p. 218, gives the essential facts. Richard J. H. Sidney, *In British Malaya Today*, London, Hutchinson, n.d. (1926?), pp. 79–92, tells the story (with fictitious names) at length. Presumably Sidney, who was in Malaya at the time, drew on contemporary newspaper reports. Before his madness was triggered off by the discovery that he had lost his parcel, the killer had had a dispute with a ship's officer over the cabin allocated to him. He must have been in a state of some tension before the killing began.

25. R. J. Wilkinson, *A Malay–English Dictionary*, Singapore, Kelly & Walsh, 1901 (revised as *A Malay–English Dictionary (Romanised)*, Mytilene, Salavopoulos & Kinderlis, 1932), Part 1, p. 25. John Crawfurd, *A Descriptive Dictionary of the Indian Islands and Adjacent Countries*, London, Bradbury & Evans, 1856, reprinted Kuala Lumpur, Oxford University Press, 1971, p. 12, says: 'In Malay it means a furious and reckless onset, whether of many in battle, or of an individual in private.'

26. J. Low, *Dissertation*, p. 296; his book was published in 1836 although he did not retire from the SS until 1850.

27. N. B. Dennys, *A Descriptive Dictionary of British Malaya*, London, London and China Telegraph, 1894, p. 4. Dennys wrote his book as an updated version of Crawfurd, cited in note 25 above.

28. *AR Pahang 1897*—'the Pahang Malays who live in and about the capital are undoubtedly a somewhat turbulent people'. Again, 'at Pekan murders are common, fights which result in wounds occur every week' (SSD 3 August 1887). Then in Perak 'thieving and robbing were very common crimes about Kuala Kangsar' in 1877 (*PSCM*, 18 November 1879, *PMS*, p. 212). Quotation in text from Swettenham, *British Malaya*, p. 120. On *budak raja* see p. 50 above. As late as 1890 Kota Lama preserved its unenviable reputation for disorder (*PGG* 1890, p. 480).

29. J. F. A. McNair, *Perak and the Malays: Sarong and Keris*, London, Tinsley Bros., 1878, reprinted Kuala Lumpur, Oxford University Press, 1972, p. 115.

30. W. E. Maxwell, 'Journey to Patani', p. 30. Maxwell is here repeating the views of the semi-urbanized Province Wellesley Malays, who made up his party.

31. J. R. Logan, 'Plan for a Volunteer Police in the Muda Districts, Province Wellesley, Submitted to Government by the Late J. R. Logan in 1867', *JSBRAS*, 16, 1885, p. 174. On the use of spikes (*ranjau*) by robbers, see J. D. Vaughan,

'Notes on the Malays of Pinang and Province Wellesley', *JIA*, n.s., 2, 1858, p. 160.

32. Report by H. C. Syers on police organization in Selangor enclosed with SSD 1 August 1878; J. M. Gullick, 'Syers and the Selangor Police Force 1875–1897', *JMBRAS*, 51(2), 1978, pp. 22–7; P. Morrah, 'The History of the Malayan Police', *JMBRAS*, 36(2), 1963, pp. 56–88; E. Sadka, *The Protected Malay States 1874–1895*, Kuala Lumpur and Selangor, University of Malaya Press, 1968, pp. 237–49. The enclosures to SSD 28 May 1883 are various memoranda on police organization, including one by Swettenham, who argued at length against deploying police detachments into *kampung* in Perak, as likely to cause a conflict with the *penghulu* and villagers. He seems to have changed his mind when he observed the success of Syers' policy in Selangor. Gullick, 'Syers', analyses the issue. Cheah Boon Kheng, 'Social Banditry and Rural Crime in North Kedah 1909–1929', *JMBRAS*, 54(2), 1981, provides some interesting comparative material from Kedah at a later time but in rather similar circumstances.

33. Clifford, *Studies in Brown Humanity*, pp. 127–8. He goes on to say that Malay villagers had an even more intense dislike of the Sikh element in the colonial police. See sources in note 32 above on police generally. In 1889 the recruits to the Perak Police were 'decidedly poor . . . and are of little use' (*AR Perak Police 1889* in *PGG* 1890, p. 130). In 1890 112 recruits to the Perak Police were not of the desired standard (*AR Perak 1890*). It was, in part, a prejudice of the Perak European police officers, recruited from the Indian regular army, who much preferred Sikhs and other North Indian recruits with a military background. Syers was almost alone in raising a predominantly Malay force in Selangor.

34. Swettenham, *Malay Sketches*, p. 26. Keyser, *Trifles and Travels*, p. 92, tells how the body of a murdered woman was thrown into the river. As it floated downstream it was now and again caught against the piles of a projecting bathhouse (*jamban*). The householder merely pushed the body out into the stream to float on—no concern of his.

35. *AR Pahang 1889*. Gullick, 'Syers', pp. 34–5.

36. See p. 169 above.

37. J. H. M. Robson, *People in a Native State*, Singapore, Singapore Free Press, 1894, p. 23. See p. 169 above.

38. Ibid., p. 28.

39. *AR Kedah 1905–1906*, referring to villages in Kedah. Clifford, *Studies in Brown Humanity*, pp. 132–3, describes a local defence effort which went sadly wrong.

40. H. Norman, *The Peoples and Politics of the Far East: Travels and Studies in the British . . . Colonies and Malaya*, New York, Scribner, 1895, p. 584, referring to villages on the Kelantan plain.

41. *AR Kedah 1906–1908*. In practice few villagers did open fire but it may have been a deterrent.

42. *PSCM*, 5 September 1878, *PMS*, p. 171.

43. M. L. Wynne, *Triad and Tabut*, Singapore, Government Printing Press, 1941, especially pp. 208–34 and pp. 336–46, examines the evidence in considerable detail. *PSCM* (printed in *PMS*) has references to secret societies in Perak—see minutes of 5 September 1878, *PMS*, p. 172; 20 October 1879, p. 203; 20 February 1880, p. 218; 5 January 1881, p. 235; and 19 October 1882, p. 261. On Melaka, see O. Cavenagh, *Reminiscences of an Indian Official*, London, W. H. Allen & Co., 1884, p. 26. Logan, 'Volunteer Police', p. 185, equates 'Mahomedan *jumahas*' with Chinese

secret societies. Wilfred Blythe, *The Impact of Chinese Secret Societies in Malaya—A Historical Study*, London, Oxford University Press, 1969, is the authoritative study of secret societies, Chinese and also Malay. It is a specialist topic with religious undertones examined later: see p. 291 below.

44. *PGG* 1890, p. 147; *PGG* 1899, p. 16, reports from Kinta. *Swettenham Journal*, p. 291. A bank note forger escaped from the local gaol at Krian by using his wooden pillow to prise apart the bars of his cell window (*PGG* 1899, p. 98, report from Krian).

45. Swettenham, *British Malaya*, p. 120.

46. *Birch Journal*, p. 305.

47. Cavenagh, op. cit., p. 313, cited in R. O. Winstedt, 'A History of Johore', *JMBRAS*, 10(3), 1932, p. 97.

48. Clifford, in Kratoska (ed.), op. cit., p. 232. At p. 233 he gives a number of specific instances. See also his contemporary reports of 1887 enclosed with SSD 3 August 1887 and 15 October 1887. But see comments in note 1 above. At a meeting of the Pahang State Council on 10 June 1887 'it was decided . . . to promulgate a penal code based on Islamic law modified by the Pahang version of the laws known as the *kanun*' (Linehan, 'Pahang', pp. 113 and 118–21). A court of justice was opened on 5 March 1887 but there was interference with its decisions (p. 121). The *kanun* was 'one of the few written codes of law known to the Malays'; it dealt mainly with slavery (p. 128). These events in 1887 suggest that there was no system of law or of court hearings previously.

49. *PSCM*, 6 September 1878, *PMS*, pp. 172–3. The two Malay judges were Raja Dris (later Sultan Idris) and the Datuk Temenggong. R. J. Wilkinson, 'Introductory Sketch', *Papers on Malay Subjects, Law*, Part 1, 1908, reprinted 1922, and in M. B. Hooker (ed.), *Readings in Malay Adat Laws*, Singapore, Singapore University Press, 1970, warns the student that 'he should not take the so-called codes (*undang-undang*) too seriously. They are digests not codes of law, evidence . . . of legal theories'. Wilkinson's essay is not included in P. L. Burns (ed.), *Papers on Malay Subjects*, Kuala Lumpur, Oxford University Press, 1971, but it is reprinted in Hooker, *Readings*, and the passage quoted above is at p. 7 of Hooker.

Clifford described the *kanun* (see note 48 above) as 'more curious as an antiquity than useful as a guide for governing a country' (SSD 15 October 1887). M. B. Hooker, 'Muhammadan Law and Islamic Law', in M. B. Hooker (ed.), *Islam in South-East Asia*, Leiden, Brill, 1983, p. 166, sums up a discussion of the 'Islamized law texts (Digests) of the Malay world' with the conclusion that, with the exception of the Sarawak laws, 'none of the texts properly represents legal reality . . . there is little or no evidence of an application . . . legal reality . . . lay outside the texts'.

Newbold had difficulty in obtaining copies of the digests and surmised that their contents had been 'orally handed down' in those aristocratic families 'to whom the administration of the law is usually confided' (Newbold, op. cit., Vol. 2, p. 219).

W. E. Maxwell borrowed from Raja Dris the latter's copy of the legal digest known as *Undang2 Kerajaan*. At this time Dris (see above) was 'chief judge' of the court in Perak which dealt with Malay cases (John E. Kempe and Sir Richard Winstedt, 'A Malay Legal Digest Compiled for . . . Sultan of Pahang', *JMBRAS*, 21(1), 1948, p. 1).

C. S. Hurgronje, *The Achehnese*, translated by A. W. S. O'Sullivan, 2 vols., London, Luzac, 1906, concluded that 'we should be wandering altogether off the right track in seeking for the laws and institutions of countries such as Acheh in lawbooks of foreign (e.g. Arabic) origin' (p. 12). The whole passage, ibid., pp. 6–15, is a detailed and devastating rejection of *undang-undang* and the like as evidence of reality.

50. R. O. Winstedt, *Start from Alif, Count from One: An Autobiographical Memoire*, Kuala Lumpur, Oxford University Press, 1969, p. 130.

51. *AR Kedah 1906–1908*, p. 8; Sharom Ahmat, *Tradition and Change in a Malay State: A Study of the Economic and Political Development of Kedah 1878–1923*, MBRAS Monograph No. 12, 1984, p. 110.

52. H. C. Clifford, 'Report: Expedition to Trengganu and Kelantan', *JMBRAS*, 34(1), 1961 (originally printed for Colonial Office use in 1895 and reprinted Kuala Lumpur, Government Press, 1936), pp. 60–1, and SSD 22 September 1900; W. W. Skeat and F. F. Laidlaw, 'The Cambridge University Expedition to Parts of the Malay Peninsula 1899–1900: Personal Accounts', *JMBRAS*, 26(4), 1953, pp. 55, 69, 76, 112, 123–4, 130–1 and 135, give an account of punishment and imprisonment in the states of north-east Malaya in 1900 which shows that there was ill-treatment and overcrowding in insanitary prisons. But the picture is a great deal less horrific than Clifford's picture of Pahang and then of Terengganu some years earlier.

53. Clifford, 'Expedition', p. 61. See p. 238 above on gaol conditions.

54. M. B. Hooker, *Adat Laws in Modern Malaya*, Kuala Lumpur, Oxford University Press, 1972, in discussing some specific points of modern practice, remarks that '*adat* Islam disputes were later settled by compromise' (p. 211). The quotation in the text is from ibid., p. 246. This is the author's impression of what the practice was in the formative period of the late nineteenth century.

55. SSD 17 November 1909.

56. J. Low, 'Observations on Perak', *JIA*, 4, 1850, p. 502.

57. P. Favre, *An Account of the Wild Tribes Inhabiting the Malayan Peninsula, Sumatra and a Few Neighbouring Islands*, Paris, Imperial Printing Office, 1865; including a reprint of 'A Journey in the Menangkabaw States of the Malay Peninsula', *JIA*, 3, 1849, pp. 168–9.

58. 'Notes of a Trip to Kedah', *Malay Mail*, 20 April 1900.

59. *AR Kedah 1906–1908*. The deponent swore 'By God, or by the word of God', or he might recite the same passage from the Kuran many times (J. Low, *Dissertation*, p. 273).

60. J. Low, *Dissertation*, p. 272. He adds that when this procedure was used in the Malay states there was 'a greater degree of solemnity'.

61. Ibid., p. 279.

62. Clifford, 'The Nature of an Oath', *Malayan Monochromes*, pp. 159–86, tells a story of the resolution of a dispute over the ownership of buffaloes. It was accepted that divine retribution would follow perjury within thirty days (p. 174). The District Officer is a witness to the proceedings.

63. W. E. Maxwell, 'Malay Proverbs, Part 3', *JSBRAS*, 3, 1879, pp. 30–[illegible].

64. 'The men were then told to dive in the river to establish their innocence. The Sakei came up first but the trial was not deemed a good one' (Douglas Diary, 22 June 1878). Both were employed by a Sumatran to collect gutta percha and the issue was which one had taken his property.

65. *Negeri Sembilan Gazette* 1897, p. 203. See also W. E. Maxwell, *Notes and Queries*, issued with *JSBRAS*, 14, 1884, p. 22, on a form of ordeal known as '*ganju*'.

66. See note 3 above.

67. Swettenham, *The Real Malay*, pp. 141–2.

68. Swettenham, *Malay Sketches*, p. 122.

69. Swettenham, *The Real Malay*, p. 160.

70. *Straits Settlements Legislative Council Proceedings, 1878, Paper No. 5*, 'Report showing the Constitution of the Court of Justice in Perak, Selangor and Sungei Ujong', p. 30. Sadka, *Protected Malay States*, pp. 113, 171, 262–5, and 269–72. See also p. 76 above.

71. Sadka, *Protected Malay States*, pp. 257–9.

72. SSD 7 June 1892. See Chapter 5, notes 105–7 on the background.

73. W. E. Maxwell, 'Journey to Patani', p. 16.

74. *AR Perak 1909*, citing Winstedt as District Officer, Matang. See p. 110 above.

75. Clifford, *In a Corner of Asia*, p. 107—a most entertaining account of the experiences of a Malay peasant in a colonial prison. See also Clifford, *Studies in Brown Humanity*, p. 125.

76. Clifford, *In a Corner of Asia*, p. 107.

77. Keyser, *People and Places*, p. 106.

78. Swettenham, *The Real Malay*, pp. 156–7 and 161.

79. Clifford, *In a Corner of Asia*, pp. 114–16.

11
New Influences: Medicine and Education

LIKE imprisonment in a royal or a colonial gaol, illness was a misfortune to be avoided if possible, or endured with stoicism if it did not respond to the available methods of treatment. There was no comprehensive Malay theory of illness but there was a variety of remedies to be applied in appropriate cases.[1] The *pawang* often filled the role of healer, using herbal and other treatments. If these practical methods failed, he 'fell back upon charms, spells, incantations and exceedingly noisy devil dances'.[2] A later chapter on the uses of magic deals with its application to illness. What follows here is a brief consideration of illness in its social context.

There was little understanding of hygiene as a precaution against disease. Personal cleanliness was deemed essential. A Malay 'performed his morning ablutions with scrupulous care' as the start to each day.[3] It was usual to build a house on the bank of a river or stream so that a bathhouse (and latrine) could be close at hand. If there was no clean water for washing, a Malay would go in search of it. Thus, when Ibrahim Munshi was in west Johor, 'when we wanted a bath . . . we would go to one place after another, and even so we could not find good water. The wells were the same. However, there was one stream where the water was a little clearer and there we bathed, though even that water was red.'[4] Yet, the same river or stream was often used as a lavatory and as a washing place for clothes and utensils and as a source of drinking water. It must often have been polluted. Domestic refuse was dropped or poured through the slatted floor of the house, where the fowls and ducks scratched for food and also defecated. In consequence, the ground beneath the house was often 'the embodiment of dirt and insanitariness'.[5] As a result, intestinal disorders such as diarrhoea, and skin diseases such as yaws (*puru*) were prevalent and epidemics of cholera not infrequent.[6]

When an epidemic disease such as cholera or smallpox spread across the countryside, the population often fled to escape it—and thereby carried it further. It had been discovered by experience that isolation gave some measure of protection. When, for example, Logan visited Kedah in 1850, he found on arrival at the mouth of the Kedah River that the ruler and his entourage had withdrawn to an up-river village because of an outbreak of smallpox. There was also a ban on movement along the river.[7] If an individual fell sick of such a disease, his village segregated him from the community.[8]

There were conventional signals to indicate a quarantine. Braddell at Segamat in Johor in the early 1850s encountered a *pucuk*, 'that is two sticks are set up and from a string hung across them, a number of "putchoh" or leaves are hung, as a sign interdicting the approach of any one'.[9] When Skeat was in Biserat in southern Siam in 1899, he came on houses surrounded by fences—'the gates had several strands of white thread (*benang Jawa*) drawn tightly across the top from post to post, and a rope of jungle grass similarly arranged with pendant slip-knots of coconut fronds, the rope and threads being fastened in the middle'. This quarantine had been imposed ten days before by a Malay medicine-man (*bomoh*) under the authority of the local ruler, who exacted a fine of $5 from anyone who crossed the line.[10]

European medical treatment offered by the colonial regime was at first available only in the towns. Hence it was necessary to move a sick person, either by carrying him 'in a *sarong* slung over a pole' or later, when there were roads, by bullock-cart.[11] Malay villagers came in time to accept the efficacy of European medicine. Their attitude in this—as in much else—was essentially pragmatic. It worked. However, they continued to show reluctance to enter hospitals for treatment as in-patients. Apart from an understandable distrust of being shut up in a strange institution, they refused to be tended and supplied with food by hospital staff who were predominantly non-Muslim. They were also particularly averse to the drastic remedy of surgery.[12]

The major encounter in this period between traditional Malay attitudes and Western medicine, was the campaign for mass vaccination against smallpox (*ketumbuhan* or *cacar*), which the Malays regarded with dread. It was often brought to remote villages by pilgrims returning from Mecca.[13] The first campaign was launched in the SS in the early 1870s. The initial response in Province Wellesley was disappointing. The Malays, it was said, believe 'that it is a disease they are doomed to contract at some time during their lives and that consequently, the sooner they get it over the better. They much prefer being attacked by smallpox to having themselves or their children vaccinated. Hence no precaution whatever is taken and all the members of the family sleep in the same close confined room with the infected.'[14]

A decade later, there was similar resistance to vaccination in the western Malay states. W. E. Maxwell said, 'I have known vaccination resisted on religious grounds by a conservative chief who declared it to be contrary to the law of the Koran to make punctures in the skin of the human body.'[15] However, this attitude was not general among the Malay upper class, many of whom were prepared to acquiesce if not to co-operate. In 1880 the Perak State Council, with Raja Muda Yusuf—an arch conservative—presiding, unanimously authorized compulsory vaccination in infected areas with fines of up to $5 as a sanction against refusal.[16] Raja Bot of Selangor went so far as to be trained as a vaccinator to work among his community in Kuala Lumpur.[17] The real breakthrough came with the smallpox epidemic of 1885–6, in which vaccination was generally accepted. By the early 1890s, an outbreak of smallpox would prompt a village to apply for the immediate dispatch of vaccinators.[18] Yet in a few communities there was still resistance to other measures against infection. In 1899, it was necessary to send in a detachment of troops with fixed bayonets to overawe a village which had been resisting by force an attempt to fumigate the body of a woman who had died of smallpox and to burn her house.[19]

Leprosy is a story less creditable to European medicine. The disease was brought to Malaya by Chinese migrants and in the late nineteenth century it had spread, though still on a small scale, even to distant parts of the Malay states. In three remote *mukim* of Upper Perak, there had been about 20 known cases in the late 1870s but the number had increased to between 40 and 50 in 1893. In 1899 Pahang had 168 reported cases of leprosy and all but two of them were Malays.[20] Villagers regarded this terrible scourge with horror and reacted, as with smallpox, by isolating the sufferer together with those members of his family who stayed with him. Yet they did not drive him out altogether—he was usually allowed to live on the outskirts of the village and the villagers sometimes helped by cultivating his fields.[21]

Malays could recognize that leprosy spread by proximity—one theory was that mosquitoes carried it—and the limited quarantine, described above, was a compromise between fear of the disease and pity and affection for a neighbour of kinsman afflicted with it. The state governments, advised by their doctors, concluded that to contain the spread of leprosy it was best to isolate the sufferers, and proposed to transfer them to the quarantine station which the SS government had established on Pulau Jerejak, near Penang. However, the removal of about 100 cases, some of whom were reluctant, would require compulsory powers. The Colonial Office, advised by the Royal College of Physicians in London, refused to approve the necessary legislation since the prevalent medical view was that leprosy was not contagious. The Malay members of the Perak State Council responded by suggesting that their lepers should be transferred to England—if the disease were not contagious they would do no harm there.[22] It was only fifteen years later that medical opinion in Europe caught up with the observed fact that leprosy does spread by contact, and compulsory segregation was eventually approved.[23]

Insanity was commonly diagnosed as due to possession by a malevolent spirit. The *pawang* did his best to exorcise the demon. If this failed, and the patient was violent, he was confined by force. In Kedah in 1900, a man who had attacked his father was kept in stocks on the family verandah. In Melaka in 1885, a dangerous lunatic had been confined in a cage, 6 feet by 5 feet in size, some 20 or 30 yards from his father's house. He had been held in this fashion for the past three years and was in a filthy and unwashed state.[24] If the sufferer was not violent, his relatives put up with the inconvenience and treated him as incurable. They were usually reluctant to hand over the insane to European care or treatment.[25]

Abnormal mental states, including spirit mediumship, often take culturally determined forms. Members of a society go over the narrow line between normal and abnormal behaviour in the fashion which has come to be regarded as 'normal'. In Chapter 10, it has been suggested that there were cultural elements in *amuk* cases. Another such category of mental instability in a traditional form is the condition known in Malay as '*latah*'. In non-technical terms a person subject to *latah* could suffer temporary mental derangement, not caused by organic disease, and would then behave or react in an abnormal but stylized manner. *Latah* was found among Indonesians as well as Malays; it was generally confined to adults. Some local communities had a much greater incidence of *latah* cases than others. Certain forms were particularly common among women.[26]

A brief medical description of *latah* is 'a great increase of susceptibility to stimulus from without, especially when the subject is in a fit of absentmindedness'.[27] A sudden shock, such as a loud noise or a peremptory word of command, could so disturb a person (if susceptible to attacks of *latah*) that he began to behave abnormally. Such behaviour included outbursts of obscene language which the sufferer would never use when in a normal condition, or a mechanical imitation of every gesture or movement of the person whose act had induced the attack.

Susceptibility to *latah* may have hereditary and environmental elements. It has been suggested that the central element in *latah* is a 'condition of abstraction . . . a temporary dissociation of conscious thought'[28] in a person who is already susceptible. This 'absent-mindedness' is a reflection of the quietude of Malay life. In previous chapters, Clifford's observation of Malay life has provided examples of this disposition. The Malay sits on the steps of his house 'and looks out patiently at life'; on the bank of the river 'the sleepy villager, whose patient eyes watch life indolently from the water's brink, wonders why the land has fallen to sleep'.[29] A sudden noise or interruption of this condition catches a Malay otherwise disposed to *latah* when he is likely to react.

There is evidence to the same effect in some aspects of Malay manners and etiquette. Abdul Majid wrote that 'a Malay gentleman of high breeding . . . never scolds his servants in public'.[30] McNair wrote that 'a Malay, as a rule, speaks slowly' and quickly loses respect for anyone who is 'boisterous . . . impulsive and rude'.[31] Zainal Abidin adds that 'it is bad manners to speak in an unnecessarily loud voice. It amounts to shouting at the person addressed.'[32] It is not of course suggested that noisiness always induced *latah*, to which only a small number of Malays were subject. But these comments do indicate the cultural background of the dreamy abstraction to which a *latah* case was normally addicted.

If this is the explanation, in part, of attacks of *latah*, does it serve also to provide a reason for the indisputable decline in the incidence of *latah* in this century? Dr Galloway, whose theory has been summarized above, finds the explanation in 'the gradual hardening of the conditions of life . . . no leisure for abstraction or introspection' in the Malay environment of more recent times. He also points out that *latah* does not occur among Malays who live in the more strenuous and noisy environment of the towns.[33] Further evidence to the same effect is provided by Richmond Wheeler's experience of teaching Malay students at the Sultan Idris Training College in the 1920s. 'The usual method of asking questions in order to test progress often failed utterly.' The student to whom the sudden question was addressed was 'hopelessly upset' and gave oral answers which were far below the standard of his written work. Wheeler relates this behaviour to *latah*, arguing that 'the obvious forms of *latah* are only extreme cases of a mental attitude which is very widespread'.[34]

To sum up, it was only a small number of Malays who were constitutionally susceptible to attacks of *latah*. Where the individual had such a disposition, the circumstances and tempo of Malay life—which have changed significantly in modern times—created situations in which an attack might be caused by sudden interruption of a state of absent-mindedness. The behaviour of a *latah* case took culturally determined forms.

In the opening paragraph of this book, it was suggested that Malay acceptance of education in vernacular schools and the impact of the system on Malay life began in the early years of the twentieth century. Yet these were changes which had their origins as far back as the 1860s in the SS, and so they fall within the limits of the present study. In time, an alien and unwelcome intrusion took root, first in the rural areas of Province Wellesley and Melaka, and later in the Malay states—both the FMS and also Kedah and Johor, though in these cases on a very restricted scale.[35] It was a very slow and gradual process, in which the real momentum began no earlier than 1890.[36] As a result, the pupils who passed through the schools were still too few and too young to achieve prominence in Malay society of the late nineteenth and early twentieth centuries. In this study, the main interest lies in the changing attitudes of parents and pupils to the schools as an experience and a preparation for life.

In the traditional Malay way of life, only religious education was provided by formal teaching. Of other fields Wilkinson, the first Inspector of Schools FMS, wrote that 'education was based upon a sort of apprenticeship. Most boys picked up a good deal of industrial knowledge by assisting their parents in the work of agriculture, fishing and trapping.' In this way, a boy did none the less acquire manual skills, absorb a good deal of useful knowledge, especially about plants and animals, and in some cases learn the techniques of a carpenter, a metal-worker or a magician. A few might become trained fighting men, or literate for the practical purposes of reading or writing spells, letters, etc. A girl was similarly an informal apprentice to her mother or other older women in the work of her sex, which ranged from cooking and the care of young children to padi planting and sometimes a mastery of the tales, proverbs and popular verse in which women were often better instructed than men.[37]

A boy of the upper class learnt in a similar way, by example rather than precept, but he would absorb less of the manual skills, since men of his class did not do general work with their hands, though some of them became good craftsmen of the dilettanti type.[38] He had the opportunity but often lacked the inclination to learn to read and write. J. W. W. Birch in Perak in 1875 made a literacy count of eight chiefs with whom he was dealing at the time; half were literate and half were not.[39] Abdullah Munshi found that most of the upper class in Pahang and in Kelantan were illiterate and adds that 'If in Malay countries the people would exert themselves to get a good teacher for their children, all those countries would be full of people knowing how to read and write'. However, 'people do not value the art of writing and do not work hard with the assistance of teachers'. Yet even in 1838 there were signs that the ruling class was coming to recognize that literacy was a useful accomplishment. Abdullah's Kelantan informant said that 'he wished I would stay in Kelantan and teach him'. Few, however, were prepared to apply themselves to the task—'these people think that it is quite simple and easy to attain the writer's art, just by listening and imitating'.[40]

With due allowance made for a professional teacher's prejudice in favour of his own profession, Abdullah had identified the root of the problem. Good teaching would stimulate the pupil's efforts and, to achieve literacy, there must be organized instruction; 'listening and imitating', the basis of other forms of learning, was not enough. The SS could supply a limited number of Malays, who had been educated in mission schools or in government schools or abroad, to fill the position of tutor to the sons of a ruler or chief, or to serve as master of a small school under aristocratic patronage. Hugh Low came across one such teacher in Perak in 1877. Shaik Hashim—'he seemed a good old man and keeps a school for which he is very poorly paid, he has been *guru* to all the rajas of Perak'.[41] He was evidently one of the class whom Vaughan described as 'highly educated and intelligent Malays ... who are usually of Arabic extraction'.[42]

A boy might also be sent away to be educated. Patani, for example, was able to attract pupils from neighbouring states, though probably more for religious than lay education.[43] A few boys were sent to schools in the SS. One such was Raja Bot, the son of Raja Jumaat, the progressive chief of the important mining district of Lukut. In 1857 Raja Bot's father sent him to Melaka to be in the care of the Resident Councillor and to attend the English school there.[44]

In the villages, Koran teaching was the only form of instruction. When Cavenagh began to experiment with Malay schools in the rural areas of the SS, he invited the 'village priest' to act as teacher whenever he appeared to be 'qualified' for the task.[45] There were advantages in building on the foundation of Islamic teaching. A man who could teach the children to recite the Koran in Arabic, was likely to be literate in that script at least.[46] The parents would have more confidence in a familiar and respected figure than 'spick and span town-bred gentlemen, whose hands had never been soiled in a rice-field and who were adepts at composing love quatrains and flowery letters'.[47] Under Cavenagh's scheme, the Koran teacher gave his familiar instruction in reciting the Koran for 2 hours each morning and afternoon and devoted the rest of his time to 'Malay instruction'. Except in some parts of rural Melaka, this system proved unsatisfactory but A. M. Skinner, who took charge of Malay education in 1871, persevered nevertheless.[48]

The first school in the western Malay states was established at Klang in 1875. It was not a great success but it led Douglas, the Resident, to a decision to open another school at Kuala Selangor in 1877. Douglas 'had an interview with the *imam* and a talk with him about a school for Selangor. He says he can only teach the *Kuran* himself and knows of no one competent to teach boys to read and write and cipher.'[49] It seems that teachers were found from elsewhere. When *Hari Raya* was celebrated at Klang in 1878, 'the school children with the *guru* and some four or five teachers etc. came to a "feast"—the boys nicely dressed and very well behaved. One of the ushers read an address to me—nicely worded and of course complimentary in the extreme.'[50] This passage suggests that Douglas had recruited one of the SS teachers 'adept at composing . . . flowery letters'. However, all was not well with basic instruction. A report of 1879 on the Klang school disclosed that the head teacher employed his pupils in 'cutting firewood, running errands etc.'[51] By this means, the teacher had his own children available to supplement the family income by the sale of fruit.

There was a shortage of textbooks and other school equipment. When Dr Mohamed Said went to the village school at Linggi in Negeri Sembilan in the second decade of the twentieth century, the three more senior classes sat on benches and wrote in exercise books in pencil, but the two junior classes squatted on the floor and wrote on slates, using slate pencils purchased from the local shops.[52] A generation earlier the equipment must have been even scantier. It is not surprising that the teachers, inadequately trained and lacking essential apparatus, opted for practical subjects.

The parents were at first very reluctant to send their sons to the new schools. In Selangor and Sungei Ujong the government made regulations under which school attendance was compulsory but it was difficult to enforce these rules. One of the many tasks of the *penghulu* was to persuade parents to send their children to school. Among other inducements offered were a midday meal, a football pitch, and the opportunity to attend a Koran class at the school in the afternoon.[53] In the early days of the school at Klang, Douglas decided that he would 'give a huge children's feast after bulan puasa to all who could come decently dressed. I shall . . . only admit those children who go to school.'[54]

Even in 1896 the District Officer at Kuala Langat wrote that 'the difficulty in a district like this is to convince parents that it is for their good that their boys should be educated. They complain that the staple industries of the district, i.e. cutting *ataps*, clearing jungle or working fish stakes do not require that their sons should be able to read or write, and that on leaving school their boys are flung back on their hands without any knowledge of woodcraft such as might enable them to earn their living or any prospect of obtaining a living by means of their acquirements.'[55]

Literacy offered little advantage if it was neither used in work nor in recreation. There was nothing to read. Logan, visiting Naning in 1849, 'enquired for books . . . but he did not think that anybody but the *imam* possessed one. At last he recollected that he himself had a manuscript and invited me to go to his house to see it. . . . It was a little volume which had remained in the family from time immemorial, and of which the nucleus had been some prayers in Arabic. To this various additions in Malay on different subjects and with a curious diversity and defectiveness of handwriting, had been made from time to time . . . neither the present head of the family nor any of its members could read or write. The book was nevertheless . . . highly respected and prized.'[56]

Abdullah Munshi made a similar enquiry in Kelantan in 1838. 'He said he had a bundle of Malay manuscripts put away belonging to a relative. . . . Then he went home, and later came with a basket wrapped in cloth. I opened it and found manuscripts on the subject of religion and prayer.' While at Kuala Terengganu, Abdullah noted that 'there are a few people among them who write an excellent Arabic hand; they write out the *Kuran* and Arabic religious books. A *Kuran* written out in Terengganu is highly esteemed even in the outer world. About two out of three cannot read the *Kuran* and about four out of five cannot read Malay.' In Pahang, 'with few exceptions the letters of Malays and Malay *rajas* are badly constructed and badly spelt, letters wrongly joined and misplaced'.[57]

The supply of reading material was much improved by the appearance of the first Malay newspaper, *Jawi Peranakan*, which was published for about twenty years from 1876 onwards. Percipient Europeans, like Ernest Birch, recognized its importance.[58] It was not controversial but devoted most of its space to social and literary material, information of the weather, advertisements, and official announcements. It was, however, contemporary reading material written to inform and entertain the reader. Far away from the editorial office in Singapore, a Malay clerk in the Resident's office in Klang, came to Douglas to ask for permission to act as the local correspondent of the newspaper. The autocratic Douglas replied that 'I was quite agreeable to their giving any information of interest to *Jawi Peranakan*—that Englishmen were not afraid of honest criticism, that we were anxious to have our acts made public'.[59]

Real progress came only after 1900 when the rapidly increasing number of Malay schools were provided with a range of 'Malay literary works of worth and popular appeal'; these were placed in school libraries open to adult members of the village community'[60] This development came in the period in which Dr Mohamed Said recollects, from his childhood, that the older women of the family were 'avid readers' of Malay literary works.[61] Although the effect of literacy was slow in appearing, it encouraged the habit of reading.

As the governments became increasingly paperbound, they recruited clerks, who were required to be literate in Malay, preferably the *Rumi* (roman) rather than the *Jawi* (Arabic) script. With this inducement, there was general acceptance of the introduction of *Rumi* Malay into the curriculum in the 1890s.[62] The *Rumi* Malay newspaper, *Bintang Timur*, was founded to meet the needs of the Straits Chinese community but it was a useful addition to reading matter for Malays when it came their way.[63]

Yet class teaching in Malay schools was a sort of voyage into 'never never land', where sums were done in pounds, shillings and pence or in pounds and ounces; maps showed Tierra del Fuego in South America but not Singapore; and readers had titles such as 'Mary's Little Lamb'.[64] Even the 'three R's' taught in this fashion were a mystery, and parents began to ask for something better as they came to value education.[65] There were similar absurdities in the teaching of geography. 'Geographical terms and features are known verbally but frequently not understood.' Pupils would point to places on a map without knowing which was north and south, which land and which sea.[66] These were problems which R. J. Wilkinson tackled energetically during his brief but immensely creative tenure of the post of Inspector of Schools FMS (1903–6).[67] They had been building up since the Malay attitude to schools swung from rejection to active demand from about 1890 onwards.[68]

The Malay schoolmasters of this period were a mixed bag. There were some exotic specimens—one was 'dressed in European clothes, with tremendously big blue spectacles as his most prominent feature and with a huge umbrella tucked under his arm'.[69] The majority, however, were homegrown products of the pupil-teacher system which, as the title suggests, retained a number of pupils under a form of teaching apprenticeship. It was not a satisfactory system and was later replaced by teacher training colleges. Yet it marked the beginning of a new occupation in village society—the respected and often influential figure of the village schoolmaster—finding its recruits from the sons of village worthies such as *penghulu*, *haji* and so on. To them were still added a sprinkling of migrant teachers from the SS and a few drawn from the upper class of Malay society.[70]

Education for girls made much slower progress. Even if parents could be persuaded to send their young daughters to school, they often took them away at about the age of ten, since this was the time at which it was considered necessary to 'lock up your daughters' and keep them secluded until they could be safely married as virgins.[71] The argument that an educated woman made a better wife and mother fell on stony ground. At Tanjong Karang in Selangor in 1897, 'the people are a little disposed still to stand by their old customs and religious teaching, which they consider may be influenced to their detriment by such an innovation as a girls' school'.[72] However, in Selangor, Raja Muda Sulaiman became an energetic promoter of female education. Under his auspices, a girls' school was opened at Bandar, the royal capital, in 1895. The curriculum was Koran teaching, reading and writing, weaving, sewing, knitting, crocheting, beadwork, ornamental work with gold thread, gold stamping on cloth, and cookery. The Raja Muda bore the expense of running the school, and to reassure anxious parents he had the girls transported to and from school in a bullock-cart. It flourished briefly while the royal patron could supervise it himself, but when he ascended the throne in 1898, it, like a number of other girls' schools, suffered poor attendance and inadequate teaching.[73] The majority of girls' schools were closed down within a few years at most of their establishment.

Although education was gradually finding acceptance in the villages, there were often mixed feelings. It disturbed the parent that the children would have a different upbringing from his own. 'The elder Malay has a vague fear of the new education, fear for his *kampungs* and *padi* fields at the hands of his educated children, and, perhaps, even a tinge of jealousy that his sons should have greater advantages than he.'[74] With girls the doubts were still stronger. The *penghulu* and village elders 'profess their desire for the education of their daughters' but did not send them to school.[75] As the village schoolmaster, a young man at this time, grew into a village elder the distrust would pass. But that carries the story through to about 1920.

In the upper class there was less parental mistrust of European education. Even a Malay of the traditional type, such as Raja Mahmud of Selangor, could see that his sons would have a better prospect of a career if they were educated in the new fashion.[76] Many of the sons of the upper class were sent to English-medium schools in the towns, when these schools were established. Yet an élite required that some more exclusive form of education should be provided than the mixed classes of the secondary schools in the main towns. From this tendency came the Malay College at Kuala Kangsar, established in 1905.[77] However, the Selangor Raja School, which had a brief life between 1890 and 1894, falls within the period of this study and gives some insights into the Anglo-Malay approach to the education of young aristocrats.

On the Malay side in Selangor, there was a willing acceptance of this new opportunity and about a dozen pupils, including the Raja Muda, a married man in his twenties, attended at one time or another.

The first and only headmaster of the Selangor Raja School was a young Englishman, new to Malaya, who spoke no Malay and had no teaching experience, except perhaps as a school chaplain. He did little to introduce an appropriate curriculum and gave priority to inculcating the moral and ethical values of the English Victorian society from which he came. The experiment was abandoned in 1894 since it was an expensive method of educating a dozen boys. Moreover, by this time F. W. Haines had assumed other duties as chaplain and inspector of schools in Selangor. The remaining pupils, if they wished to continue their education, were transferred to the newly opened Victoria Institution, the premier English secondary school of Selangor for many years to come.[78]

There is a little to suggest that the Malay aristocrats, who sent their sons to the Selangor Raja School and later to the Malay College at Kuala Kangsar, accepted the view that they were a community in need of what Swettenham called 'regeneration'.[79] They did, however, regard a pilgrimage to Mecca as a means of extricating oneself for a time from some embarrassment or even disgrace. It was perhaps in that spirit that they came to treat a boarding school, imbued with notions of higher things, as a useful expedient. When Wilkinson, who had taken a leading part in founding the Malay College, became Resident of Negeri Sembilan in 1910, he was moved to write that 'there is an idea prevalent in the state that the Malay College—which makes a point of training the character as well as the intelligence—was really a sort of reformatory for idle and refractory boys of good family'.[80]

1. J. D. Gimlette and H. W. Thomson, *A Dictionary of Malayan Medicine*, London, Oxford University Press, 1939, reprinted Kuala Lumpur, Oxford University Press, 1971 and 1983, and J. D. Gimlette, *Malay Poisons and Charm Cures*, London, Churchill, 1916 (3rd ed. 1929), reprinted Kuala Lumpur, Oxford University Press, 1971, and Singapore, Oxford University Press, 1985, are the most important sources. I. H. Burkill, *A Dictionary of the Economic Products of the Malay Peninsula*, 2 vols., London, published on behalf of the SS and FMS Governments, Crown Agents, 1935, gives much information on Malay use of particular vegetable products for medicinal purposes.

2. *AR Pahang 1894*, para. 28.

3. H. C. Clifford, *In a Corner of Asia being Tales and Impressions of Men and Things in the Malay Peninsula*, London, Fisher Unwin, 1899, p. 78. In 18[illegible]5 Perak Malays bathed twice a day (J. Low, 'Observations on Perak', *JIA*, 4, 1850, p. 503). But in Terengganu in 1838 'the people's clothes were poor and dirty and their persons were unclean' (Abdullah bin Abdul Kadir, Munshi, *Kesah Pelayaran Abdullah*, translated by A. E. Coope, *The Voyage of Abdullah: A Translation from the*

Malay, Singapore, Malaya Publishing House, 1949, p. 21).

4. Mohamed Ibrahim bin Abdullah, Munshi, *The Voyages of Mohamed Ibrahim Munshi*, translated by A. Sweeney and Nigel Phillips, Kuala Lumpur, Oxford University Press, 1975, p. 11.

5. F. A. Swettenham, *British Malaya: An Account of the Origin and Progress of British Influence in Malaya*, London, John Lane Bodley Head, 1907 (revised editions 1929 and 1948, London, Allen & Unwin), p. 151. SSD 11 December 1894, report by Clifford.

6. J. W. W. Birch, *The Journals of J. W. W. Birch First British Resident to Perak 1874–1875* (hereafter cited as *Birch Journal*), edited by P. L. Burns, Kuala Lumpur, Oxford University Press, 1976, p. 82.

7. J. R. Logan, 'Notes at Penang, Kedah etc.', *JIA*, 5, 1851, p. 57. When Birch arrived in Perak in November 1874 he found that Sultan Abdullah was upstream 'having deserted Batak Rabit on account of the cholera' (SSD 26 April 1875 with report of 2 April 1875 by Birch, para. 10, reprinted in *Birch Journal*, p. 389). W. W. Skeat and F. F. Laidlaw, 'The Cambridge University Expedition to Parts of the Malay Peninsula 1899–1900: Personal Accounts', *JMBRAS*, 26(4), 1953, p. 40, found that 'the *raja* of Jalor had run away from danger taking his entire household and his followers with him'. To Gajah, one of the most famous of the Pahang fighting captains (see p. 72 above), had a dread of smallpox (W. Linehan, 'A History of Pahang' (hereafter cited as 'Pahang'), *JMBRAS*, 14(2), 1936, p. 98).

8. *PGG* 1897, p. 524, report from Matang. In Jelebu neighbours were exempt from the customary courtesy of attending a funeral if the deceased had died of smallpox (A. L. Keyser, *Trifles and Travels*, London, Murray, 1923, p. 89).

9. T. Braddell, 'Notes of a Trip to the Interior of Malacca', *JIA*, 7, 1853, p. 98. Braddell was told that about 30 per cent of the population of Muar, including the Temenggong, had contracted smallpox. '*Pucuk*' denotes a shoot of bamboo or some other plant used for medicinal purposes (Burkill, op. cit., p. 1969; Gimlette and Thomson, op. cit., p. 189).

10. Skeat and Laidlaw, op. cit., p. 42. Skeat was told that in Kelantan whole villages rather than individual houses were quarantined in this fashion. See also Keyser, *Trifles and Travels*, p. 98—'a palm leaf across the threshold'.

11. In 1874 Swettenham came on the aged Datuk Bandar of Sungei Ujong being carried in this way (F. A. Swettenham, *Sir Frank Swettenham's Malayan Journals 1874–1876* (hereafter cited as *Swettenham Journal*), edited by P. L. Burns and C. D. Cowan, Kuala Lumpur, Oxford University Press, 1975, p. 172).

12. Swettenham, *British Malaya*, p. 155; *The Real Malay: Pen Pictures*, London, John Lane Bodley Head, 1900, p. 26. In the 1890s it was suggested that Malays should be recruited and trained as hospital dressers and attendants to staff wards specially reserved for Malay patients (*PGG* 1896, p. 818, report from Education Department). According to Winstedt, Malay hospital inmates feared 'the vengeful spirits of dead patients' who haunted the place (*Start from Alif, Count from One: An Autobiographical Memoire*, Kuala Lumpur, Oxford University Press, 1969, p. 136). Keyser, *Trifles and Travels*, p. 98.

13. As an example, a returning pilgrim brought smallpox to the Kuala Kangsar district in 1891; there were 34 cases and 10 were fatal (*PGG* 1891, p. 1016). In another instance, the village isolated the pilgrim as soon as it was realized that he had smallpox, but reported the outbreak only four days later (*PGG* 1897, p. 524, report from Matang).

14. SS Medical Department Annual Report for 1871 enclosed with SSD 24 August 1872. However, the Director of Medical Services SS was more optimistic than his colleague on the spot in Province Wellesley. He believed that Malays 'if properly treated [are] rather amenable to reason than otherwise . . . very willing to have their children vaccinated as a rule'.

15. W. E. Maxwell, 'The Malay Peninsula: Its Resources and Prospects', in P. H. Kratoska (ed.), *Honourable Intentions: Talks on the British Empire in South-East Asia Delivered at the Royal Colonial Institute 1874–1928*, Singapore, Oxford University Press, 1983 (reprinted from the *Proceedings of the Royal Colonial Institute* 1891), p. 154. The chief was Raja Mahmud, with whom Maxwell had clashed on another issue: see p. 83 above. J. M. Gullick, *The Story of Kuala Lumpur 1857–1939*, Singapore, Eastern Universities Press, 1983, p. 95. At a meeting of the Selangor State Council in 1883 Raja Muda Musa, another arch conservative, unsuccessfully opposed the issue of instructions to *penghulu* for mass vaccination (Mohamed Amin Hassan, 'Raja Muda Musa ibni Sultan Abdul Samad', *Peninjau Sejarah*, 1 (1), 1966).

16. *PSCM*, 20 February 1880, *PMS*, p. 219.

17. Gullick, cited in note 15 above.

18. *AR Pahang 1894* and *AR Pahang 1898*. *AR Kuala Selangor 1898*, para. 57, in *SGG* 1899. *PGG* 1893, p. 12, report from Kinta.

19. *Malay Mail*, 23 March 1899, reporting an episode from Parit Buntar in Perak; it may be surmised that the village was an immigrant community new to official quarantine measures.

20. *PGG* 1894, p. 126, a report by the Datuk Seri Adika Raja on his subdistrict (see p. 78 above). *AR Pahang 1899*, para. 65.

21. Clifford, *In a Corner of Asia*, pp. 139–68 (and *The Further Side of Silence*, New York, Doubleday, Page & Co., 1927, pp. 187–214), tells a story of a leper and his devoted wife (on whom see p. 230, note 24 above).

22. Swettenham, *British Malaya*, p. 269. In 1891 the 186 patients in the settlement at Pulau Jerejak included a few volunteers from Perak and Selangor (SSD 21 April 1891).

23. *PGG* 1899, pp. 646–50, publishes the conclusions of the international medical conference on leprosy held at Berlin in 1897.

24. 'Notes of a Trip to Kedah', *Malay Mail*, 20 April 1900, and 'A Trip to Malacca', *Straits Times*, 12 March 1885; this report mentions that there was another such case a few miles away. *PSCM*, 28 February 1880, *PMS*, p. 223, deals with a man shut up as a lunatic.

25. Swettenham, *The Real Malay*, p. 250.

26. H. A. O'Brien, 'Latah', *JSBRAS*, 11, 1883, and 'Latah', *JSBRAS*, 12, 1883, gives a lengthy description of *latah* cases and offers some suggested explanation. See also Gimlette and Thomson, op. cit., pp. 141–2, for another good description by medical experts, and F. A. Swettenham, *Malay Sketches*, London, John Lane Bodley Head, 1895, pp. 64–82, for Malay and European theories of the time. A. B. Rathborne, *Camping and Tramping in Malaya: Fifteen Years' Pioneering in the Native States of the Malay Peninsula*, London, Swan Sonnenschein, 1898, reprinted Singapore, Oxford University Press, 1984, p. 57. L. R. Wheeler, *The Modern Malay*, London, Allen & Unwin, 1928, pp. 219–21. Keyser, *Trifles and Travels*, p. 112.

27. Gimlette and Thomson, op. cit., p. 141.

28. David J. Galloway, 'A Contribution to the Psychology of *Latah*', *JSBRAS*, 85, 1922, p. 143. Galloway's essay is the most convincing explanation of *latah* known

to the author; he writes with the authority of a medical expert but relates his analysis and conclusions to the sociological background.

29. H. C. Clifford, *Studies in Brown Humanity being Scrawls and Smudges in Sepia, White and Yellow*, London, Grant Richards, 1898, pp. 49 and 154, already quoted above at pp. 186 and 160.

30. Abdul Majid bin Zainuddin, *The Malays in Malaya: By One of Them*, Singapore, Malaya Publishing House, 1928, p. 76.

31. J. F. A. McNair, *Perak and the Malays: Sarong and Keris*, London, Tinsley Bros., 1878, reprinted Kuala Lumpur, Oxford University Press, 1972, p. 203.

32. Zainal Abidin bin Ahmad, 'Malay Manners and Etiquette', *JMBRAS*, 23(3), 1950, p. 58.

33. Galloway, op. cit., p. 149.

34. Wheeler, op. cit., p. 221. Galloway also suggests that education was a powerful force in reducing Malay susceptibility to *latah*—especially among women. He argues that schooling induces 'powers of restraint' over a tendency to daydream. Gimlette and Thomson, op. cit., p. 142, confirm that *latah* was (in 1939) 'less common in the Malay states than it was fifty years ago'. Gimlette had begun his medical career in Malaya in Pahang in 1896.

35. R. Stevenson, *Cultivators and Administrators: British Educational Policy towards the Malays 1875–1906*, Kuala Lumpur, Oxford University Press, 1975, is the leading study of Malay education in the FMS between 1875 and 1906. The present writer has found his Chapter 6, 'Malay Reactions and Attitudes to Education', particularly useful in writing this passage but has found much relevant information and ideas throughout the book. D. D. Chelliah, *A Short History of Education in the Straits Settlements*, Kuala Lumpur, Government Press, 1947; reprinted Singapore, G. H. Kiat, 1960, is another useful, basic study. The text of the major official reports on education of this period is made available in F. H. K. Wong and Gwee Yee Hean (eds.), *Official Reports on Education: Straits Settlements and the Federated Malay States 1870–1939*, Singapore, Pan Pacific Book Distributors, 1980. H. R. Cheeseman, 'Education in Malaya, 1900–1941', *MHJ*, 2(1), 1955, writes with the authority of a man whose career began in 1906 and carried him to the position of Director of Education after World War II. *Special Reports on Educational Subjects*, Vol. 14, 1905, Cmd. 2379 includes 'The System of Education in the F.M.S.' and 'The System of Education in the S.S.'. R. J. Wilkinson, 'The Education of Asiatics', appears in the same series of *Special Reports on Educational Subjects*, Vol. 8, 1902, Cmd. 835; Datuk Mahmud bin Mat, 'The First Malay School in Pahang', *MHJ*, 1(2), 1954, and Datuk Mohamed Said, *Memoirs of a Menteri Besar: Early Days*, Singapore, Heinemann, 1982, record personal experiences of pupils in Malay schools of this period.

The first Malay school was established in Kedah at Alor Star in 1861 (Muhammad Hassan bin Dato' Kerani Muhammad Arshad, *Al-Tarikh Salasilah Negeri Kedah*, Kuala Lumpur, Dewan Bahasa dan Pustaka, 1968 (previously published in *Jawi*, 1926), p. 210). The first Malay school in Kelantan dates from 1904 (*AR Kelantan 1904* and W. A. Graham, *Kelantan—A State of the Malay Peninsula—A Handbook of Information*, Glasgow, James MacLehose & Sons, 1908, p. 116). On Johor see p. 86 above and C. A. Trocki, *Prince of Pirates: The Temenggongs and the Development of Johor and Singapore 1784–1885*, Singapore, Singapore University Press, 1979, p. 109. In 1909 Terengganu had one school for the sons of chiefs (SSD 22 September 1909). Sutherland says it was founded in 1908 (H. Sutherland, 'The Taming of the

Trengganu Elite', in R. T. McVey (ed.), *Southeast Asian Transitions: Approaches through Social History*, New Haven, Yale University Press, 1978, p. 50).

In the SS and FMS, education was generally in the hands of administrators, whose reports contain many interesting comments and snippets of information. Much criticism has been levelled at them for the inadequacy and misdirection of their efforts. But they were Victorian Englishmen, drawn from a society in which primary education for all had been introduced in 1870. Hence they took a close interest in such schools as there were.

36. Stevenson, op. cit., p. 43.

37. R. J. Wilkinson, 'The Incidents of Malay Life', *Papers on Malay Subjects, Life and Customs*, Part 1, 1908, reprinted in *JMBRAS*, 30(4), 1957, p. 46.

38. See p. 57 above. In Raman, for example, Cameron noted that 'the raja makes very handsome howdahs of wrought *rotan* for his elephants' ('On the Patani', *JSBRAS*, 11, 1883, p. 130).

39. *Birch Journal*, p. 259.

40. Abdullah Munshi, op. cit., pp. 10 and 41. 'The Malay aristocracy ... were by tradition disdainful of book learning' (Stevenson, op. cit., p. 147).

41. H. Low, 'The Journal of Sir Hugh Low, Perak 1877' (hereafter cited as 'Low Journal'), edited by E. Sadka, *JMBRAS*, 27(4), 1954, p. 86. He had been in Perak for fifty-four years.

42. J. D. Vaughan, 'Notes on the Malays of Pinang and Province Wellesley', *JIA*, n.s., 2, 1857, p. 122. Brian Harrison, 'The Anglo-Chinese College and Early Modern Education', in K. S. Sandhu and P. Wheatley (eds.), *Melaka—The Transformation of a Malay Capital c.1400–1980*, 2 vols., Kuala Lumpur, Oxford University Press, 1983, Vol. 1, p. 305, summarizes the development of education in Melaka between 1815 and 1840. See also C. M. Turnbull, *The Straits Settlements 1826–1867: Indian Presidency to Crown Colony*, London, Athlone Press, 1972, p. 226.

43. *AR Kelantan 1903–1904*; *AR Pahang 1905*.

44. Mohamed Amin Hassan, 'Raja Bot bin Raja Jumaat', *JMBRAS*, 40(1), 1967, p. 69. Raja Bot was about ten years old at this time. He remained in Melaka to learn commercial practice from the Chinese merchant who did business with his father—very unusual at that time for a Malay aristocrat.

45. O. Cavenagh, *Reminiscences of an Indian Official*, London, W. H. Allen & Co., 1884, p. 263.

46. Some Koran teachers, however, were illiterate and relied on memory to enable them to recite the text of the Koran. *Special Reports on Educational Subjects*, cited in note 35 above, and Vaughan, op. cit., p. 121.

47. Winstedt, *Start from Alif*, p. 68. On his contact with Malay teachers see p. 185 above.

48. Chelliah, op. cit., p. 62.

49. Douglas Diary, 5 June 1877; Stevenson, op. cit., pp. 24–5.

50. Douglas Diary, 30 September 1878.

51. Sel. Sec. 108/80 quoted by Stevenson, op. cit., p. 25.

52. Mohamed Said, op. cit., p. 46.

53. Stevenson, op. cit., pp. 25 and 38–43. 'Koran classes have a very beneficial effect on the attendance' (*AR Education Department Perak 1893* in *PGG* 1894, p. 207). On football see p. 332 below.

54. Douglas Diary, 23 August 1878. *Bulan puasa* is the Muslim month of fasting (see Glossary).

55. *AR Kuala Langat 1896* in *SGG* 1897, p. 456.

56. J. R. Logan, 'Five Days in Naning', *JIA*, 3, 1849, p. 285.

57. Abdullah Munshi, op. cit., pp. 10, 21 and 42. Although the final comment on poor handwriting is included in his account of Pahang, it may have been intended to be a general comment.

58. E. W. Birch, 'The Vernacular Press in the Straits', *JSBRAS*, 4, 1879, reprinted *JMBRAS*, 42(1), 1969. Nik Ahmad bin Haji Nik Hassan, 'The Malay Press', *JMBRAS*, 36(1), 1963.

59. Douglas Diary, 20 April 1878.

60. Stevenson, op. cit., p. 106.

61. Mohamed Said, op. cit., p. 78.

62. Stevenson, op. cit., p. 71, citing Rodger in *AR Perak 1891*, states that Malay reaction to the introduction of *Rumi* Malay into the curriculum had been generally favourable. It was expected to assist Malays in dealing with members of other communities who, if literate in Malay, read and wrote *Rumi* but not *Jawi*. Apart from *Rumi*, Malay candidates for government posts were sometimes required to be able at least to speak English.

63. Nik Ahmad bin Haji Nik Hassan, op. cit., pp. 41–2.

64. *AR Kuala Kangsar 1896* in *PGG* 1897, p. 138; *AR Education Department Selangor 1898*, para. 9, in *SGG* 1899; *AR Education Department Perak 1889* in *PGG* 1890, p. 272.

65. *AR FMS Education Department 1898* in *SGG* 1899, Supplement.

66. *SGG* 1896, p. 403, report from Ulu Langat, by Skeat who argued that it was preferable to teach English in Malay schools rather than *Rumi* Malay; *AR Education Department FMS* in *PGG* 1899; *AR Education Department Selangor 1898* in *SGG* 1899.

67. Stevenson, op. cit., pp. 103–14, rightly gives this chapter the title 'A New Era'.

68. In 1891 Perak had 51 Malay schools, of which no less than 42 had been established since 1889 (*AR Education Department Perak 1891* in *PGG* 1892, p. 638). The new tempo was in part due to a change of Residents. Hugh Low, who was succeeded as Resident by Swettenham in 1889, was more interested in English than Malay schools. Swettenham reversed those priorities. Stevenson, op. cit., pp. 30 and 43.

69. This apparition was observed at the school sports held at Jugra as part of the *Hari Raya* celebrations (*SJ*, 3 May 1895).

70. Stevenson, op. cit., pp. 35–6 and 92.

71. Ibid., pp. 92–4.

72. *SGG* 1897, p. 294, report from Kuala Selangor. Stevenson, op. cit., p. 93, quotes a spirited statement by Skeat on the need to educate Malay girls if there was to be real progress.

73. *SGG* 1896, p. 353, report from Kuala Langat. Stevenson, op. cit., pp. 92–3.

74. *AR Pahang 1905*, para. 52, citing a report from Temerloh.

75. *Special Reports on Education 1905*, p. 9. See note 35 above.

76. Stevenson, op. cit., Chapters 7 and 8, 'Early Attempts at Educating the Malays in English 1876–1903' and 'The Establishment of the Kuala Kangsar Malay College 1903–1906' respectively, cover this theme very fully. On Raja Mahmud's sons, see ibid., p. 152. On the Selangor Raja School generally, ibid., pp. 148–54.

77. See p. 227 above.

78. Ibid., pp. 150–2 and 170, note 29. A. Wright and H. A. Cartwright (eds.), *Twentieth Century Impressions of British Malaya: Its History, People, Commerce, Industries and Resources*, London, Lloyds, 1908, p. 283. In his later years F. W. Haines, the former headmaster of the Selangor Raja School, was chaplain at Penang. On his background and career see Stevenson, op. cit., p. 170, note 29, and many other references to his activities in Selangor.

79. J. de V. Allen, 'Two Imperialists: A Study of Sir Frank Swettenham and Sir Hugh Clifford', *JMBRAS*, 37(1), 1964, pp. 55–8, analyses Swettenham's passage in *The Real Malay*, pp. 258–66, and other relevant passages in Swettenham's writings. See also F. A. Swettenham, 'British Rule in Malaya', in Kratoska, op. cit., pp. 186–90; *Malay Sketches*, London, John Lane Bodley Head, 1895, pp. [illegible]–4; *Footprints in Malaya*, London, Hutchinson, 1942, p. 52; *British Malaya*, pp. 1[illegible]6–7; and *About Perak*, Singapore, Straits Times, 1890, pp. 45–50. Stevenson, op. cit., pp. 56–7, considers Swettenham's views and then (pp. 68–73) the views of other British administrators of the period. Allen, 'Two Imperialists', also analyses Clifford's opinions and attitudes.

80. *AR Negeri Sembilan 1910*. Out of 25 boys from this state sent to the College in 1910, 4 were discharged for idleness and 1 for theft the same year.

12
The Organization of Islam

EVERY Malay was a Muslim. It was a national status as much as a religion. A convert to Islam was said to become a Malay (*masuk Melayu*) though it was recognized that in Malaya there were Muslims who were not also Malays. At the same time there were anomalies and reservations in treating Islam as a national status. 'In theory', wrote Wilkinson, 'all the Muslim world was to have constituted a single nation under one elective ruler.'[1] Reality did not correspond with that theory. The Koran reflects social conditions and political ideas, norms and values, of an Arabian commercial and pastoral society of several centuries before Islam came to South-East Asia in the fifteenth century. Moreover Islam came to Malaya with accretions and modifications from Iran, India and elsewhere through which it had passed in its long journey to eastern Asia.[2] Malay society did not accept in full the civilization, for it was hardly less than that, of Islam as a world movement. Malay culture had its ancient traditions (*adat*), especially in the practice of magic and in the beliefs on which magical practice was founded. It also preserved considerable elements of Hindu practice since the Malays had been Hindus before they were converted to Islam.

For reasons to be explained in this chapter, the late nineteenth century witnessed considerable changes in the organization of Islam in Malay society, tending to give it a more dominant position in the Malay way of life as a whole.

As a Muslim, a Malay was expected to conform to the five 'Pillars of Islam' which were the bedrock of his faith. He must subscribe to the doctrine of the Unity of God (*tauhid*), pray five times a day at set hours, observe the fast between sunrise and sunset during the month of fasting (*bulan puasa*), which was the Islamic month of Ramadan, make the pilgrimage to Mecca if it was practicable for him to do so, and pay a religious tithe (*zakat*). These obligations, if duly observed, impinged upon his whole life at various times.

In a village community, the central focus of religious observance was the mosque (*masjid*) at which the men, but not the women, were expected to gather for collective prayers on Fridays. It was the practice, when Friday prayers were over, for the congregation to discuss informally any other matters of common concern to them as a community before they dispersed.

A mosque was both a building and an organization. A small settlement might have a prayer house (*surau*) for group prayers and other meetings, but only a community of forty-four families or more was a congregation large enough to have a mosque for Friday prayers.[3] The mosque was the most important communal building in the village though it was often quite unpretentious in style. Abdullah Munshi noted that the mosque at Pekan at which the ruler of Pahang went to pray on Fridays, had a stone floor and walls and a thatched roof.[4] Although a mosque was usually public property, it could be owned by an individual.[5] It might stand alone or on a site with other buildings administered by trustees as a religious endowment (*wakaf*).[6]

In the 1890s, many villages in western Malaya had so much increased in size that they became entitled to build a mosque or wished to rebuild an existing mosque on a larger scale. The colonial regime often contributed 'dollar for dollar' to building funds raised by local subscription. To build a mosque was a source of prestige both for the community and for those of its members who could contribute. In 1891 in Ulu Langat, for example, the District Officer 'had a meeting with the Mahommedans in the Kajang *mukim* in the afternoon to arrange for the building of a new mosque. The Mendilings and others, with the exception of the Menangkabau people, were inclined to be liberal. These Menangkabau people are very well off, but they all hoard their money; they will not even build respectable houses for themselves.'[7]

The new mosque might not be handsome—one such was described as 'atrociously ugly, a square wooden box of a building, with a corrugated iron roof . . . [it] approximates in appearance to one of the government halting bungalows, and is consequently considered very superior by the Malays'.[8] Yet this mosque—and others like it—was the achievement of years of patient effort by the organizers. It was first necessary to enlist general support and in particular to select a convenient and suitable site—'this alone was a matter which may have taken . . . years for in these peasant communities all moves are made slowly'. Next, it was necessary to approach the district officer for approval and his support in applying to the state council for a government subvention. 'A petition had to be drawn up setting forth the deplorable condition of the old mosque, tumble-down, riddled by white ants, small and altogether beneath the dignity of the place.'

It was often arranged that as local contributions to the building fund were received, they should be safely banked at the district office treasury in the names of the village committee until a sufficient balance had been accumulated. The district officer might also find 'a respectable contractor and I will see that the money is properly applied and good value obtained for it'.[9] As the work went on, 'every beam has been laid and every nail driven by a Chinese contractor under the close scrutiny of the village elders, the timber and materials are generally of the best. For many years to come it will serve the needs of the simple piety of generations of worshippers.' By special dispensation the organizer might perhaps be buried 'near the mosque where he may hear the blessed mutter of the Friday services for ever'. In this fashion a new mosque could be a focus of co-operation and common interest in the village, drawing the community together.

Every mosque had its 'own government and is independent of all others'.[10] It had its complement of four officials—the *imam*, the *khatib*, the *bilal*, and the village headman (*penghulu*).[11] In Vaughan's day the *bilal* (muezzin) announced the Friday call to prayer at about 11.00 a.m.; by noon the mosque was beginning to fill—each member of the congregation washed his feet at the water tank before entering the mosque; the prayers began at 1.00 p.m., with the *imam* leading the congregation. A chapter or two of the Koran was read from the pulpit though few understood the Arabic text.[12]

The mosque officials were local men who had attained their influential positions by reason of their piety and comparative degree of learning. They were often *haji* though this was not a necessary qualification. In the period before *kadi* were appointed (as explained below) to deal with legal matters, it fell to the *imam* to settle disputes and do what he could to enforce religious observances such as attendance at the mosque. Douglas has a number of entries in his diary for the period 1877–81 on the activities and problems of the *imam* of the mosque at Klang, Haji Mohamed Akil. He was 'a man of no note, merely an ordinary planter', who had been appointed *imam* ten years before, when Raja Mahdi held Klang at the beginning of the Selangor Civil War. His father and grandfather had been *haji* and they were of Bugis origin in a community where the ruling class, but not the *rakyat*, were Bugis. Douglas mentions that he delegated to the *imam* the task of informing two convicted murderers that they were to die. He also called in the *imam* to sit with him as an assessor while Douglas was trying a maintenance claim by a deserted wife. On a *Hari Raya* holiday, Douglas 'went to a cake fight (tea party) at the *imam*'s—there were a lot of *hajis*'. However, a couple of months later the *imam* was in trouble because he refused to solemnize the marriage of a woman who had been in debt-bondage to the Sultan's daughter, Raja Arfah—the reason was that 'her mistress did not give her away'. Douglas rebuked the *imam* for not recognizing that debt-bondage and its appurtenances had been abolished. One can sympathize with the *imam* caught between two opposing traditions—for Raja Arfah had a violent temper.

The *imam* of Klang fell out with his congregation and was 'rejected by the Klang people'. However, his successor proved to be even more unpopular and he was reinstated. It was stipulated that instead of an allowance, he must obtain his remuneration in fees for services to his flock. In this way, it was hoped that he would put himself out to keep on good terms with them. However, he mounted a sustained—but unsuccessful—attempt to induce the State Council to authorize him to levy fines for non-attendance at the mosque on Fridays. Swettenham mentions that the Klang *imam* tried 'cases involving religion'.[13]

Haji Mohamed Akil was obviously the wrong man to place in a difficult position of authority. Klang was the administrative capital and one of the important towns of Selangor at this time. His colleague at Kuala Selangor had a less stormy career, but Douglas mentions a dispute over the collection of coconuts—presumably as tithe—and the delivery to the *imam* of a woman caught in adultery by her husband. It seems clear that settled Malay communities were beginning to demand of an *imam* much more than his conventional function of leading the Friday prayers.

Those who attended Friday prayers were earnest in their devotions. In 1826 James Low gives a rather unsympathetic account of the Sultan of Perak, his officers and subjects, assembled in the mosque. They prayed 'with a fervour which is rendered ludicrous by the odd gestures by which it is accompanied. As they become warmed up by their devotion they nod and shake their heads violently in concert. One who has not been accustomed to such an exercise would be rendered quite giddy by it.'[14] However, it was not easy to induce the less devout to come to the mosque at all.[15] Yet the colonial regime, which had taken into its hands the enforcement of the law, was not disposed to make attendance a legal obligation.[16] Malays in the government service, such as police constables, were allowed to plead the call of duty as an excuse for their absence.[17] However, the general impression was that attendance did gradually improve.[18]

Laxity in attending Friday prayers, or other backsliding, did not denote any fundamental decline in religious belief. Swettenham wrote that although the Malay 'would suffer crucifixion sooner than deny his faith, he is not a bigot . . . he believes that the absence of hypocrisy is the beginning of religion'.[19] If he did not feel disposed to conform, he just dropped out. Maxwell wrote of his Malay companions on the journey to Patani that 'Abdul Manan was the *imam* of the party, and led the devotions when anyone could be persuaded to pray with him, which, I am afraid, was not often'.[20] Much depended on the example of one's betters. In Terengganu, for example, the ruling class set the tone, being 'very fanatical Muhammadans'.[21]

Prayer could be a recreation as well as a religious duty. When Ibrahim Munshi was visiting west Johor during the fasting month, 'Enche Wan Andak conceived the idea of holding a *maulud* recitation' and assembled the local worthies who 'recited *maulud* prayers in the house at the rear'.[22] As a boy, Dr Mohamed Said witnessed performances of the mystic practice known as *ratib* in which the participants, experts and novices alike, stood with linked hands in a circle chanting '*la-ila-ha-il-lallah*' until some of them became possessed and fainted. However, the collective chant continued until the leader clapped his hands to call a halt. These were 'austere religious exercises . . . not for the weakminded or the faint-hearted'.[23]

The purpose of the Koran classes, which every Malay attended in his boyhood, was to impart a proficiency in reading the Koran even if the Arabic text was not understood or only imperfectly. There were social occasions when a good performer could win praise. 'It will save his face and delight the ears and hearts of his parents if he can accept the challenge to take his turn when the book is read in the house after the first evening prayer.'[24] As related above, the young Abdul Majid, bidden for the first time to a feast at the *istana* at Kuala Kangsar, was discomforted by an invitation to take his turn at reading the Koran after the meal. He admits ruefully, 'I did not particularly shine as there were many brilliant *Karis*.'[25]

Swettenham whiled away time 'reading the Koran with the Punghulu; there's one comfort in it that I understand it as well as anyone else here, and that is not at all'. On another occasion Sultan Abdul Samad of Selangor settled a dispute 'and made the two parties ... shake hands, read the *Kuran*, and did everything proper'.[26] Clifford describes the well-to-do guests assembled for a village wedding 'seated gravely intoning the *Kuran*, but stopping to chew betel-nut and to gossip scandalously, at frequent intervals'.[27] Koran reading was part of the texture of Malay life.

In the fasting month 'every Mohammedan is commanded to abstain (in the daytime only) from eating and drinking, from conjugal intercourse, and even from such things as smoking, betel-nut chewing and taking snuff'.[28] Although there is some conflict of testimony, it is clear that backsliding, when it occurred, was discreet, and so no attempt was made to enforce observance by law. As with mosque attendance, the signs are that strictness of observance increased a little in the latter part of the nineteenth century.[29]

At the end of the fasting month came the feast of *Hari Raya*. Swettenham was in the royal capital of Selangor on 12 November 1874, when the great annual holiday fell due. 'As it is the custom for everyone to prostrate himself before the Sultan today, Langat is filled with people from morning to night, all got up regardless of expense. *Hari Raya* is almost identical with Xmas Day. If you meet your enemy you ought to forget all by-gones, and shake hands with him and ask him to forgive all real and imaginary wrongs done to him, and he can't refuse you. It is a day when everyone must go to the temple, when everyone wears the best dress he has got, everyone must go before the Sultan, and it is a day of general rejoicing, finishing up with a great feast after the last month's fasting.'[30] Even in the tense period before the killing of J. W. W. Birch in Perak a year later, the Maharaja Lela of Pasir Salak gave the customary feast to his people on the eve of the fatal day.[31] The same general celebrations continued in the later years of the century. In Jelebu in 1897, for example, there was 'a wholesale slaughter of buffaloes for food and large parties of people going from house to house to pay complimentary visits'.[32]

The role of the Malay ruler in a Muslim community was rather uncertain and, to that extent, uneasy.[33] Monarchy was not part of the community in which the Prophet developed his teaching, but in the course of its transmission to South-East Asia, Islam passed through societies in which there were royal rulers. The question of the Malay ruler's duty, as he perceived it, to uphold Islam as a code of conduct, will be considered later. But because of the factors just mentioned, his traditional role in Malay society did not have as much Islamic 'content' as might have been expected. At the start of his reign he was ceremonially installed with rites which did include Islamic elements but much more beside.[34] During his reign 'proper ceremonies and religious forms assisted in legitimising the incumbent's authority'.[35] He might take part in the Friday worship at the mosque in his state capital. On *Hari Raya* his subjects came to pay their respects to him.

What was lacking was an infrastructure through which the ruler might influence, if not control, the ebb and flow of Muslim activity in the community. The tribulations of the *imam* of Klang, described above, show that if there was trouble within a local congregation, no intermediate authority stood between the mosque congregation and the ruler, who might be far away. Such religious dignitaries as there were, performed their duties for the ruler at his capital.[36]

In Perak, the office of Imam Paduka Tuan, one of the eight chiefs of the second rank, became the title given to the officer of the court to whom the ruler delegated the authority and duties of a *mufti*, including making rulings (*fatwa*) on questions of doctrine.[37] Later J. W. W. Birch noted sourly 'the regular breed of Hajis ... the barnacles of Sultan Abdullah'.[38] When Clifford was in Terengganu in 1895, the dominant figure at the court was Ungku Sayid of Paloh, 'who is the Sultan's uncle and also his *guru*, or religious teacher'.[39] He was much more than a royal chaplain; he too seems to have performed the duties of a *mufti*. He was described in 1909 as 'the chief religious authority in whom is vested the interpretation of all difficult legal matters in the last instance.... He apparently has no regular active duties but is, as well as the two judges, sometimes called to the [state] council if matters affecting religion are to be discussed.'[40]

In Kelantan the village *imam*, as in Selangor, was generally left to his own devices but for some years in the 1890s the ruler's energetic chief minister, the Maha Menteri, made himself very unpopular by enforcing stricter Islamic observances of various kinds.[41] In Kedah the ruler had appointed a state *kadi*, assisted by a chief *imam*. In the villages of Kedah 'much of the *penghulu*'s work was religious' and he was supposed to 'prevent activities regarded as sinful against Allah'.[42] In Pahang there was in 1890 a Kadi's court which was believed to have had its origins in pre-colonial times.[43]

In those states where the chiefs of outlying districts had been appointed, their powers were, in theory, purely temporal. This was to be expected since the constitutional theory of Islam knows nothing of chiefs of districts. In practice the local chief took into his own hands the collection of tithes, as part of the revenues for which he acted as the ruler's representative. He may have dispensed alms to the poor, given feasts on religious holidays—like the Maharaja Lela, or assisted in the projects of building mosques.[44] Practice must have varied with the individual concerned and his circumstances.

The information given above indicates a social need for some kind of intermediate or supervisory authority standing between the ruler and the congregations of the village mosques. The variety of expedients adopted in different states suggests that there was no generally accepted model for providing such an authority. The special circumstances of the rural areas of the SS are described later—there was no Muslim ruler at the apex of the system there, of course.

Before coming to the 'bureaucratization' of Islam and the arrival of the district *kadi*, it is necessary to consider the personal activity of a ruler as a Muslim. It seems that some, but not all of the rulers, were in the habit of worshipping at the mosque in the state capital. Sultan Zainal Abidin III of Terengganu hardly ever emerged from his *istana* except for his regular attendance at Friday prayers.[45] Although James Low observed the ruler of Perak in 1825 at the mosque, there is no further mention of a Perak ruler attending Friday prayers until Sultan Idris, who came to the throne in 1887; he was a man of deep and genuine piety.[46] Sultan Sulaiman of Selangor combined two hobbies, religion and wood-carving, in his attendance at the Klang mosque and his interest in its furnishings.[47] On occasion he preached to the congregation from the pulpit which, like the prayer mats and some of the other woodwork, was of his own design.[48]

Apart from these public occasions, rulers showed a preference, perhaps influenced by the European 'private chapels' in palaces and stately homes, for establishing their own mosque for daily prayers. There was a latent doctrinal issue here since, although a mosque might be private property, its nature required that it should be available for use by a congregation of a specified size.[49] The accepted compromise was to build a mosque adjacent to the *istana* so that in practice it became a private, rather than a public, place of worship. In 1897 a new mosque was built at Bandar for the aged Sultan Abdul Samad and 'inside [was] a nicely carved chair surmounted on both sides with two tattered banners from Mecca'.[50] In Perak in the same year, a fund of $40,000 had been raised by subscription to celebrate the diamond jubilee of Queen Victoria by building a 'Jubilee Mosque' near the *istana* at Bukit Chandan. Robson, a sensitive observer of the nuances of Malay behaviour, commented that 'it will be handy to His Highness to offer his prayers in solitary state'.[51]

It was expected of a ruler that he should give alms to the poor, and generally support charitable funds of all sorts. This traditional burden on royal purses was one of the factors adduced by the rulers in asking for increases in the political allowances which they received from state funds, in substitution for the right to raise taxes in former days. At last, Sultan Idris of Perak obtained a special allowance of $12,000 annually and Sultan Sulaiman of Selangor $6,000 but Treacher doubted (in 1902) whether either ruler's drawings were 'exclusively confined to charitable and religious purposes' as had been intended when these special allowances were first given.[52]

A number of factors contributed to the rapid and extensive bureaucratization of Islam in the protected Malay states in the last years of the nineteenth century. In a passage above, it has been suggested that there was a social need of a link between the ruler, and his court advisers, and the local congregations. It was also a reaction of the rulers to their deprivation of their secular powers under the Residential system. They felt that they had a responsibility for the proper observance of Islamic rules of conduct; this was one of the tasks which the formula of the Pangkor Engagement left in their hands. On the British side, experience of leaving Malay Muslim congregations to their own devices in the rural areas of the SS had led to a number of abuses, as perceived by British administrators, notably W. E. Maxwell.[53]

In Province Wellesley there had been unsuccessful experiments in the mid-nineteenth century in establishing a 'species of hierarchy' by which a senior *kadi* at Teluk Ayer Tawar issued warrants to give recognition to the officers of local mosques. However, the SS authorities were unwilling to support the *kadi* if a congregation chose its own officers in defiance of the *kadi*'s nominations. As a result there was no control at all. Vaughan commented that 'such a course if persevered in will do much to ruin the Mahomedan religion'.[54]

Years later, in 1882, Maxwell offered a scathing analysis. He wrote: 'the office of *kadi* is one very little understood by British officers in the Straits Settlements. There is a general hazy idea that Muhammadans in the Colony are entitled to have matters in which their religious law, customs and observances are involved, decided upon by their own religious functionaries, that the religious functionary to whom application should be made in such cases is called a "*kadi*" and that he is chosen for his office by the people themselves.'

'Now, in Muhammadan countries, the *kadi* is a civil, not a religious, functionary and he derives his powers from the civil government, not from any religious body or functionary. It is true that Muhammadan, like Jewish, law and religion are, to a great extent, inseparable, and that the knowledge of one implies a knowledge of the other. But the judge must not be confused with the priest.' Maxwell goes on to describe 'men styling themselves *kadis*' in the SS who are 'practically irresponsible ... for the most part ignorant and corrupt'. These *kadi* acted under the purported authority of warrants issued to them by Muslim leaders in the towns. He continues—'a sum of money is paid for the document thus obtained, and the owner then sets up as a *kadi* in some country place, his authority being mainly confined to questions of marriage and divorce. For a payment he is ready to marry, without a *wali* or otherwise contrary to law any runaway couple; or to declare invalid a marriage in a case where a woman is tired of her husband.'

Maxwell concludes that 'all *kadis* ought to be appointed by the government. Their number should be limited, and they should be subordinate to the magistrates, who should make themselves acquainted with the principles of Muhammadan law.'[55] Here, we have the blueprint for the system later introduced into the FMS and an indication of the underlying problem, i.e. the calibre of the men appointed to be *kadi*.

The first *kadi* appointed in Perak under colonial rule took office in 1879. When the appointment came before the State Council, Hugh Low reminded the Council that there was a general demand for it 'but there is a great difficulty in his opinion in selecting a proper person to fill it'. The Council rejected the candidate proposed by the Regent, Raja Muda Yusuf, as 'he is a stranger and does not know the country or people and does not possess their confidence'. Yusuf retaliated by raising objections to Low's candidate, Sheikh Mahomed Taib. Eventually there was a compromise by which Low's candidate got the post with Yusuf's man as assistant *kadi*.[56]

In Selangor there was no *kadi* appointed during the lifetime of Raja Muda Musa, who was eccentric, difficult and very devout.[57] At his death in 1884, his position devolved on his more amenable son, Raja Sulaiman, who was no less devout and much concerned to improve the standard of Islamic organization and observance in the state. In 1885 therefore, Haji Jafar, who was a native of Selangor, became *kadi* and Raja Sulaiman undertook to arrange for assistant (*naib*) *kadi* to be appointed in the districts.[58] The duties of the new Selangor *kadi* 'consist chiefly in settling matrimonial disputes connected with Mahomedan law and customs, and in the selection of proper persons to act as *naibs*, or *imams*, in the various divisions of the state'.[59]

There was probably a change of style resulting from the new status of the *kadi* as a responsible official. In former times a *kadi* in the SS exercised a very personal authority—'his orders are generally obeyed with fear and trembling by the poor and ignorant'.[60] The *kadi*'s proceedings had been very informal—'they exercise their judicial functions in their own houses or in small sheds attached to them which they dignify with the name of *Balai Shara*'.[61] The new-style *kadi* in the FMS met a real social need and their arrival was welcomed. Raja Dris (later Sultan Idris), returning from a visit to Kinta, told the Perak State Council in 1882 that 'many complaints were made to him of the inconvenience caused by there being no judge capable of hearing matrimonial cases in Kinta, Kampar or Sungai Raya'.[62] The European administrators gratefully relinquished to the *kadi* Malay matrimonial cases—'a class of native affairs which owing to neglect were fast attaining a state of chaos'.[63]

Yet what had been an informal, if arbitrary, system hardened into bureaucracy. By 1889, Perak had a system by which a divorce decree of a *naib kadi* was to be provisional, until reported to the Sultan for approval. If a chief *kadi* gave such a decree there was a right of appeal against it during the ensuing forty days. Meanwhile neither spouse might remarry.[64]

The *kadi* was appointed in the name of the ruler. Some rulers, however, were reluctant to limit themselves to a review of the *kadi*'s divorce decrees. In Negeri Sembilan the ruler insisted that the *kadi* should hold his court in the *istana* and then sent out his 'own men' to execute the *kadi*'s warrants. In consequence the *kadi* was 'a mere figurehead'.[65] This procedure—in 1904—was a reversion to the traditional arbitrary royal justice. Bureaucracy perhaps was better. However, the spouses were free to decide whether to submit their dispute to the *kadi*.[66] *Kadi*, as salaried officials, were no longer entitled to accept the customary contributions (*zakat*) due to Muslim officials.[67]

A *kadi* was chosen on his general merits and no formal qualifications were imposed. In the early days, some *kadi* in the FMS were illiterate though they could recite lengthy passages from the Koran which they had memorized. In later times, the paperwork limited the choice to men who were literate. It became common practice—though not obligatory—to appoint only *haji* to the position of *kadi*. In the course of the pilgrimage, as will be related, a *haji* was likely to pick up a good deal of basic Islamic learning. As a *haji*, he had personal prestige to support his official authority.[68]

Another useful qualification was a period of study at one of the renowned centres of Islamic instruction, mainly in the northern states. Kelantan and Terengganu, in particular, had celebrated *pondok* schools and there were some other places where a studious and devout young man might qualify to be a *kadi* or *imam* or *ulama* in his own district at home. Thus in central Pahang in 1905 'there is annually an exodus of the youth of the district to Patani and Kedah to seek that religious instruction which is not apparently to be found to any extent in Pahang'.[69]

Clifford summed up the performance of the *kadi* of late nineteenth-century Pahang as follows: 'on the whole these men did their work well, for many of them had the fear of God before their eyes, and they hesitated to tamper with His law even for the sake of worldly profit. They often meted out punishments with brutality; they often applied the law with a too narrow regard for its letter rather than its spirit; but they acted for the most part . . . honestly.'[70] Skeat, too, found the presence of a *naib kadi* in his district very helpful.[71] It is necessary to set these comments against the indignant censure of individual *kadi* who were found wanting on grounds of incompetence, neglect of duties, or worse. One *kadi* absconded when his defalcations were discovered, and another (in Patani) took female respondents in divorce cases into his house and compelled them to resort to prostitution—'he himself pockets the profits'.[72]

The trend towards a more formal system of administration of

religious affairs was not confined to the FMS, and in Kelantan at least the sequence can be traced.[73] There had long been a state *mufti* in the royal capital. At the end of the nineteenth century he was maintaining a register of all mosques and prayer houses (*surau*) and their officials over whom he had 'nominal jurisdiction'. The 1890s in Kelantan witnessed the vigorous but controversial efforts of the Maha Menteri to enforce stricter observances.[74] This was part of the general process of establishing administrative control over the villages of the populous Kelantan River delta, of which very little is known in detail.[75] The arrival of the first European adviser—W. A. Graham appointed by the Siamese—in 1904 to advise the Kelantan government began a process of dividing lay and religious leadership. The *imam* lost his temporal authority to the local headman (*To Kweng*), and the authority of the Syariah Court in the capital was more clearly defined. Graham himself, in his memoirs, says little of these changes, confining his chapter on 'Religion' to 'animistic superstition' and the penetration of Buddhism as a consequence of Siamese influence.[76] One has the impression that in Kelantan, and also in Terengganu, the *kadi* made his appearance in local administration at a much later period.

Earlier chapters have described the disappearance of the local district chief from outlying parts of Terengganu and the decline of the influence and authority of the village headman.[77] Even if one discounts some of Clifford's picture of exploitation by court favourites and 'the evils attending this system of absenteeism', there was a real vacuum between the royal court and the village community.[78] The religious establishment of Terengganu, a state in which *ulama* had great influence, to some extent filled the gap. Around the capital were three powerful families—'religious scholarship was kept within the family so to speak, and passed down from father to son like an hereditary profession'.[79] One of them was headed by the celebrated Ungku Sayid of Paloh who dominated his nephew, the ruler.[80] In the villages the mosque officials, now 'the undisputed leaders of rural Terengganu', included many who had been students or fellow students of members of the leading *ulama* families when they attended the Islamic schools (*pondok*) in their formative years as young men. These were links which persisted and provided channels of influence and communication from the power centre around the capital to the outlying districts.[81]

In the Malay states generally, the handful of religious dignitaries at the ruler's court tended to move with the spirit of the times towards a stricter insistence on orthodoxy. They held titles such as *mufti* (jurisconsult) or *syaikh-ul-islam* (religious leader), which conferred authority to make pronouncements (*fatwa*) on contentious points such as when obtaining a reward for the use of capital was usury, proper conduct between the sexes, and religious doctrine itself.[82] The court dignitaries tended to reformulate or endorse a traditional viewpoint in contrast to—and sometimes in conflict with—the ideas of the radical reformers spreading eastwards from the homelands of Islam. Thus was born the *kaum tua–kaum muda* dichotomy of which Roff has provided an authoritative account.[83]

While the doctrinal heavyweights slogged it out over their heads, the villagers, too, could be reft by schism and divided into opposing groups. In the late 1850s the Malay community of Province Wellesley had been split into followers and opponents of an Arab, Abdul Ghani, whom Vaughan describes as 'an inoffensive man'. He seems, none the less, to have caused some unrest by preaching a fundamentalist creed. His followers bound themselves by oath to obey the teachings of the Koran. They were also to treat any who did not share their views as opponents—'to keep aloof from those that do not join them, or those that do and subsequently forsake them; they are not allowed to attend feasts held by those that are not in the league, and above all they are not to attend the funerals of those that do not join them'. These specific injunctions give an interesting insight into the formal occasions on which a village community demonstrated its solidarity or, in this case, the lack of it. Vaughan says that these rules were very effective in dividing Abdul Ghani's followers from their opponents. The latter included the wealthier peasants and were known to Europeans as 'the free thinkers'. Again, religious attitudes reflect the underlying structure of village society, the embryonic classes of richer and poorer peasants.[84]

Abdul Ghani may have exposed, rather than created, conflicts, and opposed groups through which local leaders used religious affiliations as a means to achieving power within Malay communities in north-west Malaya. When Logan drew up his scheme for a reformed local police in Province Wellesley in the 1860s he proposed that it should not be under the control of village leaders. 'There would otherwise be danger of the *jumaah* and their heads acquiring much influence and too powerful an organisation. The *jumaah* bring a strong social pressure to bear on the villagers in the interest of a stricter and more fanatical observance of Mahomedanism and a greater submission to their religious leaders.'[85] In his analysis of Malay secret society organization before and after the Penang riots of 1867, Wynne concluded that 'Abdul Gunny the priest' and the 'Freethinkers', whom he calls 'the radical party', were the precursors of the Red and White Flag societies which took part in the riots.[86]

The perversion of religious associations (*jumaah*) to semi-criminal underground movements was a feature of Malay society in Province Wellesley, where there were special problems. But it was not just a unique case of a Malay community under stress because it lacked indigenous political leadership. The Malays of Province Wellesley retained close links with Kedah, from which many of them had come to the asylum of British territory at the time of the Siamese occupation of Kedah (1821–42), and they provided the first wave of Malay settlers in Krian in north-west Perak.[87] Hence the same unrest, with religious undertones, flickers occasionally in the annals of Kedah and of Perak. In 1881, for example, the Perak State Council had occasion to discuss the practice of flying coloured flags over mosques. 'The Regent states that it has never been the custom to use flags in the mosques of Perak, and he recommends that no flags be allowed for the present.' Raja Dris and another Malay member supported this proposal. However, Sheikh Mahomed Taib, always at odds with the Regent, 'thinks that a white flag with black letters may be allowed at the mosque, but no colours should be permitted other than black and white'. In the end, the Council accepted a compromise by which the *imam* might fly a flag of any colour if he first obtain the approval of the Regent.[88] Research in this age is unlikely to arrive at an explanation of underground feuds which baffled government officials at the time.

There were other village schisms of a purely religious character. In 1878 the Perak State Council discussed 'a stranger named Haji Ismail, that is dividing villages on a religious question of the number of times for public prayer in the mosque, and wishes to introduce customs unknown formerly in Perak against the will of the principal head and religious men in the state'. The Council called for a further report.[89] Disputes of this kind still occurred and divided congregations twenty years later. In 1897, the *penghulu* of Matang submitted a petition signed by seventy-eight people at Selinsing—'it proposes a purely religious purpose—dealing with the management of the mosque, and enforcing by means of penalties a stricter observance of certain Muhammadan rites; on the other hand certain covert acts of this society made it clear that it was diverging into illegitimate paths. The present mosque board of management complained of their authority being derogated.' This allegation was supported by complaints of intimidation and violence used to secure signatures to the petition or to browbeat opponents. The ringleader, a teacher, was removed from the area.[90]

The Malay villager was normally relaxed and tolerant in his religious outlook.[91] Yet, as the episodes mentioned above show, he could be roused to vehement dispute or even violence. It was particularly likely to occur when religion was called in aid of national feeling. When, for example, the Siamese occupied Kedah between 1821 and 1842, they 'used something more than persuasion' to enforce a nominal conversion to Buddhism of 'a considerable portion' of the remaining Malay population. James Low blamed the *haji* for the reaction—'under the mask of religion they are with but few exceptions ever ready to range themselves in the ranks against the *kafir*'.[92] Low said that Malay antagonism against the infidel could extend to the Europeans. Certainly it happened in the 1890s when the trouble in Pahang overflowed into Terengganu, to which the leaders of the Pahang revolt had fled. The Ungku Sayid of Paloh 'preached a Holy War' against Clifford's expedition.[93] Clifford later wrote of Malay feeling that 'if those against whom he rebels chance to belong to any other faith, no matter what the cause of the quarrel, no matter how lax the rebel's own practice may be, his revolt is at once raised to the dignity of a *sabil Allah*, or holy war against the infidel . . . in this lies the real strength of the Muhammadan population.'[94]

Apart from this brief outburst in Terengganu in 1895, there was never any likelihood that Malaya would see Malay religious nationalism comparable with the contemporary struggle of the Acehnese against the Dutch.[95] But the mere thought of it may have prompted the colonial regime to show sympathy for the efforts of the Malay rulers to defuse the latent tensions, such as they were, among their subjects by a programme of Islamic reform. Conscientious men such as Sultan Idris of Perak and Sultan Sulaiman of Selangor were genuinely troubled.[96] Clifford wrote in 1898 that 'according to Mohammedan law the moral responsibility for not punishing certain offences falls entirely upon the Mohammedan ruler of the state . . . the government is pledged to grant all proper facilities for the performance of religious obligations. The punishments prescribed by the *Hukum Shara* are of too brutal a nature for adoption in any civilised community.'[97]

The colonial courts had taken over the punishment of crime and dealt with questions affecting property, albeit in a rather uncertain fashion as regards the property of Muslims.[98] But there were many precepts of personal conduct in the practice of Islam which fell outside the legal system of the new regime. The practice of a conventional Malay ruler in this field is illustrated by the case of Raja Muda Ali of Riau (r.1845–57)—'he never missed Friday prayers ... ordering women to be veiled ... if a Muslim were discovered gambling or cockfighting, he was punished accordingly' and so on.[99] Under a colonial regime a ruler no longer had prerogative powers to act in this fashion and the colonial laws gave him no help.

In 1892, Sultan Idris proposed to the Perak State Council that there should be legislation to prohibit and, if necessary, punish adultery and incest. Under the existing legal procedure, it had been found difficult to obtain the evidence required to prove incest. As regards adultery, the injured husband had no legal remedy against his wife's lover and so he was disposed to 'take the law' into his own hands.[100] There were, however, other problems of right behaviour according to the norms of a Muslim community which were more intractable since European opinion regarded them as matters of morality and unsuitable for legal enforcement. In 1895 Raja Muda Sulaiman (as he then was) of Selangor put forward to a rather embarrassed colonial regime his draft regulations. These covered a number of matters, mainly matrimonial. The parents of both parties were to be asked for their consent to a betrothal, and there was to be redress for breach of promise. A married woman whose husband deserted or failed to support her should have a right to apply to a court for a remedy.

Sulaiman's code also imposed on a wife a duty of marital obedience. 'If the woman does not obey any direction given her by her husband in conformity with Muhammadan law or custom she is declared to be a rebellious wife, and if she persists in disobedience to any order which may be made by a magistrate she should be punished with imprisonment until she submits to her husband.' She was also given a measure of protection against divorce. If the husband divorced his wife without cause, he was to be liable to pay her 'a reasonable allowance until she marries again'.

Adultery was to be punished by a fine. Women of bad character 'must live apart, and cannot live together or associate with persons of good character'. This rather harsh judgment indicates that a mistress was perceived as a greater threat to marital stability than a prostitute.[101]

In proposals of this kind, the rulers were adapting the basic rules of the Islamic code and modifying them for late nineteenth-century Malay society. Treacher told the Colonial Office that Sulaiman's proposals were 'merely a private compilation of what the author supposes to be Mohammedan law'. With this rather supercilious comment it was hoped to shelve such ideas.[102]

However, at the first conference (durbar) of FMS rulers in 1897 they pressed their proposals.[103] Idris then set up in 1898 what would now be called a 'working party' of *raja* and chiefs to draw up a Muslim Code. In the fullness of time this produced the uniform Mohammedan Laws Enactment of 1904 passed in each of the FMS. In addition to the familiar matrimonial issues, the rulers' proposals of 1903 included compulsory attendance at mosque on Fridays for all males living within three miles of a mosque and a licence to be issued by the ruler, to anyone who wished to teach 'religious doctrine' outside his family circle. To teach without a licence or to teach 'false doctrine' was to be an offence punishable by a fine.[104]

This protracted episode illustrates the difficulties of Muslim rulers under a non-Muslim colonial regime. An earlier chapter has described how an autocrat like Baginda Omar of Trengganu, or the ruler of Kelantan acting through his chief minister, or even the distinctly secular ruler of Kedah, by issuing decrees, could make the law and incorporate in it as much of Islamic rules as he recognized and wished to adopt.[105] The ruler of a Federated Malay State, although guaranteed by treaty that matters of religion were reserved to his unfettered discretion, was obliged in fact to proceed by persuasion of the colonial regime to operate its law-making process.

The attitude to drinking alcohol was rather more relaxed—perhaps because, where it occurred, the offenders were often members of the upper class.[106] The main concern was that decorum should be observed by refraining from taking alcoholic drink in public.[107] A rather brash Australian visitor to Upper Perak in 1882 wrote afterwards that 'I gave the *imam* and the *penghulu* a glass of brandy, and though good Mohammedans they both took their tipple, but they seemed to appreciate a bundle of cigars more, and when I offered the *imam* some biscuits he asked to be allowed to take them home, as he had no teeth.'[108] One senses here that Malay politeness made it difficult to refuse the hospitality of this over-powering stranger. When Ibrahim Munshi went to Klang in 1872 in company with a European, their Malay host, Tunku Kudin, offered them a glass of sherry. Ibrahim, however, politely but firmly declined 'a drink of that liquid which I have never touched' and had rose syrup instead.[109] When Ibrahim's patron, Sultan Abu Bakar of Johor, entertained European guests to dinner he, and the other Malays, did not partake of the fine wines which the ruler produced. They drank water, and on other occasions tea.[110] The one exception to the general observance—in public at least—of the ban on alcohol was the Kedah royal family, who adopted a very European life-style and made no pretence of being abstainers. The glass of sherry which Ibrahim Munshi declined was offered by Tunku Kudin of Kedah.[111] This trend in Kedah reached its climax in 1907 with the death of Raja Muda Abdul Aziz, who at the end of a bout of drinking at the house of the European Adviser 'swallowed a large piece of opium' of which he died.[112]

Excesses of this kind were unusual, but there was concern at the slow erosion of proper standards of behaviour. In 1921 Sultan Iskander of Perak privately expressed his concern at 'seeing the way in which young men were drifting away from religion'. In public he said that 'young Malays should be educated to be first of all ornaments of their faith, and secondly trained as Malays'.[113] It was not easy, however, to enforce stricter standards when members of the upper class were so often a bad example. In Kedah in 1908, perhaps in reaction to the death of the Raja Muda, 'there has been a great "revival" . . . of the outward forms of religion. Attendance at mosque is compulsory, and offences against morality are punished with imprisonment of one year. This of course applies only to the *rakyats*; the Tunkus and others in high position can be as immoral as they like without let or hindrance. Gambling and opium smoking are rather encouraged than otherwise by the authorities as they are profitable vices and provide amusement for the influential Malays.'[114] An unduly cynical European view perhaps, but some weight must be given to it.

Clifford liked to say that 'after several centuries of conversion to the Faith, they continue to be Malays first and Muhammadans afterwards'.[115] It was a superficial comment. Elsewhere he made a more perceptive distinction between faith and works—'for all their laxness these people remained firmly convinced of their own sanctity ... they knew themselves to be Muhammadans—the special *proteges* of Allah and His Prophet ... the freethinker would probably have been lynched'.[116]

In all parts of Malaya, not just the SS and FMS, Malay society in this period was exposed to the permeation, pressure and—for some Malays at least—the temptation of a different way of life. Some succumbed—Emily Innes wrote that the manners of the Westernized Tunku Kudin 'were not in all respects improved by contact with Europeans'.[117] Yet the more profound reaction of the majority was a deeper sense of their identity as members of the community of Islam. The spokesmen of this reaction included the new profession of Malay journalists of whom Abdul Majid wrote that they were 'the leading lights among the Malays ... to hear them talk was really a treat; and their philosophy was always Islamic! Western ideas and western ideals had not touched them.'[118] This was a process which has been aptly described as 'the growth of an awareness' of a problem for Malays of adaptation in line with 'the transformation taking place in the country'. It was called *perjuangan*, i.e. 'a commitment to or involvement in a noble cause'.[119] It was partly a debate on social reform and partly 'an ideal of ... uniting all Islam ... to make it once more a great world-power'.[120]

These trends built up their momentum in the early years of this century and to that extent they lie beyond the limits of this study. Yet there were two institutions—Islamic education and the pilgrimage to Mecca—which made a significant contribution towards that movement in the latter part of the nineteenth century.

The basic intellectual preparation of Malay youth, in general, was instruction at a Koran class. He learnt by rote certain Arabic formulae, then studied the alphabet 'as a sort of guide to reading Arabic prayers and texts ... he would in time succeed in being able to read the Koran and the principal prayers from end to end ... the general drift of the text was explained to him, but not ... the meaning of the Arabic words.... A slight amount of dogma was also imparted.... Every prayer represented one more step to the good; it was a milestone on the way to wisdom ... the cleverer boys went on and studied more. Learning took on a strong religious tinge and became rather fanatical, but it was never stifled by the form in which instruction was given.'[121] It was a mechanical method of teaching, though hardly more so than the instruction in 'Mary's Little Lamb' and so on, to which the Malay vernacular schools subjected the Malay pupil in their turn. Yet there was this difference that the European style of education was by intention—however imperfectly executed—aimed at developing understanding as well as knowledge. In time, the leading Islamic teachers, notably the celebrated To Kenali, adopted a similar approach, using the Malay vernacular press as teaching material.[122]

The latter part of Wilkinson's account of Islamic education above indicates that a minority—'the cleverer boys'—having completed their basic instruction at a village Koran class, went on to pursue further and more intense studies at a residential *pondok* school.[123] The buildings of such a school included 'students [*sic*] quarters, buildings where teaching public prayer and other religious activities take place and the houses of the *guru* and other teachers and of the families and single individuals living in the *pondok*'. 'Teaching, praying and other communal activity takes place either in the mosque or more often in school buildings (*madrasah*).' The standard subjects of instruction were commentaries on the Koran (*taufsir*) law (*fikh*), philosophy (*tasauf*), grammar (*nahu*) and the traditions and sayings of the Prophet (*hadis*). The *pondok* school was both a means of instruction for the majority of its students and a 'way of life' lasting perhaps ten years for the small minority who aspired to become Islamic scholars. In the north-east of Malaya the *pondok* schools were a major influence. The number of students drawn from other parts of Malaya was probably not large enough to make the schools a significant element of the Islamic culture of those remoter areas.

In the nineteenth century, only a very small number of Malays made the pilgrimage to Mecca. Yet the pilgrimage was the most pervasive intellectual influence of its time in the Malay community.[124] Among the Five Pillars (*rukun*) of Islam it was the duty of every Muslim to make the pilgrimage, if he could afford the expense and could also provide for his dependants, either by taking them along or supporting them while he was away. Hence the pilgrimage became a major factor in the accumulation of capital. Malay peasants saved for years in the hope of eventually getting to Mecca.[125] However, a man could not work more land than he and his family could cultivate nor could he herd large numbers of buffaloes. Hence he had sometimes to entrust his capital to others. In this he must keep on the right side of the line which divided profit (*untung*) from usury (*riba*). If he invested his savings in jewellery for his wife, would she give it up when he wished to turn it back into money? Was it justifiable to sell inherited land to raise money for the expenses of the pilgrimage? If his savings made him conspicuously well-to-do, could he avoid the envy and reject the requests for help in hard times of his hard-pressed neighbours? The 'long haul' through a working life, until he could at last set off, was thus full of complications.[126]

To go on the pilgrimage offered a number of worldly rewards. The pilgrim had the title and prestige of being a *haji*. This might open for him avenues to such activities as teaching Islamic doctrine or holding office at the local mosque. If he had been involved in scandal or had suffered some setback or disgrace, absence on the pilgrimage would allow the memory of it to fade in his circle, and he would return purged by spiritual grace of his temporal embarrassments. This was a particularly important factor in aristocratic life. But the concept of shame (*malu*) pervades Malay culture at every level.[127] There could be adversities as well. The pilgrim usually had a hard time in Arabia, and if he was fleeced of the money set aside for his return passage, he might be repatriated at the expense of Syed Alsagoff or some other Singapore merchant. He would then have to work as a labourer on his return until he had paid off the debt.[128]

It is impossible to extract from the total number of pilgrims, mainly Javanese or other Indonesians, the exact figure of pilgrims who started from Malaya itself. It seems likely, however, that there were only a few hundred each year.[129] In the 1860s many pilgrims travelled in Arab sailing vessels in conditions which were compared to slave ships.[130] The introduction of steamships was a great improvement since the duration of the voyage was reduced from two or three months to three weeks. Nevertheless, in the 1870s and 1880s there was often appalling overcrowding. In 1869, for example, the *Daydream* sailed from Singapore with 223 pilgrims on board. This slightly exceeded her permitted maximum complement of 216, but the situation aboard became much worse as she picked up 393 more passengers at Sumatran ports. 'The people were stowed away in the hold, in the cabins, in a house on deck and on the deck itself, and the ship was so full that it was impossible to keep it clean or for the people to move or even to lie down.'[131] Ships left the United Kingdom loaded with coal for discharge at bunkering ports such as Singapore; in some instances their owners sent them in to Jeddah to pick up a deck cargo of returning pilgrims, in spite of the squalor and fire risks of a coal carrier.[132] These were conditions to test the stamina of healthy adults but many pilgrims 'go on board very old and at times broken down in health and with the knowledge that they will never reach Mecca; but as long as they are on the way and die they have the most implicit faith that they are obeying the laws of Mahomed, and doing the correct thing for their salvation'.[133] Epidemic disease spread easily among pilgrims on board ship and mortality was high.

The authorities in the SS ports made sustained efforts to improve conditions on pilgrim ships leaving Singapore and, by liaison with Jeddah, to prevent abuses during the voyage.[134] As the nineteenth century drew to its close, the volume of criticism dwindled. It must be assumed that standards became tolerable though still uncomfortable. From the 1880s the number of pilgrims increased, but the period of rapid expansion began only in the twentieth century.[135]

Escorting pilgrims had become an established business in Arabia. It was in the hands of an unofficial, but well-organized, body of Arab *syaikh*. These men divided the pilgrims between themselves according to the countries from which they came. A Malay pilgrim would be allocated to a party conducted by a *syaikh* who specialized in the South-East Asian pilgrim trade. The *syaikh* would have learnt to speak Malay or Javanese, either by previous residence in the region or by taking a wife from among the Malay–Indonesian community settled in Jeddah. He recruited each year's intake through brokers in Singapore, or paid a commission to pilgrims returning to their homes in the previous season to induce them to recommend him to their neighbours. The *syaikh* co-operated with the local officials in Jeddah and other Arabian centres and shared with them the profits of their trade.[136]

In this organized tourist industry pilgrims from South-East Asia had 'a great reputation for piety' and made 'an impression of naivety'.[137] Under the charge of the *syaikh*, each party moved on from Jeddah to Mecca for the ceremonies in and around the holy city, visited Medina if possible, and returned a few weeks later to Jeddah. 'In fairly large throngs they are urged day after day through the town, from one holy place to another, the ceremonies are very carefully rehearsed to them; the repetition of the prayer formulas is less conscientious, as strangers in any case understand almost nothing of them.'[138]

They crossed the hot, dusty desert in camel convoys. On first arrival, they were kitted out for the tour and later they bought the *haji's* garb of turban (*serban*), robe (*jubah*), and vest (*antari*). On each annual *Hari Raya Haji* festival after their return, they would don this raiment to celebrate their pilgrimage and show their status. If, while in Arabia, they had money to spare they might spend it —with the *syaikh*'s help—on religious articles such as a rosary or an embroidered white cap. It was well known among the *syaikh* that South-East Asian pilgrims often came with 'a money bag which they mean to empty there'.[139]

Most of these simple, pious people took home with them 'a very confused memory in which horrible crowds, crushing and shouting, heat and thirst play a considerable part'. They might also acquire an 'improvement of their Kuran recitation'.[140]

As might be expected the 'spiritual gain' of the experience varied with the individual. The older ones wished 'to devote their last days to religious practices on pure soil; younger ones devote themselves to religious studies'. Some were 'desirous of mystic blessings'. A few, especially among the young, had an eye for material advantage, either in Arabia or on their return home.[141] The experience also widened the outlook of pilgrims and imparted a sense of belonging to an Islamic society. Hurgronje noted among pilgrims 'a deep impression of a hitherto unknown world' and a sense of the 'politico-religious might of Islam'. This impression they drew from gathering at the very centre of the Islamic world in company with a vast number of pilgrims from other countries. Hurgronje also wrote that among the pilgrims from British India 'the contemptuous and insulting attitude of most of the English to the "natives" gave rise to hate . . . a few draw from the pilgrimage the seeds of raw fanaticism'. Many more brought back a sense of 'the might which Islam seems to spread from its spiritual centre [from] active intercourse with fellow pilgrims from the entire Archipelago'. At the very least, they 'first become habituated in Mecca to their daily ritual duties and return home as well disciplined faithful'.[142]

A small proportion of each year's flow of pilgrims stayed on at the end of the brief season, and settled permanently, or for a long period of years, in Mecca or Jeddah. For example, the famous To Kenali of Kelantan went to Mecca at the age of eighteen in 1886 and applied himself there for years to the study of Islam. Since he could not afford to buy books, he listened and committed to memory the teachings of the famous divines whose lectures he attended. If reference to a written text became essential, he begged booksellers to allow him to read their books in the shop, or he used the libraries at the mosques. With his teacher he visited Egypt in

1903. Eventually, after an absence of twenty-two years, he returned to Kelantan in 1908. He had become, by this unremitting course of study, the greatest Islamic teacher of his day in Malaya, perhaps its leading scholar.[143]

In this fashion, a dedicated student could prepare the way to a career when he returned to his native state. He might establish a *pondok* school and draw to it students from far away eager to sit at the feet of a renowned scholar. He might obtain an official position as a *penghulu*, an *imam* or a *kadi*. If the local mosque held property in trust (*wakaf*), he might become one of the trustees and receive an income from that source, or by sharing in the *zakat* contributions of the faithful. These 'graduates' of long-term study in Arabia were the mainstay of Islam in South-East Asia 'with a much more vivid consciousness of the unity of their islamised race than the short stay can produce among the *hajis*'.[144]

1. R. J. Wilkinson, 'Malay Beliefs', 1906, reprinted in 'Papers on Malay Customs and Beliefs', *JMBRAS*, 30(4), 1957, p. 9. Where theology 'represents all morals, science and civilisation it can no more be shaken off than race or nationality' (p. 4).

2. M. B. Hooker (ed.), *Islam in South-East Asia*, Leiden, Brill, 1983, especially the essays by Hooker himself and by A. C. Milner (note 33 below), deal at length with these aspects of South-East Asian Islam.

3. 'Malayan custom requires forty-four families' (T. Braddell, 'Notes of a Trip to the Interior of Malacca', *JIA*, 7, 1853, p. 81). 'Over forty houses' (J. F. A. McNair, *Perak and the Malays: Sarong and Keris*, London, Tinsley Bros., 1878, reprinted Kuala Lumpur, Oxford University Press, 1972, p. 228). See S. Husin Ali, *Malay Peasant Society and Leadership*, Kuala Lumpur, Oxford University Press, 1975, p. 56, on the use of a *surau*.

4. Abdullah bin Abdul Kadir, Munshi, *Kesah Pelayaran Abdullah*, translated by A. E. Coope, *The Voyage of Abdullah: A Translation from the Malay*, Singapore, Malaya Publishing House, 1949, pp. 10 and 20.

5. J. D. Vaughan, 'Notes on the Malays of Pinang and Province Wellesley', *JIA*, n.s., 2, 1857, p. 154. See p. 219 above on the unsuccessful claim by Toh Puan Halimah to the ownership of the mosque at Matang.

6. *PGG* 1898, p. 344.

7. *SGG* 1891, p. 834, report from Ulu Langat. In the neighbouring *mukim* of Beranang the *penghulu* had already collected $350 and hoped to get an additional $500 for a new mosque at that village (ibid.). See also *SGG* 1895, p. 187, report from Ulu Langat on a new mosque at Semenyih.

8. C. W. Harrison, *The Magic of Malaya*, London, John Lane, 1916, p. 186. Harrison's account of the long effort of a villager to get a mosque built is the source of the passage which follows, and of the quotations except as indicated in note 9 below (finding a contractor).

9. *SGG* 1891, p. 834.

10. Vaughan, op. cit., p. 152. He is describing the situation in Province Wellesley, *c.*1850 but his statement is probably of general application.

11. T. J. Newbold, *Political and Statistical Account of the British Settlements ... with a History of the Malayan States on the Peninsula in the Straits of Malacca*, 2 vols., London, Murray, 1839, reprinted as *British Settlements in the Straits of Malacca*, Kuala Lumpur, Oxford University Press, 1971, p. 247. Vaughan's list is *imam*, *khatib*, *bilal*, *siak* (mosque caretaker—R. J. Wilkinson, *A Malay–English Dictionary*, 2 parts, Singapore, Kelly & Walsh, 1901 (revised as *A Malay–English Dictionary (Romanised)*, 2 parts, Mytilene, Salavopoulos & Kinderlis, 1932), Part 2, p. 467) and *lebai* (mosque elder—ibid., p. 31). 'The *imam* leads the congregation in prayer ... the *khatib* faces the congregation and addresses them either in set formulae or in his own words' (ibid., Part 1, p. 593). On the religious duties of the *penghulu*—in some cases—see p. 112 above.

12. Vaughan, op. cit., p. 156.

13. F. A. Swettenham, *Sir Frank Swettenham's Malayan Journals 1874–1876* (hereafter cited as *Swettenham Journal*), edited by P. L. Burns and C. D. Cowan, Kuala Lumpur, Oxford University Press, 1975, p. 154. Douglas Diary, 1, 6 and 8 November 1877, 13 April, 23 and 26 August and 31 October 1878, 1, 25 and 27 February, 6 May, 29 August, 1, 5 and 6 September 1879, 10, 11 and 28 May and 21 December 1881. E. Innes, *The Chersonese with the Gilding Off*, 2 vols., London, Richard Bentley & Son, 1885, reprinted (1 vol.) Kuala Lumpur, Oxford University Press, 1974, Vol. 1, pp. 92–5, tells a story of Raja Arfah's brutality towards a bondswoman.

14. J. Low, 'Observations on Perak', *JIA*, 4, 1850, p. 502. He also contrasts the 'grave and respectable character' of Malay religious ceremonial with the less restrained practices of Indian Shi'ite Muslims which he had no doubt witnessed at Penang.

15. In the 1890s the Maha Menteri of Kelantan 'insisted upon attendance at the Friday congregational prayers, even to the breaking of heads of recalcitrant church-goers' (H. C. Clifford, *Studies in Brown Humanity being Scrawls and Smudges in Sepia, White and Yellow*, London, Grant Richards, 1898, p. 24). William R. Roff, 'The Origins and Early Years of the Majlis Ugama', in W. R. Roff (ed.), *Kelantan: Religion, Society and Politics in a Malay State*, Kuala Lumpur, Oxford University Press, 1974, p. 108. The Malay was 'not a regular attendant at the mosque' (F. A. Swettenham, *British Malaya: An Account of the Origin and Progress of British Influence in Malaya*, London, John Lane Bodley Head, 1907 (revised editions 192[illegible] and 1948, London, Allen & Unwin), p. 145; see also his *Footprints in Malaya*, London, Hutchinson, 1942, p. 50). O. Cavenagh, *Reminiscences of an Indian Official*, London, W. H. Allen & Co., 1884, pp. 343–4.

16. H. Low, 'The Journal of Sir Hugh Low, Perak 1877' (hereafter cited as 'Low Journal'), edited by E. Sadka, *JMBRAS*, 27(4), 1954, p. 85.

17. J. H. M. Robson, *People in a Native State*, Singapore, Singapore Free Press, 1894, p. 25.

18. R. J. Wilkinson, 'The Incidents of Malay Life', *Papers on Malay Subjects, Life and Customs*, Part 1, 1908, reprinted in *JMBRAS*, 30(4), 1957, p. 62; L. R. Wheeler, *The Modern Malay*, London, Allen & Unwin, p. 177.

19. F. A. Swettenham, *Malay Sketches*, London, John Lane Bodley Head, 1895, pp. 4–5.

20. W. E. Maxwell, 'A Journey on Foot to the Patani Frontier in 1876 being a

Journal Kept during an Expedition Undertaken to Capture Datoh Maharajah Lela of Perak', *JSBRAS*, 9, 1882, p. 16. 'The Malays are extremely lax in the observance of the daily prayers' (Wilkinson, 'Malay Beliefs', p. 5).

21. *AR Pahang 1894*, para. 46.

22. Mohamed Ibrahim bin Abdullah, Munshi, *The Voyages of Mohamed Ibrahim Munshi*, translated by A. Sweeney and Nigel Phillips, Kuala Lumpur, Oxford University Press, 1975, p. 11.

23. Mohamed Said, *Memoirs of a Menteri Besar: Early Days*, Singapore, Heinemann, 1982, p. 12.

24. Swettenham, *British Malaya*, p. 135.

25. Abdul Majid bin Zainuddin, *The Wandering Thoughts of a Dying Man: The Life and Times of Haji Abdul Majid bin Zainuddin*, edited by William R. Roff, Kuala Lumpur, Oxford University Press, 1978, p. 74, and see p. 226 above. A *Kari* (or *Qari*) was a person learned in the Koran or a Koran reader (Wilkinson, *1932 Dictionary*, Part 1, p. 512).

26. *Swettenham Journal*, pp. 56 and 204.

27. H. C. Clifford, *In Court and Kampung, Being Tales and Sketches of Native Life in the Malay Peninsula*, London, Grant Richards, 1897 (2nd ed. with autobiographical preface, London, Richards Press, 1927), p. 128.

28. Wilkinson, 'Malay Beliefs', p. 5.

29. Swettenham, *British Malaya*, p. 145, and *Malay Sketches*, p. 233, twice states that Malay observance of the fast was lax. However, he also wrote that 'usually he makes an effort to keep the forty days fast' (*Footprints*, p. 50). (Surely the fast was for the lunar month of twenty-nine or thirty days of *Ramadan*; forty days was the period of mourning). Clifford said that the fast was observed since villagers feared supernatural penalties if they broke it (H. C. Clifford, *Malayan Monochromes*, New York, Dutton, 1913, p. 160). Wilkinson's judgement (for early in this century) is that 'on the whole, this injunction is loyally observed' ('Malay Beliefs', p. 5). Mohamed Said, also referring to this later period, tells of an uncle who smoked secretly but adds that the rest of his family 'never flinched from rigidly observing the extremely austere Islamic month of fasting' (*Memoirs*, p. 95).

30. *Swettenham Journal*, pp. 147–8. He decided to postpone a call at the *istana* as it 'was so full of people, men and women and children from morning till night'.

31. SSD 11 January 1877 in CO 273/90, p. 180. See p. 195 above.

32. *Negeri Sembilan Gazette* 1897, p. 111.

33. A. C. Milner, 'Islam and the Muslim State', in M. B. Hooker (ed.), *Islam in South-East Asia*, Leiden, Brill, 1983, deals at length with the political aspects of Islamic kingship in Malaya. An earlier version of Milner's study is 'Islam and Malay Kingship', *Journal of the Royal Asiatic Society*, 1981, pp. 46–61.

34. See p. 33 above; R. O. Winstedt and R. J. Wilkinson, 'A History of Perak', *JMBRAS*, 12(1), 1934, appendices (g), (h) and (j); R. O. Winstedt, 'Kingship and Enthronement in Malaya', *JMBRAS*, 20(1), 1947, and *The Malays: A Cultural History*, Singapore, Kelly & Walsh, 1947, pp. 55–6; Wilkinson, 'Some Malay Studies', *JMBRAS*, 10(1), 1932, pp. 82–8; W. R. Roff, *The Origins of Malay Nationalism*, New Haven, Yale University Press, 1967, p. 68.

35. G. P. Means, 'The Role of Islam in the Political Development of Malaysia', *Comparative Politics*, 1(2), 1969, p. 268. 'Islam was not a pillar of royal authority' (ibid. p. 269). The essays of Means and of Yegar (note 36 below) have been very helpful to the author in writing this passage.

36. M. Yegar, *Islam and Islamic Institutions in British Malaya*, Leiden, Brill, 1979, p. 20; Means, op. cit., p. 274; E. Sadka, *The Protected Malay States 1874–1895*, Kuala Lumpur and Singapore, University of Malaya Press, 1968, p. 187.

37. J. W. W. Birch, *The Journals of J. W. W. Birch First British Resident to Perak 1874–1875* (hereafter cited as *Birch Journal*), edited by P. L. Burns, Kuala Lumpur, Oxford University Press, 1976, p. 126, editorial note; and evidence of Che Mida to PCE in CO 273/88, p. 104; Roff, *Origins of Malay Nationalism*, p. 46. On the duties of the *mufti* see notes 38 and 82 and p. 289.

38. *Birch Journal*, p. 363. The testimony of British observers on Islam in pre-colonial Malay states is suspect on account of bias and often misapprehension. As in the remark by Birch quoted in the text the bias may be obvious; the failure to comprehend the nature of Islam is more pervasive and less easy to recognize—all the more so because of the paucity of Malay information on the subject and the subsequent modifications of Islamic structure under the impact of British rule.

In addition to the sources cited in note 36 above Roy F. Ellen, 'Social Theory Ethnography and the Understanding of Practical Islam in South-East Asia', in M. B. Hooker (ed.), *Islam in South-East Asia*, pp. 80–1, traces the effects of colonial rule and religious reform on the later development of the offices of *mufti*, *kadi* and *imam*, noting that these factors were 'instrumental in the further institutionalization of Islam'. But it is easier to note that there were changes than to work back to the original social situation.

Another commentator remarks that the exclusion of 'Malay religion and custom' from the ambit of British control 'fortified the theory of the secular state based on the divorce of what was reckoned to be religion from politics' (A. M. M. Mackeen, *Contemporary Islamic Organisation in Malaya*, Monograph No. 13, Yale University Southeast Asia Studies, New Haven, 1969, p. 29). Islam, instead of being part of the seamless fabric of a Muslim society, became a 'reserved subject' requiring its own apparatus.

The old situation lasted longer in Terengganu than in most other states. A European administrator who had been there in the 1920s wrote that 'there is—strictly speaking—no priesthood in orthodox Islam. The *imams* do not even today form a caste apart. There were no *kadis* (as separate officials) in Terengganu in the 1920's because the judge and magistrates (Malays) were expected to know the Islamic Law and apply it where appropriate. Perhaps it was only when British judges and magistrates began to be appointed that it became necessary to have special officials to administer Islamic law on marriage, divorce and inheritance' (M. C. Hay, Review of J. M. Gullick, *Indigenous Political Systems of Western Malaya*, *Journal of the Royal Asiatic Society*, 1959, p. 170).

Whatever the pre-colonial situation, however, the text in this passage seeks to demonstrate how bureaucratization of Islam ensued.

39. H. C. Clifford, 'Report: Expedition to Trengganu and Kelantan', *JMBRAS*, 34(1), 1961 (originally printed for Colonial Office use in 1895, and reprinted Kuala Lumpur, Government Press, 1936), p. 68.

40. SSD 22 September 1909, journal of British Agent, Terengganu, for July/August 1909: CO 273/351, p. 221. The Sayid died in 1918 at an age of more than 100 years (Shaharil Talib, *After Its Own Image: The Trengganu Experience 1881–1941* (hereafter cited as *The Trengganu Experience*), Singapore, Oxford University Press, 1984, p. 146; Shaharil Talib Robert, 'The Trengganu Ruling Class in

the Late Nineteenth Century', *JMBRAS*, 50(2), 1977, p. 43).

41. Roff, 'Majlis Ugama', p. 104; Clifford, *Studies in Brown Humanity*, pp. 22–30. See also Roff, 'Majlis Ugama', at p. 108.

42. Muhammad Hassan bin Dato' Kerani Muhammad Arshad, *Al-Tarikh Salasilah Negeri Kedah*, Kuala Lumpur, Dewan Bahasa dan Pustaka, 1968 (previously published in *Jawi*, 1926), p. 221. Sharom Ahmat, *Tradition and Change in a Malay State: A Study of the Economic and Political Development of Kedah 1878–1923*, MBRAS Monograph No. 12, 1984, p. 81.

43. Sadka, *Protected Malay States*, p. 265, citing *AR Pahang 1890*. Linehan's account of this period does not mention it (W. Linehan, 'A History of Pahang' (hereafter cited as 'Pahang'), *JMBRAS*, 14(2), 1936, pp. 118–20).

44. Roff, *Origins of Malay Nationalism*, p. 69; Wilkinson, 'Malay Beliefs', p. 6.

45. SSD 17 November 1909: British Agent's report for October 1909: CO 273/351, p. 395.

46. See note 14 above. Abdul Majid bin Zainuddin, *Wandering Thoughts*, p. 74.

47. R. O. Winstedt, *Start from Alif, Count from One: An Autobiographical Memoire*, Kuala Lumpur, Oxford University Press, 1969, p. 5.

48. *Singapore Sunday Times*, 9 September 1934—an article on the Sultan's life-style and character. He had reigned since 1898.

49. See note 3 above.

50. 'Jugra Revisited', *Malay Mail*, 18 May 1897, probably by Robson who had been district officer there a few years before. The article mentions that Raja Muda Sulaiman (see note 48 above) had arranged 'the carving on the chair, the moulding of the pillars, the stained glass windows, the cement floor'. On the exterior wall of the mosque was an inscription to record that the Raja Muda had made these contributions and that the Sultan had formally inaugurated the building for worship. It would appear that in this—as in some other cases—European practice had been adopted in these matters.

51. *Malay Mail*, 16 June 1897.

52. SSD 30 October 1894, 1 September 1904. Treacher's comment: SSD 22 October 1902. See p. 61 above on royal finances.

53. Yegar, *Islam and Islamic Institutions*, p. 93, and pp. 33 and 115 above.

54. Vaughan, op. cit., p. 153. Teluk Ayer Tawar seems to have been the leading Malay settlement in Province Wellesley. It was the headquarters of the Kedah Malay resistance during the Siamese occupation (1821–43) of Kedah (J. M. Gullick, 'Kedah 1821–1855: Years of Exile and Return', *JMBRAS*, 56(2), 1983, p. 41).

55. SSD 7 June 1892 enclosing a memorandum which Maxwell had written ten years before—dated 8 July 1882. On Maxwell see p. 123, note 107, and note 38 on general issues. In the same collection of papers Hugh Low commented that Maxwell's account did not reflect conditions in Perak (CO 273/181 p. 77). In support of his case, Maxwell mentions that the chief *kadi* of Province Wellesley had received a sentence of imprisonment for forging an entry in the register of marriages. In 1892 Singapore was rocked by a case which had considerable similarities to the Maria Hertogh case, which led to serious riots (C. M. Turnbull, *A History of Singapore 1819–1975*, Kuala Lumpur, Oxford University Press, 1977, pp. 247–8). In the 1892 case an English girl of thirteen either was abducted by or eloped with a Malay, who took her off to a *kadi* by whom she was instantly converted to Islam so that she might marry the Malay. The *kadi* said afterwards, 'I made her a Mahomedan by reading the *kalimah* to her.' He then immediately married them and issued a

marriage certificate. The prosecution of the Malay 'caused a considerable sensation' but did not, like the 1950 case, lead to a riot. The Court recognized the marriage by ruling that the girl, as the wife of the accused, was not a competent prosecution witness (SSD 13 June 1892). The *dua kalimah syahadat* are the basic statements of the Islamic creed (Wilkinson, *1932 Dictionary*, Pt. 1, p. 499).

56. *PSCM*, 4 March 1879 and 4 May 1879, *PMS*, pp. 195–6 and 198. On Sheikh Mahomed Taib see p. 225 above. On the feud between Yusuf and Mat Taib see Sadka, *Protected Malay States*, pp. 112 and 182. For a clash between the powers in Aceh see note 82 below.

57. J.M. Gullick, 'Selangor 1876–1882: The Bloomfield Douglas Diary', *JMBRAS*, 48(2), 1975, pp. 11–12. Mohamed Amin Hassan, 'Raja Muda Musa ibni Sultan Abdul Samad', *Peninjau Sejarah*, 1(1), 1966.

58. *AR Selangor 1885*, para. 14. *SGG* 1896, p. 494, report from Kuala Langat. A successor was appointed to the post of state *kadi* in 1898 (*SGG* 1898, p. 525).

59. *AR Selangor 1885*. *SGG* 1897, p. 150, report from Kuala Langat.

60. Vaughan, op. cit., p. 154. Means, op. cit., p. 274.

61. J.R. Logan, 'Plan for a Volunteer Police in the Muda Districts, Province Wellesley, Submitted to Government by the Late J.R. Logan in 1867', *JSBRAS*, 16, 1885, p. 191. He mentions that *kadi* dealt with matrimonial matters, including restitution of conjugal rights to either spouse and applications by the wife for 'maintenance, dower, cohabitation and divorce'. As regards the volume of this work the *naib kadi* at Krian dealt with 40 cases in 1896 (*PGG* 1897, p. 341).

62. *PSCM*, 26 October 1882, *PMS*, p. 264.

63. *SGG* 1897, p. 457, a report from Kuala Langat by Skeat.

64. *PSCM*, 16 February 1889, *PGG* 1889, p. 477.

65. SSD 3 March 1904.

66. A petition was presented in 1878 for a system of compulsory registration of Muslim marriages in the SS; presumably there would also have been compulsory registration of divorces. The government, however, preferred to continue with the optional registration system (SSD 24 August 1878).

67. *PSCM*, 28 February 1880, *PMS*, p. 224.

68. Vaughan, op. cit., pp. 122 and 154.

69. *AR Pahang 1905*, citing a report from Temerloh. A list of the leading pupils of the Kelantan Islamic teacher, To Kenali, includes two from Province Wellesley and Johor respectively (Abdullah Al-Qari bin Haji Salleh, 'To Kenali: His Life and Influence', in W.R. Roff (ed.), *Kelantan: Religion, Society and Politics in a Malay State*, p. 96. On To Kenali see below, p. 300; the significance of *pondok* (hut) in connection with religious schools is explained in the Glossary.

70. H.C. Clifford, 'Life in the Malay Peninsula: As It Was and Is', in P.H. Kratoska (ed.), *Honourable Intentions: Talks on the British Empire in South-East Asia Delivered at the Royal Colonial Institute, 1874–1928*, Kuala Lumpur, Oxford University Press, 1983 (reprinted from the *Proceedings of the Royal Colonial Institute*, 1899), p. 237.

71. *AR Kuala Langat 1896* in *SGG* 1897, p. 457.

72. *AR Selangor 1890*, para. 192, records that the state *kadi*, Syaikh Ahmad of Province Wellesley, had been compulsorily retired following complaints against him. For other reports see *PGG* 1897, p. 22, report from Krian; *SGG* 1896, p. 717, report from Ulu Selangor; SSD 14 October 1908, report from British Vice-Consul at Singgora (Songkhla) in Siam.

73. Roff, 'Majlis Ugama', pp. 104–32, covers the sequence of events down to 1915.

74. See note 41 above.

75. Roff, 'Majlis Ugama', p. 109, and see p. 114 above.

76. W. A. Graham, *Kelantan—A State of the Malay Peninsula: A Handbook of Information*, Glasgow, James MacLehose & Sons, 1908, pp. 32–3; Roff, 'Majlis Ugama', p. 112.

77. See pp. 87 and 113 above.

78. Clifford, 'Expedition', pp. 69 and 71.

79. Shaharil Talib Robert, 'The Trengganu Ruling Class', p. 37.

80. See note 40 above.

81. Shaharil Talib, *The Trengganu Experience*, p. 27.

82. There was some uncertainty about the functions of a *syaikh-ul-islam* (Khoo Kay Kim, 'Malay Society 1874–1920', *JSEAS*, 5(2), 1974, p. 185). From the mid-nineteenth century if not before there was a *mufti* both in Kelantan and in Kedah (Roff, 'Majlis Ugama', p. 106; and Muhammad Hassan, op. cit., p. 221, where the appointment of a *mufti* in Kedah in 1870 is recorded). See also Khoo Kay Kim, 'Malay Society', *passim*. Shaharil Talib, *The Trengganu Experience*, p. 27, refers to a *mufti*, a *syaikh-ul-islam* and a *syaikh-ul-ulama* in Terengganu. See also Roff, *Origins of Malay Nationalism*, p. 67; Means, op. cit., p. 56. Hurgronje has an interesting passage on the role of the leading *ulama* in Aceh, Habib Abdurrahman. The ruler of Aceh 'found himself constrained . . . to establish a new kind of court of justice in which the *habib* should decide all questions relating to religion'. There was conflict about the extent of the court's jurisdiction. However, 'the centralisation of power' under the *habib* was 'nothing short of prodigious'. He had the support of a 'guild' of lesser *ulama* (C. S. Hurgronje, *The Achehnese*, translated by A. W. S. O'Sullivan, 2 vols., London, Luzac, 1906, Vol. 1, pp. 159–64).

83. Roff, *Origins of Malay Nationalism*, Chapter 3.

84. Vaughan, op. cit., p. 153. See also pp. 101 and 214 above.

85. Logan, 'Volunteer Police', p. 176. *Jumaah* were religious associations; in north-west Malaya some had developed undesirable political aspects (see p. 244 above).

86. M. L. Wynne, *Triad and Tabut*, Singapore, Government Printing Press, 194 , p. 220. Wynne suggests that the 'free thinkers' were followers of Haji Makawi, who had taken part in the risings against the Siamese in Kedah in the 1830s. But Wynne acknowledges that Vaughan makes no such identification.

87. See pp. 108 and 112 above. C. M. Turnbull, *The Straits Settlements 1826–1867: Indian Presidency to Crown Colony*, London, Athlone Press, 1972, pp. 91 and 97. On Kedah see Cheah Boon Kheng, 'Social Banditry and Rural Crime in North Kedah 1909–1929', *JMBRAS*, 54(2), 1981, and Gullick, 'Kedah', pp. 36 and 64. On Malay settlement in Krian see R. D. Hill, *Rice in Malaya: A Study in Historical Geography*, Kuala Lumpur, Oxford University Press, 1977, pp. 94, 99–100, 108–15, and Gullick, 'Kedah', pp. 56 and 66.

88. *PSCM*, 5 January 1881, *PMS*, p. 235. Wynne, op. cit., p. 343. W. Blythe, *The Impact of Chinese Secret Societies in Malaya: A Historical Study*, London, Oxford University Press, 1969, describes the activities, so far as they were discovered, of the Malay societies in Perak between 1879 and 1882, but does not suggest any Islamic background to this unrest.

89. *PSCM*, 19 December 1878, *PMS*, p. 178.

90. *PGG* 1897, p. 834, report from Matang.

91. 'He is not a bigot' (in Swettenham, *Malay Sketches*, p. 5, and *Footprints*, p. 50). 'He cannot be called devout' (Swettenham, *British Malaya*, p. 1[illegible]). 'Their religion sat lightly enough upon these simple villagers' (Clifford, *Malayan Monochromes*, p. 160). In the north-east, however, there was a more intense attitude. It was Clifford's opinion that in Terengganu, unlike most other states, the ruling class were 'very fanatical Muhammadans' (*AR Pahang 1894*). In neighbouring Kelantan 'the religious fanaticism of the late Maha Menteri had a certain temporary effect. . . . The bulk of the Kelantan natives however are far too ignorant to be capable of any great enthusiasm for the faith they profess but do not understand' (Clifford, 'Expedition', pp. 116–17). Both Clifford and Swettenham had visited the north-eastern states but there is an element of condescension in the tone of these remarks by Victorian Englishmen, who were likewise not conspicuously devout in their faith. But if that be disregarded the gist of their judgement is apparently correct.

92. J. Low, *A Dissertation on the Soil and Agriculture of the British Settlement of Penang or Prince of Wales Island in the Straits of Malacca including Province Wellesley on the Malayan Peninsula . . ., with . . . Incidental Observations, etc.*, Singapore, Singapore Free Press, 1836, reprinted as *The British Settlement at Penang*, Singapore, Oxford University Press, 1972, p. 273. See also J. Low, 'Retrospect of British Policy in the Straits of Malacca . . . and the neighbouring Native States', manuscript in CO 273/1, printed in *The Burney Papers*, Vol. 5, Part 1, Siam Society, Bangkok, 1914, p. 145, and Gullick, 'Kedah', *passim*. Governor Bonham wrote 'they object to seeing a Mussulman population subject to a nation following another religion. This failing is engendered and studiously kept alive by the Arabs residing at Penang and by all Mohamedans who have performed the pilgrimage to Mecca to whom simple Malays pay unbounded respect, which of course is not extended to them by the Siamese' (IOL Board's Collections, Vol. 1807, Item 74268, p. 51). Bonham (Governor SS 1836–43) was writing in 1839 at the end of the bitter struggle of the Kedah Malays to drive the Siamese out of their country.

93. Clifford, 'Expedition', p. 45.

94. Clifford, *Studies in Brown Humanity*, p. 229.

95. The Colonial Office files (CO 273 series) of this period contain fragmentary but interesting material on British official perceptions of the risk of a 'holy war' against them. On the war in Aceh see Anthony Reid, *The Contest for North Sumatra: Atjeh, The Netherlands and Britain 1858–1898*, Kuala Lumpur, Oxford University Press, 1969, *passim*. For a shorter account see D. G. E. Hall, *A History of South-East Asia*, London, Macmillan, 1955, pp. 594 and 617–21.

From time to time there was correspondence between Singapore and Batavia (Jakarta), and consultation between the Foreign and Colonial Offices in London, and between the Foreign Office and the British Ambassador in Constantinople, on Turkey as a centre of pan-Islamic influence, which might make mischief for the colonial powers in South-East Asia. As one example there was concern over the appointment of 'a hot fanatic in religious matters' as Turkish consul in Singapore (CO 273/118, p. 474, dated 15 September 1882). The Maharaja of Johor dipped a toe in these turbulent waters by sending his brother to Constantinople with the Singapore Arab merchant, Syed Mohamed Alsagoff, but he was unable to obtain an audience with 'any one of distinction' (which was always the prime objective of Johor contacts with foreign courts) (SSD 29 December 1884). See p. 76 above on the sharp treatment of two Negeri Sembilan chiefs who addressed a petition to a Turkish admiral visiting Singapore in 1892. When British was at war with Turkey in 1914 even the Sultan of Selangor, as mild and faithful a Malay ruler as might be found, had to protest his loyalty to the British Crown (SSD 3 December 1914). In Terengganu during the war it was said that 'there is a considerable pro-Turkish party in this state, chiefly among the Arabs' (SSD 15 December 1918).

Papers on these subjects are found in volumes (followed by page numbers) in the CO 273 series as follows: 42/379, 108/487, 112/240, 113/89, 118/474, 126/626, 130/515 and 517, 131/377 and 597, 246/133, 253/359 and 418, and 305/111. This may not be all of them.

96. Although Sultan Sulaiman did not come to the throne of Selangor until 1898, the great age and retiring disposition of his predecessor (and grandfather), Sultan Abdul Samad, brought Sulaiman as Raja Muda well to the fore in the earlier 1890s. In so far as the royal family participated in the activities described, it was he who took the leading part.

97. *AR Pahang 1897*, a passage in which Clifford is commenting on the first durbar of FMS rulers held at Kuala Kangsar in 1897—see note 103 below. Mackeen, *Contemporary Islamic Organisation*, p. 32, points out that in theory the ruler's power to legislate is much restricted by the existence of '*fiqh*, the substantive law of Islam', i.e. the law already exists and a ruler may not make his own. However, in the 1890s this conundrum does not seem to have troubled royal consciences. As Mackeen points out, 'In practice however the Muslim sovereigns have not infrequently tended to rule by arbitrary interventions in neglect of the *sharia*' rulings' (ibid.).

98. M. B. Hooker (*The Personal Laws of Malaysia*, Kuala Lumpur, Oxford University Press, 1976; *Adat Laws in Modern Malaya*, Kuala Lumpur, Oxford University Press, 1972; *Readings in Malay Adat Laws*, Singapore, Singapore University Press, 1970; *Islam in South-East Asia*; and *Islamic Law in South-East Asia*, Singapore, Oxford University Press, 1984) has contributed an immense and authoritative corpus of commentary and analysis on these topics. In earlier years W. E. Maxwell, with 'Land Tenure' and 'Slavery' monographs, and a large number of shorter essays, published mainly in *JSBRAS*, and later E. N. Taylor ('Malay Family Law: An Essay on the Law and Custom Relating to the Distribution of Property on Dissolution of Marriage among the Peninsular Malays—With Illustrative Cases', *JMBRAS*, 15(1), 1937) went deeply into these subjects. (There is additional writing on the special aspects of matrilineal *adat perpatih* society in Negeri Sembilan.) M. B. Hooker, 'A Note on the Malayan Legal Digests', *JMBRAS*, 41(1), 1968, reviews the more important Malay digests. Although it lacks the scholarship of the weightier studies, R. J. Wilkinson, 'Introductory Sketch', *Papers on Malay Subjects, Law*, Part 1, 1908, reprinted 1922 and again in M. B. Hooker (ed.), *Readings in Malay Adat Laws*, is a most percipient short study. Wilkinson also wrote the Preface to J. Rigby (ed.), 'The Ninety-nine Laws of Perak', *Papers on Malay Subjects, Law*, Part 2, 1908, reprinted 1929 and again in Hooker, *Readings*. Among modern sociological studies is Judith Djamour, *The Muslim Matrimonial Court in Singapore*, London, Athlone Press, 1966. Although the present author is a lawyer by profession he has always found much difficulty in relating studies written mainly from the legal standpoint to the society with which this book is concerned. In the English legal system the theory and the practice are linked through case-law and precedent. Malay legal theory seems to him to be far away on the moon when one considers what happened in Malay legal proceedings.

99. Raja Ali Haji ibn Ahmad, *Tuhfat al-Nafis*, translated and annotated by

Virginia Matheson and Barbara Watson Andaya, *The Precious Gift*, Kuala Lumpur, Oxford University Press, 1982, p. 283.

100. *PSCM*, 9 December 1891, *PGG* 30 March 1892; *PSCM*, 4 June 1894, *PGG* 14 September 1894. See *Malay Mail*, 25 October 1898, on the move towards legislation. On marital violence see p. 216 above.

101. Pamphlet enclosed with SSD 25 September 1894. In this male-dominated society the disobedient wife seems to have been particularly objectionable. In 1912 the Kedah State Council rejected a proposal by the chief *kadi* that fines should be imposed at his discretion for the offence of *nusus* (or *nushuz*), defined as 'the offence of a disobedient wife'. Wilkinson translates the word to mean 'recalcitrant'—'of a wife who refuses to co-habit with her husband and may therefore be divorced with the loss of her marriage settlements (*mahar*)'—in *1932 Dictionary*, Part 2, p. 178. Refusal to cohabit is a much more specific—and serious—matter than marital disobedience. It may be that in his own *istana* Sulaiman was already at odds with his first and principal wife, Tunku Maharum. When he made a second, polygamous marriage in 1898 she deserted him for two years (see p. 225 above).

At this stage there does not seem to have been such acute preoccupation with improper proximity (*khalwat*) between the members of the two sexes as appeared later.

In 1898 a man and a woman caught in the act of adultery were sentenced to four and two months' imprisonment respectively. The maximum sentences under Regulation 11 of 1894 (*SGG* 1894, p. 686) were two years and one year (*Malay Mail*, 4 June 1898). There was similar legislation in Perak (*Malay Mail*, 25 October 1898). This was said to be 'in conformity with modern ideas' (ibid.).

102. CO minute on SSD 25 September 1894.

103. *AR Pahang 1897*. Much of the discussion at the durbar was taken up with this subject. The ruler of Negeri Sembilan made his mark by taking an active part in the debate (SSD 20 August 1897).

104. Sadka, *Protected Malay States*, p. 172, citing Sel/Sec 111/99. The draft legislation was forwarded to London under cover of SSD 19 March 1903. The end result was the Mohammedan Laws Enactment passed by each FMS state council in 1904. (Hooker, *Islamic Law in South-East Asia*, p. 140).

105. Clifford, 'Expedition', p. 60. See also pp. 246 and 283 above.

106. Wilkinson, 'Malay Beliefs', p. 7, says that Malay public opinion treated drinking spirits as 'a much less serious sin' than, for example, eating pork.

107. 'Pahang Notes', *Malay Mail*, 17 August 1900. 'Some of the rich Malays, Sayids and others, will drink beer and even wine but they seldom do it publicly' (J. Low, *Dissertation*, p. 294).

108. 'A Few Weeks among the Malays', *Straits Times*, 4 April 1883. The writer was Henry Copeland, a British immigrant who rose to membership of the New South Wales Assembly. He was notorious for his heavy drinking (as the episode in the text may indicate) and lost his post as a Minister in the New South Wales Government after appearing very drunk indeed at a public occasion. He was Agent-General for New South Wales in London at the time of his death in 1905.

109. Mohamed Ibrahim Munshi, op. cit., p. 74. He came to Klang in April 1872 as interpreter to C. J. Irving.

110. F. Caddy, *To Siam and Malaya in the Duke of Sutherland's Yacht 'Sans Peur'*, London, Hurst & Blackett, 1889, p. 239, and see p. 56 above.

111. Both Tunku Kudin (see above) and his elder brother, Sultan Ahmad

Tajuddin II of Kedah, drank alcohol regularly. It is said that Ahmad's son, Sultan Abdul Hamid, in his young days included a case of whisky in his baggage when on tour. After a bout of *delirium tremens*, however, he became an abstainer. W. G. Maxwell, writing of the ruler's medical history, refers to his 'insane indulgence in spirits and women' in his early years (SSD 16 April 1913). Maxwell of course had no firsthand knowledge of these excesses since, although he visited Kedah in 1889, he did not reside there until 1909. Abdul Majid refers to 'the drinking habits of high class Malays in Kedah' (*Wandering Thoughts*, p. 109). Mubin Sheppard, *Tunku: A Pictorial Biography 1903–1957*, Petaling Jaya, Malaysia, Pelanduk Publications, 1984, p. 7 (on Abdul Hamid).

112. Report of 2 June 1907 by the British Vice-Consul in Kedah (Meadows Frost) in CO 273/333, p. 469. It appears that Raja Muda Abdul Aziz took the opium with the idea of going to sleep, but he must have been too fuddled to know what he was doing.

113. Khasnor Johan, *The Emergence of the Modern Malay Administrative Elite*, Singapore, Oxford University Press, 1984, pp. 174 and 183, citing the *Times of Malaya*, 31 March 1921, for the speech. The earlier remarks were made in conversation with Laurence Guillemard. Although these public and private thoughts were expressed long after the end of the period of this study, one senses that they express a longstanding concern.

114. Report of 27 July 1908 in diary of British Vice-Consul in Kedah, in CO 273/343, p. 514. At the FMS rulers' durbar of 1903 the ruler of Negeri Sembilan proposed that there should be a system of fines for Muslims who drank alcohol. The proposal was referred to the state councils (*Malay Mail*, 30 September 1903).

115. Clifford, *Malayan Monochromes*, p. 121—'she was a Malay first and a follower of the Prophet accidentally'. See also, *In a Corner of Asia*, p. 155.

116. Clifford, *Malayan Monochromes*, pp. 160–1.

117. Innes, op. cit., Vol. 1, p. 88.

118. Abdul Majid, *Wandering Thoughts*, pp. 59–60; Roff, *Origins of Malay Nationalism*, Chapters 2 and 3; Nik Ahmad bin Haji Nik Hassan, 'The Malay Press', *JMBRAS*, 36(1), 1963; Abdul Rahman al-Ahmadi, 'Notes towards a History of Malay Periodicals in Kelantan', in W. R. Roff (ed.), *Kelantan: Religion, Society and Politics in a Malay State*.

119. Khoo Kay Kim, 'Malay Society', p. 184.

120. Wilkinson, 'Malay Beliefs', p. 9. V. S. Naipaul, *Among the Believers: An Islamic Journey*, London, Deutsch, 1981, has an interesting chapter on these trends in contemporary Malaysia, and see Judith Nagata, *The Reflowering of Malaysian Islam: Modern Religious Radicals and Their Roots*, Vancouver, University of British Columbia Press, 1984.

121. Wilkinson, 'Incidents', pp. 47–8. The complete passage from which the key phrases only are abstracted here is worth reading. He warns that 'it is never safe to condemn a system that has proved acceptable to a large section of humanity'. He adds that attempts to teach Arabic as a language to Malay boys had been 'found wanting' since it was beyond the ability of the teachers as well as the pupils.

122. Khoo Kay Kim, 'Malay Society', p. 187. Abdullah Al-Qari, op. cit., *passim*.

123. This passage is derived, and contains phrases from, R. L. Winzeler, 'Islamic Schools in Kelantan', *JMBRAS*, 48(1), 1975, particularly pp. 93–4.

It is an account of the situation in our day which, so far as one can judge in respect of a traditional institution, probably gives a fair picture of the same centres of instruction at the turn of the century. There is no data on the number of pupils at that earlier time nor where they came from.

124. C. S. Hurgronje, *Mekka in the Latter Part of the 19th Century*, translated by J. H. Monahan, Leiden, Brill, 1931, and J. Vredenbregt, 'The Haddj: Some of Its Features and Functions in Indonesia', *BKI*, 118, 1962, have been invaluable sources in writing the passage which follows. As the Malay and Indonesian pilgrims were treated as one group there is no reason to think that a description of the Indonesian experience is not equally applicable to the Malays. Abdul Majid bin Zainuddin, 'A Malay's Pilgrimage to Mecca', *JMBRAS*, 4(2), 1926, was written after that articulate man had become the Malayan governments' Pilgrimage Commissioner, who went each year to Arabia.

125. M. G. Swift, 'Economic Concentration and Malay Peasant Society', in M. Freedman (ed.), *Social Organisation: Essays Presented to Raymond Firth*, London, Frank Cass, 1967, p. 249, wrote that 'it is said to have been common in the past for people to use everything they possessed to get to Mecca, hoping that they would die there'. See p. 253, note 53, above on the ex-Menteri of Larut who, when his health was failing, decided to spend 'the rest of his days' in Mecca—though he died in Singapore before leaving (SSD 5 September 1894).

In 1896 the cost of a return passage was $48; $55 in 1899 (SSD 17 March 1896 and 3 August 1899). The *syaikh* often charged much more than this, ostensibly on account of the cost of official exit permits, etc. (SSD 3 August 1899).

126. Swift, 'Economic Concentration'; 'Capital, Saving and Credit in a Malay Peasant Economy', in R. W. Firth and B. Yamey (eds.), *Capital, Saving and Credit in Peasant Societies: Studies from Asia, Oceania, the Caribbean and Middle America*, London, Allen & Unwin, 1964; 'Malay Peasants', in R. D. Lambert and B. Hoselitz (eds.), *The Role of Savings and Wealth in Southern Asia and the West*, Paris, UNESCO, 1963; and *Malay Peasant Society in Jelebu*, London, Athlone Press, 1965. These four studies by Swift are invaluable to an understanding of economic factors in Malay society.

127. 'Abdul Majid has gone to Mecca to lay down the burden of his sins at the holy places' (Clifford, *Malayan Monochromes*, p. 186). 'The pilgrimage to Mecca is the cure for the errors of the Muhammadan world' (F. A. Swettenham, *The Real Malay: Pen Pictures*, London, John Lane Bodley Head, 1900, p. 161). See also Swettenham, *Malay Sketches*, p. 254, and *Swettenham Journal*, p. 316.

128. 'The ring of corrupt people in Arabia which at present exploits pilgrims for its own advantage' was almost beyond the control of the authorities in Constantinople, London or Singapore (SSD 30 July 1896).

129. An appendix to the notes to this chapter offers some background information. See p. 313 below.

130. Cavenagh, op. cit., p. 298.

131. SSD 273/35, pp. 103–4, report of the Emigration Board.

132. SSD 19 May 1877.

133. SSD 20 April 1876, report by Master Attendant, Singapore.

134. See p. 314 below.

135. Vredenbregt, op. cit., p. 93.

136. SSD 30 July 1896 and Hurgronje, *Mekka*, and Vredenbregt, op. cit., *passim*.

137. Hurgronje, *Mekka*, pp. 220 and 225.

138. Ibid., p. 239. Abdul Majid, 'Pilgrimage', describes the sequence of events in detail.

139. Hurgronje, *Mekka*, pp. 220 and 222.

140. Ibid., p. 240.

141. Ibid., pp. 220–1 and 241. Wilkinson, 'Some Malay Studies', pp. 103–6, is a good short account of Malay Islamic mysticism. A. H. Johns, 'Malay Sufism as Illustrated in an Anonymous Collection of 17th Century Tracts', *JMBRAS*, 30(2), 1957, is an extended study related to a collection of Malay documents. Hooker, *Islam in South-East Asia*, includes in his bibliography (pp. 225–6) a list of the publications, down to 1979, of Johns, the leading authority on this subject.

142. Hurgronje, *Mekka*, pp. 248–9. See Governor Bonham, cited in note 92 above, on the role of *haji* in rousing national feeling. In 1881 a British official wrote of the 'demoralisation' of pilgrims by their experiences. Possibly disaffection was intended (SSD 5 March 1881). The pilgrims from Malaya were reluctant to travel on the passports offered to them by a solicitous colonial regime. Hardship added to the merit gained from the pilgrimage. Conversely merit was lost by accepting the aid of a 'Christian agency' (SSD 30 July 1896). In 1896 only three passports had been issued (ibid.). However, at an earlier period Douglas records that seventeen pilgrims had 'signed bonds' (Douglas Diary, 20 May 1881).

143. Abdullah Al-Qari, op. cit., p. 90. In another less celebrated case a teacher first spent twenty years (1879–99) as a young man in Arabia. On his return to Malaya in 1899 he held high positions in Perak and then in Johor and helped to found the *Al Imam* newspaper: Mohamed Sarim bin Haji Mustajab, 'Syeikh Muhammad Tahir Jalaluddin al-Falaki, Pelopor Gerakan Islah Islamiyyah di Tanah Melayu', *Malaysia in History*, 20(2), 1977.

144. Hurgronje, *Mekka*, p. 256. R. L. Winzeler, 'The Social Organization of Islam', in W. R. Roff (ed.), *Kelantan: Religion, Society and Politics in a Malay State*, illustrates the avenues open to a returned *haji*.

Supplementary Note on the Pilgrim 'Traffic'

In the 1880s it was estimated that about seven-eighths of the pilgrims who embarked at Singapore were Javanese or other Indonesians (SSD 21 February 1887). The Javanese came to Singapore, partly to earn money there to pay for their passages, and partly because the Dutch, anxious about the political effects of the pilgrimage (see note 95 above and also note 142), imposed restrictions on their departure for direct transit to Arabia. Later, however, the Dutch changed their policy in an effort to divert to Javanese ports the profitable steamer trade in carrying pilgrims. During most of the nineteenth century it seems that a large number of Indonesian, mainly Javanese, pilgrims embarked at Singapore. On arrival the authorities at Jeddah treated all pilgrims from South-East Asia as *'orang Jawa'*. The following arrivals were reported for 1889 and 1890:

	From Singapore		*From Batavia*	
Year	*Ships*	*Pilgrims*	*Ships*	*Pilgrims*
1889	4	3,225	2	718
1890	3	7,281	2	1,112

Source: FO to CO 1 June 1891, report from British Embassy at Constantinople, based on information from the consulate at Jeddah: CO 273/177, p. 540.

As illustrated by the figures of the *Daydream* in the text above, the less scrupulous shipmasters, no doubt under orders from their owners, evaded the Singapore regulations, which imposed a maximum number of passengers, by stopping at Sumatran ports to pick up many additional passengers (SSD 19 December 1873 and 9 June 1869). The prescribed scale, which was not in itself very satisfactory, related the maximum to the size of the vessel in shipping tons. It was 2 pilgrims to 3 tons.

For the leading Singapore shipping companies the pilgrim trade was a substantial business. In 1898, for example, the Ocean Steamship Co. alone carried 1,574½ pilgrims (the half passenger was presumably a child) (SSD 27 February 1899).

In 1899 an improved scale of permitted loading was introduced by which each pilgrim was to have 16 'superficial feet' and 96 'cubic feet' of space (SSD 27 February 1899). For some reason, the pilgrims took with them so much baggage that the ships reckoned that they had to provide 25 tons of space in the hold for each 100 passengers (SSD 28 December 1875).

The SS government was under constant pressure to improve its control of the trade. The consular staff at Jeddah made unfavourable comparisons between the conditions on ships arriving from Singapore and those from Indian ports. In this they may have failed to make due allowance for the much longer voyage from South-East Asia. It would appear that by the end of the nineteenth century the combined efforts of authorities in several countries had effected some improvements.

The other main social problem arising from the movement of pilgrims, was the indebtedness of some pilgrims to Singapore shipowners, notably Syed Mohamed Alsagoff, who had repatriated them as far as Singapore when they were stranded without money at Jeddah. In this respect at least, the pilgrims from South-East Asia fared better than those from India who, in similar circumstances, died of starvation in Jeddah (Board of Trade to CO 6 December 1875, CO 273/82, p. 461).

In spite of the official policy of abolishing slavery and debt-bondage in the Malay states it was allowed to continue, in a covert fashion, in Singapore. There is an interesting report on this situation in SSD 2 February 1875 and its enclosures. Most of those in bondage were Javanese or Boyanese, though a number of them remained in Singapore and Malaya and were absorbed into the Malay population. See p. 113 above.

The problem of the destitute pilgrim who sold himself into bondage was more a Javanese than a Malay question. Out of 107 pilgrims repatriated in 1898, only 17 were British subjects or protected persons (SSD 27 February 1899). However, it was often difficult to obtain accurate information from them of their place of birth.

When a destitute pilgrim needed help he signed a promissory note. As the pilgrims travelled in family groups many notes were jointly signed by two or three men (in some cases as many as seven or eight). The pilgrim needed an advance of about $50 (for each member of his party) to escape from Jeddah and get back to Singapore. Only part of the money went in passage costs; the rest went in bakshesh to local officials and *syaikh*. By the terms of the note the pilgrim undertook to pay off his debt by work to be done on his return to Singapore. Syed Mohamed Alsagoff, the Singapore merchant who put up much of the money through his associates in Jeddah, admitted that he had lent $100,000 in three years (1884–7) (SSD 7 May 1887).

The SS authorities tried to prevent pilgrims from getting into this situation by asking the Singapore shipping companies to issue return tickets to Jeddah from Singapore and back. The Grand Sharif of Jeddah, however, countered this interfeence with his exactions by detaining pilgrims, even if they had tickets, until his customary baksheesh was paid (report of 9 May 1899 from British Consul at Jeddah CO 273/253, p. 550).

Syed Mohamed Alsagoff sent the returning pilgrims to his estate on Kukub Island, off the coast of Johor. See p. 176, note 74, above. There were reports of abuses. In 1896, for example, the *Glenfalloch* brought to Singapore 320 pilgrims said to be under contract to Alsagoff. On investigation, it was found that about a quarter had not signed any agreement to work for him, and that many more had been deprived of the travel passes issued to them by the Dutch at the time of departure. This had been done to give Alsagoff 'an additional hold over them'. It was also very doubtful whether Alsagoff was entitled to require the pilgrims to work outside Singapore, and therefore beyond the supervision of the Singapore authorities. CO 273/215 and 217 contain several papers on this matter. SSD 30 July 1896 is the most important.

The bulk of the papers on the whole subject are in the CO 273 volumes of inter-departmental correspondence (FO–CO) over the 1880s and 1890s. It includes (volume and page number) 109/123 and 128, 126/629, 199/268, 205/99, 247/186, 248/18■ and 253/410.

13
The Use of Magic

THE austere monotheism of Islam was an insufficient reassurance that by godliness and divine favour all would go well. The Malays retained and cherished, as part of their pre-Islamic cultural tradition, practices which can be called 'magic' for dealing with the local forces which they believed could work good or ill for them.

To achieve success in growing padi or catching fish or collecting jungle produce or felling timber, to preserve one's health, to live in a stable and prosperous community, the peasant made skilful use of a variety of techniques, which had been acquired in the past by experience and experiment and had been handed down by one generation to the next as custom (*adat*). Both skill, for which the basic word was '*pandai*', and the established way of doing things (*adat*) were highly valued in the Malay scheme of things.

Yet there was a large area of uncertainty. A man might cultivate his padi, using all the skill and technique imparted to him by tradition, and yet lose his crop owing to some uncontrollable disaster such as a flood or a drought. When epidemic disease spread across the country it killed many without respect for their status. In 1845, the ruler of Kedah, and in 1888, the ruler of Negeri Sembilan, died during an epidemic. Hence, it was necessary to safeguard the state as much as the village community.

These calamities were attributed to the malign influence of supernatural forces and beings, whom it was possible to placate or to restrain by the appropriate procedure. No one could be sure of success, but if he resorted to these safeguards he felt more confident. It would be a false dichotomy to draw a clear line of division between the proper exercise of skill and mediation with the supernatural. The Malay mind at this time did not make that distinction, nor provide a scientific basis for what may seem to a later age to be rational, as distinct from magical procedure. It was an integrated whole, in which the essential requirement was to follow custom in all its elements at every stage. 'Cook rice in a rice pot', runs one of the several Malay sayings which recognize that the groundwork of success is the selection of the correct method.[1] The correct method was the traditional method.

By implication, the use of magic recognized the existence of minor supernatural powers and was a departure from the monotheism of Islam. But in some fashion, which did not require deep analysis, custom and religion were compatible. This is a theme for consideration later in this chapter.

In a study of Malay society it is essential to consider traditional practices, magical or otherwise, in their social context. It is not so much what was done, as how those who did it or witnessed it viewed the matter. In a study of social change, it is also necessary to consider, whether, in the period covered, those views were changing, in the light of deeper scientific knowledge or religious belief.[2]

In an earlier chapter it has been shown that the cultivation of padi, although not a universal practice, was a central element of village life to which more than economic importance attached.[3] It was therefore necessary to protect the rice cultivation cycle against adverse supernatural powers. For this purpose there was a mock battle in the rice-fields known as '*berpuar*'.[4] 'Two parties were formed, the *pawang* leading the attacking one, the other was gradually driven from one end of the *sawah* to the other. Small sheds had been erected here and there, and a little food and a few cents placed in each; round each a great battle was fought with *keladi* spears, and on the *pawang*'s party driving the other clear of the *sawahs* there was great rejoicing.'[5] In Perak in earlier times there had been a different kind of ceremony but with the same purpose. It was organized by the *Sultan Muda*, the state magician, to drive the devils down-river to the sea (*menghilirkan sumbang*). At Chigar Galah, the village which was furthest upstream on the Perak River, a raft was launched. It floated downstream, stopping at each large village, where there was a ritual ceremony and a feast, until it was finally dispatched into open waters at the estuary.[6] The symbolism of both rituals explains itself.

This Perak ritual has an obvious resemblance to a more common ritual known as '*tolak bala*' (to expel ill fortune). Thomson, writing in 1850, says 'they cause a model of a *perahu* to be constructed complete with masts and sails, in which they place rice and other eatables; into this the friends assembled beseech the unruly imps to be so good as to enter and leave the body of their friend . . . they carry the *perahu* out from the dwelling and cast it into the sea so that it may sail away with the imps and never return.'[7] In this instance the purpose of the ceremony was to remove evil spirits from the body of a sick man. However, when Skeat was in the north-east of the Peninsula in 1899, he came across the same ritual in five different places as an annual ceremony (still called '*tolak bala*') for driving the 'mischief' out of the villages down-river to the sea. In one elaborate description, he notes that the model vessel was now equipped with a rudder 'of the stern-hung European type'.[8] Elsewhere Skeat describes a different kind of ceremony, with significant Islamic elements, which was used for the same purpose in Melaka and in Selangor.[9]

Running through the different rituals is the single theme. At intervals, a village felt the need to rid itself of the evil influences which might accumulate and attack the community or its basic foodstuff.

In contrast to these precautionary rites of spiritual hygiene was the ceremony, variously known as '*main berhantu*' or '*main puteri*', which was essentially a seance in which a medium communicated with spirits for the purpose of curing an existing ill. It was most usually applied to the cure of a sick person but it could be held to relieve a 'great difficulty' of any kind.[10] It was essentially a remedy.

The most celebrated occasion of a *main berhantu* was in Perak in 1875 when, as the ruler and the chiefs perceived it, the body politic was beset by the 'great difficulty' of alien control, represented before their eyes by the earnest but overbearing British Resident, James Wheeler Woodford Birch. To relieve the state of this incubus, Sultan Abdullah held a seance which lasted for three nights. Its purpose was to consult the protective deities of Perak on the best means of ridding Perak of the obnoxious Birch. It was magic played upon the stage of public life.

First, as constitutional convention required, the ruler consulted a meeting of the Perak chiefs and propounded the question, 'If there be any prophets or spirits left in Perak let us look into Mr Birch's future, and see if there is any means by which he may die and his steamer be wrecked on the bar of Kuala Perak.'[11] The chiefs said, with no less constitutional propriety, 'Very good. Let us try.'[12]

In the seance which followed, the principal performers were the Raja Kecil Muda, deputy to the Sultan Muda, and his son, Raja Ahmad. The latter was the leading medium and put questions to the spirits while he himself was in a trance. Later on Sultan Abdullah himself became 'possessed of a devil' to whom he put questions. On the third night 'the Sultan got possessed of seven devils and when he got possessed of the seventh devil he drew his *keris* and danced about and fell down several times as if the devil had thrown him down'. Finally, Raja Ahmad made a manikin of moistened flour which he and the Sultan both stabbed. When it was over Sultan Abdullah said, 'See, in a month Mr. Birch will be dead.' The chiefs said, 'Very good.'

When he wrote that a seance might be held in times of 'great difficulty', Swettenham adds, 'say the dangerous illness of a personage of importance'.[13] This is a reference to another seance which was an act of state. It was held when the Regent, later Sultan, of Perak, Raja Yusuf, fell ill in 1885. Yusuf had a tumour of the brain and seemed likely to die; however, he made an unexpected though temporary recovery and died two years later. Both Swettenham and Clifford wrote colourful accounts of the affair in which the sick man, who was cordially disliked by everyone, tricked various persons who hoped to obtain favours from him on what they supposed was his deathbed.[14]

In this case the medium was a woman of aristocratic birth. 'The *pawang*, who was now supposed to be "possessed" and no longer conscious of her actions . . . made obeisance to the taper, sprinkling the floor round it with saffron-coloured rice and perfumed water; then, rising to her feet and followed by the attendant, she performed the same ceremony before each male member of the reigning family present in the room, murmuring all the while a string of gibberish addressed to the spirit. This done, she resumed her seat on the mat, and, after a brief pause, the minstrels struck up a different air, and, singing the praises of another *jin*, called upon him to come and relieve the king's distress.'[15] To the satisfaction of his magicians and the consternation of the court circle, the ruler made an almost instantaneous recovery though he was to die later 'in the odour of iniquity'.[16]

Although a village seance was not a grand occasion, it employed essentially the same method, i.e. the use of a medium to cajole or negotiate with the spirits for the recovery of a sick man.[17] It was particularly appropriate to the treatment of someone who had become delirious or mentally disturbed, since the outward symptoms suggested that the patient was no longer himself but was under the control of alien forces. Even a village seance required considerable preparations. 'A large feast is prepared for the neighbourhood at the house of the sick person, where he is laid in the centre of the room or hall. Dancing girls are engaged to dance around him to the music of tom toms, gongs and *suling*, when much noise and mirth is indulged in. A miniature mosque is at the same time prepared which being carried to a solitary place, they deposit some grains of rice for the spirits to feed upon and though it is allowed that the grain is not consumed still they believe that they appropriate the essence.'

It seems likely that Thomson's 'dancing girls' were in fact female practitioners.[18] Skeat, in describing a seance in Kuala Langat in 1896, says that 'the medicine man appeared and took his seat beside the censer, his wife, an aged woman, whose office it was to chant . . . struck up the invocation (*lagu pemanggil*) and we listened in rapt attention as the voice, at first weak and feeble with age, gathered strength and wailed ever higher and shriller up to the climax at the end of the chant'. Meanwhile the *pawang* made his preparations which included inhaling incense and covering his face with his *sarung*. 'The moment of possession arrived, and with a violent convulsive movement . . . the spasm being strangely followed by a dry and ghostly cough.' After much ritual action the medium was possessed by a 'tiger spirit', mimicking the growl and movement of a tiger. 'Then the evident excitement of the onlookers was raised to fever pitch as the bizarre . . . and strangely brute-like form . . . slowly licked over as a tigress would lick its cub, the all but naked body of the patient.' Later the medium took a dagger and 'engaged in a fierce hand-to-hand combat with his invisible foe (the spirit whom he had been summoned to exorcise)'. When the rite ended the *pawang* returned to his normal condition 'in a state of complete exhaustion [and] experienced a severe attack of nausea'.[19]

In a description of another similar seance which he saw at Biserat in southern Siam in 1899, Skeat comments that 'it was a dynamic piece of acting, every muscle of the medicine-man's body twitching convulsively in turn'.[20]

In his analysis of ceremonies of this kind, Firth emphasizes the social aspects. The seance serves as 'a bridge between the ideas, emotions and behaviour of the sick person and those of the people who surround him. . . . [It] takes the brake off the speech conventions of ordinary discourse' since the medium is not answerable for what he says.[21] To that extent it is a kind of catharsis of the frustrations and inhibitions of social life, which may have their psychosomatic effects. There is also, as Skeat's description shows, a strong element of drama and of entertainment. A good seance is a splendid show, which will draw onlookers despite the Islamic disapproval to which it is exposed in modern times.

That disapproval was already beginning to make itself felt in the last years of the nineteenth century. Thomson asked the *imam* whether he could reconcile belief in Tuan Allah, as the one and only God, with belief in spirits. 'To this he replied, "It is very wrong certainly but we must respect the customs of men of old who had converse with these demigods, a thing denied us ignorant children of the present age".'[22] Respect for ancient tradition (*adat*) was one of the stock justifications of a period in which custom was still revered.

The society in which one lived, including its temporal rulers, feared these supernatural forces and wished to placate them. So long as there was a general compliance, it was difficult for an individual to obtrude his personal objections. When Abdullah Munshi, that pioneer of the Malay enlightenment, was in Pahang in 1838, 'I asked some of the people whether these bad customs and ways could not be altered, and they said that such customs had existed from ancient times, and if they were changed or broken, the wrath of the dead rulers would fall upon the country'. Later on, when Abdullah's party reached Kelantan, he was pressed to conform to what he regarded as 'a silly custom' since otherwise ill fortune would befall all concerned. He gave in, saying, 'I reflected that if I did not do as they asked and we were to meet with any misfortune they would attribute it to my omission.'[23]

In a conflict between religious conviction and social disapproval, the individual could sometimes extricate himself by withdrawing from public view. It is clear that some of the chiefs who were at the scene of Sultan Abdullah's seance in August 1875, described above, distanced themselves from a public ceremony, to which they had given their formal approval in the preliminary consultation. They disapproved of it but it was not proper (*patut*) to display open disagreement with the ruler's conduct. Thus, on the first night of the three-day seance, 'Orang Kaya Mat Arshad who was well instructed in the *Kuran* refused to be present, and remained in his boat'. On the following day, Mat Arshad's father, the Datuk Laksamana of Perak, arrived on the scene in response to an earlier summons from the Sultan. He, too, 'remained in his boat' when the performance was resumed on the second night.[24] His absence could hardly have gone unremarked since he was one of the most influential chiefs in Lower Perak and a close associate of the Sultan. Yet he was also a man known for his learning in Islamic law. J. W. W. Birch wrote of him that he was 'the only person I know in the country really fitted for ... principal *hakim* or judge'.[25]

Another witness was Syed Mashhor, who had taken refuge in Perak after the defeat of Raja Mahdi's faction, of which Mashhor was a prominent leader, in the Selangor Civil War. He was 'living on charity, having no followers and no money'.[26] It was not possible for him to be conspicuously absent but he said afterwards, 'I never saw such a performance before.'[27] The Sultan's secretary was in a rather similar situation; he said afterwards that 'most of the Perak Malays believe in this devil raising but strict Mahomedans will not have anything to say to them'.[28] A third unwilling witness of the seance was the Sultan's cousin and crony, Raja Dris. At this stage, Birch regarded him as 'rather a debauchee' but he matured to become Sultan Idris, a pillar of Islamic orthodoxy in later years.[29]

In those times under the colonial regime—but not as a direct consequence of it—orthodox opinion could express its disapproval without constraint. The attitude of Malay society was altering. Swettenham tells how the chaplain ('spiritual teacher') of Sultan Idris of Perak came in 'to lead the evening prayer'. He found the ruler and his Resident in discussion of 'various superstitions' of which Idris, as a great authority on Malay custom, had extensive knowledge. The story continues that 'the *guru*, or teacher, no doubt heard the end of our conversation, and was duly scandalised'. Swettenham does not say whether he later rebuked his royal master; granted Malay conventions, it seems unlikely. He did, however, send a stern letter of reproof to Swettenham, saying—'I wish to enquire about the practice of *berhantu*, as has been the custom of *rajas* and chiefs in this state of Perak. Is it right according to your religion, Mr. Resident, or is it not? For that practice is a deadly sin to the Muhammadan Faith, because those who engage in it lose their reason and waste their substance to nothing.'[30] It must have taken some determination to throw down the gauntlet to a man who was an autocrat as well as a personal friend of the ruler.

It is also worth noting that the chaplain made his objection, not to the worship of false gods, but against the unbridled licence ('lose their reason') which a seance gave to the baser elements of human nature.[31]

Religious orthodoxy could not eliminate these practices—they continue to this day. However, their status altered. Instead of being performed openly, with no more objection than the silent absence of those who disapproved, magical practice was expelled from state ritual. In Perak, there was no repetition of the 1885 seance held in time of 'great difficulty' when the ruler seemed to be dying.

Other ceremonies which recognized the existence of the genii of the state continued a little longer, since they did not involve spirit possession—a 'loss of reason'. As related in an earlier chapter, when Sultan Idris was installed in 1889 there was an ancient lustration ceremony performed in a temporary building with the significant name of *balai hantu*. However, there was nothing of that kind in the installation ceremonies of a ruler of Johor in 1895 and of Selangor in 1903.[32] Both included substantial elements of European ceremonial practice, but little or nothing which can be identified as an invocation of supernatural forces or pagan deities. Such things were no longer admissible.

In the villages it was no longer proper to be openly associated with the ceremonies of the *pawang*. Shaw, who first came to Malaya in 1900, observed that when the *tolak bala* raft descended the Perak River and made its periodic stops at important villages, the local worthies were not present 'while the *pawang* is holding converse with the spirits but they arrive on the scene as soon as this part of the ceremony is over and partake freely of the *kenduri*'. However, he adds that 'still the old formularies have not been forgotten; in times of trouble they are much relied on'.[33]

With the decline in the prestige of magic, the standing of the practitioner, the *pawang*, suffered a corresponding fall. In his heyday the *pawang* (also called *bomoh* when treating the sick) had been a real authority in his community. His function was to co-ordinate and lead the villagers in the sequence of activities of padi growing from the opening of the season through to the reaping of the harvest; in the dangerous work of felling jungle trees to clear new land; in fishing at sea; and in the search for tin and other minerals. In this work mere skill could be defeated by the malign influence of the spirit world. It was necessary to ward off such misfortune by the appropriate ceremony, which was organized by the *pawang*.[34] Yet it was more than a process of reassurance. The co-ordination which resulted from following the lead of the *pawang* could have beneficial practical effects. It was no coincidence that in padi planting the government had to take other measures to establish a common programme or timetable in replacement for the *pawang*.

In most cases the *pawang* was a shrewd, practical man who had learnt his ritual and his incantations from an older practitioner, without perhaps understanding some of it. In many villages the office of *pawang* passed from father to son. With the knowledge the apprentice *pawang* also inherited the necessary apparatus (*kebesaran*) for the practice of magic. Those magicians who could perform as spirit mediums must have been endowed with a temperament for that demanding role. One such, Siputum, was among the men implicated in the killing of J. W. W. Birch in 1875—'a medicine man, a sorcerer . . . a wilder looking creature it would have been hard to find'.[35] He must have been a fey figure who genuinely 'heard voices'.

Although the *pawang* gradually ceased to be a prominent personality in his community, he did not abandon his practice but continued to perform for those who required his services. One of the most remunerative activities was assisting the Chinese miners in finding and producing tin. The latter readily accepted that the *pawang* was a useful intermediary in dealing with the local genii, who could make or mar their operations.[36] There was an elaborate set of taboos on tin mines; failure to find tin at a place chosen by the *pawang* could readily be explained by supposing that someone had broken these rules. As in other fields, the *pawang* on a tin mine combined practical skill with magic—'an intimate knowledge of the district enables the *pawang* to shrewdly guess the most likely places for tin to be found'.[37] As already stated in an earlier chapter, the medical services of the *pawang* or *bomoh* were often a combination of practical herbal remedies and, it these failed, magical rites.[38]

As late as 1923 the young gentlemen at the Malay College at Kuala Kangsar engaged a *pawang* to ensure that the College football team would win the big match of the season against the Penang Free School team. The College team was none the less beaten 5–0. The *pawang*, after the fashion of his kind, explained that a candle, 'over which he had muttered appropriate incantations . . . had been blown out by the wind during the match contrary to his injunction that it must be kept alight'.[39]

In spite of education and religious teaching, a community could still lose its collective head in a moment of tension. In the 18[illegible]0s, a village in Jelebu in Negeri Sembilan was seized by panic when a *pawang* predicted a 'period of total darkness, when water would become solid, and no fire could be lit'. The villagers abandoned their daily work and began 'a frantic collection of provisions' against the apocalyptic disaster. The resourceful district officer, however, enlisted 'the services of a rival holy man . . . to explain that, in the face of such a stupendous calamity, precautions were useless and the only wise thing to do was to . . . wait'. They did—and nothing happened.[40]

Places could inspire vague fears. It could be the grave of a famous forbear or just some abnormality, such as a conspicuous boulder or a deformed tree. Such places were centres of supernatural power (*keramat*) and on occasion propitiatory rites might be performed there. This earned disapproval 'by the more strictly Muhammedan Malays of the towns and especially by those that are partially of Arab descent'. But a compromise was found. Such practices 'might be consistent with Muhammedan orthodoxy on the understanding that the prayers were addressed solely to the Deity, but the invocation of spirits or deceased saints and their propitiation by offerings could not be regarded as otherwise than polytheistic idolatry'.[41]

Through it all, as Abdullah Munshi perceived, ran the force of tradition. It is unnecessary to propound a reason for what we, and our fathers before us, do and have done. It was often difficult to distinguish between what was believed to be lucky (*bertuah*), and what was regarded as good form (*patut*). Both were achieved by following the traditional practice (*adat*). In so far as it implied a recognition of lesser gods and powers, it was not at first regarded as a dereliction from the belief in the unity of the one God. These were different compartments in the outlook upon those things which are beyond human control. Logically, of course, it was not a tenable position. At first among the small but influential minority of the Malay intelligentsia and religious teachers, later among the larger group who followed the lead of that minority, the dominance of the *adat* was eroded by disapproval of its magical aspects.

1. C. C. Brown, *Malay Sayings*, London, Routledge & Kegan Paul, 1951, p. 181: '*Tanak dalam periok.*' He gives three equivalent expressions for the concept of the right method.

2. W. W. Skeat, *Malay Magic: Being an Introduction to the Folklore and Popular Religion of the Malay Peninsula*, London, Macmillan, 1900, reprinted Singapore, Oxford University Press, 1984, is an excellent ethnographic description of Malay beliefs and ceremonies of the late nineteenth century. After serving as a district officer in Selangor, Skeat headed the Cambridge expedition of 1899–1900 to North-east Malaya, including the Malay states of southern Siam; see W. W. Skeat and F. F. Laidlaw, 'The Cambridge University Expedition to Parts of the Malay Peninsula 1899–1900: Personal Accounts', *JMBRAS*, 26(4), 1953, which includes much useful data. On Malay custom R. J. Wilkinson ('The Incidents of Malay Life', *Papers on Malay Subjects, Life and Customs*, Part 1, 1908, reprinted in *JMBRAS*, 30(4), 1957), is an excellent source, especially on rites of passage. His 'Malay Beliefs', 1906, reprinted in 'Papers on Malay Customs and Beliefs', *JMBRAS*,

30(4), 1957, and 'Some Malay Studies', *JMBRAS*, 10(1), 1932, are also useful. R. O. Winstedt, *The Malay Magician—Being Shaman, Saiva and Sufi*, London, Routledge & Kegan Paul, 1951, is a revised version of his *Shaman, Saiva and Sufi*, London, Constable, 1925. This and *The Malays: A Cultural History*, Singapore, Kelly & Walsh, 1947, are Winstedt's major essays in this field, on which he wrote a large number of essays and notes on a variety of subjects, many of them published in *JSBRAS* and *JMBRAS*. Many other lesser contributions appear in issues of that Journal from its first appearance in 1878 onwards. The leading modern study of Malay magic is Kirk Michael Endicott, *An Analysis of Malay Magic*, Oxford, Oxford University Press, 1970, reprinted Kuala Lumpur, Oxford University Press, 1981. This is an attempt—not wholly persuasive to the present writer—to give a systematic account of Malay magic in terms of modern anthropological theory. On this subject, as on much else, this author is a disciple of Firth, whose pupil he once was, in deprecating 'a monolithic view of Malay magic' (Raymond Firth, 'Faith and Scepticism in Kelantan Village Magic', in W. R. Roff (ed.), *Kelantan: Religion, Society and Politics in a Malay State*, Kuala Lumpur, Oxford University Press, 1974, p. 190). See also Raymond Firth, 'Ritual and Drama in Malay Spirit Mediumship', *Comparative Studies in Society and History*, 9, 1967, pp. 190–207, where he analyses the seance (*main puteri*).

3. See p. 129 above.

4. The *berpuar* ritual derives its name from '*puar*', the stem of the wild ginger plant, sometimes used as a mock spear or javelin in these fights. R. J. Wilkinson, *A Malay–English Dictionary*, 2 parts, Singapore, Kelly & Walsh, 1901 (revised as *A Malay–English Dictionary (Romanised)*, 2 parts, Mytilene, Salavopoulos & Kinderlis, 1932), Part 2, p. 281; I. H. Burkill, *A Dictionary of the Economic Products of the Malay Peninsula*, 2 vols., London, published on behalf of the SS and FMS Governments, Crown Agents, 1935, p. 133.

5. *SGG* 1892, p. 562, report from Ulu Langat with a footnote by E. W. Birch, Resident of Selangor, that similar ceremonies took place in Naning (Melaka) at three-year intervals. C. O. Blagden, 'Notes on the Folklore and Popular Religion of the Malays', *JSBRAS*, 29, 1896, describes it as 'a sort of mock combat'.

6. G. E. Shaw, 'Rice Planting', *Papers on Malay Subjects, Malay Industries*, Part 3, 1911, p. 8.

7. J. T. Thomson, 'Pulau Aur', *JIA*, 4, 1850, p. 194.

8. Skeat and Laidlaw, op. cit., pp. 22, 43, 50, 74 and 78. The long description is at p. 74. W. E. Maxwell, *Notes and Queries*, issued with *JSBRAS*, 15, 1885, p. 54, adds a footnote to a description of this ritual that 'such a boat or raft is called *lanchang* in Perak'.

9. Skeat, *Malay Magic*, p. 220, citing Muhammad Ja'afar, 'An Account of the Cultivation of Rice in Malacca', *JSBRAS*, 30, 1897, and Skeat, 'Some Records of Malay Magic, by an Eyewitness', *JSBRAS*, 31, 1898.

10. F. A. Swettenham, *Footprints in Malaya*, London, Hutchinson, 1942, p. 52.

11. Evidence of Kulup Mat Rouse to PCE CO 273/86, pp. 519–33. He was the Sultan's secretary. Extracts from his evidence, and that of others, are reprinted in R. O. Winstedt and R. J. Wilkinson, 'A History of Perak', *JMBRAS*, 12(1), 1934, Appendix (i), pp. 172–4.

12. See p. 23 above on the conventions of royal consultation of chiefs. 'Sultan Muda' was the title held by the 'State Medicine-man' (Winstedt and Wilkinson, op. cit., p. 135).

13. Swettenham, *Footprints*, p. 52.

14. F. A. Swettenham, *Malay Sketches*, London, John Lane Bodley Head, 1895, pp. 152–9. H. C. Clifford, *Malayan Monochromes*, New York, Dutton, 1913, pp. 70–80: his brain tumour is mentioned at p. 73.

15. Swettenham, *Malay Sketches*, p. 155.

16. H. C. Clifford, *Bushwhacking and Other Asiatic Tales and Memories*, New York, Harper, 1929, p. 177.

17. Skeat, *Malay Magic*, pp. 436–44; W. E. Maxwell, 'Shamanism in Perak', *JSBRAS*, 12, 1883.

18. Thomson, 'Pulau Aur', p. 194. A *suling* is a fife, pipe or flageolet (Wilkinson, *1932 Dictionary*, Part 2, p. 497).

19. Skeat, *Malay Magic*, pp. 436–44.

20. Skeat and Laidlaw, op. cit., p. 47.

21. Firth, 'Ritual and Drama', pp. 194 and 200.

22. Thomson, 'Pulau Aur', p. 197.

23. Abdullah bin Abdul Kadir, Munshi, *Kesah Pelayaran Abdullah*, translated by A. E. Coope, *The Voyage of Abdullah: A Translation from the Malay*, Singapore, Malaya Publishing House, 1949, pp. 12 and 66.

24. Evidence of Kulup Mat Rouse to PCE CO 273/86, pp. 529–30.

25. Report by Birch of 14 December 1874 enclosed with SSD 14 December 1876, para. 60, reprinted in J. W. W. Birch, *The Journals of J. W. W. Birch First British Resident to Perak 1874–1875* (hereafter cited as *Birch Journal*), edited by P. L. Burns, Kuala Lumpur, Oxford University Press, 1976, p. 388. The Datuk Laksamana was never appointed to this office; he was exiled to the Seychelles in the aftermath of Birch's death (SSD 18 May 1877).

26. F. A. Swettenham, 'Some Account of the Independent Native States of the Malay Peninsula especially the Circumstances which Led to the More Intimate Relations Recently Adopted towards Some of Them by the British Government', *JSBRAS*, 6, 1880, p. 189.

27. Evidence of Syed Mashhor to PCE CO 273/88, p. 84.

28. Evidence of Kulup Mat Rouse to PCE CO 273/86, p. 529.

29. Ibid., p. 520, and also evidence of Syed Mashhor, loc. cit., at p. 84, both say that Raja Dris was present at the seance. There is no suggestion that he took any active part in it. An opium smoker and a debauchee: *Birch Journal*, p. 58.

30. Swettenham, *Malay Sketches*, pp. 208–9.

31. The antithesis between rationality (*akal*) and carnal instinct (*hawa nafsu*) is fundamental in the Islamic view of proper conduct. R. F. Ellen, 'Social Theory, Ethnography, and the Understanding of Practical Islam in South-East Asia', in M. B. Hooker (ed.), *Islam in South-East Asia*, Leiden, Brill, 1983, pp. 71 and 87; J. L. Peacock, *Muslim Puritans: Reformist Psychology in Southeast Asian Islam*, Berkeley, University of California Press, 1978, p. 135; J. T. Siegel, *The Rope of God*, Berkeley, University of California Press, 1969, pp. 33 and 37; C. S. Kessler, *Islam and Politics in a Malay State: Kelantan 1838–1969*, Ithaca, Cornell University Press, 1978, p. 221.

32. The Perak and Selangor installations are described at pp. 33–6 above. The 'curious mixture of oriental and European customs' at the Johor ceremony of 1895 included a ritual sprinkling of rice-flour (*menepuk tepung tawar*) but nothing else identifiable as pre-Islamic Malay custom (SSD 4 November 1895).

33. Shaw, op. cit., p. 9. Shaw's comment has remained true down to our time. When

the present author arrived in Sungei Ujong (Seremban) in September 1945 there was a *tolak bala* drive to the sea in progress on the Linggi River in the territory (down-river from Seremban) of the Datuk Shahbandar—prompted by a severe outbreak of smallpox, which added to the tribulations of late 1945. As an eager anthropologist the author asked the Datuk whether he might be an unobtrusive witness of this interesting event. However, the Datuk, who was a man of Western life-style, declined the request—firmly but politely—with some evident embarrassment over the whole affair. In a similar situation a century earlier J. T. Thomson (*Some Glimpses into Life in the Far East*, London, Richardson, 1864, reprinted as *Glimpses into Life in Malayan Lands*, Singapore, Oxford University Press, 1984, p. 172) wrote that 'they avoided letting me see the rites, being ashamed of my unbelief and their own superstition, which latter was contrary to their own professed religion (the Mahometan)'. In the 1920s Wheeler remarked that 'elaborate tabus (*pantang*) . . . are completely neglected nowadays' (*The Modern Malay*, London, Allen & Unwin, 1928, p. 93), but 'the old beliefs will prevail in times of stress' (ibid., p. 94).

34. Blagden, op. cit., p. 6. Wilkinson, 'Incidents', p. 46, describes the *pawang*'s activities as 'the relic of an old agricultural religion'. See pp. 126 and 130 above on the role of the *pawang* in regulating the agricultural timetable.

35. Swettenham, *Malay Sketches*, p. 245.

36. A. Hale, 'On Mines and Miners in Kinta', *JSBRAS*, 16, 1885, pp. 306–7; F. A. Swettenham, *British Malaya: An Account of the Origin and Progress of British Influence in Malaya*, London, John Lane Bodley Head, 1907 (revised editions 1929 and 1948, London, Allen & Unwin), p. 229. See *SJ* 17 May 1895 for description of the working procedure of a Malay *pawang* on a mine.

37. A. B. Rathborne, *Camping and Tramping in Malaya: Fifteen Years' Pioneering in the Native States of the Malay Peninsula*, London, Swan Sonnenschein, 1898, reprinted Singapore, Oxford University Press, 1984, pp. 131–2.

38. See p. 258 above.

39. Datuk Mohamed Said, *Memoirs of a Menteri Besar: Early Days*, Singapore, Heinemann, 1982, p. 173.

40. A. L. Keyser, *People and Places: A Life in Five Continents*, London, Murray, 1922, p. 152.

41. Blagden, op. cit., pp. 2 and 11; R. O. Winstedt, 'Keramat: Sacred Places and Persons in Malaya', *JMBRAS*, 2(3), 1924. Skeat, *Malay Magic*, has many references and an appendix, at pp. 673–4, on *keramat*. It is also one of the key concepts examined by K. M. Endicott, op. cit., especially at pp. 90–5. Wilkinson, as usual, finds words to express the matter simply as 'the idea of special sanctity attaching to weird or abnormal objects. Exceptional things, thinks the Malay, must have exceptional soul-personalities, so that . . . he is very careful to respect anything that is quite out of the common. Trees of unusual size, rocks of peculiar shape, animals with strange deformities . . . all such things are sacrosanct' ('Malay Beliefs', p. 11).

14
Sports, Amusements, and Recreations

'At night sitting amongst palm and banana and other rich tropical foliage, intermingled with scarves and flags and quaint devices, on the banks of a mountain river lit by a full moon in a cloudless sky we witnessed a series of dances and performances and listened to the chants of wild Sakais, the Malays, the Menangkabau men and the Chinese—we had scarf dances and shawl dances and saucer dances and a monkey dance and besides singing, Malay and Chinese instrumental accompaniments all the performers being men.'[1] Thus Governor Weld spent a memorable night on tour at Kajang, in Selangor, in July 1883.

The sheer richness, variety, and aesthetic appeal of the element of entertainment in Malay culture absorbed the attention of those who described it in the nineteenth century—as it continues to do in our own age. This was a sector of Malay culture in which borrowing from foreign sources was not uncommon, though still only a small part of the whole. Amusements were also an integral part of Malay life, often associated with events such as a wedding or a state ceremony. Hence, it is a subject which needs to be examined in its social context. Many Malay amusements were displays of skill for public entertainment, ranging from the sport known as *sepak raga* which was essentially athletic, to the intellectual pastimes of good story-telling or a contest of capping one pithy proverb or verse with another. It is also possible that, in the more physical kinds of amusement, there was a sublimated form of the strain of violence which lay below the surface in village life and was too easily released in aristocratic life.[2] It is not entirely a coincidence that Raja Mahmud, 'equally noted for his cruelty and for his fighting qualities', was also an accomplished performer in the mock duel with daggers known as *main silat*.[3]

The social context determined the form and quality of a set-piece entertainment. The performers who enchanted Weld were villagers, the best dancers and singers in their community, but essentially amateurs. On the other hand 'a Malay chief would consider himself shamed if he regaled his guests with amateur performances of a bucolic type'.[4] Hence, professional troupes lived as dependants of royal courts and the households of great men or made visits to them. Weld noted that all the performers at Kajang were men. Malay, or at least Islamic convention, generally disapproved of women dancers and the like. A ruler might have palace dancers who were girls raised at his court, and there were professional troupes which included female performers, but a woman of good reputation did not appear in public as an amateur.

In the entertainments which formed an essential and much appreciated part of a social event, it is sometimes difficult to separate the element of recreation from the event itself. In aristocratic life a wedding was celebrated with 'Malay theatrical performances, shadow plays, chess or gambling in one form or another'.[5] However, one cannot easily distinguish ritual from entertainment in, say, the bridegroom's procession to the bride's house, or the ensuing *bersanding* ceremony, at a village wedding. Even a grimly serious ritual, such as a seance to cure a sick person, contained in itself an element of drama which attracted and excited the onlookers.[6]

Islam was an austere religion which did not permit idols or representations of living things, though in the course of passing through Iran and India, it had picked up some dancing and acting of a limited kind. Its main contribution to Malay amusements was the celebration of *Hari Raya*.[7] Orthodox Islam disapproved of a number of traditional Malay amusements. When the Maha Menteri imposed his authority on Kelantan in the 1890s, he 'endeavoured to suppress the travelling theatres to which the people are so much attached'. He also 'put down cock-fighting, bull matches, prize-fights, hunting and the keeping of dogs'.[8]

The great traditional sport was cock-fighting (*sabung ayam*) between birds armed with metal spurs (*taji*). Such contests 'furnished food for discussion for weeks, even months, before, and everyone of standing has visited and examined the cocks and has made a book on the event'.[9] It also had its ritual and magical aspects. The owner of a fancied bird would be careful to choose a propitious time when favourable forces were in the ascendant.[10] There were other superstitions, too—'they will not bet upon a bird with black plumage that is matched against one with yellow and white'.[11] Cock-fighting was thus at the centre of a network of related elements of Malay culture—local competition, ritual and magic, strict rules of procedure (Newbold's summary of a Malay treatise on cock-fighting extends over five pages of print), gambling, and the excitement of a spectacle of savage skill and courage, which ended all too often with the death or maiming of one or both birds.

'On the day fixed for the fight, a crowd collects before the palace and some of the king's youths set up a cock-pit, which is a ring about three feet in diameter, enclosed by canvas walls, supported by stakes driven into the ground. Presently the *juara*, or cock-fighters, appear each carrying his bird under his left arm. They enter the cock-pit, squat down, and begin pulling at and shampooing the legs and wings of their birds, in the manner which Malays believe loosens the muscles, and gets the reefs out of the cock's limbs. Then the word is given to start the fight, and the birds, released, fly straight at one another, striking with their spurs, and sending feathers flying in all directions. This lasts for perhaps three minutes, when the birds begin to lose their wind, and the fight is carried on as much with their beaks as their spurs . . . the Malays herald each stroke with loud cries of approval . . . and the birds are exhorted to make fresh efforts . . . presently time is called . . . at the word each cock-fighter seizes his bird, drenches it with water . . .' and so on through perhaps ten rounds until one bird admits defeat.[12]

No reason is given for the gradual loss of popular appeal of cock-fighting in the latter part of the nineteenth century. Yet it did undeniably decline. At the installation of a Raja Muda of Perak in 1908, an attempt was made to hold a cock-fight but it was a fiasco due to the lack of trained fighting cocks. 'The cocks of Kuala Kangsar were a miscellaneous assembly of roosters who could neither crow nor fight.'[13]

The mock duel with the dagger or sword (*main silat*) may originally have been a war-dance to demonstrate martial skill or a duel to the death. In the nineteenth century it had become a formalized type of fencing. In Wilkinson's time at the end of the century it was losing its appeal. He says that 'a performance may be followed with breathless interest by the seniors among the spectators . . to the younger generation of Malays the dance is unintelligible'.[14] Yet when a man, like Raja Mahmud, who had in his day fought in real combat with these weapons, took the stage, he could impart to the stylized movements the lethal menace of the real contest—'the four cuts and single thrust of native swordsmanship were exhibited with their accompanying guards', while the drums and trumpets sounded in accompaniment.[15] Skeat, who saw a performance in Patani at about the same time, wrote that 'their fencing was just a piece of acting, an exhibition of proficiency in the use of the *keris*'.[16]

The other traditional Malay contest, *sepak raga*, was a pure display of dexterity and skill, with the excitement of a contest but lacking any element of fighting to the death. In this game a circle of players kick a ball, made a woven plaited material, in the air. As the ball falls a player kicks it up again so that it does not touch the ground. A contest between teams, consists in putting each team into the ring to see whether it can achieve a higher number of kicks than its opponents before the ball is missed and falls to the ground. The kick is given with the side of the foot and the entire game calls for much practice and skill. This game, too, lost its vogue towards the end of the nineteenth century. When Wilkinson was writing his essay on Malay amusements in 1910 he invited a Perak Malay to supply him with a list of traditional sports. The list provided did not include *sepak raga*. He surmised that *sepak raga* had given place to the superior attraction of football matches, which possess 'the excitement of having players divided into sides' contesting control of the ball. A proficient team of *sepak raga* players was mustered to perform as part of the celebrations of the inaugural meeting of the FMS Federal Council in December 1909.[17] But the game had become—for the time being at least—an antiquarian pastime like morris dancing on the village green in England. It was no longer a game played spontaneously by the young men as their choice of casual amusement.

Association football—'soccer'—came to Malaya in the 1880s as a game played by Europeans.[18] However, it soon spread like wildfire through the Malay community. At a time when it was difficult to induce Malay boys to come to the new schools 'one of the greatest incentives to attendance at school is the proximity of a football ground . . . their enthusiasm over a game of association football is extraordinary'.[19] When a new school was planned it became official policy to offer two attractions—a football pitch to bring in the boys and a Koran teacher at $8 per month to take afternoon classes in his subject. The latter was a 'never failing remedy for a poorly attended school' when parental reluctance was the problem.[20]

At first, the Europeans made fun of Malay soccer—'the natural gravity and dignity of the Malay is noticeable. No preliminary horseplay or turning of somersaults as among English schoolboys can be seen. After a lot of talking, which is shared equally by all the players, the ball is started. The game reminds one of the description one reads of ladies' football matches in England. The players make apologetic charges and stand around in picturesque attitudes. The full-back may be seen stretched at full length smoking a cigarette, whilst a mildly fierce battle is being waged near his opponents' goal . . . the costumes worn by the players are very *chic*.'[21]

However, as Wilkinson had realized, the Malays took to soccer as a substitute for the traditional martial arts like *main silat*. The urge to compete and to win spurred them on. They began to field teams which played hard and well. By 1912 the Selangor Football Association included eight teams of which three were Malay. When a Malay team was playing, its supporters lined the touch-line 'cheering them on with shouts of *bunuh* (kill) and *tendang* (strike)'.[22] This atmosphere of conflict led to incidents between Malay and European players and to other friction.

Malay dancing was a display for the entertainment of an audience, not a recreation in which the latter could participate. When Swettenham visited Pèkan in Pahang in 1875, he witnessed what he called 'a royal nautch'. He describes how four women dancers, permanent members of the ruler's household, took their places in a sitting position but rose slowly to their feet—'the arms hands and body being the real performers whilst the feet are scarcely noticed and for half the time not visible'. Each of the half dozen dances represented a theme such as rice cultivation or war. It was a form of ballet, with shamanistic undertones, lasting about half an hour for each dance. Towards the end, two dancers became possessed and were removed. The audience of about two hundred was entirely male; the performance took place during the small hours of the night.[23] Dancers of this professional type and expertise were not found in every royal household and were not often seen.

In the towns and villages there were women who performed the *joget* or *ronggeng* dances as professional entertainers. It was not a socially approved profession. Strictly, *joget* was pure dancing and *ronggeng* a combination of dancing and singing. The *joget* 'is a dance by two persons who keep in step with one another' as they advance and retreat across the dance floor. 'It is danced by two girls but it is common for one of them to step aside and for a male spectator to take her place. It is then the other's duty to copy his steps exactly, and by her skill in this respect her skill is judged.'[24]

The history of the *ronggeng* illustrates the effect of European and Islamic influence on an indigenous Malay art-form. The emphasis on steps rather than movements of the hands and arms; the European style of melody; and the use of instruments such as the violin or the bamboo flute (*seruling* or *suling*) were probably adopted by imitation of the Portuguese. In the remote past, the dancers had been Malay maidens but Islam vetoed such indecorous practices and professional dancing girls took the stage.[25] Those dancers who had the talent could command large fees in the towns. As their charms faded they earned much less from performing before village audiences.[26]

Amateur dancing by male performers, such as Weld had seen, continued to the end of the century at least. In 1890, for example, on the occasion of *Hari Raya* the District Officer of Lower Perak had a gathering of 300–400 people at his house 'and there was the usual dancing'.[27] Two factors may have kept the practice going. British officials were sometimes enthusiastic students of Malay culture; it is striking how often the reports relate to festivities at a district officer's house. Among immigrant communities there was an element of competition. 'Now we, men of Menangkabau, will entertain you with one of our traditional dances' is implicit in Weld's account of the entertainment provided on the occasion of his visit to Kajang. A seance seems to have required dancing on the part of the medium or those who assisted him.[28]

The only dance of Islamic origin was the *hadzrah* or *hithrah*, in which a line of a dozen Malay youths moved in single file to the beat of drums.[29] The drummers chanted verses in Arabic and between each verse the dancers sang a chorus. Wilkinson describes it as 'a long line of boys who sing, sway and prostrate themselves before the religious pundit who instructs them in religious chants. The words are largely Arabic; the sentiment is religious; the professed object is to glorify God.' In modern times, this dance has been modified to a less religious style by dressing the performers in gaudy costumes as 'princesses', and giving them secular verses to sing to a violin accompaniment. But it is not clear whether this decline from grace had begun as early as the beginning of this century; it may have come later.[30]

Drama was an entertainment of foreign origin and some of it had only recently been imported into Malay culture. There is an extensive literature on the shadow-play (*wayang kulit*).[31] It was—and still is—performed by projecting on to a screen the shadow outlines of leather silhouette figures, manipulated between a bright lamp, which is behind the screen, and the screen itself. The operator (*dalang*) also speaks the dialogue. The plays are based on traditional Rama legends and other tales. The shadow-play is generally believed to have originated in Java, but it entered northern Malaya by way of Siam and Cambodia, with elements taken from the culture of those countries, which appear both in the puppets and in the repertoire.[32] In southern Malaya, however, the shadow-play was a direct import from Java. The two different categories are referred to as '*wayang Siam*' and '*wayang Jawa*'.

In West Johor and in Selangor immigrants of Javanese descent performed the *wayang Jawa* under the patronage of princes and chiefs as an entertainment for the upper class. But by the end of the nineteenth century, there was only a handful remaining of the aristocratic patrons of this type of play, and lack of support sent it into a decline. The skill of the *dalang* was lost for lack of practice.[33]

The *wayang Siam* of Patani, Kelantan, Kedah, and some parts of Terengganu had a wider base since it was part of the popular culture of the *rakyat*. It had a vitality which has preserved it down to modern times. Yet in the course of time, there were significant changes in the arrangements for giving performances.

The *dalang* learnt his craft, including his repertoire, from an older, established practitioner. There was more to it than just practice; only a man with an aptitude could become proficient. Perhaps for that reason it was not a hereditary occupation passing from father to son. A would-be *dalang* was sometimes drawn into the profession by discovering, as a member of an audience, that it made a strong appeal to him. He went on to gain entry by becoming one of the instrumentalists who accompanied the *dalang* in his performance. If the pupil had talent, and the *dalang* was willing, he might become an apprentice to him. Yet it was more than just a training contract. There are elements of ritual in the performance, especially in the invocations and rites which begin the night's session. In the same tradition the initiation of a new *dalang* was marked by a kind of 'laying on of hands' (*peturun dalang*) in which the master invoked supernatural aid for the proper instruction of the pupil.[34]

In the nineteenth century, a *dalang* was invited to give a performance. On some domestic occasion such as a wedding or a feast for a rite of passage such as circumcision, a villager would engage a *dalang* to perform. So also an entire village might call him in. The promoter(s) paid the fee to the *dalang* and the audience could witness a 'free performance' (*main peri*). Perhaps patrons of this kind gradually became more difficult to find in sufficient numbers. At all events, the *dalang* became his own promoter; he set up an enclosure and charged individuals for admission to it. In a subtle way this changed the social ambience of the performance. It was still an entertainment with traditional and religious aspects, but it was now commercial entertainment and not part of a social event.[35] Under either arrangement the *dalang* earned a modest sum by his skill. In the heyday of the traditional *wayang kulit* as part of the social life of the community the *dalang* was a 'skilled puppeteer . . . revered and privileged [for] his dexterity, his memory and his versatile voice . . . word perfect and flawless in manipulation of his puppets.[36] His skill did not diminish with the change of role but he declined into a travelling showman.

The other 'traditional' Malay theatrical entertainment was the *ma'yong*, which had come into Malaya from Ligor in Siam some centuries ago.[37] In its original form in the states of the north-east of Malaya it was an aristocratic entertainment given by royal troupes to rulers and their palace circle. This type of *ma'yong* lasted into the early years of the twentieth century.[38] The performance was given in the royal hall (*balai*) with the members of the court sitting round the stage on three sides. There was no written script; the actors improvised in the context of traditional stories of adventure, interspersed with comic and musical interludes. Sheppard writes that 'the music which emerges from the *rebab* to accompany the song is an arabesque woven round a melody which is very seldom directly stated either instrumentally or vocally'. Until the Maha Menteri of Kelantan led the puritan reaction of the 1890s in Kelantan, the actresses wore only minimum clothing by Malay standards, i.e. a *sarung* tucked in under the armpits leaving the shoulders bare. The whole company were part of the household who had quarters at the back of the *istana* and were sometimes given rice-fields to till on the royal lands.[39]

The *ma'yong* which permeated through to the West Coast was essentially the same kind of performance, but it was given in a very different, more demotic milieu. Swettenham, writing in 1878, described it as 'a kind of theatrical performance, with some dancing and much so-called singing, the performers, as a rule, being a travelling company of three or four men and perhaps one woman, who make their living by their performances, and play either at the invitation of the *raja* in his own house or before the public on a stage erected in the middle of a street'.[40] There are two references to *ma'yong* performances in Perak villages in 1875 which imply that the audience was or included the *rakyat*.[41] To these villages the travelling players brought the tinsel glamour of the stage, a break in the humdrum routine of village life. Vaughan, writing in 1857, describes the *ma'yong* as 'exhibited by men and boys, the latter disguise themselves so successfully [as women] that Malay youths have been known to fall in love with them, forsake their *kampungs* and wander for days in the train of the actors'. It may have been tawdry, but there was a richness of aesthetic elements which explains the impact of the *ma'yong*. 'Music composed of drums and brass instruments accompany the performance,' continues Vaughan, 'the former are beaten incessantly and the latter are struck at intervals, the brass instruments are simple hollow utensils, but emit exceedingly pleasing sounds when struck. The actors dress in rich colours and resemble Hindu gods; red is the principal colour of the clothing, and the head-dresses and skirts are covered with gold and silver tinsel. The performance consists of all the actors moving about to the sound of music and contorting their bodies into a variety of postures far from pleasing; they do not speak in the dance but recitations take place during the evening's performance.'[42]

The colour and music made less appeal to a European observer, who was attuned to Western entertainment. When Weld, visiting Perak, was entertained to a *ma'yong*, he was bored with 'dancing girls, though they could hardly be said to dance. The principal actors were a girl and her husband, who kept up a kind of dialogue—he being a clown and rather funny. It was eminently decorous and rather slow, and we all got rather sleepy.'[43] Skeat was equally unenthusiastic about the performance which his host arranged for him in Kelantan in 1899. In this case all the roles, except those of two clowns, were taken by women. The plot was a conventional story, using the same legends as the shadow-play. A magic prince (*raja sakti*) pursued a golden roe-deer, who was a princess in disguise. The performance was interrupted by a heavy downpour of rain. 'The *rebab* player was instructed to hand over his instrument to another player (*gilir rebab*) to stop the rain and it did after an uncomfortable interval.' Skeat also describes the costumes—'the two clowns wore long white trousers, with a cloth girt about their waists. The women who were acting mens' [*sic*] parts wore a sarong (extending halfway down the calf of the leg) over long trousers, like those of the clowns. Above they had a cloth swathed tightly about their breasts, and over it a short, loose jacket. A head-cloth, a *keris* (worn under the sarong but with the ivory hilt exposed) and a shoulder-cloth (*tetampan*) completed their attire.'[44]

By this time the *ma'yong*, as popular entertainment, was becoming rather bedraggled and down-at-heel, though still a social occasion for the audience. A performance was given in Kuala Lumpur in October 1894 in a Malay house near the railway station. 'The stage was mud floor, the players sat or lounged on the ground within the barricade about 12 feet square in the middle of the house, the barricade bring surrounded outside by chairs and benches, which were occupied by audience. There were about fourteen male and three female performers.' The audience of about 150 filled the house. They came 'in their very best clothes' and 'one side of the house was reserved for Malay ladies'.[45]

The cast took stock parts—a prince (*pa'yong*), a clown (*peran*), a princess (*ma'yong* or *puteri*) and her duenna (*mek sni* or *ma'inang*).[46] In the rather shabby company which appeared in Kuala Lumpur in 1894 some of the male actors 'wore vests and some didn't but none wore coats . . . there was the heavy father, the light comedian, and the "*pawang*" who seemed to be the leading actor . . . melodrama, comedy and burlesque followed each other in quick succession; the greatest hit of the evening was when two of the actors put on masks and gave a burlesque which might have been entitled "playing at being a *raja*!" The heavy lady talked at intervals, filling up her time eating *sirih* . . . the other two ladies came down a ladder from the loft clad in gorgeous apparel, belted with belts of silver buckled with gold and powdered thickly all over the head. Then having placed glistening spikes upon their fingers they sang and moved about in what the Malays consider graceful rhythm.' The troupe was a very mixed bag—one was from Melaka and another from Java—but in keeping with fashion they proclaimed themselves a Kelantan company, with one actress from Patani.[47]

There was a distinct sub-variety of the *ma'yong* called the *menora* which had a Thai cast and performed plays about King Phor[illegible].[48]

The *ma'yong*, like the shadow-play, began with ritual invocations 'to drive away evil spirits'.[49] It straddled uneasily between 'eminently decorous' traditional entertainment, and the vulgarity which the Hollywood film was soon to bring to Malaya. As related in Chapter 3, even Sultan Zainal Abidin III of Terengganu was taken to see a film in Singapore in 1912—though what he saw and whether he liked it we do not know.[50] The *ma'yong* was probably destined to disappear under the impact of the cinema. But between them came another form of Malay entertainment, the *bangsawan*. Indeed the rather unsympathetic account of the 1894 *ma'yong* in Kuala Lumpur suggests that it had begun to move towards the broad humour of the *bangsawan*.

For a time the *bangsawan* was 'the most popular form of theatrical entertainment in the country'.[51] It was of Indian origin, though its repertoire included much adapted versions of the plots of *Hamlet*, *Romeo and Juliet*, *Ali Baba* and *Genevieve of Brabant*. Rather like an English traditional pantomime, the actors, performing within the loose context of these stories, made topical allusions and offered clever mimicry of stock Malayan stereotypes of the period.

The success of the *bangsawan* at the turn of the century was due to the superior quality of one company named after its proprietor, the '*wayang Kassim*'. Kassim must have been a gifted actor-manager who 'attracted excellent comedians, encouraged them to jest on the topics of the day, improved the scenery and accessories, and chose his actresses with a keen eye for beauty'.[52] Although the success of one manager is by its nature ephemeral, the *bangsawan* survived the competition of the cinema and lasted, as popular entertainment, into the 1920s.[53] Richard Sidney's account of a performance of *Hamlet*, which he saw in 1923, probably gives an exact enough picture of the essential nature of the *bangsawan* in earlier years. Sidney describes the opening scene on the battlements of Elsinore as follows: 'We do not have to wait for the humour until the gravediggers' scene, for it begins as soon as the first clown (the sentry) meets the ghost! . . . a telephone has been introduced into the castle grounds at Elsinore . . . by means of which the sentry tries his best to call up the rest of the guard. The ghost, however, will stand none of this nonsense, and continually frightens the sentry, so much so that he falls down on the stage, kicking up his legs in the air. (Loud laughter and cheers from the audience).' Sidney noted that 'the dresses must have cost a great deal of money—many being of gorgeous velvet, and almost too hot to think about so far as this climate is concerned. The make-up is patchy . . . I once noticed a girl who was made up with a beautiful pink and white face but who still had black legs . . . characters announce what they are going to do and who they are; and very often they will sing a song in Malay but with the words set to old English or American popular songs.'[54]

In spite of it broad humour and alien origin, the *bangsawan* met with acceptance in aristocratic circles. In the course of the 1903 durbar of Malay rulers in Kuala Lumpur, Kassim's *wayang* troupe performed *Hamlet* or *Macbeth* (there was some doubt as to which it was) for the guests at an evening levee. A couple of days later the same company enlivened a 'water fete' in the Lake Gardens with its version of 'Bluebeard'. This included a Malay version of the drawing-room song 'And Her Golden Hair'. Three months later, Malay high society gathered again in Kuala Lumpur for the installation (at Klang) of Sultan Sulaiman. Kassim's *wayang* company was performing in Campbell Street on the edge of the newly established Malay settlement at Kampung Bharu. There is a report (of some disorder among the audience at a performance) which mentions incidentally that the Raja Muda of Kedah and his party were in the front row of seats.[55]

The other attraction which drew the crowds at this time was the travelling circus, an entirely imported entertainment. On 8 April 1891, for example, at Klang 'a circus company with dogs, monkeys and horses gave a very good performance and afforded great amusement to the people. Their Highnesses the Raja Muda and Tunku Dia Udin with their families, and a large crowd of natives attended and to the latter it will no doubt form the subject of talk for the rest of their lives.'[56] One may infer from the final comment that a circus was a novelty at this time.

The entertainment known as the *boria* had its own peculiar history and was really confined to Penang.[57] In the early days of the British presence in Penang, the local garrison consisted of detachments of Indian regiments sent across by the East India Company to protect their dependency. Indian Muslims from the garrison performed as minstrels in fancy dress during the month of Muharam. They visited the houses of prominent citizens to sing topical songs and present sketches. In their original form in India, these had been performances to celebrate the memories of Hassan and Hussein, the grandsons of the Prophet Mohamed, but that aspect did not appear in their presentation in Penang.

The *boria*, as a form of commentary on topical events, proved versatile, like the *ma'yong*. When Skeat returned from his arduous attempt to ascend Gunung Tahan, 'our Malays recited a *boria*, a descriptive poem consisting of numerous stanzas chanted by the author, with a chorus following each stanza. The poem gave an account of the travels of the expedition from its beginning, together with comments, polite but evidently humorous, on the leaders of the party.'[58]

Dancing, singing and drama, with orchestral accompaniment or songs, were an incidental means of giving to the audience the pleasure of listening to music of one kind or another. There is much evidence of Malay appreciation of music for its own sake. An accompaniment to a dance or other activity was often dominated by rhythm, produced by drums or other percussion instruments. In some instances, however, harmony was the key to the aesthetic pleasure of the performance—'the strangely languid music of the Malays, which surges forward, falters as if too tired to continue, picks up again, and so on to the last dying cadence, whilst the voice of the singer follows the same pattern, starting on a certain note, then falling a tone or a half or quarter tone as if too tired to maintain the original note, or perhaps with a desperate effort actually rising a tone before wearily dying away again'.[59] This account of modern Malay film music may over-emphasize its languid effect, but it well describes the attraction of the harmony to the European as much as the Malay ear.

The harmonic structure of Malay music is so much akin to that of Europe that the Malays readily adopted foreign tunes. Sidney, whose account of the *bangsawan* has been quoted above, says that many of the tunes used for the songs were taken from musical comedies of the early twentieth century such as 'The Belle of New York'.[60] Another observer, too, bears testimony to Malay pleasure in singing, relating that Malay seamen 'in the evening gather around one of their number who is beating a drum or tambourine and singing some martial or amorous song or recitation in the chorus of which they all join with the greatest glee and animation'.[61]

Music was often the accompaniment to some other activity—'a boat's crew will pull seventy miles, with scarcely any cessation, if allowed to sing, and the notes of a fiddle will keep Malay lascars at work for several days and nights without murmur'.[62] Vaughan, from whom that quotation comes, is one of the best sources on Malay music-making. 'The Malays are exceedingly fond of music and many have acquired a tolerable knowledge of the violin and they play their national tunes and many European airs correctly; the drum appears to be the only native instrument, and for hours will a party of Malays amuse themselves by reciting verses accompanied by its monotonous tones. On the violin they will execute by ear all their own tunes and English jigs and Portuguese fandangos and will dance to the tunes with as much spirit as an Englishman at a fair; reels and jigs they manage well and will go through the figures of a quadrille tolerably.' Vaughan adds at this point, however, that his comments relate more to the Malays of the Straits ports than to 'the stolid country Malays'. He continues—'they have numerous songs called *lagu*, sung to different airs, in which each verse is concluded by a chorus . . . the subject always has some reference to passing events, and each verse is sung by a different person, which is followed by a chorus . . . the airs are plaintive and consist of numerous semitones . . . at festivals the drums and cymbals are the usual instruments employed, shrill pipes resembling the clarinet are introduced but they are always played by natives of India . . . Malayan tunes are capable of being easily adapted to European music'.

Vaughan is probably not correct when he implies that the violin was not a 'native instrument'. The Malay word '*biola*' is indeed of Portuguese origin though it had been used in Malay contexts for centuries.[63] The Malay stringed instrument played with a bow was the *rebab*, to which Skeat refers as a 'spike-fiddle'; it was used at an entertainment which he attended in Kelantan in 1899.[64] There is also a reference in 1892 from Selangor to a 'Malay type of violin—the bridge and head of the instrument being carved in the orthodox fashion . . . the strings were nothing but fishing-line and the bow simply knitting cotton; it emitted some very satisfactory sounds'.[65] The *rebab* was not one of the instruments of the traditional royal band (*nobat*) but it was the mainstay of the orchestra which accompanied a *ma'yong* performance. Some Malay aristocrats, notably Sultan Ahmad Tajuddin II of Kedah, learnt to play the European violin.[66]

There was music in the background of Malay life in many contexts besides entertainment. Thus, in Perak in the 1860s, 'there was a Terengganu man, who had such a sweet voice, that when he read the *Kuran* all who heard him were charmed with it'.[67] Kite flying was a favourite Malay pastime, and 'many of the kites had instruments attached to them that hummed a loud tone when acted upon by the air'.[68] It was also a Malay practice in the mid-nineteenth century to suspend long bamboos (*buluh ribut* or *buluh perindu*) in the jungle near their villages. These tubes were 30–40 feet long, perforated by holes and suspended vertically. They made flute-like noises when the wind blew. Logan came across these instruments while visiting Naning in rural Melaka.[69] Vaughan says that 'when a number of such contrivances are erected of different sizes they produce a chord of musical noises nearly perfect; their taste and ear is so correct that discordant notes are seldom heard'.[70] These bamboo pipes may have been set up for magical purposes—to charm or divert the spirits of the jungle. The striking aspect of the practice is the exactness of Malay musicianship in their use.[71]

Like musical bamboos, kites may have had some ritual significance in their origin. Wilkinson had some doubts whether the kite was an indigenous Malay artefact since in his time the sail of the kite was made of paper. It may be, however, that the earliest Malay kites were made with broad leaves. Whatever their origin, kite flying was a popular pastime among Malays in the nineteenth century. 'Now was the season for flying paper kites,' wrote Thomson, 'a pastime in which both old and young engage—in fact an old Malay is a very child in this respect. Hundreds of kites of various forms, from the serpent to the turtle, were sporting in the air.' Much later, when Florence Caddy was at Muar in 1889, she wrote 'nearer me is a girl at play, wearing a white jacket, red cap and a long sarong. I thought she was dancing by the way she waved her arms; she is flying her kite.' Again, Skeat in Perlis in 1900 saw men and boys flying kites: 'in one field the end of the kite string had been made fast to a bent-down rice-stalk so that the kite flew itself, kept steady, without the least attention, by the regularity of the monsoon wind'.[72]

Malay artistry developed the kite (*layang-layang*) into a splendid and ingenious thing. The largest were 6 feet high and 7 feet across. The different shapes were given fanciful names—'fighting dragon' (*naga berjuang*), 'crescent' (*sahari bulan*), 'eagle' (*rajawali*), and 'bird of paradise' (*cenderawasih*). There was much skill in the design. 'The peculiarity of the Malay kite is that it presents a convex instead of a concave surface to the wind, and no tail is required, the kite being steadied by means of a beak which projects forward at the top of the framework.' Skeat also mentions a thin strip of bamboo (*dengung*) which 'hums loudly in the wind'. The season of flying of kites was the hot, dry spell following the rice harvest; the empty fields offered an open space and there was often a steady wind. Apart from these practical considerations it is possible that originally kites were flown as a magical rite in association with the ripening of the padi. However, in Skeat's time kite flying was essentially a recreation and 'grown-ups will fly them with quite as much zest as children'.[73]

Many of the indoor games played by Malays were of foreign origin. Wilkinson mentions rolling marbles (*main guli*), chess (*main catur*), which he thought had come to Malaya from India, draughts, whose Dutch origin is disclosed in the Malay name of *main dam*, backgammon—another Indian import and a game played only by women—*main cuki*—a game played like draughts on a board marked with 120 positions and probably imported from Java—and *main congkak*, an Acehnese game played with cowrie-shells on a boat-shaped board.[74]

In Malay chess 'the chessmen are seldom carved figures but are mere draughtsmen with Arabic characters, representing the various classes, cut on them.'[75] European enthusiasts found no difficulty in attracting Malay chess-players to their contests; one may assume that some Malays at least were addicts. In 1894 the district officer at Kuala Kangsar organized an open-air game of chess, using Malays as pieces to stand on a chess-board marked out on his lawn. He and his assistant matched themselves against two leading Perak chiefs, the Temenggong and the Seri Adika Raja. This contest drew an audience of several hundred spectators who watched attentively as the game took its slow course over a period of three hours, but whether they understood the moves or came to witness the curious activities of the powers that be is not recorded.[76] Two years later, a more conventional chess tournament at Kuala Kangsar attracted 32 entries, who were divided into two classes—'those who considered themselves adepts and those who did not'. The district officer notes that 'it was surprising the amount of interest the Malays all over the district took in it'. The Seri Adika Raja took first place in the master class. In the novices' competition two small boys from Kota Lama emerged as winners, 'beating several elderly Malays, who were very much chaffed'.[77]

Chess was a game of skill which did not attract side-bets on the outcome. One of the attractions of the traditional sport of cock-fighting was the opportunity it afforded of gambling on the result. Betting on these contests was an ancient practice to which customary rules could apply. In 1830, for example, the paramount ruler of Negeri Sembilan demanded payment of a 2½ per cent tax on the sums which the Datuk Klana of Sungei Ujong had won from betting on cock-fights at the royal capital. 'This was too much for the very small reserve of patience possessed by Datuk Klana Kawal' and the ensuing dispute over the tax led to the downfall of the ruler. In later years one of the reasons why orthodox Islamic opinion disapproved of cock-fighting was the betting associated with it.[78]

As a general rule, the Malays were not addicted to games of chance played mainly for the winnings which they produced.[79] But there was a minority who played at cards, using either European or Chinese packs of cards. These were pure games of chance. Games such as bridge, or even whist, in which there was a degree of skill to affect the outcome, were not popular; 'patience' was unknown.[80] Gambling was not socially respectable. When Raja Bot, a pillar of the Selangor establishment—a member of the state council and one of the ruler's advisers—could not resist the urge, he slipped away to Singapore to play the Chinese game of chance known as *chap ji kee*. At his death in 1916, he owed about $9,000, due mainly to betting losses.[81]

Social disapproval was not a sufficient deterrent. The temptation was close at hand, since the Chinese were inveterate gamblers for whom their employers provided the facilities, at a profit to themselves. In pre-colonial days, for example, Old Market Square in Kuala Lumpur held 'a huge gambling booth of jungle rollers roofed with *ataps* in which literally all day and all night, gambling is pursued by a crowd of often excited Chinese and Malays'.[82] In Perak, as in Selangor, no attempt was made to exclude Malays from these gambling centres.[83] The colonial regime permitted the system to continue since it had no means of suppressing it in the Chinese mining centres, and it was an important source of state revenue.[84] The state councils were later much concerned at the growing problem of Malay gambling and secured a ban on the admission of Malays to licensed gambling-houses.[85] It was difficult to enforce but it had some effect. When the Colonial Office ruled that licensed 'gambling farms' must end since it was improper for colonial governments to obtain revenue in this way, Sultan Idris was moved to make one of his very rare protests. Without the system of licensing and supervision, it would be impossible to prevent Malays from taking part in Chinese gambling, which would inevitably continue, however unlawful. In the ruler's view this was 'a matter purely affecting Asiatics and internal policy' and it was contrary to the spirit of the Pangkor Treaty that the protecting power should overrule a state council on such a matter.[86]

The short-lived Islamic 'revival' in Kedah in 1908 led the British

Vice-Consul to identify gambling and opium-smoking as 'profitable vices' provided for the amusement of 'influential Malays'.[87] In 1913 the Kedah State Council was discussing a proposal to ban the import of playing cards owing to 'the natural tendency of people to gamble'.[88] The Perlis State Council, too, was moved to discuss the prevalence of gambling among Malay women, especially members of the royal family (*kaum raja*).[89] In Kelantan there was betting on the bullfights which were a feature of that state. At the other end of the Peninsula and twenty years earlier, Florence Caddy found that Johor Bahru 'is considered an Asiatic Monte Carlo' with Chinese gambling-houses to which the ruler took his European house guests for an evening's entertainment.[90] Gambling was a minor but intractable problem.

Malays traditionally hunted or trapped wild animals for food or, in cases such as wild elephant, for profit, or, in the case of crocodiles, to eliminate a danger to themselves. It could be dangerous and it always required much skill. George Maxwell and other European writers tell stories of hunting, with Malay parties, rhinoceros, deer, *seladang*, crocodile, tapir, wild goat, elephant and tiger, as well as several forms of fish drive.[91] Trapping and domestication of wild elephants has been described in a previous chapter.[92] The Malays undoubtedly enjoyed the excitement, the exercise of skill and the concerted effort of hunting animals, but it was left to the Europeans to make it into a sport or entertainment for its own sake.

As accurate firearms became available to them, Malay hunters began to use them to escape the obvious dangers of close encounters using spears, etc. Yet the new weapons brought a different kind of danger. 'The Malays are very careless with firearms at any time, but particularly so when they are hunting and excited.' This comment relates to an account of the accidental shooting of one member of a hunting party by another. The Malay who had fired the shot explained that his companion 'had the appearance of a large stag, of which he could distinguish quite clearly both the hide and the antlers, and it was not until the latter fell wounded that he assumed his natural form'.[93]

As the jungle became safer and less filled with unknown terrors, the Perak aristocracy could indulge a taste for picnics. Swettenham gives a long account of such an expedition by river barge to dig for turtles' eggs or to net fish, with an interlude for discreet bathing in the river. 'The ladies are in their smartest garments and wear their costliest jewels . . . the rowers seize their paddles and with beat of gong and the musical notes of the silver *serunai*, with jest and laughter, pennons waving . . . the picturesque flotilla glides on its course down the long sunny reach.'[94] The special recreation of the Kuala Kangsar court circle was the rock-slide (*menggeluncur*) down into a pool below. The entertainment of the visitors to the first durbar of FMS rulers at Kuala Kangsar in 1897 included 'an extremely successful picnic' at the rock-slide; 'nearly all the chiefs present joined in sliding down the rock and seemed to immensely enjoy an entertainment that was quite novel to the visitors'.[95]

The lavishness of these occasions was made possible by the new affluence of royal courts under the colonial regime. As related in Chapter 2, when Raja Muda Yusuf received Weld he came with elephants 'most gorgeously and artistically decorated and caparisoned in gold and embroidery and silk and flowers'.[96] But this was an elaboration of an existing taste for movement, colour and a throng of people, which lay deep in Malay culture. In the hard times of 1877 in Perak, Raja Muda Yusuf and other notables came to welcome Hugh Low and with 'a following of about 400 people marched along the bank on the opposite side in procession with flags and music'.[97]

This kind of recreation was not confined to Perak. In Kelantan, too, there is a 'season when everyone who is anyone goes down to the mouth of the river, camps on the great stretches of sand, which divide the fresh waters of the river from the salt waters of the sea, and there they disport themselves after their own fashion . . . sea-bathing, boat-sailing, fish-catching, and general junketing'.[98] Graham, too, noted that 'the people are expert boatmen, and many large racing canoes and crews are kept by the aristocracy. They occasionally compete with each other at festivals.'[99]

Only a small number of Malays went as far afield as Europe. Some, like the Seri Adika Raja, disliked the experience cordially. For many, however, it was an enjoyable adventure in which they put their existing accomplishments to new uses and learnt some new ones. Arthur Keyser took his two Malay servants to England when he went on leave in the 1890s. 'On weekends the pair in white clothes with yellow turbans and yellow *sarungs* round their waists would meet me at Maidenhead and paddle side by side in a punt. . . . At Henley they guided their boat in and out of the crowd as if we had a regatta at Jelebu every day.' On a later leave he spent Christmas at Wilton, one of the English stately homes, and Yusuf 'was accorded the honour of opening the Servants Ball as the partner of our gracious hostess in the Lancers. "I cannot dance the Lancers," he said, "but I will try", and under kind guidance he went through the performance with credit. After we left he wrote to the housekeeper and expressed his fear that he would never meet his kind friends again in this world, but hoped to do so in the next.'[100] In socially less demanding circumstances the two Malays 'passed many happy hours on their bicycles in Battersea Park'.[101]

In Malaya itself, English festive occasions such as a district agricultural show took root in Malay life, after a period of trial. In 1895, 10,000 people came to the Krian and Selama agricultural show. The exhibits included padi, vegetables and fruit, coffee, palm sugar, pepper and spices, needlework, *atap*, fishing and agricultural implements. Only the poultry and livestock exhibits were poor and scanty.[102]

There were quieter and more solitary amusements as well. Braddell saw a Malay boy 'playing bubbles' using a padi straw to suck up a gum solution from a half coconut shell.[103] Ibrahim Munshi on his travels walked along a beach 'collecting sea-shells which were of attractive appearance and various types'. On another occasion he writes that 'I had relieved my weariness by picking various orchids; I had a basketful, which my servant carried. I eventually managed to take them back to my house in Teluk Belanga.'[104]

Above all else 'the Malays', said Vaughan, 'have a very pleasant way of whiling away an hour by relating stories to each other'.[105] Ibrahim Munshi tells of an evening when the party listened to music and singing; 'When we were tired of that Engku Abdul Rahman would call for the "treasury of tales", and he would come forward clearing his throat and tell various stories.'[106] When W. E. Maxwell made his long journey overland from Province Wellesley to Patani his Malay companions 'enlivened the evening by relating all sorts of adventures, the point of the stories being generally the perfidy of the Perak Malays, or the iniquity of the Malay *rajas*'.[107] When Keyser returned with his Malay servants from leave in England, 'Salleh's adventures lost nothing in the telling when we got back, and I often, when supposed to be asleep in the hut constructed for me in the jungle, listened to the stories told to an admiring audience round the camp fire'.[108]

There were also professional story-tellers who recited Malay traditional tales 'intoning the words in a monotonous chant as if [they] were reading aloud from a book'.[109] This was a stylized presentation, sometimes with musical accompaniment, of a performer's stock of tales. It was a traditional craft which, like the shadow-play, had a ritual opening ceremony. The story-teller did not memorize the exact text of material but told the story time and again, finding his own words on each occasion for the familiar material. He had usually acquired his repertoire and his skill from the instruction given by a story-teller of a previous generation, to whom he was related or had been apprenticed. The degree of stylization of language and presentation varied with the professional standing and expertise of the individual performer. In some cases he followed a regular occupation and travelled round the towns and villages as a professional. In others, a noted and respected village amateur gave an occasional performance to a local audience.[110]

Europeans usually encountered a story-teller at the house of a ruler or chief whom they were visiting. When, for example, George Maxwell stayed with the ruler of Setul, in southern Siam, in 1889, 'after dinner two reciters or story-tellers were introduced for our amusement'.[111] They were sometimes known as '*penglipur lara*'—literally, 'those who sweep away care'—but Wilkinson translates it as 'wandering rhapsodist'.[112] W. E. Maxwell said that they 'wandered like minstrels among Malay villages as did Homer among the Greek cities'.[113] It kept the Malay classics alive in a society where few could read. In the 1830s Newbold found that the *Hikayat Hang Tuah* 'is still in much esteem with the Malays who delight in hearing recited the exploits of their celebrated [hero]'.[114] However, the repertoire was much wider than the classics of Malay literature. Clifford wrote of Pahang in the 1890s that the story-tellers 'learn by rote some old world tale . . . and they wander from village to village, singing it for pay to the unlettered people, to whom these songs and stories represent the only literature which comes within their experience'.[115]

As Malay society moved into a new age it had less need of a story-teller. Clifford called them 'a class of men which is fast dying out in the Peninsula' and Wilkinson, writing a generation later, said that 'the modern Malay reads books where his ancestors listened to rhapsodists'. However, he continues that 'present day education rarely carries a native boy to the point at which reading becomes a pleasure'. Another reason for the disappearance of the story-teller was that 'it is very doubtful whether the ancient minstrels ever earned enough money to pay their way. A hearty welcome and a good dinner represented the most they could expect for their services.'[116]

Although the story-teller spoke at a rapid pace, he told his story with sufficient deliberation to enable his audience to keep up with the narrative as it unfolded. Stock phrases and padding help the performer himself to recollect what comes next and move on without hesitation. For this reason, efforts to record in writing what was said are self-defeating. Either the *verbatim* text in print seems diffuse—as it communicates to the eye, not the ear—or the recorder finds it necessary to edit the text so that it reads as prose.[117]

An earlier chapter on education has made the point that the habit of reading as a recreation necessarily awaited the time when reading matter, the Malay newspaper and the printed book, became readily available in the twentieth century.[118] Once the habit had gained hold, the reader tended to be omnivorous. Dr Mohamed Said, writing of the period around 1920, tells of a fellow schoolboy at the Malay College who was introduced to English literature by reading Walter Scott's *Quentin Durward* as a set book in Standard VII. Then he became an 'avid reader of Sexton Blake detective stories, which were then sold at Seremban railway station bookstall'. He also bought at auctions 'sloppy sentimental love stories' by English novelists and political essays by educated Indians.[119]

Another product of the educational system was an awareness of history in a new way. The traditional culture—the plays, the recitations, the singing, the great public ceremonies—was an invocation of the past as an ancient and almost mythical period. It has been suggested that Malay awareness of 'the meaning of history as distinct from legend' began with the publication in 1921 of a history by Winstedt *written in Malay*.[120] However, one may respectfully doubt whether this claim is justified. Serious Malay history of the recent past is at least as old as the *Tuhfat al-Nafis*, written in the late 1860s.[121] A number of state chronicles of individual states, such as Kedah, Selangor and Johor, were written early in this century. These were both the product and the cause of the awakening of Malay interest in their own history.[122]

There are other signs of the same trend. Swettenham wrote in 1890: 'the other day a Malay lady from Kuala Kangsar told me she was going to see the [Taiping] Museum for the third time'.[123] He goes on to say that, 'on average, about 150 people visited the museum each day and that few of them were Europeans'. Wilkinson, too, refers to 'a few Malay dilettanti . . . who are devoted to hobbies like local customary law or ceremonial or history or folklore'.[124] An earlier chapter has mentioned the growing preoccupation of Malay rulers and their courts with the revival of ancient ceremonies.[125]

In the first instance, this trend appeared mainly among the upper class of Malay society, whose forebears had made the history of their time, and among the small but influential minority of teachers, journalists and others whose professional work drew them to look at the history of their country. Wilkinson said that 'native scholars are few' and that they tend to compose 'pedantic poetry lamenting the dismal doom of persons condemned to live like orphaned strangers in the midst of an uncongenial world'.[126] It is probable that the widening horizons and intellectual stimulus of closer acquaintance with Islam and the Middle East had a parallel effect.

By the end of the nineteenth century the Malay upper class and intelligentsia had begun to feel a sense of unease at the situation in which they found themselves in their own Malay states. The European justification for taking control into their own hands was the alleged incapacity to provide good government and economic progress of the Malays during the pre-colonial period. But was this a true reading of the events of the recent past? A closer study of history might give the answer.

The changing Malay taste in amusements and recreations is not the main highway into an understanding of themes of that serious kind. Nevertheless, it opens up some paths through which one can learn something more of Malay society of this period.[127]

1. SSD 29 July 1883.

2. See pp. 238 and 83 above.

3. A. B. Rathborne, *Camping and Tramping in Malaya: Fifteen Years' Pioneering in the Native States of the Malay Peninsula*, London, Swan Sonnenschein, 1898, reprinted Singapore, Oxford University Press, 1984, p. 91. *Malay Mail*, 14 April and 30 June 1902, cited at p. 81 above.

4. R. J. Wilkinson, 'Malay Amusements', *Papers on Malay Subjects, Life and Customs*, Part 3, 1910 (hereafter cited as 'Malay Amusements'), p. 24. Wilkinson's essay and Mubin Sheppard, *Taman Indera: Malay Decorative Arts and Pastimes*, Kuala Lumpur, Oxford University Press, 1972, reprinted as *A Royal Pleasure Ground*, Singapore, Oxford University Press, 1986, are invaluable sources on the main themes of this chapter.

5. F. A. Swettenham, *British Malaya: An Account of the Origin and Progress of British Influence in Malaya*, London, John Lane Bodley Head, 1907 (revised editions 1929 and 1948, London, Allen & Unwin), p. 149. Swettenham is here referring to 'festal occasions' such as 'a wedding, ear-piercing, the appointment of officers by the Sultan . . . it is the invariable practice to give great entertainments to large numbers of people'.

6. See p. 320 above. The *bersanding*, at which the bride and groom are seated side by side in the public view, is usually the social climax of the traditional Malay wedding ceremony.

7. See p. 282 above.

8. H. C. Clifford, 'Report: Expedition to Trengganu and Kelantan', *JMBRAS*, 34(1), 1961 (originally printed for Colonial Office use in 1895; and reprinted Kuala Lumpur, Government Press, 1936), p. 117; *Studies in Brown Humanity being Scrawls and Smudges in Sepia, White and Yellow*, London, Grant Richards, 1898, p. 24. On the Maha Menteri see p. 289 above.

9. H. C. Clifford, *In Court and Kampong, being Tales and Sketches of Native Life in the Malay Peninsula*, London, Grant Richards, 1897 (2nd ed. with autobiographical preface, London, Richards Press, 1927), p. 48.

10. Wilkinson, 'Malay Amusements', p. 66.

11. T. J. Newbold, *Political and Statistical Account of the British Settlements ... with a History of the Malayan States on the Peninsula in the Straits of Malacca*, 2 vols., London, Murray, 1839, reprinted as *British Settlements in the Straits of Malacca*, Kuala Lumpur, Oxford University Press, 1971, Vol. 2, p. 182.

12. Clifford, *In Court and Kampong*, pp. 48–50; Newbold, op. cit.; J. D. Vaughan, 'Notes on the Malays of Pinang and Province Wellesley', *JIA*, n.s., 2, 1857, p. 162; W. Cameron, 'On the Patani', *JSBRAS*, 11, 1883, p. 337; Rathborne, op. cit., p. 307; P. Favre, *An Account of the Wild Tribes Inhabiting the Malayan Peninsula, Sumatra and a Few Neighbouring Islands*, Paris, Imperial Printing Office, 1865, including a reprint of 'A Journey in the Menangkabaw States of the Malay Peninsula', *JIA*, 3, 1849, p. 161; J. F. A. McNair, *Perak and the Malays: Sarong and Keris*, London, Tinsley Bros., 1878, reprinted Kuala Lumpur, Oxford University Press, 1972, p. 265. There are incidental references to cock-fighting in J. W. W. Birch, *The Journals of J. W. W. Birch First British Resident to Perak 1874–1875* (hereafter cited as *Birch Journal*), edited by P. L. Burns, Kuala Lumpur, Oxford University Press, 1976, p. 304; F. A. Swettenham, *Sir Frank Swettenham's Malayan Journals 1874–1876* (hereafter cited as *Swettenham Journal*), edited by P. L. Burns and C. D. Cowan, Kuala Lumpur, Oxford University Press, 1975, pp. 191, 268 and 302; Swettenham, *British Malaya*, pp. 136, 139 and 314; and *Also and Perhaps*, London, John Lane Bodley Head, 1912, pp. 267–8; PCE evidence CO 273/86, pp. 453, 499 and 540, CO 273/88, pp. 29 and 80.

13. Wilkinson, 'Malay Amusements', p. 69. There were also fights, arranged as entertainment, between bulls or buffaloes, and between a buffalo and a tiger. C. C. Brown, 'Kelantan Bull-fighting', *JMBRAS*, 6(1), 1928; W. W. Skeat and F. F. Laidlaw, 'The Cambridge University Expedition to Parts of the Malay Peninsula 1899–1900: Personal Accounts', *JMBRAS*, 26(4), 1953, pp. 117–18; J. Low, *A Dissertation on the Soil and Agriculture of the British Settlement of Penang or Prince of Wales Island in the Straits of Malacca including Province Wellesley on the Malayan Peninsula ..., with ... Incidental Observations, etc.*, Singapore, Singapore Free Press, 1836, reprinted as *The British Settlement at Penang*, Singapore, Oxford University Press, 1972, p. 106; H. M. Tomlinson, *Tidemarks: Some Records of a Journey to ... the Forest of Malaya*, London, Cassell, 1924, pp. 244–6. European observers found fights between buffaloes or bulls rather tame affairs—though it seems that the Malay spectators were often wildly excited (Skeat and Laidlaw, op. cit., p. 117).

A duel between a buffalo and a tiger was a more serious matter though the outcome was not in doubt: the buffalo gored the tiger to death on its horns. Such contests are described in F. A. Swettenham, *Footprints in Malaya*, London, Hutchinson, 1942, p. 18; J. Low, *Dissertation*, p. 106; McNair, op. cit., p. 268; and H. C. Clifford, *Malayan Monochromes*, New York, Dutton, 1913, pp. 305–7. Both Swettenham and McNair recount fights organized by the ruler of Johor, on two different occasions, for the entertainment of visiting European royalty. McNair comments that 'this was one of the rare exhibitions of the kind . . . rapidly dying out before the advance of European civilisation'.

14. Wilkinson, 'Malay Amusements', p. 28. Clifford to the same effect—'inane sword dances which are so dear to the Malays' (*In Court and Kampong*, p. 127).

15. *Malay Mail*, 30 June 1902—see p. 83 above. Even more exciting was a duel in real earnest such as Clifford describes in *Malayan Monochromes*, pp. 289–91. But a mere 'imitation war dance' could get out of hand if the opponents became 'warm with excitement' so that third parties had to separate them before serious harm was done (McNair, op. cit., p. 263).

What is generally called '*main silat*' perhaps needs analysis. In the 1932 edition of his dictionary, but not in the original 1901 edition, Wilkinson defines '*main silat*' as 'a fencing-dance without weapons . . . if weapons are held in the hand the dance is known as *main pencak*' (R. J. Wilkinson, *A Malay–English Dictionary*, 2 parts, Singapore, Kelly & Walsh, 1901 (revised as *A Malay–English Dictionary (Romanised)*, 2 parts, Mytilene, Salavopoulos & Kinderlis, 1932), Part 2, p. 273). Winstedt recognizes the distinction but reverses the terms by defining '*main pencak*' as 'a sword-dance, especially unarmed' (R. O. Winstedt, *An Unabridged Malay–English Dictionary*, Singapore, Kelly & Walsh, 1954, p. 245).

Sheppard mentions a third category, i.e. 'unarmed combat', called '*main silat buah*' (Sheppard, *Taman Indera*, p. 140). See also Mubin Sheppard, 'Main Gayong', *Straits Times Annual*, 1971.

The following distinctions may be over-elaborate. In particular what Skeat witnessed in Patani in 1899 seems to have been an introductory mime leading to an unarmed combat—see below. But one can distinguish: (1) a real duel—Clifford, *Malayan Monochromes*, (2) a mock duel with weapons as demonstrated by Raja Mahmud in 1902, (3) unarmed combat in a stylized form—'when they began to box in earnest . . . they could hit pretty hard' (Skeat and Laidlaw, op. cit., p. 76), and (4) pure mime—'one would suggest the stab of a poniard (*badik*) by pointing downwards with his outstretched fore-finger. The other in reply would go through the motion of warding it off' (ibid.).

The author is much indebted to Dr Sheppard for information and comment in correspondence but any imperfections of this analysis should be laid at his own door. Sheppard, *Taman Indera*, provides a fascinating account of the art of *main silat*, illustrated with diagrams. He also recounts two celebrated encounters at Kota Bharu in 19■0 and at Pekan *c.*1905 as related by Malay informants. The first ended with general fighting among the spectators, one of whom drew a loaded revolver (ibid., p. 143).

Wilkinson is probably right in attributing the decline of Malay interest in *main silat*, until revived in modern times, to the abandonment of the wearing of weapons. The finer points of fencing were no longer of practical use (Wilkinson, 'Malay Amusements', p. 28). See p. 238 above on carrying arms.

16. Skeat and Laidlaw, op. cit., p. 76, referring to the mime.

17. Wilkinson, 'Malay Amusements', p. 16. In 1874, however, Swettenham saw young *raja* playing *sepak raga* for their own amusement (*Swettenham Journal*, p. 79).

See also Newbold, op. cit., Vol. 2, p. 184; J. T. Thomson, *Some Glimpses into Life in the Far East*, London, Richardson, 1864, reprinted as *Glimpses into Life in Malayan Lands*, Singapore, Oxford University Press, 1984, p. 80; Rathborne, op. cit., p. 322; McNair, op. cit., p. 263.

18. Although the Selangor Club, founded in 1884, included organized games in its activities, little is known of it until *SJ* began publication in 1892 (J. G. Butcher, *The British in Malaya 1880–1941: The Social History of a European Community in Colonial South-East Asia*, Kuala Lumpur, Oxford University Press, 1979, pp. 59 and 63). There were European soccer teams in Singapore from 1889 (W. Makepeace, G. E. Brooke and R. St. J. Braddell (eds.), *One Hundred Years of Singapore being Some Account of the Capital of the Straits Settlements ... to the 6th February 1919*, London, Murray, 1921, Vol. 2, p. 333). Kicking a ball about without organized teams had begun much earlier. C. B. Buckley, *An Anecdotal History of Old Times in Singapore 1819–1867*, 2 vols., Singapore, Fraser & Neave, 1902; reprinted Kuala Lumpur, University of Malaya Press, 1965, and Singapore, Oxford University Press, 1984, p. 500, describes an 'exciting ... game of football in which all joined' on the Padang on New Year's Day, 1849.

19. *AR Selangor 1902*. See p. 266 above on problems of school attendance.

20. *AR Education Department Perak 1893*, para. 35 in *PGG* 1894, p. 207.

21. *SJ*, 13 December 1895. 'Some Malays at Kuala Selama have started football and play with great keenness but not much skill' (*PGG* 1896, p. 734).

22. Butcher, op. cit., p. 119. Golf and cricket were not played by Malays until much later. In his last years Yam Tuan Mohamed of Negeri Sembilan (r.1888–1933) used to play a round of golf with his wife on Sundays on the 6-hole course of the Kuala Pilah Club (W. A. Gordon-Hall, 'Yam Tuan Mohamed', *Malaya*, 1954, p. 625). When Raja (later Sultan) Sulaiman of Selangor, then a youth of sixteen, visited Klang in May 1879 and was entertained, with his grandfather, Sultan Abdul Samad, at the Residency, he 'joined in the game of tennis' (Douglas Diary, 5 May 1879). Douglas does not say whether he showed any aptitude. A few years later Emily Innes encouraged the Tunku Panglima Raja to play tennis with her; see p. 206, note 92, above. These were isolated episodes; Malay aristocrats did not play tennis at this time as a normal recreation.

23. F. A. Swettenham, 'A Malay Nautch', *JSBRAS*, 2, 1878; and *Malay Sketches*, London, John Lane Bodley Head, 1895, pp. 44–52; Sheppard, *Taman Indera*, pp. 82–4.

24. Wilkinson, *1932 Dictionary*, Part 1, p. 475, and Part 2, p. 347.

25. Sheppard, *Taman Indera*, p. 89. See p. 319 above for Thomson's account of dancing girls at a seance to cure a sick man.

26. R. J. H. Sidney, *Malay Land—Tanah Melayu: Some Phases of Life in Modern British Malaya*, London, Palmer, 1926, p. 139, writing in the 1920s, states that a first-rate dancer in her late teens could earn as much as $500 for a single night's performance. He is describing an entertainment at the house of a 'rich Malay', probably in Kuala Lumpur. He ascribes the origin of the *ronggeng* to 'Egyptian harem dancing'.

27. *PGG* 1890, p. 515. *SGG* 1891, p. 834, and *Sungei Ujong Gazette* 1895, p. 3, also describe performances by male dancers at a gathering at the house of the district officer on *Hari Raya* or some other Islamic holiday.

28. See p. 319 above.

29. Wilkinson, 'Malay Amusements', pp. 33 and 93 (a description by Winstedt).

Sheppard, *Taman Indera*, gives '*rodat*' as a synonym. Wilkinson, whose dictionary does not include '*rodat*', relates *hadzrah* to *sedati*, which he describes as an Acehnese 'choric dance and song by boys . . . brought into disrepute through the character of the performers and the nature of the dialogue and songs'. The *sedati* gets its name from the Arabic '*ya sedati*' ('Oh my masters') which was part of the refrain (*1932 Dictionary*, Part 1, p. 386, and Part 2, p. 399). Sheppard states that the *rodat* or *hadzrah* was performed only in Terengganu and Kedah, both notable centres of Islamic instruction (*Taman Indera*, p. 91).

30. *PESTA Official Souvenir Programme*, Kuala Lumpur, Department of Information Services, 1956. This was the annotated programme of the festival of traditional culture held in the Lake Gardens. See also Wilkinson and Sheppard, cited in note 29 above. Sheppard also mentions another Arabic dance, the *zapin*, in which four pairs of dancers, male and female, dance to a faster rhythm than the *ronggeng*. This is unknown to Wilkinson and may be a modern introduction.

31. The authoritative modern study is P. L. Amin Sweeney, *The Ramayana and the Malay Shadow-play*, Kuala Lumpur, National University of Malaya Press, 1972. See also Anker Rentse, 'The Kelantan Shadow-play (Wayang Kulit)', *JMBRAS*, 14(3), 1936; Sheppard, *Taman Indera*, pp. 69–81; A. H. Hill, 'Wayang Kulit Stories from Trengganu', *JMBRAS*, 22(3), 1949; articles by Sheppard or Sweeney in *JMBRAS*, 38(1), 41(1) and 45(1), and the works cited by Sweeney in the bibliography to his *Ramayana* above; P. L. Amin Sweeney, *Authors and Audiences in Traditional Malay Literature*, Berkeley, Center for Southeast Asian Studies, University of California, 1980, Chapter 4, analyses the structure of a *wayang kulit* performance given on Malaysian television in 1971.

32. Sweeney, *Ramayana*, p. 22.

33. Skeat's *Malay Magic: Being an Introduction to the Folklore and Popular Religion of the Malay Peninsula*, London, Macmillan, 1900, reprinted Singapore, Oxford University Press, 1984, is a compendium of information which he had collected during his time in Selangor in the 1890s. It is probably a significant omission that he makes no reference to *wayang kulit* performances other than by including them (p. 521) in a list of types of Malay theatrical performance obtained from a Malay informant. However, the *Malay Mail*, 15 May and 15 June 1897, mentions performances. One company came from Kelantan and the other was Javanese. See also *SGG* 1897, p. 421, to the same effect.

34. Sweeney, *Ramayana*, Chapter 3.

35. Ibid., p. 26. It is surprising that Skeat and Laidlaw, op. cit., includes no mention of a *wayang kulit* performance witnessed during a year (1899–1900) spent in North-east Malaya.

36. Sheppard, *Taman Indera*, pp. 80–1.

37. Wilkinson, 'Malay Amusements', p. 42, and *1932 Dictionary*, Part 2, p. 118. Sheppard, *Taman Indera*, p. 58, says that the *ma'yong* came from Patani, which had been dismembered in the 1830s and incorporated in the province of Ligor as a number of small states.

38. Sheppard, *Taman Indera*, p. 58.

39. Ibid., pp. 59–67.

40. Swettenham, 'A Malay Nautch', p. 161. Wilkinson, who was in Malaya between 1889 and 1916, wrote that the *ma'yong* was 'performed usually under a shed (*bangsal ma'yong*) the audience being in the open air'—which is consistent with Skeat's account cited in note 44 below (*1932 Dictionary*, Part 2, p. 118).

41. There was a *ma'yong* at Pasir Salak as part of the celebrations of the ear-piercing of the daughter of the Maharaja Lela (SSD 11 January 1877, CO 273/90, p. 143). Villagers giving evidence to PCE mentioned having seen a *ma'yong* at Bandar Bahru on the Perak River (PCE CO 273/86, p. 472).

42. Vaughan, op. cit., p. 134.

43. A. Lovat, *The Life of Sir Frederick Weld: A Pioneer of Empire*, London, Murray, 1914, p. 300. Weld had only been three months in the country and would certainly not have understood the Malay dialogue or the finer points.

44. Skeat and Laidlaw, op. cit., pp. 119–20. The *rebab* player led the orchestra and played the melody which they accompanied. There were usually four other musicians—two played drums (*gendang*) and two, gongs (*tawak*) (Sheppard, *Taman Indera*, p. 58).

45. *SJ* 5 October 1894.

46. Wilkinson, *1932 Dictionary*, Part 2, p. 118.

47. *SJ* 5 October 1894.

48. Sheppard, *Taman Indera*, p. 65.

49. *PESTA Official Souvenir Programme*, cited in note 30.

50. See p. 59 above.

51. Wilkinson, 'Malay Amusements', p. 55.

52. Ibid.

53. At the *Pesta* of 1956 a *bangsawan* performed three plays, one of which, entitled '*Taming Sari*', was presumably an adaptation of Shakespeare's *The Taming of the Shrew*.

54. Sidney, *Malay Land*, p. 143. Sidney himself, as Headmaster of the Victoria Institution, Kuala Lumpur, produced orthodox versions of Shakespeare's plays, with schoolboys and teachers, including himself, in the cast (*In British Malaya Today*, London, Hutchinson, n.d. (1926?), Chapters 10 and 11); he includes some photographs. The plays were put on in public in Kuala Lumpur and taken on tour to Singapore and Penang.

55. *Malay Mail*, 21 and 23 July 1903 and 23 October 1903. On the Selangor installation see p. 36 above.

56. The Raja Muda was the future Sultan Sulaiman who had married the daughter of Tunku Kudin (or Dia Udin), the former Viceroy of Selangor. Kudin had a house and property at Klang. See *SGG* 1891, p. 398, on the circus.

57. Mubin Sheppard, editorial note in *Malaya in History*, 10(1), 1965, p. 39; H. T. Haughton, 'Boriah', *JSBRAS*, 30, 1897. Later the *boria* fell into disrepute. In 1922 a *Jawi Pekan* clerk in the Education Department at Penang wrote that it was 'an ignorant and degrading performance' imported to Malaya by Indian convicts, especially those convicted of thuggery (in the technical Indian sense) (M. L. Wynne, *Triad and Tabut*, Singapore, Government Printing Press, 1941, p. 195).

58. Skeat and Laidlaw, op. cit., p. 153; A. L. Keyser, *Trifles and Travels*, London, Murray, 1923, p. 112.

59. Duncan Forbes, *The Heart of Malaya*, London, Robert Hale, 1966, p. 88. Sheppard writes that 'priority is given to skilled striking of drums and gongs, which are played in a group; wind and stringed instruments are few and wind is allotted only a minor part in the over-all sound effect' (*Taman Indera*, p. 47). He goes on to describe Malay musical instruments in detail (pp. 47–56). They were the work of 'specialist craftsmen' using simple tools but were 'of high quality both in workmanship and musical quality' (p. 57). The standard of performance was not always high.

J. W. W. Birch describes how 'men and women joined in tomtoms and music' (*Birch Journal* p. 72—one of the few references to women joining in amateur dancing—it was an improvised entertainment 'to amuse us during a shower, at the *Maharaja*'s house') Swettenham and Birch at Blanja in April 1874 were entertained to 'a Malay *soiree musicale*, not as good as it might have been chiefly owing to the feebleness of the first (and only) violin' (*Swettenham Journal*, p. 76).

60. Sidney, *Malay Land*, p. 143.

61. D. J. Macgowan, 'Notes on the Maritime Malays', *JIA*, 4, 1850, p. 691.

62. Vaughan, op. cit., pp. 135–6. Vaughan first came to Malaya in the 1850s as an officer of a vessel of the East India Company navy. He then served the SS government as master attendant and as police magistrate. Finally he resigned to go into private legal practice. He died at sea in 1891 (C. M. Turnbull, *The Straits Settlements 1826–1867: Indian Presidency to Crown Colony*, London, Athlone Press, 1972, p. 103). There is a longer account of his many-sided activities in Makepeace, Brooke and Braddell (eds.), op. cit., pp. 223–4. As might be expected from his comments quoted here, he was very musical—'a fine singer'.

When the crew of the vessel carrying Abdullah Munshi rowed the vessel out of the Kelantan River estuary he sang them a 'chanty' of *pantun* and they responded with a chorus between each of his verses (Abdullah bin Abdul Kadir, Munshi, *Kesah Pelayaran Abdullah*, translated by A. E. Coope, *The Voyage of Abdullah: A Translation from the Malay*, Singapore, Malaya Publishing House, 1949, pp. 60–4, where the 'chanty' is given in full). His son, Ibrahim Munshi, mentions that in the evenings at Padang 'the fiddle, *kecapi* and *rebana* would sound . . . just as on the cutter' (Mohamed Ibrahim bin Abdullah, Munshi, *The Voyages of Mohamed Ibrahim Munshi*, translated by A. Sweeney and Nigel Phillips, Kuala Lumpur, Oxford University Press, 1975, p. 10). A *kecapi* is a four-stringed lute, which Wilkinson says was 'not in modern use'. A *rebana* was a tabor or tambourine 'used for beating time for dancers' (Wilkinson, *1932 Dictionary*, Part 1, p. 522, and Part 2, p. 322).

The quotations in the remainder of the paragraph of the main text are from Vaughan, op. cit.

63. Wilkinson, *1932 Dictionary*, Part 1, p. 144.

64. Skeat and Laidlaw, op. cit., p. 153. '*Rebab*' (rebeck), like '*biola*' is a word of foreign (Arabic) origin (Wilkinson, *1932 Dictionary*, Part 2, p. 321). See note 44 above on the leading role of the *rebab* player in the orchestra.

65. *SGG* 1892, p. 728, report from Kuala Selangor.

66. See p. 56 above on Sultan Ahmad and p. 29 on the instruments of the *nobat*.

67. F. A. Swettenham, 'Some Account of the Independent Native States of the Malay Peninsula especially the Circumstances which Led to the More Intimate Relations Recently Adopted towards Some of Them by the British Government', *JSBRAS*, 6, 1880, p. 178. Ibrahim Munshi says that in his party 'the expert in the art of the *pantun* was the blind man. He sang in a sweet, well-modulated voice, with a gentle and graceful style' (Ibrahim Munshi, op. cit., p. 12). In a similar fashion Logan tells how 'a boat crowded with Malays passed in front of Klebang, slowly pulling towards the town, with musical instruments, a fine-toned gong, and the voices of the joyous Malays uniting in a pleasing air' (J. R. Logan, 'Journal of an Excursion from Singapur to Malacca and Pinang', *Journal of the Royal Geographical Society*, 16, 1846, p. 312). Clifford, in one of his rhapsodic passages, wrote: 'amid the rhythmical thud of the drums, the droning of verses from the *Kuran* . . . another *sampan*, bright with gorgeous silks and glittering with tinsel, passes by, bearing the

bridegroom and his relations to the hut where the little frightened bride awaits their coming' (*Studies in Brown Humanity*, p. 155). Music was always an enjoyable adjunct of any social occasion.

68. J. T. Thomson, *Glimpses*, p. 48.

69. J. R. Logan, 'Five Days in Naning', *JIA*, 3, 1849, p. 35.

70. Vaughan, op. cit., p. 136.

71. '... semi-legendary bamboo regarded as a precious love-charm' (Wilkinson, *1932 Dictionary*, Part 1, p. 163). This aspect is discussed by L. Wray, 'Malay Aeolian Pipes', *Perak Museum Notes*, Vol. 3, reprinted in *SJ* 16 November 1894, and in his 'Journal of a Collecting Expedition to the Mountain of Batang Padang Perak', *JSBRAS*, 21, 1890. See also I. H. Burkill, *A Dictionary of the Economic Products of the Malay Peninsula*, 2 vols., published on behalf of the SS and FMS Governments, London, Crown Agents, 1935, p. 299.

In his 'Aeolian Pipes' Wray describes the instrument as a bamboo at least an inch in diameter with a hole cut between each joint on alternate sides. The holes are 'spaced at different parts of the joints to give different notes, and the shapes of the holes are varied with the intention of altering the timbre of the notes, in the same way as is done with organ pipes. The holes are square, round, triangular, besides segments and sectors of circles and many irregular shapes.... The *buluh perindu*, being prepared, is stuck upright into the ground, large end downwards or tied on to a tree-top near a house, so that its music can be heard. Living bamboos are sometimes cut and made aeolian, and they will remain alive for some time afterwards. A clump so treated will produce musical notes whenever the wind blows through it ... weird and plaintive.'

The bamboo used for this purpose is the *Bambusa magica* (Wilkinson, op. cit., and Burkill, op. cit.).

W. W. Skeat and C. O. Blagden, *Pagan Races of the Malay Peninsula*, 2 vols., London, Macmillan, 1906, Vol. 2, p. 310, cite Skeat (*SJ*, 6 August 1897) to record that 'in former days members of the travelling theatrical troupes' would put minute slivers of this kind of bamboo between their teeth, believing that it would make their singing voices 'irresistably [*sic*] melodious' and give them a magical power over their audience to obtain whatever the singer might demand. This form of magic was so much feared that 'in some parts of the Peninsula the mere possession of a splinter of the "yearning bamboo" was formerly an offence punishable by death'.

The interesting—but unanswered—question is how the skill to make these pipes, with their exactly placed and shaped holes, was acquired and by whom. Presumably it was part of the stock-in-trade of some *pawang*.

72. Wilkinson, 'Malay Amusements', p. 20; Thomson, *Glimpses*, p. 48; F. Caddy, *To Siam and Malaya in the Duke of Sutherland's Yacht 'Sans Peur'*, London, Hurst & Blackett, 1889, p. 270; Skeat and Laidlaw, op. cit., p. 138. For an account of kite-flying which ended in a tragic quarrel, see p. 239 above.

73. Skeat, *Malay Magic*, pp. 484–5. On the magical aspect Skeat noted that both on the East Coast and in Perlis 'men formerly habitually flew kites ... as part of their ceremonies at the ripening of the crop' (Skeat and Laidlaw, op. cit., p. 138). He compared this with a Siamese rite 'in aid of the rice crops' and a similar rite of the ancient Greeks (ibid.). The analogy is apparently between the 'swinging' movement of ripening padi and a similar movement of the kite. Skeat also noted the use of a small and roughly made kite for unspecified 'fishing purposes' in Singapore (Skeat, *Malay Magic*, p. 484).

In modern times, however, the kite has become exclusively a child's toy except in Kelantan and Terengganu (Sheppard, *Taman Indera*, pp. 171–9). Dr Mohamed Said remembers flying kites with other boys at Linggi around 1915 (*Memoirs of a Menteri Besar: Early Days*, Singapore, Heinemann, 1982, p. 48).

74. Wilkinson, 'Malay Amusements', pp. 57–61 and 94. See also his *1932 Dictionary*, Part 1, p. 192 (*chatur*), p. 251 (*dam*), p. 239, (*chukur*), and p. 234 (*chongkak*). Rathborne, op. cit., p. 322, saw 'Malay boys . . . tossing coppers into a small hole in the ground, and watching the result of each throw . . . with much eagerness and interest'. Vaughan, op. cit., p. 162, also describes this Malay variety of 'pitch and toss'.

75. Vaughan, op. cit., p. 164.

76. *PGG* 1894, p. 295. On the Seri Adika Raja see p. 78 above. In Terengganu in 1917 the British Agent (Humphreys) and the Malay judge 'defeated Tunku Long and his brother, Tunku Hitam, in a chess match' (SSD 19 June 1917). McNair describes the Malay chess-board and gives the names of the chessmen (op. cit., p. 264).

77. *PGG* 1896, p. 677.

78. R. J. Wilkinson, 'Notes on the Negri Sembilan', *Papers on Malay Subjects, History*, Part 5, 1911; reprinted in P. L. Burns (ed.), *Papers on Malay Subjects*, Kuala Lumpur, Oxford University Press, 1971, p. 300. 'The Raja objects to cock-fighting and gambling' (*Swettenham Journal*, p. 268), referring to Kelantan in 1875.

79. Betting on the result of cock-fights was the only traditional Malay form of gambling (Vaughan, op. cit., p. 162).

80. Wilkinson, 'Malay Amusements', pp. 60–1, describes the card games played occasionally by Malays. See also Skeat, *Malay Magic*, pp. 487–93, for an extended description, citing W. E. Maxwell's material in *Notes and Queries*, issued with *JSBRAS*, 14, 1884, p. 24; and *SJ* 3 March 1897.

81. Mohamed Amin Hassan, 'Raja Bot bin Raja Jumaat', *JMBRAS*, 40(2), 1967, pp. 89–90.

82. S. M. Middlebrook, 'Yap Ah Loy', *JMBRAS*, 24(2), 1951, p. 93, citing a report by Swettenham. Clifford, *In Court and Kampong*, p. 32, tells the story of Raja Mahmud's raid—to steal the winnings—on 'the great Klang gambling house'.

83. H. Low, 'The Journal of Sir Hugh Low, Perak 1877' (hereafter cited as 'Low Journal'), edited by E. Sadka, *JMBRAS*, 27(4), 1954, p. 80.

84. E. Sadka, *The Protected Malay States 1874–1895*, Kuala Lumpur and Singapore, University of Malaya Press, 1968, p. 136.

85. Ibid., pp. 191 and 298. *PGG* 1898, p. 401, report from Batang Padang on Malays in gambling-houses after the controlled monopoly system had been ended.

86. SSD 12 October 1894.

87. Report of 27 July 1908, CO 273/343, p. 514. See p. 295 above.

88. SSD 31 March 1913.

89. SSD 26 June 1912.

90. *AR Kelantan 1903–1904*, CO 273/314, p. 21. Caddy, op. cit., pp. 236 and 246. Singapore society came across to indulge in the gambling facilities at Johor Bahru which were no longer available in Singapore. But Florence Caddy does not say that there were Malays at the tables.

91. W. G. Maxwell, *In Malay Forests*, Edinburgh, Blackwood, 1930; C. Mayer, *Trapping Wild Animals* (and see p. 198 above for his account of trapping elephants); W. T. Hornaday, *Two Years in the Jungle: The Experiences of a Hunter and Naturalist*

in India, Ceylon, the Malay Peninsula and Borneo, New York, Scribner, 1885, Part 3; Newbold, op. cit., Vol. 2, pp. 188–90; McNair, op. cit., Chapters 11 and 12; W. Cameron, op. cit., p. 346. The flesh of the male crocodile was believed to have medicinal properties (Burkill, op. cit., p. 683). H. C. Syers was a notable hunter of Malayan big game and was killed by a *seladang* in 1897 (J. M. Gullick, 'Syers and the Selangor Police Force 1875–1897', *JMBRAS*, 51(2), 1978, pp. 47–8). *SJ*, 1892, contains articles by Syers on his exploits.

92. See p. 198 above.

93. *PGG* 1892, p. 70, report from Kuala Kangsar.

94. Swettenham, *Malay Sketches*, pp. 211–26, for the expedition to obtain turtles' eggs; quotations from p. 215 and p. 217. Ibid., pp. 19–30, for an account of a 'Fishing Picnic'. See also *Footprints*, p. 99, on both topics.

95. Swettenham, *Malay Sketches*, pp. 31–7. SSD 20 August 1897 (the durbar excursion). In later years '*menggeluncur* picnics had ... become part and parcel of college life' at Kuala Kangsar (Mohamed Said, op. cit., p. 194, and J. M. Gullick, 'The Malay Administrator', *Merdeka Outlook*, 1(1), 1957, p. 78). Wilkinson, however, scoffs at the idea that this was a traditional sport and says that it was invented by a British district officer 'as a combination of aquatic sport with curry tiffins' ('Malay Amusements', p. 71). We shall never know. Undoubtedly the Malays enjoyed it.

96. SSD 21 September 1881, and see p. 31 above.

97. 'Low Journal', p. 44. These passages may reflect the local tastes and circumstances of Perak. But in Kedah, Sultan Abdul Hamid, who had a marked addiction for public procession and display, used to make royal progresses through his state.

98. Swettenham, *British Malaya*, pp. 314–15.

99. *AR Kelantan 1903–1904*.

100. See p. 78 above on the Seri Adika Raja's unhappy visit to London. A. L. Keyser, *People and Places: A Life in Five Continents*, London, Murray, 1922, pp. 142–4. He remarks (p. 141) that 'it is a great mark of confidence for a Mahomedan to leave his country with one not of his own religion'. On the experience of Raja Alang Iskander of Perak in London, leading Clifford to write his Saleh stories (*A Prince of Malaya*), see p. 69, note 91, above. One of the earliest and oddest episodes of a Malay visiting London, is the story of Tunku Mohamed Ariffin, 'a clever pushing young man' from Sumatra, who persuaded Baginda Omar, the aged ruler of Terengganu, to send him on a mission to London bearing the ruler's gifts to Queen Victoria in return for her present to him (see p. 27 above). He managed to secure an interview with the Prince of Wales (the future King Edward VII) and the Foreign Secretary (Lord Clarendon); as his funds were running low he tried to borrow £200 from the Prince of Wales for his return passage. See SSD 22 December 1869, 1 January 1870 and 24 January 1870 and various letters between the FO and CO in CO 273/34. It was this affair which led Governor Ord, much exasperated, to agree with the Consul-General in Bangkok that Terengganu was under the suzerainty of Siam—so that the Queen's letter of acknowledgement was sent via Bangkok (SSD 24 January 1870 and M. C. ff. Sheppard, 'A Short History of Trengganu', *JMBRAS*, 22(3), 1949, Chapters 4 and 5).

101. Keyser, *People and Places*, p. 140.

102. *PGG* 1895, p. 528, report from Krian.

103. T. Braddell, 'Notes of a Trip to the Interior of Malacca', *JIA*, 7, 1853, p. 96.

104. Ibrahim Munshi, op. cit., pp. 10 and 19.

105. Vaughan, op. cit., p. 168.

106. Ibrahim Munshi, op. cit., p. 10.

107. W. E. Maxwell, 'A Journey on Foot to the Patani Frontier in 1876 being a Journal Kept during an Expedition Undertaken to Capture Datoh Maharajah Lela of Perak', *JSBRAS*, 9, 1882, p. 15.

108. Keyser, *People and Places*, p. 143.

109. 'Penglipur Lara: The Soother of Cares', English translation of a Malay text entitled (in English) 'Sri Rama: A Malay Fairy Tale founded on the Ramayana', *JSBRAS*, 17, 1886. See also Amin Sweeney, 'Professional Malay Story-telling—Part 1—Some Questions of Style and Presentation', *JMBRAS*, 46(2), 1973; and Amin Sweeney 'The Pak Pandir Cycle of Tales', *JMBRAS*, 49(1), 1976.

110. This passage is derived from Sweeney's meticulous and perceptive analyses (especially his essay on 'Malay Story-telling'), of which it is a very brief and inadequate summary.

111. SSD 17 May 1889.

112. Wilkinson, *1932 Dictionary*, Part 2, p. 23. Whatever may have been the practice in Maxwell's time, the expression '*penglipur lara*' is no longer used by or about the professional story-tellers of our time (Sweeney, 'Malay Story-telling', pp. 6–7).

113. W. E. Maxwell, 'Sri Rama', p. 88.

114. Newbold, op. cit., Vol. 2, p. 88.

115. Clifford, *In Court and Kampong*, pp. 153–4.

116. Ibid.; Wilkinson, 'Malay Amusements', p. 71.

117. Sweeney, 'Malay Story-telling', p. 23.

118. See p. 267 above.

119. Mohamed Said, op. cit., p. 89.

120. Zainal Abidin bin Ahmad, 'Modern Developments' (Chapter 14), in R. O. Winstedt, 'A History of Malay Literature', *JMBRAS*, 17(3), 1940, p. 151. He refers to 'an introduction to Malay history proper called *Tawarikh Melayu* (1918) by Dr. Winstedt in collaboration with Daing Abdu'l-Hamid bin Tengku Haji Mohamed Salleh, the first scientific work on general Malay history ever produced in the Malay language'. He also emphasizes the distinction between '*tawarikh*', as 'history proper' and '*hikayat*', which were mere stories—'there had been no clear distinction in the Malay mind between fact and fiction'. Much depends on how much weight is given to the word 'scientific' in this judgement. But the earlier Malay *hikayat* cited in note 121 below (including of course the *Tuhfat al-Nafis*) do offer a *factual* narrative of events of the recent past.

121. A Malay text of the *Tuhfat al-Nafis* is printed in *JMBRAS*, 10(2), 1932; for the recent English translation by Matheson and Andaya, see Raja Ali Haji ibn Ahmad, *Tuhfat al-Nafis*, translated and annotated by Virginia Matheson and Barbara Watson Andaya, *The Precious Gift*, Kuala Lumpur, Oxford University Press, 1982. The Kedah and Selangor works referred to are cited in these notes as Muhammad Hassan bin Dato' Kerani Muhammad Arshad, *Al-Tarikh Salasilah Negeri Kedah*, Kuala Lumpur, Dewan Bahasa dan Pustaka, 1968 (previously published in *Jawi*, 1926), and Wan Mohamed Amin bin Said, *Pesaka Selangor*, edited by Abdul Samad Ahmad, Kuala Lumpur, Dewan Bahasa dan Pustaka, 1966. The *Hikayat Pahang* has not been published but Linehan reproduces material—and in some places translated passages—from it in his 'A History of Pahang', *JMBRAS*, 14(2), 1936. A. C. Milner, *Kerajaan: Malay Political Culture on the Eve of Colonial Rule*, Tucson,

University of Arizona Press, 1982, also makes considerable use of it and (p. 37) opines that it was written 'in the early years of this century'. It will be clear from Milner's summary (*Kerajaan*) that it does give a detailed narrative of events from 1857 to 1889—'a great deal of information about people and events'. But 'it tells us nothing of the psychological or intellectual development' of Sultan Ahmad, who is the central figure.

There is also an unpublished Malay history of Sungei Ujong written in 1910: see Wilkinson, 'Notes on the Negri Sembilan', in Burns (ed.), *PMS*, p. 295. A copy of this was extant in the hands of Datuk Klana Ma'amur of Sungei Ujong at his death in 1945 and passed through the present author's hands as District Officer, Seremban.

122. On internal evidence the author believes that these Malay texts of the early twentieth century were written mainly to present an authorized view of the recent past, as perceived by the ruler and his advisers. To that extent they must be regarded as partly propaganda rather than objective records. But they do contain a great deal of factual material, much of which appears to be accurate. As such they seem to provide clear evidence that the distinction between fact and myth existed in the minds of Malay writers concerned with nineteenth-century history, long before Winstedt's book appeared in 1918. One must, of course, accept Zainal Abidin's view that the authority of Winstedt induced much wider acceptance of the distinction.

123. *AR Perak 1890*. The museum evidently held a varied collection of exhibits, not all of which were historical. Its acquisitions in 1898, for example, included two snakes, various mineral specimens, a forged $100 note, samples of black and white pepper, and two Mexican dollars of 1870 and 1871. Average daily admissions in 1898 were 122. *PGG* 1899, p. 28, Perak Museum notes for December 1898.

As another small example, road construction work in 1876 led to the discovery of a tomb near Kamunting in the Larut district. W. E. Maxwell says that 'the Menteri and the ladies of his family went on elephants to see it and it has been the object of much prestige ever since'. W. E. Maxwell, 'A Malay Kramat', *JSBRAS*, 2, 1878, p. 237. As the Menteri was sent off to the Seychelles in 1877, this event must have happened before that year.

When Weld visited Perak at the beginning of 1881 Raja Muda Yusuf took him on a 'visit to the tomb of a Malay princess, the ancestress of the Perak *Rajas*' (SSD 23 February 1881).

124. Wilkinson, 'Malay Amusements', p. 72.

125. See pp. 31–6 above.

126. Wilkinson, 'Malay Amusements', p. 71.

127. W. R. Roff, *The Origins of Malay Nationalism*, New Haven, Yale University Press, 1967, and Khoo Kay Kim, 'Malay Society 1874–1920', *JSEAS*, 5(2), 1974, have analysed the stirrings of new ideas in Malay society. All which the author seeks to suggest here is that, even in recreations and amusements, one can find slight but significant indications of a new mood.

15
The Stability of Malay Society

A hundred years ago traditional societies in many parts of the world were under severe pressure from the industrialized countries of the West. Colonial expansion, economic penetration and the cultural impact of an alien way of life which asserted its superiority by missionary proselytization, a new style of education, and a demonstration of technical expertise all affected traditional societies directly by inducing, if not enforcing, rapid change, and also indirectly by offering an alternative set of habits and values associated with political and economic dominance.

Under this pressure, some societies disintegrated to a greater or lesser extent. Malay society, however, did not do so. One of the main themes of this study is that social change did begin in this period, albeit in a slow, uncertain and uneven fashion. But—even in the western Malay states where the alien impact was strongest—Malay society preserved its essential character and institutions.

No one factor can be identified as the sole or even the main cause of this comparative stability combined with a degree of slow change. The political system imposed on the Malay states between 1874 and 1914 professed, and, to some extent, practised a policy of non-intervention in 'Malay religion and custom'.[1] Although the initial collision of the 'Perak War' and other lesser conflicts left their mark on Malay communities, it also became a warning to British administrators of the potentially serious consequences of pushing Malay society to the point at which a kind of collective *amuk*, or war against the infidel, was perceived as the only practicable response.[2]

Both colonial rulers and Malay monarchs of the still independent states tended to oust the ruling class from its traditional function of court office and district government. However, the same change obliged the ruler or state government, in which power was reconcentrated after its mid-nineteenth century dispersion, to organize a state civil service or circle of royal appointees to assist in the new method of government. This development opened up new avenues of advancement and new careers to members of the ruling class. Thereby they recovered status even if they had suffered a loss of power.[3] The bureaucratization of the aristocracy really gathered momentum only in the twentieth century, but it had its beginnings in the period of this study.

Economic penetration by Chinese tin miners had begun in the second quarter of the nineteenth century. In those states, such as Perak and Selangor, where mining became a major industry it had severe disruptive effects on Malay society at every level. To some extent this was self-induced. It is too often overlooked that in 1874 the Chinese, though only as temporary sojourners, probably outnumbered the Malays in Perak and Selangor. Like the sorcerer's apprentice, Malay government had released a tidal wave which it could not contain.[4]

The economic development which continued under colonial rule tended, as before, to bypass rather than penetrate the Malay economy. The immigrant Chinese were concentrated in areas which the Malays did not occupy. Their presence provided markets for Malay produce and thereby gave some stimulus to Malay agriculture, leading to an increase in the value of Malay smallholdings.[5] To that extent—one should not exaggerate the overall effect—Chinese economic activity stabilized rather than disrupted Malay land settlement and agriculture.

In so far as the new regimes sought to expand the production of commercial crops, they encouraged plantation development rather than peasant agriculture. The planters who arrived to open coffee estates in the 1880s and 1890s came mainly from Ceylon, where they had been accustomed to working estates with Tamil labour imported from South India. They found it much easier and more congenial to continue that practice rather than recruit Malay labourers to work on their estates.[6] It is true that, as an earlier chapter has shown, the immigrant Malay settlers sought part-time employment as wage-labourers. However, this need was met by offering temporary work on government road-building and the like. It had no widespread effect of drawing Malay men into the commercial economy as labourers.[7]

An incidental by-product of plantation agriculture was a system of registered ownership of land. This novelty was extended to a somewhat reluctant Malay peasantry as a means of extracting revenue from them as 'quit-rent'. In so doing, the regime created a new form of Malay property, i.e. valuable and saleable smallholdings. It was a change which was to be of great significance when Malay smallholders came to plant rubber on a wide scale from about 1910 onwards—and its consequences led to the protective Malay Reservations Enactment of 1913. In the latter part of the nineteenth century, however, Malay ownership of land as a transferable asset probably stabilized Malay villages rather than displaced them.[8]

Apart from external factors, there was a general recognition that Malay 'character' had a considerable effect on the pace of change. In addition to the numerous European commentaries, Malay writers, such as Abdul Majid bin Zainuddin, were disposed to theorize about this topic.[9] Still more the advocates of change perceived the problem as a need for effort (*perjuangan*) or, in Swettenham's terminology, 'regeneration' of Malay character.[10]

This is an area where European writers display a marked degree of cultural bias and distorting preconception of the superiority of their own social values. It is more useful to attempt to identify the accepted 'values' of Malay society itself. There was the concept of status (*taraf*).[11] This led to competition for high status in upper-class society and an all-pervading sense of class structure—ruling class and subject class—which did not disappear in the brave new world after 1874. There was the authority of tradition (*adat*) and the need to conform to what was proper (*patut*) in one's conduct. The right course was generally to do what one's father did and the local community considered correct.[12]

Yet these collective constraints could impose bonds which were too tight. If one's own folly or the injustice of others induced a sense of shame (*malu*) or of resentment (*sakit hati*) the individual might react with an initial calm, arising from the conventional quietism of Malay life, until the bonds suddenly snapped in some bloodbath of *amuk* or disorientation of *latah*. In times of 'great difficulty' for the family or the community reassurance and relief were obtained by invoking supernatural aid through a *main berhantu*.[13]

Malay observance of the outward forms and practices of Islam, attendance at Friday prayers and the like, was sometimes lax or combined with continued acceptance of pre-Islamic rites and beliefs. This factor may have led European observers to underrate the strong and pervasive effect of Islam on Malay life. It probably became stronger as the nineteenth century moved towards its close, and contacts with the Middle Eastern heartland of the faith became closer. It was a powerful reassurance to a community under pressure. The sense of belonging to a world-wide community of believers helped the Malay to retain his conviction that his way of life, which—significantly—he equated with Islam, was not inferior to the culture of the dominant European regime. As we have seen, Hurgronje noted that this sense of Islamic 'solidarity' was one of the most important spiritual experiences of the small number of Malays and Indonesians who made the pilgrimage. Abdul Majid found that the rising group of Malay journalists and intelligentsia, who provided the intellectual leadership of the new generation, discussed the Malay situation in terms of Islamic, not European, ideas. It was the visible 'alternative' and the Malays had identified themselves with it.[14]

Another feature of Malay temperament, which imposed a restraint to check the acceptance of change, was the disposition to think carefully and slowly over the merits of a proposed innovation. In a more perceptive assessment than appears elsewhere in his writings, Swettenham noted that 'when the value of a change which may at first have been viewed with suspicion, or even fear, dawns on the Malay, it takes deep root, and his confidence and regard for it will grow with years, whilst the same measure introduced too hastily, perhaps too zealously, startles and frightens him and fills him with resentment which leaves no room for calm consideration and reflection'.[15] McNair too refers to the 'staid and retiring ways' of the Perak Malays and their dislike of anyone who behaves in an 'impulsive' fashion, adding that 'a Malay as a rule, speaks slowly, giving to every word a distinct emphasis'.[16]

Wheeler, whose work in teaching at the Sultan Idris Training College in the 1920s brought him into close contact with perhaps the most progressive element in Malay village society of a rather later period, noted that 'intense conservatism is a fundamental characteristic . . . and, as such, may be modified but not easily destroyed . . . it must always be considered in connection with the opposite property of adaptability, for Malays possess both to a high degree'.[17] This does not convey a picture of obdurate resistance to change, but of a national temperament in which there was a balance.

Conservatism was more than a determinant of one's own reactions to change. It could be a brake on others. There was an element of fatalism in Malay character which was expressed in the concept of an allotted or ascribed lot (*rezeki*) in life. It was not omnipotent since a man might, by his own efforts, emerge from the ruck. But if he did so, he became 'the target of hostility and envy' of his neighbours. 'Pressures of mockery criticism and thinly veiled hostility can work effectively in a village because of Malay sensitivity to the opinion of others.'[18] Here one comes back to the sense of shame (*malu*). Malay society gave little credit and imputed some reproach to the man who bettered himself.[19]

Themes of this kind are by their nature difficult to extricate from the vague cloud of generalization in which they appear in the sources. It is hardly useful to pursue them further here. But one is left with the impression that the strong and enduring norms and values of Malay life gave stability to Malay society without putting it into a strait-jacket. 'I cannot dance the Lancers,' said Yusuf, 'but I will try.'[20]

1. Pangkor Engagement Clause 6 (J. de V. Allen, A. J. Stockwell, and L. R. Wright (eds.), *A Collection of Treaties and Other Documents Affecting the States of Malaysia 1761–1963*, 2 vols., New York, Oceana Publications, 1981, Vol. 1, p. 391). The formula was generally adopted in all Malay states as they came under British control, whether or not there was a treaty provision to that effect. See p. 33 above.

2. *Instructions to the British Residents and Others Papers Relating to the Protected Malay States*: Cmd. 2410 of 1879. In 1901 the Raja of Patani, then as now under Siamese rule, came to Swettenham to protest against Siamese interference in his small state. Swettenham wrote that 'he appeared to me to be in that frame of mind when Malays become desperate and resort to violent measures, in the belief that others have failed, and life is not worth living under existing conditions' (SSD 3 September 1901).

3. See p. 88 above.

4. J. M. Gullick, *Indigenous Political Systems of Western Malaya*, London, Athlone Press, 1958, pp. 23–4, extracts the following contemporary estimates for the period around 1870:

State	*Malays*	*Chinese*
Perak	30,000	40,000 (at Larut)
Selangor	5,000	10,000

Sources: J. F. A. McNair, *Perak and the Malays: Sarong and Keris*, London, Tinsley Bros., 1878, reprinted Kuala Lumpur, Oxford University Press, 1972, p. 156; SSD 27 April 1875; SSD 3 August 1879; SSD 6 November 1872. As the Chinese, and to some extent the Malay population also, was prone to take flight to escape disorder, and no head count was attempted until 1879, any such figures are not very reliable.

5. See p. 157 above.

6. R. N. Jackson, *Immigrant Labour and the Development of Malaya 1786–1920*, Kuala Lumpur, Government Printer, 1961, pp. 94–5 and elsewhere.

7. See p. 106 above.

8. See p. 107 above.

9. Abdul Majid bin Zainuddin, *The Malays in Malaya: By One of Them*, Singapore, Malaya Publishing House, 1928.

10. J. de V. Allen, 'Two Imperialists: A Study of Sir Frank Swettenham and Sir Hugh Clifford', *JMBRAS*, 37(1), 1964, *passim*, and see p. 11 above.

11. A. C. Milner, *Kerajaan: Malay Political Culture on the Eve of Colonial Rule*, Tucson, University of Arizona Press, 1982, Chapters 5 and 6, on the concepts of '*patut*' and '*malu*'. Swettenham wrote in his journal (*Sir Frank Swettenham's Malayan Journals 1874–1876* (hereafter cited as *Swettenham Journal*), edited by P. L. Burns and C. D. Cowan, Kuala Lumpur, Oxford University Press, 1975, p. 213): 'and as the Malays say when they have no other reply to give, they were *malu* and they did not care if they died for it, they must have some satisfaction'. Again, 'when he felt that some injury—or even some fancied slight—had put him to shame, he would brood over the wrong and suddenly seize a weapon ...' (F. A. Swettenham, *Footprints in Malaya*, London, Hutchinson, 1942, p. 52).

12. As illustrations of custom overriding the views of the individual see p. 321 above (Abdullah Munshi) and p. 223 (Abdul Majid).

13. On *amuk* and *sakit hati*, see p. 240 above; on *latah*, see p. 261 above; on *main berhantu*, see p. 318 above.

14. See pp. 296 and 300 above.

15. SSD 6 March 1879. This comment gains weight from the fact that it is made in the context of a working report (he was on tour in Sungei Ujong) and not as one of his later expansive and retrospective general comments. 'Malays cannot be dealt with hurriedly; they must have time to consider what is required of them' (A. E. Anson, *About Others and Myself*, London, Murray, 1920, p. 312).

16. J. F. A. McNair, op. cit., p. 203. See also W. T. Hornaday, *Two Years in the Jungle: The Experiences of a Hunter and Naturalist in India, Ceylon, the Malay Peninsula and Borneo*, New York, Scribner, 1885, p. 312; J. D. Vaughan, 'Notes on the Malays of Pinang and Province Wellesley', *JIA*, n.s., 2, 1857, pp. 124–5.

17. L. R. Wheeler, *The Modern Malay*, London, Allen & Unwin, 1928, p. 250. Apart from the passage quoted in note 15 above Swettenham tends to stress simple conservatism—'long established custom has a strong hold on a very conservative race' (*Footprints*, p. 52); 'conservative to a degree' (*Malay Sketches*, London, John Lane Bodley Head, 1895, p. 3).

18. M. G. Swift, 'Malay Peasants', in R. D. Lambert and B. Hoselitz (eds.), *The Role of Savings and Wealth in Southern Asia and the West*, Paris, UNESCO, 1963, p. 240, and 'Economic Concentration and Malay Peasant Society', in M. Freedman (ed.), *Social Organisation: Essays Presented to Raymond Firth*, London, Frank Cass, 1967, p. 261.

19. See p. 225 above.

20. See p. 348 above for the context. Keyser's account of the experiences of the two Malays in London is interesting reading: A. L. Keyser, *People and Places: A Life in Five Continents*, London, Murray, 1922, pp. 136–46; and *Trifles and Travels*, London, Murray, 1923, pp. 26 and 87. They had to put up with some hostility from Londoners (*People and Places*, p. 140). Yusuf, though long settled in Malaya, was a

Javanese. On one of his local leaves Keyser took him to Java and they went back to his village to find his mother (A. L. Keyser, *From Jungle to Java*, London, Roxburghe Press, 1928). In Singapore Keyser took Yusuf to the Alhambra cinema (the same one as had entertained Sultan Zainal Abidin III in 1913—see p. 59 above) but Yusuf was shocked and refused to go a second time, saying 'I do not like to see so much naked' (*People and Places*, p. 136).

Appendix

Notes on Individuals as Sources

THE purpose of this Appendix is to supplement the general discussion in Chapter 1 of the interaction of personality and perception of historical material. The notes which follow are brief introductions to the circumstances and temperament of individuals from whose recollections a significant amount of material has been taken in the writing of this book. A number of the books written by these authors have been reprinted in modern times with biographical introductions which the reader may find a useful source of additional background information if he requires it. The names are arranged in alphabetical order and the titles referred to will be found in the bibliography.

Abdul Majid bin Zainuddin (b. 1887) was first a schoolmaster and then the Malayan Pilgrimage Commissioner. Although he could never quite outstrip his rival, Zaba (see below), he was an earnest Malay 'intellectual' of the colonial period and a considerable literary figure.

Abdullah bin Abdul Kadir, Munshi, who lived in the first half of the nineteenth century, is generally regarded as the father of modern Malay writing. He first wrote in a modern, non-traditional style, which has attracted some criticism. His readiness to accept the European view of perceived shortcomings of Malay character also jars a little in present times. In this book the material cited comes mainly from Abdullah's account (the *Voyage*) of his East Coast trip to Kelantan in 1838. His best-known work is his Autobiography.

John Anderson's pamphlet was written in 1824 but was reprinted in *JMBRAS*, 35(4), 1962. It is an excellent account of the West Coast states in his time. Its anti-Siamese tenor does not detract from its usefulness in that respect.

Peter J. Begbie was an Indian Army officer who took part in the episode of 1831–2 known as 'the Naning War'. His book combines his personal experiences in Melaka at that time with a general account of the Malay States.

James W. W. Birch was transferred from Ceylon to become Colonial Secretary, Straits Settlements, in 1870. He was killed in 1875 while serving as the first British Resident of Perak. Although a controversial figure, he was a careful, thorough administrator, whose reports and journal written in Perak are a useful source of factual information.

Isabella Bird (Mrs. Bishop) was a celebrated lady traveller and author of travel books. She spent a few weeks in Malaya in the first half of 1879 and later published an account of her experiences in Sungei Ujong, Selangor and Perak, which shows that she was an acute observer as well as a practised writer.

C.F. Bozzolo was employed in Perak, initially as superintendent of government plantations and later as District Officer, Upper Perak, around 1890. In that latter capacity he made an overland journey to Kelantan in 1888 to obtain elephants. His unpublished account of his journey (a printed enclosure to SSD 31 January 1889) gives a very detailed picture of the situation in Kelantan as he observed it.

Thomas Braddell came to Malaya in 1844 to manage a sugar estate in Province Wellesley. He became the head of the government legal service in Singapore in 1864 (Attorney-General from 1867). He acquired a detailed knowledge of the western Malay States, which he visited from time to time. He went with Sir Andrew Clarke to the negotiations in Perak and Selangor in 1874, and wrote the official reports thereon. He was legal adviser to Sultan Abu Bakar of Johor and a contributor to *JIA*.

Florence Caddy was a society journalist who visited Malaya briefly in 1889. During that time she stayed as the guest of Sultan Abu Bakar of Johor, of whose life-style she wrote a fascinating description.

John Cameron settled in Singapore in 1861, after some years at sea. He edited the *Straits Times* until his death twenty years later. His book is one of the classic accounts of the Straits Settlements of his time.

Sir Orfeur Cavenagh was Governor of the Straits Settlements from 1859 to 1867. He was a genial, popular figure, whose detachable wooden leg (he had lost a leg while serving in the Indian Army) astonished the Malays of the rural areas of Province Wellesley and Melaka, in the course of his tours. The Malayan chapters of his autobiography are good reading.

Sir Hugh Clifford first came to Malaya at the age of 17. He served as an administrator in Perak and then in Pahang until 1901. He returned as Governor for a short period in 1927–9. He had also visited Terengganu and Kelantan in 1895. His knowledge of the Malay States, especially Pahang, was unrivalled. He was a gifted writer whose stories and sketches are a vivid picture of Malay life and customs. By temperament a romantic, he was often preoccupied with the more horrific episodes of his experiences.

Noel Dennison was an administrator in Sarawak and later in Perak, where he had charge of the Krian District from 1877 to 1881, and he then moved to Lower Perak until his death a few years later. In those districts he was deeply involved in encouraging and assisting Malay settlers to take up new lands. His official reports (including material reproduced in the *Rice Cultivation Report 1893*) are first-rate sources of information.

Bloomfield Douglas was Resident of Selangor from 1876 to 1882. His unpublished diary is a useful record of the routine of administration, including 'Malay affairs', during his time. See *JMBRAS*, 48(2), 1975, where some extracts are published.

George W. Earl spent much of his working life in North Australia and in the Straits Settlements. He first settled in Singapore after a period as master of ships trading from Singapore to ports in what is now Indonesia. In his later years he was in a law practice with J. R. Logan (see below) and then a government magistrate at Penang. *The Eastern Seas* is the best-known of his numerous works (there is a list of them in *JMBRAS*, 32(1), 1959, pp. 148–51).

David J. Galloway was in medical practice in Singapore from 1885 until the early years of the twentieth century. He was a prominent figure in social and public life. At various times he was an unofficial member of the Straits Settlements Legislative Council and of the Johor State Council. In this book his explanation of the sociology of the ailment known as *latah* is most useful.

William T. Hornaday was an American zoologist who visited Malaya in 1878 in the course of a two-year (1876–8) field expedition to collect specimens in various Asian countries. His book is a vivid, breezy account of his experiences.

C. Snouck Hurgronje was a senior Dutch official in the Netherlands East Indies around 1900. For some years from 1898 he was adviser on native affairs to the Governor of Aceh. He was an outstanding scholar, well known in Malaya as the author of books on Aceh and on the pilgrimage to Mecca, which he had observed at first hand.

Emily Innes lived in Sarawak (1875) and then from 1876 to 1882 in Selangor and in Perak, as the wife of a district officer. She wrote her book to set her experiences against the impressions gained by Isabella Bird (above) during the latter's short visit. Emily Innes's bitterness does not detract from the value of her description. But on Malay society she is sometimes rather superficial.

Charles J. Irving held senior official appointments in the Straits Settlements from 1867 to 1887. In the early 1870s he made a number of visits to Selangor and to Perak. His official memoranda (unpublished) display his vaunted expertise on Malay affairs. He undoubtedly made himself well-informed on these matters.

Arthur L. Keyser served for a short time (in 1888) as private secretary to Swettenham in Selangor. In the early 1890s he was District Officer, Jelebu (in Negeri Sembilan), before moving on to become British Consul in Brunei (in 1901). His two major books deal with much else besides Malaya. But the chapters on his Malayan experiences, mainly in Jelebu, are a racy and vivid picture of Malay rural life (and of the experiences of his Malay servants in England when he went on leave).

James R. Logan is one of the outstanding figures in the history of English writing about the Malays in the nineteenth century. He arrived about 1840 as a planter but for most of his life thereafter (he died in 1869) he practised law and wrote as a journalist (there is a short biographical note in *JSBRAS*, 7, 1881). He is best known as the founder, editor and a frequent contributor to *JIA* (1847–59). Many of his articles are accounts of what he observed during visits to the Malay States.

Sir Hugh Low, after many years in Labuan, served as British Resident of Perak from 1877 until his retirement in 1889. Apart from his brief journal for part of 1877 (*JMBRAS*, 27(4), 1954), his reports and memoranda are unpublished sources. His immense success as architect of the 'Residential system' was based on his clear and sympathetic understanding of Malay society in his time.

James Low came to Malaya in the 1820s as an Indian Army officer but remained until 1850 in a civilian capacity. In the 1830s he had administrative charge of Province Wellesley. He was also concerned in British dealings with Kedah, Perak and Siam. He was a controversial figure, much criticized for alleged abuse, to his own advantage, of his position in Province Wellesley. He wrote a book on Penang and various articles and memoranda. His information is always useful but it needs to be appraised with care, for possible bias.

J.F A. (Fred) McNair was another Indian Army officer who became a government official. He was Colonial Engineer, i.e. head of the Public Works Department, from 1867. In 1875–6 he was Chief Commissioner in Perak, i.e. head of the civil government liaison team with the military forces engaged in the so-called Perak War. Finally, he was Resident Councillor, Penang until his retirement in 1884. He wrote his book (*About Perak*) in defence of British intervention in the Malay States, in which he had played a leading part. But the book, like his extant official reports, reflects his knowledge of the Malay way of life in his time.

Datuk Mahmud bin Mat was a member of one of the leading Malay families of east Pahang. His recollections of his boyhood experiences of the period following the abolition of debt-bondage in Pahang are a valuable record of the changing circumstances of Malay aristocratic life around 1900. After a distinguished career in the Malayan Civil Service he was Chief Minister of Pahang and then Speaker of the Federal Council in the period after 1948.

Sir William E. Maxwell became an administrator, in Province Wellesley and Melaka, from the late 1860s. In the period after the Perak War of 1876 he was for a time Assistant Resident of Perak. In the mid-1880s he became the leading government expert on the introduction of the Torrens system of registered title to land. He was then Resident of Selangor (1889–92) and Colonial Secretary Straits Settlements before going (in 1895) to West Africa to be Governor of the Gold Coast, where he died in 1897. Maxwell was a first-rate scholar, who collected Malay manuscripts and other material. He played a leading part in establishing the Straits Branch of the Royal Asiatic Society in 1878 and for some years edited its journal (*JSBRAS*), to which he contributed many notes and longer essays on a wide range of subjects. He was an autocrat with definite, and sometimes controversial, views on Malay affairs among other things. His Memorandum on the Land Code of 1894 was part of his long-running dispute with Swettenham over Malay land tenure. One cannot always accept Maxwell's opinions as correct but there is no doubt that he was a brilliant scholar and one of the ablest men of his time in the government service.

Sir W. George Maxwell was, like his father (Sir William), a controversial administrator but able and successful. He retired in 1926. In the context of this book he is useful mainly as a source of information on Malay methods of hunting big game and handling elephants, on which he was very knowledgeable.

Charles Mayer came to Singapore as the manager of the menagerie which formed part of a travelling circus. He established himself as a trapper of Malayan wild animals for export to zoos and menageries abroad. He gives a particularly useful account of trapping and taming elephants.

Mohamed Ibrahim bin Abdullah, Munshi was the son of Abdullah Munshi (above). He rose to a senior position in the service of Sultan Abu Bakar of Johor towards the end of the nineteenth century. Earlier in his career he accompanied senior Johor or European officials on various trips to the western Malay States in the period 1871–2. His book (the *Voyages*) on these journeys is an excellent source on conditions in the areas which he visited, particularly Selangor in 1872.

Thomas J. Newbold was an Indian Army officer who was stationed for three years (1832–5) in Melaka. He was by disposition a scholar and he collected Malay manuscripts as well as obtained oral information. His book (on the British Settlements) is not very satisfactory as an account of the Straits Settlements but it is an excellent source on the Malay States in the 1830s. In later years he served in India but died at an early age in 1850.

Sir Henry Norman was a British politician and journalist with definite 'imperialist' views. His book was written after a period of four years' travel in various countries of the Far East. The fifty odd pages on Malaya include an interesting account of an overland trip from Perak to Kelantan, of which he gives a very vivid description. His detailed information is useful but allowance should be made for his bias.

Sherard Osborn served as a young naval officer in the blockade of Kedah in 1838–9. During that time he had command of a small vessel with a Malay crew. His reminiscences are both readable and informative.

Raja Bot bin Raja Jumaat, unlike most Malay aristocrats of his time, had had a spell at an English school in Melaka in the early 1860s followed by a short apprenticeship in the office of a Chinese merchant. In later years he acquired some influence as elder statesman and adviser to his young kinsman, Sultan Sulaiman of Selangor (r.1898–1938). As a source Raja

Bot's main contribution is his letter written to the *Malay Mail* in 1902 on Selangor history (see p. 128 above). There is a biographical sketch in *JMBRAS*, 40(2), 1967.

Ambrose B. Rathborne was an Australian mining engineer who carried on business in partnership with the leading planter of the time, Thomas H. Hill, in various agricultural and construction enterprises between 1882 and 1898. These activities brought him into contact with Malay villagers, of whose way of life he wrote a perceptive account in his reminiscences.

John H. M. Robson lived for more than 50 years (1889–1941) in Selangor. In the 1890s he was a district officer. He founded and edited first the *Selangor Journal* (1892–7), a fortnightly journal, and then the *Malay Mail*, which from 1896 was the English language newspaper in Kuala Lumpur. To these publications Robson contributed articles based on his experience of Malay life in the 1890s. His first book (*People in a Native State*) is a reprint of articles which he had written for the *Singapore Free Press*. In later years he was a prominent businessman and for a time an unofficial member of the Federal Council. He was an excellent observer and a gifted writer.

Richard J. H. Sidney came to Malaya originally to be headmaster of the Victoria Institution in Kuala Lumpur. At that period (1924–6) he wrote newspaper articles which, combined with other material, were published in 1926 as two books. Later he held other positions in Malaya as a teacher and a journalist. Like Robson, he wrote well, though Malay life was not his main interest.

Walter W. Skeat was an administrator in the Selangor Government service in the 1890s. In this period he collected the material for his book on *Malay Magic*. In 1899–1900 Skeat and F. F. Laidlaw were joint leaders of the 'Cambridge University expedition', i.e. a party of scientists, in an extensive tour of the Malay states of the north-east, including those in southern Siam. Their narrative of the expedition (*JMBRAS*, 26(4), 1953) is a valuable source, and incidentally it is prefaced by a short biography of Skeat. He was invalided out of the service in 1900 and never came back to Malaya again, although he lived on until 1953.

Sir Frank A. Swettenham came to the Straits Settlements as an administrative cadet in 1870 and retired as Governor of the Straits Settlements in 1904. In the period from 1882 to 1901 he held a sequence of senior posts in the western Malay States, of which he had an unrivalled knowledge. He shared with Hugh Low the role of creating the 'Residential system' and with Hugh Clifford the work of literary description, in sketches and stories as well as official reports, of life in the States in his time. His *British Malaya* is avowedly an exposition of the system which he had helped to develop. Like much else which he wrote, it includes a full description of Malay life and character. He was inclined to be dogmatic and patronizing on some aspects of these topics but there is no question about the depth of his knowledge.

John T. Thomson was a surveyor in Penang and Singapore over the years from 1838 to 1853. He learnt to speak Malay and developed friendships with Malays, which gave him a useful knowledge of life in Province Wellesley in his time.

Jonas D. Vaughan served in the East India Company's navy before becoming master attendant at the port of Singapore in 1856. He was later a magistrate and a practising lawyer. His essays published in *JIA* are a valuable source. His talent as a musician gave him a particular interest in that aspect of Malay culture.

L. Richmond Wheeler was a lecturer at the Sultan Idris Teacher Training College at Tanjong Malim in the 1920s. The College was one of the main centres of Malay intellectual and literary activity in Wheeler's time. His experiences prompted him to write a book about the impact of social change on Malay society. It is not an entirely successful effort but it is a pioneer study in this field.

Richard J. Wilkinson was a member of the Malayan Civil Service from 1889 to 1916, when he became Governor of Sierra Leone in West Africa. His *Dictionary*, the *Papers on Malay Subjects*, which he edited and for which he wrote some outstanding studies, and his brief period (1903–6) as head of the FMS Education Department are the main features of his outstanding contribution to Malay history, literature and education, which he did much to revitalize. Among British colonial officials who interested themselves in Malay culture Wilkinson ranks as the most outstanding—and understanding—figure. There is an obituary by Winstedt in *JMBRAS*, 20(1), 1947.

Sir Richard O. Winstedt was a member of the Malayan Civil Service from 1902 until 1935. During the 1920s he was Director of Education and a major influence, not always in the right direction, on the development of Malay education. As a scholar he made an enormous contribution to many fields of Malay studies. A Malay once said that 'Allah gave us a language and Winstedt gave us a grammar'. He also compiled dictionaries, wrote histories of Malaya and of individual Malay States, and contributed innumerable essays to *JMBRAS* on a variety of subjects. In the context of this book however he is most useful in his record of Malay village leadership in Perak in the early years of his service, when Winstedt was a district officer, and in his account of Malay houses, dress and other material artefacts.

Zainal Abidin bin Ahmad ('Zaba'), born in 1895, was one of the leading figures in Malay education, literature and intellectual life in the first half of the twentieth century. He wrote extensively in both English and Malay in newspapers and journals. His essays, cited in the bibliography of this book, touch on only a part of his literary output. It was a period when the Malay intelligentsia wrote at length on issues of progress, social reform and kindred topics. Zaba was pre-eminent among them—though he was an 'establishment' figure rather than a radical.

Glossary

In the text, Malay words and phrases are reproduced in the modern spelling except in quotations and in the footnotes and bibliography where titles of books and other publications appear in their original form, in so far as they include Malay words.

Where a figure appears in brackets after the short translation in the glossary below, this is a reference to the page of the text where a fuller explanation is given—in those cases where this may be needed to understand the term in question.

abdi	slave
adat	custom, tradition
adat perpatih	local custom of Negeri Sembilan based on Menangkabau tradition and matrilineal social organization
air	water, liquid
akal	intelligence, reason (in contrast to *hawa nafsu*)
amuk	reckless attack: running amok (240)
ampun	royal pardon or favour
ampun kurnia	royal bounty, gift of revenue from a specific source
anak	child, young (of animals), small part of a larger thing
anak buah	kinsmen or community under a headman (*penghulu*)
anak dagang	foreign Malay, i.e. one not a native of the state (226)
anak raja	prince, person of royal descent, aristocrat
anakenda/ayahanda	child/father—reciprocal forms of address especially between rulers of unequal status (40 note 18)
angin besar	great wind, tornado (104)
anjung	projecting front room, verandah
antari	inner vest worn under a pilgrim's gown
asah gigi	filing down the teeth (196)
atap	thatch: roof of any material (such as tiles)
ayam	fowl (cock or hen)
badik	dagger, poniard
bahara	measure of weight comprising 300 *kati*, i.e. approximately 400 lb or 181½ kg.
bahru (or *baharu*)	new, fresh (spelt '*bharu*' in 'Kota Bharu', capital of Kelantan)

baju	jacket (189)
baju belah/ baju kurung	types of jacket worn by women (190)
balai	hall of audience: office
balai hantu/ balai mandi	hall for ritual lustration (34)
bangsal	shed, booth
bangsal ma'yong	covered stage for open air theatrical performance (355 note 40)
bangsawan	type of theatrical performance (339)
bapa	father
batas	limit, boundary of a section of a padi-field (125)
bekas	box, storage receptacle
belabas (or *kain belabas*)	fabric with some gold and silver threads
belacan	shrimp paste, prawn paste
belacu (or *kain belacu*)	unbleached cotton cloth
belanja	expense; money with which to meet expense
belat	fish-trap (136)
beliung	Malay axe (164)
benang	thread
berhantu	haunted, connected with spirits (see *main berhantu* below)
bendang	wet padi-field (especially in North Malaya)
bergelar	possessing a title, office-holder (see *orang bergelar* below)
berjuang	charging (in battle), fighting (see *perjuangan* below)
berpuar	ritual mock-fight to drive spirits from fields (217)
bersanding	seated side by side (of spouses at wedding ceremony)
bersila	sitting cross-legged (proper male posture) (192)
bertam	palm (*Eugeissona tristis*)—its leaves are plaited to provide a thatch for houses (183)
bertangkap mangmang	ordeal by immersion (248)
bertimpoh	sitting with legs drawn back to one side (proper female posture)—contrast *bersila* above (194)
bertuah	fortunate, auspicious
bilal	*muezzin*, caller to prayer at the mosque
biola	violin (342)
biram	elephant (literary) (207 note 105)
bomoh (or *bomor*)	village doctor or medicine man
boria	band of musicians or their song (340)
buah	fruit (see also *anak buah* above)

budak	young boy or girl, youth
budak dalam	palace attendants (either sex)
budak raja	royal pages, bodyguards (50)
budu	pickled anchovy
bukit	hill
bulan	moon, lunar month (of Islamic calendar), calendar month
bulan puasa	month of fasting (*Ramadan*) (282)
buluh	bamboo
buluh perindu/ buluh ribut	bamboo pipes blown in the wind, aeolian harp (342)
bunuh	to kill
buruk	rotten (of materials), shabby, inferior
cacar	smallpox
cangkul	draw-hoe
cawi (or *kain cawi*)	kind of cloth
cenderawasih	bird of paradise
cindai (or *kain cindai*)	Indian cloth used in making sashes
ciri	formula spoken at the installation of a ruler or chief, especially at the installation of a Sultan of Perak
cunam	prepared lime used in making a betel-quid for chewing (195)
daerah	district, territorial division of a state
dalang	manipulator and reciter in a shadow-play (*wayang kulit*) (335)
damar	resin, torch made with resin
dapur	cooking hearth, kitchen
daulat	majesty, supernatural quality which invests a ruler
dedap	kind of tree (*Erythrina*)
dengung	humming sound, humming device attached to a kite-string
durian	thorny fruit (*Durio zebethinus*) celebrated for its creamy flesh and distinctive smell
dusun	orchard, fruit grove
fatwa	legal ruling (of a Muslim jurist) (290)
fikh	law based on Islamic doctrine
gajah	elephant
gambir	gambier (*Uncaria gambir*)—ingredient in betel-quid and exported for use in tanning leather
ganju	ordeal, test of guilt (256 note 65)

gantang	gallon or bushel as a measure of volume—a *gantang* of rice weighs about 5 *kati*, say 7 lb.
gelaran	title of nobility or of office
gendang	drum, especially for signals
getah	sap, latex—as in '*getah taban*' (gutta-percha)
gilir	to rotate, take in turns
giruf	steep (of a roof) (183)
gotong-royong	working together, co-operation in a village
gundik	secondary wife of a ruler: concubine (49)
guru	teacher, schoolmaster
hadis (or *hadith*)	tradition about the Prophet—source of doctrine (297)
haji	pilgrim to Mecca, respectful prefix to name of a pilgrim
hakim	judge
halaman	open space or lawn around a house
hamba	slave, bondsman—*hamba berhutang*: a debt-bondsman; *hamba datuk*: your lordship's servant (in addressing a chief)
hari	day, daytime
hari raya	holiday often meaning *Hari Raya Besar* below
Hari Raya Besar	holiday at the end of the month of fasting (also called *Aidilfitri* (Arabic))
Hari Raya Haji	the feast of the pilgrims to celebrate the anniversary (tenth day of the twelfth month) of the pilgrimage (also called *Aidiladha* (Arabic))
harta	wealth, property
harta pesaka	inherited property (in contrast to property acquired by purchase or development) (130, 298)
hati	heart or liver, seat of sensation (see *sakit hati*)
hawa nafsu	lusts of the flesh, sensual (in contrast to rational) elements of personality (327 note 31)
hikayat	romance, tale, chronicle (361 note 120)
hithrah (or *hadzrah*)	boys' dance (Islamic) (334)
hukum	judicial sentence or decision: divine decree
hukum syarak	Muslim law (in contrast to *adat* or custom)
hulam	uncooked vegetables
ibu	mother; largest item of a class
ibu-bapa	parents; junior tribal headman (Negeri Sembilan) (111)
ibu rumah	central or main room of a house
ikan	fish (*anak ikan*—small fish)
ikat diri	to bind oneself (249)

imam	leader, especially of congregation at a mosque (279)
istiadat	customary ceremonial
istana (or *astana*)	palace, residence of a ruler
jagung	maize
jala	casting net (for fish)
janda	widow or divorcee
jawi	Malay or Indonesian—*huruf Jawi* (often abbreviated to *Jawi*) denotes the traditional Malay script adapted from Arabic letters in contrast to *huruf Rumi* (abbreviated to *Rumi*) meaning the romanized script introduced in teaching Malay to schoolchildren in the 1890s (267, 275 note 62)
jawi pekan (or *peranakan*)	townsman of mixed Malay–Indian descent, especially at Penang (5)
jin	genie, spirit
joget	form of dance (333)
jubah	pilgrim's gown
jumaah (or *jumaha*)	assembly, society (291)
junjung	to carry on the head; execute a royal command (78)
kadi	registrar of (Muslim) marriage and divorce (286)
kafir	non-Muslim, infidel
kain	cloth, waist-cloth (*sarung*) (202 note 50): a generic word often prefixed to particular kinds of cloth
kalimah	sentence—*dua kalimah syahadat*: the Muslim declaration of Faith (305 note 55)
kampung	group, especially of houses; village or hamlet
kangchu	district headman (Chinese—Johor only) (112)
kanun	Muslim law made in exercise of his authority by a ruler; code of law (Pahang) (255 note 49)
kari (or *qari*)	person learned in the Koran or proficient in reading it aloud (303 note 25)
kati	measure of weight equivalent to 1⅓ lb. or 0.605 kg
kaum muda/kaum tua	opposed radical/conservative groups (290)
kebaya	woman's gown (191)
kebesaran	insignia of a ruler; magician's apparatus
kebulatan	unanimity
keladi	root crop (*Colocasia esculentum*)—the *taro* of the South Pacific
keledek	sweet potato (*Ipomoea batatas*); term of disparagement as in *loyar keledek* below
kembung (or *kepuk*)	rice-bin, granary
kemuning	tree (*Murraya paniculata*) whose yellow wood was used in making *keris* handles, etc.

kenduri	feast, especially on religious or ritual occasions
keping	piece; small coin (140)
kerabat am/ kerabat diraja	more distant/close relatives of ruler, especially in Terengganu (71)
kerah	corvée, i.e. compulsory service by customary obligation (99)
kerajaan	rule by a *raja*, monarchy, government as a system
keramat	person, place or thing with supernatural powers (325)
kereta sombong	express train (197)—literally 'haughty carriage'
keris	Malay dagger, typically with wavy edges
keruing	tree (*Dipterocarpus*) from which an oil (*minyak keruing*) can be extracted (155)
kerusi	chair
ketua kampung	village headman lower in status and responsibility than a *penghulu* (110)
ketumbuhan	smallpox (also *cacar*)
khalwat	proximity of a man and a woman suspected of immorality (in its primary sense—retirement from the world)
khatib	reader, mosque official
kincir	waterwheel for irrigating padi-fields (125)
koyan	measure of weight or capacity—usually 40 *pikul* or 800 *gantang*
kupang	coin (sometimes a 10-cent piece) (140)
Kuran	Koran, Muslim holy book
ladang	forest clearing for growing dry padi or other crops (125)
lading	short sword, chopper—with a blade which narrows near the hilt
lagu	tune, chant
lagu pemanggil	invocation to spirits at a seance (320)
lancang	vessel to carry away evil spirits (326 note 8)
latah	form of hysteria (261)
lauk	cooked meat or fish eaten with rice as a supplement to it
layang-layang	kite
lebai	man of piety, mosque elder
lembaga	ancient beginnings—*adat lembaga*: ancient custom; tribal headman (guardian of custom) in Negeri Sembilan (111)
lepau	kitchen (56); *orang lepau*: cook
lesung	mortar for pounding rice
lombong siam	mine pits (170 note 6)

lopak	section of a wet padi-field bounded by *batas*
loyar buruk/ loyar keledek	an unqualified agent acting in a legal matter; a lawyer who takes cases for very small fees (249)
luak	territory of an *Undang* (district chief) in Negeri Sembilan
madrasah	religious school (297)
maha menteri	chief minister
mahar	property settled on the wife by the husband which she retains if divorced without good cause
main berhantu/ main puteri	seance to contact or drive away spirits (318)
main catur	chess
main congkak	game played with cowrie shells (344)
main dam	draughts—the *dam* (queen) may move along any line on the board disregarding any other pieces on the same line (344)
main guli	game of rolling marbles (344)
main peri	theatrical performance (*wayang kulit*) without admission charge, i.e. free (336)
main silat/ main pencak	fencing, with or without weapons, unarmed combat, dance in imitation of fencing (353 note 15)
ma'inang/mek sni	female role (duenna to heroine) in *ma'yong* (338)
malu	shame, ashamed, shy, modest
masjid	mosque
masuk Melayu	to be converted to Islam—literally 'to enter the Malay [community]'
mata-mata	policeman—literally 'eyes'
Maulud	Prophet's birthday
ma'yong	theatrical performance (336); princess in the play (338)
menepuk tepung tawar	to sprinkle rice-flour as a ritual act (327 note 32)
menggeluncur	rock-slide (347)
menghilirkan sumbang	to drive evil down-river to get rid of it (317)
mengkuang	pandanus (screwpine) whose leaves are used for plaiting mats
menora	theatrical performance with Thai elements related to *ma'yong* (338)
menteri	minister
merampas	expropriate, confiscate (73)
merdeka	free man (in contrast to a slave); a debt-bondsman (*orang berhutang*) ranked as free (228 note 4)

mimbar	lectern, pulpit of a mosque
muda	young, junior; '*raja muda*' is either, according to local practice, a brother or other relative of a ruler who is appointed to assist him or a son of the ruler designated as his heir
mufti	Muslim consultant or jurist (283)
Muharam	first month of the Islamic year (340)
mukim	parish, area served by a mosque; (later) subdistrict (110)
naga berjuang	fighting dragon (type of kite)
nahu	grammar (297)
naib	assistant, especially *naib kadi*
nakhoda	master of a trading vessel; title given to a trader with seafaring connections
nebeng	village headman in Kelantan (Thai '*nai-ban*') equivalent to *ketua kampung* elsewhere—subordinate to *To Kweng*, Kelantan equivalent of *penghulu* (114)
nibung	palm (*Oncosperma*), whose hard but elastic wood was used in flooring houses
nipah	palm (*Nypa fruticans*) whose leaves were the main source of material for plaited palm thatch (*atap*) in the coastal districts where it flourished (155)
nobat	principal drum of royal band; royal band itself (29)
nusus (or *nushuz*)	refusal of wife to cohabit, disobedience to husband (310 note 101)
orang balai	servants of royal household
orang bergelar	title-holder, man of rank
orang berhutang	debt-bondsman (228 note 4)
orang besar	literally 'great man'; notable or chief of non-royal descent
orang hulur	slave-debtor to a *raja* for an unpaid fine (Pahang); man surrendered in compensation for a man killed (Negeri Sembilan)
orang kaya	literally 'wealthy man'; aristocrat
orang keistimewaan	royal favourite (Terengganu)
orang merdeka	free man (see *merdeka* above)
orang tebusan	indentured labourer, especially Javanese (113)
orang tua	old man, village elder
orlong (or *relong*)	measure of length or of area—240 feet or 73 metres approximately in length or 1⅓ acres or 0.6 hectare approximately in area
padi	rice plant; unhusked rice grain as harvested
padi bukit	dry padi grown on a *ladang* (clearing)

padi paya/ padi sawah	wet padi
paduka	honorific prefix to certain titles and forms of address, e.g. '*paduka ayahanda*' to a respected senior ruler (40 note 18)
pandai	clever, skilful
panglima	warrior, fighting captain
panjang	long
pantang	ritual prohibition, taboo
pantun	four-line verse with precise structural features (357 note 62)
para	attic used as sleeping place of unmarried daughters (181)
parang	chopper, general-purpose cutting tool
patek	word used by a subject (*rakyat*) to refer to himself when he addresses a ruler or other royal personage (73)
patut	fitting, proper
pawang	magician, practitioner of magical rites
paya	swamp (for wet padi cultivation) (125)
pa'yong	prince (in *ma'yong*) (338)
pekan	market, small town; (place name) royal capital of Pahang
penghulu	headman of a village or (later) of an administrative subdistrict (*mukim*)
penghulu istiadat	master of ceremonies (at a ruler's court)
penglipur lara	literally 'soother of care'—applied to traditional story-teller (361 note 112)
peon (or *piun*)	messenger, office-boy, especially with reference to such staff at government offices
perahu	boat, vessel, ship (anglicized as 'prow', 'prahu'): strictly it means an *undecked* vessel only
peran	stock role (clown) in *ma'yong*
perjuangan	struggle, moral reform (296)
perut	stomach, literally womb; sub-clan (Negeri Sembilan) (111)
petak	synonym of *lopak* above
peturun dalang	initiation of an apprentice to his craft by an established *dalang* (shadow-play operator)
peterana	mat of honour on which a ruler sat on his dais (33)
pikul	measure of weight, 100 *kati*, 133⅓ lb. or 60.5 kg
pinang	areca palm and its fruit, used in making a betel quid; '*Pulau Pinang*' is Penang Island
pinding	waist buckle (Bugis)
pisang	banana

pitis	small coin with hole in the centre (140)
pondok	hut, especially of student accommodation at a religious school (297)
puan	lady; married woman; honorific prefix to some name and titles of aristocratic women or a royal consort (64 note 25)
puasa	fasting—(see also *bulan puasa* above)
pucuk	shoot, especially of bamboo (259)
pulang belanja	to reimburse expenses, especially with reference to the price paid for developed land, i.e. a repayment to the seller of his investment (108)
pulut	glutinous rice (195)
puru	skin disease, yaws
raja	ruler; honorific prefix indicating royal descent in the male line of men or women (71)
raja sakti	role in *ma'yong*, magic prince (337)
rajawali	eagle, sparrowhawk (type of kite)
rakyat (or *raiat*, *ryot*)	subject of a ruler, peasant
ranjau	caltrop, spikes of bamboo or of metal set in a path as a trap (192, 242)
ratib	repetition of a religious formula as a mystic practice (281)
rawai (or *rawei*)	line of unbaited hooks drawn across the path of fish to trap them in the current of an estuary
raya	great, large, special, as in '*hari raya*'
rebab	viol, Malay fiddle (342)
relap	literally 'the shining streamers attached to a line and drawn through the water to frighten fish in a fish drive'; colloquially '*relap besar*' denotes the fish drive itself (136)
rezeki	primarily food, livelihood, income; the allotted fortune of an individual, his station in life, etc. (366)
riba	interest, usury
rodat	synonym for *hithrah* above
rokok	cigarette (160)
ronggeng	type of dance (333)
rotan	rattan (*Calamus*)
rukun	basic principle, article of faith (277)
rumi	romanized (of Malay script) (see also *jawi* above)
sabil Allah	literally 'path of God'; holy war against the infidel (292)

sabit	sickle (in contrast to *tuai* below)
sabung ayam	cock-fight (330)
sakit hati	anger, grievance, ill will (365)
sambal	condiments eaten with a curry such as peppers, grated coconut, salt fish and other foodstuffs to give flavour to the curry and rice
sampan	boat, dinghy
saputangan	handkerchief, head-cloth (see also *tengkolok* below)
sarung	sheath; waist-cloth (on this usage 202)
saudagar	merchant, wholesale dealer
sawah	wet padi-field, especially in South Malaya (see *bendang* above)
sayur	vegetables
sedati	Islamic dance (355 note 29)
sehari bulan	new moon, crescent (of a kite)
seladang	wild ox (*Bos gaurus*), perhaps the most dangerous of Malayan big-game
selendang	shawl worn over the head by women and over the shoulder by men
seluar	trousers (189)
seorang	one person by himself, a single person, individual
sepak raga	Malay ball game (332)
serah	to hand over, deliver
serambi	open verandah at the front of a house
serban	turban as worn by pilgrims (299)
serunai	trumpet, clarinet with bell mouth, instrument of the *nobat*
siak	caretaker of a mosque
singgasana	raised dais, throne of a ruler (33)
sirih	betel vine (*Piper betle*), betel leaf
songkok	Malay headgear (193)
songkok leleng	ceremonial Malay headgear (Bugis) (46 note 65)
sudu	spoon
suku	quarter; one of four tribes in Negeri Sembilan
suling (or *seruling*)	fife, flageolet, pipe
sumbang	devil, abomination
sungai	river, stream (spelt '*sungei*' in Sungei Ujong, part of Negeri Sembilan)
sungai korok	man-made channel for irrigation, drainage or as a canal for movement of boats
surau	prayer-house (278)
syahadat	testimony (see *kalimah syahadat* above)
syaikh (or *sheikh*)	title of a Hadramaut Arab who does not claim

	descent from the Prophet with the title *Syed*; agent (with reference to Arab agents, e.g. in pilgrim contexts)
syaikh-ul-islam	head of a local Muslim community, title given to a leading Muslim dignitary in a Malay state (307 note 82)
taban	tree (*Pallaquium*) from which gutta-percha (*getah taban*) is extracted
tahun	year—usually solar or lunar, but see below
tahun jagung	literally 'maize year', i.e. the three or four months in which a crop of maize grows to maturity (131)
tahun padi	literally 'rice year', i.e. six or seven months' growing season of padi (131)
tajak	slashing tool used for clearing off-season weeds which spring up on a padi-field between one harvest and the start of the next planting season
taji	metal spur attached to the foot of a fighting-cock
talak	formula by which a man may divorce his wife; if pronounced three times (*talak tiga*) an irrevocable divorce
tali air	irrigation channel to carry water from a pool or stream to the field
tanah	state (as in *Tanah Melayu*), land as property, soil
tara	level (in a literal sense or of status); applied to a flat roof of less than 45° angle
taraf	rank, position
tasauf	philosophy (Islamic)
taufsir	Islamic religious commentary
tauhid	doctrine of the unity of God
tawak	gong used for summons or signal
tawarikh	history, annals (361 note 120)
telaga	pool, well
telaga ikan	fish-pond
tembaga	brass, copper or similar metal
tembaga puteh	alloy used in Terengganu metalware (166)
tengah rumah	synonym for *ibu rumah* above
tendang	to kick
tenggala	plough
tengkolok	headkerchief (190)
terasul	correspondence, the art of letter-writing
tetampan	shoulder scarf worn by those attending a royal court (338)
tingkat	storey of a house or other structure (34)

titah	royal command
tolak bala	ceremony to drive out evil (317)
tongkat	walking-stick, stave; instrument in royal *nobat* (29)
tua	old, senior (in contrast to *muda* meaning 'junior')
tuai	Malay reaping knife (126)
tuba	poison obtained fron *Derris elliptica* or other plants and poured into a stream to stupefy the fish so that they float to the surface and may be caught; fishing by this method (136)
tudung	veil
tumbuk lada	small dagger—literally a 'pepper crusher'—often carried by women as a concealed weapon (239)
tunku (or *tengku*)	prince or princess of royal descent; honorific prefix (alternative to '*raja*' in some states) to indicate that status (71)
tunku puan	title of the principal wife of a ruler if she herself is of royal descent; if not the appropriate title is '*raja permaisuri*' (64 note 25)
ulama	theologians, men of Islamic erudition—a collective noun for this class as a group—the singular, less often used, is '*alim*' meaning 'a man of learning'
Undang	literally 'Lawgiver'; title of the four major territorial chiefs of Negeri Sembilan
undang-undang	laws, digest of laws (245)
untung	commercial profit or gain, in contrast to usury (*riba*), i.e. interest on loan of money (297)
usaha	effort, diligence (141)
wakaf	religious endowment, especially of land held for charitable and religious purposes (273)
wali	guardian of an unmarried girl who acts for her at the wedding ceremony (286)
wayang	theatrical performance
wayang kulit	shadow-play (335)
zakat	tithe, religious contribution (277)
zapin	modern dance of Arab origin (355 note 30)

Bibliography

THE sources of material used in this book fall broadly into two main categories—official papers, most of them held at the Public Records Office in London, and published books and articles. Many of the articles have appeared in the *Journal of the Straits Branch/Malayan/Malaysian Branch Royal Asiatic Society* since it first appeared in 1878.

Chapter 1 of this book includes a general discussion of the sources and their usefulness and reliability. This bibliography is provided to assist the reader who may require it to identify the specific source given in a footnote.

Official Papers

Official Reports: Periodic

ANNUAL REPORTS

British Residents and Advisers, heads of departments and district officers submitted formal annual reports. Most of this material was published in the official *Gazettes* of the SS (until about 1890) and then in the similar gazettes of state governments (in Perak and Selangor at least). In this century the reports appear as sessional papers of the state, federal or legislative councils as part of their proceedings. The Colonial Office records include bound volumes of annual reports of British Residents and Advisers.

JOURNALS AND MONTHLY REPORTS

Residents and district officers kept official journals. This is the origin of the journals of Hugh Low (1877), J. W. W. Birch (1874–5) and Frank Swettenham (1874–6), which have been edited and published in book form in recent years (see 'Books and Articles' below). The diary of Bloomfield Douglas (1876–82) was probably a personal record from which he wrote up his official journal.

In Perak and Selangor in the 1890s, lengthy extracts from the monthly reports of district officers were published in the official *Gazettes* of the two state governments. There was a similar practice in Sungei Ujong, though on a more restricted scale. In the early 1890s the *Sungei Ujong Gazette* was printed and published as a supplement to the *Selangor Gazette*, with which it is bound in the PRO files.

From 1909 onwards, the British Agent in Kuala Terengganu sent in a monthly journal which was forwarded to London under cover of a despatch from the Governor SS.

Council Proceedings and Papers

State councils were established in 1877–8 in Perak and Selangor, rather later in Sungei Ujong and Pahang.

The contemporaneous publication of council minutes began in the early 1890s when the governments of Perak and Selangor took the opportunity, arising from the establishment of their own official *Gazettes*, to include minutes of council meetings in the *Gazettes*.

The minutes of the Perak State Council for 1877–82, which are of great historical interest, were published in 1907–9 in the *Papers on Malay Subjects* series. These minutes (with some abridgement) have been reprinted in the 1971 selection of *Papers on Malay Subjects*, edited by P. L. Burns.

From 1909 onwards the British Advisers in Kedah and Perlis made their monthly reports to the Governor SS by sending to him a copy of the minutes of the meetings of the state council with a commentary. These minutes were in turn forwarded to the Colonial Office under cover of despatches.

The discussions in the SS Legislative Council in the latter part of the nineteenth century contain little which is pertinent to this study. But the proceedings of the SS Legislative Council fall into three parts—minutes, verbatim record of discussion, and sessional papers. A few of the sessional papers are very useful. These are:

Paper	*Title/Subject*
No. 5 of 1878	'Report Showing the Constitution of the Court of Justice in Perak Selangor and Sungei Ujong'
No. 23 of 1883	'Criminal Procedure Code [Local Rural Administration and Penghulus]'
No. 6 of 1893	'Reports Furnished by Order of His Excellency the Governor upon the Best Means of Encouraging the Cultivation of Rice in the Malay Peninsula'
No. 22 of 1917	'Report by Mr. R. O. Winstedt . . . on Vernacular and Industrial Education in the Netherlands East Indies and the Philippines'

The proceedings of the Federal Council of the FMS, established in 1909, are on similar lines but, apart from Hugh Clifford's statement of policy on the Malay states in 1927, begin too late to be relevant.

Official Correspondence

The CO 273 series at the Public Records Office comprises the despatches (cited as 'SSD' and date) from the Governor SS to the Colonial Office, and the CO minutes and draft replies. The final CO 273 volumes of each year contain Colonial Office correspondence on Malayan subjects with the

Foreign Office and other UK departments, and with individuals, including officials on leave from Malaya.

The main interest of this material is the abundant mass of memoranda and reports submitted to the Governor and forwarded by him in support of his despatches.

Each year or two the Colonial Office printed and laid before Parliament a number of important despatches, with their enclosures. These are particularly important for the 1870s and early 1880s. They are:

Command Paper	*Title*
466 of 1872	*Papers Relating to Salangore*
1111 of 1874	*Correspondence Relating to the Affairs of Certain Native States in the Malay Peninsula*
1320 of 1875	*Further Correspondence Relating to the Affairs of Certain Native States in the Malay Peninsula*
1503 of 1876	*Further Correspondence Relating to the Affairs of Certain Native States in the Malay Peninsula*
1505 of 1876	*Further Correspondence Relating to the Affairs of Certain Native States in the Malay Peninsula*
1512 of 1876	*Further Correspondence Relating to the Affairs of Certain Native States in the Malay Peninsula*
1709 of 1877	*Further Correspondence Relating to the Affairs of Certain Native States in the Malay Peninsula*
2410 of 1879	*Instructions to the British Resident and Other Papers Relating to the Protected Malay States*
3095 of 1881	*Papers Relating to the Protected Malay States*
3285 of 1882	*Correspondence Respecting Slavery in the Protected Malay States*
3428 of 1882	*Correspondence Respecting Slavery in the Protected Malay States*
3429 of 1882	*Further Correspondence Respecting Slavery in the Protected Malay States*

The publication of these papers continues through the 1880s and 1890s. Its main content is the annual reports submitted from Singapore, despatches reporting gubernatorial tours of the states, etc.

At times when the situation in the Malay States was causing concern, and generating voluminous correspondence, e.g. the period 1874–7, the Colonial Office printed the papers for its own use in the 'Eastern Pamphlets' series. The correspondence laid before Parliament was a selection of most, but not all, of the papers printed within the Colonial Office. The Eastern Pamphlets are held at the Public Records Office in the series CO 882 (previously CO 819).

Special Reports and Memoranda

The following printed papers or despatches deserve mention:

1. 'Enquiry as to the Complicity of Chiefs in the Perak Outrages'. Under cover of SSD 14 December 1876 the Governor SS forwarded the record of evidence, working papers and summaries and findings of the commission established to enquire into the events leading up to the death of J. W. W. Birch in Perak in November 1875. This is a vivid picture of Malay aristocratic life in Perak (and is cited in this book as 'PCE'). It fills three bulky volumes (CO 273/86–88) at the Public Records Office.
2. Command Paper 835 of 1905 in Special Reports on Educational Subjects, vol. 8, 'The Education of Asiatics', by R. J. Wilkinson.
3. Command Paper 2379 of 1905 in Special Reports on Educational Subjects, 'The System of Education in the FMS'.
4. *Report of the Commission Appointed by His Excellency the High Commissioner to Enquire into Certain Matters Relating to the State of Trengganu* ('The Bucknill Report'), Singapore, Government Printing Office, 1918.
5. *Malaya: A Report on the 1947 Census of Population*, by M. V. del Tufo, London, Crown Agents for the Colonies, 1949.

Books and Articles

Abdul Majid bin Zainuddin, Haji, 'A Malay's Pilgrimage to Mecca', *JMBRAS*, 4(2), 1926.

_____ *The Malays in Malaya: By One of Them*, Singapore, Malaya Publishing House, 1928.

_____ *The Wandering Thoughts of a Dying Man: The Life and Times of Haji Abdul Majid bin Zainuddin*, edited by William R. Roff, Kuala Lumpur, Oxford University Press, 1978.

Abdul Rahman al Ahmadi, 'Notes towards a History of Malay Periodicals in Kelantan', in William R. Roff (ed.), *Kelantan: Religion, Society and Politics in a Malay State*, Kuala Lumpur, Oxford University Press, 1974.

Abdullah Al-Qari bin Haji Salleh, 'To Kenali: His Life and Influence', in William R. Roff (ed.), *Kelantan: Religion, Society and Politics in a Malay State*, Kuala Lumpur, Oxford University Press, 1974.

Abdullah bin Abdul Kadir, Munshi, *Kesah Pelayaran Abdullah*, translated by A. E. Coope, *The Voyage of Abdullah: A Translation from the Malay*, Singapore, Malaya Publishing House, 1949.

Allen, J. de V., 'Two Imperialists: A Study of Sir Frank Swettenham and Sir Hugh Clifford', *JMBRAS*, 37(1), 1964.

_____ 'The Ancien Regime in Trengganu 1909–1919', *JMBRAS*, 41(1), 1968.

_____ 'The Elephant and the Mousedeer—A New Version: Anglo-Kedah Relations 1905–1915', *JMBRAS*, 41(1), 1968.

_____ 'Sultan Zainal Abidin III of Trengganu', *Malaya in History*, 1, 1968.

Allen, J. de V., Stockwell, A. J. and Wright, L. R. (eds.), *A Collection of Treaties and Other Documents Affecting the States of Malaysia 1761–1963*, 2 vols., New York, Oceana Publications, 1981.

Aminuddin bin Baki, 'The Institution of Debt-Slavery in Perak', *Peninjau Sejarah*, 1(1), 1966.

Andaya, B. W., 'The Installation of the First Sultan of Selangor in 1766', *JMBRAS*, 47(1), 1974.

_____ 'The Indian "Saudagar Raja" (The King's Merchant) in Traditional Malay Courts', *JMBRAS*, 51(1), 1978.

_____ *Perak: The Abode of Grace*, Kuala Lumpur, Oxford University Press, 1979.

Anderson, J., *Political and Commercial Considerations Relative to the Malayan Peninsula and the British Settlements in the Straits of Malacca*, Penang, 1824; reprinted in *JMBRAS*, 35(4), 1962.

Annandale, N. and Robinson, H. C., *Fasciculi Malayenses: Anthropological and Zoological Results of an Expedition to Perak and the Siamese Malay States 1901–1902, Anthropology—Part 1*, The University Press of Liverpool, 1903.

Anon., 'Journal Kept on Board a Cruiser in the Indian Archipelago in 1846', *JIA*, 8, 1854.

Anson, A. E., *About Others and Myself 1745–1920*, London, Murray, 1920.

Bastin, J., 'Problems of Personality in the Reinterpretation of Malayan History', in J. Bastin and R. Roolvink (eds.), *Malayan and Indonesian Studies—Essays Presented to Sir Richard Winstedt on His Eighty-fifth Birthday*, London, Oxford University Press, 1964.

Bastin, J. and Roolvink, R. (eds.), *Malayan and Indonesian Studies: Essays Presented to Sir Richard Winstedt on His Eighty-fifth Birthday*, London, Oxford University Press, 1964.

Begbie, P. J., *The Malayan Peninsula Embracing the History, Manners and Customs of the Inhabitants, Politics, Natural History, etc. from Its Earliest Records*, Madras, Vespery Mission Press, 1834; reprinted as *The Malayan Peninsula*, Kuala Lumpur, Oxford University Press, 1967.

Birch, E. W., 'The Vernacular Press in the Straits', *JSBRAS*, 4, 1879; reprinted *JMBRAS*, 42(1), 1969.

Birch, J. W. W., *The Journals of J. W. W. Birch First British Resident to Perak 1874–1875*, edited by P. L. Burns, Kuala Lumpur, Oxford University Press, 1976.

Bird, I. L. (Mrs Bishop), *The Golden Chersonese and the Way Thither*, London, Murray, 1883; reprinted Kuala Lumpur, Oxford University Press, 1967 and 1980.

Blagden, C. O., 'Notes on the Folklore and Popular Religion of the Malays', *JSBRAS*, 29, 1896.

Blythe, W., *The Impact of Chinese Secret Societies in Malaya: A Historical Study*, London, Oxford University Press, 1969.

Braddell, R. St. J., 'The Good Old Days', in W. Makepeace, G. E. Brooke and R. St. J. Braddell (eds.), *One Hundred Years of Singapore*, London, Murray, 1921.

Braddell, T., 'Notes of a Trip to the Interior of Malacca', *JIA*, 7, 1853.

Brown, C. C., 'Kelantan Bull-fighting', *JMBRAS*, 6(1), 1928.

_____ *Malay Sayings*, Routledge & Kegan Paul, London, 1951.

Buckley, C. B., *An Anecdotal History of Old Times in Singapore 1819–1867*, 2 vols., Singapore, Fraser & Neave, 1902; reprinted Kuala Lumpur, University of Malaya Press, 1965, and Singapore, Oxford University Press, 1984.

Burdon, T. W., 'The Fishing Methods in Singapore', in T. W. Burdon and M. L. Parry (eds.), 'Papers on Malayan Fishing Methods', *JMBRAS*, 27(2), 1954.

Burdon, T. W. and Parry, M. L. (eds.), 'Papers on Malayan Fishing Methods', *JMBRAS*, 27(2), 1954.

Burkill, I. H., *A Dictionary of the Economic Products of the Malay Peninsula*, 2 vols., London, published on behalf of the SS and FMS Governments, Crown Agents, 1935.

Burney, H., *Burney Papers*, 5 vols., Bangkok, Siam Society, 1910–14.

Burridge, K. O. L., 'The Malay Composition of a Village in Johore', *JMBRAS*, 29(3), 1956.

_____ 'Managerial Influences in a Johore Village', *JMBRAS*, 30(1), 1957.

Butcher, J. G., *The British in Malaya 1880–1941: The Social History of a European Community in Colonial South-East Asia*, Kuala Lumpur, Oxford University Press, 1979.

Buyong bin Adil, Haji, *Sejarah Selangor*, Kuala Lumpur, Dewan Bahasa dan Pustaka, 1971.

Cadby, F., *To Siam and Malaya in the Duke of Sutherland's Yacht 'Sans Peur'*, London, Hurst & Blackett, 1889.

Cameron, J., *Our Tropical Possessions in Malayan India: Being a Descriptive Account of Singapore, Penang, Province Wellesley, and Malacca, their Peoples, Products, Commerce and Government*, London, Smith, Elder & Co., 1865; reprinted as *Our Tropical Possessions in Malayan India*, Kuala Lumpur, Oxford University Press, 1965.

Cameron, W., 'On the Patani', *JSBRAS*, 11, 1883.

Cant, R. G., *An Historical Geography of Pahang*, MBRAS Monograph No. 4, 1973.

Cavenagh, O., *Reminiscences of an Indian Official*, London, W. H. Allen & Co., 1884.

Chai Hon-Chan, *The Development of British Malaya 1896–1909*, Kuala Lumpur, Oxford University Press, 1964.

Chandra, M., *Protector? An Analysis of the Concept and Practice of Loyalty ... within Malay Society*, Penang, Aliran, 1979.

_____ 'Continuity and Change in Malay Ideas of the Melakan Period', in K. S. Sandhu and P. Wheatley (eds.), *Melaka: The Transformation of a*

Malay Capital c.1400–1980, Kuala Lumpur, Oxford University Press, 1983.

Cheah Boon Kheng, 'Social Banditry and Rural Crime in North Kedah 1909–1929', *JMBRAS*, 54(2), 1981.

Cheeseman, H. R., 'Education in Malaya, 1900–1941', *MHJ*, 2(1), 1955.

Chelliah, D. D., *A Short History of Education in the Straits Settlements*, Kuala Lumpur, Government Press, 1947; reprinted Singapore, G. H. Kiat, 1960.

Cheng Siok Hwa, 'The Rice Industry of Malaya: A Historical Survey', *JMBRAS*, 42(2), 1969.

Chiang Hai Ding, 'The Origins of the Malayan Currency System', *JMBRAS*, 39(1), 1966.

Clifford, H. C., *In Court and Kampong, Being Tales and Sketches of Native Life in the Malay Peninsula*, London, Grant Richards, 1897 (2nd ed. with autobiographical preface, London, Richards Press, 1927).

_____ 'A Journey through the Malay States of Trengganu and Kelantan', *The Geographical Journal*, 9(1), 1897 (a shortened version of 1961 item below—with additional introductory material).

_____ *Studies in Brown Humanity being Scrawls and Smudges in Sepia, White and Yellow*, London, Grant Richards, 1898.

_____ *In a Corner of Asia being Tales and Impressions of Men and Things in the Malay Peninsula*, London, Fisher Unwin, 1899.

_____ *Malayan Monochromes*, New York, Dutton, 1913.

_____ *A Prince of Malaya*, New York, Harper, 1926; originally published as 'Sally' in *Blackwoods Magazine*, February 1904, and *Saleh: A Sequel*, London, Blackwood, 1908.

_____ *In Days that are Dead*, London, Murray, 1926.

_____ *The Further Side of Silence*, New York, Doubleday, Page & Co., 1927.

_____ *Bushwhacking and Other Asiatic Tales and Memories*, New York, Harper, 1929.

_____ 'Report: Expedition to Trengganu and Kelantan', *JMBRAS*, 34(1), 1961; originally printed for Colonial Office use in 1895; reprinted Kuala Lumpur, Government Press, 1936.

_____ *Stories by Sir Hugh Clifford*, edited by William R. Roff, Kuala Lumpur, Oxford University Press, 1966.

_____ 'Life in the Malay Peninsula: As It Was and Is', in P. H. Kratoska (ed.), *Honourable Intentions: Talks on the British Empire in South-East Asia Delivered at the Royal Colonial Institute, 1874–1928*, Singapore, Oxford University Press, 1983; reprinted from the *Proceedings of the Royal Colonial Institute*, 1899.

_____ 'British and Siamese Malaya', in P. H. Kratoska (ed.), *Honourable Intentions: Talks on the British Empire in South-East Asia Delivered at the Royal Colonial Institute, 1874–1928*, Singapore, Oxford University Press, 1983; reprinted from the *Proceedings of the Royal Colonial Institute*, 1902.

Coope, A. E., 'The *Kangchu* System in Johore', *JMBRAS*, 14(3), 1936.

Copeland, H., 'A Few Weeks among the Malays', *Straits Times*, 4 April 1883.

Cowan, C. D., *Nineteenth Century Malaya: The Origins of British Political Control*, London, Oxford University Press, 1961.

Crawfurd, J., *A Descriptive Dictionary of the Indian Islands and Adjacent Countries*, London, Bradbury and Evans, 1856; reprinted Kuala Lumpur, Oxford University Press, 1971.

Crookewit, H., 'The Tin Mines of Malacca', *JIA*, 8, 1854, translated from Dutch.

Davison, W., 'Journal of a Trip to Pahang with H. E. the Governor', *JSBRAS*, 20, 1889.

De Bruijn Kops, G. F., 'Sketch of the Riau-Linggi Archipelago', *JIA*, 8, 1854.

De la Croix, J. E., 'Some Account of the Mining Districts of Lower Perak', *JSBRAS*, 7, 1881.

Dennys, M. B., *A Descriptive Dictionary of British Malaya*, London, London and China Telegraph, 1894.

Djamour, J., *The Muslim Matrimonial Court in Singapore*, London, Athlone Press, 1966.

Dodge, N. N., 'Population Estimates for the Malay Peninsula in the Nineteenth Century with Special Reference to the East Coast States', *Population Studies*, 34(3), 1980.

Earl, G. W., *The Eastern Seas: Or Voyages and Adventures in the Indian Archipelago in 1832–33–34 . . . Commercial Resources of the Archipelago*, London, W. H. Allen & Co., 1837; reprinted as *The Eastern Seas*, Singapore and Kuala Lumpur, Oxford University Press, 1971.

Ellen, R. F., 'Social Theory, Ethnography and the Understanding of Practical Islam in South-East Asia', in M. B. Hooker (ed.), *Islam in South-East Asia*, Leiden, Brill, 1983.

Endicott, K. M., *An Analysis of Malay Magic*, Oxford, Oxford University Press, 1970; reprinted Kuala Lumpur, Oxford University Press, 1981.

Evans, I. H. N., 'Ethnological Miscellanea: Setting up the Posts of a Malay House', *Journal of the FMS Museum*, 7(4), 1918.

_____ *Papers on the Ethnology and Archaeology of the Malay Peninsula*, Cambridge, Cambridge University Press, 1927.

Fauconnier, H., *The Soul of Malaya*, translated from French by E. Sutton, London, Elkin, Mathew & Marrot, 1931, originally published as *Malaisie*, Paris, Librairie Stock, 1930; reprinted Singapore, Oxford University Press, 1985.

Favre, P., *An Account of the Wild Tribes Inhabiting the Malayan Peninsula, Sumatra and a Few Neighbouring Islands*, Paris, Imperial Printing Office, 1865; including a reprint of 'A Journey in the Menangkabaw States of the Malay Peninsula', *JIA*, 3, 1849.

Firth, R. W., *Malay Fishermen: Their Peasant Economy*, London, Kegan

Paul, 1946 (revised edition 1966).

_____ 'Ritual and Drama in Malay Spirit Mediumship', *Comparative Studies in Society and History*, 9, 1967.

_____ 'Faith and Scepticism in Kelantan Village Magic', in William R. Roff (ed.), *Kelantan: Religion, Society and Politics in a Malay State*, Kuala Lumpur, Oxford University Press, 1974.

Firth, Rosemary, *Housekeeping among Malay Peasants*, London, Athlone Press, 1943 (revised edition 1966).

Forbes, D., *The Heart of Malaya*, London, Robert Hale, 1966.

Fraser, T. M., *Rusembilan: A Malay Fishing Village in Southern Thailand*, Ithaca, Cornell University Press, 1960.

Freedman, M. (ed.), *Social Organisation: Essays Presented to Raymond Firth*, London, Frank Cass, 1967.

Fukui, H., 'An Agro-environmental Consideration', in M. Kuchiba, Y. Tsubouchi, and N. Maeda (eds.), *Three Malay Villages: A Sociology of Paddy Growers in West Malaysia*, translated by P. Hawkes and S. Hawkes, Honolulu, University Press of Hawaii, 1979.

Galloway, D. J., 'A Contribution to the Psychology of *Latah*', *JSBRAS*, 85, 1922.

Gardner, G. B., *Keris and Other Malay Weapons*, Singapore, Progressive Publishing Co., 1936.

Gibson-Hill, C. A., 'The Boats of Local Origin Employed in the Malayan Fishing Industry', *JMBRAS*, 27(2), 1954.

Gimlette, J. D., *Malay Poisons and Charm Cures*, London, Churchill, 1915 (3rd ed. 1929); reprinted Kuala Lumpur, Oxford University Press, 1971, and Singapore, Oxford University Press, 1985.

Gimlette, J. D. and Thomson, H. W., *A Dictionary of Malayan Medicine*, London, Oxford University Press, 1939; reprinted Kuala Lumpur, Oxford University Press, 1971 and 1983.

Gordon-Hall, W. A., 'Yam Tuan Mohamed', *Malaya*, 1954.

Graham, W. A., *Kelantan—A State of the Malay Peninsula: A Handbook of Information*, Glasgow, James MacLehose & Sons, 1908.

Grist, D. H., 'The Rice Problem', *Journal of Tropical Geography*, 5, 1955.

Gullick, J. M., 'A Careless, Heathen Philosopher?', *JMBRAS*, 26(1), 1953.

_____ 'Kuala Lumpur 1880–1895', *JMBRAS*, 28(4), 1955.

_____ 'The Malay Administrator', *Merdeka Outlook*, 1(1), 1957.

_____ *Indigenous Political Systems of Western Malaya*, London, Athlone Press, 1958.

_____ 'Selangor 1876–1882—The Bloomfield Douglas Diary', *JMBRAS*, 48(2), 1975.

_____ 'The Tampin Succession', *JMBRAS*, 49(2), 1976.

_____ 'Syers and the Selangor Police Force 1875–1897', *JMBRAS*, 51(2), 1978.

_____ 'Isabella Bird's Visit to Malaya: A Centenary Tribute', *JMBRAS*, 52(2), 1979.

_____ *The Story of Kuala Lumpur 1857–1939*, Singapore, Eastern Universities Press, 1983.

_____ 'Kedah 1821–1855: Years of Exile and Return', *JMBRAS*, 56(2), 1983.

_____ 'The Entrepreneur in Late 19th Century Malay Peasant Society', *JMBRAS*, 58(1), 1985.

_____ 'Kedah in the Reign of Sultan Ahmad Tajuddin II (1854–1879)', *JMBRAS*, 58(2), 1985.

_____ 'The Elephants of Syed Zin', *JMBRAS*, 59(1), 1986.

_____ 'Tunku Kudin in Selangor 1868–1878', *JMBRAS*, 59(2), 1986.

Hale, A., 'On Mines and Miners in Kinta, Perak', *JSBRAS*, 16, 1885.

Hall, D. G. E., *A History of South-East Asia*, London, Macmillan, 1955 (4th ed. 1981).

Harrison, B., 'The Anglo-Chinese College and Early Modern Education', in K. S. Sandhu and P. Wheatley (eds.), *Melaka: The Transformation of a Malay Capital c.1400–1980*, 2 vols., Kuala Lumpur, Oxford University Press, 1983.

Harrison, C. W., *The Magic of Malaya*, London, John Lane, 1916.

_____ *Some Notes on the Government Services in Malaya*, London, Government Information Agency, 1929.

Hashimah Roose, 'Changes in the Position of Malay Women', in B. Ward (ed.), *Women in the New Asia: The Changing Social Roles of Men and Women in South and South-East Asia*, Paris, UNESCO, 1964.

Haughton, H. T., 'Boriah', *JSBRAS*, 30, 1897.

Hay, M. C., Review of J. M. Gullick, *Indigenous Political Systems of Western Malaya*, *Journal of the Royal Asiatic Society*, 1959, p. 170.

Hill, A. H., 'Wayang Kulit Stories from Trengganu', *JMBRAS*, 22(3), 1949.

Hill, R. D., *Rice in Malaya: A Study in Historical Geography*, Kuala Lumpur, Oxford University Press, 1977.

_____ 'The History of Rice Cultivation in Melaka', in K. S. Sandhu and P. Wheatley (eds.), *Melaka: The Transformation of a Malay Capital c.1400–1980*, 2 vols., Kuala Lumpur, Oxford University Press, 1983.

Hilton, R. N., 'The Basic Malay House', *JMBRAS*, 29(3), 1956.

Hooker, M. B., 'A Note on the Malayan Legal Digests', *JMBRAS*, 41(1), 1968.

_____ *Readings in Malay Adat Laws*, Singapore, Singapore University Press, 1970.

_____ *Adat Laws in Modern Malaya*, Kuala Lumpur, Oxford University Press, 1972.

_____ *The Personal Laws of Malaysia*, Kuala Lumpur, Oxford University Press, 1976.

_____ 'Muhammadan Law and Islamic Law', in M. B. Hooker (ed.), *Islam in South-East Asia*, Leiden, Brill, 1983.

_____ (ed.), *Islam in South-East Asia*, Leiden, Brill, 1983.

_____ *Islamic Law in South-East Asia*, Singapore, Oxford University Press, 1984.

Hornaday, W. T., *Two Years in the Jungle: The Experiences of a Hunter and Naturalist in India, Ceylon, the Malay Peninsula and Borneo*, New York, Scribner, 1885.

Hurgronje, C. S., *The Achehnese*, translated by A. W. S. O'Sullivan, 2 vols., London, Luzac, 1906.

_____ *Mekka in the Latter Part of the 19th Century*, translated by J. H. Monahan, Leiden, Brill, 1931.

Hussain bin Mahmud, 'Sultan Idris of Perak', *Malaya in History*, 13(1), 1970.

Innes, E., *The Chersonese with the Gilding Off*, 2 vols., Richard Bentley and Son, London, 1885; reprinted (1 vol.) Kuala Lumpur, Oxford University Press, 1974.

International Bank for Reconstruction and Development, *The Economic Development of Malaya*, Baltimore, Johns Hopkins, 1955.

Jackson, J. C., *Planters and Speculators: Chinese and European Agricultural Enterprise in Malaya 1786–1921*, Kuala Lumpur and Singapore, University of Malaya Press, 1968.

_____ 'Rice Cultivation in West Malaysia: Relationship between Culture History, Customary Practices and Recent Developments', *JMBRAS*, 45(2), 1972.

Jackson, R. N., *Immigrant Labour and the Development of Malaya 1786–1920*, Kuala Lumpur, Government Printer, 1961.

Jones, S. W., *Public Administration in Malaya*, London, Royal Institute of International Affairs, 1953.

Johns, A. H., 'Malay Sufism as Illustrated in an Anonymous Collection of 17th Century Tracts', *JMBRAS*, 30(2), 1957.

Kempe, J. E. and Winstedt, R. O. (eds.), 'A Malay Legal Digest Compiled for ... Sultan of Pahang', *JMBRAS*, 21(1), 1948.

Kessler, C. S., *Islam and Politics in a Malay State: Kelantan 1838–1969*, Ithaca, Cornell University Press, 1978.

Keyser, A. L., *People and Places: A Life in Five Continents*, London, Murray, 1922.

_____ *Trifles and Travels*, London, Murray, 1923.

_____ *From Jungle to Java*, London, Roxburghe Press, 1928.

Khasnor Johan, *The Emergence of the Modern Malay Administrative Élite*, Singapore, Oxford University Press, 1984.

Khoo Kay Kim, 'Johor in the 19th Century: A Brief Survey', *Journal of the Historical Society, University of Malaya*, 4, 1967–8.

_____ 'Malay Society 1874–1920', *JSEAS*, 5(2), 1974.

_____ *The Western Malay States 1850–1873: The Effects of Commercial Development on Malay Politics*, Kuala Lumpur, Oxford University Press, 1972.

_____ 'Raja Lumu—Sultan Salehuddin: The Founding of the Selangor Dynasty', *JMBRAS*, 58(2), 1985.

Kratoska, P. H. (ed.), *Honourable Intentions: Talks on the British Empire in South-East Asia Delivered at the Royal Colonial Institute 1874–1928*, Singapore, Oxford University Press, 1983.

Kuchiba, M., Tsubouchi, Y. and Maeda, N. (eds.), *Three Malay Villages: A Sociology of Paddy Growers in West Malaysia*, translated by P. Hawkes and S. Hawkes, Honolulu, University Press of Hawaii, 1979.

Lake, H., 'Johore', *The Geographical Journal*, 3, 1894.

Lambert, R. D. and Hoselitz, B. (eds.), *The Role of Savings and Wealth in Southern Asia and the West*, Paris, UNESCO, 1963.

Lim Teck Ghee, *Peasants and Their Agricultural Economy in Colonial Malaya 1874–1941*, Kuala Lumpur, Oxford University Press, 1977.

Linehan, W., 'Reinstatement of an *Orang Hulur*', *JMBRAS*, 4(2), 1926.

_____ 'The Bendaharas of Pahang', *JMBRAS*, 4(3), 1926.

_____ 'A History of Pahang', *JMBRAS*, 14(2), 1936.

Logan, J. R., 'Journal of an Excursion from Singapur to Malacca and Pinang', *Journal of the Royal Geographical Society*, 16, 1846.

_____ 'Five Days in Naning', *JIA*, 3, 1849.

_____ 'The Manners and Customs of the Malays: Dress', *JIA*, 3, 1849.

_____ 'The Manners and Customs of the Malays: Meals', *JIA*, 4, 1850.

_____ 'Notes at Penang, Kedah etc.', *JIA*, 5, 1851.

_____ 'Plan for a Volunteer Police in the Muda Districts, Province Wellesley, Submitted to Government by the Late J. R. Logan in 1867', *JSBRAS*, 16, 1885.

Loh Fook Seng, P., 'The British Approach to Slavery in the Straits Settlements and the Malay States 1819 to 1910', *Journal of the Historical Society, University of Malaya*, 3, 1964–5.

_____ *The Malay States 1877–1895—Political Change and Social Policy*, Kuala Lumpur, Oxford University Press, 1969.

Lovat, A., *The Life of Sir Frederick Weld—A Pioneer of Empire*, London, Murray, 1914.

Low, H., 'The Journal of Sir Hugh Low, Perak 1877', edited by E. Sadka, *JMBRAS*, 27(4), 1954.

Low, J., *A Dissertation on the Soil and Agriculture of the British Settlement of Penang or Prince of Wales Island in the Straits of Malacca including Province Wellesley on the Malayan Peninsula ..., with ... Incidental Observations, etc.*, Singapore, Singapore Free Press, 1836; reprinted as *The British Settlement at Penang*, Singapore, Oxford University Press, 1972.

_____ 'Observations on Perak', *JIA*, 4, 1850.

_____ 'Retrospect of British Policy in the Straits of Malacca ... and the Neighbouring Native States', manuscript in file CO 273/1 at the Public Records Office, printed in H. Burney, *Burney Papers*, Vol. 5, Pt. 1, Bangkok, Siam Society, 1914.

Macgowan, D. J., 'Notes on the Maritime Malays', *JIA*, 4, 1850.

Mackeen, A. M. M., *Contemporary Islamic Organisation in Malaya*, Monograph No. 13, New Haven, Yale University, Southeast Asia Studies, 1969.

McNair, J. F. A., *Perak and the Malays: Sarong and Keris*, London Tinsley Bros., 1878; reprinted Kuala Lumpur, Oxford University Press 1972.

McVey, R. T. (ed.), *Southeast Asian Transitions: Approaches through Social History*, New Haven and London, Yale University Press, 1978.

Mahmud bin Mat, Datuk, 'The Passing of Slavery in East Pahang', *MHJ*, 1(1), 1954.

_____ 'The First Malay School in Pahang', *MHJ*, 1(2), 1954.

_____ 'Some Features of Malay Life in East Pahang at the Close of the 19th and the Beginning of the 20th Centuries', *Malaysia*, May 1964.

Makepeace, W., Brooke, G. E. and Braddell, R. St. J. (eds.), *One Hundred Years of Singapore being Some Account of the Capital of the Straits Settlements ... to the 6th February 1919*, 2 vols., London, Murray 1921.

Maxwell, W. E., 'A Malay Kramat', *JSBRAS*, 2, 1878.

_____ 'Malay Proverbs, Part 3', *JSBRAS*, 3, 1879.

_____ 'A Journey on Foot to the Patani Frontier in 1876 being a Journal Kept during an Expedition Undertaken to Capture Datoh Maharajah Lela of Perak', *JSBRAS*, 9, 1882.

_____ 'Shamanism in Perak', *JSBRAS*, 12, 1883.

_____ 'The Law and Customs of the Malays with Reference to the Tenure of Land', *JSBRAS*, 13, 1884.

_____ 'The History of Perak from Native Sources', *JSBRAS*, 14, 1884.

_____ *Notes and Queries*, issued with *JSBRAS*, 14, 1884.

_____ *Notes and Queries*, issued with *JSBRAS*, 15, 1885.

_____ 'Penglipur Lara: The Soother of Cares', English translation of a Malay text entitled (in English) 'Sri Rama: A Malay Fairy Tale founded on the Ramayana', *JSBRAS*, 17, 1886.

_____ *Notes and Queries*, issued with *JSBRAS*, 17, 1886.

_____ 'The Law Relating to Slavery among the Malays', *JSBRAS*, 22, 1890.

_____ 'The Malay Peninsula: Its Resources and Prospects', in P. H. Kratoska (ed.), *Honourable Intentions: Talks on the British Empire in South-East Asia Delivered at the Royal Colonial Institute 1874–1928*, Singapore, Oxford University Press, 1983; reprinted from the *Proceedings of the Royal Colonial Institute*, 1891.

_____ *Memorandum on the Introduction of a Land Code in the Native States in the Malay Peninsula*, Singapore, Government Printer, 1894.

Maxwell, W. G., 'Mantra Gajah', *JSBRAS*, 45, 1906.

_____ *In Malay Forests*, Edinburgh, Blackwood, 1930.

_____ 'Memories of the First British Adviser Kedah', *Malaya in History*, 4, 1958.

Mayer, C., *Trapping Wild Animals in Malay Jungles*, London, Fisher & Unwin, 1922.

Means, G. P., 'The Role of Islam in the Political Development of Malaysia',

Comparative Politics, 1(2), 1969.

Middlebrook, S. M., 'Yap Ah Loy', *JMBRAS*, 24(2), 1951.

Mills, L. A., 'British Malaya 1824–1867', *JMBRAS*, 3(2), 1925; reprinted *JMBRAS*, 33(3), 1960.

Milner, A. C., 'Islam and Malay Kingship', *Journal of the Royal Asiatic Society*, 1981, pp. 46–70.

_____ *Kerajaan: Malay Political Culture on the Eve of Colonial Rule*, Tucson, University of Arizona Press, 1982.

_____ 'Islam and the Muslim State', in M. B. Hooker (ed.), *Islam in South-East Asia*, Leiden, Brill, 1983.

Mohamed Amin Hassan, 'Raja Muda Musa ibni Sultan Abdul Samad', *Peninjau Sejarah*, 1(1), 1966.

_____ 'Raja Bot bin Raja Jumaat', *JMBRAS*, 40(2), 1967.

Mohamed Ibrahim bin Abdullah, Munshi, *The Voyages of Mohamed Ibrahim Munshi*, translated by A. Sweeney and Nigel Phillips, Kuala Lumpur, Oxford University Press, 1975.

Mohamed bin Nik Mohamed Salleh, 'Kelantan in Transition 1891–1910', in W. R. Roff (ed.), *Kelantan: Religion, Society and Politics in a Malay State*, Kuala Lumpur, Oxford University Press, 1974.

Mohamed Said, Datuk, *Memoirs of a Menteri Besar: Early Days*, Singapore, Heinemann, 1982.

Mohamed Salleh bin Perang, Datuk, *Reputations Live On: An Early Malay Autobiography*, edited and translated by A. Sweeney, Berkeley, University of California Press, 1980.

Mohamed Sarim bin Haji Mustajab, 'Syeikh Muhammad Tahir Jalaluddin Al-Falaki Pelopor Gerakan Islah Islamiyyah di Tanah Melayu', *Malaysia in History*, 20(2), 1977.

Morrah, P., 'The History of the Malayan Police', *JMBRAS*, 36(2), 1963.

Mubin Sheppard (formerly M. C. ff. Sheppard), 'A Short History of Trengganu', *JMBRAS*, 22(3), 1949.

_____ 'Boria', *Malaya in History*, 10(1), 1965.

_____ 'Main Gayong', *Straits Times Annual*, 1971.

_____ *Taman Indera: Malay Decorative Arts and Pastimes*, Kuala Lumpur, Oxford University Press, 1972; reprinted as *A Royal Pleasure Ground*, Singapore, Oxford University Press, 1986.

_____ *Tunku: A Pictorial Biography 1903–1957*, Petaling Jaya, Malaysia, Pelanduk Publications, 1984.

Muhammad Hassan bin Dato' Kerani Muhammad Arshad, *Al-Tarikh Salasilah Negeri Kedah*, Kuala Lumpur, Dewan Bahasa dan Pustaka, 1968; previously published in *Jawi*, 1926.

Muhammad Ja'afar, 'An Account of the Cultivation of Rice in Malacca', translated by C. O. Blagden, *JSBRAS*, 30, 1897.

Murton, H. J., 'Notes on Gutta and Caoutchouc in the Malay Peninsula', *JSBRAS*, 1, 1878.

Nagata, Judith, *The Reflowering of Malaysian Islam: Modern Religious*

Radicals and Their Roots, Vancouver, University of British Columbia Press, 1984.

Naipaul, V. S., *Among the Believers: An Islamic Journey*, London, Deutsch, 1981.

Newbold, T. J., *Political and Statistical Account of the British Settlements . . . with a History of the Malayan States of the Peninsula in the Straits of Malacca*, 2 vols., London, Murray, 1839; reprinted as *British Settlements in the Straits of Malacca*, Kuala Lumpur, Oxford University Press, 1971.

Nik Ahmad bin Haji Nik Hassan, 'The Malay Press', *JMBRAS*, 36(1), 1963.

Noone, R. O., 'Notes on the Kampong, Compounds and Houses of the Patani Malay Village of Banggul Ara, in the Mukim of Batu Kurau, Northern Perak', *JMBRAS*, 21(1), 1948.

Norman, H., *The Peoples and Politics of the Far East: Travels and Studies in the British . . . Colonies and Malaya*, New York, Scribner, 1895.

Norton-Kyshe, J. W., *Cases Heard and Determined in H. M. Supreme Court of the Straits Settlements 1808–1884*, 4 vols., Singapore, Singapore and Straits Printing Office, 1885.

O'Brien, H. A., 'Latah', *JSBRAS*, 11, 1883.

_____ 'Latah', *JSBRAS*, 12, 1883.

_____ 'Jelebu', *JSBRAS*, 14, 1884.

Ooi Jin-Bee, *Land, People and Economy in Malaya*, London, Longmans, 1963.

Osborn S., *Quedah: Or Stray Leaves from a Journal in Malayan Waters*, London, Routledge, 1857 (revised 1860 and 1861 and published as *My Journal in Malayan Waters, or the Blockade of Kedah*); reprinted as *The Blockade of Kedah in 1838: A Midshipman's Exploits in Malayan Waters*, Singapore, Oxford University Press, 1987.

Papers on Malay Subjects, First Series, *Literature* (1907), *Law* (1908), *History* (1907–11), *Life and Customs* (1908–10), and *Malay Industries* (1909–11), Kuala Lumpur, Federated Malay States Government Press, and reprinted individually at various dates (1922–39); selected papers reprinted in P. L. Burns (ed.), *Papers on Malay Subjects*, Kuala Lumpur, Oxford University Press, 1971; M. B. Hooker (ed.), *Readings in Malay Adat Laws*, Singapore, Singapore University Press, 1970; and R. J. Wilkinson, 'The Incidents of Malay Life', *JMBRAS*, 30(4), 1957. Individual papers in this series, are listed here and cited in notes by reference to the author. Citations under *PMS* relate to the Burns edition unless otherwise indicated.

Pasqual, J. C., articles published in the *Singapore Sunday Times*, 14 and 28 October 1934.

Peacock, J. L., *Muslim Puritans: Reformist Psychology in Southeast Asian Islam*, Berkeley, University of California Press, 1978.

PESTA Official Souvenir Programme, Kuala Lumpur, Department of Information Services, 1956.

Pridmore, F., *Coins and Coinages of the Straits Settlements and British Malaya, 1786 to 1951*, Singapore, Memoirs of the Raffles Museum, Singapore, No. 2, 1955; reprinted Singapore, National Museum of Singapore, 1975.

Raja Ali Haji ibn Ahmad, *Tuhfat al-Nafis*, translated and annotated by Virginia Matheson and Barbara Watson Andaya, *The Precious Gift*, Kuala Lumpur, Oxford University Press, 1982.

Raja Bot bin Raja Jumaat, 'Rice Cultivation in the States', letter in the *Malay Mail*, 14 November 1902, reprinted in *Peninjau Sejarah*, 1(2), 1966.

Rathborne, A. B., *Camping and Tramping in Malaya: Fifteen Years' Pioneering in the Native States of the Malay Peninsula*, London, Swan Sonnenschein, 1898; reprinted Singapore, Oxford University Press, 1984.

Reid, A. J. S., *The Contest for North Sumatra: Atjeh, the Netherlands and Britain 1858–1898*, Kuala Lumpur, Oxford University Press, 1969.

Rentse, A., 'A History of Kelantan', *JMBRAS*, 12(2), 1934.

——— 'The Kelantan Shadow-play (Wayang Kulit)', *JMBRAS*, 14(3), 1936.

——— 'The Origin of the Wayang Theatre', *JMBRAS*, 20(1), 1947.

Rigby, J. (ed.), 'The Ninety-nine Laws of Perak', *Papers on Malay Subjects, Law*, Part 2, 1908, reprinted 1929, and partly reprinted in M. B. Hooker (ed.), *Readings in Malay Adat Laws*, Singapore, Singapore University Press, 1970.

Robert, Shaharil Talib, *see* Shaharil Talib.

Robson, J. H. M., *People in a Native State*, Singapore, Singapore Free Press, 1894.

——— *Records and Recollections 1889–1934*, Kuala Lumpur, Kyle Palmer, 1934.

Roff, W. R., 'The Life and Times of Haji Othman Abdullah', *Peninjau Sejarah*, 1(2), 1966.

——— *The Origins of Malay Nationalism*, New Haven, Yale University Press, 1967.

——— 'The Origins and Early Years of the Majlis Ugama', in W. R. Roff (ed.), *Kelantan: Religion, Society and Politics in a Malay State*, Kuala Lumpur, Oxford University Press, 1974.

Sadka, E., 'The State Councils in Perak and Selangor 1877–1895', in K. G. Tregonning (ed.), *Papers on Malayan History*, Singapore, University of Malaya Press, 1962.

——— *The Protected Malay States 1874–1895*, Kuala Lumpur and Singapore, University of Malaya Press, 1968.

Sejarah Melayu or Malay Annals, Raffles MS 18, translated by C. C. Brown, *JMBRAS*, 25(2–3), 1952.

Shaharil Talib (formerly Shaharil Talib Robert), 'The Trengganu Ruling Class in the Late Nineteenth Century', *JMBRAS*, 50(2), 1977.

_____ *After Its Own Image: The Trengganu Experience 1881–1941*, Singapore, Oxford University Press, 1984.

Sharom Ahmat, 'The Political Structure of the State of Kedah 1879–1905', *JSEAS*, 1(2), 1970.

_____ 'The Structure of the Economy of Kedah, 1879–1905', *JMBRAS*, 43(2), 1970.

_____ *Tradition and Change in a Malay State: A Study of the Economic and Political Development of Kedah 1878–1923*, MBRAS Monograph No. 12, 1984.

Shaw, G. E., 'Rice Planting', *Papers on Malay Subjects*, *Malay Industries*, Part 3, 1911, reprinted 1926.

Sheppard, M. C. ff., *see* Mubin Sheppard.

Short, D. E. and Jackson, J. C., 'The Origins of an Irrigation Policy in Malaya', *JMBRAS*, 44(1), 1971.

Sidney, R. J. H., *In British Malaya Today*, London, Hutchinson, n.d. (1926?).

_____ *Malay Land—Tanah Malayu: Some Phases of Life in Modern British Malaya*, London, Palmer, 1926.

Sidhu, J. S., *Administration in the Federated Malay States 1896–1920*, Kuala Lumpur, Oxford University Press, 1980.

Siegel, J. T., *The Rope of God*, Berkeley, University of California Press, 1969.

Skeat, W. W., 'Some Records of Malay Magic, by an Eyewitness', *JSBRAS*, 31, 1898.

_____ *Malay Magic: Being an Introduction to the Folklore and Popular Religion of the Malay Peninsula*, London, Macmillan, 1900, reprinted Singapore, Oxford University Press, 1984.

_____ and Blagden, C. O., *Pagan Races of the Malay Peninsula*, 2 vols., London, Macmillan, 1906.

_____ and Laidlaw, F. F., 'The Cambridge University Expedition to Parts of the Malay Peninsula 1899–1900: Personal Accounts', *JMBRAS*, 26(4), 1953.

Stevenson, R., *Cultivators and Administrators: British Educational Policy towards the Malays 1875–1906*, Kuala Lumpur, Oxford University Press, 1975.

Stoney, B. O., 'The Malays of British Malaya', in A. Wright and H. A. Cartwright (eds.), *Twentieth Century Impressions of British Malaya: Its History, People, Commerce, Industries, and Resources*, London, Lloyds, 1908.

Sullivan, P., *Social Relations of Dependence in a Malay State: Nineteenth Century Perak*, MBRAS Monograph No. 10, 1982.

Sutherland, H., 'The Taming of the Trengganu Elite', in R. T. McVey (ed.), *Southeast Asian Transitions: Approaches through Social History*, New

Haven and London, Yale University Press, 1978.

Sweeney, P. L. A., *The Ramayana and the Malay Shadow-play*, Kuala Lumpur, National University of Malaya Press, 1972.

_____ 'Professional Malay Story-telling—Pt. 1—Some Questions of Style and Presentation', *JMBRAS*, 46(2), 1973.

_____ 'The Pak Pandir Cycle of Tales', *JMBRAS*, 49(1), 1976.

_____ *Authors and Audiences in Traditional Malay Literature*, Berkeley, Center for Southeast Asia Studies, University of California, 1980.

_____ 'Introduction' and 'Commentary on the Text', *Reputations Live On*, Mohamed Salleh bin Perang, Datuk (q.v.).

_____ 'Introduction', *The Voyages of Mohamed Ibrahim Munshi* (q.v.) (with N. Phillips).

Swettenham, F. A., 'A Malay Nautch', *JSBRAS*, 2, 1878.

_____ 'From Perak to Slim and Down the Slim and Bernam Rivers', *JSBRAS*, 5, 1880.

_____ 'Some Account of the Independent Native States of the Malay Peninsula especially the Circumstances which led to the More Intimate Relations Recently Adopted towards Some of Them by the British Government', *JSBRAS*, 6, 1880.

_____ 'Journal Kept during a Journey across the Malay Peninsula', *JSBRAS*, 15, 1885.

_____ *About Perak*, Singapore, Straits Times, 1890.

_____ *Malay Sketches*, London, John Lane Bodley Head, 1895.

_____ *Unaddressed Letters*, London, John Lane Bodley Head, 1898.

_____ *The Real Malay: Pen Pictures*, London, John Lane Bodley Head, 1900.

_____ *British Malaya: An Account of the Origin and Progress of British Influence in Malaya*, London, John Lane Bodley Head, 1907 (revised editions 1929 and 1948, London, Allen & Unwin).

_____ *Also and Perhaps*, London, John Lane Bodley Head, 1912.

_____ *Footprints in Malaya*, London, Hutchinson, 1942.

_____ 'Sir Frank Swettenham's Perak Journals 1874–1876', edited by C. D. Cowan, *JMBRAS*, 24(4), 1951.

_____ *Sir Frank Swettenham's Malayan Journals 1874–1876*, edited by P. L. Burns and C. D. Cowan, Kuala Lumpur, Oxford University Press, 1975.

_____ *Stories and Sketches by Sir Frank Swettenham*, edited by W. R. Roff, Kuala Lumpur, Oxford University Press, 1967.

_____ 'British Rule in Malaya', in P. H. Kratoska (ed.), *Honourable Intentions: Talks on the British Empire in South-East Asia Delivered at the Royal Colonial Institute 1874–1928*, Singapore, Oxford University Press, 1983; reprinted from the *Proceedings of the Royal Colonial Institute*, 1896.

Swift, M. G., 'Men and Women in Malay Society', in B. Ward (ed.), *Women in the New Asia*, Paris, UNESCO, 1963.

_____ 'Malay Peasants', in R. D. Lambert and B. Hoselitz (eds.), *The*

Role of Savings and Wealth in Southern Asia and the West, Paris, UNESCO, 1963.

_____ 'Capital, Saving and Credit in a Malay Peasant Economy', in R. W. Firth and B. Yamey (eds.), *Capital, Saving and Credit in Peasant Societies: Studies from Asia, Oceania, the Caribbean and Middle America*, London, Allen & Unwin, 1964.

_____ *Malay Peasant Society in Jelebu*, London, Athlone Press, 1965.

_____ 'Economic Concentration and Malay Peasant Society' in M. Freedman (ed.), *Social Organisation: Essays Presented to Raymond Firth*, London, Frank Cass, 1967.

Syed Husin Ali, *Social Stratification in Kampong Bagan: A Study of Class, Status, Conflict and Mobility in a Rural Malay Community*, MBRAS Monograph No. 1, 1964.

_____ *Malay Peasant Society and Leadership*, Kuala Lumpur, Oxford University Press, 1975.

Syed Hussein Alatas, 'The Grading of Occupational Prestige amongst the Malays of Malaysia', *JMBRAS*, 41(1), 1968.

Taylor, E. N., 'Malay Family Law: An Essay on the Law and Custom Relating to the Distribution of Property on Dissolution of Marriage among the Peninsular Malays—With Illustrative Cases', *JMBRAS*, 15(1), 1937.

Thio, E., *British Policy in the Malay Peninsula*, Vol. 1: *The Southern and Central States*, Kuala Lumpur and Singapore, University of Malaya Press, 1969.

Thomson, J. T., 'Pulau Aur', *JIA*, 4, 1850.

_____ *Some Glimpses into Life in the Far East*, London, Richardson, 1864; reprinted as *Glimpses into Life in Malayan Lands*, Singapore, Oxford University Press, 1984.

_____ 'A Sketch of the Career of the Late James Richardson Logan of Penang and Singapore', *JMBRAS*, 7, 1881.

Tomlinson, H. M., *Tidemarks: Some Records of a Journey to . . . the Forest of Malaya in 1923*, London, Cassell, 1924.

Tregonning, K. G. (ed.), *Papers on Malayan History*, Singapore, University of Malaya, 1962.

Trocki, C. A., 'The Johore Archives and the Kangchu System 1844–1910', *JMBRAS*, 48(1), 1975.

_____ *Prince of Pirates: The Temenggongs and the Development of Johor and Singapore 1784–1885*, Singapore, Singapore University Press, 1979.

Turnbull, C. M., *The Straits Settlements 1826–1867: Indian Presidency to Crown Colony*, London, Athlone Press, 1972.

_____ *A History of Singapore 1819–1875*, Kuala Lumpur, Oxford University Press, 1977.

Vaughan, J. D., 'Notes on the Malays of Pinang and Province Wellesley', *JIA*, n.s., 2, 1857.

Vetch, R.H., *Life of Lieutenant General Sir Andrew Clarke*, London, Murray, 1905.

Vredenbregt, J., 'The Haddj; Some of Its Features and Functions in Indonesia', *BKI*, 118, 1962.

Wan Mohamed Amin bin Said, *Pesaka Selangor*, edited by Abdul Samad Ahmad, Kuala Lumpur, Dewan Bahasa dan Pustaka, 1966.

Watson, J.G., 'Rattans', in I.H. Burkill, *A Dictionary of the Economic Products of the Malay Peninsula with Contributions by . . . J. G. Watson*, 2 vols., London, published on behalf of the SS and FMS Governments, Crown Agents, 1935.

Westerhout, J.B., 'Notes on Malacca', *JIA*, 2, 1848.

Wheeler, L.R., *The Modern Malay*, London, Allen & Unwin, 1928.

Wicks, P.C., 'The Malayan Novels of Sir Hugh Clifford', *Malaya in History*, 27, 1984.

Wilkinson, R.J., *A Malay–English Dictionary*, 2 parts, Singapore, Kelly & Walsh, 1901 (revised as *A Malay–English Dictionary (Romanised)*, 2 parts, Mytilene, Salavopoulos & Kinderlis, 1932).

_____ 'The Education of Asiatics', *Special Reports on Educational Subjects*, Cmd. 835, Vol. 8, 1902.

_____ 'Malay Beliefs', 1906; reprinted in 'Papers on Malay Customs and Beliefs', *JMBRAS*, 30(4), 1957.

_____ *Papers on Malay Subjects*, Kuala Lumpur, Government Press, 1907–11: 'Letter Writing', *Malay Literature*, Part 3, 1907; 'Introductory Sketch', *Law*, Part 1, 1908, reprinted 1922 and again in M.B. Hooker (ed.), *Readings in Malay Adat Laws*, Singapore, Singapore University Press, 1970; 'The Incidents of Malay Life', *Life and Customs*, Part 1, 1908, reprinted in *JMBRAS*, 30(4), 1957; 'Malay Amusements', *Life and Customs*, Part 3, 1910; 'Notes on the Negri Sembilan', *History*, Part 5, 1911.

_____ 'Some Malay Studies', *JMBRAS*, 10(1), 1932.

Wilson, P.J., *A Malay Village and Malaysia*, New Haven, HRAF Press, 1967.

Winstedt, R.O., *Papers on Malay Subjects*, Kuala Lumpur, Government Press, 1907–11: 'The Circumstances of Malay Life: The Kampong—The House—Furniture—Dress—Food', *Life and Customs*, Part 1, 1909; 'Arts and Crafts', *Malay Industries*, Part 1, 1909; 'Fishing, Hunting and Trapping', *Malay Industries*, Part 2, 1911.

_____ 'Report by Mr. R.O. Winstedt . . . on Vernacular and Industrial Education in the Netherlands East Indies and the Philippines', *Proceedings of the Legislative Council Straits Settlements*, Paper No. 22 of 1917; reprinted in F.H.K. Wong and Gwee Yee Hean (eds.), *Official Reports on Education: Straits Settlements and the Federated Malay States 1870–1939*, Singapore, Pan Pacific Book Distributors, 1980.

_____ 'The Hadramaut Saiyids of Perak and Siak', *JSBRAS*, 79, 1918.

——— 'Keramat: Sacred Places and Persons in Malaya', *JMBRAS*, 2(3), 1924.

——— 'A History of Malay Literature', *JMBRAS*, 17(3), 1940.

——— *The Malay Magician: Being Shaman, Saiva and Sufi*, London, Constable, 1925, revised edition London, Routledge & Kegan Paul, 1951.

——— 'A History of Johore', *JMBRAS*, 10(3), 1932.

——— 'A History of Selangor', *JMBRAS*, 12(3), 1934.

——— *The Malays: A Cultural History*, Singapore, Kelly & Walsh, 1947.

——— 'Kingship and Enthronement in Malaya', *JMBRAS*, 20(1), 1947.

——— *An Unabridged Malay–English Dictionary*, Singapore, Kelly & Walsh, 1954.

——— *Start from Alif, Count from One: An Autobiographical Memoire*, Kuala Lumpur, Oxford University Press, 1969.

Winstedt, R. O. and Daing Abdul Hamid bin Tengku Mohamed Salleh, *Kitab Tawarikh Melayu*, Singapore, 1918.

Winstedt, R. O. and Wilkinson, R. J., 'A History of Perak', *JMBRAS*, 12(1), 1934.

Winzeler, R. L., 'Islamic Schools in Kelantan', *JMBRAS*, 48(1), 1975.

——— 'The Social Organization of Islam in Kelantan', in W. R. Roff (ed.), *Kelantan: Religion, Society and Politics in a Malay State*, Kuala Lumpur, Oxford University Press, 1974.

Wong, D. S. Y., *Tenure and Land Dealings in the Malay States*, Singapore, Singapore University Press, 1975.

Wong, F. H. K. and Gwee Yee Hean (eds.), *Official Reports on Education: Straits Settlements and the Federated Malay States 1870–1939*, Singapore, Pan Pacific Book Distributors, 1980.

Wong Lin Ken, *The Malayan Tin Industry to 1914*, Tucson, University of Arizona Press, 1965.

Wray, L., 'Journal of a Collecting Expedition to the Mountain of Batang Padang Perak', *JSBRAS*, 21, 1890.

——— 'Malay Aeolian Pipes', *Perak Museum Notes*, 3; reprinted in *SJ*, 16 November 1894.

Wright, A. and Cartwright, H. A. (eds.), *Twentieth Century Impressions of British Malaya—Its History, People, Commerce, Industries and Resources*, London, Lloyds, 1908.

Wynne, M. L., *Triad and Tabut*, Singapore, Government Printing Press, 1941, distributed 1957.

Yegar, M., 'The Abolition of Servitude in British Malaya: An Historical Analysis', *Israeli Yearbook on Human Rights*, 5, 1975.

——— *Islam and Islamic Institutions in British Malaya*, Leiden, Brill, 1979.

Zaharah Haji Mahmud, 'The Pioneering of Wet-rice Growing Traditions in West Malaysia: A Restudy with Special Reference to the State of Kedah', *Geographica*, 5, 1969.

_____ 'The Period and Nature of "Traditional" Settlement in the Malay Peninsula', *JMBRAS*, 43(2), 1972.

Zainal Abidin bin Ahmad, 'Modern Developments', in R. O. Winstedt, 'A History of Malay Literature', *JMBRAS*, 17(3), 1940; *not* included in the reprint of Winstedt, 'A History of Classical Malay Literature', *JMBRAS*, 31(3), 1958.

_____ 'Malay Manners and Etiquette', *JMBRAS*, 23(3), 1950.

Newspapers

Bintang Timor
Jawi Peranakan
Malay Mail
Selangor Journal
Singapore Free Press
Singapore Sunday Times
Straits Times
Times of Malaya

Unpublished papers

Douglas, W. Bloomfield, Diary 1876–1882 (incomplete), xerox copy at Rhodes House Library, Oxford.

Hikayat Pahang—anon.—see Chapter 1, note 17.

Khasnor Johan, 'The Administrative Élite in the Federated Malay States: An Aspect of Malaysian Social History', Ph.D. thesis, Monash University, 1974 (published in 1984 in revised form: see p. 400 above).

Index

ABDUL AZIZ, RAJA MUDA OF KEDAH, 60, 295, 311 n. 112
Abdul Ghani, Sheikh, 35, 46 n. 65, 290
Abdul Hamid, Sultan of Kedah, 37, 56, 58, 60, 63 n. 20, 311 n. 111, 360 n. 97
Abdul Majid bin Zainuddin, Haji, 222–3, 226, 235 n. 68, 311 n. 111, 370
Abdul Mohet, Sheikh, 184, 225
Abdul Rahman (of Johor), 86
Abdul Rahman (To Bahman), 89 n. 12
Abdul Rahman bin Mohamed Al-Idrus (Ungku Sayid of Paloh), 283, 289, 292
Abdul Samad, Sultan of Selangor: interest in agriculture, 32, 52, 57; character, 21, 32, 38, 40 n. 13, 45 n. 53, 49, 55, 58, 66 n. 52, 205 n. 83; *istana*, 188, 202 n. 43; political, 21, 26, 38, 83, 193, 239, 282, 285; wealth, 54, 66 n. 44; wives, 52, 188
Abdullah, Sultan of Perak: family and household, 49, 91, 186; *main berhantu* (1875), 318, 321; political, 22, 35, 38, 40 n. 12, 44 n. 50, 79, 102, 138, 205
Abdullah bin Abdul Kadir, Munshi, 5, 7, 264, 266, 321, 325, 370
Aborigines, 13, 99, 151, 171 n. 13
Abu Bakar, Sultan of Johor: lifestyle, 6, 14 n. 12, 22, 42, 55, 58, 193, 295; political, 5, 37, 46 n. 63
Adat perpatih, 4, 13, 111, 222
Adultery, 6, 216, 240, 249, 280, 293, 310 n. 101
Agriculture, *see* Padi *and* other crops
Ahmad, Sultan of Kelantan, 37
Ahmad, Sultan of Pahang: character, 21, 30; household, 28, 31, 50, 63 n. 12, 65 n. 32, 69 n. 91, 188; political, 23, 26, 28, 31, 38, 43 n. 39, 44 n. 49, 63 n. 20, 64 n. 27
Ahmad, Sultan of Terengganu 38
Ahmad Tajuddin I, Sultan of Kedah, 26, 42
Ahmad Tajuddin II, Sultan of Kedah: household, 64 n. 27; lifestyle, 42, 56–7; political, 24, 37, 84
Ali, Haji, 82, 102
Ali, Raja Muda of Riau, 293
Alsagoff, Syed Mohamed, *see* Mohamed Alsagoff
Amuk, 83, 240–1, 253 n. 24, 365
Amusements, *see* Entertainments; Games and Pursuits; Sports and Contests
Anderson, J., 370
Anson, A. E., 15 n. 20
Antah, Yam Tuan of Negeri Sembilan, 38, 316
Arabs, 5, 71, 88 n. 4
Arfah, Raja, 220, 280

BAHMAN, To, *see* Abdul Rahman
Balai, 21–6, 74, 188, 336
Band, *see* Nobat
Begbie, P. J., 8, 370
Betel nut, 29, 158, 169, 194–5, 206 n. 94, 282
Birch, J. W. W., 8, 81, 195 282, 370
Bird, I. (Mrs Bishop), 9, 371
Bot, Raja, 35, 260, 264, 345, 374
Bozzolo, C. F., 371
Braddell, T., 8, 15 n. 20, 371
British rule, effects of: on crafts, 163f; courts, 249; economic, 74f, 153f; education, 263f; Islam, 285f; law and order, 239f; medical, 259f; political, 23f; settlement (of land), 103f, 129f; social, 181f
Bugis, 4, 36, 128

CADDY, F., 371
Cameron, J., 371
Camphor, 172 n. 24

Cars, *see* Roads
Cattle and buffaloes: economic importance, 133f, 157; padi cultivation, 126f
Cavenagh, O., 265, 371
Character (Malay), 240–1, 262, 269, 316–17, 363–7; *see also* Swettenham, F. A.
Chiefs: debt-bondsmen, 210f; economic position, 79f; matrimonial alliances, 215; political, 24, 30, 35, 43 n. 46, 71f, 245f; under colonial rule, 75f, 91 n. 42, 245f
Chinese: Sino-Malay relations, 13, 156, 240, 364; tin miners, 53, 128, 170 n. 1
Chulalongkorn, King of Siam, 27, *see also* Siam
Chulan, Raja, 70 n. 94, 91 n. 42, 237 n. 93
Clifford, H., 210, 371
Clothing: aristocratic, 31, 205 n. 83; fighting dress, 192; holiday, 282; nautical 192; stage, 337f; traditional, 58, 189f; Western, 25, 55–6, 193, 268
Coconuts, copra and coconut oil, 132–3, 147 nn. 56–61
Coffee growing, 107, 161–2
Corvée, *see Kerah*
Court ceremonial: traditional, 21–6; under colonial rule, 33–7
Crafts and village industries, 162–7; metal work, 57, 163–6; pottery, 165; shipbuilding, 57, 166; weaving, 163, 166, 211; woodwork, 57

Damar, 124, 155
Dancing, 329, 333–4
Davidson, J. G., 16 n. 20
Debt-bondage and slavery, 11, 48, 99, 210–14, 228 n. 4, 314–15; aborigines, 13, 210; European attitude, 11, 210; termination, 7, 49, 74, 210–14
Dennison, N., 371
Dhiauddin (Kudin), Tunku, 26, 63 n. 19, 70, 90 n. 26, 176 n. 74, 185, 193, 220, 234 n. 60, 235 n. 81, 295
Douglas, B., 16 n. 24, 265, 371

Earl, G. W. 372
Economic factors: aristocrats and, 32, 85, 138, 211–14; external, 2, 4, 124, 127, 167; markets, 128f, 137, 139–40, 167; shops, 139; traders, 101–3, 128, 159, 240; wage earning, 106, 162; *see also* Land settlement and use; Land tenure
Education: attitudes to, 269; curriculum, 268; female, 268; Islamic, 263, 296–7; reading material, 266–7, 350; teachers, 265, 268; traditional 263–4; upper class, 60, 70 n. 95, 88, 199, 226, 264, 269–70, 324; vernacular, 265–6
Elephants, 31, 54, 56, 80, 158–9, 197–9, 207 nn. 109–28
Entertainments: cinema, 59, 339, 369 n. 20; circus, 340; dancing, 319–20, 329, 331, 333–4, 355 nn. 26–30; music, 341–3; story telling, 348–50; theatre, 195, 334–40

Federated Malay States (FMS): Chinese population, 13, 367 n. 4; Education Department, 268; federal council, 199, 210, 228 n. 3, 332; Islamic organization, 287; Malay population, 4, 14 n. 7; *see also* individual States
Firth, R. W., 320, 326 n. 2
Fish and fishing: as food, 124, 136–8, 194; fishing methods, 133–6, 140
Followers and domestic staff: economic role, 151, 212f; male followers, 42 n. 34, 50f, 63 n. 19, 98; royal, 26, 48f, 188; upper class, 7, 212f
Food and cooking: cooking, 181: European, 54–5; foodstuffs, 29, 43 n. 43, 124, 138, 157, 159; meals and feasts, 48, 194–6, 222, 317; utensils and implements, 194, 206 n. 92, 222
'Foreign' Malays *see* Migrants (*anak dagang*)
Funerals, 47 n. 68, 193, 196
Furniture and household utensils, 22–3, 39 n. 9, 185; European, 55, 59; lamps, 138, 155, 185; utensils, 124, 184f

Gajah, To, *see* Rasu
Galloway, D. J., 272 n. 28, 372
Gambier, 124, 138, 160, 174 n. 63
Games and pursuits: agricultural shows,

348; chess, 344; collecting sea-shells, etc., 348; European sports, 332, 354 n. 22; gambling, 345; hunting, 31, 198, 346; indoor games, 344, 359 n. 80; kite flying, 343, 358 n. 73; reading and story telling, 348–50; travels, picnics and outdoor trips, 28, 55, 57–60, 346–7, 360 n. 100
Garden produce, 157, 364
Gold mining, 152

HAINES, F. W., 270, 276 n. 78
Hajar, Wan, 84, 233 n. 60
Halimah, Toh Puan, 75, 211, 218–20
Hall, D. G. E., 12
Hamid, Syed, ruler of Tampin, 22, 188, 202 n. 46
Hamidah (Che Mida), 218, 232 n. 4, 221
Hikayat, 8, 15 n. 19, 26, 350, 361 n. 121
Hornaday, W. T., 183, 222, 372
Houses, 74, 165, 181–8, 219, 232 n. 46, 258
Hurgronje, C. S., 255 n. 48, 312 n. 124, 372

IBRAHIM, SULTAN OF JOHOR, 37, 46 n. 63, 60, 69 n. 89
Idris, Haji, 212
Idris, Sultan of Perak: character and circumstances, 60, 70 nn. 95 and 96, 75, 189, 205 n. 83; household and family, 40 n. 19, 46 n. 62, 52, 64 n. 26, 91 n. 42, 229 n. 10, 234 n. 60; piety, 34, 287, 293; political, 33, 45 n. 56, 59, 226, 240, 245, 255 n. 49
Illness: attitude to, 258; European medicine, 259, 271 n. 12; *latah*, 261–2; magic as treatment, 318–20; smallpox vaccination, 259–60; *see also* Insanity
Indonesians: immigrants, 5, 14 n. 7, 105f, 127f, 225–7, 272 n. 19; pilgrims, 298–301, 313–15; traders, 98, 101–2, 154, 225–6; *see also* Bugis; Migrants
Innes, E., 194, 206 n. 92, 220, 372
Insanity, 240–1, 261–2
Insignia (*kebesaran*), 21, 28–9, 33, 35–6, 43 n. 40, 45 n. 62, 46 n. 65, 324
Irrigation, 80, 85, 131–2, 163, 178 n. 117
Irving, C. J., 15 n. 20, 22
Iskander, Sultan of Perak, 69 n. 91, 199, 295, 311 n. 113
Islam: bureaucratization, 280, 284f, 293f, 304 n. 38; conduct and beliefs, 6, 32, 112, 190, 203 n. 61, 237 n. 97, 280f, 293f, 303 n. 29, 308 n. 91, 310 nn. 101–11, 334, 340, 346; doctrine, 277, 290f, 307 n. 86; fasting month, 282; *Hari Raya*, 195, 265, 330; Indian Muslims, 5; *Holy War*, 292; *kadi*, 115, 217, 224, 285f, 304 n. 38, 305 n. 55; Koran reading, 265, 269, 282, 296f, 311 n. 121; legal and property aspects, 5, 13, 66 n. 44, 215, 217, 246, 287, 293f, 306 n. 66, 309 nn. 97–8, 346; attitude to magic, 34, 182, 321f; Muslim world, 28, 277, 292, 308 nn. 92 and 95, 365; mysticism, 281, 313 n. 141; observances, 26, 277f; schools and teachers, 263f, 288, 296, 301, 306 n. 69, 313 n. 142; state ceremonies, 26, 34, 283, 303 n. 35; state officials and *ulama*, 5, 72, 87, 114, 289f, 304 n. 38, 307 n. 82; tithes, 117 n. 5, 281, 285; *see also* Mosques; Pilgrimage
Ismail, Sultan of Perak, 35, 38, 75, 198
Istana, 21, 36–7, 48f, 52, 55, 59, 64 n. 29, 188, 226, 228, 249, 282, 285, 303 n. 30, 331, 333

JAFFAR, NGAH, MENTERI OF LARUT, 22, 74, 84 n. 3, 132, 218–20, 233 n. 53
Jervois, W., 42 nn. 34 and 37, 234 n. 62
Johor, conditions in, 5, 14 n. 7, 85–6, 112–13, 244
Journal of the Indian Archipelago (*JIA*), ix, 8
Journal of the Straits/Malayan/Malaysian Branch of the Royal Asiatic Society, ix, 8
Jungle produce: atap, 150, 155–6; camphor, 172 n. 24; *damar*, 155; gutta percha, 154, 171–2 nn. 20–3; rattan,

152–3, 171 n. 11; timber, 153, 171 n. 17; wood oil, 155

KARIM, CHE, CHIEF OF SELAMA, 79, 90 n. 26, 187, 225
Kedah, conditions in, 4, 14 n. 7, 21, 57, 84–5, 108, 111–12, 127, 132, 143 n. 17, 155–7, 172 n. 34, 214, 244, 246–7, 273 n. 35, 283
Kelantan, conditions in, 3, 6, 14 n. 7, 21, 67 n. 67, 87, 104, 113–14, 116 n. 1, 139–40, 156, 264, 273 n. 35, 283, 289, 29?, 321, 347
Kenali, To, *see* Mohamed Yusof bin Ahmad
Kerah (corvée labour), 48–9, 54, 63 n. 20, 73f, 85, 99–100, 198
Keyser, A L., 347, 372

LAKSAMANA OF PERAK, *see* Mohamed Amin
Land settlement and use, 98, 104–9, 116 n. 3 157
Land tenure: colonial (Torrens) system, 11, 109f, 214, 364; Malay traditional, 11, 19 n. 37, 87, 98, 107f
Language and literacy, 25, 40 n. 19, 60, 264–9
Latah, *see* Illness
Legal system: colonial, 249; Malay traditional, 4, 244–9; *see also* Islam
Letters and literature, 7, 25–6, 350; *see also* Newspapers
Logan, J. R., 8, 21, 242, 290, 372
Low, H., 8, 16 n. 20, 69 n. 92, 75, 79, 373
Low, J., 6, 13, 373

MCNAIR, J. F. A., 9, 15 n. 20
Magic: agricultural, 126, 130, 317f; holy places, 32?; housebuilding, 182; treatment of illness, 258–9, 318f; Islam and, 34, 321f; *pawang*, 13, 126, 130, 151, 182, 258–9, 334; state ceremonies, 7 314, 318; theatrical, 355, 358 n. 71; theories of, 13, 325 n. 2
Maharum, Tunku, 225, 235 n. 81
Mahdi, Raja, 54
Maheran, Wan, 233 n. 60
Mahmud bin Mat, Datuk, 7, 212, 229 n. 13, 214, 273 n. 35
Mahmud bin Raja Saman, Raja, 10–11, 81–4, 187, 260, 269, 272 n. 15, 331
Mahmud ibni Sultan Mohamed, Raja, 46 n. 64, 233 n. 60
Mansur, Sultan of Kelantan, 21, 38
Marriage: aristocratic and royal, 50f, 73–4; arranged, 215; ceremonies, 195–6, 280; divorce, 216f, 220; Islamic factors, 286f, 293–4; 'modern', 222; polygamy, 52, 64 nn. 25–7, 217, 223–5; remarriage, 235 n. 79, 234–44, 287; settlements of property, 217
Mashhor, Syed, 73, 322
Mat, *see* Mohamed
Maxwell, W. E., 10, 373; land policy, 11, 117 n. 5; Malay village society, 115, 123 n. 107, 249, 286; slavery, 228 n. 4
Maxwell, W. G., 374
Mayer, C., 374
Medical, *see* Illness
Melaka, conditions in, 5, 14 n. 7, 115, 157, 249, 286
Menangkabau, *see Adat perpatih*
Menteri (ministers), 21, 72, 85–6, 283, 289
Menteri of Larut, *see* Jaffar, Ngah
Mida, Che, *see* Hamidah
Migrants (*anak dagang*), Malay, 3, 50, 98, 101f, 129f, 168f, 178 n. 117, 225–7
Mohamed, Sultan of Selangor, 38, 42 n. 37, 128, 233 n. 60
Mohamed, Yam Tuan of Negeri Sembilan, 38, 287, 310 n. 103
Mohamed II, Sultan of Kelantan, 37
Mohamed III, Sultan of Kelantan, 37
Mohamed Amin, Datuk Laksamana of Perak, 74, 218, 321
Mohamed Amin, Wan, 15 n. 19, 235 n. 81
Mohamed Ibrahim bin Abdullah, Munshi, 41 n. 21, 86, 258, 281, 295, 348, 374
Mohamed Isa, Wan, 76, 220, 232 n. 45
Mohamed Salleh, Wan, 77–8, 344

Mohamed Salleh bin Perang, 86
Mohamed Saman (Mat Saman), Wan, of Kedah, 84–5, 132
Mohamed Taib, Sheikh, 225, 236 n. 85, 287, 291
Mohamed Yusof bin Ahmad (To Kenali), 297, 300
Mosques: attendance, 26, 280f; building, 62, 277–9, 285, 298, 301; officials, 297, 301f
Mukim, 85, 110–11
Musa, Raja Muda of Selangor, 70 n. 95, 287
Musa, Syed, 79–80

NANING, 13
Negeri Sembilan, conditions in, 4, 14 n. 7, 41 n. 3, 74, 76, 92 n. 45, 111, 221, 247, 265, 287
Newbold, T. J., 374
Newspapers, Malay, 267
Nobat (band), 29, 36, 49, 326, 341–2
Norman, H., 22, 374

OMAR, BAGINDA, SULTAN OF TERENGGANU, 6, 38, 48, 57, 87, 246, 248, 294
Opium, 124, 138, 159, 295, 346
Ord, H., 57
Osborn, S., 124, 374

PADI: cultivation, 4, 100f, 124f, 143 n. 21, 317f; rice as food, 124, 157, 194f
Pahang, conditions in: economic, 53, 127f, 157; political, 4, 31, 72, 240f, 255 nn. 48–9, 283; social, 7, 14 n. 7, 65 n. 32, 260, 278, 288, 321, 333
Panglima, 72, 239, 242
Patani, 3, 104, 157, 264, 332, 367 n. 2
Penang, 5, 14 n. 7, 42 n. 37; *see also* Province Wellesley
Penghulu: appointment, 76–7, 82, 218, 220; duties, 87, 106, 110f, 247, 250, 266, 272 n. 15; personality, 79, 110f; religious role, 112, 114, 279, 281, 283
Pepper, 80, 107, 161, 175 n. 66
Perak, conditions in: economic, 14 n. 7, 65 n. 35, 105f, 121 n. 67, 127, 133; political, 24, 33–5, 44 n. 50, 75, 77, 286; social, 3–4, 226, 244, 260–1, 293, 331, 347
Perlis, 4, 14 n. 7, 346
Pilgrimage, 6, 99, 113, 166, 210, 233 n. 53, 250, 259, 271 n. 13, 297–301, 312–15
Police, 51, 169, 178 n. 125, 242–4, 254 nn. 32 and 33, 281
Population, 3–5, 14 n. 7, 364, 367 n. 4
Poultry, 134, 157, 173 n. 38, 182, 186, 258
Prisons, 238, 246, 250, 251 n. 1
Province Wellesley, 5, 8, 108, 112, 242, 249–50, 259, 285–6, 290–1, 305 n. 55
Punishment, 6, 246, 248f, 280, 292–3

RAILWAYS, 106, 160, 168, 177, 207 n. 104
Rasu (To Gajah), 72, 89 n. 12
Rathborne, A., 375
Recreations, upper class, 35, 37, 54f, 56, 59; *see also* Games and pursuits
Riau, 28, 36, 42 n. 37
River communications, 43 n. 39, 98, 116 n. 3, 124, 130, 138, 157–8, 169, 173 n. 46, 179–80, 240, 318, 323, 346–7
Roads and vehicles: bicycles, 56; bullock-carts, 65 n. 32, 160, 169, 259; carriages, 37, 56–7, 60, 66 n. 51; footpaths, 43 n. 39, 159; motor vehicles, 1, 6, 59; roads, 155–7
Robson, J. H. M., 9, 178 n. 125, 242, 375
Rubber, 1
Rulers, role and activities: ceremonial, 3, 20f, 317; economic, 53f, 61–2; family and domestic, 45f, 71, 221, 225, 333; European contact, 4–6, 27, 55, 58; mutual relations, 6, 25, 55, 59; personality, 30f, 326; public role, 3, 20f, 72, 210, 245f; religious role, 26, 277, 282, 284f; travels, 28, 59f

SAMAN, RAJA, TUNKU PANGLIMA RAJA, 81, 83, 93 n. 77, 206 n. 92
Selangor, conditions in: economic, 128; political, 35–6, 46 n. 54, 63 n. 20,

81, 83; social, 3, 14 n. 7, 243, 266f, 287
Ships and shipbuilding, 57, 67 n. 70, 166
Siam, influence of, 2, 4, 8, 26–7, 40 n. 15, 56, 87, 207 n. 105, 289, 292, 335–6
Sidney, R. J. H., 375
Singapore, 5, 14 n. 7, 28, 154
Skeat, W. W., 8, 325 n. 2, 375
Slavery, *see* Debt-bondage and slavery
Societies, secret, 291
Society, Malay, 3, 12, 71, 75, 79, 87, 101, 210, 225f, 269, 351, 366
Sports and contests: cock-fighting, 330–1, 344; football, 324; *sepak raga*, 332
State councils, general aspects, 24, 30, 75, 90 n. 26
Straits Settlements, *see* Melaka; Penang; Province Wellesley; Singapore
Sugar cane, 134
Sulaiman, Sultan of Selangor, 35, 57–8, 60–2, 66 n. 44, 193, 225, 269, 285, 287, 293, 309 n. 96, 340
Sumatra, *see* Indonesians
Sungei Ujong, *see* Negeri Sembilan
Swettenham, F. A., 10f, 15 n. 20, 98, 117 n. 5, 270, 366, 375

TAHIR, HAJI, 162, 175 n. 70, 225
Taxes, 53, 109, 124, 138, 150
Teh Sapiah, Wan, 218, 234 n. 60
Terengganu, conditions in: economic, 65 n. 32, 87, 113, 165–7; political, 27, 42 n. 34, 86, 113, 246–7, 290; social, 3, 14 n. 7, 214, 273 n. 35, 267, 284f
Theft, 240, 242, 244
Thomson, J. T., 376
Tin, 74, 79–80, 83, 102, 124, 150–2, 170 n. 1, 324
Titles, 71–2
Tobacco, 53, 124, 138, 160
Tools, 164
Trade links, 5, 101–3, 138, 148, 150, 156f

UNGKU SAYID OF PALOH, *see* Abdul Rahman bin Mohamed Al-Idrus
Uteh, Che, 64 n. 25, 234 n. 60, 290, 357 n. 62

VAUGHAN, J. D., 290, 357 n. 62, 376
Victoria, Queen, 7, 27, 33, 285
Violence, 74, 81–2, 187, 216, 235–44, 253 n. 28, 329

WEAPONS: personal, 163, 187, 238f; trade in, 102, 163–4; types, 238–9
Weld, F., 38 n. 2, 42 n. 34, 58, 221
Wilkinson, R. J., 10, 18 n. 33, 24, 66 n. 49, 117 n. 5, 196, 263, 268, 295–7
Winstedt, R. O., 10, 18 n. 33, 376
Women: aristocrats, 36, 64 nn. 25–6; dancers, 31, 330, 333; domestic and court attendants, 31, 49–50, 98, 188, 330; dress, 190–2; *rites de passage*, 196, 206 n. 101; social position, 1, 210, 214–25, 263, 268, 293–4

YUSUF, SULTAN OF PERAK, 31–2, 38, 40 n. 19, 44 n. 50, 45 n. 62, 54, 65 n. 40, 260, 286, 291, 319, 347

ZAINAL ABIDIN III, SULTAN OF TERENGGANU, 5, 25, 28, 32, 38, 49, 59, 65 n. 32, 86–7, 246, 338
Zainal Abidin bin Ahmad (Zaba), 376
Zainal Rashid II, Sultan of Kedah, 37

EAST ASIAN HISTORICAL MONOGRAPHS

British Mandarins and Chinese Reformers: The British Administration of Weihaiwei (1898–1930) and the Territory's Return to Chinese Rule
Pamela Atwell

The Emergence of the Modern Malay Administrative Elite
Khasnor Johan

The Federal Factor in the Government and Politics of Peninsular Malaysia
B. H. Shafruddin

Malay Society in the Late Nineteenth Century: The Beginnings of Change
J. M. Gullick

The Origins of an Heroic Image: Sun Yatsen in London, 1896–1897
J. Y. Wong

The Structure of Chinese Rural Society: Lineage and Village in the Eastern New Territories, Hong Kong
David Faure

A Wilderness of Marshes: The Origins of Public Health in Shanghai, 1843–1893
Kerrie L. MacPherson